Geopolitical and Economic Consequences of Trade Policies and Tariffs

Renata Thiébaut
https://orcid.org/0000-0003-1529-3451
AI Global Exchange Forum, Canada

Marc Selgas-Cors
Universitat de Barcelona, Spain

IGI Global
Scientific Publishing
Publishing Tomorrow's Research Today

Vice President of Editorial	Melissa Wagner
Director of Acquisitions	Mikaela Felty
Director of Book Development	Jocelynn Hessler
Production Manager	Mike Brehm
Cover Design	Jose Rosado

Published in the United States of America by
IGI Global Scientific Publishing
701 East Chocolate Avenue
Hershey, PA, 17033, USA
Tel: 717-533-8845 | Fax: 717-533-7115
Website: https://www.igi-global.com E-mail: cust@igi-global.com

Library of Congress Cataloging-in-Publication Data

LCCN: 2025029838 (CIP Data Pending)
ISBN13: 9798337338354
Isbn13Softcover: 9798337338361
EISBN13: 9798337338378
British Cataloguing in Publication Data
A Cataloguing in Publication record for this book is available from the British Library.

Table of Contents

Detailed Table of Contents

The trade war initiated by Donald J. Trump against China during his first term has taken on a global character in 2025. While the main goal was to decrease trade deficits, his administration sought to increase industrialization in the country by promoting American-first protagonism. This book chapter's primary objective is to understand the main reasons that led to the ongoing trade war, as well as to examine the growing challenges to the legitimacy of the WTO and existing international trade rules, which are founded on the core principles of non-discrimination, National Treatment, and fairness. Finally, it examines the increasing significance of new international actions in global trade like the BRICS+, not only to comprehend its key aspects of trade wars but also to lay the groundwork for future discussions, such as new compliance mechanisms, and WTO reform.

In the complex web of global economics, few concepts have sparked as much debate, policy intervention, and public interest as trade. Trade—the exchange of goods, services, and capital across international borders—has long been championed as a driver of economic growth, innovation, and international cooperation. Since the end of World War II, the global economic order has largely trended toward liberalization, fostering a rules-based system designed to reduce tariffs, eliminate trade barriers, and integrate markets across continents. Institutions like the General Agreement on

and digital trade barriers. In conclusion, it outlines key principles for a WTO TFA 2.0 that reflects the realities of modern, trust-based, and sustainable global trade.

The trade war between the United States and China has opened strategic opportunities to expand economic markets in Asian countries. The United States' trading partners are expected to retaliate to protect domestic industries and recover nominal income. This would cause further harm to U.S. economic growth and income, slowing global economic growth, with the negative impact intensifying when tariffs extend to free trade agreement partners and prompt retaliation. This study uses the literature research method. It analyzes information about the trade war between the United States and various Asian countries, especially China, which has a long history of trade conflict with the U.S., and discusses the effect of U.S. reciprocal tariffs on trade policies and tariffs in Asian countries. Trump's program would not only cause grave damage to the U.S. economy; these policies would actually benefit other countries, including most in Asia.

This chapter examines the African Continental Free Trade Area (AfCFTA) as a crucial instrument for addressing global trade challenges, including the surge in protectionist policies observed during the COVID-19 pandemic. This analysis employs geoeconomics, strategic trade theory, and new regionalism to examine how the AfCFTA can enhance Africa's economic strength and independence. The chapter examines policy frameworks and case studies from Ghana, South Africa, Nigeria, and Kenya, as well as insights from various regional trade agreements, including RCEP, USMCA, and MERCOSUR. The chapter suggests that the AfCFTA could enhance Africa's position in global trade negotiations, foster regional value chains, and consolidate the continent's markets. The chapter concludes with a helpful framework that policymakers, development partners, and institutions can utilize to safeguard Africa against external shocks through the AfCFTA.

Oil prices are the outcome of a highly integrated, dynamic global system. With geopolitical risk and trade policy uncertainty contribute to the volatile world markets, the study analyses the impact of geopolitical risk, trade policy uncertainty on crude oil price globally. It considers data from 2000 to 2023 and finds out systematic link between the three variables. The data proved a long run impact of trade policy uncertainty and geopolitical risk on the crude oil. This enhances the influence of the variables and leads to implementation of policy measures in global markets. The data are tested through Auto Regressive Distributed Lag (ARDL) model and checked for long run cointegration and short run association. The policy, thus, has been suggested as to improve the transition towards sustainability globally. Though the impact of geopolitical risk and trade policy uncertainty is not strong on crude oil price in world market, it can affect the short run volatility. Thus, mitigation, diversification and transparency are the key factors to strengthen the existing situation in world.

This chapter examines the geopolitical dimensions of China's trade policy by analyzing how the People's Republic of China strategically leverages trade as an instrument of power to achieve greater strategic autonomy and expand its global influence in a rapidly shifting international order, particularly in the face of escalating tensions with the United States; it explores core policy instruments such as the Belt and Road Initiative, the Dual Circulation Strategy, and the Digital Silk Road, while also evaluating China's engagement with multilateral institutions, its efforts to securitize key supply chains, and its ambitions to reform global trade governance, concluding that China's trade strategy should be understood not merely as economic policy but as an integrated component of a grand geopolitical strategy aimed at reshaping the global order in line with its normative preferences and long-term interests.

The story of modern China can be traced back to Deng Xiaoping, who challenged the Chinese people to do even better than Japan did with the Meiji Restoration. The end result has been over forty years of extraordinary economic growth and China rising to become the second-largest economy in the world with hundreds of millions of people lifted out of poverty. Its share of global trade has also risen significantly over the past four decades with the help of special economic zones being established, along with becoming a member of the World Trade Organization and more recently the Belt and Road Initiative. But the rise of China has not occurred without suspicions and concerns along the way. From cyber espionage and stealing trade secrets to Taiwan and the militarization of the South China Sea, questions remain about China's true intentions and if it is trying to rise peacefully or overturn the liberal order. This chapter explores the history of China's rise to global superpower status and if China can be considered an honest trade broker and member of the global community under Xi Jinping.

This chapter analyzes the geopolitical and economic implications of China's critical mineral and electric vehicle (EV) exports to the United States and Brazil amidst rising tariffs. Critical minerals are essential for the global green energy transition, particularly for EV batteries and renewable energy infrastructure. China has become the dominant force across the entire critical minerals supply chain, from raw material extraction to high-tech component manufacturing, and is the world's largest exporter of EVs. The U.S. has imposed substantial tariffs on Chinese imports. Brazil, with its significant critical mineral reserves, has adopted a phased import tax system for EVs. The intensifying competition for critical minerals, exacerbated by the U.S.-China trade war, presents a "Green Paradox," where the pursuit of clean energy risks environmental degradation. Ultimately, unilateral trade measures are insufficient to address supply chain vulnerabilities and environmental costs, underscoring the necessity for multilateral cooperation.

In a world increasingly defined by great-power rivalry and economic coercion, the European Union (EU) is reshaping its trade policy to serve not only economic growth but strategic geopolitical objectives. Anchored in a realist international relations framework, the analysis traces how the EU is transitioning from a normative promoter of global trade rules to a more assertive, interest-driven actor capable of wielding economic tools to defend sovereignty, exert influence, and mitigate external

economic governance and disproportionately impacting developing nations through 'reciprocal' tariffs. The protectionist measures announced by Trump included an increase in customs duties on goods imported from different countries. Therefore, this chapter proposes to study the relationship between logistics and trade. Indeed, the objective is to better understand the effect of the logistics sector on trade, and then to study the repercussions of U.S. trade wars, especially the impact of Trump's tariffs on global logistics and supply chains.

The return of Donald Trump has marked a key moment for the international system. The establishment of a system of reciprocal tariffs has had an impact on the international economy. This paper aims to identify the main effects of the trade war between the United States and China on the international economic system. The concept of trade war is rescued, as well as some trends on trade policy (Ripsman, 2006), globalization (Rodrik, 2007) and securitization (de Goede, 2017) to understand the economic dynamics of the international system. The proposed methodology is a network analysis (Granovetter, 2012) based on the exports and imports of the world's 40 main economies. With this, a series of categories are proposed to identify the adaptability of economies to the reciprocal tariffs imposed by the United States. The categories are commercial diversification, specialization of exportable supply, strategic industries and position within global value chains. Among the findings, it discusses the role of China, India, Japan and South Korea as key Indo-Pacific nodes.

Two of the world's largest democracies United States and India have a robust and progressing trade partnership, which has deepened over the years. This paper investigates the evolving dynamics of their global trade under the influence of protectionism and populism. In recent years both the countries are focusing more on their national interests and economic self reliance, rather than heavily relying on global trade or free market globalisation. However there is an increased skepticism towards liberal economic globalisation, because both the nations have witnessed drastic political and economic shifts driven by the populist leaders and their strategic directives. This research takes on a comparative approach on exploring the political economy of both the nations. This study underlines how domestic political narratives shape international trade participation, through scrutinizing key trade policies, institutional rhetoric and economic data related to the shifts in government both India (from 2014-2024) and U.S (from 2018-2024).

Foreword

When countries engage in trade with one another, they build not only economic interdependence but also mutual trust and cooperation. Historically, trade has served as a powerful tool for diplomacy. In today's globalized world, strengthening trade relationships is essential for maintaining global stability. When approached strategically, trade should not be a precursor to conflict, but rather a foundation for long-term peace and sustainable international partnerships.

Although not without flaws, the World Trade Organization (WTO) plays a vital role in promoting global trade and maintaining a balanced distribution of goods and services among its member nations. Over the past decade, the global shift from open markets toward protectionism has generated considerable uncertainty for both Global North and Global South nations. Its relevance is now jeopardized with increased protectionism.

The United States and China, two of the world's largest economies, were among the first to be embroiled in a trade war, primarily due to a substantial trade imbalance between the two countries. While this imbalance appears significant on paper, it is not an insurmountable issue. The prolonged nature of the dispute underscores its geopolitical underpinnings, rather than being solely driven by geoeconomic concerns. The current trade war goes beyond China and the U.S., resulting in a systematic change and even reset of the global trade systems.

The book 'Geopolitical and Economic Consequences of Trade Policies and Tariffs' offers a comprehensive analysis of the ongoing trade war from various perspectives. Each chapter, while unique in focus, is cohesively connected to the broader narrative. The understanding of the impact of trade war to countries like Vietnam, Tunesia, Brazil and India give it a broad (and interesting) analysis of how these countries are responding to the trade war.

Another interesting aspect of the book is the fact that recommendations were presented based on two-fold approach: first, how the WTO can continue to be a relevant stakeholder in global trade; and two, how diverse countries can better tackle the current shifts and impacts of the trade war.

Dr. Renata Thiébaut, Dr. Marc Selgas-Cors, and their co-authors have produced a commendable work in creating such a thorough and insightful volume. The book not only elucidates the profound shifts occurring in the global economic landscape but also proposes practical solutions to these complex challenges.

In an increasingly fragmented world, it is imperative to harness the power of trade to foster cooperation among nations. Should global leadership embrace this path, we may yet achieve widespread prosperity. Otherwise, we risk facing a more turbulent and uncertain future.

Shahid Hussain
AI Global Exchange Forum, Saudi Arabia

Preface

In January 2025, Donald J. Trump began his second term as U.S. President. On February 1, 2025, the Administration announced tariff actions under IEEPA affecting Mexico, Canada, and China, subsequently expanded and adjusted over 2025, marking the continuation of his distinctive "America First" approach. His administration swiftly initiated a trade war with neighboring countries Mexico and Canada, driven by concerns over the fentanyl crisis and persistent trade imbalances. This was followed by the imposition of tariffs on imports from China, Australia, and several other countries, justified by rhetoric emphasizing trade imbalances and the need for the U.S. to reconstruct its manufacturing capabilities. These actions signaled a significant escalation in protectionist trade policies, reshaping relations with traditional allies and resulting in far-reaching implications for global economic stability. The trade war has now gained global attention, being a multidisciplinary topic that impacts the historical achievements of international trade, posing challenges to existing frameworks of global trade.

The evolution of global trade was marked by the inauguration of the World Trade Organization (WTO) in 1995. The organization plays a critical role in safeguarding trade rules based on core principles: (a) non-discrimination (Most-Favored-Nation and National Treatment); (b) reciprocity; (c) binding and enforceable commitments; (d) transparency; and (e) safety valves to protect domestic industries. The current model of international trade, however, is under strain due to protectionist headwinds and institutional gridlock. In Adam Smith's own words:

> *"It is the maxim of every prudent master of a family, never to attempt to make at home what it will cost him more to make than to buy."*
>
> *– Adam Smith, The Wealth of Nations, Book IV, Chapter II*

This sentiment reflects the growing disillusionment with the uneven benefits of globalization, particularly as trade wars expose the vulnerabilities and inequities inherent in the global trade system, which ultimately impact consumers.

KEY CHALLENGES AND REFLECTIONS

During the development of this book, multiple shifts in the global trade war were observed, rendering its outcome and effects on the trade balances of individual nations difficult to predict. It was indeed a challenge to keep all facts up to date in order to provide current and in-depth analysis of the trade war and its implications across the globe.

This underscores the importance of this work as a multidisciplinary study that approaches the subject from diverse perspectives. Despite the increasing significance of such trade conflicts, few comprehensive studies have focused on this topic within the current global trade environment. This book is not only timely but also presents a wide range of topics impacted by current trade dynamics, written by authors with core expertise across various industries.

This book aims to fill a notable gap in the existing literature on contemporary trade wars, particularly in the geopolitical and economic consequences of the United States' trade policies under Trump's second term. It explores not only the immediate consequences of these conflicts but also their long-term implications for global trade dynamics, international alliances, and economic governance.

The book also illuminates potential future trajectories of global trade, providing nuanced policy recommendations designed to navigate and mitigate escalating trade tensions. By integrating rigorous analysis with strategic foresight, it aims to equip policymakers and scholars with actionable insights for fostering resilient and equitable international trade relations.

CONCEPTUAL FOUNDATION

The authors bring extensive knowledge and diverse perspectives on the trade war. Dedicated chapters focus on regions such as Asia, and Africa to provide an in-depth understanding of geoeconomic strategies and the potential effects of trade wars on their economies, amid a significant shift in their trade relations with the United States.

The authors provide a rich and multifaceted exploration of the trade war, particularly in terms of how countries intersect with geopolitics, economic policy, regional responses, supply chains, and global institutions. The book begins with the historical background of trade developments, the importance of the WTO, and then discusses the current global trade war initiated by Donald J. Trump with most countries around the globe.

Examining the trade war through various lenses is crucial to understanding its complex and far-reaching impact. This volume offers a regional perspective, with chapters examining how diverse countries have responded to global trade tensions. For instance, Africa's approach is explored through the lens of the African Continental Free Trade Area (AfCFTA), highlighting efforts to strengthen intra-continental trade and reduce reliance on external partners. In Asia, the focus shifts to how U.S. tariff policies have reshaped trade strategies and political alignments, particularly in China and emerging Asian economies.

China is given particular attention due to its central role in the contemporary trade war landscape. Several chapters delve into China's geopolitical strategy, its approach to critical mineral exports, and its broader efforts to strike a balance between strategic autonomy and global influence. These analyses offer insight into how China has transitioned beyond reactive trade policy and established itself as a proactive, rule-setting power.

A sectoral breakdown of the trade war reveals its varied impact across industries. The book examines the impact on oil prices, logistics, and supply chain disruptions, particularly in the context of global uncertainties. It also investigates how media narratives and public opinion shape trade policy debates, reinforcing nationalistic economic agendas. Theoretical foundations of trade wars are critically examined through chapters on the political economy of protectionism and the evolving role of global institutions, such as the WTO, considering potential future developments in international trade governance.

This book is intended for a diverse audience, including academics, policymakers, trade professionals, and graduate students in the fields of international trade, political economy, international relations, and international law studies. As it covers a wide range of topics, it provides readers with a comprehensive overview of the current state of international trade.

Its innovative aspect makes a meaningful contribution to the ongoing discourse on trade wars, offering both theoretical insights and real-world case studies, while challenging conventional narratives and proposing critical reflections on the future of trade governance. It indeed serves as a valuable resource for those shaping, studying, or navigating the complexities of global trade policy in the 21st century.

OVERVIEW OF CHAPTERS

Chapter 1: The Evolution of Global Trade in the 21st Century

Renata Thiébaut

The trade war initiated by Donald J. Trump against China during his first term has taken on a global character in 2025. While the main goal was to decrease trade deficits, his administration sought to increase industrialization in the country by promoting American-first protagonism. This book chapter's primary objective is to understand the main reasons that led to the ongoing trade war, as well as to examine the growing challenges to the legitimacy of the WTO and existing international trade rules, which are founded on the core principles of non-discrimination, National Treatment, and fairness. Finally, it examines the increasing significance of new international actions in global trade like the BRICS+, not only to comprehend its key aspects of trade wars but also to lay the groundwork for future discussions, such as new compliance mechanisms, and WTO reform.

Chapter 2: The Political Economy of Trade Wars

Ann Cherian, Kamal Kumar Rajagopalan, Sumanta Bhattacharya, Satish Pawar, Nilesh Anute, Selvakumar P, Manjunath T.C.

In the complex web of global economics, few concepts have sparked as much debate, policy intervention, and public interest as trade. Trade—the exchange of goods, services, and capital across international borders—has long been championed as a driver of economic growth, innovation, and international cooperation. Since the end of World War II, the global economic order has largely trended toward liberalization, fostering a rules-based system designed to reduce tariffs, eliminate trade barriers, and integrate markets across continents. Institutions like the General Agreement on Tariffs and Trade (GATT), and later the World Trade Organization (WTO), were created to promote free trade principles and resolve disputes within a structured framework. This post-war period of globalization ushered in unprecedented levels of economic interdependence, transforming domestic economies and reshaping geopolitical alliances. In the intervention, and public interest as trade.

Chapter 3: The Empire Strikes Back: U.S. Hegemony and its Influence on the WTO

Juliana Florentina Fernandes Leao, Roberto Alexandre Zanchetta Borghi

This chapter analyzes the transformation of U.S. trade policy from 2016 to 2025, focusing on the erosion of its multilateral leadership, particularly within the World Trade Organization (WTO). Drawing from Giovanni Arrighi's theory of global hegemony, it explores the ideological and material foundations of American dominance and the systemic contradictions exposed by rising protectionism. Emphasizing the role of China's ascent and institutional strain, the study argues that the U.S. shift reflects a structural reconfiguration of global trade governance rather than a temporary deviation. The analysis traces historical developments, theoretical foundations, and recent policy shifts under Donald Trump's two administrations.

Chapter 4: Beyond WTO TFA: Building Digital Trust and Transparency in Fragmented Trade

Aleksandr Orel, Aleksei Bondarenko, Anton Kozhankov

This chapter examines why, in an era of trade fragmentation, regulatory divergence, and the shift toward data-driven commerce, it has become necessary to move beyond the WTO Trade Facilitation Agreement (TFA). It analyzes how geopolitical tensions, ESG disclosure requirements, export controls, and differences in rules of origin increase compliance complexity and costs. The chapter highlights the limitations of the current TFA, which was designed for a pre-digital era, and argues for the creation of trusted, interoperable digital trade frameworks, cross-border data exchange, and the use of verifiable digital credentials to ensure transparency, predictability, and inclusion in trade. Drawing on examples from various regions, the chapter demonstrates how emerging technologies can help reduce both physical and digital trade barriers. In conclusion, it outlines key principles for a WTO TFA 2.0 that reflects the realities of modern, trust-based, and sustainable global trade.

Chapter 5: U.S. Trade Policy and Reciprocal Tariffs: The Trade War and Its Impact on Future Trade Policies in Asian Countries

Susanna Hartanto

The trade war between the United States and china has opened strategic opportunities to increase the economic market in Asian countries. United States trading partners are expected to retaliate to protect domestic industries and recover nominal income. This would cause further harm to United States economic growth and income, slowing global economic growth with the negative impact intensifying when tariffs extend to free trade agreement partners and prompt retaliation. This study used the literature research method. The research analyzes information about the trade war that happened between the United States of America and other Asian countries, especially with China, which has a long history of trade war and discussed the effect of United States reciprocal tariff on trade policies and tariff to Asian countries. Trump's program would not only cause grave damage to the United States economy. These policies would actually benefit other countries, including most countries in Asia.

Chapter 6: AfCFTA as a Strategic Response to Trade Wars: Reinventing Africa's Role in the Global Economy

Beryl OLubandwa

This chapter examines the African Continental Free Trade Area (AfCFTA) as a crucial instrument for addressing global trade challenges, including the surge in protectionist policies observed during the COVID-19 pandemic. This analysis employs geoeconomics, strategic trade theory, and new regionalism to examine how the AfCFTA can enhance Africa's economic strength and independence. The chapter examines policy frameworks and case studies from Ghana, South Africa, Nigeria, and Kenya, as well as insights from various regional trade agreements, including RCEP, USMCA, and MERCOSUR. The chapter suggests that the AfCFTA could enhance Africa's position in global trade negotiations, foster regional value chains, and consolidate the continent's markets. The chapter concludes with a helpful framework that policymakers, development partners, and institutions can utilize to safeguard Africa against external shocks through the AfCFTA.

Chapter 7: Geopolitical Risk, Variability of Oil Price and the Global Trade Uncertainty: An Economic Perspective

Piyali Roy Chowdhury

Oil prices are the outcome of a highly integrated, dynamic global system. With geopolitical risk and trade policy uncertainty contribute to the volatile world markets, the study analyses the impact of geopolitical risk, trade policy uncertainty on crude oil price globally. It considers data from 2000 to 2023 and finds out systematic link between the three variables. The data proved a long run impact of trade policy uncertainty and geopolitical risk on the crude oil. This enhances the influence of the variables and leads to implementation of policy measures in global markets. The data are tested through Auto Regressive Distributed Lag (ARDL) model and checked for long run cointegration and short run association. The policy, thus, has been suggested as to improve the transition towards sustainability globally. Though the impact of geopolitical risk and trade policy uncertainty is not strong on crude oil price in world market, it can affect the short run volatility. Thus, mitigation, diversification and transparency are the key factors to strengthen the existing situation in world.

Chapter 8: China's Geopolitical Strategy in Trade Policy: Navigating Strategic Autonomy and Global Influence

Marc Selgas-Cors

This chapter examines the geopolitical dimensions of China's trade policy by analyzing how the People's Republic of China strategically leverages trade as an instrument of power to achieve greater strategic autonomy and expand its global influence in a rapidly shifting international order, particularly in the face of escalating tensions with the United States; it explores core policy instruments such as the Belt and Road Initiative, the Dual Circulation Strategy, and the Digital Silk Road, while also evaluating China's engagement with multilateral institutions, its efforts to securitize key supply chains, and its ambitions to reform global trade governance, concluding that China's trade strategy should be understood not merely as economic policy but as an integrated component of a grand geopolitical strategy aimed at reshaping the global order in line with its normative preferences and long-term interests.

Chapter 9: Is China an Honest Trade Broker?

Jeremy Levine

The story of modern China can be traced back to Deng Xiaoping, who challenged the Chinese people to do even better than Japan did with the Meiji Restoration. The end result has been over forty years of extraordinary economic growth and China rising to become the second-largest economy in the world with hundreds of millions of people lifted out of poverty. Its share of global trade has also risen significantly over the past four decades with the help of special economic zones being established, along with becoming a member of the World Trade Organization and more recently the Belt and Road Initiative. But the rise of China has not occurred without suspicions and concerns along the way. From cyber espionage and stealing trade secrets to Taiwan and the militarization of the South China Sea, questions remain about China's true intentions and if it is trying to rise peacefully or overturn the liberal order. This chapter explores the history of China's rise to global superpower status and if China can be considered an honest trade broker and member of the global community under Xi Jinping.

Chapter 10: China's Critical Mineral and EV Exports to the U.S. and Brazil: Geopolitical and Economic Implications Amid Rising Tariffs

José Floriano Lima Filho

This chapter analyzes the geopolitical and economic implications of China's critical mineral and electric vehicle (EV) exports to the United States and Brazil amidst rising tariffs. Critical minerals are essential for the global green energy transition, particularly for EV batteries and renewable energy infrastructure. China has become the dominant force across the entire critical minerals supply chain, from raw material extraction to high-tech component manufacturing, and is the world's largest exporter of EVs. The U.S. has imposed substantial tariffs on Chinese imports. Brazil, with its significant critical mineral reserves, has adopted a phased import tax system for EVs. The intensifying competition for critical minerals, exacerbated by the U.S.-China trade war, presents a "Green Paradox," where the pursuit of clean energy risks environmental degradation. Ultimately, unilateral trade measures are insufficient to address supply chain vulnerabilities and environmental costs, underscoring the necessity for multilateral cooperation.

Chapter 11: The European Union's Geopolitical Role in the Era of Trade Wars

Marc Selgas-Cors

In a world increasingly defined by great-power rivalry and economic coercion, the European Union (EU) is reshaping its trade policy to serve not only economic growth but strategic geopolitical objectives. Anchored in a realist international relations framework, the analysis traces how the EU is transitioning from a normative promoter of global trade rules to a more assertive, interest-driven actor capable of wielding economic tools to defend sovereignty, exert influence, and mitigate external threats. The paper examines this shift through five interrelated domains: (1) the internal foundations of the EU's single market and regulatory power; (2) its strategic posture vis-à-vis the United States, China, and Russia; (3) its emerging instruments of economic statecraft, such as the Carbon Border Adjustment Mechanism and the Anti-Coercion Instrument; (4) the geopolitical implications for the Global South; and (5) its attempts to stabilize a fragmented multilateral order. Drawing on official EU documents, think tank reports, and recent academic literature (2022–2025).

Chapter 12: The 'Newest Great Game': West-Russia Rivalry over Trade Tariffs in Central Asia

Ahmet Turan

The ongoing rivalry among major powers in Central Asia is driven by the region's strategic importance and abundant natural resources. Recent tensions between Russia and the West over trade tariffs have led to the emergence of a new arena for economic and political struggle in the region. The present study examines the dynamics of this competition, which is referred to as 'The New Great Game' and analyses the impact of trade policies on regional alliances and economic dependency relationships. The imposition of protectionist tariffs by Russia, implemented through the Eurasian Economic Union (EAEU), and the adoption of free trade and investment strategies by the West, targeting the region, are among the primary strategies that are deepening this competition. This article examines how Central Asian countries navigate great power competition through balancing strategies and explores the potential impact of global trade wars on regional economies. It argues that this contest will significantly shape the region's geopolitical future beyond trade tariffs.

Chapter 13: Global Trends in Logistics: The Impact of the U.S. Trade War on Supply Chains

Ahlem Hamri, Rafaa Mraihi

Global Conflicts are major factors contributing to supply chain disruptions. In the one hand countries works to improve transport and logistics infrastructures to promote trade and world connections, in the other hand, they implement export bans, tariffs, or embargoes, trade restrictions and sanctions come into effect, limiting access to essential resources and materials. Trump's tariff measures give a significant collapse of the multilateral trading framework, revealing the vulnerability of global economic governance and disproportionately impacting developing nations through 'reciprocal' tariffs. The protectionist measures announced by Trump stipulated an increase in customs duties on goods imported from different countries. Therefore, this chapter proposes to study the relationship between logistics and trade. Indeed, the objective is to better understand the effect of the logistics sector on trade. Then to study the repercussions of US Trade Wars especially the impact of Trump's tariffs on global logistics and supply chains.

Chapter 14: Trade War: Trump's Trade Policy and Its Impact on the International Economy

Raquel León De La Rosa, Misael González Ramírez

The return of Donald Trump has marked a key moment for the international system. The establishment of a system of reciprocal tariffs has had an impact on the international economy. This paper aims to identify the main effects of the trade war between the United States and China on the international economic system. The concept of trade war is rescued, as well as some trends on trade policy (Ripsman, 2006), globalization (Rodrik, 2007) and securitization (de Goede, 2017) to understand the economic dynamics of the international system. The proposed methodology is a network analysis (Granovetter, 2012) based on the exports and imports of the world's 40 main economies. With this, a series of categories are proposed to identify the adaptability of economies to the reciprocal tariffs imposed by the United States. The categories are commercial diversification, specialization of exportable supply, strategic industries and position within global value chains. Among the findings, it discusses the role of China, India, Japan and South Korea as key Indo-Pacific nodes.

Chapter 15: The Dynamics of Global Trade Under Protectionism and Populism: A Comparative Study of United States and India

Safa Ahmad

Two of the world's largest democracies United States and India have a robust and progressing trade partnership, which has deepened over the years. This paper investigates the evolving dynamics of their global trade under the influence of protectionism and populism. In recent years both the countries are focusing more on their national interests and economic self reliance, rather than heavily relying on global trade or free market globalisation. However, there is an increased skepticism towards liberal economic globalisation, because both the nations have witnessed drastic political and economic shifts driven by the populist leaders and their strategic directives. This research takes on a comparative approach on exploring the political economy of both the nations. This study underlines how domestic political narratives shape international trade participation, through scrutinizing key trade policies, institutional rhetoric and economic data with the shift in government in both India (from 2014-2024) and U.S (from 2018-2024).

FINAL ACKNOWLEDGEMENTS

The Editors, Dr. Renata Thiébaut and Marc Selgas-Cors, with their wealth of knowledge and expertise in global trade, have curated the chapters to provide readers with in-depth information throughout the exploration of case studies in diverse sectors and in diverse regions. They challenge readers to envision a future of global trade where robust and fair mechanisms uphold the principles of global trade, ensuring a world where sustainable, equitable, and enduring countries' trade relations are not just aspirations, but realities that safeguard prosperity for generations to come.

Dr. Renata Thiébaut and Dr. Marc Selgas-Cors, would like to extend their sincere appreciation to all authors for their esteemed contributions. Their diverse backgrounds were paramount in providing a holistic understanding of the global trade war through multiple parameters, which greatly contributed to the significance, uniqueness, and international scope of this book. Appreciation is extended to all institutions involved, particularly to IGI Global, for embracing our project and providing invaluable support throughout the publication of this book.

Chapter 1
The Evolution of Global Trade in the 21st Century

Renata Thiébaut
https://orcid.org/0000-0003-1529-3451
AI Global Exchange Forum, Canada

ABSTRACT

The trade war initiated by Donald J. Trump against China during his first term has taken on a global character in 2025. While the main goal was to decrease trade deficits, his administration sought to increase industrialization in the country by promoting American-first protagonism. This book chapter's primary objective is to understand the main reasons that led to the ongoing trade war, as well as to examine the growing challenges to the legitimacy of the WTO and existing international trade rules, which are founded on the core principles of non-discrimination, National Treatment, and fairness. Finally, it examines the increasing significance of new international actions in global trade like the BRICS+, not only to comprehend its key aspects of trade wars but also to lay the groundwork for future discussions, such as new compliance mechanisms, and WTO reform.

1. INTRODUCTION

While historically shaped by the divides of colonization, Global South countries are increasingly leveraging bilateral and multilateral mechanisms to pursue new pathways for economic growth. Benefiting from lower overall operational costs, including raw materials, inputs, and labor compared to Global North countries, those that invested in developing export-oriented manufacturing capabilities in the 20th century have been better positioned to emerge as prominent players in global trade.

DOI: 10.4018/979-8-3373-3835-4.ch001

It could be argued that World War II was the cornerstone of modern global trade as well as its new configurations through the formation of regional and global alliances.

According to Ortiz-Ospina et al. (2014), global trade expanded in two distinct waves: the first ranging from the 19th century to the period preceding World War II, and the second wave from the beginning in the post-war era and continuing to the present day. Both periods were influenced by globalization.

In the 19th century, trade was shaped by imperialism and intra-European exchange. Intra-European trade primarily involved the exchange of manufactured goods as countries would build their trade capabilities based on their competitive advantage. Moreover, with the rise of European imperialism, global trade followed a colonial pattern that created structural imbalances, as colonized countries were relegated to the production of raw materials and commodities. This model was increasingly undermined by the rise of economic nationalism, contributing to a decline in commodity prices and exports, and ultimately leading to a period of post-war economic austerity (Ortiz-Ospina et al., 2014).

The second wave aligned with the emergence of the 'Golden Age of Capitalism', where the Bretton Woods adjustment period suggested the 're-set' of the finance system, alongside global economic and trade reconstruction. It was within this context that Bretton Woods institutions, such as the World Bank and International Monetary Fund were founded. During the Bretton Wood Conference held in the United States in 1944, global trade was a widely discussed topic, and the institutionalization discussions through the International Trade Organization (ITO) was short-lived. The ITO did not come into existence due to its complex scope, however, which was replaced by the GATT (General Agreement on Tariffs and Trade), which was formed through rounds of negotiations, having thus limited capabilities and provisional agreement to expedite the trade governance (Dadush & Dominguez Prost, 2023). The GATT came into force on January 1, 1948, under a "Protocol of Provisional Application". The need to regulate global trade became increasingly important to support global economic growth, while supporting the premise that developing countries were passive to trade disadvantages.

Table 1. Economic Development Stages

Economic Development Stages	Characteristics
Early stage	● Agriculture and/or resource-based economy. Countries often lack significant capital for industrialization and/or have scored low in the Human Development Index (HDI).
Economic take-off	● Agriculture and/or resource-based economy, beginning of industrialization. ● Countries may be accumulating capital for industrialization and are likely to still scoring relatively low in the Human Development Index (HDI), though improvements may be starting.
Economic moving towards maturity	● Higher economic diversification with the shift from dependence on one sector. ● Higher level of technological advancements.
Advanced stage of economic development	● Economic transition to Service and Knowledge-Based Economies based on innovation-driven growth. ● High levels of technological advancement, significant human capital development, and high Human Development Index (HDI) scores.

Source: Own author (adapted from Rostow's Five Stages of Economic Growth and Development)

In economies facing lower levels of development, the export of low-value goods, such as natural resources and agricultural commodities, has historically been a dominant economic activity. Several of these countries faced the consequences of colonization, having most of their trade activities built upon the relations with their colonizers (Acemoglu & Robinson, 2017), and "(...) forced into foreign market structures" (Han, 2023). This reliance characterized them as 'developing economies,' contributing to a consequential delay in their industrialization and broader economic diversification due to trade reliance, lack of infrastructure and technological costs.

Economic take-off countries have on the other hand, experienced periods of 'economic boom' as a result of strong government policies that drove export-oriented industrialization. Taiwan, South Korea, Hong Kong, and Singapore (named as Asian Tigers) faced economic and societal transformations between 1970 and 1990 which led to increased GDP growth, which, according to Han (2023) encompassed social, cultural, historical contexts. Confucianism has also largely contributed to a propitious business-oriented environment, which posits that Confucianism and its core values, such as "stability, diligence, loyalty, and respect for authority-influencing corporate and political institutions to support developmentalism" (Han, 2023). Amsden (1990) underscores that "(...) exports have been pivotal in the rapid economic expansion of all the East Asian countries". They have now moved from the Economic take-off stage and to the Advanced stage of economic development, due to early investments in export-oriented manufacturing and technological developments.

The United States is an example of a service-oriented economy. Fordism, one of the main systems of industrial production with global implications, was responsible for an era of mass production in the country in 1913/1914 (Amsden, 1990). This shift was paramount for the country to achieve an advanced stage of economic development resulting in increasing efficiency. The combination of a growing middle class and consumerism led the country to become the largest economy globally.

An in-depth study of the evolution of the American economy is crucial to understand the global trade dynamics in the 21st century and the creation of a linkage with the current global trade war. Fordism was characterized by vertically integrated companies that controlled most or all aspects of production. This industrial model was later applied to 'offshoring' manufacturing and implemented in developing economies that were in the early stages of building their own manufacturing capabilities. These countries benefited from inexistence or weak labor laws as well as lower operational costs compared to more developed economies. As a consequence, companies from developed countries shifted their production to leverage these factors.

2. THE CHINESE ECONOMIC MODEL

China has become an 'example to follow' in the Global South. After years of economic challenges and widespread famine caused by civil war, the "Reform and Opening Up" policies announced by Deng Xiaoping in late 1978 signaled the start of China's transition toward a market-oriented economy. Some key items have contributed to trade developed in the countries, that then became lessons learned in other countries.

First, a series of reforms initiated during the Mao Zedong era that encompassed "land reform and redistribution, substantial investments in heavy industry, public health, literacy, electrification, and transportation (that) gave China a substantial leg up" (Kuo, 2025). These initiatives were crucial to reduce the reliance on state-owned enterprises (SOEs) (Dorn, 2023), enabling more private enterprises to emerge.

Second, the 'Four Modernizations' focused on advancing agriculture, industry, national defense and science and technology. The attraction of direct investments (FDIs) facilitated by tax incentives, contributed to increasing the country's foreign capital (Kuo, 2025). The Special Economic Zones (SEZs) became catalysts of FDIs, also serving as 'export hubs'.

Third, the strengthening of the manufacturing industry to be export oriented. One of the core pillars of manufacturing in China was the level of specialization the country achieved in order not to rely on the manufacturing of a single product.

Hollweg (2019) adds that

"The increase in China's domestic value added in exports arose from an expansion of fabrication activities in provinces such as Guangdong, Jiangsu, and Zhejiang (...) However, there is a clear sub-national variation in domestic value added

from activities in exports. Richer provinces increasingly specialized in higher value added activities including R&D and sales and marketing, particularly Beijing, Tianjin, and Shanghai (...) (Hollweg, 2019).

China has become the main exporter globally due to the combination of diverse factors namely effective policies, low costs of production, productivity growth and access to technology through initial technology transfer (ESCAP, 2019). They served global and domestic demands: while China built robust industries, the economy gradually transitioned from being agricultural-based to an innovation-driven one. It is worth noting that China is a Global South, however, as pointed out in literature, its 'unprecedented economic development' resulted in the country becoming one of the main 'rivals' of the United States in global trade.

3. THE EXPORT RELIANCE CHALLENGE

The structural transformation of national economies is intrinsically related to their integration into the global trading system. As the world became increasingly globalized, with an eventual decrease in trade barriers, countries enjoyed better chances to enhance their export capabilities to increase foreign exchange earnings. It is for this reason that several developing countries were and still are reliant on exports to be one of the largest contributors to their GDP growth.

Table 2. Exports of goods and services (% of GDP) - Above 70%

Country Most Recent Year	Most Recent Value
Luxembourg 2024	215.5
San Marino 2022	197.4
Hong Kong SAR, China 2024	181.7
Singapore 2024	178.8
Djibouti 2024	160.8
Ireland 2024	147.6
Malta 2024	123.5
United Arab Emirates 2023	108.6
Virgin Islands (U.S.) 2022	97.4
Cyprus 2024	96.7
Macao SAR, China 2024	89.8
Aruba 2023	88.3
Bahrain 2023	87.4

continued on following page

Table 2. Continued

Country Most Recent Year	Most Recent Value
Viet Nam 2023	86.5
Slovak Republic 2024	85.2
Seychelles 2024	85.2
Guyana 2005	84.6
Netherlands 2024	84.1
Slovenia 2024	81.5
Belgium 2024	79.2
Armenia 2024	76.3
Estonia 2024	76.3
Libya 2024	74.8
Hungary 2024	74.7
Maldives 2023	74.4
Brunei Darussalam 2024	74.3
Lithuania 2024	74.1
Papua New Guinea 2004	72.2
Switzerland 2024	72.2
Cambodia 2024	71.4
Malaysia 2024	71.4
Thailand 2024	

Source: Country official statistics, National Statistical Organizations and/or Central Banks; National Accounts data files, Organisation for Economic Co-operation and Development (OECD); Staff estimates, World Bank (WB)

The high percentage of exports of goods and services as a proportion of GDP indicates that the country is highly reliant on international trade. As presented in the list, developed and developed countries have a percentage higher than 70%. The basket of exports is what defines domestic technological capabilities and exports of low or value-added products. Nonetheless, the global trade war and implication of tariffs by the United States directly affect their trade surplus with the United States, strongly affecting their GDP growth if there is a strong reliance on the exports to the American market.

There is the need to analyze data through microscopic lenses of a series of datasets, such as bilateral data between individual countries and the U.S., the imposition of tariff percentages also applied to individual countries, and the trade basket, among others; to understand the importance of trade and how the trade war can disrupt current trade scenario.

In addition, a study published by the World Trade Organization underscored the upsurge of global value chains as the main pillar to the integration of developing countries in their economic growth as well as being a contributor for their relevance in global trade (Hollweg, 2019). Trade growth was possible due to a reduction in transaction costs resulting from technological advances and the improvement of productivity (Ortiz-Ospina et al., 2014).

The changes of trade dynamics which contributed to American companies relocating to developing countries, the growing importance of China to the global stage, which dethroned the U.S. as the largest exporter globally.

Figure 1. World trade of Merchandise and Services

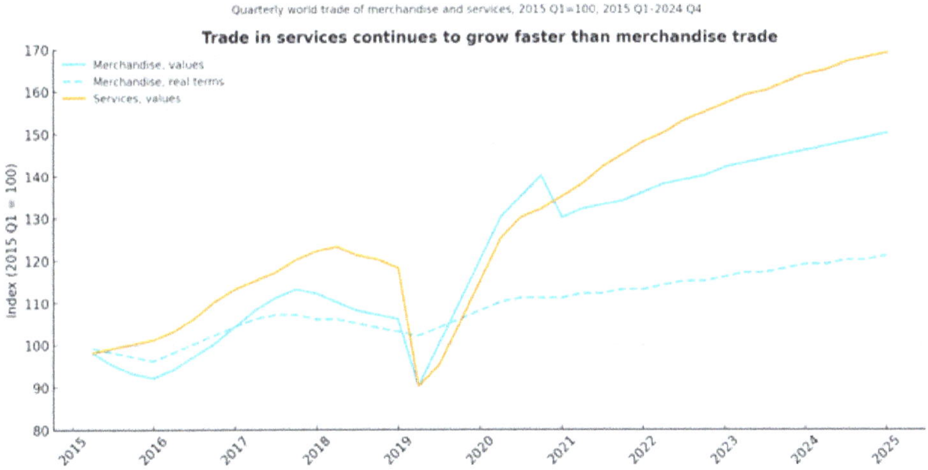

Source: UN Trade and Development (UNCTAD) calculations based on UNCTADstat database

Developing countries relied on export-led manufacturing growth trade, but trade in services, on the other hand, is projected to expand faster and bring a higher impact to global trade. In other words, developed economies which are leading in artificial intelligence will be at advantage, jeopardizing the development of developing countries "(...) to advance from low- to high-productivity economic activities" (UNCTAD, 2024).

3.1 Trade Relations Through Alliances

Regional and global alliances have provided emerging markets with new trade opportunities. Their legitimacy would include the formation of a designated zone with lower or higher levels of integration specified through an agreement. The European Union is today the most economically integrated bloc, allowing free mobility and the adoption of a common currency after the accession process is concluded. The latest and largest alliance globally, the Comprehensive and Progressive Agreement for Trans-Pacific Partnership (CPTPP), promotes free trade among its eleven members, which differs from the European Union which adopts regional characteristics and serves countries across continents (Dadush & Dominguez Prost, 2023). These economic blocs allow members to harmonize trade policies, unified tariff schemes and promote cooperation in fields beyond trade. These are only two examples of several economic blocs existing across the globe. However, following the success of the Asian Tigers and eventually China and other emerging economies to gain momentum in global trade, several informal alliances arose along the years. Below is a list of informal alliances (or acronyms) coined by banks and economists during the 2000s-2010s:

1. MIST: Mexico, Indonesia, South Korea, Turkey.
2. MINT: Mexico, Indonesia, Nigeria, Turkey.
3. Next 11: Bangladesh, Egypt, Indonesia, Iran, Mexico, Nigeria, Pakistan, Philippines, Turkey, South Korea, Vietnam.
4. EAGLEs: Brazil, China, Egypt, India, Indonesia, South Korea, Mexico, Russia, Taiwan, and Turkey.
5. CIVETS: Colombia, Indonesia, Vietnam, Egypt, Turkey, South Africa.
6. SANE: South Africa, Algeria, Nigeria, Egypt.
7. TIMPs: Turkey, Indonesia, Mexico, Philippines.
8. BBVA EAGLEs (Emerging and Growth-Leading Economies): countries expected to contribute significantly to global economic growth over the next decade (excluding developed economies).
9. VISTA: Vietnam, Indonesia, South Africa, Turkey, Argentina.

Since 2009, the BRIC has been in the spotlight, due to the growing GDP of Brazil, Russia, India and China as well as their relative importance on the global stage. South Africa, the last member to join the BRICS, is a strategic member that represents the Africa continent, rich in resources and essential for the BRICS influence (Carducci & Bruno, 2014, 49).

The inauguration of the BRICS Bank in Shanghai in 2015 allowed the members to enhance cooperation in trade as well as investments in infrastructure, among others. Fast forward to 2025, the now BRICS+ has gained several more members and partner countries, totaling nearly 20. The BRICS+ now corresponds to nearly 55% of the world's population and 46% of global GDP based on purchasing power parity (Holtzmann & van der Voort, 2025). The Bank became the most important institution, allowing the purchase of green bonds as well as trade in currencies other than the American dollar, including the Chinese yuan.

Initially the BRICS does not possess legal personality, being purely based on political motivation to enhance cooperation. Its informal aspect was responsible to minimize impediments of cooperation dynamics.

BRICS involves members with different levels of economic development, being an example of transnational cooperation. The Trump administration has frequently voiced protectionism practices against American products by the economic blocs like the European Union, but the BRICS+, alongside China, have become the main rhetoric of the trade war, due to the fact that the alliance challenges the dominance of the U.S. dollar.

Holtzmann & van der Voort (2025) state that

"Just before his inauguration, US President Trump warned that BRICS countries attempting to replace the dollar as a trading currency would face 100% tariffs on their trade with the United States. This threat was made against the backdrop of the BRICS countries' efforts to reduce their dependence on the dollar and promote alternative currencies in international trade. This makes clear the stance that Trump is taking towards the group of states. Russia and China have taken steps in the past to increase the use of national currencies and thus reduce the influence of the dollar (Holtzmann & van der Voort, 2025).

Notably, BRICS+ is the main platform of Global South countries, and the trade war has had the opposite effect, which is to unite them. It is expected that the BRICS+ will issue a statement against Trump's policies in the upcoming 17th BRICS summit held in Brazil (Iglesias, Cele, & Viotti Beck, 2025).

3.2 The role of the World Trade Organization

International trade was propelled by increased globalization, which, in modern history, enabled post-World War economic reconstruction. These periods underscore the importance of maintaining multilateral cooperation platforms. Notwithstanding, intertemporal dynamics should be key contributors to thorough reform to avoid ontological insecurity and eventual irrelevance. Indeed, trade wars such as these pose significant constraints to the survival of normative frameworks, undermining the foundational principles of international trade law as described in the GATT and other binding agreements presented with the WTO preamble.

With the institutionalization of global trade, particularly with the inclusion of provisions that acknowledged the need to better support these countries, they were able to lever from support from the United Nations and World Trade Organization (WTO) through trade-related technical assistance and capacity building programs, as well as enjoying the Special and Differential Treatment (S&D) present in WTO Agreements. Lower tariffs and support to help them build the infrastructure became essential to building a robust trade sector (World Trade Organization, Understanding the WTO: Developing Countries. Overview). The path to development slowly became intertwined with trade exports, generating higher Gross domestic product (GDP).

It goes without saying that protectionist policies, tariff escalations and a trade war have been on the increase. Any attempt to address the protectionism risks associated require an adequate understanding of the multifaceted challenges emerging in the new global economic order. Such challenges can be classified into mainly four categories:

- The challenge of reforming the World Trade Organization (WTO) to ensure greater inclusivity, transparency, and responsiveness to contemporary trade realities.
- The challenge of establishing fair and equitable trading systems that address the structural disadvantages faced by countries in the Global South.
- The challenge of adopting a new approach to international trade that integrates environmental sustainability and digital trade norms.
- The challenge of effectively enforcing international trade rules and upholding the rule of law in an era of increasing unilateralism and geopolitical tension.

By thoroughly investigating Trump's trade policies and the responses from affected countries, this book offers a critical analysis of the current state of global trade and the potential trajectories it may take amid rising protectionism.

4. THE 2025 GLOBAL TRADE WAR AND BEYOND

The founding of GATT and WTO marked an important milestone in international trade. The compliance mechanism implemented at the organization reinforced the commitment to abide by the binding agreement to trade liberalization. For Matto & Staiger (2019), non-compliance with the WTO charter can "(...) pose an existential threat to the rules-based multilateral trading system" (Mattoo & Staiger, 2019).

Tariff increases began during Trump's first term, with $380 billion in tariffs imposed between 2018 and 2019. The Biden administration maintained most of these tariffs and, in May 2024, announced an additional $18 billion in tariffs on Chinese goods, including semiconductors and electric vehicles (Wiley, 2024). Under the second Trump administration, tariffs expanded to cover $1.4 trillion in imports. Overall, the average U.S. tariff rate is expected to rise from 2.5% in 2024 to 8.4% by 2026, the highest level since 1946 (York & Durante, 2025).

The revenue generated from these tariff hikes is projected to increase after-tax incomes by 1% in 2026. Due mainly to the tariffs, the OECD has downgraded economic growth forecasts for several countries:

- Canada: Expected to grow by 0.7% in 2024 and 2026, down from the previous estimate of 2%.
- Mexico: Projected to contract by 1.3% in 2024 and shrink another 0.6% in 2025, compared to previous growth estimates of 1.2% and 1.6%.
- U.S.: Growth revised to 2.2% in 2024 and 1.6% in 2026, down from 2.4% and 2.1% (OECD, 2025).

Currently, the EU has only been affected by tariffs on steel and aluminum. However, these tariffs are significant enough that the EU has announced countermeasures, which will take effect by mid-April (April 13th). Most countries, including the EU, China, and especially Canada, have announced countermeasures and will continue to raise their tariffs in response to U.S. actions. This escalation has significant economic implications, but what does it mean for the AI industry? Currently, the EU significantly relies on the U.S. for various critical sectors, with artificial intelligence (AI) being a prominent example. Most leading technology companies are based in the U.S., and these companies are increasingly engaging with AI, thereby concentrating a substantial portion of the global AI industry within the US. This dynamic has led to a situation where most of the world's major AI companies are headquartered in the U.S.

The Trump administration aimed to disrupt these established global supply chains and incentivize companies to reshore production to the United States. While the trade war was first initiated against China in 2018 to detain China's trade imbalance and dominance, during his second mandate, trade war gained global aspects, reconsidering its strategies with most countries that the U.S. has trade deficits with.

While at the present moment it is not possible to predict its outcomes, the respect to internal trade laws abiding by all members of the WTO is crucial to the future of the institute as the main body to safeguard trade activities, as well as giving continuity to the promotion of fair-trade practices.

5. CONCLUSION

After World War II, countries sought to develop and form diverse arrangements, resulting in the emergence of economic trade blocs, initially regional-based, that gained a more international shape, as seen in the Comprehensive and Progressive Agreement for Trans-Pacific Partnership (CPTPP) case. Furthermore, in the early 2000s, several trade alliances emerged, contributing to the evolution of trade and creating new possibilities through informal settings, as opposed to institutionalized economic blocs. BRICS (and now BRICS+) is a notable example of successful trade cooperation. When Goldman Sachs first coined the term, the emerging markets (Brazil, Russia, India, China, and then the addition of South Africa) leveraged their economic growth to form a platform for cooperation based on mutual interest in sustainable development. The BRICS Bank played and still plays a crucial role in increasing the number of members (both full members and partners) in search of investments.

The fact that BRICS countries have now strengthened trade cooperation, including the possibility of using currencies other than the U.S. dollar, it became one of Trump's primary 'targets' in the trade war. Additionally, China, its economic rival and largest exporter globally, has become one of the prominent members and advocators of the now BRICS+. The opposition of new trade arrangements infringes the free will of countries to form alliances if they do not oppose the WTO charters.

Trade wars challenge existing frameworks, particularly the legitimacy and relevance of the World Trade Organization (WTO), which is the primary organ responsible for safeguarding trade rules. The non-compliance with trade principles, which are binding among its members, can cause an even more profound institutional crisis than what was achieved since the General Agreement on Tariffs and Trade (GATT) came into force in the post-war context.

Currently, the world is more integrated, and economies are more competitive. For this reason, any factor that causes trade disruption through unlawful and unilateral actions means must be regarded as a priority topic for discussions accordingly.

REFERENCES

Acemoglu, D., & Robinson, J. A. (2017, January 30). *The economic impact of colonialism*. VoxEU.org. https://cepr.org/voxeu/columns/economic-impact-colonialism

Amsden, A. H. (1990). Third World industrialization: 'Global Fordism' or a new model? *New Left Review, (I)*/182, 5–31. https://newleftreview.org/issues/i182/articles/alice-h-amsden-third-world-industrialization-global-fordism-or-a-new-model.pdf

Carducci, M., & Bruno, A. S. (2014). The BRICS countries between justice and economy: Methodological challenges on constitutional comparison. *Sociology and Anthropology (Alhambra, Calif.)*, *2*(2), 46–58. https://www.hrpub.org/download/20140105/SA4-19601777.pdf. DOI: 10.13189/sa.2014.020204

Dadush, U., & Dominguez Prost, E. (2023). Preferential trade agreements, geopolitics, and the fragmentation of world trade. *World Trade Review*, *22*(2), 278–294. DOI: 10.1017/S1474745623000022

Dorn, J. A. (2023, October 10). *China's post-1978 economic development and entry into the global trading system*. Cato Institute. https://www.cato.org/publications/chinas-post-1978-economic-development-entry-global-trading-system

Han, D. (2023, January 14). *Economic Grrrowth in the East: Asian Tiger Economies*. JSTOR Daily. https://daily.jstor.org/economic-grrrowth-in-the-east-asian-tiger-economies/

Hollweg, C. H. (2019). *Global value chains and employment in developing economies.*, https://www.wto.org/english/res_e/booksp_e/gvc_dev_report_2019_e_ch3.pdf

Holtzmann, H.-D., & van der Voort, A. (2025, January 28). *BRICS - What are the key issues for 2025?* Friedrich Naumann Foundation for Freedom. https://www.freiheit.org/brics-what-are-key-issues-2025

Iglesias, S., Cele, S., & Viotti Beck, M. (2025, July 3). *BRICS aspires to occupy ground vacated by US under Trump*. Bloomberg. https://www.bloomberg.com/news/articles/2025-07-03/brics-aspires-to-occupy-global-ground-vacated-by-us-under-trump

Kuo, K. (2025, June 19). *How China got rich: A deep dive into China's 40-year history of economic transformation*. World Economic Forum. https://www.weforum.org/stories/2025/06/how-china-got-rich-40-year-history-of-economic-transformation/

Mattoo, A., & Staiger, R. W. (2019, April). *Trade wars: What do they mean? Why are they happening now? What are the costs?* (NBER Working Paper Series, No. 25762). National Bureau of Economic Research. https://www.nber.org/papers/w25762

OECD. (2025, June 3). *OECD Economic Outlook, Volume 2025 Issue 1: Tackling Uncertainty, Reviving Growth.* https://www.oecd.org/en/publications/2025/06/oecd-economic-outlook-volume-2025-issue-1_1fd979a8/full-report/general-assessment-of-the-macroeconomic-situation_3e68d1e3.html

Ortiz-Ospina, E., Beltekian, D., & Roser, M. (2014, April). *Trade and globalization.* Our World in Data. https://ourworldindata.org/trade-and-globalization

UNCTAD. (2024, October 29). *The reshaping of global trade: How developing countries can strategize.* United Nations Conference on Trade and Development. https://unctad.org/news/reshaping-global-trade-how-developing-countries-can-strategize

United Nations Economic and Social Commission for Asia and the Pacific (ESCAP). (2019). *China's economic transformation: Impacts on Asia and the Pacific* (ST/ESCAP/2836). United Nations. https://www.unescap.org/sites/default/files/China%27s%20economic%20transformation_impacts%20on%20Asia%20and%20the%20Pacific.pdf

World Bank. (n.d.). *Exports of goods and services (% of GDP).* World Bank Open Data. Retrieved July 4, 2025, from https://data.worldbank.org/indicator/NE.EXP.GNFS.ZS?end=2024&most_recent_value_desc=true&start=2024&view=map

World Trade Organization. (2015). *Understanding the WTO* (5th ed.). Information and External Relations Division. https://www.wto.org/english/thewto_e/whatis_e/tif_e/understanding_e.pdf

York, E., & Durante, A. (2025, June 2). *Trump tariffs: Tracking the economic impact of the Trump trade war.* Tax Foundation. https://taxfoundation.org/research/all/federal/trump-tariffs-trade-war/

Chapter 2
The Political Economy of Trade Wars

Ann Mary Cherian
https://orcid.org/0009-0002-1452-8941
Christ College, India

Kamal Kumar Rajagopalan
https://orcid.org/0000-0001-8833-0554
P.P. Savani University, India

Sumanta Bhattacharya
https://orcid.org/0000-0003-2563-2787
Asian International University, India

Satish Pawar
https://orcid.org/0000-0003-0098-935X
Balaji College of Arts, Commerce, and Science, India

Nilesh Anute
https://orcid.org/0000-0001-6599-813X
Sri Balaji University, India

P. Selvakumar
https://orcid.org/0000-0002-3650-4548
Department of Science and Humanities, Nehru Institute of Technology, Coimbatore, India

T. C. Manjunath
https://orcid.org/0000-0003-2545-9160
Rajarajeswari College of Engineering, India

ABSTRACT

In the complex web of global economics, few concepts have sparked as much debate, policy intervention, and public interest as trade. Trade—the exchange of goods, services, and capital across international borders—has long been championed as a driver of economic growth, innovation, and international cooperation. Since the end of World War II, the global economic order has largely trended toward liberalization, fostering a rules-based system designed to reduce tariffs, eliminate trade barriers, and integrate markets across continents. Institutions like the General Agreement on Tariffs and Trade (GATT), and later the World Trade Organization (WTO), were created to promote free trade principles and resolve disputes within a structured

DOI: 10.4018/979-8-3373-3835-4.ch002

framework. This post-war period of globalization ushered in unprecedented levels of economic interdependence, transforming domestic economies and reshaping geopolitical alliances.In the intervention, and public interest as trade.

1. INTRODUCTION

In the complex web of global economics, few concepts have sparked as much debate, policy intervention, and public interest as trade. Trade—the exchange of goods, services, and capital across international borders—has long been championed as a driver of economic growth, innovation, and international cooperation. Since the end of World War II, the global economic order has largely trended toward liberalization, fostering a rules-based system designed to reduce tariffs, eliminate trade barriers, and integrate markets across continents. Institutions like the General Agreement on Tariffs and Trade (GATT), and later the World Trade Organization (WTO), were created to promote free trade principles and resolve disputes within a structured framework.

This post-war period of globalization ushered in unprecedented levels of economic interdependence, transforming domestic economies and reshaping geopolitical alliances. In the intervention, and public interest as trade. Trade—the exchange of goods, services, and capital across international borders—has long been championed as a driver of economic growth, innovation, and international cooperation. Since the end of World War II, the global economic order has largely trended toward liberalization, fostering a rules-based system designed to reduce tariffs, eliminate trade barriers, (Aguilera R. et al. 2021) and integrate markets across continents. Institutions like the General Agreement on Tariffs and Trade (GATT), and later the World Trade Organization (WTO), were created to promote free trade principles and resolve disputes within a structured framework. This post-war period of globalization ushered in unprecedented levels of economic interdependence, transforming domestic economies and reshaping geopolitical alliances.

Yet, despite decades of globalization and economic integration, a new wave of protectionism has surged in recent years, challenging the orthodoxy of free trade. Nations around the world are reasserting control over their trade policies, often resorting to tariffs, quotas, and other restrictive measures in an effort to shield domestic industries from foreign competition. This phenomenon—termed “the rise of protectionism”—has catalyzed a resurgence of trade wars, whereby countries retaliate against each other's trade barriers in a spiraling sequence of economic confrontation. Trade wars are not new. History provides several examples of how economic nationalism and protectionist policies have led to intense commercial rivalries between nations, often with damaging consequences.

The Smoot-Hawley Tariff Act of 1930, enacted by the United States during the Great Depression, stands as a stark reminder of how protectionist impulses can backfire, provoking retaliatory tariffs and exacerbating economic downturns. Yet the current wave of trade conflicts is shaped by new dynamics: the growing economic influence of emerging markets like China and India, the strategic competition between the United States and China, rising populism in Western democracies, and concerns over national security, technological supremacy, and economic sovereignty.

In recent years, the U.S.–China trade war has come to symbolize this new era of protectionism. Initiated in 2018 with the imposition of tariffs on billions of dollars' worth of Chinese goods by the United States—ostensibly to address trade imbalances, intellectual property theft, and forced technology transfers—the conflict quickly escalated. China responded in kind, targeting U.S. agricultural products, automobiles, and industrial machinery. The consequences rippled across global supply chains, disrupted markets, and introduced a new era of economic uncertainty (Aguilera R. et al. 2021).

Companies began rethinking supply routes, investors recalibrated risks, and governments reconsidered long-standing trade policies. Underlying the return of trade wars is a complex interplay of economic, political, and ideological forces. Protectionist policies are often justified by their proponents as necessary measures to preserve domestic jobs, support struggling industries, and correct perceived unfair trade practices. In democratic nations, these arguments resonate strongly with voters who feel left behind by globalization and who perceive foreign competition as a threat to their livelihoods.

In authoritarian or state-led economies, trade restrictions may serve broader strategic aims—bolstering national champions, advancing technological independence, or enhancing geopolitical leverage. Moreover, the rise of protectionism reflects deeper shifts in the global order. The post-Cold War consensus favoring liberal economic policies is increasingly under strain. The COVID-19 pandemic accelerated this trend, exposing vulnerabilities in global supply chains and prompting many countries to re-evaluate their dependence on foreign production, especially in critical sectors such as pharmaceuticals, semiconductors, and medical equipment. In parallel, climate change and the push for green technologies have prompted nations to consider trade policies as tools for environmental objectives, sometimes resulting in "green protectionism."

2. THE POLITICAL ECONOMY OF TRADE POLICY: A FRAMEWORK FOR ANALYSIS AND DISCUSSION

The 21st century has ushered in a transformative era for global trade, reshaping the dynamics of international commerce in ways that are both promising and perplexing. With the dawn of the new millennium, globalization intensified, bringing with it rapid economic integration, technological advancement, and the proliferation of cross-border trade. Nations became more interconnected than ever before, (Akkermans J. et al. 2020) forming intricate supply chains that spanned continents and created unprecedented opportunities for growth, innovation, and poverty reduction. Trade liberalization, driven by multilateral agreements and supported by international institutions such as the World Trade Organization (WTO), fostered a system in which goods, services, capital, and ideas could flow more freely across national borders. Yet, even as global trade expanded, new and evolving challenges emerged—testing the resilience, equity, and sustainability of the international trading system.

The 21st century began with considerable optimism regarding the benefits of globalization. Developing countries, especially in Asia, experienced rapid growth due in large part to export-led strategies. China's accession to the WTO in 2001 marked a pivotal moment in global trade, signaling the deeper integration of the world's most populous nation into the global economy. This integration brought vast opportunities: consumers in developed countries gained access to affordable goods, multinational corporations expanded into new markets, and hundreds of millions of people in emerging economies were lifted out of poverty. Simultaneously, technological innovations—particularly in information and communication technologies—lowered transaction costs, enabled real-time trade operations, and made e-commerce a central pillar of modern commerce.

However, the expansion of global trade has not been without controversy or consequence. As the benefits of globalization became more visible, so too did its shortcomings. In many developed nations, segments of the population began to feel that the gains from trade were unevenly distributed. While some industries thrived and consumers enjoyed lower prices, others—particularly traditional manufacturing sectors—struggled in the face of foreign competition.

The resulting job (Akkermans J. et al. 2020) displacements, wage stagnation, and perceived erosion of national sovereignty contributed to a growing backlash against trade liberalization, fueling protectionist sentiment and challenging the political consensus that had underpinned global trade policy for decades. The 2008 global financial crisis marked a turning point in the trajectory of international trade. The crisis not only exposed the vulnerabilities of deeply integrated financial systems but also dampened global demand and led to a significant contraction in trade flows. In its aftermath, governments around the world reassessed the risks of over-dependence on foreign markets. The momentum behind multilateral trade negotiations—such as the Doha Round—slowed dramatically, giving way to a surge in bilateral and regional trade agreements.

Notable examples include the Comprehensive and Progressive Agreement for Trans-Pacific Partnership (CPTPP) and the African Continental Free Trade Area (AfCFTA), both of which reflect a growing diversification in trade alliances beyond traditional Western-led institutions. Compounding these structural shifts are newer and more complex challenges that have surfaced in the 21st century.

The emergence of geopolitical rivalries, particularly between the United States and China, have profoundly influenced global trade patterns. What began as disputes over trade imbalances and intellectual property rights quickly escalated into broader confrontations over technology, national security, and global influence. These rivalries have led to the imposition of tariffs, export controls, and investment restrictions—policies that challenge the open-market ideals that have defined the post-war trading system.

3. ECONOMIC IMPACTS OF TARIFFS AND TRADE BARRIERS: AN ANALYTICAL PERSPECTIVE

Trade policy lies at the intersection of economics and politics, shaped as much by markets and efficiency considerations as by interest groups, institutions, ideologies, and national priorities. While traditional economic theory often advocates for free trade based on comparative advantage and the pursuit of overall welfare maximization, the reality of trade policymaking is far more complex (Alessandria G. et al. 2017). In practice, governments rarely implement purely free trade regimes. Instead, trade policy is frequently marked by a mixture of liberalization and protectionism, informed by strategic calculations, domestic political pressures, historical legacies, and global power dynamics.

Understanding the political economy of trade policy thus requires a multidisciplinary framework—one that integrates economic models with insights from political science, international relations, and institutional theory. Trade policy refers to the set of rules, regulations, tariffs, subsidies, and agreements that governments use to manage international trade.

These instruments are intended to influence the flow of goods, services, capital, and labor across borders, with the goal of achieving specific economic or political outcomes. While economists often measure trade policy by its impact on aggregate welfare—such as gross domestic product (GDP), employment, or consumer surplus—policymakers must also consider the distributional consequences of trade (Alessandria G. et al. 2017).

Liberalizing trade may benefit consumers and export-oriented firms, but it can also impose significant costs on import-competing industries and workers, generating domestic resistance and political backlash. The political economy framework recognizes that trade policy decisions emerge from a contest of interests between various stakeholders: producers and consumers, workers and employers, exporters and importers, large multinational corporations and small businesses, urban and rural populations, and organized interest groups.

These actors exert pressure on policymakers through lobbying, campaign contributions, public opinion, and voting behavior. In democratic systems, elected officials must weigh the preferences of constituents who are directly affected by trade. In authoritarian regimes, trade policy may be more insulated from popular demands but still influenced by elite coalitions and state priorities.

A central concept in this analysis is the idea of concentrated versus diffuse interests. The costs and benefits of trade policies are often unevenly distributed. For example, while the overall gains from free trade may be substantial, they are typically spread thinly across a broad consumer base, making them less visible or politically salient. Conversely, the costs of trade liberalization—such as factory closures or job losses—tend to be highly concentrated in specific sectors or communities, generating vocal and organized opposition. This asymmetry helps explain why protectionist policies, though economically inefficient, persist in many countries (Alessandria G. et al. 2021).

Politicians may respond to pressure from well-organized interest groups, such as labor unions or industry associations, who have a strong incentive to influence trade policy in their favor. Institutional arrangements also play a pivotal role in shaping trade outcomes. In federal systems, for instance, subnational governments may advocate for policies that reflect regional economic interests. Parliamentary systems may enable or constrain trade reform depending on the configuration of party politics and coalition dynamics.

At the international level, membership in trade organizations—such as the WTO, regional trade agreements (RTAs), or customs unions—imposes legal and normative constraints on unilateral trade actions. These institutions not only provide mechanisms for dispute resolution and coordination but also serve as forums for negotiating trade rules and standards. Yet, institutional effectiveness varies widely depending on enforcement capabilities, political will, and the relative power of member states.

4. PROTECTIONISM AND NATIONALISM: THE POLITICAL FORCES SHAPING ECONOMIC POLICY

Tariffs and trade barriers are among the most visible and influential instruments of trade policy, with far-reaching implications for national economies, global commerce, and international relations. While often justified on grounds of protecting domestic industries, generating government revenue, or correcting trade imbalances, their economic impacts are complex and multifaceted. Tariffs—taxes imposed on imported goods—and non-tariff barriers (NTBs), such as quotas, import licenses, subsidies, technical standards, and regulatory requirements, can significantly reshape trade flows, alter production and consumption patterns, and influence macroeconomic performance. Understanding their effects requires a nuanced analysis that considers both their intended outcomes and unintended consequences.

At a basic economic level, tariffs raise the price of imported goods, making them less competitive relative to domestically produced (Alessandria G. et al. 2021) alternatives. This price distortion encourages consumers to buy domestic products and helps protect domestic producers from foreign competition. In the short term, this can lead to increased output, higher profits, and job preservation in protected industries. However, these benefits are often outweighed by broader economic costs. Consumers face higher prices, reducing their purchasing power and welfare. Import-dependent industries that rely on foreign inputs may experience increased production costs, diminishing their competitiveness. As a result, tariffs can inadvertently harm other sectors of the economy, leading to misallocation of resources and efficiency losses.

The classic economic model of tariffs illustrates a "deadweight loss"—an efficiency loss resulting from the deviation of prices and quantities from free market equilibrium. In graphical terms, tariffs create two distinct deadweight loss triangles: one representing the loss in consumer surplus not captured by domestic producers or the government (due to decreased consumption), and another representing the inefficiency of producing domestically at higher costs than the world market. While the government may collect tariff revenue, this gain is typically smaller than the (Alessandria G. et al. 2021) combined losses experienced by consumers and the broader economy. In essence, tariffs transfer wealth from consumers to domestic producers and the state, but in doing so, they shrink the overall economic pie.

Non-tariff barriers, while less overt than tariffs, often have comparable or greater economic effects. Technical standards, health and safety regulations, and licensing requirements can serve legitimate policy purposes, such as protecting consumers or the environment. However, when applied in a discriminatory or excessively burdensome manner, they act as de facto protectionist tools. For example, a country might require foreign products to meet complex certification processes that domestic goods are exempt from, effectively raising the cost of imports and shielding domestic producers. Unlike tariffs, the costs of NTBs are harder to quantify and often less transparent, which can make them more politically palatable but equally distortionary.

4.1 Global Value Chains: Trade Wars and Their Effects on Supply Networks

Protectionism and nationalism have re-emerged in the 21st century as powerful forces shaping global trade policy and international relations. Though these concepts are not new, their resurgence in contemporary politics has reignited debates about the role of the state in regulating markets, the meaning of economic sovereignty, and the legitimacy of global institutions. Protectionism refers to the economic policy of restricting imports through measures such as tariffs, quotas, subsidies, and regulatory barriers, with the goal of shielding domestic industries from foreign (Alessandria G. et al. 2024) competition.

Nationalism, in this context, represents a political ideology that prioritizes national interests, identity, and autonomy over international cooperation and global integration. Together, these forces constitute a potent ideological and political framework that challenges the liberal, rules-based international order that has defined global commerce since the mid-20th century. The political appeal of protectionism and nationalism lies in their ability to mobilize public sentiment around themes of economic insecurity, cultural identity, and perceived threats to national sovereignty. In many advanced economies, deindustrialization, job outsourcing, stagnant wages, and rising inequality have fostered a sense of disillusionment with globalization.

Large segments of the population, particularly in traditional manufacturing regions, feel left behind by technological change and international trade. Political leaders have responded to these concerns by invoking nationalist narratives that blame foreign competitors, immigrants, or supranational institutions for domestic economic woes. Protectionist policies are thus framed not only as economic tools but as acts of national self-defence—restoring control, dignity, and fairness to domestic markets.

The politics of protectionism are particularly evident in electoral democracies, where politicians often exploit public anxieties to gain support. Campaigns that emphasize "buying local," restoring lost industries, or punishing "unfair" trade practices resonate with voters who have experienced economic dislocation. Political rhetoric around "America First" in the United States, Brexit in the (Alessandria G. et al. 2024) United Kingdom, and the rise of populist movements in Europe and Latin America reflect a broader global trend toward economic nationalism.

These movements often oppose free trade agreements, question the legitimacy of global governance institutions like the World Trade Organization (WTO), and advocate for greater state intervention in the economy. The strategic deployment of protectionist narratives enables leaders to consolidate power by appealing to patriotism, historical grievances, and a nostalgic vision of national prosperity. However, the relationship between protectionism, nationalism, and politics is not confined to populist democracies. In state-led economies or authoritarian regimes, protectionist policies are frequently used to advance national development goals, maintain regime stability, or assert geopolitical influence.

For instance, China's industrial policies and strategic trade practices are part of a broader vision to achieve technological self-sufficiency and global leadership in key sectors such as artificial intelligence, semiconductors, and green energy. Similarly, India has implemented a "Make in India" initiative to encourage domestic manufacturing and reduce dependency on imports. These policies are underpinned by nationalist ideologies that emphasize economic independence as a cornerstone of national strength and resilience.

4.2 The US-China Trade War: Origins, Economic Fallout, and Global Implications

In the modern global economy, production is no longer confined within national borders. Instead, goods and services are increasingly produced through complex networks known as global value chains (GVCs)—interconnected systems in which different stages of production are located across multiple countries. (Soundariya A. et al. 2025) From raw material extraction and intermediate goods manufacturing to final assembly and distribution, value is added in different geographical locations, based on comparative advantages such as labor costs, resource availability, technology, and infrastructure.

Over the past three decades, GVCs have become the backbone of international trade and industrial organization, driving efficiency, lowering costs, and enabling unprecedented economic integration. However, the rise of trade wars in the 21st century has disrupted these finely tuned networks, challenging their resilience and reshaping the geography of global production. GVCs are a defining feature of globalization. Companies no longer manufacture entire products in one location; instead, they "slice up the value chain," outsourcing or offshoring specific tasks to regions that can perform them more competitively or cost-effectively.

A smartphone, for example, may involve software development in the United States, microchip production in Taiwan or South Korea, rare earth extraction in Africa, screen manufacturing in Japan, and final assembly in China.

These distributed systems have allowed firms to scale quickly, access new markets, and reduce production costs, while enabling developing economies to integrate into the global economy through specialized tasks, even if they cannot produce complete products on their own. However, the efficiency of GVCs also comes with significant vulnerabilities (Soundariya A. et al. 2025).

They rely on the free and predictable flow of goods, services, data, and capital across borders. Trade wars—characterized by tariffs, export controls, investment restrictions, and other retaliatory measures—disrupt this flow and generate uncertainty in global supply chains. The U.S.–China trade war, which began in 2018, exemplifies how geopolitical tensions can ripple through GVCs. As tariffs were imposed on hundreds of billions of dollars' worth.

5. EU-U.S. TRADE DISPUTES: TARIFFS, RETALIATORY MEASURES, AND ECONOMIC CONSEQUENCES

The U.S.–China trade war stands as one of the most significant geopolitical and economic conflicts of the 21st century, reflecting a deeper structural rivalry between the world's two largest economies. Emerging prominently in 2018 during the administration of President Donald Trump, the trade war was initially framed as a response to America's long-standing trade deficit with China and concerns about unfair trade practices. However, beneath the surface lay a broader contest for economic dominance, technological leadership, and global influence. The causes of the trade war are rooted in a complex matrix of economic grievances, political ideologies, and strategic anxieties, and its consequences have been far-reaching—impacting global trade flows, corporate supply chains, market dynamics, and international diplomacy (Kaur M. et al. 2025). The primary causes of the US–China trade war revolve around several persistent tensions.

First, the trade imbalance: for decades, the United States has run a substantial trade deficit with China, importing far more than it exports. While economists often argue that such imbalances are macroeconomic in nature—driven by savings and investment patterns—many American policymakers and businesses saw this as evidence of asymmetry in market access.

Second, the U.S. raised strong objections to intellectual property (IP) theft, forced technology transfers, and the lack of adequate protection for foreign firms operating in China. American firms claimed they were compelled to share proprietary technologies as a condition of doing business in China, giving rise to accusations of coercive industrial policy and unfair competitive advantage.

Third, the U.S. criticized state subsidies and China's state-led economic model, particularly the dominance of state-owned enterprises (SOEs) and the opaque nature of government support for sectors targeted by China's "Made in China 2025" strategy.

This program aimed to position China as a global leader in high-tech industries such as robotics, aerospace, biotechnology, and artificial intelligence—sectors that the U.S. considers critical to its own economic and national security.

In response to these concerns, the Trump administration enacted a series of escalating tariffs beginning in 2018, targeting over $360 billion worth of Chinese goods. China retaliated with tariffs on over $110 billion in American exports, particularly agricultural products like soybeans and pork, which struck at key political constituencies in the United States.

This tit-for-tat escalation created volatility in financial markets, disrupted global supply chains, and forced companies on both sides to reconsider their international sourcing and investment strategies. The U.S. imposed tariffs in phases, with early rounds focusing on steel, aluminum, and high-tech goods, and later rounds expanding to consumer electronics, clothing, and household products. China's retaliatory measures (Kaur M. et al. 2025) were equally strategic, designed not only to inflict economic damage but also to exert political pressure ahead of U.S. elections.

The economic consequences of the trade war were widespread. For both countries, the tariffs functioned as a tax on businesses and consumers. Multiple studies estimated that U.S. consumers bore a significant portion of the cost of the tariffs through higher prices, particularly on goods that had limited domestic substitutes. American farmers suffered significant losses as China shifted its imports to alternative suppliers in Brazil, Russia, and other emerging markets. U.S. manufacturers faced rising input costs due to tariffs on intermediate goods, which in turn weakened their global competitiveness.

In China, while the overall economic growth slowed, the government enacted counter-cyclical measures, such as tax cuts and stimulus programs, to cushion the impact. Yet Chinese exporters also faced reduced access to one of their largest markets, leading to job losses and declining business

6. TRADE WARS IN HISTORICAL CONTEXT: KEY LESSONS FROM PAST ECONOMIC CONFLICTS

The trade relationship between the European Union (EU) and the United States, two of the world's largest and most advanced economies, has long been characterized by both close cooperation and recurring disputes. While they share deep economic ties, mutual investment flows, and similar commitments to open markets and democratic governance, trade tensions between the EU and the US have periodically flared due to differences in regulatory standards, industrial policy, and geopolitical priorities. Over the past few decades, and particularly in the 21st century, the EU–US trade relationship has been punctuated by a series of high-profile disputes involving tariffs, subsidies, and retaliatory measures (Samal A. et al. 2025).

These conflicts underscore the fragile balance between economic integration and national interest, and they illustrate how even allied nations can struggle to align their commercial policies in a globalized and competitive environment. One of the most prolonged and emblematic trade disputes between the EU and the US has been the Boeing–Airbus subsidy conflict—a case that illustrates the complexity and strategic importance of state support in the aerospace industry.

Dating back to the early 2000s, both the US and the EU accused each other of illegally subsidizing their respective aerospace champions, Boeing and Airbus, in ways that distorted competition in global aircraft markets. The dispute was brought before the World Trade Organization (WTO), which after years of investigation ruled that both parties had indeed provided improper subsidies.

The U.S. objected to launch aid and low-interest loans extended by European governments to Airbus, while the EU challenged tax incentives and military contracts that allegedly benefited Boeing. As a result of these rulings, the WTO authorized both sides to impose retaliatory tariffs: in 2019, the U.S. implemented tariffs on $7.5 billion of EU goods, including wine.

6.1 Trade Wars and Economic Growth: Assessing the GDP Consequences

Throughout history, trade wars have surfaced as recurring episodes in the complex interplay of economics, politics, and national rivalry. Although global trade is often viewed as a force for prosperity and peace, the history of trade relations reveals a pattern of protectionist policies, retaliatory tariffs, and economic nationalism that periodically disrupt international commerce. Studying historical trade wars provides valuable insight into the motivations behind such conflicts, their economic and political consequences, and the long-term lessons they offer for managing present-day disputes (Samal A. et al. 2025).

From the mercantilist rivalries of early modern Europe to the tariff battles of the 20th century, past trade wars underscore the dangers of escalation, the unintended costs of economic retaliation, and the crucial importance of cooperative institutions in maintaining global trade stability. One of the most infamous examples in modern history is the Smoot-Hawley Tariff Act of 1930, enacted during the early stages of the Great Depression in the United States.

Aimed at protecting American farmers and manufacturers from foreign competition, the act raised U.S. tariffs on over 20,000 imported goods to historically high levels. Though intended to shield domestic industries and reduce unemployment, the policy backfired spectacularly. Major trading partners—including Canada, France, and other European nations—responded with retaliatory tariffs, leading to a sharp contraction in global trade. World trade volume fell by over 60% between 1929 and 1934, exacerbating the global economic crisis. Rather than fostering recovery, the tariff war deepened the Depression and contributed to rising political extremism, protectionism, and international tension in the lead-up to World War II. The Smoot-Hawley episode remains a cautionary tale about the perils of unilateral trade barriers and the domino effect of retaliatory protectionism.

Even earlier, the 17th and 18th centuries witnessed intense mercantilist trade conflicts among European colonial powers, particularly between Britain, France, Spain, and the Netherlands. Under mercantilist doctrine, wealth was believed to be finite, and nations sought to accumulate precious metals and positive trade balances through high tariffs and colonial expansion. Trade wars during this period were often intertwined with military conflicts, such as the Anglo-Dutch Wars, which revolved around control of shipping lanes, overseas markets, and access to raw materials (Samal A. et al. 2025). These early trade rivalries laid the foundation for the global trading system but were also marked by violence, monopolization, and zero-sum thinking that suppressed competition and stifled innovation.

In the 19th century, the world witnessed a gradual shift toward liberalization with the British repeal of the Corn Laws in 1846, an event that marked a turning point in modern trade policy. The Corn Laws had imposed tariffs on imported grain, raising food prices and protecting landowners at the expense of consumers and industrial workers.

Their repeal, driven by rising pressure from industrialists and free-trade advocates like Richard Cobden and John Bright, signaled a new era of liberal economic thought in Britain and inspired similar reforms across Europe. Yet even as liberal trade principles took root, conflicts persisted. The Franco-Prussian rivalry in the late 1800s, for instance, included tariff disputes over agricultural and industrial goods, which fueled broader geopolitical antagonism in Europe.

6.2 Trade Wars and Labor Markets: Examining Employment Shifts and Economic Consequences

Trade wars, defined as economic conflicts resulting from extreme protectionist policies wherein countries impose tariffs or other trade barriers against each other, have far-reaching implications on global and domestic economic growth. At their core, trade wars disrupt the free flow of goods and services, leading to inefficiencies in global supply chains, increased production costs, and ultimately, reduced gross domestic product (GDP) growth in both the initiating and retaliating economies.

Historically, trade wars have demonstrated their capacity to hinder economic growth (Dahiya R. et al. 2025). The U.S.-China trade war that began in 2018 is a prime example. The imposition of tariffs on hundreds of billions of dollars worth of goods led to increased prices for consumers and businesses, uncertainty in markets, and shifts in supply chain strategies. For instance, U.S. GDP growth slowed from 2.9% in 2018 to 2.3% in 2019, partly due to declining business investment and lower exports. Similarly, China's GDP growth decelerated from 6.6% in 2018 to 6.1% in 2019, as its export-driven economy faced a decline in demand from one of its major trade partners.

From a theoretical perspective, trade wars contradict the principle of comparative advantage, a cornerstone of classical economic theory. When nations impose tariffs, they effectively discourage specialization and efficiency. This leads to a misallocation of resources, where countries may produce goods they are less efficient at producing, thereby lowering overall productivity and economic output. Moreover, firms exposed to global markets tend to innovate more and exhibit higher productivity; protectionism may stifle these benefits, reducing long-term GDP potential. In the short term, some industries may benefit from trade protection, experiencing a temporary boost in production and employment due to reduced foreign competition (Dahiya R. et al. 2025).

However, these gains are often outweighed by broader economic costs. Retaliatory tariffs from trade partners can damage export-dependent industries, reduce foreign market access, and trigger job losses. For example, in the U.S.-China trade war, American soybean exports to China plummeted, adversely affecting farmers and leading the U.S. government to provide billions in subsidies to offset the losses. Trade wars also create significant uncertainty in the global economy, which can dampen investment and consumption.

Businesses may delay capital expenditures due to unpredictable costs and shifting trade policies, while consumers may face higher prices for imported goods, reducing their purchasing power. This uncertainty can be particularly damaging for emerging markets that rely on trade and foreign investment for growth.

6.3 Tariffs and Their Impact on Inflation: Price Dynamics in a Trade War

Trade wars profoundly affect employment and labor markets, introducing both immediate disruptions and long-term structural changes. By altering the flow of goods and services across borders, these conflicts trigger shifts in production, investment, and consumption patterns, all of which directly influence job creation, wages, and labor force dynamics. Although proponents of protectionist policies argue that trade wars can shield domestic industries from foreign competition and protect jobs, empirical evidence suggests that their overall impact on employment is far more complex and often adverse. In the short term, trade wars can provide relief to industries (Chib S. et al. 2025) vulnerable to foreign competition, such as steel or textiles.

Tariffs imposed on imports can create temporary boosts in domestic production, potentially safeguarding jobs or even leading to marginal employment gains in targeted sectors. For instance, during the U.S.-China trade war that began in 2018, U.S. tariffs on Chinese steel led to increased domestic steel production and a modest uptick in steel industry employment. However, these gains were limited and came at a steep cost to other parts of the economy, particularly industries that rely on steel as an input—such as automotive, construction, and machinery manufacturing—which faced higher input costs, reduced profitability, and job losses.

The broader impact of trade wars on labor markets is overwhelmingly negative. Retaliatory tariffs from trade partners often target key export sectors, leading to job losses in industries reliant on foreign markets. In the case of the U.S., Chinese retaliatory tariffs significantly reduced demand for American agricultural products, particularly soybeans. As a result, many American farmers saw their incomes decline sharply, leading to layoffs in agricultural support industries and rural job losses.

The federal government responded with over $28 billion in aid to farmers through subsidy programs, attempting to mitigate the damage. However, such transfers do not create sustainable employment and may distort labor market signals in the long run. Trade wars also increase uncertainty, which tends to depress business investment and hiring decisions (Chib S. et al. 2025).

Employers may delay expansions or cut back on hiring due to unpredictability in trade policies and market access. This hesitancy can reduce job growth, especially in sectors tied to global value chains. Moreover, companies facing higher costs due to tariffs might respond by automating more functions or offshoring production to non-targeted countries, reducing the demand for domestic labor even further.

7. MULTILATERALISM VS. BILATERALISM: SHAPING THE FUTURE OF GLOBAL TRADE AGREEMENTS

Tariffs, a central instrument in trade wars, exert a significant and often immediate influence on inflation and consumer prices. When a country imposes tariffs—taxes on imported goods—those additional costs frequently cascade through the supply chain, raising prices for raw materials, intermediate inputs, and final consumer goods. While the stated objective of tariffs is often to protect domestic industries or correct trade imbalances, their economic impact is multifaceted and frequently includes inflationary pressures that can ripple across the entire economy (Limbore N.V. et al. 2025).

The basic economic mechanism is straightforward: when a tariff is applied to an imported product, the cost of that product rises. In theory, the foreign exporter could absorb the cost, but in practice, the burden is often shared—or fully passed on—to domestic importers, retailers, and ultimately consumers. For example, when the U.S. imposed tariffs on Chinese goods during the 2018–2019 trade war, empirical studies showed that over 90% of the tariff costs were borne by U.S. businesses and consumers, not Chinese exporters.

This direct cost transmission mechanism led to higher prices for a wide range of goods, from washing machines and electronics to apparel and furniture. These price increases contribute to overall inflation, measured by indices such as the Consumer Price Index (CPI) and the Producer Price Index (PPI).

As input costs rise for businesses, producers either absorb the losses, reducing profit margins, or pass the costs onto consumers through higher prices. In many cases, businesses initially attempt to maintain pricing stability but eventually adjust prices upward as tariffs persist, embedding inflationary pressures into the economy. The inflationary effects are particularly pronounced in sectors that are heavily reliant on imports and have few (Limbore N.V. et al. 2025) alternative sources of supply.

U.S. tariffs on steel and aluminum caused prices of these materials to spike, which then increased production costs in industries like construction, automotive manufacturing, and machinery. Moreover, the impact of tariffs on prices is not isolated to directly taxed goods. Because many industries rely on complex global supply chains, the effects of tariffs can propagate indirectly.

A single tariff on an imported component can increase the price of a final assembled product. This phenomenon is especially critical in high-tech and automotive sectors, where intermediate goods cross multiple borders before final assembly. Even goods produced domestically can see price hikes if their production depends on imported inputs now subject to tariffs.

Beyond specific goods, tariffs can also affect overall inflation expectations. When households and businesses anticipate higher costs in the future due to trade restrictions, they may alter their consumption and pricing behavior accordingly.

Consumers may accelerate purchases in anticipation of future price hikes, temporarily increasing demand and prices. Simultaneously, firms may raise prices preemptively or adjust wages upward, further contributing to inflationary momentum. These shifts can introduce volatility and complicate monetary policy. The inflationary impact of tariffs can also depend on the elasticity of demand and supply for the affected goods.

For goods with inelastic demand—where consumers have few substitutes, such as electronics or medical devices—tariffs tend to result in more significant price increases because consumers cannot easily switch to alternatives. Conversely, when domestic substitutes are readily available, (Limbore N.V. et al. 2025) the inflationary effect may be muted, though this often requires time for producers to scale up, during which prices remain elevated. In the short term, the lack of sufficient domestic production capacity can exacerbate supply constraints and push prices even higher.

Tariffs also influence inflation differently depending on the macroeconomic context. In an already tight economy, where demand is strong and capacity utilization is high, tariffs can accelerate inflation sharply. On the other hand, in a sluggish or deflationary environment, tariffs may have a more muted effect or contribute to stagflation—where inflation rises despite weak economic growth. This was a concern during parts of the U.S.-China trade war, where inflationary pressures from tariffs coincided with declining business investment and slowing global demand.

8. TRADE POLICY AND NATIONAL SECURITY: NAVIGATING THE ECONOMIC AND POLITICAL CROSSROADS

The evolving global trade landscape is increasingly shaped by the tension and interplay between multilateralism and bilateralism—two distinct yet overlapping approaches to international trade agreements (Li & Lu, 2020). Multilateralism, rooted in collective decision-making and standardized rules, seeks to unify a broad group of countries under common economic principles, as exemplified by the World Trade Organization (WTO) and its predecessor, the General Agreement on Tariffs and Trade (GATT). Bilateralism, by contrast, refers to trade agreements negotiated between two countries or economic blocs, allowing more tailored, reciprocal arrangements that reflect the specific interests of the involved parties.

As trade policies adapt to emerging economic, geopolitical, and technological realities, the debate over which approach best serves global economic development and stability has become increasingly prominent. Multilateralism has historically been seen as the most effective way to reduce global trade barriers, enhance predictability, and promote fairness among trading nations.

The WTO, for instance, has provided a comprehensive framework to resolve disputes, encourage transparency, and support global economic integration. It has helped establish norms that reduce the risks of trade protectionism, prevent trade wars, and provide a level playing field for both developed and developing nations. Moreover, multilateral agreements often include provisions for capacity building, development assistance, and special treatment for least developed countries (LDCs), making them more inclusive and equitable.

However, in recent years, the multilateral approach has faced increasing criticism and stagnation. One of the primary challenges has been the difficulty of achieving consensus among a growing and diverse membership. The WTO now includes over 160 members, each with varying levels of development, political priorities, and economic interests. Reaching agreement on complex issues such as agricultural subsidies, intellectual property, digital trade, and environmental standards has proven exceptionally difficult.

The failure of the Doha Development Round, launched in 2001 and effectively stalled by the 2010s, underscores the limitations of multilateralism in delivering timely and substantive outcomes in a rapidly changing world. This perceived ineffectiveness has led many nations to pursue bilateral and regional agreements as more pragmatic alternatives. Bilateral agreements allow countries to negotiate terms that are tailored to their specific needs and priorities, often achieving results more quickly than the (Li & Lu, 2020) cumbersome multilateral process. These deals can address modern trade issues—such as data governance, digital services, labor standards, and environmental protection—that are often too contentious for broad multilateral consensus.

The U.S.-Mexico-Canada Agreement (USMCA) modernized the earlier NAFTA agreement to reflect contemporary trade realities, including e-commerce and digital copyright protections. Regional and bilateral agreements have also become instrumental tools for geopolitical strategy. Countries use these agreements not only to strengthen economic ties but also to build political alliances and increase their influence in specific regions. China's Belt and Road Initiative (BRI), which includes numerous bilateral trade and investment agreements, exemplifies the use of economic engagement for strategic positioning. Similarly, the European Union leverages bilateral deals with countries in Africa, the Middle East, and Asia to reinforce its regulatory standards and political values abroad.

8.1 The Role of International Institutions

In the 21st century, the boundaries between trade policy and national security have become increasingly blurred. Once considered separate spheres—trade as an economic tool and national security as a defense concern—these domains are now deeply interconnected. Governments around the world are recognizing that the flow of goods, services, data, and capital across borders can directly influence their national security posture.

As a result, trade policy has evolved beyond a mere instrument for economic growth and competitiveness to a strategic mechanism used to safeguard national interests, secure supply chains, and project geopolitical power (Li & Lu, 2020). This intersection of economics and politics introduces a complex landscape in which trade decisions are no longer governed solely by principles of efficiency or market liberalism, but also by concerns over sovereignty, resilience, and strategic autonomy.

The integration of trade policy into national security strategy is driven by several global developments. First, the increasing reliance on global supply chains for critical goods—such as semiconductors, pharmaceuticals, rare earth elements, and defense-related technologies—has exposed vulnerabilities in times of geopolitical tension or crisis. The COVID-19 pandemic starkly revealed these dependencies, as countries scrambled for essential medical equipment and vaccines, prompting a re-evaluation of what constitutes national security. Similarly, the Russia-Ukraine conflict underscored the dangers of energy dependence on geopolitically unstable regions. These crises have catalyzed a global push toward supply chain diversification, domestic production capacity, and friend-shoring—policies where trade relationships are steered toward politically aligned partners.

Investment policy has also become an area where trade and national security converge. Governments have strengthened foreign direct investment (FDI) screening mechanisms to prevent foreign entities, particularly those linked to rival states, from acquiring sensitive technologies, infrastructure, or data assets.

The U.S. Committee on Foreign Investment in the United States (CFIUS) has expanded its mandate to review a wider range of transactions, while similar bodies in the EU, (Li & Lu, 2020) Japan, and Australia have tightened oversight of foreign investments. These policies aim to prevent the erosion of technological leadership and protect critical industries from foreign influence, even if it means restricting capital inflows that would otherwise boost economic activity.

Another key dimension is the use of sanctions and export restrictions as tools of economic statecraft. Sanctions regimes—targeting nations, corporations, or individuals—are designed not only to punish but also to shape behavior by restricting access to global markets, financial systems, and strategic technologies. These measures can have wide-ranging effects on global trade, creating ripple effects across sectors and countries. For instance, sanctions on Russia's energy and banking sectors have reshaped global energy markets and financial flows, while restrictions on Chinese tech firms have affected global semiconductor supply chains. The growing use of sanctions highlights the dual-use nature of trade policy—serving both economic and strategic ends.

8.2 Navigating Trade Wars: Policy Challenges and Strategic Responses

International institutions have played a fundamental role in shaping the modern global trade order. Among these, the World Trade Organization (WTO) stands as the cornerstone of multilateral trade governance, guiding the rules, norms, and dispute resolution mechanisms that facilitate international commerce. However, the effectiveness of these institutions is increasingly under scrutiny as the (Li J.

et al. 2019) global trade environment becomes more complex, fragmented, and politically charged.

The growing tensions between economic interdependence and national sovereignty, the rise of geopolitical rivalries, and the rapid advancement of technology have all challenged the traditional architecture of trade governance. As a result, the role of international institutions must evolve—beyond the WTO—to address contemporary issues such as digital trade, climate change, supply chain resilience, and economic inequality, while preserving the foundational principles of openness, predictability, and fairness in global trade.

The WTO was established in 1995, succeeding the General Agreement on Tariffs and Trade (GATT), with the primary aim of promoting free trade by reducing barriers, ensuring transparency, and providing a legal and institutional framework for negotiating and enforcing trade agreements. Its core functions include administering WTO agreements, serving as a forum for trade negotiations, monitoring national trade policies, providing technical assistance to developing countries, and resolving trade disputes through its Dispute Settlement Body (DSB). For decades, the WTO helped underpin a rules-based global trading system that reduced tariffs, encouraged liberalization, and integrated developing economies into the global market. It contributed to significant growth in trade volumes and played a key role in supporting economic globalization.

Yet, despite these achievements, the WTO has faced mounting criticism for its perceived ineffectiveness in adapting to contemporary trade challenges. One major issue is the paralysis of the WTO's dispute resolution system, particularly the Appellate Body, which ceased functioning effectively in 2019 due to a U.S.-led blockade of judicial appointments. Without a functioning appellate mechanism, the credibility and enforceability of WTO rules have been undermined.

Member states are now increasingly resorting to unilateral trade actions or bilateral solutions, bypassing WTO procedures and eroding its central role in global trade governance. Furthermore, the WTO's consensus-based decision-making model—where all 164 member states must agree on major decisions—has become a significant barrier to timely reforms and progress.

Diverse economic interests among developed, developing, and least-developed countries make it exceedingly difficult to achieve consensus on critical issues such as agricultural subsidies, fisheries regulation, digital trade, and intellectual property rights. The failure of the Doha Development Round, launched in 2001 to address the needs of developing countries, exemplifies this challenge.

Although some incremental agreements have been reached—such as the Trade Facilitation Agreement in 2013—comprehensive multilateral progress remains elusive. The rise of preferential trade agreements (PTAs), regional trade blocs, and bilateral deals has further shifted the locus of trade governance away from multilateralism. (Li J. et al. 2019) Agreements such as the Comprehensive and Progressive Agreement for Trans-Pacific Partnership (CPTPP), the Regional Comprehensive Economic Partnership (RCEP), and the African Continental Free Trade Area (AfCFTA) demonstrate how countries are increasingly relying on smaller, more flexible platforms to negotiate modern trade rules.

These arrangements often address issues that the WTO has struggled to incorporate, including e-commerce, data governance, environmental standards, and labor protections. While these agreements can be more responsive to member needs, they also contribute to regulatory fragmentation and create challenges for coherence across the global trade system.

9. CONCLUSION

Trade wars represent one of the most contentious and complex instruments in the realm of economic policy. Characterized by the imposition of tariffs, quotas, and other trade barriers in retaliation to perceived unfair trade practices or imbalances, trade wars can have profound and far-reaching effects on national economies, global markets, and international relations.

The policy implications of engaging in or responding to trade wars are multifaceted, involving a delicate balance between domestic economic objectives, geopolitical strategy, and the global rules-based trade system. In today's interconnected world, where supply chains span continents and digital flows are integral to commerce, the blunt instrument of trade protectionism carries both short-term political appeal and long-term risks.

Effective policy design requires a nuanced understanding of the drivers, consequences, and strategic considerations of trade wars, coupled with mechanisms to mitigate their most damaging effects while advancing national and global interests. At the core of trade war policy is the motivation to correct perceived trade imbalances or respond to unfair practices such as intellectual property theft, forced technology transfers, state subsidies, or currency manipulation.

Policymakers may use tariffs as leverage to force trading partners into negotiations or behavioral change. For example, the U.S.-China trade war initiated in 2018 aimed to address a broad range of issues, from the massive U.S. trade deficit with China to broader concerns about technological dominance and industrial espionage. While such motivations may be legitimate, the use of tariffs often results in unintended consequences. Policy responses must therefore be evaluated not just on the basis of their stated objectives but also in terms of their ripple effects on prices, employment, investment, consumer behavior, and global economic stability. One of the most immediate policy implications of trade wars is the impact on consumer prices and inflation.

Tariffs imposed on imported goods typically raise input costs for domestic producers and prices for consumers. These cost increases can erode purchasing power, reduce business margins, and lead to inflationary pressures that complicate macroeconomic management. Central banks may be forced to adjust interest rates in response to trade-induced inflation, potentially slowing economic growth or exacerbating recessions.

Therefore, policymakers must weigh the short-term gains of protection against the macroeconomic risks of cost-push inflation, especially in a global environment already strained by supply chain disruptions or energy shocks. The employment and labor market consequences of trade wars also demand close policy attention. While tariffs may protect jobs in specific industries—such as steel, aluminum, or textiles—they often lead to job losses in downstream sectors that rely on imported components or face retaliatory tariffs abroad.

American farmers and automotive manufacturers experienced significant financial distress during the trade war with China due to retaliatory duties and disrupted export markets. Policymakers must anticipate such distributional effects and consider implementing support mechanisms—such as worker retraining programs, sector-specific subsidies, or unemployment benefits—to cushion affected populations.

A failure to address these disparities can fuel economic dislocation, social unrest, and political polarization.

REFERENCES

Aguilera, R., Duran, P., Heugens, P. P. M. A. R., Sauerwald, S., Turturea, R., & VanEssen, M. (2021). State ownership, political ideology, and firm performance around the world. *Journal of World Business, 56*(1), 101113. Universitat Ramon Llull+2IDEAS/RePEc+2DOI: 10.1016/j.jwb.2020.101113

Akkermans, J., Richardson, J., & Kraimer, M. L. (2020). The COVID-19 crisis as a career shock: Implications for careers and vocational behavior. *Journal of Vocational Behavior, 119*, 103434. PMC+2espace.curtin.edu.au+2DOI: 10.1016/j.jvb.2020.103434

Alessandria, G., Kaboski, J. P., & Midrigan, V. (2017). Trade integration and the trade balance in China. *IMF Economic Review*, *65*(4), 642–668. DOI: 10.1057/s41308-017-0036-2

Alessandria, G., Kaboski, J. P., & Midrigan, V. (2021). Trade adjustment dynamics and the welfare gains from trade. *Journal of International Economics*, *131*, 103450. DOI: 10.1016/j.jinteco.2021.103458

Alessandria, G., Kaboski, J. P., & Midrigan, V. (2024). Taking stock of trade policy uncertainty: Evidence from China's pre-WTO accession. *Journal of International Economics*, *150*, 103938. DOI: 10.1016/j.jinteco.2024.103938

Alessandria, G., Kaboski, J. P., & Midrigan, V. (2024). Trade-policy dynamics: Evidence from 60 years of U.S.-China trade. *Journal of Political Economy*.

Chib, S., Mehta, A. K., Selvakumar, P., Saravanan, A., Mishra, B. R., & Manjunath, T. C. (2025). Mental health challenges and solutions in high-pressure work environments. In Harriott, S. (Ed.), *Innovative Approaches to Managing Conflict and Change in Diverse Work Environments* (pp. 247–272). IGI Global. DOI: 10.4018/979-8-3693-9556-1.ch011

Kaur, M., Selvakumar, P., Dinesh, N., & Chandel, P. S. Mohit, & Manjunath, T. C. (2025). Reconstruction and preservation strategies for cultural heritage. In S. Oflazoğlu & M. Dora (Eds.), *Preserving Cultural Heritage in Post-Disaster Urban Renewal* (pp. 385–412). IGI Global.

Li, J., Li, P., & Wang, B. (2019). The liability of opaqueness: State ownership and the likelihood of deal completion in international acquisitions by Chinese firms. *Strategic Management Journal*, *40*(2), 303–327. DOI: 10.1002/smj.2985

Li, S., & Lu, J. W. (2020). A dual-agency model of firm CSR in response to institutional pressure: Evidence from Chinese publicly listed firms. *Academy of Management Journal*, *63*(6), 2004–2032. DOI: 10.5465/amj.2018.0557

Limbore, N. V., Anute, N., Ahluwalia, G. K., Chordiya, P. B., Kalshetti, P., & Selvakumar, P. (2025). Ethical leadership and corporate responsibility. In Harriott, S. (Ed.), *Innovative Approaches to Managing Conflict and Change in Diverse Work Environments* (pp. 193–218). IGI Global. DOI: 10.4018/979-8-3693-9556-1.ch009

Soundariya, A., Behera, N. K., Selvakumar, P., Chandel, P. S., Gupta, S., & Manjunath, T. C. (2025). AI and environmental ethics: The role of AI in addressing climate change – ethical considerations in AI-driven environmental solutions. In Chakraborty, S. (Ed.), *Human Values, Ethics, and Dignity in the Age of Artificial Intelligence* (pp. 321–346). IGI Global. DOI: 10.4018/979-8-3693-9035-1.ch013

Chapter 3
The Empire Strikes Back: U.S. Hegemony and Its Influence on the WTO

Juliana Florentina Fernandes Leao
https://orcid.org/0009-0003-8447-8916
Faculty of Economics and Business Administration, Ghent University, Belgium

Roberto Alexandre Zanchetta Borghi
https://orcid.org/0000-0001-5471-9705
Institute of Economics, UNICAMP, Brazil

ABSTRACT

This chapter analyzes the transformation of U.S. trade policy from 2016 to 2025, focusing on the erosion of its multilateral leadership, particularly within the World Trade Organization (WTO). Drawing from Giovanni Arrighi's theory of global hegemony, it explores the ideological and material foundations of American dominance and the systemic contradictions exposed by rising protectionism. Emphasizing the role of China's ascent and institutional strain, the study argues that the U.S. shift reflects a structural reconfiguration of global trade governance rather than a temporary deviation. The analysis traces historical developments, theoretical foundations, and recent policy shifts under Donald Trump's two terms in office.

1. INTRODUCTION

U.S. tariffs raised by Donald Trump since his first administration, especially on China, amid the slogan "Making America Great Again" pose key challenges to the current international order, which the United States has paradoxically shaped over the post-Cold War decades. Multilateral institutions, such as the World Trade

DOI: 10.4018/979-8-3373-3835-4.ch003

Organization (WTO), have been important channels through which American leadership has been exerted by promoting trade and globalization; however, they have been more recently questioned by the American presidency. The economic rise of China and its quest for greater representation in global governance increase the tensions among the two largest world economies and the role of international institutional bodies.

In the international landscape, the interactions between global actors constantly shape the balance between cooperation and conflict. Amid this dynamic, a singular position of leadership holds the key to influencing momentum and outcomes. However, a nation's ability to command this leadership is intricately linked to the very forces it seeks to control. This is a complex interplay of influence among major powers as they navigate the complexities of shaping global order.

The essence of such leadership is described by Giovanni Arrighi (1994), who builds on Antonio Gramsci's concept of hegemony, yet expands it globally. Through a Marxist dialectical approach, Arrighi (1994) explains how a nation's position is determined not only by military, economic, financial, and political supremacy but also by its ability to disseminate a dominant cultural and intellectual ideology. His framework highlights the dual nature of global leadership, encompassing both material and ideological aspects, emphasizing that power disputes unfold across multiple dimensions and must be understood within the context of historical and geopolitical factors.

Leadership entails more than exerting influence; it involves shaping the system within which power is exercised and contested (Arrighi, 1994). This concept is essential to understanding the U.S. position in global politics. Since the early 20th century, the United States has positioned itself at the helm of the evolving international order, grounded in multilateral cooperation and free trade principles (Börzel & Zürn, 2021).

The development of the U.S.-shaped order was reinforced through the consolidation of economic, security, and legal institutions. As Douglass North (1990) described, institutions are the "rules of the game," and their legitimacy depends on actors capable of maintaining them. The United States, while creating the international framework, embedded its strategic interests within it, guaranteeing that institutional power remained tied to its hegemony. However, as its influence expanded, it became clear that the functionality of these institutions was conditional upon their alignment with American objectives (Foot, MacFarlane, & Mastanduno, 2003). The core of the institutionalist analysis lies in understanding the dynamic layers of interaction between states and institutions in shaping international operations.

In the realm of trade, this is seen in the sustained relationship between the United States and the World Trade Organization. Even before its establishment in 1995, following the roots of its predecessor, the General Agreement on Tariffs and

Trade (GATT), the United States played a key role in fostering cooperation among member states. Based on free trade principles, the WTO operates through multiple mechanisms: (i) serving as a negotiation forum, (ii) regulating trade rules, and (iii) resolving commercial disputes (Vangrasstek & Pascal, 2013).

Within this landscape, Chang and Evans (2005) emphasize the evolutionary nature of institutions from a historical perspective. They argue that institutions not only constrain action but also enable and shape it, highlighting a reciprocal relationship between social structures and individual agencies. Regarding U.S. dominance, this phenomenon becomes particularly evident as interaction reveals the inherent ambiguity of the functional multiplicity of institutions.

Taking the WTO case, Chang and Evans (2005) explain that shifts in global power dynamics since the 1990s have altered the pace of trade liberalization and the system's effectiveness. A clear indication of these challenges is seen in formal disputes before the WTO. Over the organization's 30-year history, 631 cases have been registered, compared to 488 under GATT (Vangrasstek & Pascal, 2013). Additionally, changes in the economic agenda of developed countries, particularly the idea that the domestic market belongs to producers and citizens, have contributed to disruptions, as nationalist rhetoric has grown more prevalent.

In recent years, the conduct of the WTO has come under greater scrutiny, particularly following Donald Trump's presidency and shifts in U.S. foreign policy. The "America First" doctrine became the foundation of U.S. policy, reinforcing protectionist measures and efforts to reduce the trade deficit with major partners. These shifts largely responded to the growing U.S. trade imbalance with China, intensified since China's entry into the WTO in 2001 (Hopewell, 2021). Ultimately, these changes played a pivotal role in triggering a trade war between the two economic giants.

In 2018, the U.S.-China trade war erupted under the pretext of national defense. Despite reaching a deal in early 2020, the effects of the COVID-19 pandemic from that year onwards caused a sharp decline in global trade and the reinforcement of protectionist policies. Even beyond Trump's administration, subsequent events, including Russia's invasion of Ukraine in 2022, exacerbated U.S. protectionist tendencies (Bounds, 2022). By 2025, with Trump's return to the White House for a second term, his protectionist stance became even more pronounced.

On April 2, 2025, Trump declared "Liberation Day", during which he announced an extensive set of tariffs. These included a flat 10% tariff on all U.S. imports, as well as country-specific tariffs based on perceived trade imbalances. In total, more than 60 countries were affected by this secondary measure, followed by bilateral negotiations or retaliatory actions – further weakening the economic multilateralism once championed by the world's leading power (Ignatenko et al., 2025).

Although the U.S. remains the most influential force shaping the WTO and the broader multilateral trade system, the declining competitiveness of its industrial exporting sectors, coupled with dissatisfaction over the effectiveness of multilateral dispute resolution mechanisms, has fostered a hostile relationship between the U.S. and the very institution it helped create. As Chang and Evans (2005, p. 45) note, "distrust of government in any form combined with deep-seated xenophobia turns any institution of global governance into the enemy".

Under this context, the evolving nature of the U.S. trade policy raises a crucial question: has the post-Cold War U.S. role as a hegemonic leader and advocate of economic multilateralism undergone a fundamental transformation? Is this shift part of a broader trend or merely an isolated episode? The proposed chapter argues that recent shifts in the U.S. trade policy reflect a structural realignment rather than a temporary deviation. While Trump's policies have accelerated this trend, the retreat from multilateralism is not confined to his administration but represents a broader shift in the U.S. global strategy, which can be examined in more detail regarding the U.S position toward the WTO.

After decades of developing the multilateral trade system under U.S. leadership, the rise of new global powers, particularly of China, and the growing discontent within the U.S. itself, evidenced by the resurgence of protectionism, unilateral sanctions, and treaty withdrawals, have shaken the foundations of the multilateral order. Considering these evolving international dynamics and the pursuit of answers to these critical questions, the present study gains significance.

This chapter is divided into three key subsections that collectively explore the intricate relationship between U.S. hegemony and trade multilateralism. The first section establishes the theoretical framework, examining the U.S. pivotal role within the multilateral system. Building on this foundation, the second section delves into the historical evolution of the WTO and its predecessor, the GATT. It highlights the significant impact of U.S. influence on their development. Finally, the third section provides a contemporary analysis of U.S. policy towards the WTO from 2016 to 2025, focusing on protectionism and the institution's responses to major global challenges like the U.S.-China trade war, the COVID-19 pandemic, the war in Ukraine, and the introduction of new tariffs under Trump's second administration.

2. THE ROLE OF INSTITUTIONAL AND GLOBAL POWER DYNAMICS

2.1 Systemic Cycles of Accumulation: Arrighi's Theory of Hegemony

The definition of hegemony takes its concrete form in the field of political science in the 20th century, through the studies of the Marxist dialectical thinker Giovanni Arrighi (1994), whose contribution stemmed from the Gramscian and Braudelian approaches regarding the idea of systemic cycles of accumulation (SCA). Arrighi's (1994) hegemonic theory allowed for the analysis of a nation's international position based on the articulation of its supremacy in military, economic, financial, and political terms, as well as its capacity to disseminate a cultural and intellectual ideology to others (Pires & Mattos, 2016; Silvestre, 2019).

The theory of Systemic Cycles of Accumulation (SCA), originally rooted in Fernand Braudel's historical analysis, was further developed by Giovanni Arrighi (1994) to explain long-term transformations in global power dynamics. According to this framework, capitalism evolves through successive cycles marked by two distinct phases: material expansion, characterized by productive investment and economic growth, and financialization, in which capital shifts toward speculative activities. Each cycle is led by a hegemonic state that reorganizes the global order to sustain its dominance. The SCA theory thus provides a powerful lens for understanding historical shifts in international leadership and anticipating future transitions within the capitalist system.

Arrighi (1994) contributes to the Braudelian approach by emphasizing that phases of financial expansion intensify competition between states, resulting in both hyper-accumulation and political instability. Through this lens, hegemonic states not only influence systemic change but also become vulnerable to emerging challengers. He also introduces a layered notion of leadership, where hegemonic powers are both emulated and expected to steer global development; yet this notion is fraught with contradictions (Arrighi & Silver, 2001).

While hegemonic states act in their national interest, they often frame their leadership as serving a collective global good. According to the author, hegemony is only credible when a power can claim it contributes to the general expansion of collective global power. However, the dominance of one nation often sparks conflict and opposition, leading to periods of "systemic chaos", marked by international rivalry, social unrest, and shifts in the distribution of global power (Arrighi, 1994).

After World War II, the United States assumed hegemonic leadership by supporting global recovery and countering Soviet influence (Mazzucchelli, 2009). This involved institutional innovations, such as the IMF and UN, and a new gold-dollar monetary regime. Roosevelt's vision of a unified "one-world" order gave way to Truman's "free-world" doctrine, which underpinned a liberal capitalist framework (Pecequilo, 2012). This new framework was spread across various dimensions of the U.S. leadership.

In the commercial domain, American leadership solidified its hegemonic role by spearheading the Liberal International Order, an arrangement designed to promote free trade and interstate cooperation. This vision materialized through the early establishment of a Multilateral Trading System under the General Agreement on Tariffs and Trade (GATT) in 1947, which played a pivotal role in restoring and regulating international trade relations (Ikenberry, 2015; Hopewell, 2021).

As Arrighi (1994, p. 72) observes, this system became "the main instrument for the formation of the world market under North American hegemony," with the U.S. state assuming a central role in setting the trajectory and pace of global commercial liberalization. The post-war economic landscape was thus not merely reconstructed; it was deliberately steered by institutional innovations designed to entrench U.S. influence in global governance. Understanding the institutional infrastructure crafted during this period is essential for grasping how the U.S. operationalized its hegemonic power.

2.2 Institutions and Global Economic Governance

The study of institutions and their effect on the global economy has evolved over a century. Early Institutionalists, such as Thorstein Veblen (1988), emphasized how markets arise from complex institutional interactions. This "Old Institutionalism" gave way to a renewed approach in the 1980s. Led by Douglass North, the New Institutional Economics (NIE) refocused the debate on development by exploring how institutions shape economic performance through reducing transaction costs and uncertainty.

North (1990, 1992) defined institutions as the "rules of the game," distinguishing between two types: (i) informal and (ii) formal. Informal institutions include codes of conduct, norms, and conventions derived from socially transmitted cultural information (North, 2018). Formal institutions encompass political, economic, and contractual rules; despite their diversity, both aims to reduce transaction costs and uncertainties, ensuring predictable economic decision-making, which directly impacts growth. By embedding economic processes over an institutional framework, North moved beyond neoclassical assumptions of perfect information and rationality, showing that development depends on evolving institutional structures.

North's insights are especially relevant for the United States, which shaped global economic governance in the post-Cold War era. He argued that even with equal trade opportunities, as Ricardian theory suggests, institutional differences cause asymmetries in outcomes. From the NIE perspective, U.S. institutions related to property rights, contract enforcement, and political stability have historically lowered transaction costs, fostering an environment conducive to sustained growth and reinforcing U.S. dominance in global markets (North, 2018).

North (1990) viewed institutions as key to explaining why some nations grow while others stagnate despite similar market access or trade policies. However, critics argue that NIE oversimplifies institutional evolution, leading scholars like Ha-Joon Chang and Peter Evans (2005) to establish the historically grounded and interdisciplinary framework of the Institutional Political Economy (IPE).

IPE challenges the knowledge that strong institutions automatically cause development, emphasizing a bidirectional and context-dependent relationship between institutional change and economic growth. Economic development can itself drive institutional evolution through new social actors and political demands (Chang, 2010).

IPE also critiques NIE's static view of institutions as mere "restrictions" securing market efficiency. Instead, Chang (2010) and Evans (2014) argue that institutions are constitutive, meaning that they shape, create, and enable markets rather than simply constrain them. This expanded view recognizes institutions as embedded in power relations, ideologies, and histories. This perspective is vital to understanding the construction of global institutions like the WTO and the U.S. central role in shaping their design.

The rise of U.S. hegemony after the Cold War was aligned with a global push for liberal economic governance. Pecequilo (2012) notes the U.S. leveraged its power to structure global institutions to reflect and reinforce its interests. The WTO, established in 1995 to replace GATT, exemplifies this. While promoting multilateral trade liberalization, it embeds institutional rules that favor countries with strong legal and administrative capacities, such as the United States (Chang & Evans, 2005).

A key example is the WTO's Dispute Settlement Understanding (DSU). Chang and Evans (2005) argue that although the DSU universalizes norms, potentially empowering developing nations, it also exposes them to vulnerability. DSU assumes an even playing field, but in practice, the economic and legal power of countries grants them disproportionate influence. These reveals institutions are not neutral rule enforcers but are shaped by global power structures, which in turn shape economic outcomes worldwide (Chang & Evans, 2005).

Hence, the U.S. credibility in sustaining global institutions is a double-edged sword. On the one hand, it anchors trust in the system; on the other, it poses risks when national sovereignty clashes with international institutional constraints. Chang and Evans (2005) note that the legitimacy of institutions like the WTO depends not only on rule enforcement but also on the perception of fairness and inclusion, a standard that is often questioned when powerful nations act unilaterally or obstruct collective decision-making.

A clear illustration of this is the inherent contradiction between the DSU's commitment to multilateralism and GATT's Article XXI, the security exception. This provision was deliberately included in the original GATT to ensure that the U.S. and other major powers could prioritize their security interests, even if it meant breaching core trade obligations. Article XXI explicitly allows members to act in the name of security, effectively serving as a strategically placed escape clause for the hegemonic power (Lapa, 2020).

For decades, the security exception clause was considered "off-limits" for WTO panels due to its sensitive, political nature. This hands-off approach was a crucial part of the compromise: countries would abide by the trade rules, but the hegemonic power would retain a sovereign, unilateral right to act when it deemed its security was at risk. This dynamic reveals how the WTO, despite its multilateral facade, ultimately contains provisions that accommodate the interests of its most powerful member, validating the link between institutional design and the presence of U.S. hegemony (Lapa, 2020).

This historical reality challenges universalist assumptions often found in NIE, which can suggest a single, optimal institutional formula for growth. Instead, it aligns with historical analyses, such as the work of Gerschenkron (2015), which reinforce the idea that institutional development is path dependent. Late industrializers often cannot replicate the trajectories of developed nations like the U.S., as their institutional environments differ due to unique historical, political, and social legacies. This challenges the NIE tendency to universalize a specific institutional formula for growth, particularly one modeled after the American experience. Institutional change, therefore, must be context-sensitive and historically informed.

This critique underscores a broader skepticism toward global governance as currently structured. Far from being neutral or universally beneficial, it tends to favor nations that already hold power within the system, most notably the United States. IPE scholars urge for a more nuanced understanding of institutions as historically contingent and ideologically charged, rather than as static tools for enforcing market primacy (Gerschenkron, 2015).

While New Institutional Economics has significantly advanced the understanding of how institutions influence development, especially through the lens of transaction costs and formal/informal rule structures, it remains limited in capturing the full complexity of institutional dynamics in a globalized world. In this regard, the critiques and contributions from IPE, especially those examining U.S. influence and global governance, offer a more nuanced and historically grounded perspective. Institutions, rather than being neutral or fixed, are both shaped by and shape the socio-political environments in which they operate, particularly in systems where hegemonic powers, such as the United States, play a central role.

The historical narrative and theoretical frameworks, from Arrighi's (1994) hegemonic cycles to the institutional dynamics highlighted by Chang and Evans (2005), provide a foundation for understanding the evolving nature of U.S. leadership. The United States is undergoing a fundamental realignment of its global strategy, shifting away from the liberal multilateralism it championed towards a more unilateral approach. In the following sections, we will investigate how this shift correlates with a reliance on protectionist measures and a corresponding decline in the use of formal WTO dispute settlement mechanisms.

3. THE EVOLUTION OF THE MULTILATERAL TRADING SYSTEM

3.1 The Birth of Global Trade Governance: GATT and the Cold War Context

With the end of the Second World War, the world faced the challenge of reconstructing a new global order (Arrighi, 1994). European countries, especially the United Kingdom, were weakened by the war's devastation and lacked the capacity to reclaim their previous leadership roles. This uncertain international scenario sparked debates on recovery mechanisms, and which powers would lead the process. The Bretton Woods Conference marked a turning point, establishing a bipolar world order centered on the United States and the Soviet Union (Arrighi, 1994).

The geopolitical rivalry between the U.S. and the Soviet Union quickly shaped the postwar global framework (Mazzucchelli, 2009). While the Soviets consolidated control over Eastern Europe, the U.S. projected its influence across the Atlantic through what became known as Pax Americana (Van der Wee, 1986; Cohrs, 2018). This ideological competition accelerated the formation of separate economic blocs and defined competing legitimacy criteria.

Europe's urgent need for reconstruction fostered stronger international relations, largely driven by the asymmetric growth of the U.S. economy (Mazzucchelli, 2009). By 1945, the United States had seen rapid growth, with a 70% increase in per capita GDP since 1939, and its share of global production rose from under 40% to around 65% (Mazzucchelli, 2009). The U.S. also extended significant credit and military support to its allies, cementing its leadership in the postwar order.

The shift from centuries of Eurocentric dominance to American hegemony was marked by important changes in global dynamics. While both British and U.S. hegemonies promoted liberalism, their approaches differed. Britain pursued unilateral free trade, whereas the U.S. favored an intergovernmental model based on bilateral and multilateral agreements, as exemplified by the Bretton Woods Agreement and the creation of key international institutions (Arrighi, 1994).

The post-1945 institutional framework reflected the U.S. vision of multilateral cooperation and strategic economic interests, including a sharp rise in exports (Mazzucchelli, 2009). However, this multilateral ideal faced resistance due to tensions between Europe's British-led trade legacy and the emerging U.S. leadership (Vangrasstek & Pascal, 2013; Van der Wee, 1986).

In 1947, President Harry Truman promoted free trade through a UN conference, proposing the creation of an International Trade Organization (ITO). This agency would oversee tariff reductions, eliminate quotas, and prevent discrimination, aiming to consolidate a U.S.-led multilateral trading system (Vangrasstek & Pascal, 2013).

The Havana Charter, drafted in 1948 by over 50 countries, was to establish the ITO. However, the U.S. Congress refused to ratify it, citing national security concerns during the early Cold War (Arrighi, 1994; Vangrasstek & Pascal, 2023). In the meantime, the GATT was created in 1947 as a provisional framework to reduce tariffs and promote trade openness, eventually becoming de facto the global trade institution (Vangrasstek & Pascal, 2013).

Over 47 years, GATT held eight negotiation rounds that reflected shifts in global power, expanding its scope beyond tariffs to non-tariff barriers and dispute settlement (Vangrasstek & Pascal, 2013). The early rounds focused on institutionalizing multilateralism, while later rounds, such as the Dillon Round (1960–1961), addressed new realities, like the European Economic Community (Oliveira, 2007).

The collapse of Bretton Woods in the 1970s exposed industrial asymmetries, prompting the U.S. to adopt more protective "fair trade" policies during the Tokyo Round (1973–1979). The Quad (U.S., Canada, EU, Japan) resisted developing countries' demands, slowing consensus but achieving tariff cuts and new rules (Oliveira, 2007).

The Uruguay Round, launched in 1987 amid shifting power dynamics, addressed GATT's limitations by introducing a single undertaking and a dispute settlement system. With the end of the Cold War, U.S. leadership helped consolidate a liberal global order focused on openness and multilateralism, culminating in the 1994 Marrakesh Agreement and the 1995 founding of the WTO (Ikenberry, 2015).

3.2 The World Trade Organization: Institutional Strengthening and New Geopolitical Challenges

For the past 75 years, the Multilateral Trading System has aimed to expand free trade principles among global economies. Since the World Trade Organization was established in 1995, it has formalized this system by setting clearer rules and limits on trade agreements, fostering a competitive environment that supports innovation and economic growth worldwide (Vangrasstek & Pascal, 2013; European Commission, 2022). The WTO's framework integrates universal rules to govern member countries, enabling stability and smooth operation of global markets through negotiations, dispute resolution, rule administration, and policy review (Thorstensen, 1999).

Significant changes occurred when the WTO replaced GATT. Key principles were updated, such as rebranding contracting parties as member countries, enforcing the most-favored-nation rule to apply trade concessions universally (except in free trade zones), ensuring national treatment for foreign products, adopting a single undertaking requiring full commitment from members, and creating a faster dispute settlement mechanism (Thorstensen, 1999). These changes strengthened the WTO's legal authority and made consensus decision-making the institution's foundation (Vangrasstek & Pascal, 2013).

In its early years, the WTO expanded global trade, reduced tariffs, and broadened negotiation topics. However, the Doha Round, launched in 2001, remained unresolved due to disagreements that hamper dispute resolution and full trade liberalization (Vangrasstek & Pascal, 2013). The growing complexity within the WTO reflects a redistribution of global power and the challenges of reaching consensus among 164 member countries, reviving conflicts seen in the GATT era as nations defend their domestic trade interests.

Political dynamics within the WTO have become even more complicated, partly due to the consensus mechanism that allows any member to veto initiatives, slowing liberalization efforts and fostering legalistic hurdles (Vangrasstek & Pascal, 2013). Pressure from powerful member countries to reform the organization's legislative structure is ongoing. Trade disputes, especially between developed powers like the United States and the European Union, further complicate negotiations, as domestic political considerations often take precedence over international cooperation (Hopewell, 2021).

Notably, the U.S. Congress plays a crucial role in shaping American trade policy through the Constitutional Commercial Clause, which grants it veto power over WTO proposals and dispute resolutions, often prioritizing domestic interests (Vangrasstek & Pascal, 2013). This illustrates how global institutions influence national strategies and vice versa, with some countries joining the WTO later and adapting their approaches accordingly. Such dynamics underscore Chang's concept of institutional "perversion," where institutions evolve in ways that may undermine their original goals (Chang, 2010).

With the accession of China in 2001 and Russia in 2012, initially seen as essential to the global integration of the World Trade Organization, disputes and controversies involving major powers such as the United States and the European Union intensified. China's accession to the WTO reflected its rising prominence in the global geopolitical landscape and marked a broader economic transformation, characterized by a sharp increase in international trade participation. This shift complemented ongoing efforts from the Uruguay Round, contributing to the decline in trade barriers for developing countries, with the share of their exports facing tariffs above 15% projected to drop from 9% to 5% (WTO, n.d.-a).

Initially, China focused on understanding the institution's functioning and rules, guided by its bargaining power within the global economy. Later, it shifted toward defending its commercial competitiveness, especially through the Dispute Settlement Understanding (DSU), a legal mechanism of the WTO used by member countries to resolve trade disputes – as illustrated in Figure 1.

Figure 1. Number of disputes initiated, and original panels established

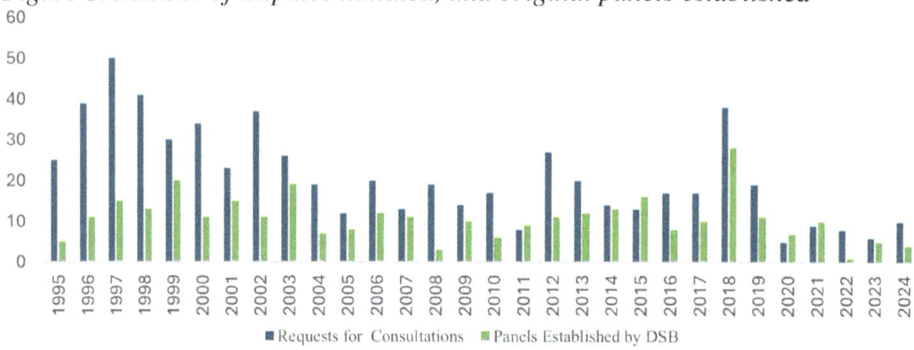

Note. In the figure, the Dispute Settlement Body (DSB) refers to the decision-making arm of the WTO that manages the legal process for resolving trade disputes among member countries. It operates under the DSU, the legal mechanism that provides the rules and procedures for these resolutions.

Source: Adapted from "Dispute settlement activity — some figures" by the World Trade Organization (n.d-b)

China's engagement with the WTO's dispute mechanism was strategic, aiming to preserve its economic position while asserting influence within the organization (Bekkers & Schroeter, 2020). As China gained prominence, tensions escalated, particularly with the U.S., which began questioning the legitimacy of WTO mechanisms. This trend is particularly evident in China's increasing role as both a complainant and a respondent, as illustrated by the continuous increase in the number of disputes initiated or original panels established by the DSB between 2001 and 2018.

This led to an increase in the use of the DSU by other member states pursuing economic and political objectives. Since 1995, 639 dispute cases have been registered since the WTO's creation in 1995 (WTO, n.d.-c). When consultations between parties fail, the dispute may proceed to a panel and, if necessary, to the Appellate Body.

The number of new consultations fell between 2019 and 2021 compared to the late 2010s, but pending appeals continued to grow (WTO, n.d.-b). In 2018, marked by the onset of the U.S.–China trade war, there was a surge in consultations, the highest since 1998, triggered by U.S. tariffs on Chinese goods like steel and aluminum (Figure 1). Between April and August 2018, China opened five consultations against the U.S., with only one reaching the Appellate Body, while the U.S. opened eight against various countries (WTO, n.d.-c). However, during Trump's first administration, the Appellate Body was rendered inoperative as the U.S. blocked new appointments, leading to institutional paralysis (Bekkers & Schroeter, 2020).

Due to the limitations of the dispute mechanism and the blocking of the Appellate Body, several members, particularly China and the U.S., resorted to retaliatory measures without awaiting final rulings, further escalating global tensions. This highlighted institutional weaknesses and reinforced calls for reform (Vangrasstek & Pascal, 2013). The global context evolved further with the COVID-19 pandemic, Biden's election in 2020, and the outbreak of the war in Ukraine in 2022, all of which renewed debates on the role of multilateralism and the WTO's relevance.

Biden reversed Trump's opposition to the appointment of Ngozi Okonjo-Iweala as WTO Director-General, signaling a more cooperative stance. Okonjo-Iweala emphasized a shift with coordinated responses to the economic impacts of the pandemic and the Ukraine war as a central mission (WTO, 2022). Yet, challenges such as intensifying global competition, rising protectionism, and institutional deadlocks continue to complicate the WTO's role.

An analysis of U.S. policy across Trump's two administrations and Biden's term, during the trade war, pandemic, and Ukraine crisis, invites reflection on whether shifts in the U.S. position on multilateralism represent isolated episodes or a broader reorientation of global governance.

4. FROM LEADER TO CHALLENGER: THE UNITED STATES AND THE WTO

4.1 Trump's First Administration (2017–2020): Trade War with China and Early COVID-19 Challenges

The trade relationship between the United States and China must be understood within the context of the post-Bretton Woods international economic order and Asia's development at the end of the 20th century. This era observed a surge in trade and investment flows to Asian countries, in particular China, and a modernization of their export bases. These shifts fueled greater regional integration and established China as a key global supplier, especially to the U.S., amid a restructuring of American capital that intensified outsourcing and offshoring (Cintra & Pinto, 2017).

To better illustrate the chronological sequence of events and their impact on U.S. hegemonic positioning towards the WTO, the timeline in Table 1 outlines key milestones discussed in this section.

Table 1. Chronology of Key Events in U.S. Hegemonic Positioning Towards the WTO (2018–2025)

2018	Under the pretext of national defense, the U.S.–China trade war begins
Early 2020	The U.S. and China reach a trade deal. The COVID-19 pandemic begins, leading to a sharp decline in global trade and the reinforcement of protectionist policies
2021	A return to diplomacy and multilateralism is expected with the Biden administration.
2022	Donald Trump begins his second term in the White House, and his protectionist stance becomes even more pronounced.
2025	Donald Trump begins his second term in the White House, and his protectionist stance becomes even more pronounced.
April 2, 2025	Trump declares "Liberation Day" and announces an extensive set of tariffs, including a 10% flat tariff on all U.S. imports and country-specific tariffs.

Source: Authors' compilation based on archival and secondary sources (e.g., Hopewell, 2021; Bounds, 2022; Mena, 2025)

By the early 2000s, China had overtaken Japan as the U.S.'s leading net exporter. A dual-pole configuration in the global economy emerged: the U.S. increasingly imported Chinese goods, while China's demand for regional inputs boosted Asian trade. This system made American consumption a key engine not only for China's exports but also for neighboring economies (Madeiros, 2016).

These trends reshaped global trade and shifted power dynamics, fueling debates over the role of institutions like the WTO. Under the Trump administration, the U.S. adopted protectionist rhetoric that challenged post-WWII multilateral norms (Hopewell, 2021). The U.S. total trade deficit with the world, illustrated in Figure 2, grew sharply from the early 2000s.

Figure 2. U.S. trade deficit in goods and services (US$ millions)

Source: Adapted from "International Trade Data" of the United States Census Bureau (n.d.)

The increase in the U.S. trade deficit was significantly driven by trade with China, an imbalance shaped by China's accession to the WTO, the 2008 financial crisis, and the subsequent U.S.-China trade war. The growing deficit, of which China was a major driver, became a key justification for a more aggressive U.S. trade posture.

Though trade frictions existed under Bush and Obama, they escalated dramatically under Donald Trump (2017–2020). While earlier administrations favored multilateralism, Trump embraced unilateralism. His "America First" policy prioritized national interests over global cooperation (Hopewell, 2021; Elms, 2021). Consequently, the administration began to more frequently invoke the GATT Article XXI security clause, reinterpreting it as a broad justification for actions that would otherwise breach international trade rules. This shift was not merely a change in rhetoric but was underpinned by a willingness to challenge the very foundations of the multilateral trading system.

As for the 2018 U.S.–China Trade War, it was more than a tariff dispute; it was a clear reflection of this new posture and a deep-seated American frustration with the WTO. The Trump administration withdrew from the Trans-Pacific Partnership and imposed tariffs on steel and aluminum under the claim of national security, triggering widespread concern.

In June 2018, the European Union requested a consultation by a WTO panel after the U.S. imposed tariffs of 25% on steel and 10% on aluminum imports. More than ten other countries joined the consultation, reflecting the widespread impact of the tariffs.

In a broader move to elevate trade protectionism, the Trump administration targeted countries with large trade surpluses, most notably China, and criticized the WTO for allegedly favoring developing countries (Elms, 2021). This period marked a clear shift from a rules-based system to a power-based approach in global trade.

Although U.S. dissatisfaction with the WTO predated Trump, it became more pronounced during his term. The U.S. criticized the WTO's dispute settlement system, despite generally winning most of its cases. However, it also frequently lost in disputes brought against it, fueling resentment (Hopewell, 2021).

Historically, the U.S. balanced free trade with protectionism, defending sectors like textiles and agriculture. But under Trump, this balance shifted sharply toward protectionism. The Office of the United States Trade Representative (USTR), a government agency responsible for developing and promoting American international trade policy, played a central role in implementing retaliatory measures, taking a more combative stance (Hopewell, 2021; Zoellick, 2022).

Under Trump, the USTR was empowered to launch investigations into Chinese trade practices, particularly regarding violations of intellectual property rights. These investigations were conducted under Section 301 of the Trade Act of 1974 and Section 232 of the Trade Expansion Act of 1962, the latter allowing retaliatory tariffs in cases deemed a threat to national security (Adekola, 2019; USTR, 2018a; Nelson, 2019).

Following a Section 301 investigation, China was accused of unfair trade practices. In July 2018, the U.S. imposed 25% tariffs on $34 billion of Chinese goods (USTR, 2018b), prompting immediate retaliation from China. The U.S. soon extended tariffs to another $16 billion in imports, again met with a reciprocal response (USTR, 2018c).

In September 2018, the U.S. imposed 10% tariffs on $200 billion in Chinese goods, later raised to 25% in 2019. China retaliated with 5–10% tariffs on $60 billion worth of U.S. goods (USTR, 2018d). By mid-2019, the U.S. raised tariffs on the $200 billion list and added another $300 billion in imports, effectively covering nearly all Chinese goods (USTR, 2018b). The main tariff exchanges are outlined in Table 2.

Table 2. Tariffs Imposed on Goods during the Trade War (in US$ Billion)

Stage	**Date**	**Tariff Imposer**	**Product per Segment**	**Tariffs**	**Value (US$ Billions)**
First wave	January/2018	U.S.	Solar panels	30% and 20%	$ 10,00
	March/2018	U.S.	Steel and aluminum	25% and 10%	$ 17-29
Second Wave	April/2018	China	Diverse products	15% -25%	$ 2,40

continued on following page

Table 2. Continued

Stage	Date	Tariff Imposer	Product per Segment	Tariffs	Value (US$ Billions)
Third wave	July/2018	U.S.	Diverse products	25%	$ 34,00
	July/2018	China	Diverse products	25%	$ 34,00
Fourth Wave	August/2018	U.S.	Diverse products	25%	$ 16,00
	August/2018	China	Diverse products	25%	$ 16,00
Sixth Wave	September/2018	U.S.	Diverse products	10%	$ 200,00
	May/2019	U.S.	Diverse products	Between 10% and 15%	$ 200,00
	June/2019	China	Diverse products	Between 10% and 25%	$ 60,00
Final Stage	September/2019	U.S.	Diverse products	15%	$ 126,00
	September/2019	China	Diverse products	Between 5% and 10%	$ 75,00
	February/2020	U.S.	Diverse products	10%	$ 126,00
	February/2021	China	Diverse products	3%	$ 75,00

Source: Adapted from Elms (2021). The table outlines the chronological stages of the U.S.-China tariff war. The brief, short-lived fifth wave of tariffs, which had a minimal impact on the overall timeline, is not included in this table.

The impact of the trade conflict reached beyond the U.S. and China, disrupting global supply chains and challenging the WTO's authority. By invoking unilateral "self-help" measures under Sections 301 and 232, both countries undermined WTO rules, particularly Article 23, which prohibits unilateral retaliation outside its framework (Nelson, 2019; Bhuimali & Chakraborty, 2018). These actions raised doubts about the WTO's capacity to resolve high-level disputes.

Although both countries continued to engage in the WTO, they often bypassed its rulings. China filed a formal complaint in 2018 but also imposed countermeasures without awaiting a decision (Nelson, 2019). The WTO only ruled in September 2020—after three complaints from China.

From 2018 to 2020, disputes at the WTO surged, with the U.S. and China each responsible for 14% of new cases. In 2018 alone, dispute filings reached their highest number since 1998 (WTO, n.d.-b). This reflected members' growing impatience with the WTO's slow resolution process and preference for immediate retaliation.

Table 3 summarizes strategies adopted by major powers during the period, with the U.S. largely undermining the system, while the EU and China sought to preserve a functional alternative. This divergence can be explained by two key institutional dynamics: the practice of appealing into the void, which refers to the practice of a party appealing to a panel ruling to the now-defunct Appellate Body, and the rise of the Multi-Party Interim Appeal Arbitration Arrangement (MPIA).

Table 3. WTO DSU Filings and Outcomes by Key Players (2018–2025)

	2001-2006	2007-2012	2013-2017	2018-2024	Key Issues	Participated in MPIA	Cases Appealed into the Void?
China	4	26	7	16	Non-agricultural products	Yes. The EU was one of the founding members of the MPIA, which was created in April 2020.	Yes. China has also been a respondent in cases appealed into the void, as the MPIA only applies when both disputing parties are members.
European Union	26	17	10	16	Agricultural products		No. As a member of the MPIA, the EU has committed to not appealing cases into the void when the other party is also an MPIA member.
United States	46	23	12	10	Commercial resources (antidumping, etc.)	No. The U.S. has actively chosen not to join and has expressed criticism of the arrangement.	Yes. The U.S. has been a user of the "appeal into the void" practice, appealing panel reports that have gone against it.
Others	61	32	52	54	Commercial resources among developing countries and agricultural products among developed ones.	-	-

Note. This table summarizes the dispute settlement activity of key WTO members, based on data from the World Trade Organization (n.d.-b). The data shows the number of cases and highlights each player's strategy in response to the WTO Appellate Body's impasse, which has led to a practice of "appealing into the void." The table also shows each member's participation in the Multi-Party Interim Appeal Arbitration Arrangement (MPIA), a temporary alternative to the defunct Appellate Body.

The MPIA was created to function as a temporary alternative to the paralyzed Appellate Body, allowing a group of WTO members, including the European Union and China, to "work around" disputes, maintaining a two-tiered, rules-based dispute settlement system (Starshinova, 2021). The WTO ultimately sided with China, ruling that U.S. tariffs violated WTO rules. This outcome was widely expected, as legal experts had long argued that U.S. measures breached fundamental trade principles (Elms, 2021; Nelson, 2019; Adekola, 2019; Bhuimali & Chakraborty, 2018).

Nevertheless, the U.S. rejected the ruling, claiming that its actions were justified under WTO exceptions. The panel disagreed, stating that the measures did not meet the necessary conditions. The USTR responded by accusing the WTO of failing to confront China's alleged IP theft (USTR, 2018e; 2018f). This reinforced the Trump administration's narrative that the WTO was ineffective in defending American interests.

The ruling had no practical impact. By then, the U.S. and China had already negotiated a bilateral agreement, rendering the WTO's decision symbolic (Nelson, 2019; Adekola, 2019). Furthermore, with the WTO Appellate Body paralyzed since late 2019, the U.S. could have appealed the decision, effectively suspending enforcement (Elms, 2021).

This case highlights the erosion of the WTO's authority and the urgent need for reform. The use of unilateral tools like Sections 301 and 232, coupled with disregard for the DSU, reshaped how countries perceive the WTO's legitimacy (Nelson, 2019; Adekola, 2019; Elms, 2021). The conflict did not remain confined to trade. The global outbreak of COVID-19 in early 2020 marked a new phase in international relations with wide-ranging economic and political effects (WHO, 2020).

The pandemic emphasized the critical need for international cooperation, yet responses were uneven between developed and developing countries. Many nations implemented lockdowns, social distancing, and rigorous monitoring while pursuing vaccine development, prompting international organizations such as the WHO, WTO, G7, and G20 to revise their strategies (Starshinova, 2021).

The WTO's role became especially significant given disparities in countries' development levels, financial capacities, and dependence on imports of medical goods. Although the WTO sought to foster equitable production of essential pandemic-related goods through early measures and conferences, many countries instead adopted nationalist and protectionist policies, restricting exports of medical supplies and food products, which exacerbated health system collapses in developing nations (WTO, 2020).

As Figure 3 shows, the total global merchandise export volumes from 2010 to 2024 experienced a significant, although short-lived, drop in 2020 before a rapid recovery began in 2021. This quick rebound can be attributed to improved health prospects and more effective pandemic control in key economies. The recovery took place alongside another crucial factor: rising prices caused by supply chain disruptions, which were further exacerbated by the Ukraine war and a commodity price shock in 2022 (IMF, 2022).

Figure 3. Total Global Merchandise Exports (US$ trillion)

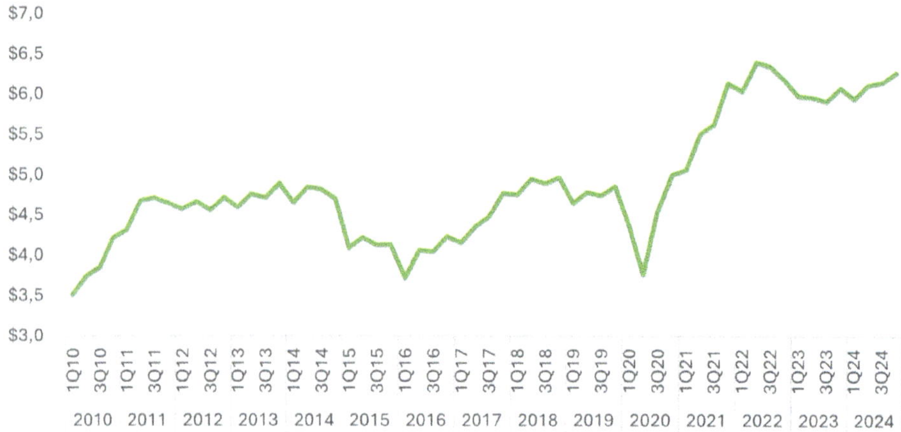

Source: Adapted from "WTO statistics database" by the World Trade Organization (n.d.-d)

After the pandemic was brought under control, but amid international conflicts such as the war in Ukraine, global trade flows began to stabilize. Although recovery rates became evident starting in 2021 due to low 2020 levels, average export growth rates remained below global levels, except for Asia, which saw exports rise by 13.8% during the period (WTO, n.d.-d).

Geoeconomic tensions also intensified during this period, notably between the United States, still under the Trump administration, and China, despite the Phase One agreement signed in January 2020. The impasses from the Trade War episode worsened during the pandemic, reinforcing issues around strategic control of key sectors, reducing external dependencies, and the technological race, thus pressuring the current rules-based system defended by multilateral institutions (Schoenbaum, 2023).

This period also saw the WTO face leadership challenges with Director-General Roberto Azevedo's resignation in August 2020, followed by a transitional period until Ngozi Okonjo-Iweala's appointment in early 2021, coinciding with shifts in U.S. administration. Despite difficulties, the WTO, supported by members like the EU, took steps to mitigate the pandemic's economic fallout and protect food security during the crisis (Schoenbaum, 2023).

4.2 Biden Administration (2021–2024): Pandemic Response and Geopolitical Turmoil

With Joe Biden's arrival at the White House, the United States intensified its support for multilateral actions and international cooperation, highlighting issues vital to the prosperity of U.S. foreign relations. In one of his first speeches, Biden (2021) declared that "America is back, [and with it] diplomacy returns to the center of our foreign policy." This approach contrasts sharply with the unilateral stance of the previous administration, which largely rejected parts of the multilateral institutions' actions. Biden's renewed multilateralism is visible not only in response to the COVID-19 pandemic but also in climate negotiations related to the Paris Agreement, NATO involvement, and strategic ties with the European Union (Haar, 2021).

Seeking to reestablish a central role for the U.S., the Biden administration aimed to redirect multilateral cooperation towards greater credibility and international recognition. In international trade, this was reflected in trying to strengthen ties with key partners, maintaining pressure on China's trade practices, and reinforcing the WTO's dispute settlement mechanisms (Patrick, 2021). Nevertheless, despite the global crisis and governmental change, trade tensions have persisted, indicating that structural conflicts remain unresolved.

Although the U.S. continues to be the most influential actor in shaping the WTO and the multilateral trading system, declining competitiveness in U.S. exporting sectors, combined with frustration over the effectiveness of multilateral conflict resolution mechanisms amid China's rise, has fostered a hostile environment between the U.S. and the institution (Chang & Evans, 2005).

Beyond the WTO, the role of informal forums such as the G20 and G7, which include the U.S., is noteworthy. During the 2008 financial crisis, the G20 acted decisively under U.S. and European leadership, coordinating efforts to manage risks and mitigate economic fallout (Schoenbaum, 2023). Expectations were high that a similar response would emerge during the COVID-19 pandemic; however, growing U.S. trade disputes with China and the EU, largely influenced by protectionist measures introduced under Trump and partially sustained by Biden, caused delays and diminished the G20's effectiveness in promoting international cooperation.

This lack of active engagement challenges the legitimacy and effectiveness of these forums. While Biden's administration has shifted the G20's focus to pandemic response, ongoing tensions between the U.S. and multilateral institutions have led to a cautious, often neutral stance. Despite the change in rhetoric, Biden's early months in office revealed a continuation of protectionist trade policies, maintaining unresolved frictions in the global economic order (Schoenbaum, 2023).

The defense of competitiveness and employability of American workers remained a key agenda for the Democratic Party, especially amid the growing influence of China's economy globally. Early in his term, President Biden appointed Katherine Tai as USTR, who pledged to tackle the economic challenges posed by China's rise through policies confronting its trade practices (Schoenbaum, 2023).

Although Washington initially expressed support for WTO initiatives during the COVID-19 pandemic, such as the intellectual property waiver for vaccines, Tai remained cautious and neutral during 2021, failing to present formal proposals. This posture has fueled perceptions that the U.S. has not made concrete advances in defending multilateralism under Biden, preserving a protectionist trade agenda justified as a national security issue amid geopolitical tensions (Schoenbaum, 2023).

Beyond the pandemic and the U.S.-China trade tensions, the February 2022 Russian invasion of Ukraine introduced significant global economic and trade disruptions. The conflict caused a sharp reduction in supplies of essential commodities such as grains and energy from Ukraine and Russia, driving commodity prices sharply upward in 2022 and forcing importers worldwide to seek alternative sources (Krueger, 2022a).

Europe faced severe energy shortages, particularly in Germany and Italy, heavily reliant on Russian gas. European nations responded by substituting Russian gas with liquefied natural gas, despite paying prices up to four times higher. These high energy costs, along with pandemic-related fiscal and monetary policies and persistent disruptions in production chains, collectively contributed to significant inflation (Krueger, 2022a).

In response to these challenges, major central banks worldwide raised interest rates to control inflation. Although initially ineffective, these measures gradually influenced commodity prices, further increasing exports. Contrary to expectations of a significant trade volume contraction due to war and pandemic disruptions, global trade volumes grew by 4.3% in the first quarter of 2022, reflecting remarkable resilience as illustrated in Figure 3 (WTO, n.d.-d). This performance underscored the adaptability of global trade networks despite ongoing crises.

Regarding Russian trade, numerous financial and commercial sanctions were imposed. The G7 and European Union proposed revoking Russia's Most Favored Nation tariff treatment, enabling them to sharply raise tariffs on Russian imports. This shift led countries like the United States to boost domestic production and become alternative suppliers of key inputs such as wheat and palladium. Additionally, the U.S. and Qatar increased short-term gas supplies to European economies to offset disruptions (WTO, n.d.-d).

Despite signaling a return to multilateral cooperation, the U.S. pursued protectionist trade policies by imposing sanctions on Russian goods and restricting foreign competition to protect domestic producers (Krueger, 2022a). Through the National Emergency Act and International Emergency Economic Powers Act, the U.S. executive branch issued Executive Orders regulating trade with Russia. Notably, Executive Orders 14066 and 14068, approved shortly after the Ukraine invasion, banned imports of fossil fuels, seafood, and other Russian products while restricting luxury goods exports to Russia (U.S. SENATE, 2022a; 2022b). Further legislative measures were unanimously approved to suspend broader trade ties with Russia.

The U.S. approach drew criticism from the European bloc, which viewed heavy investments in Ukraine and retaliatory trade laws as favoring the American defense industry at Europe's expense. In 2022, the Biden administration also passed the Inflation Reduction Act and the CHIPS and Science Act to subsidize sectors like chips and electric vehicles, with domestic content requirements reducing competitiveness in technology sectors important to Europe (Krueger, 2022b). This reflects a continuation of protectionist tendencies first seen during the U.S.-China trade conflict starting in 2018.

This emphasis on domestic industry aims to provide short-term cost advantages and attract foreign manufacturing to the United States, but strains relations with other countries and the WTO, especially as the WTO's dispute resolution system remains inactive (Krueger, 2022a; 2022c). These crises highlight the critical role of international engagement and the complex interplay between U.S. foreign policy and the multilateral trading system. Overall, the Biden administration, while promoting allied cooperation, maintained a trade agenda that balances diplomacy with protectionism justified by national security concerns.

4.3 The Trump Return: Political Dynamics and Trade Policy (Dis)Continuities

Economic factors did not support Biden's campaign, despite diplomacy and cooperation being at the core of his administration, leading to widespread public discontent and to the reelection of Donald Trump as president. The former president returned to the White House in January 2025, and since then, the American political climate, hoping to recapture America's golden period, has been marred by uncertainty. Marked by a flurry of daily actions, Trump's new term has unfolded in ways that diverge significantly from the expectations set during his initial campaign.

At the core of this new administration lies a focus on tariffs, implemented in a far more widespread manner. Additionally, the president has exercised his authority to conduct changes, ranging from renaming geographic locations, such as changing the "Gulf of Mexico" to the "Gulf of America", to promoting executive orders associated with migration, the federal government, climate, and the economy. Overall, in the first 100 days, Trump issued about 217 executive orders (Mena, 2025).

Given that inflation was a primary concern for voters during Biden's administration, early indications suggest that Trump's policies have yet to demonstrate effectiveness in curbing rising prices. With tariffs becoming the centerpiece of the new administration's strategy, domestic prices were expected to rise. The president announced plans to reignite the tariff dispute with China as part of an effort to overhaul U.S. trade policy and strengthen American industry (Financial Times, 2025; Feingold & Botwright, 2025).

In February 2025, Donald Trump announced a 10% increase in tariffs on all Chinese imports, followed by an additional 10% hike in March. What initially began as targeted measures against China soon escalated into a global campaign after the president introduced the "Liberation Day" tariffs. On April 2, 2025, he unveiled a reciprocal tariff increase: a universal 10% tariff on all imported goods, followed by further increases in selected countries starting on April 9. The new set of tariffs targeted a 34% rate on Chinese products, 20% on goods from the European Union, and up to 46% on imports from Vietnam. The administration justified this move as a corrective measure addressing perceived asymmetries in the U.S. open market and as a revenue-raising mechanism (Financial Times, 2025; Feingold & Botwright, 2025).

However, tariffs also brought significant challenges, including retaliation by trading partners and the downstream impact of higher costs on consumers. Within hours of the reciprocal tariffs package, governments began to respond to Trump's actions, with China and the European Union being the two main economic blocs suggesting countermeasures. The U.S. then established a 90-day pause on the reciprocal tariffs to reach negotiations.

Hence, the U.S. president continued to push for a new trade framework, threatening to impose 50% "reciprocal" tariffs on the EU if an agreement was not reached by August 1. After intense negotiations, a deal was announced on July 27, 2025, which averted the threatened tariffs. This agreement sets a new baseline 15% tariff on most EU exports to the U.S. and includes EU commitments to purchase large quantities of U.S. energy and to make significant investments in the U.S. (The Economist, 2025). While the agreement prevented a full-blown trade war, analysts have described it as "asymmetric" and a significant capitulation by the EU, leaving Europe in a more vulnerable position (The Economist, 2025).

In the private sector, the implications of this breakdown in the WTO's DSU system can also be observed. This shift introduces a new layer of uncertainty and risk for businesses engaged in international trade and investment, compelling firms to adapt by increasing compliance costs, re-routing supply chains, and decreasing cross-border investment. The decline of multilateral cooperation thus forces companies to prioritize political and geopolitical risk management alongside their core business strategies.

The U.S. and China engaged in a rapid tariff war following the U.S. "Liberation Day" announcement. After the U.S. imposed its initial tariffs, China responded by announcing a 34% tariff on U.S. imports, which it soon increased to 84% in the face of further U.S. threats. The tit-for-tat escalation peaked on April 10, when total U.S. tariffs on Chinese goods reached 125%, a level that China quickly matched (Lederer, 2025).

Diplomatic efforts successfully led to a meeting on May 10 in Geneva, where both sides agreed to de-escalate and roll back tariffs to 10%. This de-escalation marked a new phase of the conflict, as both nations shifted their focus to non-tariff barriers, with China restricting mineral exports and the U.S. imposing new technology and visa restrictions (Feingold & Botwright, 2025; Lederer, 2025).

Despite the easing of some tariffs, negotiations between the U.S. and China remain uncertain. The current environment of the global trading system highlights the far-reaching consequences of trade policy decisions. Before Donald Trump's return to the presidency in 2025, WTO economists had projected continued growth in global trade, driven by an expected increase in merchandise trade volumes. However, the announcement of new tariff measures prompted a reassessment of these expectations (WTO, 2025).

As of April 2025, the WTO revised its forecast for global merchandise trade growth to -0.2%, a sharp downgrade from the previous estimate of 2.7%. North America is expected to bear the brunt of the impact. This reversal in expectations underscores the fragility of trade flows to abrupt policy shifts. Moreover, the escalation of tariff wars between major economies has placed considerable strain on the WTO's rules-based system (WTO, 2025).

Needless to say, WTO members began filing complaints under the DSU against the United States, with China being the first to respond to the initial executive order issued in February. The central allegation concerned violations of the Most-Favored Nation obligation within the WTO. As anticipated, the United States invoked Article XXI of GATT, commonly referred to as the national security exception, as its defense. Following the implementation of the "Liberation Day" tariffs, China formally requested WTO consultations. Nevertheless, retaliation was seen as the most immediate and effective course of action, as the dispute panels, if established, would not be able to issue rulings on time (Wolff, 2025).

Despite these legal actions, the United States continues to avoid adverse panel rulings by appealing to the "void". In practical terms, the most concrete responses have come from member states using their domestic legislation, which permits retaliation when a respondent fails to comply under specific circumstances. This breakdown in multilateral cooperation raises serious questions about the future of international trade governance and the ability of existing institutions to manage conflict in an increasingly fragmented global trade system (McElwee, Bartels, & Carr, 2025).

5. CONCLUSION

As global competitiveness grows and geopolitical and economic tensions arise, the challenges faced by the WTO intensify, exposing the limits of its foundational principles. As the leading country in building and developing this system, the U.S.

coordinated it to facilitate cooperation among member countries. Multilateralism has consistently been seen as a crucial tool to promote economic development, as highlighted by IPE. This theoretical approach, which revisits the concept of institutions, seeks to better understand economic development challenges linked to the emergence of formal global institutions embedded in international organizations.

In the post-Cold War context, marked by strengthened U.S. hegemony and the establishment of the WTO, there was a more robust imposition of liberal institutions on other geopolitical actors. These institutions emphasize property rights and economic freedom as keys to development (Chang & Evans, 2005). Institutional theorists also stress the role of national interests in global geopolitics. The legitimacy of international organizations arises mainly from the alignment of geopolitical actors' interests. The WTO's history highlights U.S. dominance and its influence on the organization's power dynamics.

Since the GATT era, power dynamics have deeply influenced international trade governance. The U.S. played a key role in establishing the WTO and quickly used it to advance its interests, especially after the Soviet Union's collapse, integrating Eastern Europe and Asia into the system.

Yet, with growing complexity in global trade and the rise of new powers like China, dissatisfaction from the U.S. toward the WTO also grew. China's accession in 2001 and Russia's in 2012 sparked disputes led by the U.S. and the EU, encouraging bilateral negotiations and stalling the WTO's Doha Round. Furthermore, challenges faced by the WTO's appellate body reduced the organization's credibility in conflict resolution (Vangrasstek & Pascal, 2013).

Trump's presidency marked a shift in the U.S. trade policy, moving away from the core principles of the multilateral system. In 2018, the U.S. initiated a trade war with China, citing national defense concerns, and in 2020, protectionist measures were introduced in response to the COVID-19 pandemic. With the Biden administration in 2021, a return to diplomacy and multilateralism was expected, but the continuation of the pandemic and geopolitical conflicts like Russia's invasion of Ukraine intensified protectionism, even under a Democratic government (Bounds, 2022). Trump's return to the White House and the increasing number of executive orders make it unlikely that the U.S. will revert to its former position.

This calls for an examination of the U.S. role in shaping global institutions. As Zoellick (2022) noted, effective leadership involves adapting old systems to new challenges, which can lead to the "creative destruction" of multilateralism. After decades of U.S.-led multilateral trade governance, emerging powers and U.S. unilateral protectionism signal strains in the free trade-based system. This tension highlights the contradictory nature of U.S. foreign policy vis-à-vis earlier multilateral commitments.

The history of international institutions, especially the Multilateral Trading System, reflects U.S. interests that can both support and undermine the system. Understanding how hegemonic interests align with global challenges and individual advantages is key to grasping changes and obstacles in global governance today.

REFERENCES

Adekola, F. (2019). The WTO and US-China Trade Disputes: Legal and Strategic Dimensions. *Journal of International Economic Law*, *22*(4), 685–706.

Arrighi, G. (1994). *The Long Twentieth Century: Money, Power, and the Origins of Our Times*. Verso.

Arrighi, G., & Silver, B. J. (2001). *Chaos and Governance in the Modern World System*. University of Minnesota Press.

Bekkers, E., & Schroeter, S. (2020). *An economic analysis of the US–China trade conflict* (WTO Staff Working Paper ERSD-2020-04). World Trade Organization. https://www.wto.org/english/res_e/reser_e/ersd202004_e.htm

Bhuimali, A., & Chakraborty, P. (2018). WTO Under Stress: The Crisis of Multilateralism and Trade Dispute Resolution. *Economic Affairs*, *63*(4), 975–981.

Biden, J. (2021, February 4). *Remarks by President Biden on America's place in the world*. The White House. https://www.whitehouse.gov/briefing-room/speeches-remarks/2021/02/04/remarks-by-president-biden-on-americas-place-in-the-world

Börzel, T. A., & Zürn, M. (2021). Contestations of the liberal international order: From liberal multilateralism to postnational liberalism. *International Organization*, *75*(2), 282–305. DOI: 10.1017/S0020818320000570

Bounds, A. (2022). The WTO's lonely struggle to defend global trade. Financial Times. Retrieved October 15, 2022, from https://www.ft.com

Chang, H.-J. (2010). Institutions and Economic Development: Theory, Policy and History. *Journal of Institutional Economics*, *7*(4), 473–498. DOI: 10.1017/S1744137410000378

Chang, H.-J., & Evans, P. (2005). The Role of Institutions in the Economic Development of Nations. In Haque, U. M., Kanbur, R., & Venables, A. P. (Eds.), *Institutional Development and Economic Growth* (pp. 87–111). UNU-WIDER.

Cintra, M. A. M., & Pinto, A. C. (2017). The Asian Development Model and Its Impacts on Global Trade. *Revista de Economia Política*, *37*(4), 812–828.

Cohrs, P. O. (2018). *The new Atlantic order: The transformation of international politics, 1860–1933*. Cambridge University Press.

Elms, D. K. (2021). The U.S.–China Trade War: Impacts on Global Trade Governance. *World Economy*, *44*(5), 1214–1232.

European Commission. (2022). *The WTO: A multilateral trading system.* https://policy.trade.ec.europa.eu/eu-and-world/wto-multilateral-trading-system_en

Evans, P. (2014). The Role of Institutions in the Economic Development of the Global South. United Nations Development Programme (UNDP) Working Paper Series.

Feingold, S., & Botwright, K. (2025, June 25). *Tracking tariffs: Key moments in the US–China trade dispute. World Economic Forum.* Retrieved June 26, 2025, from https://www.weforum.org/stories/2025/06/trumps-us-china-trade-tariffs-timeline/

Financial Times. (2025, June 24). *EU readies retaliatory tariffs to secure better trade deal with Trump. Financial Times.* https://www.ft.com/content/3d336a84-ac59-45ee-b857-8a01fc7cd806 en.wikipedia.org+9ft.com+9reddit.com+9

Foot, R., MacFarlane, S. N., & Mastanduno, M. (2003). *US hegemony and international organizations: The United States and multilateral institutions.* OUP Oxford. DOI: 10.1093/0199261431.001.0001

Gerschenkron, A. (2015). *Economic Backwardness in Historical Perspective.* Belknap Press.

Haar, R. (2021). The Biden administration's incompatible views on multilateralism. [JSTOR.]. *Atlantisch Perspectief, 45*(5), 20–24.

Hopewell, K. (2021). Trump and Trade: The Crisis in the Multilateral Trading System. *New Political Economy, 26*(2), 271–282. DOI: 10.1080/13563467.2020.1841135

Ignatenko, A., Lashkaripour, A., Macedoni, L., & Simonovska, A. I. (2025). Making America Great Again? The Economic Impacts of Liberation. *Journal of International Economics, 157*, 104138.1-104138.12.

Ikenberry, G. J. (2015). The Future of the Liberal World Order: Internationalism After America. *Foreign Affairs, 90*(3), 56–68.

International Monetary Fund. (2022, April). Global Trade and Value Chains during the Pandemic. *World Economic Outlook.*

Krueger, A. (2022a). Will the Ukraine war revive the WTO? *Project Syndicate.* Retrieved April 15, 2023, from https://www.project-syndicate.org/commentary/wto-dispute-settlement-new-trade-issues-friend-shoring-by-anne-o-krueger-2022-05?barrier=accesspaylog

Krueger, A. (2022b). The false promise of America's CHIPS Act. *Project Syndicate.* Retrieved April 15, 2023, from https://www.project-syndicate.org/commentary/chips-act-will-not-keep-us-semiconductor-industry-on-top-by-anne-o-krueger-2022-11?barrier=accesspaylog

Krueger, A. (2022c). Sleepwalking into a global trade war. *Project Syndicate*. Retrieved April 15, 2023, from https://www.project-syndicate.org/commentary/trade-world-war-us-subsidies-protectionism-by-anne-o-krueger-2022-12?barrier=accesspaylog

Lapa, V. (2020). The WTO Panel Report in Russia – Traffic in Transit: Cutting the Gordian Knot of the GATT Security Exception? *Questions of International Law / Questions de Droit International*, 40, 15–38. https://www.qil-qdi.org/the-wto-panel-report-in-russia-traffic-in-transit-cutting-the-gordian-knot-of-the-gatt-security-exception/

Lederer, E. (2025, May 28). *U.S. says it will start revoking visas for Chinese students. Reuters*. Retrieved June 26, 2025, from https://www.reuters.com/world/us/rubio-says-us-will-start-revoking-visas-chinese-students-2025-05-28/ washingtonpost.com+10reuters.com+10staradvertiser.com+10

Madeiros, C. (2016). China and the Global Division of Labor: A Structural Perspective. *Estudos Avançados, 30*(88), 25–44.

Mazzucchelli, F. (2009). Estados Unidos e a reconstrução da ordem mundial do pós-guerra: Entre a ordem liberal e o mundo livre. *Revista Brasileira de Política Internacional, 52*(1), 98–117.

McElwee, M., Bartels, L., & Carr, C. (2025, April 9). *Trump's tariffs: WTO consultations requested by China, Canada and the European Union*. Freshfields Risk & Compliance. Retrieved June 26, 2025, from https://riskandcompliance.freshfields.com/post/102k86k/trumps-tariffs-wto-consultations-requested-by-china-canada-and-the-european-un

Mena, B. (2025, April 2). Key takeaways from Trump's Liberation Day tariffs. CNN. https://edition.cnn.com/2025/04/02/economy/key-takeaways-from-trumps-liberation-day-tariffs/index.html

Nelson, M. (2019). *U.S. Trade Policy: Section 301 and 232 Investigations and the Role of the WTO*. Congressional Research Service (CRS) Report R45529. https://crsreports.congress.gov

North, D. C. (1990). *Institutions, Institutional Change and Economic Performance*. Cambridge University Press. DOI: 10.1017/CBO9780511808678

North, D. C. (1992). *Transaction Costs, Institutions, and Economic Performance*. ICS Press.

North, D. C. (2018). *Entendendo o processo de mudança econômica* (3rd ed.). Editora Senac.

Office of the United States Trade Representative (USTR). (2018a). *Findings of the investigation into China's acts, policies, and practices related to technology transfer, intellectual property, and innovation under section 301 of the Trade Act of 1974*. Washington, DC. Retrieved May 10, 2022, from https://ustr.gov/sites/default/files/Section%20301%20FINAL.PDF

Office of the United States Trade Representative (USTR). (2018b). *USTR finalizes tariffs on $200 billion of Chinese imports in response to China's unfair trade practices*. Washington, DC. Retrieved April 28, 2021, from https://ustr.gov/about-us/policy-offices/press-office/press-releases/2018/september/ustr-finalizes-tariffs-200

Office of the United States Trade Representative (USTR). (2018c). *Rebalancing United States-China trade*. Washington, DC. Retrieved June 30, 2022, from https://ustr.gov/phase-one

Office of the United States Trade Representative (USTR). (2018d). *$300 billion trade action (List 4)*. Washington, DC. Retrieved May 15, 2022, from https://ustr.gov/issue-areas/enforcement/section-301-investigations/section-301-china/300-billion-trade-action

Office of the United States Trade Representative (USTR). (2018e). *Section 301 investigations*. Washington, DC. Retrieved May 15, 2022, from https://ustr.gov/issue-areas/enforcement/section-301-investigations

Office of the United States Trade Representative (USTR). (2018f). *USTR finalizes second tranche of tariffs on Chinese products in response to China's unfair trade practices*. Washington, DC. Retrieved May 15, 2022, from https://ustr.gov/about-us/policy-offices/press-office/press-releases/2018/august/ustr-finalizes-second-tranche

Oliveira, G. (2007). O sistema multilateral de comércio: Da Rodada Uruguai à OMC. *Revista de Economia Contemporânea*, *11*(2), 305–327. DOI: 10.1590/S1415-98482007000200006

Patrick, S. (2021, February 4). *The Biden administration and the future of multilateralism*. Observer Research Foundation. https://www.orfonline.org/expert-speak/biden-administration-future-multilateralism

Pecequilo, C. S. (2012). *O poder e a nova ordem global*. Saraiva.

Pires, L. S., & Mattos, C. (2016). A crise estrutural do capital: Elementos teóricos e implicações para a economia mundial contemporânea. *Revista de Economia Contemporânea*, *20*(2), 207–230.

Schoenbaum, T. J. (2023). The Biden Administration's Trade Policy: Promise and Reality. German Law Journal, 24(Special Issue 1), 102-124. DOI: 10.1017/glj.2023.7

Silvestre, L. (2019). Ciclos hegemônicos e transições sistêmicas: Arrighi e a China como potência emergente. *Revista Brasileira de Política Internacional*, *62*(1), e004. DOI: 10.1590/0034-7329201900104

Starshinova, O. (2021). Is the MPIA a Solution to the WTO Appellate Body Crisis? *Journal of World Trade*, *55*(5), 787–803. DOI: 10.54648/TRAD2021033

The Economist. (2025, July 28). *EU-US trade deal explained.* Retrieved from https://shows.acast.com/theeconomistmorningbriefing/episodes/eu-us-trade-deal-takes-shape-israels-new-negotiations-with

Thorstensen, V. (1999). O Brasil e a OMC: Desafios e oportunidades. *Revista Brasileira de Comércio Exterior*, *59*, 3–11.

United States Census Bureau. (n.d.). *International trade data* [Data set]. Retrieved May 27, 2025, from https://www.census.gov/foreign-trade/data/index.html

U.S. Senate. (2022a). Roll call vote #131, 117th Congress, 2nd session. Retrieved April 7, 2023, from https://www.senate.gov/legislative/LIS/roll_call_votes/vote1172/vote_117_2_00131.htm

U.S. Senate. (2022b). Roll call vote #132, 117th Congress, 2nd session. Retrieved April 7, 2023, from https://www.senate.gov/legislative/LIS/roll_call_votes/vote1172/vote_117_2_00132.htm

Van der Wee, H. (1986). Prosperity and upheaval [Penguin.]. *World Economy*, 1945–1980.

Vangrasstek, C., & Pascal, L. (2013). *The history and future of the World Trade Organization.* World Trade Organization. https://www.wto.org/english/res_e/booksp_e/historywto_e.pdf

Veblen, T. (1988). *The Theory of the Leisure Class.* Penguin Classics. (Original work published 1899)

Wolff, A. W. (2025, April 10). *The WTO at 30: The return of higher tariffs.* Peterson Institute for International Economics. Retrieved June 26, 2025, from https://www.piie.com/commentary/speeches-papers/2025/wto-30-return-higher-tariffs

World Health Organization. (2020, March 11). WHO Director-General's opening remarks at the media briefing on COVID-19 – 11 March 2020. https://www.who.int/director-general/speeches/detail/who-director-general-s-opening-remarks-at-the-media-briefing-on-covid-19---11-march-2020

World Trade Organization. (2020). World Trade Report 2020: Government policies to promote innovation in the digital age. https://www.wto.org/english/res_e/booksp_e/wtr20_e/wtr20_e.pdf

World Trade Organization. (2022, December 20). DG Okonjo-Iweala: WTO can help strengthen global food security and resilience. https://www.wto.org/english/news_e/news22_e/dgno_20dec22_e.htm

World Trade Organization. (2025, April). *Global Trade Outlook and Statistics: Outlook for world trade in 2025 and 2026* [PDF]. Retrieved June 26, 2025, from https://www.wto.org/english/res_e/booksp_e/trade_outlook25_e.pdfwto.org+9wto.org+9wto.org+9

World Trade Organization. (n.d.-a). Understanding the WTO: The agreements – Goods: Rules on trade in goods. Retrieved May 15, 2025, from https://www.wto.org/english/thewto_e/whatis_e/tif_e/agrm2_e.htm

World Trade Organization. (n.d.-b). *Dispute settlement activity — some figures.* Retrieved June 10, 2025, from https://www.wto.org/english/tratop_e/dispu_e/dispustats_e.htm

World Trade Organization. (n.d.-c). Dispute settlement. Retrieved June 29, 2025, from https://www.wto.org/english/tratop_e/dispu_e/dispu_e.htm

World Trade Organization. (n.d.-d). WTO statistics database. Retrieved June 29, 2025, from https://stats.wto.org/

Zoellick, R. B. (2022). Before the next shock: How America can build a more adaptive global economy. *Foreign Affairs*, *101*, 86.

Chapter 4
Beyond WTO TFA: Building Digital Trust and Transparency in Fragmented Trade

Aleksandr Orel
https://orcid.org/0009-0004-8045-6135
Competence Center for Trade Facilitation, M. Ryskulbekov Kyrgyz Economic University, Russia

Aleksei Bondarenko
United Nations Economic and Social Commission for Asia and the Pacific, Thailand

Anton Kozhankov
Moscow State Institute of International Relations, Russia

ABSTRACT

This chapter examines why, in an era of trade fragmentation, regulatory divergence, and the shift toward data-driven commerce, it has become necessary to move beyond the WTO Trade Facilitation Agreement (TFA). It analyzes how geopolitical tensions, ESG disclosure requirements, export controls, and differences in rules of origin increase compliance complexity and costs. The chapter highlights the limitations of the current TFA, which was designed for a pre-digital era, and argues for the creation of trusted, interoperable digital trade frameworks, cross-border data exchange, and the use of verifiable digital credentials to ensure transparency, predictability, and inclusion in trade. Drawing on examples from various regions, the chapter demonstrates how emerging technologies can help reduce both physical and digital trade barriers. In conclusion, it outlines key principles for a WTO TFA 2.0 that reflects the realities of modern, trust-based, and sustainable global trade.

DOI: 10.4018/979-8-3373-3835-4.ch004

1. INTRODUCTION: TRADE FRAGMENTATION AND THE FAILURE OF OLD INSTRUMENTS

International trade is undergoing a profound transformation driven by both geopolitical and technological shifts. In recent years, the intensification of geopolitical fragmentation has undermined established mechanisms of global commerce. Strategic rivalry among major powers, waves of sanctions, politically motivated trade barriers, and the reconfiguration of global production networks are fundamentally reshaping the international trade landscape.

One of the most visible manifestations of this fragmentation has been the escalating trade and economic confrontation between the United States and China. Since 2018, both countries have introduced hundreds of new tariff and non-tariff barriers, leading to a widespread restructuring of supply chains. Under the second administration of President Donald J. Trump, beginning in 2025, protectionist trade policy has gained new momentum (CRF, "Trump's Economic Disruption: The World Adapts, Council of Councils"). Beyond China, restrictive measures have also targeted all countries, including allies, such as Canada, Mexico, Australia, and even the European Union. While the stated rationale includes national security, combating illicit drug flows, and correcting trade imbalances, the broader effect has been to accelerate destabilizing trends in the global system.

Concurrently, trade regionalization is accelerating. The proliferation of regional and bilateral trade agreements, such as Comprehensive and Progressive Agreement for Trans-Pacific Partnership (CPTPP), Regional Comprehensive Economic Partnership (RCEP), ASEAN+1 frameworks, and European Union (EU) Free Trade Agreements (FTAs), has produced overlapping and sometimes conflicting obligations. According to the Organisation for Economic Co-operation and Development (OECD) (2023), this "regulatory layering" increases trade compliance costs by 5–10% depending on the sector, complicating cross-border operations for businesses engaged in multi-jurisdictional trade (OECD, 2021).

Another critical dimension of fragmentation has been the tightening of export control regimes. Between 2022 and 2024, the number of restrictions on the export of dual-use goods, advanced technologies, and software increased significantly. Group of Seven (G7) countries, the EU, the U.S., and their partners have strengthened oversight of supply chains to prevent the misuse of sensitive technologies for military or illicit purposes (European Commission, Report highlights EU's approach to export controls of dual-use items, 2025). While such actions respond to growing security threats, they also contribute to the legal fragmentation of global trade.

Furthermore, the shift towards reshoring, nearshoring, and friendshoring—driven by political risk and compliance pressures is restructuring production geography. Corporations are increasingly relocating operations to politically aligned or geographically proximate locations. According to the World Bank Logistics Report (2023), this trend increases logistical costs, especially for developing countries that risk being excluded from global value chains (World Bank Blogs, "Improving Resilience and Economic Efficiency in Global Supply Chains to Counter Shocks").

The role of the private sector is also evolving. Firms are increasingly expected not only to comply with technical customs procedures but also to meet growing transparency and accountability obligations tied to Environmental, Social and Governance (ESG) performance, forced labor regulations, and dual-use controls (European Commission, "Corporate Sustainability Due Diligence Directive (CSDDD)", 2024). European Commission. These new requirements introduce new challenges such as transaction costs and legal uncertainties, particularly for small and medium enterprises (SMEs) in developing economies.

At the same time, a new paradigm of data-driven trade is emerging. As paper-based documentation gives way to structured, machine-readable data flows, data itself becomes the core asset of modern trade operations. Trust in these digital transactions (trust in data accuracy, origin, security, and legal recognition) is becoming essential. This "trust layer" is foundational for the seamless functioning of cross-border digital trade.

Technologies such as artificial intelligence, blockchain, and big data analytics are rapidly transforming trade processes by automating decisions, verifying authenticity, and improving supply chain visibility. However, the legal frameworks required to support the use of these technologies in cross-border contexts remain fragmented and underdeveloped. Key questions about legal equivalence, data privacy, liability, and interoperability persist, creating uncertainty for governments and businesses alike.

As digital trade expands, the need for harmonized legal standards and trust mechanisms becomes more urgent. Addressing these legal and institutional gaps will be essential for ensuring that innovation supports, not undermines, transparency, security, and resilience in global commerce.

1.1. Key Dimensions of Trade Fragmentation

1.1.1 Diverging Rules of Origin (ROO)

One of the most visible consequences of trade fragmentation is the increasing complexity of rules of origin. The simultaneous proliferation of overlapping FTAs has resulted in inconsistent criteria and documentation requirements. For example:

- Under RCEP, cumulation of origin is allowed across all parties, yet these rules diverge significantly from those used in CPTPP, complicating the use of preferential tariffs under multiple agreements (Byrnes, CETA European opportunity for Canadians).

- In the EU, rules of origin vary across its FTAs with Canada (CETA), Japan, and the Caribbean countries, requiring different certificates, origin calculation methods, and verification procedures—even for the same product (Byrnes, CETA European opportunity for Canadians).
- The AfCFTA presents another example where ROO are still being negotiated and may not align with existing national trade regimes or African bilateral agreements with external partners (The African Continental Free Trade Area Secretariat Rules of Origin Manual, 2022).

This growing divergence increases the administrative burden on businesses and creates barriers to full utilization of tariff preferences, particularly in sectors with complex supply chains.

Table 1. Comparative table of ROO under RCEP, CPTPP, and EU FTAs

Feature	**RCEP**	**CPTPP**	**EU FTAs (e.g., CETA, Japan, Caribbean EPA)**
Cumulation of Origin	Diagonal cumulation across all RCEP members	Full cumulation allowed across all CPTPP parties	Bilateral or diagonal cumulation depending on each FTA
Certificate of Origin	Form RCEP issued by competent authorities; some limited self-declaration	Self-certification by exporters (except some transitional provisions)	Varies: CETA allows self-declaration; Japan and Caribbean FTAs require Form EUR.1 or invoice declaration
Product-Specific Rules (PSR)	Harmonized rules based on HS 2017; may require tariff shifts or RVC	Detailed PSRs using tariff shift (CTC), RVC, or process-based criteria	Each FTA has distinct PSRs, even for the same product
Minimum Regional Value Content (RVC)	RVC thresholds vary (typically ~40%); limited cumulation may restrict flexibility	RVC and other criteria like CTC or process rules are widely used	RVC or substantial transformation required; thresholds vary across agreements
Verification Procedures	Conducted by importing authority or issuing body; includes post-clearance audits	Conducted by importing country's customs; exporter audits and site visits allowed	Varies: may include retrospective checks, third-party audits, and mutual administrative cooperation

continued on following page

Table 1. Continued

Feature	RCEP	CPTPP	EU FTAs (e.g., CETA, Japan, Caribbean EPA)
Digitalization of ROO	Limited digitalization; mostly paper-based with some exporter databases	Moderate: some electronic platforms, but mostly paper-based	Mixed: some FTAs (e.g., CETA) support e-declarations; others (e.g., Caribbean EPA) remain paper-based
Main Challenges	Cumulation is less flexible; divergence with CPTPP/CPTAs complicates multi-agreement use	Complex for SMEs due to multiple compliance layers; verification burdens	Fragmentation: different documentation, rules, and verification for similar products across various FTAs

This comparative analysis highlights the complexity and fragmentation of ROO across major trade agreements. While RCEP promotes regional integration through diagonal cumulation, it remains less flexible than CPTPP, which offers full cumulation and simplified self-certification. In contrast, EU FTAs present a patchwork of varying rules, certificates, and verification procedures, creating challenges for businesses operating across multiple agreements. Overall, the lack of harmonization in ROO frameworks increases compliance burdens and reduces the usability of preferential trade regimes, particularly for SMEs and exporters in developing countries.

1.1.2 Export Control

Fragmentation is also intensifying in the domain of export controls. Diverging national security interests have led to the emergence of parallel control regimes, each with distinct scope, coverage, and enforcement mechanisms:

- The United States enforces the Export Administration Regulations (EAR), which include restrictions based on destination countries, end-users, end-uses, and product categories (administered by BIS) (USA, Export Administration Regulations (EAR)).
- The European Union operates its own Dual-Use Regulation (2021/821), requiring exporters to secure licenses for the transfer of sensitive technologies outside the EU (EU, Regulation 2021/821).
- China, Russia, and other countries have introduced their own control lists and licensing systems, often with limited mutual recognition (China Briefing, China Issues New Export Control Regulations: What Businesses Need to Know?).

Figure 1. Venn diagram comparing U.S., EU, and Chinese export control regimes[1]

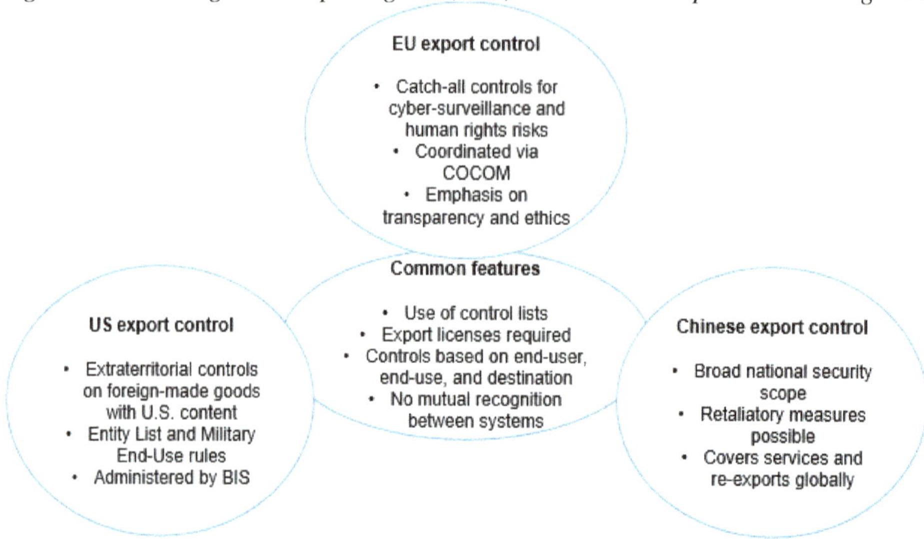

There is no mutual recognition of licenses, control lists, or enforcement procedures between export control regimes. Each jurisdiction maintains its own classification systems, restrictions, and licensing mechanisms, contributing to a growing fragmentation of global export governance. As a result, firms engaged in international trade must navigate a patchwork of incompatible control regimes, overlapping embargo lists, and multiple licensing authorities—significantly increasing the risk of non-compliance, administrative burden, and delays in cross-border transactions.

1.1.3 ESG and Sustainability Standards

A particularly acute manifestation of trade fragmentation is the rapid proliferation of incompatible ESG disclosure frameworks and sustainability standards. These divergent regulatory approaches are transforming compliance from a sectoral concern into a cross-cutting trade facilitation issue, with significant implications for transparency, interoperability, and digital trust in global supply chains.

- The EU CBAM (Carbon Border Adjustment Mechanism) introduces mandatory carbon accounting for imported products such as steel, cement, aluminum, fertilizers, and hydrogen (European Commission, Carbon Border Adjustment Mechanism). From 2026, importers must purchase carbon certificates equivalent to the EU's carbon price, effectively linking environmental performance to market access. This places a heavy compliance burden on exporters in developing countries, many of whom lack the digital infrastructure and verified emissions data to comply effectively.

- The EU CSRD (Corporate Sustainability Reporting Directive), in force from 2024, expands ESG reporting obligations to a wide range of EU and non-EU companies (Normative, EU Companies Will Have to Disclose Their Impact on the Environment to Help Consumers and Investors Make Sustainable Choices). It requires detailed, standardized disclosures on environmental, social, and governance factors across entire value chains, backed by verifiable and auditable data. Importantly, CSRD integrates digital taxonomy alignment and machine-readable data formats, raising the bar for digital trust and structured data exchange.
- In parallel, the U.S. Securities and Exchange Commission (SEC) has introduced new rules for climate-related risk disclosure, focused primarily on financial materiality and investor protection (Carbo Chain, The US SEC Climate-related Disclosure Rules Explained). Other jurisdictions—Australia, Canada, Japan, South Korea, and Singapore—are developing or refining their own ESG frameworks, each with distinct scope, timelines, and methodologies, further complicating cross-border compliance.

These unaligned regimes present growing challenges for trade facilitation:

- Lack of harmonization leads to duplicate and inconsistent reporting, raising the cost of compliance and discouraging participation by SMEs and exporters from least developed countries (LDCs).
- Absence of interoperability between national reporting systems undermines the ability to aggregate or verify ESG-related trade data across borders.
- The need to digitally verify emissions, supply chain practices, and social impact introduces a new layer of complexity in documentary compliance and risk management at the border.

From a trade facilitation perspective, ESG disclosure regimes now function as de facto non-tariff measures, affecting both market access and competitiveness. Without a coordinated response, the divergence in ESG rules may erode the principles of transparency, predictability, and fairness enshrined in the WTO Trade Facilitation Agreement (TFA).

The rise of data-driven sustainability obligations reinforces the need to build digital trust architectures that support:

- Cross-border recognition of ESG data and digital certificates (e.g., emissions reports, social audits)

- Common data models and taxonomies, allowing ESG data to be interoperable across jurisdictions
- Trusted data exchange platforms, ideally linked with national Single Window environments or regional trade digitalization frameworks

In this new landscape, the facilitation of sustainable trade requires not just faster clearance and streamlined procedures, but also reliable, verifiable, and harmonized sustainability data. ESG-driven fragmentation illustrates why the next phase of trade facilitation must move beyond forms and into trusted digital ecosystems that accommodate emerging regulatory domains.

1.1.4 SMEs and Developing Countries: Disproportionate Impact

Trade fragmentation has a disproportionately severe impact on small and medium-sized enterprises and firms in developing countries, which often lack the financial resources, technical infrastructure, and institutional capacity to navigate complex and shifting regulatory landscapes. While large multinational corporations can absorb compliance costs and dedicate entire teams to regulatory tracking, SMEs frequently operate with minimal administrative support and outdated digital systems, placing them at a structural disadvantage. Key challenges are presented in Table 2.

Table 2. Key Challenges for SMEs

Challenge	Content
1. Rising compliance costs	SMEs face growing administrative burdens as international trade becomes increasingly regulated. For example, preparing the documentation required to demonstrate origin or calculate carbon emissions may require hiring third-party consultants, auditors, or digital service providers. According to the World Bank Logistics Performance Index 2023, SMEs in developing economies may spend 5–7% of annual revenue on compliance, while large firms typically spend only 1–2% (World Bank, World Bank Releases Logistics Performance Index 2023).
2. Unpredictable market access	With the rapid introduction of uncoordinated ESG, human rights, and digital standards, SMEs often lack the capacity to respond quickly. Many are forced to withdraw from certain export markets altogether due to regulatory uncertainty, particularly when rules change mid-contract or require extensive supply chain data that is difficult to obtain.
3. Risk of border delays or rejections	Measures such as the U.S. Uyghur Forced Labor Prevention Act (UFLPA) and the EU's Carbon Border Adjustment Mechanism (CBAM) illustrate the growing enforcement of values-based trade policies. Under UFLPA, all importers regardless of size must demonstrate that their goods are not linked to forced labor in Xinjiang, or risk shipment detention or denial at the U.S. border. This poses a significant challenge for SMEs, which often lack the capacity to conduct extensive supply chain due diligence (US Customs and Border Protection, Uyghur Forced Labor Prevention Act Statistics 2025). In contrast, CBAM currently exempts most SMEs that import low volumes (under 50 tonnes annually) of targeted goods such as steel, aluminium, and fertilizers (Illuminem, EU moves to ease CBAM rules for SMEs while keeping 99% of emissions covered 2025). However, SMEs operating in these sectors at scale or as part of larger global value chains may still be subject to reporting and carbon cost obligations. Even for these firms, minor documentation errors or a lack of digital transparency can lead to delays, penalties, or reputational damage.

From the perspective of trade facilitation, this dynamic presents a critical policy challenge: traditional approaches under the WTO Trade Facilitation Agreement, such as streamlining procedures and reducing documentation, must now be complemented by mechanisms that address compliance complexity and digital asymmetry.

To ensure that SMEs and firms in the Global South are not excluded from global markets, next-generation trade facilitation must incorporate:

1) Digital trust frameworks, including verifiable credentials, digital audit trails, and blockchain-enabled traceability that allow even small firms to demonstrate compliance with origin, ESG, and labor standards in a transparent, interoperable format.
2) SME-inclusive Single Window systems. Single Windows must evolve beyond customs to integrate ESG and sustainability documentation, providing plug-and-play tools for SMEs to access, complete, and submit data with low technical barriers.
3) Targeted capacity building and digital public goods. Governments and development partners should invest in open digital tools, template registries, and

regional compliance platforms to help SMEs reduce cost and improve access to standardized reporting mechanisms.

The future of trade facilitation lies not only in reducing physical bottlenecks but also in reducing digital and regulatory frictions. As ESG, human rights, and climate-related regulations proliferate, SMEs risk being left behind unless trade facilitation frameworks are updated to ensure equity, interoperability, and digital inclusion. In this context, building trusted, digitally enabled ecosystems becomes essential to achieving both sustainable development and an inclusive global trading system.

1.1.5 Case Examples: The Cost of Fragmentation

Fragmentation in trade governance is not a theoretical concern, it has immediate, tangible impacts on exporters, especially in developing economies. The examples below illustrate how even routine trade operations now require navigating multiple regulatory regimes, each with distinct documentation, verification, and licensing procedures. These overlapping frameworks transform export compliance into a complex and resource-intensive task.

Case 1. A Vietnamese aluminium manufacturer must prepare and maintain three separate Rules of Origin (ROO) documentation packages to qualify for preferential tariffs under the CPTPP, RCEP, and EU FTAs. Each agreement applies different calculation rules, certification formats, and verification procedures, despite covering largely the same product (Hanh, 2025).

Case 2. A Thai electronics exporter shipping dual-use components to both the United States and the European Union must comply with both U.S. Export Administration Regulations (EAR) and the EU Dual-Use Regulation (2021/821). This entails separate licensing processes, classification standards, and end-user checks, significantly increasing lead times and administrative burden (Export Compliance Training Institute, A Comparison Between U.S. Export Controls and European Export Controls, 2023).

Case 3. A Hong Kong-based textile exporter, such as the Esquel Group, faces growing compliance pressure when serving Western markets. To continue shipping to the United States, the company must comply with the Uyghur Forced Labor Prevention Act (UFLPA), which prohibits the import of goods suspected of being linked to forced labor in China's Xinjiang region. Although headquartered outside mainland China, Esquel was added to the UFLPA Entity List in 2024 due to ties with cotton suppliers in Xinjiang, effectively blocking its U.S. shipments unless it can demonstrate clean supply chains. At the same time, to maintain access to the European market, the company must also meet the requirements of the EU's Corporate Sustainability Reporting Directive (CSRD), which mandates ESG disclosures across the entire supply chain, including environmental and labor practices. Complying with both frameworks requires extensive data collection, continuous monitoring of upstream suppliers, audit readiness, and often the engagement of third-party verification providers. For companies operating in global textile value chains, these overlapping obligations significantly increase the cost and complexity of compliance (The Wall Street Journal, Hong Kong's Esquel Group Added to U.S. Forced Labor Ban List).

These case examples underscore how trade fragmentation transforms traditional export transactions into multi-jurisdictional compliance exercises, often involving duplicative processes, elevated risk of shipment disruption, and substantial additional cost, particularly for SMEs and firms in developing countries. In the absence of mutual recognition or interoperable systems, the burden of reconciling fragmented regimes falls squarely on the private sector.

This section has examined the evolving landscape of trade fragmentation, emphasizing its growing complexity and tangible impact on global commerce. While fragmentation manifests in many ways, its effects are particularly pronounced in four key areas:

- Diverging Rules of Origin (ROO), which complicate the use of preferential tariffs and increase administrative burdens for exporters operating under multiple trade agreements;
- Export control regimes, where the lack of coordination between jurisdictions (e.g., the U.S., EU, China) forces firms to navigate overlapping licensing procedures and compliance frameworks;
- ESG and sustainability disclosure standards, which are emerging as powerful non-tariff barriers due to their inconsistency, lack of interoperability, and escalating reporting demands;
- The disproportionate burden on SMEs and developing countries, which often lack the institutional and technological capacity to adapt to fragmented regulatory environments.

Collectively, these dimensions of fragmentation transform international trade from a relatively rules-based system into a patchwork of overlapping obligations, disconnected standards, and regulatory uncertainty. For many firms—particularly those in developing countries—this means increased costs, delayed shipments, and lost market opportunities.

The WTO Trade Facilitation Agreement (TFA) was originally designed to reduce such barriers by streamlining border procedures and enhancing transparency. However, as trade becomes increasingly data-driven, risk-based, and sustainability-oriented, the scope and instruments of the TFA must evolve. The current fragmentation calls for a new generation of trade facilitation—one that includes digital trust infrastructure, interoperable compliance frameworks, and inclusive solutions for SMEs.

In the next section, we explore how digitalization, mutual recognition mechanisms, and trusted data exchange can help restore coherence and build a more resilient, transparent, and inclusive global trade system.

2. WTO TFA: ACHIEVEMENTS AND SHORTCOMINGS

2.1 WTO TFA - Basis of Trade Facilitation

The WTO Trade Facilitation Agreement (TFA) (WTO, Agreement on Trade Facilitation), adopted in 2013 and entering into force in 2017, marked a historic moment in the evolution of the multilateral trading system. As the first agreement concluded since the founding of the World Trade Organization, the TFA not only revived momentum in the wake of stalled Doha Round negotiations but also set a new standard for pragmatic, consensus-based cooperation in trade reform.

At its core, the TFA was designed to address the high cost and complexity of border procedures, particularly in developing and least developed countries (LDCs), by promoting more efficient, transparent, and predictable trade environments. Over the past decade, it has proven to be one of the most effective WTO instruments in terms of both adoption and impact.

The TFA has made measurable progress in three core dimensions:

(1) transparency and predictability, (2) simplification of procedures and risk-based control, and (3) flexibility in implementation with development support.

2.2.1 Transparency and Predictability: A Foundation for Trust

One of the most impactful aspects of the TFA is Article 1, which requires members to make comprehensive trade-related information publicly available. This includes:

- Customs procedures and legal requirements
- Fees and charges imposed at the border
- Rules of origin and valuation methodologies
- Administrative procedures for appeals and advance rulings

Prior to the TFA, much of this information—especially in LDCs—was either unavailable or accessible only through informal channels. For small and medium-sized enterprises, this lack of transparency created high entry barriers, often excluding them from export markets.

The OECD (2025) estimates that over the past decade, TFA-driven reforms reduced trade costs by up to 5% globally, with 3–7% improvement across regions due to faster procedures and reduced red tape (OECD, OECD Trade Facilitation Indicators).

Additionally, the TFA catalyzed the establishment of National Trade Facilitation Committees (NTFCs) in nearly all WTO members. These multi-stakeholder bodies have enhanced public-private dialogue, empowered customs authorities to engage with business communities, and supported inclusive policymaking.

2.2.2 Simplification and Risk-Based Border Controls: Speed and Efficiency

The TFA introduced a modern, performance-oriented approach to customs and border management, shifting away from exhaustive checks and paper-based systems toward risk-based and pre-arrival processing. Key provisions include:

- Pre-arrival processing (Article 7.1): Enables faster clearance by allowing customs to begin examining documentation before goods arrive.
- Risk management (Article 7.4): Encourages targeted inspections focused on high-risk consignments, reducing unnecessary delays.
- Expedited shipments (Article 7.8): Facilitates faster clearance for express and time-sensitive goods—critical for e-commerce, pharmaceuticals, and perishable agricultural exports.

According to the World Bank Doing Business 2020, the implementation of these provisions has led to an average reduction of 1.5–2.0 days in clearance times across participating developing countries (World Bank, Doing Business 2020). Moreover, The OECD Trade Facilitation Indicators (2025) study shows that globally, TFA-aligned border modernization has reduced trade costs by approximately 5% on average, and that full implementation of trade facilitation measures could potentially lead to an additional 12–14% reduction for low- and lower-middle-income countries. Specifically, the combined implementation of transparency, procedural simplification, and automation could reduce trade costs by up to 14.5% for low-income countries, 15.5% for lower-middle-income countries, and 13.2% for upper-middle-income countries (OECD, OECD Trade Facilitation Indicators: Monitoring Policies up to 2025).

In addition, the adoption of electronic data exchange, simplified documentation, and streamlined procedures has improved efficiency and increased the predictability of cross-border trade—two factors strongly associated with higher foreign investment and SME participation.

2.2.3 Development Flexibility and Capacity Support: A Model of Asymmetrical Integration

Recognizing that countries differ widely in their institutional and technical readiness, the TFA introduced a uniquely flexible three-tier implementation mechanism:

- Category A: Provisions implemented upon entry into force
- Category B: Provisions implemented after a transition period
- Category C: Provisions implemented with donor-funded technical assistance

This framework enabled countries to sequence their reforms, focusing first on low-hanging improvements while building capacity for more complex changes over time.

As of 2024, 97% of developing country WTO members have notified full implementation of their Category A commitments. In addition, more than 1,300 technical assistance projects have been supported under Category C through bilateral donors, regional initiatives, and international organizations (such as UNCTAD, World Bank, WCO, etc.) (WTO, TFAF Work Plan 2024)

In developing countries like Rwanda, Cambodia, and Georgia, TFA-related reforms have been directly linked to faster customs clearance, lower documentary requirements, and improved trade volumes and reduced informal trade. This tiered approach is now seen as a template for inclusive trade governance, balancing ambition with flexibility.

Despite these substantial accomplishments, the TFA is not a silver bullet. It was negotiated in a pre-digital era and is primarily focused on physical procedures at the border. As the global trade landscape becomes increasingly fragmented and data-driven, new challenges—such as digital trust, ESG compliance, cyber risks, and interoperability of systems—are emerging.

Nevertheless, the success of the TFA in creating a common, globally adopted platform for reform shows that multilateral cooperation on trade facilitation is not only possible—it is effective. This success should now be leveraged to build the next generation of digital, trusted, and inclusive trade facilitation frameworks, aligned with the realities of 21st-century commerce.

2.2.4 TFA's Shortcomings in the Context of New Trade Realities

Despite its widely recognized achievements, the WTO Trade Facilitation Agreement (TFA) reflects the priorities of a pre-digital, pre-fragmentation era of global trade. Designed to streamline border procedures and reduce transaction costs, the TFA was negotiated at a time when tariff barriers and physical paperwork were seen as the primary obstacles to trade. However, the realities of 21st-century commerce—characterized by digitalization, data governance, sustainability standards, and regulatory divergence—have moved far beyond the scope of what the TFA was designed to address.

As global trade policy evolves in response to shifting geopolitical, technological, and environmental dynamics, several key limitations of the TFA have become increasingly evident.

a. Limited Digital Integration: A Paper-Era Agreement in a Digital Trade World

The TFA's architecture remains primarily paper-centric, oriented toward the simplification of existing procedures rather than a transformation of trade processes through digital technologies. While certain provisions (e.g., Article 7.2 "Electronic Payment" and Article 10.2 "Acceptance of Copies") acknowledge digital tools, they fall short of setting any binding obligations or technical standards for digital interoperability.

The agreement lacks:

- Requirements for mutual recognition of e-LPCOs, such as electronic certificates of origin, phytosanitary certificates, or customs declarations;
- Guidance on cross-border Single Window connectivity, which is central to digital border management;
- Support for verifiable digital credentials, trust frameworks, or distributed ledger technologies (DLTs), all of which are emerging as foundational elements of trusted digital trade.

By contrast, some regional agreements such as the ASEAN Single Window (ASEAN, ASEAN Single Window) or the Digital Economy Partnership Agreement (DEPA) (Ministry of Trade and Industry Singapore, Digital Economy Partnership Agreement - DEPA), set much higher benchmarks for digital infrastructure, including machine-readable standards, API-based data exchange, and cross-border legal recognition of digital documents. As the result, the TFA risks becoming obsolete for countries already advancing toward fully digital trade ecosystems.

b. No Provisions for ESG, Forced Labor, or Export Control Compliance

The WTO TFA does not address the expanding and increasingly complex landscape of trade-related regulatory compliance, which today is driven not only by efficiency concerns but also by values-based governance, risk management, and geopolitical priorities.

Modern supply chains are now subject to a growing number of extra-customs requirements that govern who can trade, what can be traded, and under what conditions. Key categories of such emerging rules include:

- Environmental, Social, and Governance (ESG) reporting mandates, such as the EU's Corporate Sustainability Reporting Directive (CSRD) and Carbon Border Adjustment Mechanism (CBAM). These instruments require companies to disclose carbon emissions, labor practices, and other sustainability metrics across their global value chains. Non-compliance can lead to restricted access to EU markets or financial penalties.
- Human rights compliance regulations, including the U.S. Uyghur Forced Labor Prevention Act (UFLPA) and the EU's proposed Regulation on Prohibiting Products Made with Forced Labor, which prohibit the import of goods linked to exploitative labor conditions. Enforcement involves supply chain traceability, documentation audits, and product detentions, often with strict presumptions of guilt in high-risk regions.
- Export control regimes, such as the U.S. Export Administration Regulations (EAR) and the EU Dual-Use Regulation (2021/821), which require traders to demonstrate that sensitive goods and technologies are not being diverted for unauthorized end uses or transferred to restricted entities. These regimes increasingly demand real-time end-user screening, risk profiling, and traceability mechanisms.

These frameworks directly affect market access and impose significant operational burdens on exporters and importers, including the need for: digital document verification, third-party audits, automated screening systems, and cross-border regulatory reporting.

Yet none of these areas are explicitly covered or even mentioned in the TFA. The agreement's focus remains squarely on customs-related procedures, without acknowledging the broader set of regulatory obligations that now define cross-border trade.

As the result, trade facilitation and trade compliance have become increasingly decoupled. While the TFA aims to streamline border processes, traders are simultaneously navigating a parallel layer of regulatory requirements that are often opaque, overlapping, and jurisdiction-specific. This regulatory disconnect increases uncertainty, raises compliance costs, and undermines the effectiveness of trade facilitation reforms—particularly for SMEs and firms operating in multiple markets.

c. Insufficient Mechanisms for Regulatory Convergence and Interoperability

Although the TFA encourages cooperation and transparency (e.g., through NTFCs), it does not provide binding mechanisms for regulatory alignment. In an era where regulatory fragmentation is a key trade barrier, this is a critical omission.

Missing elements include:

- Harmonized data models (e.g., WCO Data Model or UN/CEFACT standards);
- Cross-border legal recognition of inspection results, certifications, or conformity assessments;
- Institutionalized mutual recognition frameworks for licenses, permits, and electronic documents;
- Trust infrastructure for secure cross-border regulatory data exchange.

As countries introduce data localization measures, national security restrictions, and technological standards with extraterritorial implications, the lack of common frameworks exacerbates costs, delays, and legal uncertainty. Thus, the TFA offers little support for addressing the non-tariff digital and regulatory barriers that define contemporary trade policy.

Table 3. Comparative Matrix: WTO TFA vs. Emerging Trade Challenges

Theme	WTO TFA Coverage	Contemporary Relevance
1. Paper-based procedures	Yes	Partially outdated
2. Electronic documents	Partially (non-binding)	Core challenge
3. Digital trade interoperability	No	Critical gap
4. ESG compliance	No	Key requirement for access
5. Forced labor compliance	No	Required by major markets
6. Export controls integration	No	Strategic security concern
7. Regulatory convergence	Encouraged but not binding	Urgently needed

Summary: A Foundation, But Not a Future-Proof Framework

The WTO TFA remains an essential foundation, particularly for developing and least developed countries at the early stages of customs modernization. It has delivered real progress in reducing trade frictions and strengthening border institutions.

However, as trade becomes increasingly data-driven, sustainability-focused, and risk-sensitive, the TFA's structural limitations have become more apparent. Its paper-first orientation, absence of digital legal infrastructure, and lack of alignment with broader regulatory frameworks limit its relevance for addressing the most pressing challenges of global supply chain governance.

A new generation of trade facilitation instruments is urgently needed—one that integrates digital trust, regulatory interoperability, and inclusive mechanisms for compliance with evolving global norms.

The following section introduces the conceptual framework for WTO TFA 2.0 a forward-looking agenda that builds on the TFA's success but expands its scope to meet the realities of fragmented, digitized, and sustainability-oriented global trade. This includes alignment with tools such as UNECE Recommendation 18 (ongoing work on its update), cross-border trust mechanisms, and digital mutual recognition systems.

3. BEYOND THE WTO TFA: BUILDING DIGITAL TRUST AND TRANSPARENCY IN FRAGMENTED TRADE

3.1 From Documents to Data: A Paradigm Shift

Historically, the basis for allowing goods to cross borders was a package of supporting documents: certificates of origin, export licenses, phytosanitary certificates and so on. These documents certified that the goods met the necessary requirements and could be cleared for cross-border movement.

However, in the digital age, such documents:

- are easily forged (especially unprotected PDF versions);
- are not machine-readable;
- require notarization and courier delivery;
- do not integrate with digital platforms and APIs.

Modern technologies make it possible to move from document verification to data verification, supported by cryptographic signatures, stored in decentralized registries, and available for real-time validation. This fundamentally changes the model of interaction between businesses and governments. It is no longer sufficient to trust documents; trust must be built around the integrity, security, and interoperability of the underlying trade data.

This shift towards digitalization is not merely a theoretical ideal but a practical and economically viable path, as demonstrated by recent empirical work in the Asia-Pacific region. In 2024, ESCAP conducted four comprehensive feasibility studies on cross-border electronic exchange of trade data and documents in Central Asian countries—Kazakhstan, Kyrgyzstan, Tajikistan, and Uzbekistan—providing illustrative evidence of how this paradigm shift can materialize in practice, especially for landlocked and developing economies (UNESCAP, Feasibility studies: identifying and unlocking cross-border paperless trade potential).

These feasibility studies were part of ESCAP's support to the Framework Agreement on Facilitation of Cross-Border Paperless Trade in Asia and the Pacific, offering a structured, seven-step methodology combining stakeholder interviews, national data analysis, and legal assessments. This approach enables the identification of priority documents for digitalization, relevant trading partners for pilot projects, and the design of "AS-IS" and "TO-BE" process models that map out inefficiencies and propose digitally optimized solutions.

For instance, in Kyrgyzstan (ESCAP, Feasibility study on cross-border electronic exchange of trade data and documents: Kyrgyzstan 2025), the feasibility study examined 20 trade documents to assess their level of automation, usage frequency, and interagency data exchange potential. The Certificate of Origin emerged as a priority document for digitalization, and Uzbekistan was identified as the most viable pilot partner based on trade volume, proximity, and institutional linkages. Similarly, for the exchange of phytosanitary certificates between Kazakhstan and Uzbekistan, significant bottlenecks were identified, including delays from physical document handling, risks of forgery, and lack of real-time validation mechanisms. One of the proposed TO BE models envisions cross-border data exchange directly between the relevant authorities, eliminating the need for traders to submit paper or electronic documents for these procedures.

The proposed solutions included connecting national information systems to global platforms such as the Global ePhyto Hub for automated data exchange and enhancing the Single Window systems in participating countries to enable seamless interoperability of trade-related data. For example, in the case of Tajikistan and Kazakhstan, the studies proposed integrating electronic Certificate of Origin exchange through their respective Single Window systems, enabling direct, machine-to-machine data validation.

Economic feasibility analyses further reinforced the practicality of these initiatives. The proposed pilot for exchanging electronic Certificates of Origin between Kyrgyzstan and Uzbekistan was projected to cost approximately USD 200,000, with the potential to recoup this investment within two years of implementation and generate over USD 600,000 in economic benefits within five years. These benefits stem from reduced transaction costs, faster clearance times, and decreased risks of errors or fraud, thereby delivering tangible gains to both governments and traders.

Importantly, the feasibility studies highlighted that the successful implementation of cross-border electronic data exchange requires more than just technological infrastructure. It demands legal and regulatory alignment, institutional capacity building, and interagency cooperation both domestically and internationally. Countries must harmonize their laws to accept electronic data as legally equivalent to paper-based ones and ensure interoperability between national systems and global platforms. This integrative approach fosters a trusted digital trade environment, enhancing transparency and reducing trade friction in a fragmented global landscape.

The experience in Central Asia illustrates that moving from document-based to data-driven trade facilitation is not only feasible but essential in addressing modern trade challenges, particularly for SMEs in developing countries. Paperless trade systems lower compliance burdens, reduce the need for costly intermediaries, and improve predictability in cross-border transactions. In a context where global trade fragmentation has increased regulatory complexity, adopting cross-border paperless trade solutions can mitigate fragmentation by building trust in data flows, ensuring compliance with diverse regulatory regimes (such as ESG and export controls), and promoting smoother trade operations across borders.

A complementary global perspective is offered by the UN/CEFACT White Paper on the Data Pipeline, which presents a structured model for end-to-end, data-centric supply chain management. It emphasizes that enabling trusted data sharing—from the point of origin to final destination—can significantly reduce redundant documentation, improve regulatory compliance, and increase visibility across borders. This model supports the shift from document-based to data-driven trade by establishing secure and verifiable data flows among traders, logistics providers, and regulatory agencies (UN/CEFACT, White Paper Data Pipeline). This integrative approach fosters a trusted digital trade environment, enhancing transparency and reducing trade friction in a fragmented global landscape.

The case studies in Central Asia and global perspective from White Paper on the Data Pipeline underscore that governments can achieve significant advancements in trade facilitation by strategically prioritizing the digitalization of key documents, piloting bilateral data exchanges, and gradually scaling up to multilateral frameworks underpinned by international cooperation and standards. Such initiatives align with the evolving needs of the global trading system, transitioning from a document-centered approach to one where data integrity and interoperability are at the heart of efficient and trusted trade facilitation.

In summary, moving from documents to data represents a paradigm shift in trade facilitation, aligning with the broader digital transformation in the global economy. This shift offers a pathway for countries to reduce costs, enhance compliance, and integrate into the increasingly data-driven international trade landscape.

3.2 Basic principles of the WTO TFA 2.0

a. Key enablers of "trust in data"

WTO TFA 2.0 should explicitly encourage the adoption of the following technological and governance enablers to operationalize this principle:

1) Use of machine-readable formats (XML, JSON-LD). Trade documents and related data should be structured in machine-readable, standardized formats (e.g., WCO Data Model, UN/CEFACT standards, XML, JSON-LD) to allow automated parsing, validation, and processing by customs and trade platforms.
2) Deployment of Verifiable Credentials (VCs). Verifiable Credentials, developed under the W3C standard, allow trade data (e.g., certificate of origin, test reports, licenses) to be cryptographically signed, tamper-evident, and verifiable in real time without requiring a central authority. They support privacy-preserving disclosure, enabling selective data sharing based on verification needs while protecting sensitive business information[2].

Verifiable Credentials are a promising technology for digital trade facilitation. We will explore them in greater depth in the next section.

3) Identification of data sources using Decentralized Identifiers (DIDs)

DIDs allow trusted identification of issuers (e.g., certifying agencies, laboratories) and recipients (e.g., exporters, importers) without relying on a single central registry. This supports a federated trust model, critical for international trade, where each country may maintain sovereignty over its issuing authorities while participating in a globally interoperable trust framework.

4) Internationally accessible registries of trusted issuers. WTO TFA 2.0 should promote the development of internationally recognized registries of trusted issuers (accreditation bodies, authorized certification agencies, laboratories) whose digital credentials can be validated globally by customs and border authorities. This creates a network of trust that is scalable across jurisdictions while respecting national governance structures.
    - *Practical illustration: The case of ePhyto certificates*

A clear example of "trust in data" in practice is the ePhyto system for electronic phytosanitary certificates coordinated by the International Plant Protection Convention (IPPC). Under this system:

- Data is exchanged directly between national phytosanitary authorities through the Global ePhyto Hub, ensuring authenticity and integrity.

- Certificates are structured in machine-readable XML, enabling automated verification and processing by border agencies.
- There is no reliance on insecure channels (e.g., email) or physical documents that are prone to delays and fraud.

The ePhyto example demonstrates that a secure, trusted, and scalable model for data-based trade facilitation is not only feasible but operational, providing a benchmark for broader digitalization under WTO TFA 2.0.

Thus, embedding "trust in data" in WTO TFA 2.0 will:

- Align trade facilitation with digital trade realities.
- Support automation, risk-based controls, and expedited clearance.
- Facilitate cross-border paperless trade (in line with UNESCAP's Framework Agreement or similar acts).
- Enable interoperability across regional trade initiatives (ASEAN Single Window, AfCFTA Digital Trade Protocol, EU initiatives).

Build resilience in supply chains by improving data transparency and reducing reliance on manual, paper-based processes.

In summary, "trust in data" is not merely a technological preference but a systemic shift that WTO TFA 2.0 must embrace to remain relevant in an era of digital, fragmented, and compliance-heavy global trade. It lays the foundation for seamless, secure, and scalable trade facilitation, where compliance is verified through data authenticity rather than document appearances, unlocking efficiency gains for traders and governments alike.

b. "Compliance-by-Design": Embedding Compliance into Trade Processes

Traditional compliance in international trade has relied on collecting and presenting paper-based evidence to demonstrate conformity with regulations, including:

- Environmental, Social, and Governance (ESG) standards;
- Forced labor and human rights compliance;
- Export controls and end-use restrictions;
- Technical standards and sanitary/phytosanitary measures.

This approach is reactive, document-heavy, and prone to inefficiencies. Traders spend significant resources gathering documentation from multiple sources, with verification often occurring only at the border, leading to delays, errors, and risks of non-compliance penalties.

"Compliance-by-Design" shifts compliance from being a separate, manual checkpoint to becoming an automated, integral component of trade processes. It embeds verification mechanisms directly into supply chains and digital trade platforms, enabling continuous, real-time compliance monitoring.

This approach offers:

- Proactive compliance. Automated checks during trade transactions, not after shipment or upon arrival.
- Reduced manual interventions. Decreases administrative burdens for traders and regulators.
- Higher transparency and predictability. Provides regulators with consistent, machine-verifiable data flows.
- Lower compliance costs. Minimizes the need for expensive post-facto audits and document inspections.
- Improved risk management. Customs and border agencies can focus inspections on high-risk shipments.
  - *Key components of "Compliance-by-Design"*
    1) Automated End-Use and End-User Checks

Export control regimes (e.g., US EAR, EU Dual-Use Regulation) require verifying that goods, technology, and services are not diverted to prohibited end-users or for illicit end-uses.

Using integrated databases and automated screening tools, exporters can:

- Cross-check transaction parties against denied party lists.
- Validate end-use declarations automatically.
- Flag suspicious transactions for manual review before shipment.

2) Carbon Footprint Tracking (e.g., for CBAM)

The EU's Carbon Border Adjustment Mechanism (CBAM) requires verified data on the carbon content of imported goods (e.g., steel, aluminum, cement). A mere document declaring emissions is insufficient; CBAM requires:

- Digital emissions data submission linked to production batches.
- Verification by accredited entities and centralized registry uploads.
- Customs clearance conditional on the acceptance of verified emissions data.

This is an example of "data-based compliance," where data flows replace manual document inspection.

3) Real-Time Compliance with Rules of Origin (ROO)

Rules of Origin under FTAs (e.g., CPTPP, RCEP, AfCFTA) are complex, requiring proof that products meet content or processing thresholds.

"Compliance-by-Design" allows:

- Integration of supplier declarations into manufacturers' ERP systems.
- Automated calculation of regional value content.
- Generation of machine-verifiable digital certificates of origin, simplifying customs clearance.

4) Technical Standards and SPS Compliance

Products often need to comply with technical regulations and sanitary/phytosanitary (SPS) standards, such as electronic safety, food safety, or plant health requirements. Embedding compliance enables digital submission of test results from accredited laboratories, cross-verification of lab accreditations in real-time, and linking compliance data directly to electronic customs declarations.

5) Digital Product Passport (DPP)

The Digital Product Passport is an emerging tool supported by the EU (European Data, EU's Digital Product Passport: Advancing transparency and sustainability) and UN/CEFACT (UNESCE, UN/CEFACT Solutions in Support of Digital Product Passports ECE/TRADE/481) that digitally compiles and shares structured product information (such as material composition, carbon footprint, and regulatory certifications) across the entire supply chain.

DPPs enable:

- Enhanced product-level traceability and transparency.
- Real-time access to sustainability and compliance data for regulators, customs, and consumers.
- Integration with circular economy strategies, ESG requirements, and border control systems.

By embedding DPPs into ERP and trade platforms, firms can proactively align with both market expectations and regulatory demands, fulfilling the vision of end-to-end "compliance-by-design".

- *Practical Illustration: The CBAM Example*

Under the EU CBAM, importers must submit verified carbon emissions data tied to shipments, data uploaded into a centralized CBAM registry, and payment of the appropriate carbon adjustment based on verified data.

In this system:

- A paper document alone is insufficient; importers must provide structured digital data.
- Emissions data must be third-party verified before submission.
- Customs clearance is contingent upon data validation, not just document presentation.

The CBAM model illustrates how compliance-by-design can reduce fraud, improve accuracy, and align trade with sustainability goals.

One of the key directions for the evolution of the WTO Trade Facilitation Agreement (TFA 2.0) is the shift from external verification to embedding compliance requirements directly into digital trade processes. The "Compliance-by-Design" approach means that compliance checks are no longer performed manually at the border, but automatically during the preparation and execution of trade transactions.

This approach enables trade facilitation and regulatory enforcement to function in tandem. By verifying compliance with rules—such as origin, ESG standards, or export control restrictions—before goods even arrive at the border, it reduces delays, lowers administrative burdens, and increases predictability for both traders and regulators. In a context where international trade is increasingly shaped by sustainability goals, human rights safeguards, and security considerations, such automation becomes essential.

"Compliance-by-Design" directly supports the objectives of WTO TFA 2.0 by:

- Facilitating legitimate trade while ensuring alignment with regulatory frameworks;
- Reducing clearance times through pre-arrival compliance verification;
- Supporting broader public policy goals, including emissions reduction, ethical sourcing, and secure trade in strategic goods;
- Providing real-time, trusted data for effective risk management by border agencies.

This paradigm shift is also fully aligned with global trends in digital trade. It is reflected in regional initiatives such as the ASEAN Single Window and the AfCFTA Digital Trade Protocol, which emphasize the importance of structured data exchange and system interoperability. At the same time, private-sector digital trade platforms increasingly embed compliance modules to respond to the complex and fragmented landscape of global trade regulations.

"Compliance-by-Design" is not a supplementary feature; it is becoming a foundational element of modern trade systems. It moves us beyond paper-based processes and toward ecosystems where verifiable, machine-readable data replaces traditional documents as the basis for trust and decision-making.

In this context, embedding compliance into the fabric of digital trade enables scalable, secure, and future-ready trade facilitation. It supports the simultaneous achievement of efficiency, transparency, and responsibility, goals that are essential for navigating the 21st-century trade environment.

c. Interoperability as a Global Public Good

In the age of digital trade, automation alone is not enough. The true value of trade digitalization lies not just in converting paper into electronic formats but in ensuring that digital systems across borders can speak the same language. This requires interoperability—the ability of national platforms, regulatory systems, and private sector tools to exchange data seamlessly, securely, and meaningfully across jurisdictions.

For the next generation of trade facilitation, WTO TFA 2.0 must place interoperability at its core. Without it, even the most advanced national systems risk becoming isolated silos. Interoperability transforms fragmented national reforms into an integrated global trade environment, reducing redundancy, boosting transparency, and enabling trust in cross-border transactions.

Key Enablers of Interoperability:

1) Common Data Standards

Internationally recognized data standards such as the UN/CEFACT Core Component Library (CCL) and the WCO Data Model are essential for structuring trade-related information in a consistent and machine-readable format. These standards enable regulatory, logistics, and financial systems to interpret and act on data without manual intervention or conversion.

2) API-Based System Integration

Application Programming Interfaces (APIs) enable real-time, system-to-system communication between government agencies, border control systems, and the private sector. APIs are the backbone of scalable digital trade, allowing for modular and automated exchanges of certificates, declarations, licenses, and risk data.

3) Regulatory Sandboxes and Cross-Border Pilots

To build trust and refine new digital processes, governments and stakeholders must invest in sandbox environments—controlled spaces for experimentation—and pilot projects focused on mutual recognition of electronic documents. These efforts provide evidence for broader policy harmonization and system readiness.

4) International Registries of Trusted Issuers

Trust in digital credentials depends on the ability to verify the source. Global or regional registries of trusted issuers—publicly accessible directories of verified entities—allow border agencies and trade partners to confirm that an electronic certificate (e.g., eCOO, ePhyto, eCITES) was indeed issued by a legitimate authority.

- *Practical Illustration: DEPA and TradeTrust*

In the Asia-Pacific region, the Digital Economy Partnership Agreement (DEPA) (Ministry of Trade and Industry Singapore, Digital Economy Partnership Agreement – DEPA) and Singapore's TradeTrust framework (Singapore Trade Trust) pioneered a model of trusted, cross-border document exchange. Member countries such as Singapore, Australia, Chile, and New Zealand have begun using blockchain-backed systems and verifiable credentials to exchange electronic bills of lading (eBLs) and electronic certificates of origin (eCOOs). These documents can be cryptographically verified without requiring legalization or manual authentication. Customs authorities in the importing country can instantly validate the authenticity and integrity of the document using secure APIs and digital registries dramatically reducing clearance times and fraud risk.

As supply chains grow more complex and regulatory requirements multiply, the cost of non-interoperability increases. Countries that fail to align their systems with international standards risk being excluded from fast-track processing, mutual recognition arrangements, and digital trade corridors.

Interoperability is not just a technical issue—it is a strategic imperative that affects key dimensions of international trade, including efficiency, security, trust, and sustainability, as illustrated in the figure below.

Figure 2. Benefits of Interoperability for International Trade

Efficiency	Security	Trust	Sustainability
Reduces transaction costs and processing times	Ensures data integrity and authenticity	Builds confidence in cross-border digital interactions	Supports data-driven compliance with ESG and labor standards

By embedding interoperability into the WTO TFA 2.0 framework, we can ensure that trade facilitation measures are not just faster, but smarter and more connected. This includes:

- Recommending the adoption of global data standards (e.g., WCO, UN/CEFACT).
- Encouraging international API standards for customs and trade systems.
- Supporting cross-border testing of mutual recognition pilots.
- Promoting open registries and digital trust frameworks.

In doing so, WTO TFA 2.0 can elevate interoperability from a niche technical goal to a foundational principle of 21st-century trade, positioning it as a global public good essential to resilience, inclusivity, and economic development.

d. New Institutional Models for the Digital Trade Era

While WTO TFA 1.0 emphasized the role of National Trade Facilitation Committees (NTFCs) in coordinating reforms at the domestic level (Article 23), the complexity of today's digital trade environment calls for an evolved governance framework. Enter the concept of Digital Trade and Trust Councils as a next-generation institutional model envisioned under TFA 2.0.

These councils are not simply advisory bodies, but multi-stakeholder governance platforms designed to ensure the integrity, interoperability, and scalability of digital trade systems. Their primary function would be to oversee the development, alignment, and mutual recognition of digital trust frameworks across borders.

A Digital Trade and Trust Council would typically bring together:

- Public sector agencies such as customs authorities, regulatory bodies, and central banks, who play a critical role in risk management and compliance oversight;

- Private sector actors, including logistics providers, exporters/importers, trade finance institutions, and digital trade platforms, who generate and use trade data in real-time;
- Standard-setting organizations like the International Chamber of Commerce (ICC), UN/CEFACT, and the World Customs Organization (WCO), which provide technical guidance and global standards for data exchange and trust mechanisms.

By facilitating structured dialogue and joint decision-making, Digital Trade and Trust Councils would play a critical role in addressing the institutional gaps that currently hinder seamless digital trade. One of their key functions would be to coordinate the implementation of digital trust and identity standards across jurisdictions. This includes promoting the use of decentralized identifiers (DIDs), verifiable credentials (VCs), and legally recognized digital signatures—tools that are essential for ensuring the authenticity, integrity, and legal validity of digital transactions across borders.

Moreover, these councils would work to enhance interoperability between national and regional systems, enabling the mutual recognition of electronic trade documents such as certificates of origin, phytosanitary certificates, and export permits. Without such interoperability, traders are forced to navigate fragmented digital ecosystems, leading to inefficiencies, duplicated efforts, and compliance risks. Establishing common protocols and trust anchors would allow data to flow securely between countries, reducing border delays and minimizing the need for duplicative verification.

Equally important, Digital Trade and Trust Councils would support regulatory convergence in key areas such as data governance, cross-border compliance, and cybersecurity. As countries adopt divergent policies on data localization, privacy, ESG disclosure, and supply chain transparency, the risk of regulatory misalignment grows. Councils would serve as platforms for harmonizing these frameworks or, at a minimum, enabling their interoperability through mutually agreed standards and trust mechanisms. This, in turn, would reduce regulatory friction, enhance legal certainty, and build confidence among public and private sector actors engaged in international trade.

By integrating these dimensions into a single institutional mechanism, Digital Trade and Trust Councils would not only improve the efficiency of trade processes but also reinforce the legitimacy and resilience of the emerging digital trade infrastructure.

4. VERIFIABLE CREDENTIALS AS A TOOL FOR BUILDING TRUST IN INTERNATIONAL TRADE

In the context of the rapid digitalization of international trade, there is an increasing need for reliable tools capable of ensuring trust among traders. Traditionally, this role has been fulfilled by paper documents, such as licenses, permits, certificates, and other official confirmations. However, in the digital environment, new, technically grounded mechanisms for identification and verification are required.

One promising solution in this area is the use of Verifiable Credentials (VCs)—standardized digital carriers of information that reliably confirm the authenticity and validity of various data, ranging from business reputation and authorization to the presence of specific permits (UNCEFACT, White Paper eDATA Verifiable Credentials for Cross Border Trade).

The use of Verifiable Credentials helps enhance transparency, reduce administrative burdens, and accelerate trade procedures, making this tool particularly relevant in the context of implementing the WTO Trade Facilitation Agreement and other international initiatives.

4.1 Concept and architecture of VCs

According to the World Trade Organization (WTO), the value of global merchandise trade in 2023 amounted to around USD 24 trillion (WTO, Trade growth likely to pick up in 2024 in spite of challenging environment). Each international trade transaction is accompanied by numerous documents—certificates of origin, permits, licenses, transport documents, and others—which generate significant administrative burdens and risks associated with document forgery or loss.

In the context of digitalization, trade increasingly requires universal yet decentralized solutions that ensure a balance between information accessibility and the protection of personal and corporate data. In the digital era, information becomes a key resource, and trade participants face the task of building technological infrastructure that ensures:

- data confidentiality;
- data security;
- information sovereignty;
- manageability and control by the data owner;
- support for seamless digital business processes between counterparties.

One such solution is Verifiable Credentials—standardized digital constructs that enable the secure and selective sharing of verified information between parties in a peer-to-peer format (data transmission directly between participants without intermediaries). Verifiable Credentials allow users (both individuals and legal entities) to maintain full control over their data and to grant access to third parties only when necessary.

This technology is built on open standards developed, among others, by the W3C (W3C Group Note, Verifiable Credentials Overview) and uses cryptographic methods to ensure the authenticity and integrity of information. Their architecture includes three main roles:

- **Issuer**: an organization or authority authorized to create and sign Verifiable Credentials;
- **Holder**: an individual or organization that receives and manages the Verifiable Credentials;
- **Verifier**: a counterparty requesting and verifying the authenticity of the information received.

Figure 3. Model for Exchanging VCs (W3C Group Note, Verifiable Credentials Data Model v2.0)

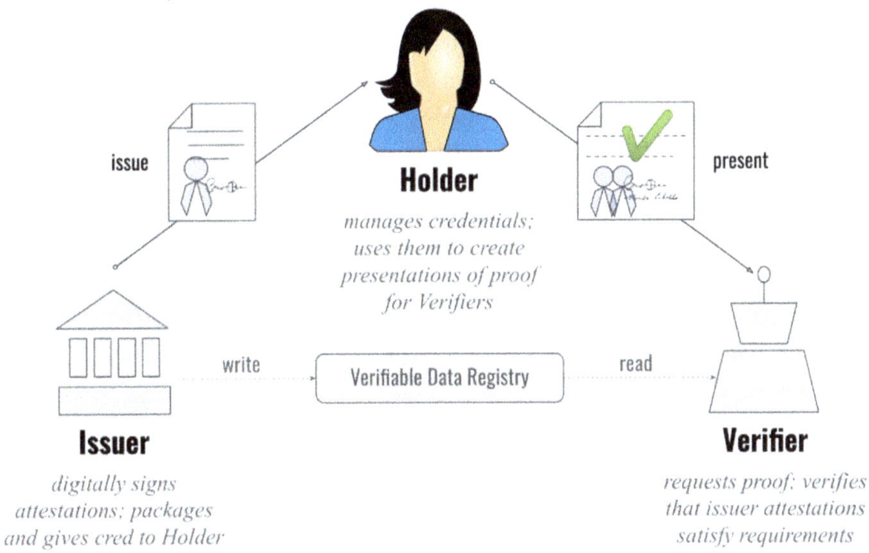

Verifiable Credentials enable real-time information verification without the need to refer to a centralized database.

Key characteristics and capabilities of VCs technology include:

- Authentication and authorization. Verifiable Credentials allow for the confirmation of the identity of an individual or organization, as well as the establishment of rights to perform specific actions.
- Integration with information systems. API interfaces enable the automated validation and status checking of digital documents by retrieving data directly from the source.
- Data integrity assurance. Cryptographic signatures certify that the data has not been altered after issuance, ensuring a high level of trust.

4.2 The Role of Verifiable Credentials in Building Trust in International Trade

The digital transformation of international trade requires new mechanisms for establishing and maintaining trust among participants in global supply chains. In an environment where counterparties often never meet in person and interactions take place through complex digital and logistics systems, ensuring the reliability and security of information becomes a key factor for the successful conclusion and execution of transactions.

Verifiable Credentials play a central role in forming the so-called "trust chain," a concept developed by the International Chamber of Commerce (ICC) and its Digital Standards Initiative (DSI) within the "Trust in Trade" document (Digital Standards Initiative, Trust in Trade). This document describes the supply chain as consisting of six interconnected layers, each performing a specific function, with layer 5—the trust chain—providing the systemic resilience of the entire model.

Figure 4. Supply Chain Layers (Digital Standards Initiative, Trust in Trade)

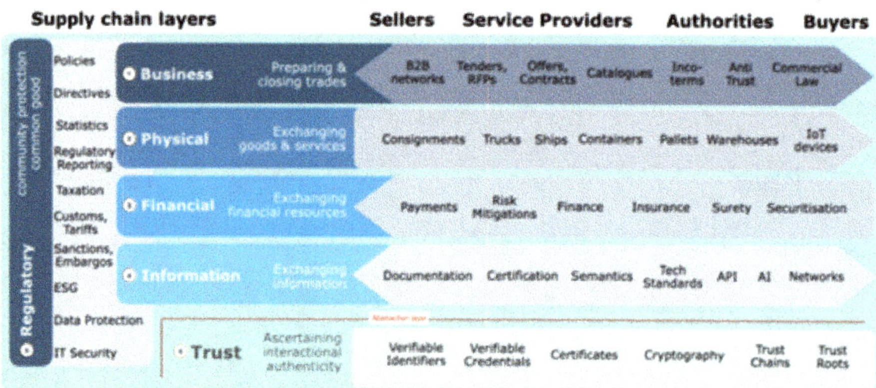

Layer 0 – Regulatory Framework

At the foundation lies the regulatory environment, shaped by governments and international legal instruments. This layer governs the rules of the game (such as customs regulations, ESG compliance mandates, and Single Window initiatives) and underpins the entire supply chain. Its influence extends through all other layers to ensure consistency with legal and institutional standards.

Layer 1 – Commercial Transactions Layer

This is where business agreements take shape. From initial procurement processes to contract signing, this layer defines the formal relationships between trade partners and the conditions under which goods and services are exchanged.

Layer 2 – Physical Operations Layer

Concerned with the actual movement and handling of goods, this layer includes transportation, warehousing, inspection, and customs clearance. It transforms contractual obligations into physical realities.

Layer 3 – Financial Transactions Layer

This layer supports the financial dimension of trade, covering payments, credit facilities, insurance, and trade finance mechanisms. It ensures that economic value is transferred securely and efficiently in line with contractual terms.

Layer 4 – Information Exchange Layer

Traditionally based on paperwork and manual processes, this layer is now undergoing digital transformation. Increasingly, information such as invoices, shipping documents, and certificates is exchanged in structured, machine-readable formats. The peer-to-peer flow of information between businesses and with governments (B2B2G) reflects a shift toward greater automation, interoperability, and traceability.

Layer 5 – Trust and Verification Layer

At the top of the digital supply chain architecture sits the trust infrastructure, essential for validating data, credentials, and actors across the system. This layer ensures that the information circulating across other layers is authentic, secure, and resistant to tampering or fraud.

A central tool enabling this trust layer is the use of Verifiable Credentials. These digital attestations allow trusted information—such as permits, licenses, or certificates of origin—to be shared in cryptographically secure formats. VCs allow not only the verification of the data itself but also the identity of the issuer and presenter, all without needing constant reference to a centralized database. This decentralized trust mechanism supports automation, reduces paperwork, and enhances security in international trade.

Ultimately, Layer 5 forms the backbone of the digital supply chain's credibility. It enables greater resilience, transparency, and efficiency across the ecosystem, unlocking the full potential of digital trade through secure, scalable, and interoperable trust mechanisms.

One practical application of Verifiable Credentials is digital identification of trade process participants. In this context, international standards such as the Legal Entity Identifier (LEI) and its digital version, the Verifiable Legal Entity Identifier (vLEI), are of particular importance.

The Legal Entity Identifier (LEI) is a 20-character alphanumeric code based on the international standard ISO 17442. It is used to uniquely identify legal entities participating in financial and trade transactions and contains ownership structure information. The LEI helps answer the critical questions of "who is who" and "who owns whom," contributing to greater transparency and trust in the global business environment. Publicly available LEI ownership data can be accessed free of charge via the international platform: https://search.gleif.org/#/search/.

The Verifiable Legal Entity Identifier (vLEI) is a digital, securely verifiable version of the LEI, created using Verifiable Credentials technology, enabling automated authenticity verification without human intervention. The vLEI allows for the real-time digital authentication of organizations and can be used in automated trade and administrative processes. This technology thus combines standardization, security, and technological interoperability, expanding the potential of Verifiable Credentials in international trade.

4.3 Problems and Challenges of Implementing VCs in Trading Processes

Verifiable Credentials are increasingly being applied across various aspects of international trade. They hold significant potential for enhancing transparency, efficiency, and trust within global supply chains. The most promising areas of application include:

1) Secure and reliable digital exchange of trade documents (invoices, transport documents, certificates of origin, etc.) in a fully digital format with guaranteed authenticity.
2) By leveraging this technology, trading and regulatory authorities can quickly and reliably verify the validity of permits and authorizations, minimizing the potential for forgery.
3) The use of Verifiable Credentials reduces the risks of fraud and errors by ensuring data integrity and verifying the sources of information.

Despite these clear advantages, the widespread adoption of Verifiable Credentials faces several technical, legal, and organizational challenges. Overcoming these challenges requires a comprehensive approach across all levels of the digital supply chain.

Table 4. Key Risks of Implementing Verifiable Credentials

Risk Title	Description
1. Technical Integration and Scalability	The implementation of Verifiable Credentials requires adaptation or a complete overhaul of existing IT systems, including document management platforms, customs, and logistics interfaces. This involves high costs, the need for staff retraining, and risks of incompatibility between the systems of different countries and organizations.
2. Legal and Regulatory Uncertainty	Legislative frameworks in most jurisdictions are either still being developed or vary significantly. Questions remain regarding the recognition of digital credentials as legally valid documents, as well as issues related to data storage and cross-border data transfer.
3. Privacy and Personal Data Protection	The use of Verifiable Credentials must consider the requirements for protecting sensitive information, particularly in the context of international exchanges. Without adequate control mechanisms, there is a risk of data leaks, unauthorized access, or monitoring of participants' activities.
4. Digital Identity Security	Vulnerabilities exist related to key management, the compromise of certification authorities, and the misuse of trusted records.

Moreover, vulnerabilities exist related to key management, the compromise of certification authorities, and the misuse of trusted records. The study "Overview of Decentralized Identifiers and Verifiable Credentials" identifies the following key risks:

- Theft of keys and credentials: If private keys are leaked, an attacker can impersonate another participant.
- Invalid or revoked credentials: The absence of effective revocation mechanisms can lead to the use of expired or revoked Verifiable Credentials.
- Privacy threats: Excessive information disclosure or the possibility of tracking user activities when multiple Verifiable Credentials are used without proper anonymization.
- Man-in-the-middle attacks: Interception and alteration of information during the transmission of Verifiable Credentials.

To mitigate these risks, **modern cybersecurity methods** can be applied, playing a critical role in protecting digital credentials and data transmitted within trade processes. In particular:

- Regular cryptographic key rotation,
- the use of multi-factor authentication (MFA), and
- storing keys in Hardware Security Modules (HSMs) significantly reduce the likelihood of digital identity compromise.

Additionally, mandatory use of digital signatures for each Verifiable Credential ensures authenticity and confirms the source of issuance, while the application of Selective Disclosure mechanisms allows only the specific data required for a particular transaction to be shared, thereby ensuring data minimization and the protection of confidential information.

Encryption and end-to-end protection technologies also play an important role during the transmission of Verifiable Credentials between parties, preventing unauthorized access or data tampering during transfer. To protect against replay attacks, one-time codes can be used to prevent the reuse of previously intercepted messages.

Taken together, these measures form the foundation for a reliable and resilient digital trust architecture. However, their effectiveness requires validation under real-world conditions and regular updates to address emerging technological and regulatory challenges.

Thus, VCs hold significant potential for transforming international trade by providing a higher level of trust among participants, reducing fraud risks, and simplifying document exchange processes. The shift from paper-based to digital solutions enables not only faster transactions but also enhances the transparency, security, and reliability of trade interactions.

To realize this potential, it is important to advance several key areas:

Firstly, scaling the technology requires the development and implementation of universal standards that will enable the use of Verifiable Credentials in international trade at a global level, ensuring interoperability across different jurisdictions and platforms.

Secondly, integration with other digital solutions—combining Verifiable Credentials with blockchain, artificial intelligence, distributed ledger technologies, and smart contracts can support more resilient, adaptive, and automated supply chain and document management systems.

Finally, cross-sectoral and cross-border cooperation involving active collaboration among government bodies, businesses, and the technology community is essential for creating a favorable regulatory and operational environment that will facilitate the widespread adoption of Verifiable Credentials.

In the context of the rapid digitalization of global trade, Verifiable Credentials can form the foundation of a new trust model—one that is more resilient, transparent, and focused on protecting the interests of all participants in trade processes.

5. CONCLUSION: TOWARDS WTO TFA 2.0 – A NEW ARCHITECTURE FOR TRUST-BASED TRADE

The traditional architecture of trade facilitation, as embodied in the WTO Trade Facilitation Agreement, was designed for an era of optimism in global integration. Its focus on streamlining customs procedures, reducing border delays, and enhancing transparency marked a major achievement for multilateralism. However, the trade landscape it was built to serve no longer exists in the same form. The fragmentation of global trade—through regionalization, export controls, rising compliance burdens, and geopolitical realignment demands a new response. TFA 2.0 must rise to this challenge.

The future of trade facilitation lies not simply in further reducing paperwork, but in building digital trust ecosystems that are scalable, interoperable, and resilient to fragmentation. In this context, "compliance-by-design" becomes a strategic imperative. This new paradigm does not treat trade facilitation and regulatory compliance as opposing goals but rather integrates them into a unified digital architecture. Automated pre-arrival checks, ESG reporting, verification of origin, and screening against export control lists must become part of the same seamless process. Instead of relying on documents as proxies of trust, tomorrow's systems will use verifiable data, transmitted securely and validated in real-time.

This shift from document-based to data-driven facilitation marks the core transformation from TFA to TFA 2.0. It entails not only technological upgrades, but institutional innovation: Digital Trust Councils involving governments, private platforms, and standards bodies should be formed to guide interoperability and ensure mutual recognition of digital documents and credentials. These councils can support the convergence of regulatory frameworks on digital identity, cybersecurity, and data governance—key pillars of a trusted trade infrastructure.

The table below summarizes this transformation and the added value of moving toward WTO TFA 2.0

Table 5. Potential Benefits of Implementing TFA 2.0

Indicator	**TFA (Current)**	**TFA 2.0 (Proposed)**
Foundation of Trust	Paper documents, signatures	Verified, machine-readable data secured by cryptography
Verification Method	Manual, paper-based, post-arrival	Real-time, automated, API-enabled pre-arrival verification
Interoperability	Partial and fragmented	Full, via international standards and trust frameworks
ESG and Export Controls	Not addressed	Embedded in digital compliance systems
Support for SMEs	Limited access, high compliance costs	Improved access, reduced transaction costs through automation
Scalability	Constrained by paper and national systems	Global, powered by interoperable digital ecosystems
Transparency and Traceability	Low visibility and fragmented reporting	High transparency across the supply chain; real-time traceability

continued on following page

Table 5. Continued

Indicator	TFA (Current)	TFA 2.0 (Proposed)
Speed and Predictability	Dependent on human processes	High-speed, automated processing with predictive clearance
Digital Technologies Used	Email, PDFs, scanned documents	APIs, Verifiable Credentials, DIDs, e-Registries, blockchain
Government Role	Supervisory, focused on document review	Proactive, co-developing digital trust infrastructure and mutual recognition regimes

Ultimately, WTO TFA 2.0 is not simply an update it is a new operating system for global trade. By embedding trust and compliance into the design of digital processes, and by promoting collaborative governance at national, regional, and global levels, it offers a blueprint for restoring predictability and fairness in an increasingly fractured trade environment. For developing countries and SMEs, this new architecture presents not just a challenge, but an opportunity—to leapfrog legacy systems and integrate directly into a smarter, more inclusive digital trade world.

REFERENCES

W3C. (2022). *Decentralized Identifiers (DID) Core*. Retrieved from https://www.w3.org/TR/did-core/

W3C. (2025). *Verifiable Credentials Data Model v2.0*. Retrieved from https://www.w3.org/TR/vc-data-model-2.0/

W3C. (2025). *Verifiable Credentials Overview*. Retrieved from https://www.w3.org/TR/vc-overview/

African Union. (2022). *Rules of Origin Manual, African Continental Free Trade Area Secretariat*. Retrieved from https://au.int/sites/default/files/documents/42397-doc-AfCFTA_RULES_OF_ORIGIN_MANUAL.pdf

African Union. *Rules of Origin Guidelines, AfCFTA*. Retrieved from https://au.int/en/documents/20230315/rules-origin-guidelines-afcfta

ASEAN. *ASEAN Single Window*. Retrieved from https://asean.org/our-communities/economic-community/asean-single-window/

Hanh, V. (2025). *An Introduction to Rules of Origin for Vietnamese Exports* (Vu Nguyen Hanh). Retrieved from https://www.china-briefing.com/china-outbound-news/introduction-rules-origin-vietnam-based-production

CarboChain. *The US SEC Climate-related Disclosure Rules Explained*. Retrieved from https://www.carbonchain.com/carbon-reporting/us-sec

Che, T., Hsieh, C.-T., & Song, Z. (2023). *Non-Tariff Barriers in the U.S.-China Trade War*. National Bureau of Economic Research (NBER). Retrieved from https://sccei.fsi.stanford.edu/china-briefs/chinas-use-unofficial-trade-barriers-us-china-trade-war

Council of Foreign Relations (CFR). (2025). *Trump's Economic Disruption: The World Adapts*. Council of Councils Global Memos. Retrieved from https://www.cfr.org/councilofcouncils/global-memos/trumps-economic-disruption-world-adapts

Digital Economy Partnership Agreement (DEPA). Retrieved from https://web.archive.org/web/20210118060435/https://www.mti.gov.sg/Improving-Trade/Digital-Economy-Agreements/The-Digital-Economy-Partnership-Agreement

European Commission. (2024). *Corporate Sustainability Due Diligence Directive (CSDDD)*. Retrieved from https://commission.europa.eu/business-economy-euro/doing-business-eu/sustainability-due-diligence-responsible-business/corporate-sustainability-due-diligence_en

European Commission. (2025). *Report Highlights EU's Approach to Export Controls of Dual-Use Items.* Retrieved from https://policy.trade.ec.europa.eu/news/report-highlights-eus-approach-export-controls-dual-use-items-2025-01-31_en

European Commission. *Carbon Border Adjustment Mechanism (CBAM).* Retrieved from https://taxation-customs.ec.europa.eu/carbon-border-adjustment-mechanism_en

European Commission. *Corporate Sustainability Reporting Directive (CSRD).* Retrieved from https://finance.ec.europa.eu/capital-markets-union-and-financial-markets/company-reporting-and-auditing/company-reporting/corporate-sustainability-reporting_en

European Union. (2021). *Regulation (EU) 2021/821 Setting up a Union Regime for the Control of Exports, Brokering, Technical Assistance, Transit and Transfer of Dual-Use Items.* Official Journal of the European Union. Retrieved from https://eur-lex.europa.eu/eli/reg/2021/821/oj/eng

Export Compliance Training Institute. (2023). *A Comparison Between U.S. Export Controls and European Export Controls.* Retrieved from https://www.learnexportcompliance.com/a-comparison-between-u-s-export-controls-and-european-export-controls

Hong Kong's Esquel Group Added to U.S. Forced Labor Ban List. (2024). *The Wall Street Journal.* Retrieved from https://www.wsj.com/articles/hong-kongs-esquel-group-added-to-u-s-forced-labor-ban-list-fec7faa9

ICC Digital Standards Initiative. (2023). *Trust in Trade.* Retrieved from https://www.dsi.iccwbo.org/_files/ugd/8e49a6_5a75a77950d7474da772bf9cfc2d985b.pdf

ICC Digital Standards Initiative. *Digital Standards for Cross-Border Trade.* Retrieved from https://www.dsi.iccwbo.org

Illuminem. (2025). *EU Moves to Ease CBAM Rules for SMEs While Keeping 99% of Emissions Covered.* Retrieved from https://illuminem.com/illuminemvoices/eu-moves-to-ease-cbam-rules-for-smes-while-keeping-99-of-emissions-covered

International Plant Protection Convention (IPPC). *ePhyto Solution.* Retrieved from https://www.ippc.int/en/ephyto/

OECD. (2021). *International Regulatory Co-operation: OECD Best Practice Principles for Regulatory Policy.* OECD Publishing., DOI: 10.1787/5b28b589-

OECD. (2025). *OECD Trade Facilitation Indicators: Monitoring Policies up to 2025.* Retrieved from https://www.oecd.org/content/dam/oecd/en/publications/reports/2025/03/oecd-trade-facilitation-indicators_0a21eb4a/fd6f27dc-en.pdf

OECD. (2025). *OECD Trade Facilitation Indicators.* Retrieved from https://www.oecd.org/en/publications/oecd-trade-facilitation-indicators_fd6f27dc-en.html

Trust, S. T. Retrieved from https://www.tradetrust.io/about/what-is-tradetrust/

UN/CEFACT. (2022). *White Paper: Verifiable Credentials for Cross-Border Trade (eDATA).* Retrieved from https://unece.org/sites/default/files/2023-08/WhitePaper_VerifiableCredentials-CrossBorderTrade_September2022.pdf

UN/CEFACT. (2023). *White Paper: Data Pipeline.* Retrieved from https://unece.org/sites/default/files/2023-10/WhitePaper_DataPipeline_Eng.pdf

UN/CEFACT. *Solutions in Support of Digital Product Passports (ECE/TRADE/481).* Retrieved from https://unece.org/trade/publications/uncefact-solutions-support-digital-product-passports-ecetrade481

UNCITRAL. (2017). *Model Law on Electronic Transferable Records (MLETR).* Retrieved from https://uncitral.un.org/en/texts/ecommerce/modellaw/electronic_transferable_records

UNCTAD. (2023). *World Investment Report 2023.* Retrieved from https://unctad.org/publication/world-investment-report-2023

UNESCAP. (2025). *Feasibility Studies: Identifying and Unlocking Cross-Border Paperless Trade Potential.* Retrieved from https://www.unescap.org/blog/feasibility-studies-identifying-and-unlocking-cross-border-paperless-trade-potential

UNESCAP. (2025). *Feasibility Study on Cross-Border Electronic Exchange of Trade Data and Documents: Kyrgyzstan.* Retrieved from https://repository.unescap.org/items/a904e9ae-be35-49df-a5b7-107756ed5ac3

U.S. Customs and Border Protection. (2025). *Uyghur Forced Labor Prevention Act Statistics.* Retrieved from https://www.cbp.gov/newsroom/stats/trade/uyghur-forced-labor-prevention-act-statistics

World Bank. (2020). *Doing Business 2020: Comparing Business Regulation in 190 Economies.* Retrieved from https://archive.doingbusiness.org/en/reports/global-reports/doing-business-2020

World Bank. (2023). *World Bank Logistics Performance Index 2023.* Retrieved from https://www.worldbank.org/en/news/press-release/2023/04/21/world-bank-releases-logistics-performance-index-2023

World Bank. (2024). *Improving Resilience and Economic Efficiency in Global Supply Chains to Counter Shocks.* World Bank Blogs. Retrieved from https://blogs.worldbank.org/en/trade/improving-resilience-and-economic-efficiency-in-global-supply-ch

Worldwide, J. *CETA – European Opportunity for Canadians.* Retrieved from https://www.jetworldwide.com/blog/european-canadian-ceta-duty-free-from-canada

WTO. (2017). *Agreement on Trade Facilitation (TFA).* Retrieved from https://www.wto.org/english/docs_e/legal_e/tfa_e.htm

WTO. (2023). *TFAF Work Plan 2024.* Retrieved from https://www.tfadatabase.org/en

WTO. (2023). *WTO Trade Monitoring Report 2023.* Retrieved from https://www.wto.org/english/res_e/publications_e/wtr23_e.htm

ENDNOTES

1 Compiled by the authors.

2 Verifiable Credentials are a promising technology for digital trade facilitation. The authors will explore them in greater depth in the next section.

Chapter 5
U.S. Trade Policy and Reciprocal Tariffs:
The Trade War and Its Impact on Future Trade Policies in Asian Countries

Susanna Hartanto
https://orcid.org/0000-0002-6936-6049
Widya Mandala Catholic University, Indonesia

ABSTRACT

The trade war between the United States and China has opened strategic opportunities to expand economic markets in Asian countries. The United States' trading partners are expected to retaliate to protect domestic industries and recover nominal income. This would cause further harm to U.S. economic growth and income, slowing global economic growth, with the negative impact intensifying when tariffs extend to free trade agreement partners and prompt retaliation. This study uses the literature research method. It analyzes information about the trade war between the United States and various Asian countries, especially China, which has a long history of trade conflict with the U.S., and discusses the effect of U.S. reciprocal tariffs on trade policies and tariffs in Asian countries. Trump's program would not only cause grave damage to the U.S. economy; these policies would actually benefit other countries, including most in Asia.

DOI: 10.4018/979-8-3373-3835-4.ch005

1. INTRODUCTION

The second term of Donald J. Trump as the president of the United States of America began in January 2025, marking the continuation of his distinctive "America First" approach (Dhar, 2025) and "Make America Great Again", a modern American political slogan made popular throughout his victorious presidential campaigns in 2016 and 2024. In a return to his first term's trade policies, he has implemented a wide range of tariff measures with most countries and traditional allies. .

According to Executive Order 14257 of April 2, 2025 - Regulating Imports with a Reciprocal Tariff to Rectify Trade Practices that Contribute to Large and Persistent Annual United States Goods Trade Deficits, in order to combat that special and exceptional threat to the United States economy and national security that comes totally or in large part from outside the nation, President Trump imposed additional ad valorem duties. He declared a national emergency in response to conditions reflected in the huge and ongoing annual United States goods trade deficits. As a result of domestic political negotiations between globalists and protectionists, who represented owners of factors unique to exporting and importing competitive industries, respectively, the United States of America Reciprocal Tariff established the country's trade policy with other nations (Bowen, T. Rene; Broz, J. Lawrence; Rosendorff, 2023).

While section 4(b) of Executive Order 14257 provided that in order to guarantee the effectiveness of this action, in the event that any trading partner retaliates against the United States in response to this action by imposing import duties on U.S. exports or taking other actions, President Trump may further amend the United States' Harmonised Tariff Schedule to increase or expand the duties imposed under this order.

Late in May, there were additional court decisions that added to the uncertainty surrounding Trump's tariff strategy. To support his reciprocal tariffs, Trump invoked a domestic legislation known as the International Economic Emergency Powers Act (IEEPA). Two different U.S. courts declared that the president had overreached himself in imposing IEEPA tariffs and demanded that all IEEPA-related duties be immediately removed. Although the lower court ruling was stayed by an expedited appeal filed by the Administration, the cases will likely to be anylsed by the Supreme Court (Elms, 2025). Meanwhile, the Trump administration is adamant that they have the power to raise tariffs as planned in July, and then changed to early August, allowing countries to negotiate.

Originlly, the increase in tariffs aimed to balance the bilateral trade deficits between the U.S. and each of its trading partners. For this purpose, it is calculated asreciprocal tariff rates, through the assumption that a mix of tariff and non-tariff factors that hinder trade from balancing are the cause of ongoing trade deficits. The tariff computation assumes that persistent trade deficits are caused by a combination of tariff and non-tariff factors resulting in trade imballances.

Trump's "America First" strategy, which prioritised the protection of American companies, is frequently cited tariffs as a key instrument for reducing reliance on imported goods, particularly from China. This approach was designed to protect American businesses from low-cost international imports, potentially revitalising United States manufacturing sectors and creating jobs within the country. As commerce between the United States and its trading partners declined, global economic growth was expected to suffer. Developing economies, especially those in Southeast Asia, may face challenges to sustain trade levels as global trade fell.

Countries that rely largely on exports to the U.S., such as those in the Asia-Pacific area, have seen their economies stagnate. Higher tariff rates, a delay in frontloading, and more onerous transhipping are all expected to discourage exports, dulling the outlook in Asia Pacific. Example for this situation is in Japan, in addition to 25 percent tariffs on automobiles and steel, the Trump administration announced reciprocal tariff surcharges in early April. The U.S. imposed a 25% tariff on imports of Japanese cars and auto parts and a 10% duty on most other goods

Exports fell 2.6% in value in July from a year earlier, sliding more than the median forecast of a 2.1% decline. The downturn, led by cars, auto parts and steel, was the biggest since February 2021. Car shipments to the US have started to decline in volume, suggesting that the impact of tariffs is finally starting to show. The Bloomberg report showed that exports to the US dropped by 10.1% last month from a year earlier, with the value of shipments of vehicles and auto parts plunging 28.4% and 17.4%, respectively. In terms of volume, exports of vehicles to the U.S. fell by 3.2%, a clear indication that carmakers are absorbing a portion of the tariffs to support sales (Yokoyama, 2025).

Regions that could see smaller downside risks than expected from the Liberation Day tariffs are those where specific sectoral tariffs have been alleviated, such as for cars and auto parts. Most importantly, Japan's auto manufacturing tariffs have almost halved from the previously announced rates to 15%, which is significant as the U.S. is Japan's largest exporting partner overall and both Japan's largest international car market. The relatively lower tariff rates on the key sector will help maintain these countries' competitiveness in the U.S. market.

The rearrangement of global supply chains posed further issues, as restructuring attempts resulted in inefficiencies and greater manufacturing costs. The economy is suffering from these higher tariff risks, and consumers will eventually pay more for goods as a result of rising production costs. This had the potential to raise consumer prices while reducing the overall competitiveness of enterprises in the impacted regions.

First, tariffs increase revenue, but the question of who will bear the costs is for debate. Historically, economists have found that foreign firms absorbed some of the burden of tariffs by lowering their prices, resulting in a combination of foreign businesses and domestic firms and consumers sharing the burden of tariffs (Rowland, 2025).

In contrast to past studies, however, recent studies have found the Trump tariffs were passed almost entirely through to American firms or final consumers. According to the United States International Trade Commission (USITC) report,, it confirmed near complete pass-through to import prices. USITC found that imported steel and aluminium prices rose by 22 percent and 8 percent, respectively, following the tariffs. For China tariffs, US importers absorbed the costs of the tariffs through a combination of less favorable margins for sellers and higher prices for consumers or downstream buyers (United States International Trade Commission, 2023).

Tariffs are generally expected to be passed on to American consumers who buy the goods that are subject to the levies. There is evidence, however, that foreign companies may occasionally reduce their prices, thereby tacitly paying a portion of the duties (Rowland, 2025). Presient Trump has suggested the use of tariffs to influence foreign nations, such as Canada and Mexico, over immigration and fentanyl smuggling, even though he has also suggested using them to help the government raise money (The White House, 2025). The concept that tariffs can level the playing field is partly based on the commonly held belief that Americans have been exploited because their market is more open than those in other countries. They are therefore seen as a multifunctional instrument (Lawrence, 2025). Brazil, for instance, has the highest tariff braket, 50% for selected products, being a bargain power of Trump's government against the home emprisionment of former president Jair Bolsonaro (Iqbal & Prazeres, 2025).

The geopolitical consequences of a protracted trade war can be severe. Countries may have begun to reorient their economic strategy, forging new trade alliances beyond the American-Chinese arena. China, in particular, attemped to enhance its position in global supply chains by reducing its reliance on American market and focussing on new trade routes.

This reorientation of economic connections would have long-term implications in new US – China trade routes, a shift in global supply chains, leading to increased costs for consumers and businesses, potential disruptions, and opportunities for other regions like Southeast Asia to become new trade hubs..

Trump's tariff policies were not designed to protect home industries and rebalance trade but also to be a tool for geopolotical interference in other countries, either from the political standpoint, to attract investment or a resource power bargain (Perez, 2025).

Key American industries such as automobile and steel producers were benefited, but on the other had, there is an increase supply chain disruptions for industries which are heavily reliant on import due to the lack of domestic insumes, which increase input costs, particulalry whenever there is aretaliation from trading partners. This two-fold impact makes it difficult for enterprises that rely on global supply chains or are downstream users of tariffed goods to thrive. However, the drawback of policy execution can cause (Wong et al., 2025):

1. Trade War Started Due to Retaliatory Tariffs

Other nations, including China, the European Union, and Canada, responded to the United States' taxes by imposing their own tariffs on their imports. Instead of fostering better trade deals, this tit-for-tat escalation hurt United States of America exporters and international supply chains. The European Union finally decided to accept a 15% tariff increase and commit to invest 600 billion dollars in the United States (Paese, 2025).

2. Increased costs for consumers and businesses

In essence, tariffs are import levies. Production costs increased as a result of American enterprises having to pay more for raw materials like steel and aluminium. Inflation without salary rises resulted from the regular pass-through of these expenses to consumers.

3. Global supply chains have been disrupted

Global supply chains are essential to contemporary manufacturing, especially in the automobile and technology sectors. This was disrupted by tariffs, which increased the cost and inefficiency of production. In order to avoid tariffs, many enterprises had to make adjustments, and some moved their operations outside of the U.S., which had the reverse effect of what was intended.

4. Inability to Lower the Trade Deficit

In several instances, the United States of America trade imbalance increased in spite of the harsh tariff tactics. Because there were limited domestic options or because American products were still less competitive in terms of both price and quality, consumers kept purchasing items from other countries.

5. International Relationships Affected

Trump's unilateral trade policies alienated important allies and threatened multilateral institutions like the World Trade Organization (WTO). Global collaboration weakened as long-term confidence in the United States as a trustworthy trading partner decreased.

6. Restricted Growth in Domestic Employment

Although the goal of the tariffs was to restore jobs to the United States, research revealed that while protected industries like steel had little job growth, companies that relied on imports or exports saw job losses.

7. Uncertainty in the World Economy

Global markets were unstable due to unpredictable tariff increases and trade conflicts, which slowed growth and investment not only in the United States but also globally. Enterprises may put off making decisions because of unstable policy environments.

2. TRADE WAR IMPLICATIONS FOR ASIAN ECONOMIES

China's response to the 2025 United States reciprocal tariffs has been to retaliate with its own tariffs on American goods, and to call for the complete cancellation of the tariffs, stating the infringement of existing trade rules. China has also expressed its disapproval of the United States tariffs, stating they violate international trade rules and are a "unilateral bullying practice" (Wu, Kurtenbach, & Tang, 2025). China has been the United States's most unbalanced trading partner since 2000, with goods trade deficit reaching \$295.5 billion in 2024, a 5.7 percent increase (\$15.9 billion) over 2023. The United States total goods trade (exports plus imports) with China was an estimated \$582.0 billion in 2024. The United States goods exports to China in 2024 were \$143.2 billion, down 3.0 percent (\$4.4 billion) from 2023. The United States goods imports from China in 2024 totaled \$438.7 billion, up 2.7 percent (\$11.5 billion) from 2023 (Office of The United States Trade Representative, 2025). Even though China is one of the main export markets for the United States, in 2024, the sheer amount of Chinese shipments to the United States exceeded United States exports to China by a factor of three (Liu, Juliana; Gan, 2025).

An additional 34% tariff on all Chinese goods imported into the United States was announced by the United States, a move that might lead to a significant reversal of ties and exacerbate trade tensions between the two biggest economies in the world (The White House, Fact Sheet: President Donald J. Trump Secures a Historic

Trade Win for the United States, 2025). According to the White House, Trump has already imposed two rounds of 10% extra taxes on all Chinese imports in an effort to stop the illegal fentanyl from entering the United States from China (The White House, Fact Sheet: President Donald J. Trump Secures a Historic Trade Win for the United States, 2025). In addition to existing duties, that implies that Chinese goods entering the United States would be subject to tariffs of more than 54% (Race, 2025).

Section 4(b) of Executive Order 14257 requires President Trump to modify the Harmonised Tariff Schedule of the United States (HTSUS) to increase the applicable ad valorem duty rate for imports from China established in Executive Order 14257. This was done in the Executive Order dated April 8th, 2025, Amendment to Reciprocal Tariffs and Updated Duties As Applied to Low-Value Imports from China. This was in response to the China's announcement that it would retaliate against the United States in response to Executive Order 14257 (Trump, 2025). The HTSUS's heading 9903.01.63 will be changed by removing "84%" from each instance where it appears and replacing it with "34%" . While there was an initial increase from 34% to 84% on April 9, 2025, and then a further increase to 125%, and back to 34%, this specific rate has been temporarily suspended until November 10, 2025. However, importers will instead be subject to the 10% reciprocal duty under HTSUS heading 9903.01.25 during the suspension period (Mohawk Global, 2025).

On the other hand, Vietnam has a different approach to United States Reciprocal Tariffs. The Trump administration claims that Vietnam "charges" the United States at a rate of 90% at the moment; this number seems to be based on the nation's present trade surplus with the U.S. The United States will therefore impose a 46 percent reduced tariff on Vietnamese goods. On April 9th, the new tariff rate was supposed to take effect (Huld, 2025).

Vietnam is implementing multiple synchronized measures to respond to the United States' 46% reciprocal tariff, aiming to cushion its negative impact on exports and the economy in general. The United States of America announcement to impose a 46% tariff on Vietnamese goods beginning on April 9th will have a significant impact on Vietnam's export activities and economic growth, according to Vietnam Deputy Minister of Industry and Trade, Truong Thanh Hoai. This is because the announcement directly affects processing and manufacturing, the attraction of foreign direct investment, domestic investment, and services. Computers, electronic components, textiles, and footwear are among the important export goods that could see a decline in export revenue.

When the United States increases tariffs, the prices of Vietnamese export products in the United States market will rise, which will affect their competitiveness compared to goods from other countries. In addition, American consumers' purchasing power will decline, leading to a decrease in demand for Vietnamese goods. Vietnam's initial reaction to the United States of America reciprocal tariffs involved seeking a postponement to negotiate a trade deal and expressing regret for the tariffs' implementation. The Vietnamese government has expressed its regret and disappointment with the tariffs but has also taken a pragmatic approach, actively engaging in negotiations, seeking to mitigate the impact on businesses, and also welcomed the temporary pause of the tariffs.

Vietnamese companies are rushing to ship goods to the United States of America before the tariffs take full effect, as the initial tariffs were set to be 46%. Some companies are even pushing back deadlines and hiring additional workers to meet the demand. While Vietnamese businesses are actively trying to expedite shipments before the full tariffs take effect, Vietnam government has sought to negotiate with the United States of America to address the tariffs, including exploring a bilateral trade agreement.

The United States of America and Vietnamese leaders have agreed to discuss the tariffs and explore a trade deal to remove them. The initial tariffs were paused for 90 days, which was seen as a positive step by Vietnam, allowing for more time to negotiate. Vietnam is hoping to reach a long-term, sustainable bilateral trade agreement with the United States that benefits both countries.

Southeast Asia, especially Malaysia, was greatly impacted by Trump's trade policy, resulting in both challenges and possibilities for the area. The disruption of global supply networks, particularly in electronics and automotive manufacturing, compelled many corporations to reconsider their production locations. Malaysia, a significant semiconductor production hub, has seen movements as corporations seek to dodge tariffs by shifting operations to Southeast Asia. As many multinational corporations relocated their production from China to Southeast Asia, trade diversion became a significant effect. Malaysia benefited from this change by increasing Foreign Direct Investment (FDI) in important industries such as electronics and automotive manufacture.

However, this increased rivalry within the area, with nations such as Vietnam and Thailand vying for similar investments, heightening the scramble for industrial projects and further complicating market dynamics. At the same time, the increase in production costs caused by the tariffs put extra strain on Southeast Asian economies such as Malaysia. As United States demand for goods increased due to tariffs on Chinese imports, Southeast Asian countries faced the simultaneous task of boosting output while controlling competition in a more crowded market. This resulted in increased tensions in the regional manufacturing scene, as countries competed for the same opportunities. While moving manufacturing operations to Southeast Asia provided chances for expansion, it also presented dangers, including increased costs and inefficiencies in production processes.

More than 75 other international trading partners, including those listed in Annex I to Executive Order 14257, have approached the United States since President

Trump signed Executive Order 14257 to address the lack of trade reciprocity in the economic relationships and the ensuing national and economic security concerns. This is in contrast to China's actions. This is a big step in the right direction for these nations to correct unfair trade agreements and sufficiently align with the United States on national security and economic issues.

On the other hand, some other Asian countries tried to wait and see the situation. The worldwide press makes it apparent that several businesses and financial experts think the order's policy may change in the near future. As a result, there is some hesitancy to commit to new tactics too quickly.

This study used the literature research method, which is a research approach that uses written sources including journals, government websites and financial website, to collect and analyze data. The qualitative research approach is used in this study. Investigating, finding, and characterising the object of study are all done using qualitative methods. Rather of depending just on one data source, qualitative researchers usually collect a variety of data sets, including observations, interviews, documents, and audiovisual material (Creswell & Creswell, 2018).

The research analyzes information about the trade war that happened between the United States of America and other Asian countries, especially with China, which has a long history of United States-China trade war. The research discussed the effect of United States reciprocal tariff on trade policies and tariff to Asian countries both for short and long term and how to overcome those effects for Asian countries.

Study limitation, the data was only collected through secondary resources. On the basis of that, the qualitative approach is generally interpretive. Qualitative data is often rich and complex, requiring careful interpretation and analysis, which can be subjective and time-consuming. The subjective nature of qualitative research can make it difficult to reproduce the same results in a different context or with a different researcher (Mwita, 2022).

3. UNITED STATES OF AMERICA VERSUS CHINA TRADE DISPUTE

In January 2018, the United States imposed tariffs and other trade restrictions (non tariff barrier like restriction of China's access to U.S. advanced technologies and restrictions on China's ability to manufacture advanced chips) on China in an attempt to alter a long-standing unfair trade practices and intellectual property theft. This marked the beginning of the economic conflict between the two countries (Swanson, 2018).

The growing trade war between China and the United States of America has led to a rise in bilateral trade tariffs since 2018. However, U.S. and Chinese producers of the goods affected by the tariffs as well as producers that use those goods as intermediate inputs, are potential losers. Diversion of trade is one way that producers are impacted. The increase in imports from other nations seems to have counterbalanced the decrease in imports from China, which is supported by aggregate bilateral US statistics that indicates trade diversion has taken place.

For example, U.S. imports from Mexico increased significantly among some goods on which the US imposed tariffs. After the $16 billion list was implemented in August, a sharp decline of nearly $850 million in imports from China was almost offset by about $850 million increase from Mexico, leaving overall U.S. imports broadly unchanged. For other countries such as Japan, Korea and Canada, one can observe smaller increases in U.S. imports relative to the levels in September-November 2017. Aggregate data could be masking other factors driving the bilateral trade patterns, such as the use of inventories. For example, there was little or no change in imports from third countries in the case of photosensitive semiconductor devices (Cerutti, Gopinath, & Mohommad, 2019).

The other channel by which producers could be affected is through market segmentation in the price of traded goods. This was most clearly observed in the case of soybeans, where U.S. exports to China fell dramatically in 2018 after China imposed tariffs. The United States was China's dominant soybean supplier, along with Brazil, in 2017. With the tariffs, the price of American soybeans fell while that of Brazilian soybeans increased, as U.S. exports to China dropped to near zero and Brazilian exports to China trended higher. Though prices have since re-converged and soybean exports to China have resumed to some extent, U.S. soybean farmers suffered, while those in Brazil benefited from trade diversion and market segmentation (Cerutti, Gopinath, & Mohommad, 2019).

Despite pledged attempts to remove tariffs, tensions still exist, and there is a risk that duties will turn into a new battle. The trade war has a detrimental effect on bilateral trade between the United States and China (Li, Chunding; He, Chuantian; Lin, 2018).

The U.S. implemented protectionist policies by applying tariffs under several provisions of the Trade Act of 1974 (Senate and House of Representatives United States of America, 1974). Section 201 imposed additional tariffs on solar cells or modules, beginning at 30% in the first year (2019) and decreasing to 15% by the fourth year (2022) (Office of The United States Trade Representative, Section 201 – Imported Solar Cells and Modules, 2022). Similarly, large home washing machines were subject to additional tariffs ranging from 20% to 50% based on a tariff rate quota (U.S. Customs and Border Protection, 2023). Tariffs were also levied on steel and aluminium imports under Section 232 of the 1962 Trade Expansion Act, claiming economic security concerns. Initially, certain economies, such as the

Republic of Korea, were spared from tariffs. However, steel and aluminium duties were finally implemented.

Furthermore, Section 301 of the Trade Act of 1974 established sweeping tariffs on products originating in the People's Republic of China. These tariffs were applied in four rounds, affecting a wide range of industries such as equipment, electronics, chemicals, agriculture, and textiles. The first wave, in July 2018, put a 25% duty on $34 billion in imports, with succeeding rounds broadening the scope and raising tariff rates. The third round included $200 billion in imports, while the fourth round, which was partially cancelled owing to a trade agreement, had an initial goal of $300 billion in goods (United States International Trade Commission, 2023).

In 2025, the U.S. initiated the trade dispute by enacting broad duties on all Chinese imports, arguing the necessity for more robust measures to combat the illegal distribution of synthetic opioids and wider trade imbalances. China reacted swiftly, focussing on important American exports including coal, liquefied natural gas, rare earth, and farm equipment before increasing tariffs on United States of America agricultural goods and imposing restrictions on United States of America enterprises (Grant Thornton, 2025). Both nations took a number of retaliatory actions as the months went by, and tariff rates increased to previously unheard of levels.

Global commerce was drastically altered in early 2025 when United States of America President Donald Trump, who had just returned to the White House, rekindled a tariff conflict with China as part of a larger initiative to restructure United States of America trade policy, which included the International Emergency Economic Powers Act (IEEPA) (Casey et al., 2024).

The trade war appears to be beneficial to the United States. This mostly stems from the United States's stronger market dominance and China's comparatively feeble retaliatory response, which is motivated by a fear of intensifying the trade war and further harming its own businesses and employment rates. Nonetheless, the impact of the trade war on United States industry is not uniform. The United States auto and agricultural sectors are more severely impacted than others.

The planned 60% tariffs on China in January 2025 are more incesive compared to his first term (York, 2024). Due to a multiplier effect, where value is added at several locations throughout global supply chains, the actual rate of these new tariffs would be higher than the suggested nominal rates. The duty is triggered by the proportion of value added in China, even if it is applied to the entire import amount.

Approximately one-third of manufacturing value added goes towards so-called "Made in China" exports (Menon, 2025). The effective tariff, which represents the tax on adding value in China, is around three times the nominal amount, or 180% . This implies that if the identical operations can be carried out in China at no more than 180% of the cost (Menon, 2025), production will probably move to other locations like Vietnam or Thailand. This gives manufacturers a strong incentive to cut China out of the supply chain (Menon, 2025).

Consumers will be negatively impacted by rising prices if the trade dispute worsens, but certain industries will also be severely harmed by broken input-output links and economic uncertainty. Policymakers who are thinking about the possible consequences of the trade tariffs proposal will find this research particularly significant. It has been demonstrated that the trading partner's retaliatory measures significantly affect the effectiveness of such protectionist policies. Before acting, a thorough analysis of the trade policy's potential impacts on the nation's supply chains, trade flows, and welfare should be conducted. After all, winning a trade war is neither nice nor simple.

However, import and retaliatory tariffs led significant decreases in imports and exports. Tariff-targeted import prices did not reduce, meaning that duties had been completely passed through to duty-inclusive prices. The consequent of 2018 tariff, losses to United States of America consumers and corporations that buy imports totalled $51 billion, or 0.27% of GDP (Azzimonti, Edwards, & Ravindranat, 2025). According to studies, the effects of these tariffs were complex and diverse While they were designed to remedy trade imbalances and defend domestic sectors, the actual results were higher consumer and company expenses, limited job growth, and considerable economic burdens. China's high-tech exports were more negatively impacted by the new U.S. tariffs than its medium- and low-tech exports (Xu et al., 2020). The usefulness of these tariffs in achieving their intended purposes is still being debated, with several research pointing to unanticipated negative outcomes.

According to the simulation results that was conducted by Fan Zhai (Zhai, 2025), a trade war under Trump 2.0 would have significant negative economic effects on all participating nations. This note has looked at the ramifications of Trump 2.0 tariffs and China's potential policy reaction to lessen their negative consequences. In particular, we examine scenarios involving tariff increases by the United States, tariff retaliation by China, and China's fiscal growth using a calibrated global dynamic general equilibrium model.

The outcomes of these scenarios' simulations indicate that President Trump's tariff policies since his second inauguration would result in a significant slowdown in economic growth and higher domestic prices in the United States. China would experience sharp drops in trade and economic losses in the interim, but fiscal stimulus and currency depreciation lessen some of these effects. There would be significant economic losses for the rest of the world as well. Overall, the U.S., China, and the world economy would suffer significant financial losses as a result of Trump's protectionist trade policies, especially if they turn into a full-scale trade war.

Directing fiscal transfers explicitly towards lower-income people can both produce economic expansion and foster more social inclusion, even while increasing government consumption can more successfully boost short-term growth. Nevertheless, the long-term negative consequences of Trump tariffs cannot be mitigated by macrostimulus measures. To lessen its susceptibility to foreign shocks,

China must shift its focus in the medium to long-term towards bolstering domestic demand drivers and improving industrial capabilities. Increasing economic connections with emerging markets, strengthening supply chain resilience, and speeding up trade diversification will all be essential in navigating a world that is becoming more protectionist. China needs to reiterate its support for the WTO and the rules-based global trading system. International trade flows would be protected and the risk of global economic fragmentation would be reduced by exhibiting leadership in promoting openness and respecting global trade norms.

On the other hand, China can use a variety of policy tools, such as structural reform, fiscal stimulus, accommodative monetary policy, and exchange rate flexibility. Short-term economic disruptions can be avoided by combining targeted fiscal stimulus with a flexible exchange rate. In a market-driven setting, allowing it to freely fluctuate will support export competitiveness in the face of unstable international trade conditions.

Amiti, Redding, and Weinstein, used difference-in-difference estimations to demonstrate that Trump tariffs had a significant negative impact on Chinese exports to the United States of America. More specifically, U.S. tariffs are nearly exclusively absorbed by United States of America businesses and consumers. There is no term of trade effect. Trade patterns changed significantly in reaction to the tariffs imposed in 2018. In the initial three months, a 10% tariff is associated with a 10% decrease in imports; however, this elasticity doubles in subsequent months (Amiti et al., 2020).

According to Amiti, Redding, and Weinstein, In 2018, the total deadweight welfare cost (real income loss) resulting from United States tariffs was around $8.2 billion. According to event study estimation, the United States total import values for Trump-listed goods, irrespective of the import partner countries (whether or not the import partners were subject to Trump tariffs), dropped by 2.5%, while the United States import values of Trump-listed goods from targeted countries fell by 31.7%. United States businesses and individuals who bought imported goods on the Trump list lost $51 trillion in actual revenue, or 0.27% of the country's GDP. An overall loss of US$7.2 trillion, or 0.04% of United States GDP (Fajgelbaum, Goldberg, & Kennedy, 2020), was caused by the combined loss of United States businesses and consumers, a gain in consumer surplus (from a slight decline in border prices), and tariff income (Fajgelbaum, P. D.; Goldberg, P. K.; Kennedy, P. J.; Khandelwal, 2020). Cavallo examined tariff pass-through at the retailer and consumer levels in the United States and discovered results that were similar to those of earlier research, including the Trump tariffs' 100% pass-through to domestic pricing in the United States. Because the retail price of consumer goods like refrigerators, handbags, and washing machines remained constant, they found that the whole burden of tariffs fell on retailers rather than consumers (Cavallo et al., 2021).

Cavallo discovered that United States enterprises faced the brunt of tariffs, with high pass-through rates to import prices and little price decreases by Chinese exporters. United States exporters dropped their prices in reaction to overseas retaliatory duties, and retail margins in United States retailers fell, demonstrating a complicated and multidimensional economic impact.

For Southeast Asia, these are concerning indicators. In the China-centered regional electronics supply chain, Malaysia, Singapore, and Thailand are major participants, while Vietnam and the Philippines are crucial at the assembly stage. Chinese and international businesses have moved their operations from China to Southeast Asia as a result of the increase of Sino-American relations.

Supply chains are more likely to split apart if the trade conflict intensifies. In keeping with Biden's most recent round of punitive measures against China, Trump is probably going to target companies based on their nationality rather than where they are located. This change in nationality is the reason for Trump's efforts to reopen the trade agreement with Canada and Mexico. Any supply chains that are reorganised geographically to get around these penalties will fail if these measures are successfully put into place. Bifurcation is more likely as the motivation to undertake expensive move declines.

For the targeted items, this might result in two supply chains: one for the United States and markets like the Eropean Union that punish value-adding in China, and one for everyone else. Although having a single supply chain is the most economical, the trade war would necessitate a supply network designed specifically to avoid tariffs. In this case, international companies in China could still relocate to Southeast Asia, but Chinese companies would no longer invest there merely to avoid tariffs.

Significant trade diversion occurs when China expands its market share in the United States, Canada, and Mexico and as exports from China to the United States are displaced by those from other nations like South Korea. For China and the United States, changing trade flows lead to slight declines in total import and export. These findings are resilient to a variety of trade elasticities (Li et al., 2020).

4. UNITED STATES OF AMERICA VERSUS VIETNAM TRADE TARIFF

Although it provides Vietnam with temporary respite, the 90-day suspension of Trump's 46% tariff on Vietnamese exports highlights how susceptible it is to United

States trade demands. Vietnam has responded by lowering tariffs on United States imports and striking energy accords, among other significant concessions.

However, Vietnam's GDP growth forecast is in jeopardy due to its limited leverage and rising protectionism. Vietnam is an intriguing prospect for United States businesses because of its young workforce and low wage costs. However, this has been impeded by Washington's 46% tariff rate, which goes into force in July (Huld, 2025). Vietnam talked with Washington for a reduction. negotiations led to a revised tariff agreement with Vietnam, with the rate significantly reduced to 20%, following the signing of a new executive order on July 31, 2025 (The White House, Further Modifying The Reciprocal Tariff Rates, 2025).

According to a World Bank research, released in March, Vietnam's GDP is expected to increase at one of the quickest rates in Southeast Asia, 6.8% by 2025 and 6.5% in 2026 (World Bank, 2025). The study attributed the predicted development to Vietnam's recovery in industries such as manufacturing exports, tourism, and foreign direct investment. The suspension of Washington's 46% tariffs on Vietnamese goods is set to expire next month. Businesses in Hanoi strive to diversify and reduce the impact of United States prohibitions (World Bank, 2025).

Vietnam is pursuing market diversification and structural changes, but its plan is complicated by its continued reliance on China and the United States. However, a agreement with Vietnam is being pushed by the possibility that United States companies may establish there if they decide to quit China, one of our main trading rivals. Additionally, investment in the communist nation has been considered by the Trump Organisation. As Vietnam strives to incorporate capitalism into its economy and pursue closer connections with the United States, the Vietnam War is a thing of the past.

4.1 Why is Trump's Tariff for Vietnam so High?

The U.S. has imposed heavy tariffs on Vietnam, citing worries that China is exploiting Vietnam as a transshipment site to avoid Washington's own high duties. Vietnam has increased measures to combat unlawful transshipment, which primarily involves products from China. Though there is no further evidence, and even Vietnamese enterprises that do not have ties with China will suffer the consequences of the trade war.

Tariffs have forced Vietnam's operations to rely on other markets throughout the world. Vietnam enterprises strive to expand their export market to other nations, such as Europe, Japan, and Korea, so that we are not completely dependent on the United States market and are less subject to any changes in the United States government.

Since the tariffs were imposed, cargo freight businesses in China have attempted to transfer their cargo to the United States via Vietnam in order to avoid the higher charges. A large number of charter flights from freight forwarders are currently flying from China to Vietnam. The ability to fly to the United States from Vietnam has expanded by around 80% (Gava Group, 2025).

4.2 Balancing United States of America demands with China Ties

Vietnam and China have a tight economic and political relationship. Beijing is Hanoi's major commercial partner, and both nations have similar political philosophies and are led by communist parties. If Vietnam decides to restrict its trade with China, it will harm the Vietnamese economy in any case. Reducing or even eliminating Chinese input materials and components will have a huge negative impact on Vietnam's economy.

Vietnam's manufacturing sector, particularly electronics and textiles, relies on imported raw materials from regional supply chains based in China. If Vietnam complies with United States demands, it will harm its relations with China, which will interpret Vietnam's compliance as joining the United States-led anti-China alliance. Vietnam is a major manufacturing hub for foreign apparel brands, but Washington has highlighted how counterfeit products have exacerbated trade worries.

The United States Trade Representative identified Saigon Square Shopping Mall as a hotspot for the sale of counterfeit fashion items from major brands. Vietnam has taken many measures to address Washington's concerns, which should lower the high tariffs imposed on them. Vietnam has been ratcheting up its assault on transshipment concerns, and it just started a new campaign to combat counterfeit items and online piracy.

No country in the world has been more proactive than Vietnam in negotiating tariff relief with the Trump administration. One of the difficulties facing the Vietnamese right now is determining how much to negotiate and give away.

Trump's tariffs also represent larger Washington worries about China's economic clout. According to United States officials, Vietnamese facilities repackage Chinese goods and act as a transhipment destination for Chinese goods looking to avoid United States duties. Vietnam's manufacturing industry, which has benefited from multinational diversification away from China, is plagued by this notion. United States trade hawks have found support in the opaqueness of certain supply lines, notwithstanding Vietnam's denials of systemic cooperation in transshipment.

Vietnam has responded by pursuing a two-pronged approach of measured diplomacy and economic concessions. A US$4.15 billion energy transaction was signed between Vietnam and United States companies during Minister of Industry and Trade Nguyen Hong Dien's March 2025 visit to Washington (Linh, 2025). In order to establish Vietnam as a dependable energy partner, this included agreements to import offshore wind technology and liquefied natural gas. Hanoi's need to keep diplomatic lines open is highlighted by General Secretary To Lam's phone call to congratulate Trump on his election victory in April 2025 (Linh, 2025).

Vietnam went beyond South Korea and Mexico's concessions by offering to lift duties on U.S. medical equipment, Boeing aeroplanes, and agricultural machinery, even though it denied U.S. claims of widespread transshipment. Despite concerns that such concessions could jeopardise emerging domestic businesses, this illustrates Vietnam's practical decision to put the short-term stability of its exports first and protect its 8% GDP growth target (Vietnam Plus, 2025).

Vietnam's efforts to expand its export markets are hampered by the delicate geopolitical balance between China and the United States. Vietnam signed the Comprehensive and Progressive Agreement for Trans-Pacific Partnership in 2018 and fully implemented free trade accords with the United Kingdom in 2021 and the European Union in 2020 in an effort to lessen its dependency on the United States.

Vietnam is not powerful enough to enforce significant countermeasures. Vietnam must use diplomatic pressure to overcome this imbalance, such as promises to buy more United States energy exports or stricter origin regulations to stop transshipment. Trump's transactional approach to trade policy, however, makes long-term concessions less likely.

However, Vietnam is still closely linked to China, which is its biggest commercial partner. Long-term hedging is made possible by these arrangements, but Vietnam's capacity to make up for short-term losses brought on by U.S. tensions is far from assured.

Vietnam's endeavours to broaden its export markets are hindered by the precarious geopolitical equilibrium between the United States and China. To reduce its reliance on the United States, Hanoi signed the Comprehensive and Progressive Agreement for Trans-Pacific Partnership in 2018 and fully implemented free trade agreements with the European Union in 2020 and the United Kingdom in 2021.

However, Vietnam is still closely linked to China, which is its biggest commercial partner. Long-term hedging is made possible by these arrangements, but Vietnam's capacity to make up for short-term losses brought on by United States tensions is far from assured.Regionally, the tariffs risk fragmenting ASEAN's production networks, potentially redirecting investment to countries such as India or Mexico. Geopolitically, the measure risks pushing Vietnam closer to China, undermining Washington's Indo-Pacific strategy.

Instead of being a resolution, the 90-day tariff respite is a tactical ceasefire. It presents a chance for Vietnam to further structural changes and deepen trust with United States trading partners. Trump's transactional worldview has positioned Vietnam as a practical negotiator. Uncertainty surrounds the long-term consequences of one-sided transparency, though. As global supply networks change, Vietnam needs to quickly adjust, diversify constantly, and get ready for a future in which trade policy can be used as a weapon as well as a shield. In the upcoming months, Vietnam's ability to transform short-term respite into long-term strategic advantage will be put to the test.

5. ROUNDABOUT TRADE OR DETOUR TRADE IN TRUMP'S TARIFFS AGAINST CHINA

Although some Asian economies have profited from the shifting of manufacturing away from China, the region as a whole has been affected in a complicated and varied fashion by the increased uncertainty and decreased levels of global trade. The economies of Asia have been significantly impacted by Trump's tariff policy, although indirectly. Here is a brief summary of the main effects:

1. Disruptions to the supply chain

Asian nations play a crucial role in international supply networks. The flow of intermediate goods has been impacted by the uncertainties and disruptions brought on by the trade war between the United States and China, which has an effect on regional production costs and efficiency.

2. "China Plus One" and Trade Diversion

Some businesses moved their production from China to Asia in an effort to reduce the risks associated with tariffs. In certain nations, such as Vietnam, Thailand, and Indonesia, this "China plus one" approach has increased foreign direct investment and job creation.

3. Market Uncertainty and Export Demand

A lot of countries in Asia rely on exports. The general slowdown in international trade and increased economic uncertainty brought on by trade conflicts sparked by tariffs have decreased export demand, which has impacted earnings across a range of industries.

4. Pressures on Costs

Supply chain disruptions may result in higher prices for components and raw materials. The integration of Southeast Asian firms into these chains may result in increased production costs and pressure from competitors in both domestic and foreign markets.

The shipping of commodities to final destination countries through third countries to get around export embargoes or exorbitant import tariffs imposed by the final destination countries is known as "roundabout trade" or "detour trade." Roundabout trading could be done in a number of ways.

For instance, a Chinese business might set up an affiliate (foreign direct investment) in Vietnam, import goods from its Chinese headquarters, and then export them back to the U.S. On the other hand, a business in a country that avoids direct trade, like Vietnam, imports products from China and then exports them back to the U.S. The middle Vietnamese company in this situation engages in indirect trade. The commodities are being reexported from Vietnam, but the Chinese company that supplied them to the Vietnamese company is not aware of this.

Free Trade Agreement (FTA) tariff rates may or may not be applied when commodities are exported through nations like Canada or Mexico that have FTAs with the U.S. The rules of origin certificate is required when U.S., importers obtain FTA tariff rates. But legally changing the label from "made in China" to "made in Mexico" and therefore qualifying the products for FTA tariffs comes at a high expense because the products need to be processed by Mexican middle-tier businesses.

However, as the difference between FTA rates and most-favored nation (MFN) rates is typically only a few percent, such as 3% for MFN rates and 0% for FTA rates (Ito, 2024), the advantages of adopting FTA rates are negligible. There was little difference in the benefits of circular commerce between MFN and FTA imports because Trump's tariffs were primarily 25% (Ito, 2024).

Many businesses have no justification for applying for FTA rates in light of this cost-benefit analysis. As mentioned in the beginning, trade data alone cannot be used to accurately identify roundabout commerce. Instead, by analysing the exceptionally high rise in Trump tariff item imports from China and the correspondingly high rise in Trump tariff item exports to the United States, this study aims to ascertain if there are wide indications of roundabout trade.

6. THE IMPACTS OF TRUMP'S TARIFFS AGAINST CHINA ON THIRD COUNTRIES

Most of countries in Asia especially in The Association of Southeast Asian Nations (ASEAN) countries are impacted by Trump tariff including:

1. Vietnam: Faces Gross Domestic Product (GDP) declines of up to 2% and possible export losses of over $30 billion. The projected growth of 6.3% is still

considered robust but is lower than the Vietnamese government's initial target of 8.3% to 8.5% (Nghi, 2025). Important industries like electronics and furnishings are suffering greatly.

2. Thailand: Expected export losses of almost $8 billion, the electronics and automotive sectors are particularly vulnerable.
3. Malaysia: The labour market and foreign direct investment are affected, and the electronics and palm oil industries are under pressure, so the impact is probably going to be minor.
4. Indonesia: Overall, it faces modest risks; even while its diverse export portfolio offers some resilience, structural improvements are still necessary for long-term competitiveness.
5. Philippines: A smaller trade base puts the agriculture and electronics industries at risk, which could result in employment losses in important export hubs.
6. Singapore: The country is nonetheless vulnerable because to its high-tech, logistics, and re-export sectors, while being mostly protected at the tariff level.

The Impacts of Trump's tariffs against China on third countries also showed in some research in Asian countries. Chor and Li (Chor & Li, 2024), A reduction in local economic activity was indicated by the greater drop in night light intensity in China's areas most susceptible to U.S. tariffs, according to satellite measurements of nighttime luminosity. Cui and Li (Cui & Li, 2021) showed that relatively lower rates of Chinese new company entrance were linked to increases in import tariffs from the United States of America.

He, Mau, and Xu (He et al., 2021) discovered that in the six months after the tariff hike, companies that were comparatively more exposed to U.S. tariffs in 2019 posted fewer job ads. On average, the decrease translated into 2.4% to 3.2% less ads for each company (He, Mau, & Xu, 2021). Other authors looked into how Trump's trade conflict with China affected global value chains. For instance, utilising data on sanctions and retaliations at the tariff-line level and incorporating it into a general equilibrium framework with global value chains, recursive dynamics, and imperfect competition.Bellora and Fontagné (Bellora & Fontagné, 2020) discovered that these value-added twists were transferred to production factors in accordance with political economy determinants, resulting in a significant increase or decrease in employment and a reallocation of capital to protected industries, primarily at the expense of their customers. Chang, who analysed data on Japanese corporations' activities in China, claims that since the trade war began, sales at Chinese affiliates have usually decreased, especially for companies with substantial exposure to trade with North America (Chang et al., 2019).

Ito (Ito, 2024) found that Trump's tariffs on China cut United States imports from China significantly, while numerous United States import partner countries raised their exports to the United States at the expense of China, generating a form of trade diversion effect. The study also found that while there was no sign of a drop in the border prices of American imports from China (i.e., no improvement in trade), there was a drop in the border prices of American imports of Trump-listed goods from other partner countries (i.e., China, specifically). Ito showed that while the import price of Chinese goods targeted by Trump decreased slightly, Japan's import quantities and values stayed the same.

To ascertain the reason for this unexpected result, the study looked into China's shipments of commodities that the Trump tariff targets to the international market. It found that China was sending more of those items to the world market. An increase in China's sales to other countries more than offset the drop in its exports to the United States of America. However, somewhat in contrast to Ito's conclusion, Hayakawa et al. (Hayakawa, 2024) asserted that the Trump tariffs' effect on China's output exports to the U.S. led to a reduction in China's imports of inputs from supplier economies, especially Taiwan.

Trump-tariff goods shipments from China to nations other than the United States of America appear to be on the rise, which may be due to tariff evading through trade through other countries. The recommendations for government policymakers and businesses in Asian countries (Wong et al., 2025). Summary of the recommendations for government policymakers are:

1. Multilateral Trade Negotiations

Retaliation frequently follows unilateral tariffs, raising tensions and interfering with international trade. Stable, rule-based frameworks are established by the World Trade Organisation, other multilateral trade agreements, and regional agreements such as the Regional Comprehensive Economic Partnership (RCEP) and the Comprehensive and Progressive Agreement for Trans-Pacific Partnership (CPTPP). These frameworks facilitate mutual benefits, resolve disputes, and reduce political risk for exporters.

2. Specific Relief Initiatives

Unexpected increases in input costs usually have a disproportionately negative impact on exporters who are industry-specific and small and medium-sized businesses. Subsidies, tax exemptions, or loan availability are examples of temporary assistance that might lessen the impact and prevent closures or layoffs, allowing companies to adapt and reorganise.

3. Invest on innovation and infrastructure

Trade resilience is a product of competition, not protectionism. A country can lower costs, increase productivity, and produce higher-value exports that are less susceptible to tariff shocks by upgrading its infrastructure (such as ports, digital systems, and innovation support through R&D and upskilling).

4. Transparent Trade Policy

One of the biggest deterrents to corporate investment is policy uncertainty. Volatility is decreased by predictable trade policy, which includes frequent reviews, open disclosures, and stakeholder interaction. It helps businesses to invest with confidence, plan ahead, and maintain supply chain stability.

Some of the recommendations for business leaders are:

1. Diversification of the Supply Chain

Businesses become more vulnerable to interruptions, strengthen their negotiating position, and maintain operations during trade shocks when they are overly dependent on a single supplier or geographic area.

2. Strategies for Cost Absorption

Cost increases brought on by tariffs may lower company profitability and price competitiveness. Organisations can maintain pricing stability without passing on all costs to customers by implementing lean operations, automation, and energy efficiency.

3. Industry Alliances

Collective action has greater weight than individual voices. Businesses may pool their resources, lobby more effectively for rational trade policy, and exchange mitigation and adaptation measures by forming or joining coalitions, particularly in fragmented industries such as manufacturing or logistics.

4. Monitor Policy Developments

Trade policy evolves throughout time. Missing a big policy shift might result in misaligned pricing, supply chain challenges, and missed opportunities in other markets. Real-time monitoring enables organisations to immediately pivot, renegotiate contracts, or capitalise on trade exclusions or new accords.

Some policies and specific recommendations for Asian countries especially in ASEAN are:

1. Asian nations' voice is provided by Collective Asian Engagement. Determine exemptions or obtain tariff deferrals by using cooperative diplomatic channels.
2. Strategy for Trade Diversification:
    a. Improve commercial ties with the EU, Middle Eastern markets, and RCEP partners.
    b. Increase trade inside Asia to increase economic participation.
3. Measures of Economic Resilience
    a. Assist the industries most impacted by trade disruptions financially.
    b. Provide focused assistance to SMEs and make investments in personnel transition plans and upskilling initiatives.
4. Enhance Asian Value Chains
    a. Develop regional production networks more quickly
    b. Encourage sourcing from within Asia to lessen reliance on the United States. avenues of commerce.
5. Put an emphasis on digital trade and services. Leverage Asia's competitive advantages in fintech, the digital economy, and cross-border services to lessen the impact of trade disruptions.

These international interests will need to be taken into account in the next stage of ASEAN's reaction. In multilateralism, it can assist in addressing a leadership void. ASEAN already operates under two guiding principles that may direct collaboration and action. First, ASEAN would support international efforts to safeguard the rules-based multilateral economic system if it acts in its own best interests and in accordance with its values. The second is to uphold and implement ASEAN centrality. ASEAN is essential to wider Asian cooperation in addition to its member states in Southeast Asia. Utilise ASEAN's centrality or risk losing it.

Southeast Asian nations' strong economic ties to China may also draw unwelcome scrutiny. Trump's administration has genuine or fictitious concerns that nations in the area are conspiring to help China get over technological limitations. The United States' recent investigation into the likelihood that China's ground-breaking artificial intelligence start-up, DeepSeek, got forbidden chips from third parties in Singapore may only be the first step. Similar scrutiny may be applied to other nations. Be prepared for a harsh trade response from the U.S. if strong evidence is found. Washington may become more suspicious of Southeast Asia's “complicity” with China as a result of its involvement in Brasil, Russia, India, China, South Africa (BRICS).

Within its own region, ASEAN will find partners who are willing. Days before Trump's tariffs were announced, the foreign ministers of China, Japan, and South

Korea met and decided to work together to respond to U.S. tariffs and "to strengthen the implementation of RCEP," which stands for the Regional Comprehensive Economic Partnership, a free trade agreement involving 15 countries that was established and is headed by ASEAN. This entails staying together as a group, taking actions in accordance with the institutions and regulations that ASEAN has agreed to, and refraining from reprisal that would only cause further economic suffering. ASEAN might fall apart if those guiding principles are broken.

Since the reciprocal tariffs have a negative effect on exports, growth, and employment, many nations affected will attempt to bargain with the United States, particularly since labour-intensive industries are typically the most affected. The ASEAN nations will want to coordinate and steer clear of agreements that hurt ASEAN as a whole, but the United States will engage with nations one-on-one.

There will be many unknowns around this plan given the circumstances surrounding Mr. Trump's tariff policy. Japan, a crucial United States ally and one of the first to initiate official discussions with the United States, has not reported much progress and is the first country to truly test the tactic of negotiation.

There are also concerns about a recession, a bad external environment, and possible negative shocks as a result of United States policy. For ASEAN economies, a two-pronged approach is the best course of action. First, the domestic economy should be strengthened by proper macroeconomic policies, tailored programs to help individuals affected, and a comprehensive package of structural and regulatory reforms in order to manage the external shocks. Working together with neighbours will boost confidence and benefit Southeast Asia more broadly. Second, the bloc can accomplish more than just safeguarding its strategic interests by using open regionalism and its centrality. To protect its interests in the international system, ASEAN can assemble a coalition of cooperative partners. Furthermore, Southeast Asia will be able to withstand the greatest danger to its political and economic stability since ASEAN's founding.

Southeast Asia's economic success is directly tied to global supply chains and export-led growth, thus the region is in a precarious position as a result of President Trump's return to a protectionist United States. Southeast Asia must immediately invest in regional economic integration, diversify its trade alliances, and create more robust trade infrastructures that are less susceptible to changes in the policies of any one market. ASEAN can not afford to wait; in a world where trade regulations are constantly changing, the region needs to move quickly and together to protect its hard-won economic victories.

As the date of July 9th, 2025 is crucial, it marks the end of Trump's tariff ceasefire against the majority of trading partners. In addition to East Asia, a number of Southeast and South Asian nations have been invited to participate in United States tariff talks. These nations are all keen to buy energy in order to lower their trade imbalances with the United States. The tariff truce in China expires on August 12. While there was an initial increase from 34% to 84% on April 9, 2025, and then a further increase to 125%, and back to 34%, this specific rate has been temporarily suspended until November 10, 2025. However, importers will instead be subject to the 10% reciprocal duty under HTSUS heading 9903.01.25 during the suspension period (Mohawk Global, 2025).

U.S. gave a reduction, negotiations led to a revised tariff agreement with Vietnam, with the rate significantly reduced to 20%, following the signing of a new executive order on July 31, 2025 (The White House, Further Modifying The Reciprocal Tariff Rates, 2025). Southeast Asian governments ought to coordinate their tariff reaction, as proposed by Malaysian Prime Minister Anwar Ibrahim. ASEAN member states should endeavour to strengthen their economic integration, reduce non-tariff barriers, and create connections between their digital economies as talks with the United States continue. In order to absorb excess exports, they should also seek to strengthen trade ties with both new and current partners, including China.

7. CONCLUSION

Initiatilly, the goal of Trump's tariff measures was to rebalance trade and safeguard American economic interests, however, it has become a barganinng mechanism to infuence politics of foreign countries, as seen Brazil. Several important trading partners including Canada and China responded with retaliatory tariffs, stating infrigement of the WTO trade rules, and disruption of international supply chains.

Additionally, because customers kept buying goods from other countries, the tariffs had little effect on the United States trade deficit. There's no strong evidence that American consumers broadly switched to purchasing goods from alternative foreign sources to dodge tariffs. Instead, behaviors leaned more toward stockpiling essential items before tariffs took effect. Nearly 49% of consumers stocked up on food (33%) and household goods (29%) anticipating future price hikes (Cahalan, 2025) or rushing to make large purchases like cars or laptops early, rather than shifting where they bought them. For example, one buyer purchased a Taiwanese laptop immediately upon news of a 32% tariff (The Economic Times, 2025). A unilateral approach to trade caused diplomatic tensions, undermined multilateral institutions such as the WTO, and resulted in long-term trust problems among allies. There was minimal total employment growth as a result of the short-term job increases in certain domestic sectors being largely offset by job losses in industries that depend on overseas trade.

Furthermore, the tariff policy's unpredictability discouraged long-term planning and investment by fostering an atmosphere of economic uncertainty on a worldwide scale. In the end, the study indicates that protectionist policies like these could impede long-term economic expansion, which would be better facilitated by cooperation, innovation, and structural changes. The thorough analysis of Trump's tariff policy shows that, despite the intention to support domestic sectors and close the trade imbalance, the wider economic effects have mostly been detrimental. The possible advantages have been weakened by the ensuing trade disputes, higher expenses, broken supply chains, and eroded global confidence.

In addition, the hazards of depending on protectionist measures in a highly interconnected global economy are underscored by the slow creation of jobs at home and the ongoing uncertainty in the world. There are opportunities and challenges associated with Trump's tariff approach. Businesses may weather these rules by investing in cost-management techniques, strengthening supply chain resilience, and actively participating in policy discussions.

In terms of policy, suggestions include moving towards multilateral trade agreements, providing targeted assistance to impacted industries, and establishing a more stable trading climate. When combined, these tactics can lessen adverse effects and put companies and legislators in a better position for future trade that is sustainable and equitable.

For Asian nations, particularly those in Southeast Asia, the Trump tariffs are a fundamental shock to the ASEAN trading framework. Nonetheless, the trade conflict between the United States and China has created advantageous chances to expand the ASEAN nations' economies. Maintaining regional stability and long-term competitiveness requires a concerted response that combines economic change, diversification, and diplomacy.

REFERENCES

Amiti, M., Redding, S. J., & Weinstein, D. E. (2020). Who's Paying for the US Tariffs? A Longer Term Perspective. *AEA Papers and Proceedings. American Economic Association, 2020*(110), 541–546. https://swh.princeton.edu/~reddings/pubpapers/ARW-May-2020. DOI: 10.1257/pandp.20201018

Azzimonti, M., Edwards, Z., & Ravindranat, S. (2025, April). *Tariffs: Estimating the Economic Impact of the 2025 Measures and Proposals*. From https://www.richmondfed.org/publications/research/economic_brief/2025/eb_25-12

Bellora, C., & Fontagné, L. (2020). Shooting Oneself in the Foot? Trade War and Global Value Chains. *CEPII Working Paper, April.*

Bowen, T. Rene; Broz, J. Lawrence; Rosendorff, B. P. (2023). A Theory of Trade Policy Transitions. *Journal of Historical Political Economy, 4*(4), 471–507. https://www.scopus.com/record/display.uri?eid=2-s2.0-105001191034&origin=resultslist&sort=plf-f&src=s&sot=b&sdt=b&s=TITLE-ABS-KEY%28US+Reciprocal+Tariff%29&sessionSearchId=cb95d1f13ec3a88216fb0a03783d5277&relpos=2

Cahalan, C. (2025, April). *Tariffs force important shift in consumer behavior.* From https://www.thestreet.com/personal-finance/tariffs-cause-an-important-shift-in-consumer-behavior?

Casey, C. A., Elsea, J. K., Casey, C. A., & Elsea, J. K. (2024). *The International Emergency Economic Powers Act : Origins*. Evolution, and Use.

Cavallo, B. A., Gopinath, G., Neiman, B., & Tang, J. (2021). Tariff Pass-Through at the Border and at the Store: Evidence from US Trade Policy. *American Economic Review: Insights, 3*(1), 19–34. DOI: 10.1257/aeri.20190536

Cerutti, E., Gopinath, G., & Mohommad, A. (2019, May 23). *The Impact of US-China Trade Tensions*. From https://www.imf.org/en/Blogs/Articles/2019/05/23/blog-the-impact-of-us-china-trade-tensions#:~:text=Evolution%20of%20trade%20in%20the%20US%20and%20China&text=The%20impact%20of%20previously%20imposed,since%20the%20trade%20tensions%20began

Chang, S. U. N., Zhigang, T. A. O., Hongjie, Y., & Hongyong, Z. (2019). The Impact of US-China Trade War on Japanese Multinational Corporations. *RIETI Discussion Paper Series, June*.

Chor, D., & Li, B. (2024). Illuminating the effects of the US-China tariff war on China's economy. *Journal of International Economics, 150*(July), 103926. DOI: 10.1016/j.jinteco.2024.103926

Creswell, J. W., & Creswell, J. D. (2018). Research Design: Qualitative, Quantitative and Mixed Methods Approaches. *Sage (Atlanta, Ga.).*

Cui, C., & Li, S. (2021). The Effect of the U.S.–China Trade War on Chinese New Firm Entry. *Economics Letters, 203*(109846).

Dhar, B. (2025). Trump's 'America First' Trade Policy. *Economic and Political Weekly, 60*(10), 18–21. https://www.scopus.com/record/display.uri?eid=2-s2.0-86000282208&origin=resultslist&sort=plf-f&src=s&sot=b&sdt=b&s=TITLE-ABS-KEY%28US+Reciprocal+Tariff%29&sessionSearchId=cb95d1f13ec3a88216fb0a03783d5277&relpos=1

Elms, D. K. (2025). *Southeast Asia in the Crosshairs: Navigating Trump's Protectionist Trade Policies.* https://techforgoodinstitute.org/blog/expert-opinion/southeast-asia-in-the-crosshairs-navigating-trumps-protectionist-trade-policies/

Fajgelbaum, P. D., Goldberg, P. K., Kennedy, P. J., & Khandelwal, A. K. (2020). The Return to Protectionism. *The Quarterly Journal of Economics, 135*(1), 1–55. https://academic.oup.com/qje/article-abstract/135/1/1/5626442. DOI: 10.1093/qje/qjz036

Gava Group. (2025, July). *Vietnam Air Cargo to U.S. Soars as Tariffs Drive Shift from China.* From https://gava.com/vietnam-air-cargo-to-u-s-soars-as-tariffs-drive-shift-from-china/#:~:text=Vietnam's%20air%20cargo%20exports%20to,air%20cargo%20momentum%20may%20continue

Hayakawa, K. (2024). Do Exports to the US Increase Imports from China during the US–China Tariff War? *IDE Discussion Papers, Institute of Developing Economies, 946*(946).

He, C., Mau, K., & Xu, M. (2021). Trade Shocks and Firms Hiring Decisions: Evidence from Vacancy Postings of Chinese Firms in the Trade War. *Labour Economics, 71*(102021), 102021. DOI: 10.1016/j.labeco.2021.102021

Huld, A. (2025, August). *The Impact of Tariffs on Vietnamese Exports: US-Vietnam Trade Relations Under Trump 2.0.* From https://www.vietnam-briefing.com/news/us-vietnam-trade-relations-trump-impact-tariff-vietnamese-exports.html/#:~:text=Trump%20imposes%20reciprocal%20tariffs%20on,not%20available%20in%20the%20US

Huld, A. (2025). *The Impact of Tariffs on Vietnamese Exports: US-Vietnam Trade Relations Under Trump 2.0.* Vietnam Briefing.

Iqbal, N., & Prazeres, L. (2025, August 15). *Bolsonaro's son praises Trump's tariff hike on Brazil.* From https://www.bbc.com/news/articles/c5yl00qlyz9o

Ito, T. (2024). Trump Tariffs and Roundabout Trade. *KDI Journal of Economic Policy*, *46*(3), 25–47.

Lawrence, R. (2025). *Explainer: How Do Tariffs Work and How Will They Impact The American and Global Economy?* https://www.hks.harvard.edu/faculty-research/policy-topics/public-finance/explainer-how-do-tariffs-work-and-how-will-they

Li, C., He, C., & Lin, C. (2018). Economic Impacts of The Possible China-US Trade War. *Emerging Markets Finance Ad Trade. Emerging Markets Finance & Trade*, *54*(7), 1557–1577. DOI: 10.1080/1540496X.2018.1446131

Li, M., Balistreri, E. J., & Zhang, W. (2020). The U.S.–China trade war: Tariff Data and General Equilibrium Analysis. *Journal of Asian Economics*, *69*(101216), 101216. DOI: 10.1016/j.asieco.2020.101216

Linh, D. K. M. (2025). *Trump's Tariff Turbulence is Reshaping Vietnam's Trade Future*. East Asia Forum. https://eastasiaforum.org/2025/06/23/trumps-tariff-turbulence-is-reshaping-vietnams-trade-future/

Liu, Juliana; Gan, N. (2025). *China imposes 34% reciprocal tariffs on imports of US goods in* retaliation for Trump's trade war.

Menon, J. (2025). *Southeast Asia at The Crossroads of Trump Tariffs 2.0.* https://eastasiaforum.org/2025/01/23/southeast-asia-at-the-crossroads-of-trump-tariffs-2-0/

Mohawk Global. (2025, August 12). *Suspension of Additional Tariffs on Chinese Imports Extended Until November.* From https://mohawkglobal.com/word-from-the-white-house/suspension-of-additional-tariffs-on-chinese-imports-extended-until-november/#:~:text=Mohawk%20Global%20Home-,Suspension%20of%20Additional%20Tariffs%20on%20Chinese%20Imports%20Extended%20Until%20November,r

Mwita, K. (2022). Strengths and Weaknesses of Qualitative Research in Social Science Studies. *International Journal Research in Business and Social Science*, *11*(September), 618–625. Advance online publication. DOI: 10.20525/ijrbs.v11i6.1920

Nghi, G. (2025, July). *ADB lowers Vietnam's GDP growth forecast to 6.3%.* From https://english.thesaigontimes.vn/adb-lowers-vietnams-gdp-growth-forecast-to-6-3/

Office of The United States Trade Representative. (2022, February). *Section 201 – Imported Solar Cells and Modules.* From https://ustr.gov/issue-areas/enforcement/section-201-investigations/investigation-no-ta-201-75-cspv-cells

Office of The United States Trade Representative. (2025). *China Trade Summary*. From https://ustr.gov/countries-regions/china-mongolia-taiwan/peoples-republic-china#:~:text=China%20Trade%20Summary&text=U.S.%20goods%20imports%20from%20China,($15.9%20billion)%20over%202023

Paese, A. (2025, July 29). *EU-US trade deal explained*. From https://ec.europa.eu/commission/presscorner/detail/en/qanda_25_1930

Perez, A. (2025, March 12). *The geopolitics of trade tariffs: The new Trump presidency*. From https://commonslibrary.parliament.uk/the-geopolitics-of-trade-tariffs-the-new-trump-presidency/

Plus, V. (2025, April). *PM calls for flexible response to US tariffs, maintaining 8% growth target*. From https://en.vietnamplus.vn/pm-calls-for-flexible-response-to-us-tariffs-maintaining-8-growth-target-post312943.vnp

Race, M. (2025, May 12). *What does the US-China tariff deal mean?* From https://www.bbc.com/news/articles/clyg2939ej2o

Rowland, B. (2025, August 21). *European Union says U.S. consumers will end up paying tariffs*. From https://www.thecentersquare.com/national/article_89123db5-c909-4bb0-8e76-69cd28a6b206.html

Senate and House of Representatives United States of America. (1974). *US Trade Act of 1974*. https://www.govinfo.gov/content/pkg/COMPS-10384/pdf/COMPS-10384.pdf

Swanson, A. (2018). *"Trump's Trade War With China Is Officially Underway*. The New York Times. https://www.nytimes.com/2018/07/05/business/china-us-trade-war-trump-tariffs.html

The Economic Times. (2025, April). *US consumers rush to buy big-ticket items before Trump's tariffs kick in*. From https://economictimes.indiatimes.com/news/international/global-trends/us-consumers-rush-to-buy-big-ticket-items-before-trumps-tariffs-kick-in/articleshow/120004178.cms?

The White House. (2025, February 1). *Fact Sheet: President Donald J. Trump Imposes Tariffs on Imports from Canada, Mexico and China*. From https://www.whitehouse.gov/fact-sheets/2025/02/fact-sheet-president-donald-j-trump-imposes-tariffs-on-imports-from-canada-mexico-and-china/

The White House. (2025, May 12). *Fact Sheet: President Donald J. Trump Secures a Historic Trade Win for the United States.* From https://www.whitehouse.gov/fact-sheets/2025/05/fact-sheet-president-donald-j-trump-secures-a-historic-trade-win-for-the-united-states/#:~:text=AMERICAN%20ACTIONS:%20The%20United%20States,and%20stop%20unfair%20trade%20practices

The White House. (2025, July). *Further Modifying The Reciprocal Tariff Rates.* From https://www.whitehouse.gov/presidential-actions/2025/07/further-modifying-the-reciprocal-tariff-rates/

Thornton, G. (2025, April). *A new tariff paradigm: How businesses can respond.* From https://www.grantthornton.com/insights/articles/tax/2025/new-tariff-paradigm-how-businesses-can-respond

Trump, D. J. (2025). *Modifying Reciprocal Tariff Rates to Reflect Trading Partner Retaliation and Alignment.* Executive Order 14257, Presidential Action, The White House. https://www.whitehouse.gov/presidential-actions/2025/04/modifying-reciprocal-tariff-rates-to-reflect-trading-partner-retaliation-and-alignment/

United States International Trade Commission. (2023). Economic Impact of Section 232 and 301 Tariffs on U.S. Industries. Washington, DC: The Commission United States International Trade Commission.

U.S. Customs and Border Protection. (2023, January). *QB 21-505 Washers and Covered Parts.* From https://www.cbp.gov/trade/quota/bulletins/qb-21-505-washers-and-covered-parts#:~:text=On%20January%2023%2C%202018%2C%20the,duty%20rates%20in%20the%20Annex

Wong, C. D., Tay, V., Homer, S. T., & Nazera, F. (2025). Impact of Trump's 2025 " Liberation Day " Tariffs on Southeast Asia. *International Journal of Research and Innovation in Social Science, IX*(June), 5556–5570. DOI: 10.47772/IJRISS.2025.905000428

World Bank. (2025). *Electrifying Journeys* (Issue March). https://openknowledge.worldbank.org/server/api/core/bitstreams/9d53a06b-7302-4f9b-b78d-fb3b45d26caf/content

World Bank. (2025, March). *Viet Nam's Economy Forecast to Grow 6.8 Percent In 2025.* From https://www.worldbank.org/en/news/press-release/2025/03/12/viet-nam-s-economy-forecast-to-grow-6-8-percent-in-2025-wb#:~:text=Share%20more,pushing%20forward%20with%20structural%20reforms

Wu, H., Kurtenbach, E., & Tang, D. (2025, April 4). *China slaps a 34% tax on all US imports in retaliation for Trump's tariffs*. From https://www.wfxrtv.com/news/business/ap-china-imposes-a-34-tariff-on-imports-of-all-u-s-products-starting-april-10/

Xu, T., Li, W., Jiang, Y., & Chen, Y. (2020). The Impact of Destination Tariffs on China's Exports: Country, Firm, and Product Perspectives. *Journal of Asian Economics*, *71*(101246), 101246. DOI: 10.1016/j.asieco.2020.101246

Yokoyama, E. (2025, August 20). *Japan's Exports Fall Most in Four Years as Tariff Pain Deepens*. From https://www.bloomberg.com/news/articles/2025-08-19/japan-s-exports-fall-most-in-four-years-as-tariff-pain-deepens

York, E. (2024, January). *Tariff of Abominations Redux: Trump Proposes 60% Tariff on Chinese Goods*. From https://taxfoundation.org/blog/trump-china-trade-war-proposal/

Zhai, F. (2025). *Macroeconomic Impacts of Trump 2.0 Tariffs on China: A Model Based Assessment*. China Economic Insights.

Chapter 6
AfCFTA as a Strategic Response to Trade Wars: Reinventing Africa's Role in the Global Economy

Beryl Njeri O. Lubandwa
https://orcid.org/0009-0000-2952-1473
Mind Shift International, Kenya

ABSTRACT

This chapter examines the African Continental Free Trade Area (AfCFTA) as a crucial instrument for addressing global trade challenges, including the surge in protectionist policies observed during the COVID-19 pandemic. This analysis employs geoeconomics, strategic trade theory, and new regionalism to examine how the AfCFTA can enhance Africa's economic strength and independence. The chapter examines policy frameworks and case studies from Ghana, South Africa, Nigeria, and Kenya, as well as insights from various regional trade agreements, including RCEP, USMCA, and MERCOSUR. The chapter suggests that the AfCFTA could enhance Africa's position in global trade negotiations, foster regional value chains, and consolidate the continent's markets. The chapter concludes with a helpful framework that policymakers, development partners, and institutions can utilize to safeguard Africa against external shocks through the AfCFTA.

1. INTRODUCTION

Africa stands at a crossroads in its development. Global trade fragmentation, in the context of economic nationalism, alongside pervasive technological disruption, is impacting the operation of international trade. The African Continental Free

DOI: 10.4018/979-8-3373-3835-4.ch006

Trade Area (AfCFTA) is a viable source to help Africa move from the fringes of international trade and become a prominent contributor to a new and equitable economic order. The AfCFTA has the potential to unite all 1.3 billion people across the continent into a single market with a total GDP of over $3.4 trillion (UNECA, 2023). The AfCFTA has been agreed upon by 54 of the 55 African Union member states, and implementation is slowly but surely underway.

To get to this stage necessitates a view of the AfCFTA that is beyond tariff and customs regulations. The AfCFTA is a very important part of Africa's objective of reducing the higher global trade friction. This effort is going to rely on cooperation with/among countries, a great deal of political capital, and a consistently followed strategy. There are great strides and changes happening in how countries trade goods and services. Recent trends against economic protectionism, the reassembling of the global value chain, and enhancing geopolitical tensions and pressure are rendering multilateralism inherently unstable and trade increasingly unpredictable. Thus, Africa's difficulties are enhanced. One figure illustrates this. More than 60% of Africa's goods are still exported outside the continent, demonstrating that Africa's entire commodity export economy is exposed to commodity price volatility and changes to global demand that it cannot control (UNECA, 2023).

This situational reality may also represent an opportunity. The AfCFTA represents the largest free trade area in the world in terms of the number of participants. Providing Africa with a strong anchor to build and restore integrity and power that can reclaim its position within the emerging global trade networks. This chapter presents the argument that the AfCFTA serves as a geopolitical shield and a means for fostering trade and driving economic growth. The AfCFTA will act as a way of safeguarding Africa's economic independence and protect it from external destabilizing influences, by reinforcing the provisions of the AfCFTA including the internal integration of markets, the support of regional value chains, and the cooperative African position for global trade regulation it to influence the establishment of new global trading rules around digital commerce, climate change trade policy and WTO reform (UNCTAD, 2022). To influence the establishment of new global trading rules on digital commerce, climate change trade policy, and WTO reform (UNCTAD, 2022). This chapter adopts a multi-theoretical approach to the AfCFTA that includes Strategic Trade Theory (Krugman & Smith, 1994), New Regionalism Theory (Söderbaum & Shaw, 2003), and concepts relating to economic sovereignty and Geoeconomics (UNCTAD, 2021) which each match, merge, and position the AfCFTA from the perspective of a navigational tool for systematizing and augmenting the long-term resilience rather than responding to change. The methodology for the chapter is presented based on findings of four major matters:

1. Africa's trade exposure is fundamentally vulnerable due to the continent's reliance on a small number of exports and external markets, such as the U.S., the EU, and China (World Bank, 2020).
2. The AfCFTA has the potential to mitigate these vulnerabilities, but how? The AfCFTA can utilize strategic incentives, such as associated tariff reductions, which could increase trade between African countries by 52% (UNECA, 2023). Similarly, creating more harmonization around regulations and increasing regional value chains are ways to make firms more competitive and find new markets for their goods.
3. Regional trade blocs strategically leverage regionalism to enhance resilience, protect regional interests, and negotiate from a stronger position in the global arena, as demonstrated by the RCEP, MERCOSUR, and USMCA (Petri & Plummer, 2020; Draper & Dadush, 2021).
4. Institutional coherence and political will will be imperative. The AfCFTA may not reach its full potential for transformation if these ongoing challenges, particularly those related to infrastructure and financing for small and medium-sized enterprises (SMEs), persist, and performance-based policies are not implemented.

This chapter outlines a step-by-step policy approach that transitions from promoting trade immediately to establishing long-term strategic independence. It is intended for governments, regional groups, and development partners. The AfCFTA's structural flexibility can help Africa go from being weak to strong. The plan must also fit with the continent's ambitions for its people, industries, and politics. If Africa works together courageously, the AfCFTA might move it from the outskirts of global trade to the core of its change.

Beyond external shocks, Africa also faces considerable challenges related to variations in infrastructure, readiness to trade, and institutional capacity. As the African Commerce Report (Afreximbank, 2023) indicates, intra-African trade (trade among African countries) accounts for less than 20% of total trade. The primary barriers to intra-African trade are inadequate transport routes, inconsistent border processes, and a lack of trade financing mechanisms. The African Continental Free Trade Area (AfCFTA) has the potential to address these barriers and lay the foundation for inclusive growth across African regions. To enhance the country's competitiveness, it will be crucial to invest in logistics infrastructure, particularly inland container depots and One-Stop Border Posts (OSBPs) (Afreximbank, 2023). Harmonizing trade standards will also be crucial.

Africa has long been described as a “rule-taker” in international trade, as its agencies have been regularly compelled to comply with or follow the rules developed by established international agencies and economies. The legacy of many structural adjustment programs from the 1980s and 1990s, as well as trade policies that leveraged aid without regional cooperation, hindered the continent's ability to negotiate effectively. With the implementation of the African Continental Free Trade Area (AfCFTA), Africa now has a strong, indigenous foundation for creating its own trade rules, establishing regional standards, and supporting companies that generate added value throughout the continent. The AfCFTA aligns with the 21st-century economy and represents a departure from many other integration strategies, as it encompasses not only tariffs but also investment, competition, intellectual property, and digital trade. This longitudinal economic power is greater than a trade agreement; it is a step towards total independence.

The COVID-19 outbreak heightened people's awareness of Africa's vulnerability in global value networks. Supply chain problems that delayed the importation of essential goods, such as industrial components and vaccines, highlighted the risks of relying too heavily on suppliers outside of Africa. The AfCFTA is a means to strengthen the regional supply chain while also enhancing public health, advancing industry, and improving digital connections. The lessons learned from the epidemic also demonstrate the importance of ensuring that Africa's institutional and physical infrastructure for commerce is prepared for future financial crises, technological advances, and climate shocks. To fully achieve the AfCFTA's potential, trade corridors, logistical hubs, customs systems, and regulatory bodies must be improved along with the policy pillars of the agreement.

The chapter argues that people should not view the AfCFTA solely as a free trade agreement, but rather as a crucial tool for transforming Africa. It's important because it serves the dual function of not only shielding Africa from external economic shocks but also of fundamentally advancing African interests in global trade negotiations. This new approach is grounded in strategic trade theory, new regionalism theory, and UNCTAD's geoeconomic framework, aiming to cluster African economies, enhance digital connectivity, strengthen industrial integration, and improve cross-border institutional functions.

The AfCFTA must not repeat the mistakes made by previous liberalisation initiatives. Concentrating solely on lowering tariffs may accelerate the deindustrialization process and reinforce the dependency that the AfCFTA aims to address. For this reason, African countries must adopt the AfCFTA implementation as part of their national development strategies, industrial policies, and investment attraction strategies. There needs to be a connection among the ministries of commerce, industry, infrastructure, and finance. The African Union Commission, UNECA, Afreximbank, and Regional Economic Communities (RECs) will also bolster their roles to optimize resource use, implement and adhere to agreements, and share information to become effective partners for policy coherence.

The AfCFTA represents an opportunity for Africa to transform its relationship with the rest of the world. Africa may hold more power when it acts together, rather than relying solely on trade, as it has traditionally operated in a deficit or donor-recipient relationship. The AfCFTA provides an opportunity to lobby for changes within the WTO, create rules for digital trade, and advocate for global environmental trade standards. Africa can utilize the AfCFTA as a foundation for enhanced trade with the Southern states, thereby creating potential strong trading linkages with the BRICS+, ASEAN, and MERCOSUR, which share similar developmental objectives.

Ultimately, it is essential to consider factors beyond trade statistics when evaluating the AfCFTA. We must also think about value in terms of job creation, poverty reduction, and increased economic autonomy. By 2050, Africa's population is expected to reach 2.5 billion, with the largest segment comprising those under 25 years old. The potential opportunity this generation represents, in stark contrast to the potential consequences of rising unemployment, is potentially monumental. This chapter examines how the AfCFTA could be a fundamental part of Africa's strategy to address trade disputes and the growing trend of protectionism worldwide. It considers AfCFTA as a geopolitical insurance policy and a mechanism to fortify the competitiveness of African economies. In this chapter, we aim to provide policymakers, academics, and development practitioners with a usable platform for framing the AfCFTA as one of the continent's flagship economic initiatives of the twenty-first century, utilizing comparative case studies, policy examinations, and scenario-based approaches.

Table 1. Policy and Institutional Recommendations

	Pillar	Key Actions	Pillar
1	Institutional Accountability	Embed performance-based frameworks at AU, REC, and national levels. Enforce compliance mechanisms.	Institutional Accountability
2	National Integration	Embed AfCFTA in national development and industrial strategies.	National Integration
3	Regional Value Chains (RVCs)	Prioritize cross-border sectoral value chains (e.g., automotive, agro-processing, digital services).	Regional Value Chains (RVCs)
4	Trade Finance Access	Expand SME and women-led enterprise financing via dedicated funds and guarantee schemes.	Trade Finance Access
5	Infrastructure Modernization	Upgrade logistics hubs (e.g., Nairobi ICD), border posts, and strategic transport corridors.	Infrastructure Modernization
6	Unified Trade Voice	Institutionalize pan-African positions in WTO, EPA, AGOA renegotiations, and emerging trade forums.	Unified Trade Voice
7	Industrialization and Liberalization Balance	Strategically liberalize while protecting and nurturing domestic industries.	Industrialization and Liberalization Balance
8	Strategic Metrics	Develop and monitor sovereignty indices (e.g., intra-African trade share, diversification metrics) to assess the impact of regional integration on African countries.	Strategic Metrics

Source: Own Author

Figure 1. ACFTA Roadmap for strategic Transformation (2025-2045)

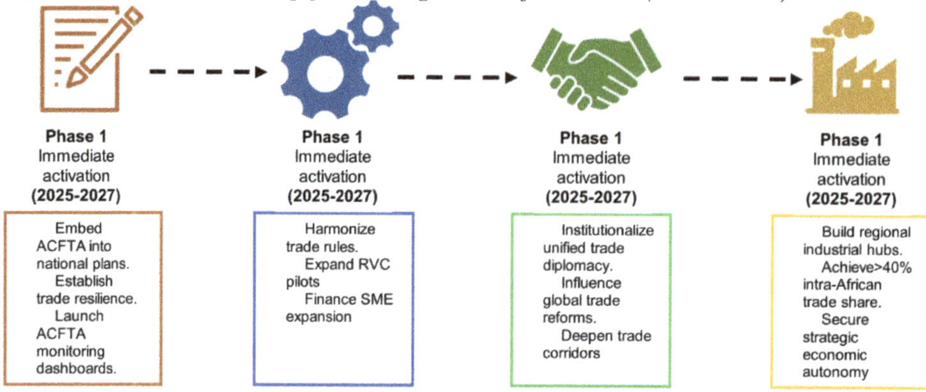

Source: Own Author

The AfCFTA presents an unprecedented opportunity for Africa; however, surviving is not enough. Africa must move away from merely responding and become a responsible participant in global commerce, developing a strong and independent economy through robust institutions. The AfCFTA will also provide Africa with a buffer against exogenous instability and enhance its voice in global trade governance. We will have to wait and be certain over the coming decade, whether Africa is still sitting on the sidelines or moving to the center of the new global trade order that is evolving. The strategy exists; now it will proceed with a degree of assertiveness and coordination.

We are witnessing a new chapter in global trade, marked by a rising tide of nationalism, strong protectionist responses, and disruptions in the global supply chain. Notably, the rise of nationalism that started with Donald Trump's re-election victory and 'America First' economic plans has increased the strain on the still fragile global trading system. These are the early contours of a new wave of trade skirmishes stemming from the erosion of global trade norms, driven by rising unilateral tariff actions and a stronger motivation for sanctioning.

Africa now faces two broad areas of concern: the emergence of a clash of great powers, and the disruption of globalization processes that create a new trading architecture and dependence on foreign states, which also factor disruption into their operational strategies. Africa has launched its most ambitious initiative to achieve greater economic self-sufficiency through the AfCFTA, with official rural integration processes being developed in all regions of Africa in 2021.

AfCFTA will be Africa's first most ambitious attempt to increase economic independence through regional integration. In other words, it presents a huge economic and geopolitical benefit by uniting 55 countries into a unified market. In this moment where protectionist trends are coalescing, it may not only provide a platform for the future but also an important syncretic point of resistance. This policy instrument will hopefully provide Africa with some insulation from any nationalism that will eventually threaten to disrupt international labour markets and increase Africa's bargaining power in international trade negotiations.

Africa's exporting regime will be resting heavily on foreign and associated markets, as the overwhelming majority of Africa's trade (greater than 60% of trade) will mainly continue to remain focused on non-African countries through external regimes.

What this means is that Africa's evolving uncertainty and unpredictability of global trade patterns present a significant and existential risk to the continent's developmental path. While Africa may have previously been ambivalent about intra-Africa trade, it can start to exploit itself as a key part of global supply chains. Figure 1 depicts Africa's reliance on its external partners both prior to (the rationale for) the AfCFTA.

Multilateralism showed us what happens when global protectionism becomes the norm in responding to the policies of the Trump administration. The U.S. tariffs on many of its emerging economies' major exports resulted in a change in the workings of some traded goods. The consequences for Africa were indirect, while steel, textiles, and agriculture appear to have had similar effects, primarily impacting China, Mexico, and the European Union (EU) countries. Figure Two depicts the range of the tariff's consequences, showing an increase. We combine the data and suggest that Africa may still be exposed to external volatilities and collectively, to move away from trade as the principal means of engagement with our countries.

The AfCFTA will allow Africa to move from an observer of global commerce to a strategic partner and to deepen our national markets. At the same time, the AfCFTA's intention is to lower tariffs on goods with a related intention of enhancing the regional value chain, ensuring closer relationships on regulatory requirements for trade management, alongside ensuring reciprocal trade relationships in international relations. Africa can develop an adaptable posture, which will demonstrate commitment to change, and it would perhaps have contributed to Africa's economic direction in a period of dislocation.

Figure 2. Tariff Escalation Intensity: Pre–Nov 2024 vs Post–Apr 2025

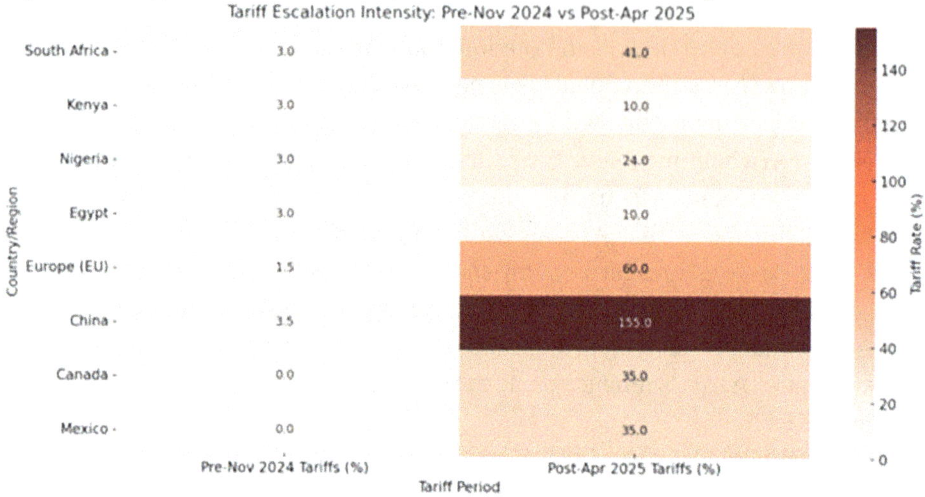

The heatmap shows that the United States had imposed tariffs on key trading partners as part of a trade policy that arose from President Trump's administration on behalf of the U.S. Government that saw a significant rise at a point in April 2025 that extended far beyond normal trading patterns. The European Union and China are also in the orange and red escalation zones, which are 155% and 60% beyond the current tariff state. For Africa, we expected price rises in South Africa at 41%, Nigeria at 24%, with both of the above being critically vulnerable, which would restrict access to AGOA benefits through trade for the two economies.

The escalation is unprecedented in deconstructing the globe's trading system and may require increases in tariffs as a financial tool. The escalations provide additional evidence of the extent to which many African economies are dependent on foreign markets that are clearly project-dependent. Sustained protectionist policy will present broader adverse implications for the economy and potentially create a disjointed economy.

The heatmap also highlights the significance of the African Continental Free Trade Area (AfCFTA) as a regulatory agency in this context. The new treaty agreement presents an unprecedented opportunity for Africa to establish a region capable of collectively developing resilient and autonomous trade systems. It constructs the trade relationship between the continent's states and parallels. These changes may be serious as Africa has possibly used the AfCFTA as a rule of protection for the continent, and free trade is very difficult to fulfill. The potential to establish global trade rules for other regions of the world presents an opportunity for Africa to create. The tariffication of South Africa to 41% and Nigeria to 24% in 2025 will leave these economies very exposed. The tariffs also limit their capacity to capitalise and benefit from the special access in AGOA. The emergence and mitigation of tariff escalations are of significant importance, demonstrating a downward trend in global trading systems, as well as an increasing reliance on tariffs as financial regulatory tools. The cases above illustrate just how much African economies rely on foreign markets; however, real economic responses will not normally occur if protectionism continues to escalate.

Figure 2 shows a heatmap in the value of AfCFTA for Africa in terms of controlling or reducing that volatility. The AfCFTA is a unique type of agreement, representing a rare opportunity for Africans to develop a more resilient and independent trade system across Africa. This development repositions the AfCFTA as a mechanism for protecting the continent of Africa and provides a potential pathway towards economic growth on the continental scale.

The AfCFTA also presents an opportunity for Africans to shape the rules of global commerce, and its Strategic Pillars of Resilience provide the framework. The AfCFTA is not only about a menu of tariff cuts; it represents a framework of protocols and tools to build greater regional economic resilience for Africa. The framework includes: (1) Trade in Goods and Services, (2) Competition Policy, (3) Investment, (4) Intellectual Property Rights, and (5) Digital Trade. Collectively, these five pillars provide a continental system of trade that not only facilitates integration but also protects the continent from external shocks. If these pillars are implemented, they will lead to increased industrialization, job creation, and economic diversification for all African countries.

2. REPOSITIONING AFRICA FROM A TRADE TAKER TO A TRADE MAKER

For too long, Africa has been perceived as a "rules-taker" in the global economy, which did not control the rules of trade within its jurisdictions but rather imposed them upon Africa from the outside by entities that dominated the continent. The African Continental Free Trade Area (AfCFTA) ought to assist Africa in becoming a trade maker where it can structure rules at the global level in areas of most importance to Africa: digital trade (including fair trade), environmental sustainability, and inclusive economic growth using a unified market approach with collective bargaining power. The growth and development narrative of Africa needs to expand from district and trade data; Africa must define its strategic intent towards transformative global economic engagement. African countries need to shift from being trade takers to trade makers, and the AfCFTA can facilitate this transition.

AfCFTA helps Africa to start its journey to becoming a trade maker and has power beyond just trade making.

The AfCFTA is crucial for Africa, particularly as the next significant step in Africa's ongoing transformation from colonial systems. Given the actual geopolitical tensions (trade wars and protectionism) and ongoing global economic crisis, the AfCFTA affords African leaders a distinctive leverage opportunity to provide protection from the degree of global political instability, and to put themselves at pare when proceeding through negotiation fields and regain the protection and independence of nations while considering Africa's global trade orientation of the future. The chapter explores how to effectively appreciate the AfCFTA in order to implement change, thereby enhancing the well-being of multiple citizens in Africa. Clear pathways are provided for politicians, institutions, and development actors to navigate uncertain economic shifts and realities, as well as the new direction towards globalization.

2.1 Research Problem

Africa is in danger of losing its position in global value chains and international trade governance. This will limit its ability to protect its interests and have a say in the rising protectionism, increasing economic nationalism (i.e., U.S., China, EU) and greater trade disputes; these challenges will be "saving challenges" for Africa, as it looks to the international system to assist in overcoming its crises - reliance on foreign markets, weak supply chains and inability to construct new trade rules. The AfCFTA was conceived as an effort to increase trade among African countries and foster regional cohesion and can also be viewed as a strategic economic and geopolitical instrument.

This research tries to offer the AfCFTA an alternate configuration and mobilizing delivery (operationalized) that aspires to go beyond improving trade in the narrow sense. Consideration of how the AfCFTA might reduce Africa's dependence on development assistance (although potentially reliant on partners), as well as leverage developing country partners' prospective negotiating capacity. The chapter primarily focuses on three aspects of how the AfCFTA may impact Africa's negotiation of trade agreements: a shift towards greater independence from historical partners, and, lastly, a focus on strengthening Africa's autonomous economies to sustain external shocks and pressures. The chapter examines the activities of the AfCFTA, identifying the potential changes required to strategic rules, institutions, and infrastructures to establish a strong foundation for the AfCFTA, thereby providing economic muscle in the iterative interdependence across Africa. The chapter also synthesizes some of the implications of AfCFTA for Africa's future positioning in global trade within a potentially multipolar economy, which entails trade competitiveness, as well as a source of financial foreign direct investment, and a role as a player in the global economy.

2.2 Research Objectives

The study will have three interconnected goals:

a) To assess AfCFTA's potential as a strategic buffer against global trade wars and protectionism.
b) To assess the possibility of enhancing Africa's economic sovereignty and changing the competitive global trade landscape.
c) To formulate actionable policy recommendations for governments, RECs, and development partners to incorporate resilience and strategic autonomy into AfCFTA's implementation.

2.3 Justification of the Study

Currently, the international trading environment is evolving, with an increase in unilateral regional economic policy, erosion of multilateral free trade agreements, and proliferation of protectionist trade policies. All of which can be seen as evolutionary forces, challenging the current instability of the international trading environment created by leadership and governance, as well as new (digital) protectionism and trade policy decisions associated with climate change. Unique evolution or new worlds for civil society organizations working with Africa, as others who engage in trade might look at Africa as a trading partner characterized by systemic value chains and regulatory anchor points.

The AfCFTA should be viewed as more than just a trade facilitation agreement – as this paper has demonstrated, the AfCFTA makes sense through this lens. Therefore, from a continental perspective, it is to be a defense-defined geoeconomic resort in a world that is increasingly becoming a world of weaponized trade. Four interdependent realities characterise this new paradigm.

Firstly, Africa's exposure to economic fragility is no longer a matter of abstraction.

The continent is subject to commodity cycles, shifts in consumer preferences, unilateral sanctions, and an uneven digital divide. Africa's economic exposure to the U.S.-China tariff war and the variety of disruptions in the supply chain exacerbated by COVID-19 are just a few examples of crises that have occurred globally, demonstrating the ease with which parts of Africa can be overlooked. This was a crisis; the AfCFTA, being a relatively young endeavor, is a once-in-a-generation opportunity to engage in safeguards policy that aligns with its central objectives: regional value chains, digital standards, and sovereign industrial policies, among others.

Second, the world is pursuing multiple poles as economic groupings systems and regionalism could be the vehicle to achieve these economies' ability to protect themselves. We already have arrangements, including the RCEP (Regional Comprehensive Economic Partnership), USMCA (United States-Mexico-Canada Agreement), and the EU (European Union). Contractors are currently working with these economic relationships for their respective countries, and strengthening borders appears to be a primary part of their overall plans. Africa faces challenges of being a geopolitical "swing state" in these relationships. The AfCFTA could play a role as a court to develop a comprehensive and independent African bloc that can define its value and not just sit passively on the outside, looking in, while others bring in strategic partners to negotiate from a better position.

Third, the AfCFTA position is unique. AfCFTA organizations are new and emergent, in contrast to the global trade deals, which have led to fairly moribund organizations due to institutional inertia. This gives Africa the opportunity to revitalize its development model, potentially achieving long-term strategic independence from the pressure of the Global North. This chapter will use the emergent AfCFTA to develop the evolving AfCFTA's policy architecture for including sovereignty, digital governance, and tracking more green/multi-faceted trade.

Finally, the force of the African population and consumer market in the emergent and much-needed area of supply and demand for 21st-century development. The AfCFTA and integrated industrial and trade policy might allow Africa to become more than a consensus breaker and participant follower of international rules, development, and become a key player in emerging areas of governance such as: AI Governance, green supply chains and possibly more broadly, data sovereignty, and digital taxes, and I think, the AfCFTA could represent, with the evolving economic ties for Africa, the most important special case for Africa's talking space of issues becoming related to these new areas of the global trade.

This chapter proposes the utilization of AfCFTA as a protective and enhancing platform for Africa; it is imperative that Africa is able to reclaim its strategic global contribution as well as navigate the negative economic shocks that all continents are going to feel. AfCFTA provides possibilities beyond the notion of classical liberalization and, through a political economy of sovereignty, new regionalism, and strategic trade theory, allows for the organization/creation of a geostrategic ecoscape. This chapter indicates how strategic foresight, intention, and probative actions are AfCFTA's best attributes. It serves as a collision of ideas that rethinks its own definition and provides actual mechanisms and trajectories for the following actors to collaboratively pursue: nations, governments, regional economic communities, financial institutions, and small business conglomerate platforms. The new discourse in operationalising the AfCFTA with concepts of sovereignty, resiliency, and future-focused industrial development is groundbreaking. In a world of geopolitically motivated markets and weaponized supply chains, Africa cannot afford to wait to recover. With AfCFTA, we have established a strategic opportunity for Africa - it can engage with a new global trade paradigm, through a rebirth of regionalism, affirming its domestic agenda in the process. However, it is critical that Africa is not merely responding to its existing reality but unambiguously announcing its capacity to define and determine the terms of its global engagement, focused and aligned towards bold coherence.

3. LITERATURE REVIEW

The African Continental Free Trade Area (AfCFTA) is one of the most ambitious regional integration efforts in the Global South. Much of the research has primarily focused on it from an economic perspective. It highlights how AfCFTA could boost intra-African trade and lower tariff barriers. However, this focus overlooks its broader strategic importance. The United Nations Economic Commission for Africa (UNECA) states that AfCFTA could increase intra-African trade by up to 52% just by removing tariffs (UNECA, 2023). Insights from the United Nations Conference on Trade and Development (UNCTAD) suggest that the AfCFTA could facilitate structural change by promoting export diversity and regional industrial growth (UNCTAD, 2022). The African Export-Import Bank (Afreximbank) discusses how the AfCFTA facilitates the harmonization of trade policies and enhances business competitiveness. It primarily focuses on establishing regional value chains and supporting small and medium-sized enterprises (SMEs) (Afreximbank, 2023). Many people now view AfCFTA as a means to make Africa less vulnerable to problems associated with global trade and other economic shocks.

3.1 Neutral Perspectives on AfCFTA's Role

While neutral opinions on the African Continental Free Trade Area (AfCFTA) generally accept the perceptions for positive change, they cautioned that achieving this requires appropriate expectations, incremental actions, and structural readiness–as mentioned again by the World Bank in its 2020 report, The African Continental Free Trade Area: Economic and Distributional Implications for Eastern and Southern Africa. According to the World Bank, AfCFTA could boost incomes by 7% and lift 30 million people out of extreme poverty by 2035, if supported by adequate trade facilitation, infrastructure investment, and a reasonable order of reforms. Similarly, in its 2023 report, entitled "Trade Integration in Africa: Unleashing the Continent's Potential in a Changing World," the International Monetary Fund reported that the benefits of the AfCFTA might not be evenly distributed unless the underlying institutional framework and capacity-building efforts are improved.

The African Development Bank's African Economic Outlook 2024 signals a prudent and temperate approach, cautioning against overambition. It argues that all African countries should focus their efforts on sectors offering economic opportunities and competitive advantages, such as agro-processing, pharmaceuticals, and logistics. (African Development Bank, 2024). Both the African Centre for Economic Transformation (ACET) and the Trade and Development Bank (TDB) emphasize that AfCFTA implementation could be piloted by starting in sub-regions that are already performing well under previous trade arrangements, like SADC, the East African Community (EAC), and Regional Economic Communities (RECs), so that they could develop contextualized models and gather practical lessons (ACET and TDB positions based on regional pilot models). Finally, as documented in the 2023 United Nations Economic Commission for Africa (UNECA) briefs and retrospectively in "Making the AfCFTA Work" (2021) and other documents, a progressive, context-sensitive integration model, supported by strong public-private partnership, industrial policy, and a phased approach, is preferable and more realistic than a single-stroke, pan-African approach, cross-national integration model. Moreover, UNECA noted that omniscient, pan-African integration or policy could undermine future economic stability and viability. In summary, based on neutral assessments of AfCFTA, all authors agree that the economic and geopolitical advantages of AfCFTA are possible if states implement disciplined governance that allows for time, patience, capacity building, and resourcing for infrastructure improvement.

3.2 Critical Arguments of AfCFTA's Strategic Positioning

While the AfCFTA is touted as a significant step towards economic integration across Africa, skeptics warn that its current weaknesses may hinder it from achieving this promise. Draper and Dadush (2021) assert that "AfCFTA has important institutional weaknesses, lax enforcement mechanisms and has unequal implementation capacities that could reduce it to an aspirational agreement rather than a transformative one". Their warning reveals broader fears that AfCFTA may also experience the same fate as many integration efforts in Africa, hindered by weak legal harmonization and enforcement, notably the various stalled efforts related to the COMESA Common Investment Area, or ECOWAS' delay in implementing a single currency.

The Economic Policy Research Centre (EPRC) in Uganda has voiced concerns about trade diversion and uneven development resulting from the AfCFTA, warning that unless weaker countries are protected through an "incremental upgrade of their industry," the AfCFTA could worsen existing inequalities towards them

(EPRC, 2023). The Friedrich Ebert-Stiftung (2022) also recognized a major blind spot within the design of AfCFTA, the lack of fish enforceable commitments on labour rights or social protection, which may exacerbate elite/oligarch capture, ultimately contributing to the exclusion of informal and/or vulnerable segments of the population (Mendez-Parra, 2022).

African participation in regional entities such as ECCAS, SADC, and IGAD indicates that "regionalism" often occurs under conditions of overlapping political memberships, a lack of political confidence, and weak implementation, suggesting that many formal arrangements do not deliver concrete changes to the regional economic landscape. Political inertia and membership interests could limit the effectiveness of AfCFTA, unless there are strong accountability measures in place. Additionally, suppose AfCFTA is implemented without regard for fairness and the rule of law, and political populations suffer increasing levels of economic inequality and instability. In that case, the entire enterprise will be at risk. To spur inclusive economic growth, AfCFTA is required to do more than establish tariffs and procedures. It must make enforceable commitments to strict rules, protections for vulnerable economies, and equity and fairness to unite the continent.

3.3 Arguments in Favour of AfCFTA's Strategic Role

An emerging line of strategic literature views the AfCFTA not just as a trade facilitation agreement but also as a strategic policy mechanism to counter trade wars and other means of building resilience, thereby asserting Africa's geopolitical agency. This school argues that the AfCFTA presents Africa with an opportunity to shift from being passive global trade marginal players to active players who can engage with the rest of the world as rule-shaping players, rather than simply rule-takers. This shift in behavior is necessary, especially as we witness the current collapse of multilateralism and the rise of protectionism from developed economies. Petri and Plummer (2020) examined the issue through the lens of Strategic Trade Theory, arguing that mega-regional trade agreements, such as the RCEP and USMCA, provide their members with insulation against global shocks. In their working paper, they highlighted that regional integration helped East Asia compensate for the losses experienced in the U.S.-China trade war. They suggested a similar path for Africa under the AfCFTA (Mattoo et al., 2020). UNECA (2023) supports this perspective, stating that the AfCFTA is "at once an economic, diplomatic and political project" to align the national development agendas of partner states with continental priorities. This perspective was further reinforced at the AfCFTA Business Forum in 2023, when the President of Rwanda, Paul Kagame, said that "AfCFTA presents Africa the opportunity to think and act strategically to boost our resilience to future shocks."

In the wake of recent developments, geoeconomics has once again proven to be the rationale for the AfCFTA. The rise in tariffs imposed by the U.S., coupled with the EU's Carbon Border Adjustment Mechanism, and disputes over digital taxation, expose African countries to fragmented regulations and supply chain vulnerability. Policy mechanisms of the AfCFTA are thus instrumental in counteracting such external forces operating at the regional bloc level, especially as international rules are increasingly weaponized. Afreximbank's African Trade Report 2023 offers compelling evidence on the importance of AfCFTA in supporting Regional Value Chains (RVCs). The consolidation of major sectors, including pharmaceuticals, textiles, and digital services, is now underway in Africa. This includes trading in intermediate goods and reducing reliance on imports from outside the continent (Afreximbank, 2023). For example, the use of digital service platforms in East Africa, particularly in Rwanda, Kenya, and Uganda, is transforming the region into an emerging hub.

The 2025 statement by the AfDB highlights the AfCFTA as the first opportunity to develop integrated infrastructure and enhance trade corridors. These corridors are currently limited by access to regional markets and industrial growth. The African Development Bank (2023) links AfCFTA with clean energy markets. Through the utilization of power pools and investments in environmentally sustainable infrastructure, this agreement has the potential to facilitate Africa's transition to low-carbon energy systems and enhance energy accessibility. An additional benefit is observed at the community level, where the International Trade Centre (ITC, 2025) indicates that the digital protocols of the African Continental Free Trade Area (AfCFTA) could diminish informal trade transaction costs by as much as 40%, yielding the most significant benefits for border communities, women, and enterprises led by youth. Such findings dilute the concentration of views that see AfCFTA as purely a macroeconomic tool championed from above into, largely, a platform for inclusive growth. From an industrial policy perspective, UNIDO (2023) describes the AfCFTA as a "continental industrialization blueprint" that can increase the manufacturing sector's GDP share from 11% to 20% by 2035. The crux lies in the implementation of strategic infrastructure initiatives such as the African Integrated High-Speed Rail Network and agro-processing clusters across these lines through the AfCFTA investment protocol.

ICTSD (2022) states that the AfCFTA gives Africa greater influence in global trade discussions, including the reform of WTO rules, subsidy programs, digital taxes, and carbon pricing. As international trade standards evolve, collaborating becomes more than just an option; it becomes essential. The World Bank estimates that fully implementing AfCFTA could generate an additional $450 billion for the continent, lift 30 million people out of severe poverty, and increase salaries for women and unskilled workers by 10% to 15%. AfCFTA is not just a business project; it is also a crucial initiative to support disadvantaged African people.

Real-world manifestations have been promising as well. In Ghana, the Integrated Customs Management System (ICUMS), which is designed to promote trade under the AfCFTA, has, according to Ghana Web, "facilitated trade with ease." The ICUMS system and technology are being rolled out in neighboring countries in collaboration with the Korea-based Universal Pass system. This may mean that it can serve as a model for West Africa (GhanaWeb, 2024). It is important to note, however, that these improvements are not inevitable. Experts (African Union's ACTA) have argued that the strategic importance of the AfCFTA will depend on reliable enforcement, investment in infrastructure, convergence in regulations, and institutional capacity. Without these prerequisites, the possibility of regionalism could be undermined by inequitable implementation, elite capture, and the disillusionment of key partners.

For instance, Rwanda has made great advances by modernising customs systems and enhancing trade logistics at the Gatuna-Katuna border with Uganda, but there are many border posts across the continent that are still struggling with the status quo. The Busia OSBP, which provides an important link between Kenya and Uganda, is significantly advanced, but it has encountered issues with delayed interoperability; at times, national agencies did not seamlessly link their systems. The Lagos-Abidjan corridor, which is an important link for trade in West Africa as well, is also facing challenges around poor road infrastructure and more trips through bureaucracy, which add time to cross-border trade. This clearly demonstrates the need to integrate cross-border infrastructure investments and work collaboratively.

It is very important to have consistent regulations. In East Africa, having some level of consensus around the standards for agricultural exports, for instance, has reduced the level of goods being rejected at the border. The lack of converged regulations for digital trade and e-commerce across SADC, on the other hand, has had serious implications for tech startups in the region. Trade challenges continue without convergence, and small and medium-sized enterprises cannot fully engage in AfCFTA.

Another important consideration is institutional capacity. For example, Ghana and Mauritius have established special units to carry out the AfCFTA, helping to ensure that changes in policy are embedded in national development plans. Many member states do not have the financial or technical capacity to meet their AfCFTA obligations, raising questions about whether the agreement will deepen the divide between reformers and laggards.

Despite the indications from this body of strategic literature about AfCFTA being best-placed as Africa's deflector shield against global volatility, as well as the vehicle for structural transformation, it is noted that the COVID-19 pandemic exposed Africa's fragility in the face of external supply chain shocks, but has fast-tracked digital payments, keener interest in intra-African air freight solutions and local production of pharmaceutical products, all focusing on the operationalization of AfCFTA. Moreover, AfCFTA has implications such as both a political agreement and an economic engine. It is credible to conclude that AfCFTA presents the most credible opportunity for Africa by rewriting its role in the global trading system, moving from fragmented trading dependencies to a recognized and assertive continental actor in global trade systems.

4. CONCEPTUAL FRAMEWORK

This chapter is grounded in an interdisciplinary conceptual framework that combines Strategic Trade Theory, New Regionalism Theory, and emerging ideas about economic sovereignty and Geoeconomics. Together, these frameworks offer a new perspective on viewing the African Continental Free Trade Area (AfCFTA) not merely as a trade agreement, but as a strategically crafted geopolitical move. As global trade becomes increasingly fragmented, tariff disputes escalate, and multilateralism wanes, this approach enables us to view the AfCFTA as a means for Africa to enhance long-term economic stability, political influence, and independence.

4.1 Strategic Trade Theory

Classical and neoclassical economic theories typically support free trade because they assume that markets are perfectly competitive. Strategic Trade Theory (STT) represents a significant departure from these theories. Paul Krugman and James Brander are the economists who developed STT. The theory suggests that when market problems arise, such as economies of scale, barriers to entry, or global factors like tariffs and subsidies, the government must intervene to assist individuals. These actions include trade deals that facilitate collaboration among businesses (Krugman, 1985), short-term protections for emerging industries, or programs that promote the growth of exports. By applying Strategic Trade Theory, this study demonstrates that the African Continental Free Trade Area (AfCFTA) constitutes a complete trade policy, designed to change the continent's role in the global economy. The AfCFTA promotes economic development across the continent by establishing a market of over 1.3 billion people. This process is superior to reacting to the chaotic competition driven by the never-ending swings in global and national markets. It supports the development of regional value chains in industries such as pharmaceuticals, automotive components, and digital services, in which the continent has a comparative advantage. The AfCFTA represents a strategic move counteracting the global protectionist tide and, less formally, supposing that future supply chain logistics or capacity concerning our dependence upon the outcome of the U.S.-China trade wars or the European Union's Carbon Border Adjustment Mechanism. Proponents of the AfCFTA hope to inoculate African economies against external trade shocks and enhance the capabilities of developed African businesses to build their presence in global value chains.

4.2 New Regionalism Theory

New Regionalism Theory (NRT) reframes regional integration as a dynamic, multi-actor process shaped by global turbulence and post-Cold War economic restructuring. Unlike "old regionalism," which was primarily state-driven and security-oriented, new regionalism views integration as a response to global disorder, driven by a mix of public institutions, private sector players, development partners, and civil society. It acknowledges overlapping memberships, political heterogeneity, and flexibility as defining characteristics of modern regionalism (Söderbaum & Shaw, 2003). Applied to AfCFTA, the New Regionalism Theory enables us to interpret the agreement as a political-economic response to the failures of the multilateral system, particularly the stagnation at the WTO, the impact of Brexit on EU-Africa trade, and the rise of unilateral tariff regimes in the Global North. The AfCFTA's architecture reflects a new regionalism in its inclusion of multiple protocols, including investment, digital trade, competition policy, and intellectual property, beyond mere tariff elimination. Its operationalization is understood within an ecology of actors, comprising the African Union Commission, regional economic communities, national customs authorities, small-to-medium enterprise (SME) coalitions, and trade finance organizations, such as the African Export-Import Bank (Afreximbank). NRT also illustrates the space of AfCFTA as a strategic hedge, affording African countries the potential for a lease or partial decoupling from external partners, while reorienting trade preferences to a regional context. As partner countries, particularly the U.S. and China, are weaponizing trade through tariffs and technology bans, the AfCFTA represents a collective approach to protecting the development and policy space available for African countries to collaborate, while simultaneously increasing regional integration. The multilayered governance and phased and staggered implementation approach is seemingly similar to those employed by other trade blocs, such as RCEP and MERCOSUR, which have successfully leveraged regional consolidation as buffers against global volatility.

4.3 Economic Sovereignty and Geoeconomics

The last part of this framework is based on the concepts of economic sovereignty and geoeconomics. Economic sovereignty is the ability of a state or region to determine its own trade, industry, and fiscal policies independently, free from excessive external influence. Geoeconomics, as defined by UNCTAD and the WEF, is the application of economic tools, including trade access and sanctions, data sovereignty, and infrastructure finance, as a means of geopolitical power. In the era of multipolarity, where supply chains are reshaped around trade with national interests and decoupled strategic digital economies, economic sovereignty is essential for development (UNCTAD, 2022; Munyati, 2024).

From this perspective, the AfCFTA is viewed as Africa's leading institutional mechanism for regaining sovereignty over its trade framework. By creating a common set of rules regarding digital trade, e-commerce, data localization, and other areas, Africa can open up its ability to be more than a passive recipient of rules from Washington, Brussels, or Beijing. In addition, AfCFTA's investment and competition protocols provide a legal basis for Africa to protect strategic sectors of its economy, such as pharmaceuticals, food security, and clean energy, from foreign predation and regulatory asymmetries.

Geoeconomically, the AfCFTA provides Africa with the opportunity to secure multilateral collectives on WTO reform, AGOA, and green trade finance negotiations. For a continent to say it will create a stronger collective is remarkable enough; increasingly, however, as the global value chains fortify towards regionalism, and climate sensitive trading regimes, the AfCFTA enables Africa to create itself as a rule-making entity than a rule-taking state, especially in contextual areas of AI governing, green technology and digital taxation.

Figure 3. Conceptual Framework of AfCFTA as Africa's Strategic Shield

Source: Own Author

The conceptual framework places the African Continental Free Trade Area (AfCFTA) as a key mechanism to promote and protect the interests of African economies in a fragmented global trade system. The conceptual framework is built on three key pillars: Strategic Trade Theory, New Regionalism Theory, Economic Sovereignty, and Geoeconomics. These viewpoints help elevate the AfCFTA from a trade liberalization policy to a regional force for industrial development and an influence on the global stage. Strategic Trade Theory considers the AfCFTA as a strategic policy tool to change Africa's position in the global market. The AfCFTA enables governments to protect nascent industries, grow domestic markets, and establish regional value chains to lead in key areas so that they can buffer the external shocks of tariff wars and protectionism.

The New Regionalism Theory recognizes AfCFTA's flexible, multi-actor nature, comprising governments, RECs, and private actors, in the face of global trading uncertainties. It reflects an African region's response to failed multilateralism and increased fragmentation. Economic Sovereignty and Geoeconomics responses acknowledge AfCFTA's role in sustaining an Africa-wide trade policy and autonomy from reliance on external economic actors. It allows for the harmonization of digital rules, coordination of industries, and collective negotiations on emerging issues, such as Artificial Intelligence (AI), data governance, and climate trade responses. As a result, the AfCFTA, as the institutional anchor, allows for the two identified theories to be recast into four specific outcomes: resilience to trade shocks; global value chain development; a unified voice in the global trade policy sphere; and reaffirmation of economic sovereignty. Ultimately, the framework will enhance the AfCFTA as a transformational tool for Africa to move from being a rule-taker to a rule-shaper in the global trade regime.

The African Continental Free Trade Area (AfCFTA) is not merely another trade agreement; it is a transformative initiative. As discussed throughout this chapter, it is emerging as the most powerful tool for Africa in an increasingly fragmented, uncertain, and competitive global trading environment. While many debates have highlighted the prospective potential for promoting intra-African trade and industrial development within the AfCFTA agreement, a survey of the literature reveals a more compelling viewpoint for AfCFTA as a geopolitical tool for sovereignty, resilience, and structural transformation. The literature, particularly policy documents, reviewed in this paper indicates that there is a significant shift in the way AfCFTA should be understood; and that 'AfCFTA' cannot be assessed solely in terms of economic growth forecasts and various tariff models. Rather, AfCFTA must be placed in a global context characterized by trade conflicts, border carbon taxes based on climate change considerations, data sovereignty-related issues, and declining multilateral governance of trade.

Within these features, AfCFTA provided Africa not only with an opportunity to coordinate its regional markets but also to present a consolidated front in global trade negotiations. UNECA, the World Bank, and key African institutions explicitly state that AfCFTA has the potential to lift millions out of poverty, improve income and employment levels, and establish continental value chains that reduce dependence on foreign markets.

Cautiously optimistic views, however, raise caution that the positive outcomes are not implicitly guaranteed through AfCFTA. Achievement of the agreement is dependent on finding an appropriate balance between ambition and a high degree of realism. There are gaps in institutional capacity, infrastructure capacity issues, and a lack of political will that threaten to halt progress if they are not addressed thoughtfully and strategically in coordination with partner states. As explained above, phased implementation, regional testing, and targeted capacity building must be at the forefront of how we roll out the AfCFTA.

It is reasonable to expect that the AfCFTA will become little more than another failed integration effort in Africa unless a fair and equitable system of enforcement can be relied on, and unless there is political will to share the outcomes. Critics point out clear and sometimes less clear fundamental defects in AfCFTA, including poor legal enforceability, inadequate labor protection, and the potential to exacerbate existing inequalities. These critiques are measured, serious, and require intentional policy planning to be considered appropriately. However, the process of strategic research represents a growing body of empirical evidence that these issues are not design defects but rather design challenges that can be met with adequate commitment to managing collaborative processes, engagement, and innovation.

What distinguishes the AfCFTA in this new era is its recognition of Africa's larger geopolitical agenda. As trade systems shift to become more multipolar and contested, Africa cannot afford to be a passive player in the new global economy; it must take an active role in shaping the rules. AfCFTA provides an institutional mechanism on which Africa can build. Its protocols on digital trade, investment, intellectual property, and competition policy provide the framework for Africa to shape its economic future. Moreover, to add even more credence to what has been said, concrete examples such as Ghana's ICUMS and the digital trade corridors in East Africa show work is already underway. The conceptual framework employed in this chapter, underpinned by Strategic Trade Theory, New Regionalism Theory, and the geoeconomics of sovereignty, confirms that AfCFTA should be viewed with both defensive and offensive motivation.

A defensive tool that provides security against shocks arising from outside sources and global policy pressure, and an offensive tool that extends Africa's productive value, institutional capacity, and bargaining power.

In summary, AfCFTA is not just a liberalization initiative; it is Africa's boldest move toward redefining its position in the global economy. When implemented with vision, patience, and determination, it can help the continent unify its fragmented markets, shield its economies from international trade conflicts, and develop a single voice in setting 21st-century trade policies. Essentially, it serves as Africa's strategic trade platform, rooted in sovereignty, driven by integration, and fueled by a shared development goal.

5. UNDERSTANDING AfCFTA IN A SHIFTING GLOBAL TRADE LANDSCAPE

The global trading system is undergoing a fundamental shift, marked by increased protectionism and a decline in the effectiveness of multilateral trade agreements. The United States, under the Trump administration, hastened these trends with the wholesale imposition of tariffs, including a 10% tariff on virtually all products, as well as targeted tariffs on its trading partners, China and the EU. The tariffs exacerbated global supply chains, raised production costs, and undermined the foundation for open trade that was lauded in the early years of the WTO. The WTO has identified protectionism as a signal of structural instability and warned (WTO,2025) that global trade growth might fall from 2.7% to as low as 0.2% by 2025, with uncertainty deriving from unresolved disputes and the stalled Appellate Body. The current wave of protectionism poses a severe challenge to African countries, many of which rely heavily on raw materials as a long-standing or incidental component of their trade with all international markets.

Significant uncertainty surrounds the reauthorization of the African Growth and Opportunity Act (AGOA) in the United States, the EU's green compliance standards, and the fragmentation of digital trade, causing severe ambiguities for African exporters. Within this context, the African Continental Free Trade Area (AfCFTA) represents the most significant opportunity for Africa to resist fragmentation resulting from these challenges and to create a more robust internal market with consequently more integrated and coordinated engagement with external trading blocs. AfCFTA can be considered a buffering mechanism against fragmentation and as an avenue of pursuing economic diplomacy and defending sovereignty.

a) Africa as Collateral: Mapping Exposure to Global Trade Shocks

Long-standing structural weaknesses make Africa more vulnerable to shocks in global trade. Most African countries rely heavily on exporting raw materials, have limited value-added chains, and are heavily dependent on a small number of outside trading partners. Africa experienced significant but indirect shocks during the U.S.-China trade war from 2018 to 2022. These shocks included price swings, rising freight costs, and supply shortages (Petri & Plummer, 2020). For instance, the U.S. could have imposed 30% tariffs on South Africa's citrus industry, which would have impacted about 35,000 jobs.

The projected U.S. tariffs on cocoa have hurt Côte d'Ivoire's economy and raised concerns that rural economies could collapse completely. Africa's dependence on China, where over 20% of all sub-Saharan exports go, and the EU only worsens these issues. The COVID-19 pandemic made it even clearer that Africa relies heavily on imports of essential medical and agricultural goods. For example, when trade partners closed their borders and halted exports, many African countries ran out of critical supplies. These crises highlight the importance of regions being self-sufficient and having a coordinated, comprehensive trade strategy. AfCFTA is an excellent example of this.

b) From Agreement to Architecture: Unpacking AfCFTA's Core Design

The AfCFTA began in 2018 with the goal of promoting industrial growth and increasing trade and economic integration. There is a Secretariat, a Council of Ministers, a Committee of Senior Trade Officials, and an Assembly made up of Heads of State that all support the AfCFTA (African Union, 2022). AfCFTA is not a fixed trade framework like the ones we have made in other places; it is in a good place to handle changes while it is being put into place.

The Agreement has a lot of rules, such as those about intellectual property, competition, investment, trade in goods and services, and trade in services. A protocol for digital trade and e-commerce is also being worked on right now. The framework's architecture is flexible so that it can include a range of modern features, such as continental standards for digital commerce, changes to rules of origin, and more environmentally friendly ways of industrialization. AfCFTA can keep changing into a trade platform that is just as useful in the 21st century as it is in line with Africa's plans because it is so flexible.

c) Stress-Tested by the World: AfCFTA as Africa's Resilience Engine

AfCFTA could do more than give people access to markets. It is a basic way to build resilience that can protect Africa from changes in the world. As global rules become more complex, including the EU's Carbon Border Adjustment Mechanism and strict data localization laws, the AfCFTA offers a way for countries to work together on a continental level.

The AfCFTA supports the growth of regional value chains in pharmaceuticals, textiles, agro-processing, and digital services. Afreximbank (2023) has noted that Africa relies more on intermediate goods from outside the continent due to the rise of African RVCs. Countries with established regional trade structures handled supply chain issues better during the COVID-19 pandemic. The AfCFTA can help Africa build this resilience by speeding up trade among member countries and simplifying business operations.

d) Strategic Repositioning: AfCFTA as Geoeconomic Leverage

While AfCFTA can act as a buffer, its main purpose is to help Africa reposition itself in global trade governance. The success of RCEP in protecting East Asia from decoupling risks, USMCA's support of North American supply control, and the EU's strategy to influence digital and climate standards highlight the power of regionalism (Petri & Plummer, 2020). AfCFTA can unite Africa as a strong group in WTO reforms, digital governance, and climate-related trade talks. The ICTSD points out that coordinated African involvement is essential for negotiating fair digital taxation and protecting data control (ICTSD, 2022). By improving internal integration, Africa can shift from being a passive player to actively shaping global trade rules.

e) Synthesis: Strategic Imperatives Going Forward

To get the most out of the African Continental Free Trade Area (AfCFTA) as a strategic tool, several priorities need to be addressed. For trade to flow smoothly across Africa, countries must work together to make sure that their customs and trade rules are the same. Also, to make it easier for people to connect and lower the cost of doing business, it is important to improve and update trade-related infrastructure, such as energy and transportation corridors. Once the digital trade and e-commerce protocol is finished, Africa will be able to compete well in the global digital economy. Setting up stronger national implementation committees will help each country work together better and enforce the rules.

In addition, member states need to make sure that their industrial, environmental, and digital policies are in line with each other in order to build a strong continental market. Achieving these goals requires strong commitment from institutions, proactive cooperation between the public and private sectors, and steady leadership at both the national and continental levels.

This chapter has shown that AfCFTA is more than a trade facilitative instrument, but a structural response to a world of uncertainty, fragmentation, and increasing economic nationalism. AfCFTA, a form of institutional flexibility in governance, will contribute to regional resilience in Africa and represents the best opportunity for the continent to redefine its position in global trade. As the world morphs into exclusive trade blocs, the evolution of intra-African collaboration under the AfCFTA scheme will determine not only the resumption of economic recovery in Africa but also shape the continent's agency and role in global governance meaningfully in the future. In the next chapter, I will examine the literature on AfCFTA, revealing the gaps within the existing bodies of scholarship, whilst outlining a conceptual framework vis-à-vis AfCFTA in the context of a theory of strategic trade, new regionalism, and economic sovereignty.

6. REPOSITIONING AfCFTA AS A DRIVER OF ECONOMIC SOVEREIGNTY AND GLOBAL COMPETITIVENESS

In the past, Africa has effectively been on the edges of global trading arrangements, primarily exporting raw commodities to developed countries and relying on devolution treaties, such as the African Growth and Opportunity Act (AGOA) and Economic Partnership Agreements (EPAs). These regimes provided access for African countries to new markets but also made their collective vulnerability apparent to global changes in public policy that were outside their control. Furthermore, all the manifestations of this vulnerability were emphasized with tariffs from the Trump administration, Britain's exit from the European Union, Europe's recent Carbon Border Adjustment Mechanism (CBAM), and the growing spread of digital protectionism (UNECA, 2024).

However, this is the time to determine and redefine Africa's economic identity in view of a world where bloc formations based on regional cooperation are currently taking shape in the form of RCEP, USMCA, and significant updates within the trade agreements of Europe. AfCFTA has enabled Africa to work as a unified player on the global scene and must be up for the task of defending its joint interests. The UN predicts that by 2050, Africa will have more than 2.5 billion people (UN-DESA, 2022); therefore, the potential for millions of consumers and workers would bring value to future trade agreements. Nigeria, Ethiopia, and Egypt are poised to play significant leadership roles as the industrial development hubs for many regions in Africa.

a) From Fragmentation to Unification: Sovereignty through Integration

The legislative and institutional architecture of the African Continental Free Trade Area (AfCFTA) has been purposefully built to respond to Africa's fragmented commercial landscape. Preceding its establishment, more than eight regional economic communities (RECs) shared overlapping areas of responsibility, inconsistent tariff schedules, and a fragmented institution (UNECA & AU, 2020). AfCFTA's clearest response is a unification of rules relating to the elimination of tariffs, trade facilitation, and rules of origin. AfCFTA also consists of rules that extend beyond trading goods and services (such as investment, intellectual property, digital trade, still under development, and competition policy). Notably, the Protocol on Investment promotes the protection of transfers of investment to Africa and a greater harmonization of national frameworks (Trade Law Centre, 2022).

Ethiopia's Industrial Parks Development Corporation (IPDC) demonstrates how a nation can commit itself to sovereign industrialization. The IPDC develops industrial parks close to borders and major trade routes to enhance market access under AfCFTA, and the AfCFTA provides more policy options for member countries. Examples include Ghana's local content requirements for its pharmaceuticals and Kenya's leather value chain strategy. Both are part of frameworks that are AfCFTA compliant, respect trade law, and assist with the development of emerging industries.

b) Building Regional Value Chains for Global Competitiveness

It is going to take a strong Regional Value Chain (RVC) development to advance Africa's industrial development. The Afreximbank African Trade Report 2023 indicates that the first steps of the AfCFTA have positively affected the trade of intermediate goods within the continent. Intermediate goods have increased by 14% in just the first steps of the AfCFTA working. The data suggests trade in intermediate goods, such as machinery and agricultural processing products, has yielded the most growth among all three categories of goods traded. The East African Community's current industrial approach exposes one of the most effective examples of RVCs.

The cross-border dairy Regional Value Chain (RVC) between Uganda and Kenya, where vertical integration was based on sanitary and phytosanitary (SPS) protocols, enhanced RVC competitiveness and reduced RVC product rejection in the regional market. With the support of ECOWAS, RVCs in West Africa have been able to attract increased investment (applying clusters and regionally simplified certification models), particularly in shea butter RVCs and Cassava RVCs. As stated earlier, physical infrastructure remains one of the main components in developing RVCs.By combining synchronized investments in digital customs platforms (like electronic cargo tracking), the Standard Gauge Railway, and one-stop border posts, the Northern Corridor (from Mombasa through Kampala to Kigali) has brought down transit delay times from 21 days to just 4–5 days and saved more than $1 million in customs costs in Uganda (TradeMark Africa, 2024). These investments are directly contributing to the AfCFTA in terms of serving its purpose of helping the efficient movement of goods within Africa and efficient logistics for intra-African trade. In terms of competitiveness, companies such as Zipline (Rwanda) and mPharma (Ghana) have expanded their regional operations from markets using AfCFTA's liberalization of services and common regulatory frameworks. These companies are developing African digital competitiveness and convincing many AfCFTA partners to shift from an aid-seeking mentality to an export-driven mentality based on innovative solutions.

c) Enhancing Africa's Voice in Multilateral Trade Forums

Building Africa's Presence in Multilateral Trade Negotiations. AfCFTA allows Africa to negotiate within international trade negotiations with a united voice. Previously, African countries were negotiating completely disconnected trade agreements individually, which resulted in cases of complicated and even at times contradictory commitments. AfCFTA allows African countries to rationalize their position in WTO negotiations, AGOA reviews, and exactly how to interpret any commitments made toward taxation on digital products.

As described by the World Trade Organization (2023), at the 2023 Public Forum, AfCFTA representatives called for simplification mechanisms for dispute-resolution for least-developed countries and for least developed and developing countries to be exempt from severe carbon-border tax conditions (World Trade Organization, 2023). This indicates that a united African voice can sway multilateral normative decision-making. Additionally, regional leaders act as facilitators for continental deliberations.

Kenya's involvement in the pilot negotiations of the Digital Economy Partnership Agreement (DEPA) provided learnings for AfCFTA's digital trade protocol, which would be impractical within individual arrangements. Nigeria's revised automotive industrial policy has attracted investments from Morocco and South Africa, forming a nascent continental auto supply chain. South Africa's presidency of BRICS has also enabled it to promote AfCFTA-aligned priorities in global investment flows and climate finance. Finally, pan-African trade diplomacy is gaining traction. The African Union Commission's Department of Economic Development, Trade, Industry and Mining is coordinating with the AfCFTA Secretariat to establish a trade diplomacy academy aimed at training negotiators across all member states.

The AfCFTA is transforming commerce in Africa and altering the continent's role in the global economy. AfCFTA facilitates Africa's capacity to operate within a multipolar framework by establishing interconnected industrial systems, aligned regulatory frameworks, and unified negotiation stances. Instances from East Africa's dairy sector, Ghana's digital health enterprises, and Kenya's leadership within the EAC illustrate that nation-state sovereignty and competitiveness need not be antagonistic; rather, they are mutually constitutive and can be concurrently advanced as components of the AfCFTA intraregional integration strategy.

This chapter shows us that economic sovereignty under AfCFTA is not only a hope but also a possibility. In the next chapter, we explore the literature and analytical frameworks that underline this change and emphasize the historical intellectual legacies and contemporary debates that underpin AfCFTA as a strategic opportunity for Africa.

7. POLICY AND INSTITUTIONAL PATHWAYS TO UNLOCK AfCFTA's STRATEGIC POTENTIAL

Achieving the full potential of AfCFTA as a geostrategic tool for Africa cannot be done without coordinated engagement across Africa's entire institutional ecosystem, defined here as the AU, RECs, UNECA, Afreximbank, and development partners. Clearly, aligning policies across member states should be largely the responsibility of the AU; however, the regional organizations, acting on behalf of discrete units of integration, are crucial in turning policy decisions into action on the ground. Entities like UNECA should focus on establishing data systems, diagnostics, and capacity development, while Afreximbank and like-minded development finance institutions (DFIs) should be concentrating on delivering trade guarantees and liquidity buffers that will facilitate transactions.

The social science frameworks underpinning this proposition represent components of Strategic Trade Theory, New Regionalism Theory, and Geoeconomics, and present AfCFTA as a continental layer of protection, an active instrument employed to buffer Africa from international trade disruptions whilst simultaneously strengthening policy independence.

Operationalizing this proposition requires that Africa operationalize a continental trade resilience framework that will include early warning systems associated with disruptions; an AfCFTA-specific contingency fund (possibly conducted by Afreximbank); and cross-border trade insurance schemes. Overall, the engagement of private sector actors, specifically SMEs, national chambers of commerce, and logistics operators, as a crosscutting issue, must be thoroughly integrated through Public-Private Partnerships (PPPs), along with national AfCFTA consultative forums to create avenues for bottom-up feedback.

a) Financing and Infrastructure for Implementation

AfCFTA's success depends on overcoming persistent infrastructure bottlenecks and mobilizing strategic financing. For instance, border harmonization and improved digital customs processes, such as issuing single clearance documents (called a joint customs clearance (JCC)), and upgrading the necessary transport corridors can jointly cut logistics costs and reduce border clearance times (e.g., Northern Corridor connects Mombasa Port to Uganda, Rwanda, and Eastern DRC).

The available evidence shows that investing in multimodal corridor improvements can deliver efficiency benefits. It is essential to focus investments on inland container depots (like the Nairobi ICD), digital trade systems to facilitate faster trade, and regional transport networks. Potential financing vehicles include public-private partnerships (PPPs), infrastructure bonds, and blends of debt and equity financing.

Development finance institutions should partner with commercial banking institutions to create credit lines for SMEs, export development funds, and guarantees for women-led enterprises. AfCFTA's digital infrastructure is also critical. The demand for integrating methods for cross-border e-commerce, digital forms of identity recognition, and pan-African payment systems (including the Pan African Payment and Settlement System-PAPSS) is rising quickly, and there means and processes need to be in place to match that demand. This will help facilitate cross-border trade in services, as their transaction frictions tend to be significant. Further, it will enhance inclusivity.

b) Strategic Pointers for the African countries and IEAs

To properly implement the AfCFTA, trade protocols should be incorporated into national development frameworks and strategy plans in alignment with Vision 2030 and Agenda 2063. It is encouraged that trade enforcement be done efficiently through trade implementation units, inter-ministerial committees, and transparency in implementation monitoring bodies. There should be a phased tariff reduction to protect industries, supported by tax incentives and R&D.

Trade facilitation tools regarding customs procedures could be done through digitising customs procedures, and regulatory reporting should be consistent across all RECs, while tariff and NTB data are easily accessible to the general public. The capacity building of SMMEs/taking the liberty to use the abbreviation, maybe also allowed, through training and simplified processes, should be complementary to supporting them with certifications and availing other groups to make cross-border trade easier and accountable.

7.1 A Roadmap for Africa's Strategic Autonomy

Achieving Africa's strategic independence through AfCFTA will be a lengthy process, similar to many other complex issues. The primary goal of the first phase, which lasts from one to two years, should be to establish institutional frameworks. Some key steps that need attention include improving customs procedures and eliminating non-tariff trade barriers that hinder business. To ensure broad participation, people must be informed about AfCFTA opportunities and have access to training programs tailored to their needs. Some economies will require more assistance than others due to shocks affecting their resilience and transition. The AfCFTA adjustment facilities will help the economy respond during these times.

As we move into the medium-term period of 3 to 5 years, it will be more important to combine continental and domestic policies with industrial planning. Changing investment laws through agreements between two countries will make it easier to get to a single set of rules for trade and investment. Infrastructure investing in updated trade corridors and border facilities that use digital customs systems increases value and lowers transaction costs. The creation of regional manufacturing clusters and continental digital frameworks will greatly improve value chains and speed up industrialization.

Long-term priorities (beyond 5 years) include developing regional value chains in critical sectors (agro-processing, health, and technology); establishing a pan-African investment protection agreement to attract and secure investment flows. At the global level, the institutionalization of Africa's role in the reform of the World Trade Organization (WTO), digital taxation frameworks, and green trade standards will elevate Africa's standing as a participant in global economic governance. Comparative insights from other regional blocs provide valuable lessons for Africa. The Regional Comprehensive Economic Partnership (RCEP) demonstrates the benefits of standardizing rules of origin and advancing digital trade frameworks. The United States-Mexico-Canada Agreement (USMCA) highlights the value of vigorous institutional enforcement and SME-focused policies. MERCOSUR illustrates how flexible sectoral liberalization can balance internal priorities with external engagement. AfCFTA can draw on these lessons while prioritising inclusive growth and Africa-specific development needs.

Monitoring progress must be evaluated using explicit and identifiable indicators. Recommended indicators are a trade diversification index, the proportion of intra-African trade, and the Logistics Performance Index (LPI) that can identify patterns of improvement on transportation and customs systems. Additional indicators, including access by SMEs to trade finance and a regional policy harmonization score, will assist in tracking the integration process and institutional alignment.

This roadmap provides an implementable framework for the AfCFTA platform to become a dynamic platform for resilience, inclusive growth, and Africa asserting itself as a global trade actor. The roadmap stresses the importance of disciplined implementation, institutional alignment, and strategic long-term commitments toward consolidating Africa's place in this evolving global trade order.

7.1.1 A Roadmap for Africa's Strategic Autonomy

To realize strategic autonomy, Africa requires a staged roadmap, addressing short-term, medium-term, and long-term policy responses. Short-term actions may include various trade facilitative reforms, capacity-development initiatives, as well as emergency financing; medium-term approaches would be more focused on reforming policy and regulations at a deeper level, building infrastructure, and institutional effectiveness.

There are regional trade blocs, such as the RCEP, USMCA, and MERCOSUR, that Africa can learn from as it operationalizes the AfCFTA. Each of the contexts may be different, but there are critical success factors that highlight flexible membership structures and regulatory harmonization, effective institutional enforcement, and strategic integration of value chains. Awareness and understanding of the strategic architectures they employed will provide useful insight into the next steps for AfCFTA to support the evolution from a market integration program through to a platform for resilience and sovereignty.

Table 2. Comparative Matrix: Strategic Regional Blocs vs AfCFTA

	RCEP	USMCA	MERCOSUR	AfCFTA
Region	Asia-Pacific (ASEAN + China, Japan, Korea, Australia, NZ)	North America (U.S., Mexico, Canada)	South America (Argentina, Brazil, Paraguay, Uruguay)	Pan-African (54 African Union member states)
Trade Objective	Deepen trade liberalization, hedge against U.S.-China tensions	Modernize NAFTA, strengthen North American manufacturing	Promote free trade and a customs union in South America	Build continental resilience, sovereignty, and strategic autonomy
Size (GDP)	~$26 trillion	~$24 trillion	~$3.4 trillion	~$3.4 trillion
Intra-Bloc Trade Share	~50% of total trade	~45% of total trade	~15% of total trade	~17% currently (Target 40%+)
Strategic Focus	Market access, supply chain integration, and digital trade rules	Labor standards, environmental standards, and dispute resolution modernization	Agricultural trade, tariff elimination	Reposition Africa as a rule-shaper in global trade (WTO, digital trade, green trade)
Global Positioning	Hedge against U.S.-China competition; the largest trade bloc by population	Deepen regional autonomy within North America vs external competitors	Balance economic liberalization with social cohesion	Execute disciplined integration, harmonize standards, and invest in regional infrastructure
Lessons for AfCFTA	Leverage flexible membership models	Embed enforceable governance resilience	Balance economic liberalization with social cohesion	Execute disciplined integration, harmonize standards

Source: Own Author

In table 2 we can see a versatile comparative approach to RCEP, USMCA, MERCOSUR, and AfCFTA through strategic areas of focus, intra-bloc trade shares, comparative global position, and transferrable lessons for Africa's trade evolution.

RCEP and USMCA are primarily focused on labor and environmental standards, as well as integrating supply chains, as illustrated in Figure 2. The significant aspect of the AfCFTA is the ability for Africa to become a rule-maker and not just a rule-taker within global trading mechanisms. However, in reaching this goal, there is a need to execute your strategies, invest in regional value chains, and confirm that governance arrangements are standardized.

The following implementation plan shows the most important actions and steps to be taken for fully unlocking the transformational opportunity presented by AfCFTA. The emphasis on full industrial development, digital transformation, and long-term integration of regional value chains should be the focus of long-term actions. It is also important to have contingency plans in place to address disruptions to external trade as a precaution. By creating a plan that allows people to be more resilient and prepared in the face of global disruptions and shocks, people can also be more useful in managing threats and achieving beneficial outcomes through effective actions, which are informed by risk-based assessments, targeted reserve planning, diversified trade portfolios, and flexible economic structures. Indicators for measuring economic sovereignty and competitiveness should be created and revised periodically to make sure they are informative and helpful in evaluations and assessments. The indicators might include, to some extent, diversification level, logistics performance, intra-African trade, investment flows, and measures to assess the extent of alignment of regional policies.

8. POLICY RECOMMENDATIONS

The AfCFTA is far more than a trade agreement. It is the most audacious economic and geopolitical initiative in the continent's 21st-century history, no other project being as ambitious or impactful. As protectionism, tariff wars, and values over digital sovereignty redefine the foundations of global trade, Africa must move from a reactive trade participant to a proactive rule-maker, which is not merely a matter of flipping a switch. Taking the continent beyond simply reacting to trade policy and practice demands strategic thinking and coordinated policy making, both based on institutional discipline and alignment.

This section outlines ten policy recommendations to retool AfCFTA so it can act as both a shield against shocks outside the continent and, more importantly, a spear to lead Africa's trade agenda. Each course of action is based on frameworks of Strategic Trade Theory, New Regionalism, and Economic Sovereignty, which each highlight the key drivers of resilience and competitiveness while acknowledging our long-standing gap in implementation. Each of the ten areas of action is connected to a core pillar of the value chain, digital harmonization, governance, and finance, to name a few, and there are other examples of progress made by other countries, such as Kenya and Nigeria. Taken together, the proposal and its ten-point action plan clearly articulate a direction towards a united, self-reliant, and globally-engaged Africa. What AfCFTA needs now is action, both brave and disciplined.

a) Institutional Accountability

For the AfCFTA to prove effective in real, tangible, impactful terms and show success, the African Union (AU), Regional Economic Communities (RECs), and national governments must establish performance-based governance. The capacity of institutional accountability will also ensure that the implementation of AfCFTA is intentional and that systematic monitoring, measuring, and enforcing compliance is not incidental. This involves specific criteria for compliance, publication of annual compliance scorecards, and linking any financial or technical support to measurable achievements. Such a culture of accountability could attenuate the inertia in implementation and fortify against political reversal. For example, the AU could design and publish a "Continental Compliance Dashboard" providing annual rankings of country compliance using relevant metrics such as ratification of the AfCFTA, customs digitization, and trade facilitation performance indicators similar to the effect the African Peer Review Mechanism has had in incentivizing governance reform.

b) National Integration

Incorporating AfCFTA into the national development and industrial strategies is critical for coherence and buying. AfCFTA should not be an adjunct project run by the trade ministries; it needs to be integrated into national economic blueprints, budget frameworks, and sectoral policies. This vertical alignment helps countries mobilise domestic resources, plan across sectors, and avoid contradictions. For example, Nigeria could include opportunities arising from AfCFTA's automotive value chain in its national industrial plan, including developing domestic assembly and parts manufacturing, and upskilling in the labour market consistent with AfCFTA investment and competition protocols. Doing so creates the necessary circumstances to ensure that AfCFTA implementation becomes a national, not continental, priority.

c) Regional Value Chains (RVCs)

AfCFTA's long-term transformational potential lies in establishing an integrated regional value chain across important sectors, including agro-processing, automotive, pharmaceuticals, and digital services. RVCs will allow African countries to optimize their comparative advantages, ramp up industrialization across the continent, and expand intra-African trade in intermediate goods. Instead of all countries competing for the same final products and markets, countries can specialize in some stages of production in the same value chains. A fantastic case study is the East African dairy industry, where Kenya, Uganda, and Rwanda developed coordinated sanitary and phytosanitary (SPS) standards and cross-border logistics to develop a regional dairy market. If successful, scaling such models across the continent can help each country reduce reliance on imported inputs and increase export competitiveness.

d) Trade Finance Access

Financial inclusion is one of the two main building blocks of a socially fair African Continental Free Trade Area (AfCFTA). Women-led businesses and many SMEs are often unable to raise capital for international trade because lenders usually ask for large amounts of collateral to issue loans to them, as well as being generally unaware of international trade, SME owners may have a limited understanding of business financing. Introducing options like tailored guaranteed schemes, SME growth funds that SMEs access at particular municipalities, or regional credit lines to raise the percentage of trade financed by undervalued transported SMEs and women-led SMEs could assist their engagement around the AfCFTA.

Afreximbank has already developed products that could be made more accessible if they were made even more tailored to their engagement with the AfCFTA, such as the MANSA compliance repository and the Intra-African Trade Fair, which reduces risks and opportunities to connect small traders. If these proposals are made to trade finance options that the RECs introduce/widgets/and position and facilitate, more underfunded women-led and SMEs who fill the AfCFTA with open market export and sales opportunities can hopefully and positively contribute to alleviating gender and financial capital divides across participation in trade.

e) Infrastructure Modernisation

Physical infrastructure is the backbone of trade. Without modern ports, roads, and border systems, the AfCFTA's protocols remain intentions on paper. Targeted improvements in transport corridors, inland ports, and “One-Stop Border Posts” (OSBP) are necessary in order to decrease transaction costs and increase the speed of trade. The example of Kenya’s Nairobi Inland Container Depot (ICD) demonstrates the replicability of successful and optimized integration between rail investments, digital customs solutions, and warehousing to reduce cargo clearance from many days to many hours.

Regional Economic Communities (RECs) should facilitate multi-country infrastructure developments, providing blended finance alongside public-private partnerships in the priority areas of connectivity for underserved regions, particularly landlocked regions and regions recovering from conflict.

f) Harmonizing Policy

The goal of creating a single African market as envisioned by the AfCFTA depends on harmonizing key regulatory areas such as customs, investment, competition policy, digital trade, and standards. Currently, varying rules and regulatory duplications cause uncertainty and delays, leading to inefficiencies.

Accelerating mutual recognition of standards, as well as aligning investment policies and customs, can significantly address non-tariff barriers (NTBs). For instance, the mutual recognition framework for agriculture in COMESA helped that regional economic community's efficiency by obviating having to do costly repeated testing and certification. Similarly, mutual recognition in digital services and the adoption of standards can free up significant regional growth for African tech start-ups, through harmonized e-invoicing, electronic signatures, and free flow of cross-border data.

g) Unified Trade Voice

Africa needs to negotiate as one to influence global trade norms. Varied positions reduce influence, especially in complicated multilateral choosing, decisions, and negotiations such as the World Trade Organization (WTO), Africa Growth and Opportunity Act (AGOA) renewals, or digital taxation conversations. Institutionalizing Pan African trade diplomacy ensures Africa prioritizes its collective trade interests in global standard-setting and related procedures.

The African Continental Free Trade Agreement (AfCFTA) Secretariat, with support from the African Union (AU) and Regional Economic Communities (RECs), should coordinate African unified positions on emerging challenges, including climate-related tariffs, data flows across borders, and subsidies reform. As an example, a unified position on special and differential treatment (SDT) or e-commerce rules at WTO Ministerial Conferences can shape negotiations in Africa’s favor, whilst helping to reverse the historical marginalization of African countries.

h) Strategic Industrialization

AfCFTA liberalization must be sequenced with industrial protectionism to avoid premature deindustrialization. A large number of African industries are nascent and vulnerable to external competition. Also, some strategic, yes, definitely strategic sectors, such as pharmaceuticals, agro-processing, or electric mobility, should be protected with intelligent tariffs, investment incentives, and R&D support until they become globally competitive.

Ethiopia's leather sector strategy is instructive, which combined temporary import restrictions with the creation of industrial parks, skills development, and export promotion. This combined approach allows Africa to liberate and industrialize simultaneously, using the AfCFTA as the basis to create jobs and diversify exports rather than a mere means to reduce tariffs.

i) Resilience systems

For Africa to compensate for the inevitable trade shocks of the future, the resilience systems will have to be built into the operational architecture of AfCFTA. By resilience systems, we mean trade early warning systems, contingency funds for vulnerable economies, and mechanisms for coordinated response to catastrophes such as pandemics or environmental disasters.

For example, during the COVID-19 pandemic, because there was no continental reserve or any coordinated logistics to expeditiously move vaccines and equipment, they arrived late. An AfCFTA Risk Resilience Fund could have been established and hosted at Afreximbank to provide quick liquidity support to affected sectors or geographies. A direct digital operational dashboard could have monitored export flows in real-time and tracked commodity price fluctuations and border delays, giving officials the opportunity to react quickly to systemic risks.

j) Strategic metrics

It is equally important to gauge progress through strategic metrics so that AfCFTA realizes its ambitions. Some of the metrics to be measured on a continuous basis include volume of intra-African trade, diversity of export levels, logistics performance, the participation of SMEs, and the degree of policy harmonization.

Frequent and careful tracking and regular public reporting of strategic metrics would assist RECs, governments, and other stakeholders in gauging performance, allowing them to adjust or act in a timely and informed manner. A proposed "Trade Sovereignty Index" could provide an indication of the level of reliance on intra-African, as opposed to external, trade across three distinct sectors. This will provide greater clarity and assist responses in the policy spaces and production. If Africa does not have strategic metrics, there is a chance it could operate in a context of obscurity as intra-African trade continues to evolve, and as the context of global trade evolves and becomes ever more complex.

8.1 Forward-thinking Innovative Recommendations

The AfCFTA Digital Sandboxes (ADS) provide a new and pragmatic model to unlock Africa's digital potential. These zones, distributed across the continent, will allow innovators to experiment in real time with cross-border e-commerce, AI, logistics, and fintech solutions, essentially eliminating long-standing regulatory barriers to digital scaling in the region. The patchy nature of African digital regulations makes it very hard for a start-up to expand outside of its home jurisdiction; this sandbox ultimately seeks to respond to that challenge.

Informed by successful innovation zones created in Singapore and the UK, these sandboxes are focused on expediting market entry for digital solutions that operate cross-border. For example, a Malawian agri-fintech could test AI-based crop insurance using data from Uganda and Ghana, and deploy mobile payments within a safe, harmonized testing space. Enabling this sandbox is the AfCFTA legal framework, and supporting this structure are the Regional Economic Communities (RECs) and national innovation hubs. The ADS could lead to a boom in Pan-African tech entrepreneurship. Already positioned to support this initiative are stakeholders such as the Kenya ICT Authority and Rwanda's Irembo platform.

The Continental Green Freight Corridor, also known as the "AfCFTA Electric Belt," has the potential to transform the continent's trade and climate initiatives. Imagine electric freight logistical routes from Lagos to Nairobi through Lusaka with solar logistics hubs, battery-swapping stations, and green customs facilities. At the moment, Africa's freight roads are old and fossil-fuel dependent, so this is an ideal time to jump directly into clean, more affordable trade logistics. Moving to electric mobility for cross-border freight will provide Africa with an opportunity to become a global role model for sustainable trade, lower transport costs, and lessen dependence on imported fuels.

Both BasiGo's leadership in e-mobility in Kenya and the pilots of Ghanaian solar mini-grid logistics have inspired the notion of a green freight corridor that might provide savings of 30% on freight costs and develop solid value of EV assembly within the SADC and EAC regions. We have a clear vision and a collective opportunity to build an AfCFTA Electric Belt to position Africa at the forefront of the global transformation towards green logistics.

The AfCFTA Trade Intelligence Engine could reshape Africa's position in global trade. This AI-enabled platform would track international trade discussions and negotiations, trade agreement negotiations, tariff changes, non-tariff barriers, national market disruptions (often referred to as "shocks" in global trade), and send contextual notifications and tailored recommendations to African negotiators and policymakers through alerts in real-time.

Current trade teams from all over Africa often spend their time chasing other participants in forums to prioritize trade that is meaningful and important, and the Trade Intelligence Engine would change this dynamic by offering a digital co-pilot that would allow them and policymakers to respond more adeptly and immediately. With a combination of data scraping techniques, sentiment analysis capabilities, and modeling with predictive analytics, the Trade Intelligence Engine would create instant "smart briefs" that reflect Africa's interests and articulate Africa's position to other stakeholders in the international trade dialogue.

Taking inspiration from platforms such as TradeNet in Kenya and Irembo Gov in Rwanda, the Trade Intelligence Engine could potentially reduce trade clearance turnaround times by as much as 60% and help save the African continent approximately $50 billion annually. With the Trade Intelligence Engine, Africa actually has an opportunity to stop being a passive participant and start being a confident rule-maker.

Table 4. Innovative Recommendation Framework

Example:	Timeline	Key Actions	Lead Actors	Expected Outcomes
Phase 1: Foundation and Commitment	2025–2027	Integrate AfCFTA into national development and industrial plans. Launch the AfCFTA Compliance Dashboard and performance-based reporting. Establish the Trade Resilience Fund via Afreximbank. Activate Digital Sandbox pilot zones for innovation. Start the harmonization of customs and investment codes	AU, AfCFTA Secretariat, National Governments, UNECA, Afreximbank	Political will embedded, foundational systems launched, and regulatory flexibility initiated
Phase 2: Systems and Scaling	2027–2030	Fast-track regional value chain pilots in sectors like agro-processing and automotive. Scale SME and women-led trade finance schemes. Launch Green Freight Corridor and digital customs pilots. Begin logistics upgrades in the top 10 intra-African trade corridors	AU, RECs, Trade Ministries, Development Partners, Private Sector	Functional intra-African trade infrastructure and access systems operationalised
Phase 3: Regional Power Consolidation	2030–2035	Institutionalize Pan-African trade diplomacy platforms. Launch AfCFTA Trade Intelligence Engine for AI-driven negotiation support. Expand strategic partnerships with ASEAN, MERCOSUR, BRICS+, and other key organisations. Promote unified African stances in WTO and global forums	AU, AfCFTA Secretariat, RECs, Regional Anchors (e.g., Nigeria, Kenya, South Africa)	Africa is recognised as a cohesive and assertive bloc in global trade governance.
Phase 4: Strategic Sovereignty	2035–2045	Consolidate regional industrial hubs with EV, pharmaceutical, and agro-processing clusters. Achieve 40%+ intra-African trade share and reduce dependence on EU/US/China. Institutionalise resilience systems and strategic trade metrics. Establish Africa as a rule-shaper in digital, green, and services trade	AU, RECs, AfCFTA Secretariat, Trade Ministries, Industry Coalitions	Africa achieves strategic autonomy and is a credible force in global trade rule-making

Source: Own Author

9. CONCLUSION

The AfCFTA is no longer merely a facilitator of trade; it is now Africa's predominant vehicle to maneuver through a chaotic global economy. The AfCFTA is central to Africa achieving two key objectives: it provides protection from unpredictable external influences and provides a forum for global trade norms and leadership. As protectionism spreads, digital separation is broadening, and the world continues to change; this is more important than ever. This chapter indicates that the AfCFTA's true potency lies not simply in its ability to open markets; it could also provide strategic autonomy, accelerate industrial development, and position the region through coordinated, deliberate action.

Delivering this promise will depend on ongoing strategic financing, firm policy environments, and institutional integrity. AfCFTA needs to be part of national industrial development, infrastructure, and innovation strategies in addition to regional trade ministries. To make sure AfCFTA remains a resilient structure to respond to future trade challenges and geo-economic disruptions, the African Union, Regional Economic Communities (RECs), the United Nations Economic Commission for Africa (UNECA), the African Export-Import Bank (Afreximbank), and the private sector all need to work together across Africa.

In this chapter, we present 10 policy ideas that could facilitate changes that arise from the African Continental Free Trade Area (AfCFTA). These ideas are varied: some aim to ensure policy coherence; others to foster infrastructure development, institutional accountability, regional value chains, or to finance small and medium enterprises (SMEs); even diplomacy. They have emerged from reality and, as Africa's positionality as a global business partner continues to evolve, all become even more important. This chapter has also illustrated new initiatives that highlight the multi-faceted nature of AfCFTA and regional trade. These were concretely illustrated with the Continental Green Freight Corridor Innovation (Untapped+ (African Import Export Bank)), a UNICEF AfCFTA Digital Sandboxes Facility, and the TDI - Trade Intelligence Engine - powered by Artificial Intelligence. These examples present a unique opportunity for Africa to become proactive in shaping its trade future instead of just being reactive.

The world is currently likely to go through a historical change in Africa that we may never see again. Technology, protectionism, and a specific style of modern extremism are polarizing the world further. In this scenario, we cannot remain idle, awaiting developments.

The AfCFTA presents an opportunity for Africa to transition from dependency to autonomy, from adhering to regulations to formulating rules and standards in global digital commerce, sustainable industrial practices, and multilateral governance. This outcome necessitates not merely goodwill; it needs robust, imaginative leadership, a culture of accountability, and a collective ambition to enhance the well-being of all individuals.

If correctly planned and executed, the AfCFTA has the ability to protect Africa from foreign economic shocks while facilitating an unparalleled era of productive, creative, and significant international influence. This is not only a policy change for Africa; it is the most significant turning point in the continent's history. The plan is established, it will be executed, and the universe will not remain stagnant. We should not either. The moment to transition from cautious optimism has come; just one imperative remains: urgent, collaborative, and sustained.

REFERENCES

Afreximbank. (2023). *African Trade Report 2023: Export manufacturing and regional value chains in Africa.* https://media.afreximbank.com/afrexim/AFRICAN_TRADE_REPORT_2023.pdf

African Development Bank. (2024). *African economic outlook 2024: Driving Africa's transformation through climate-smart investments.* https://www.afdb.org/sites/default/files/documents/publications/african_economic_outlook_aeo_2024_0.pdf

African Development Bank. (2024). *Paving the way for a stronger and more integrated Africa: African Development Bank reaffirms its commitment at Casablanca ministerial roundtable.* https://www.afdb.org/en/news-and-events/press-releases/paving-way-stronger-and-more-integrated-africa-african-development-bank-reaffirms-its-commitment-casablanca-ministerial-roundtable-81179

African Union. (2022). *6th European Union - African Union Summit: A joint vision for 2030* [Press release]. https://au.int/en/pressreleases/20220218/6th-european-union-african-union-summit-joint-vision-2030

African Union. (2022). *African Continental Free Trade Area (AfCFTA).* Retrieved July 5, 2025, from https://au.int/en/african-continental-free-trade-area

Draper, P., & Dadush, U. (2021, February 10). *Free trade in Africa is an important goal, but it is not easy to achieve.* Bruegel. https://www.bruegel.org/blog-post/free-trade-africa-important-goal-not-easy-achieve

Economic Policy Research Centre. (2023). *Leveraging the AfCFTA agreement for Uganda's export growth: Challenges and solutions.* https://eprcug.org/publication/leveraging-the-afcfta-agreement-for-ugandas-export-growth-challenges-and-solutions/?wpdmdl=17885&refresh=6859313ca9b451750675772

GhanaWeb. (2024). *ICUMS makes trade facilitation seamless – Samuel Akrofi.* https://www.ghanaweb.com/GhanaHomePage/business/ICUMS-makes-trade-facilitation-seamless-Samuel-Akrofi-1970946

ICTSD. (2022). *Africa in WTO: Towards a unified agenda.* ICTSD (IISD). https://ictsd.iisd.org/africa-in-wto-towards-unified-agenda

International Monetary Fund. (2023). *Trade integration in Africa: Unleashing the continent's potential in a changing world (Departmental Paper No. 2023/007).* https://www.imf.org/en/Publications/Departmental-Papers-Policy-Papers/Issues/2023/05/03/Trade-Integration-in-Africa-Unleashing-the-Continent-s-Potential-in-a-Changing-World-529215

International Trade Centre. (2023). *Navigating Africa's digital trade with confidence.* https://www.intracen.org/news-and-events/news/navigating-africas-digital-trade-with-confidence

ITC. (2025). *Navigating Africa's digital trade with confidence.* https://www.intracen.org/news-and-events/news/navigating-africas-digital-trade-with-confidence

Krugman, P. R. (1985). Is free trade passé? *The Journal of Economic Perspectives, 1*(2), 131–144. DOI: 10.1257/jep.1.2.131

Krugman, P. R., & Smith, A. (Eds.). (1994). *Empirical studies of strategic trade policy.* University of Chicago Press., https://www.nber.org/books-and-chapters/empirical-studies-strategic-trade-policy/introduction-empirical-studies-strategic-trade-policy DOI: 10.7208/chicago/9780226454665.001.0001

Mattoo, A., Rocha, N., & Ruta, M. (2020). *The AfCFTA and Africa's growth prospects (Working Paper No. 20-9).* Peterson Institute for International Economics. https://www.piie.com/sites/default/files/documents/wp20-9.pdf

Mendez-Parra, M. (2022). *The African Continental Free Trade Area in a global trade context: A governance perspective.* Friedrich-Ebert-Stiftung Geneva Office. https://library.fes.de/pdf-files/bueros/genf/19225.pdf

Munyati, C. (2024). *Africa and the Gulf States: A new economic partnership.* World Economic Forum. https://www.weforum.org/stories/2024/04/africa-gcc-gulf-economy-partnership-emerging

Petri, P. A., & Plummer, M. G. (2020). *RCEP: A new trade agreement that will shape global economics and politics.* Brookings. https://www.brookings.edu/articles/rcep-a-new-trade-agreement-that-will-shape-global-economics-and-politics/

Petri & Plummer. (2020). *Mega-regional trade agreements: Implications for East Asia.* https://www.pecc.org/resources/trade-and-investment-1/2639-mega-regional-trade-agreements-implications-for-east-asia/file

Söderbaum, F., & Shaw, T. M. (Eds.). (2003). *Theories of new regionalism: A Palgrave reader.* Palgrave Macmillan. https://link.springer.com/book/10.1057/9781403938794

Trade Law Centre. (2022). *AfCFTA Protocol on Investment: Key features* [Infographic]. Tralac. https://www.tralac.org/resources/infographic/16152-afcfta-protocol-on-investment-factsheet.html

TradeMark Africa. (2024). *Digital innovation and regional collaboration: Essential drivers to transforming Africa's trade future.* https://www.trademarkafrica.com/digital-innovation-and-regional-collaboration-essential-drivers-to-transforming-africas-trade-future/

UNCTAD. (2021). *Africa's free trade area can deliver considerable inclusive economic growth for the continent.* https://unctad.org/news/africas-free-trade-area-can-deliver-considerable-inclusive-economic-growth-continent

UNCTAD. (2022). *Rethinking the foundations of export diversification in Africa: The catalytic role of business and financial services.* https://unctad.org/system/files/official-document/aldcafrica2022_en.pdf

UNCTAD. (2023). *Making the AfCFTA work for Africa: Building capacities for inclusive and sustainable implementation.* https://knowledge.uneca.org/idep/sites/default/files/IDEP_Course/2023/Making-AfCFTA-Work/Brochure-AfCFTA-EN-2023.pdf

UNECA. (2023). *Implementing the AfCFTA Agreement will boost intra-African trade and industrialization.* https://www.uneca.org/stories/implementing-the-afcfta-agreement-will-boost-intra-african-trade-and-industrialization

UNECA. (2025). *COM2025 Newsletter No. 1.* https://www.uneca.org/eca-events/sites/default/files/resources/documents/com/2025/bulletins/com2025_newsletter_1.pdf

UNECA & AU. (2020). *Governing the interface between the AfCFTA and Regional Economic Communities: Issues, opportunities, and challenges (Revised November 2020).* UNECA & AU. https://archive.uneca.org/sites/default/files/uploaded-documents/RITD/2020/governing_interface_between_afcfta_and_recs_afcfta_issues_opportunities_and_challenges_revised_final_version_as_at_nov._2_2020.pdf

UNIDO. (2023). *Third Industrial Development Decade for Africa (IDDA III): Mid-term progress report.* https://www.unido.org/sites/default/files/files/2022-07/IDDA%20III%20SG%20report%202019.pdf

United Nations Department of Economic and Social Affairs (UN DESA). (2022). *World Population Prospects 2022: Summary of results.* United Nations. https://www.un.org/development/desa/pd/sites/www.un.org.development.desa.pd/files/wpp2022_summary_of_results.pdf

United Nations Economic Commission for Africa. (2024). *African perspectives of a just transition to low-carbon economies.* https://uneca.org/sites/default/files/ACPC/2024/African_perspectives_of_a_just_transition_to_Low_Carbon_economies.pdf

World Bank. (2020). *The African Continental Free Trade Area: Economic and distributional effects.* Washington, DC: World Bank. https://openknowledge.worldbank.org/server/api/core/bitstreams/ef1aa41f-60de-5bd2-a63e-75f2c3ff0f43/content

World Trade Organization. (2023). *Public Forum 2023: "It Is Time for Action"* [Conference programme]. WTO. https://www.wto.org/english/forums_e/public_forum23_e/draft_programme_e.pdf

World Trade Organization. (2025). *WTO Secretariat issues updated Global Trade Outlook and Statistics: Forecast for 2025* [Press release]. WTO. https://www.wto.org/english/news_e/news25_e/tfore_16apr25_e.htm

Chapter 7
Geopolitical Risk, Variability of Oil Price, and the Global Trade Uncertainty:
An Economic Perspective

Piyali Roy Chowdhury
https://orcid.org/0000-0002-0625-4103
School of Business and Management, Christ University, Bangalore, India

ABSTRACT

Oil prices are the outcome of a highly integrated, dynamic global system. With geopolitical risk and trade policy uncertainty contribute to the volatile world markets, the study analyses the impact of geopolitical risk, trade policy uncertainty on crude oil price globally. It considers data from 2000 to 2023 and finds out systematic link between the three variables. The data proved a long run impact of trade policy uncertainty and geopolitical risk on the crude oil. This enhances the influence of the variables and leads to implementation of policy measures in global markets. The data are tested through Auto Regressive Distributed Lag (ARDL) model and checked for long run cointegration and short run association. The policy, thus, has been suggested as to improve the transition towards sustainability globally. Though the impact of geopolitical risk and trade policy uncertainty is not strong on crude oil price in world market, it can affect the short run volatility. Thus, mitigation, diversification and transparency are the key factors to strengthen the existing situation in world.

DOI: 10.4018/979-8-3373-3835-4.ch007

1. INTRODUCTION

Geopolitical risks (GPRs) are widely studied in academics. Recently, geopolitical risks have been highlighted as a major economic driver, leading to further research on wars and economics (Alqahtani and Klein, 2021). As they affect asset prices, GPRs indicate economic and political conflicts. Economic and corporate investing behaviour is heavily influenced by domestic and international political events thoroughly throughout the world. Moreover, central banks, business investigators, and the financial press cite GPRs as a crucial investment decision factor.

Empirical studies on conflicts and economics have been influenced by GPRs' effects on economies. The question of how geopolitical actions affect asset markets is a fundamental research arena in economics. Recurrent civil wars, international wars, political turmoil, and terrorist attacks have affected many nations in the current century, and civil wars alone have affected one third of all nations (Weiss,1994). These issues need severe attention in the development of world economy, according to Bouoiyour et al. (2019), and have been exacerbated by the trade war.

The concept of GPR is associated with the global economic uncertainty that focus on different parameters. Hence, global uncertainty carries issues with respect to trade uncertainty, equity market instability, money market unpredictability, among others. In this respect, the current study focusses on finding a relationship between global uncertainty, herein focused on the trade war initiated by President Donald J. Trump and oil price fluctuations that lead to economic unpredictability in global market. Thus, the initial objective is to evaluate the impact of types of uncertainties on the oil price, as well as specific factors such as geopolitical risks, monetary policy uncertainty, trade policy uncertainty, and climate policy uncertainty.

Since oil is still the base of the world economy, that rose to 61.94 USD/Bbl in 2025, eventual changes can have broad geopolitical implications.

This book chapter aims to examine past data, identify important trends, and assess the degree to which world uncertainty impacts changes in oil prices. Focusing on both short-term shocks and long-term trends, the study seeks to offer insights that can guide investment planning in energy-dependent industries, risk management practices, and policy decisions.

2. LITERATURE REVIEW

The fluctuation of crude oil prices has been a critical subject of analysis in economics and finance because of its extensive effects on global markets and economies (Wu et al., 2023). Researchers have thoroughly investigated the determinants influencing crude oil price changes, including geopolitical risks, economic shocks, and monetary policy, to enhance understanding and prediction of these variations (Smales, 2021).

Geopolitical risks have become a significant determinant of oil price volatility (Ivanovski & Hailemariam; Zhang et al., 2022) created the Geopolitical Risk (GPR) Index, which measures geopolitical tensions and their economic impacts. This tool is essential for comprehending the relationship between geopolitical events and crude oil price variations.

Cunado et al. (2020) and Lau et al. (2023) advanced their research by examining the asymmetric effects of geopolitical risks on China's crude oil prices using a Quantile Autoregressive Distributed Lag (QARDL) methodology, revealing novel insights into the non-linear influences. The impact of trade policy uncertainty on economic activity and commodities markets has been examined. Macroeconomic consequences of trade policy uncertainty have great impacts on global commerce and market stability. The authors findings underscore the correlation between policy uncertainty and fluctuations in crude oil prices.

Macroeconomic considerations, particularly monetary policy, are essential for comprehending oil price volatility (Qian et al., 2022; Li et al., 2023) examined the impact of financial and economic policies, including interest rate modifications, on crude oil prices (Gkillas et al., 2022; Shahbaz et al., 2024) examined the correlation between oil prices and exchange rate fluctuations, elucidating the relationship between these variables.

The gap of the study is identified as the impact of geopolitical risk and trade policy uncertainty on crude oil price globally. For analysing the same, the hypotheses are defined as follows:

H_{01}: There remains no cointegration among the variables

H_{02}: There is no long run impact present in the study

H_{03}: There is no short run causality found in the study

3. METHODOLOGICAL APPROACH

West Texas Intermediate (WTI) is a benchmark grade of crude oil known for its low sulfur content and low density (Su et al., 2019; Duan et al., 2021). WTI is a key pricing standard for global oil markets, which is based primarily on the NYMEX. Supply-demand dynamics, geopolitical risks, and storage capacities influence the price of WTI. A notable event in WTI's history occurred in April 2020, when the May contract briefly traded at negative prices due to the COVID-19 pandemic, signalling severe disruptions in global oil markets.

The TPU Index quantifies uncertainty in trade policy by measuring the frequency of trade-related terms in major newspapers. Spikes in TPU have historically occurred during significant trade events, such as the Nixon-Ford shocks, NAFTA negotiations, and the 2016 U.S. election. Public reaction towards Donald Trump taking the position of president is well diversified with respect to administrative policies. In 2018, there remains a pushback with energised democratic turnouts, but in 2024, the comeback of the president is restored with civil rights, global relations along with diversified opinion. The index captures how trade policy uncertainty affects economic activity, with higher TPU correlating with reduced investment and economic slowdown. Utilizing information contained in newspapers, corporate earnings calls, and tariff rates, it draws valuable insights into how trade uncertainty is affecting global markets.

The GPR Index measures geopolitical tensions by tracking the frequency of related articles in major newspapers (Wang et al., 2021). It captures spikes in geopolitical risk during significant global events, such as the World Wars, the Cuban Missile Crisis, and 9/11. The GPR Index was constructed, which reflects the level of global instability, with higher values often correlating with reduced investment and economic uncertainty. It is very sensitive to understand how geopolitical risks affect global markets and economic activities.

Figure 1. Geopolitical Risk from 1985 to 2024

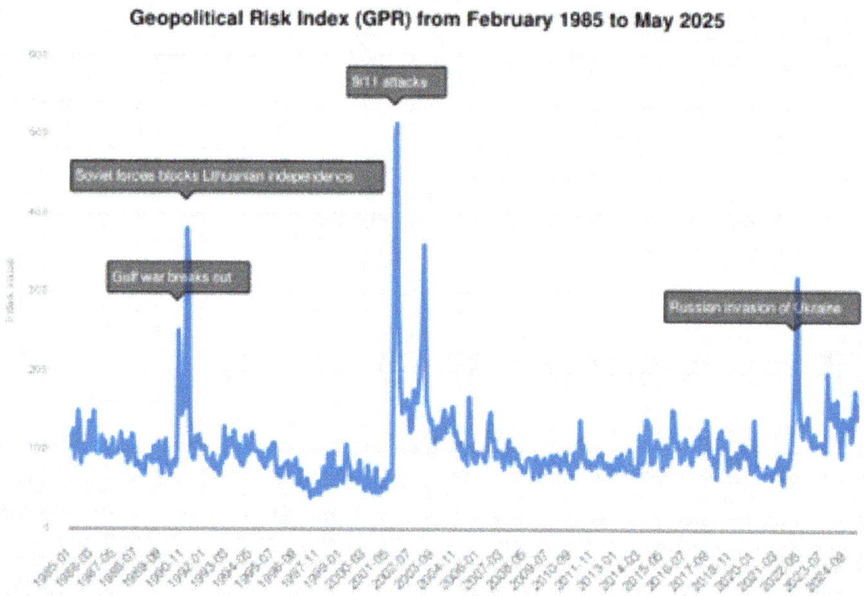

Source: Statista database

The rationale behind this inclusion of variables is summarized as follows: West Texas Intermediate is taken as a dependent variable because this has been identified as one of the global benchmarks regarding oil pricing, reflecting some dynamics within the market. Geopolitical risks are then incorporated into the analysis because the risks often disrupt oil supplies and cause significant price fluctuations on the Geopolitical Risk GPR Index. Generally, trade wars and policy shift significantly influence both global demand and supply, as captured in the TPU Index.

The ARDL (Autoregressive Distributed Lag) model is employed in this research to examine the short-run and long-run relationships between WTI crude oil prices and the selected regressors, including geopolitical risks, trade policy uncertainty, and economic factors, data ranging from 05/1/2000 to 29/12/2023. This model is beneficial for handling variables with different levels of integration, allowing for the inclusion of both short-term dynamics and long-term equilibrium relationships. By considering the lags of the independent variables, ARDL helps address potential collinearity issues and provides insights into how these factors influence oil price volatility over time.

4. RESULTS

Before analysing the data, we have organised the hypothesis as follows:

Table 1. Descriptive Statistics

Statistics	*ln*(WTI)	*ln* (TPU)	*ln* (GPRD)
Mean	1.760520	1.952269	2.009224
Median	1.787177	1.954049	2.006060
Maximum	2.162296	2.907226	3.019367
Minimum	0.949878	0.521138	0.977339
Std. Dev.	0.195212	0.286052	0.200474
Skewness	(0.461308)	(0.131133)	0.330821
kurtosis	2.389674	3.442642	4.695897
Jarque-Bera	306.8985	66.38820	831.0826
Probability	0.000000	0.000000	0.000000
Sum	10596.57	11750.71	12093.52
sum sq. Dev-	229.3331	492.4265	241.8621
Observations	6019	6019	6019

The descriptive statistics highlight distinct characteristics of the variables. WTI has a mean of 1.760520, a median of 1.787177, and low variability (SD = 0.195212), with a nearly symmetric distribution (slightly negative skewness) and moderate range, though the Jarque-Bera test strongly rejects normality (p = 0.000000). TPU, with a mean of 1.952269 and a wider range than WTI, shows moderate variability (SD = 0.286052) and a nearly symmetric distribution, but normality is also rejected (p = 0.000000). GPRD has the highest mean (2.009224), moderate variability (SD = 0.200474), and a slightly positive skew, with the highest kurtosis (4.695897) indicating significant outliers; normality is again rejected (p = 0.000000). Overall, all variables deviate significantly from normality despite differing distribution characteristics. However, the result of cointegration is depicted in table 2.

Table 2. Result of Cointegration

Test Statistic	**Value**	**Significance Level**	**I(0)**	**I(1)**
F-stat	4.609553	10%	2.63	3.35
		5%	3.1	3.87
		2.5%	3.55	4.38
		1%	4.13	5

Table 2 explains the F-Bounds Test results that evaluate the existence of a long-term connection among variables inside the ARDL framework. The null hypothesis posits the absence of a long-term association. The F-statistic is 4.609553, with critical bounds at the 10% significance level being I (0) = 2.63 and I (1) = 3.35. The F-statistic surpasses the upper bound critical value I (1) = 3.35 at the 10% level), allowing for the rejection of the null hypothesis and providing evidence of a long-run link between the variables at this significance level (acceptance of H_{11}).

Table 3. Result of Long Run and Short Run

Long Run				
Variable	**Coefficient**	**Std. Er**	**t-Stat**	**Prob.**
ln(TPU)	0.072414	0.169567	0.427051	0.6694
ln (GPRD)	-0.39278	0.253035	-1.55227	0.1207
C	2.448813	0.601374	4.070226	0
Short Run				
ECM	-0.0032*	0.000745	-4.29505	0

*signifies 5 percent level of significance

Table (3) signifies the results of long run and short run dynamics of the impact of trade policy uncertainty and geopolitical risk on crude oil prices. It is proved that the short run disequilibrium is mitigated towards long run stability with significant results. Also, the significant result of error correction term proves the long run impact of uncertainty and geopolitical risk on crude oil prices. The stability of the model is analysed through CUSUM and CUSUMQ test explained in figure 1 and figure 2.

CUSUM Test

Figure 2. Result of CUSUM at 5 percent significance

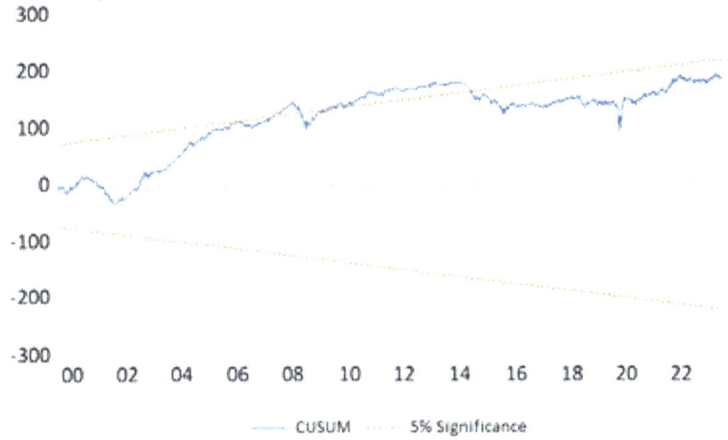

The CUSUM (Cumulative Sum) test graph (figure 2) illustrates the model's stability over time, with the CUSUM line indicating the cumulative sum of residuals and the orange lines marking the 5% significance thresholds.

The CUSUM line is consistent at 5% significance margins, indicating that the model is structurally robust and free from substantial structural fractures. This verifies that the model is appropriately described and dependable throughout the chosen time period.

CUSUM OF SQUARES

Figure 3. Result of CUSUMQ at 5 percent significance

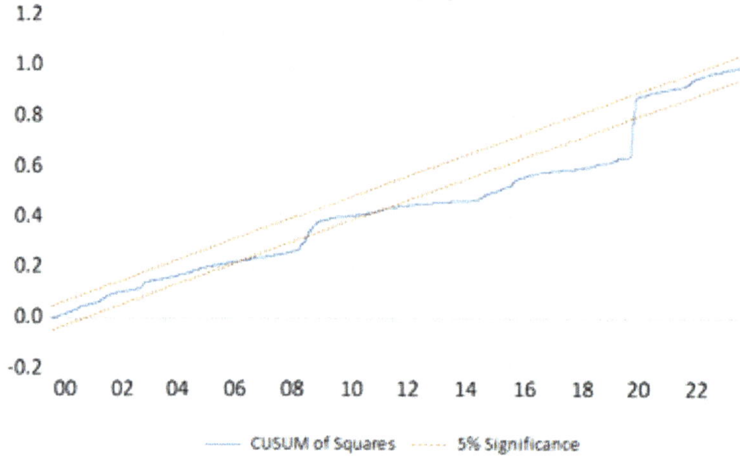

Figure 3 of the CUSUM of Squares test demonstrates the temporal stability of the model's variance, with the blue line depicting the cumulative sum of squared residuals and the orange lines denoting the 5% significant thresholds. The CUSUM of Squares line consistently remains within the significant boundaries, indicating that the model lacks structural breakdowns or instability in the variance of residuals. This verifies that the model is structurally stable, consistent, and dependable during the observed period.

5. DISCUSSION

The global trade war, reignited in 2025, has become one of the most crucial factors in international economic decisions. The trade war arises as the imposition of tariff or non-tariff barriers starts influencing global economies, their trade and overall relations with the U.S. The protectionist approach adopted by the American government affects the global supply chains, overall trade balances and consumer costs.

In 2017/2018 as there was tariff moderation on China due to technological knowledge-shifts, rare-earth metals, semiconductors and strategic technologies trade. These industries were severely affected. Still in 2025, the issues are unresolved in China due to disagreements between the countries, but the trade war contains global characteristics compared to 2018. For instance, India, has also been affected with the hike in tariffs and compensated with reduced exports. Industries like textiles, chemicals and metals are negatively affected. The ripple effects are global as the tariffs cost have pushed up inflation, and supply chain strategies are diversifying with respect to manufacturing bases in different economies.

Trade Policy Uncertainty (TPU) and the Energy Uncertainty, thus, exert a significant adverse effect on crude oil prices. Increased uncertainty in trade policies or the energy sector typically results in a decline in crude oil prices. Geopolitical Risk (GPR) exerts a positive influence, indicating that elevated geopolitical tensions result in higher crude oil prices. Factors such as currency policy uncertainty (CPU), economic policy uncertainty (EPU Monetary), and the US equities market do not significantly affect crude oil prices in this model. Asymmetric Effects of Market Shocks on Volatility shows negative shocks (adverse news) induce greater volatility than positive shocks, indicating that oil markets respond more intensely to crises or unfavourable developments. Volatility is enduring, indicating that once price variations commence, they often stay for an extended duration.

The key findings reveal that oil prices are highly sensitive to global uncertainty, but the findings reveal that crude oil prices are highly sensitive to global uncertainty, but the market responds differently to different factors, depending on it is whether geopolitical or trade related. From the figures presented, one may conclude that the Trade Policy Uncertainty (TPU) exerts downward pressure on oil prices (Wang, 2022), disrupting trade flows and weakening expectations for future demand, whereas Geopolitical Risk (GPR) contributes positively are consistent with the "risk premium" channel where heightened conflict or instability raises concerns over supply security (Kilian, Plante & Richter, 2024). This duality suggests that oil markets interpret policy-driven and conflict-driven shocks differently: trade frictions suppress consumption and investment confidence, while geopolitical shocks amplify scarcity fears.

The persistence of volatility implies that these shocks are not easily absorbed; instead, they embed long-term uncertainties. To illustrate, in the current 2025 trade war context, where tariffs gained a global projection, the compounded impact of protectionist measures (in this case, under the retaliatory tariffs umbrella) and eventually geopolitical fragmentation, it reinforced the oil's role as both a barometer of global uncertainty and a vector transmitting systemic risk across markets. As consequence, there was a growing need for policymakers to consider crude oil as not only a commodity, but also as a strategic indicator of global stability and an amplifier of economic fragility.

6. CONCLUSION

The contribution of the study focuses on suggesting policy implementations such as governments that ought to mitigate uncertainty in trade and economic policy to avert prolonged disruptions in energy markets. Efforts to achieve geopolitical stability, such as diplomatic resolutions and conflict management, can mitigate oil price volatility. Energy investors need to implement hedging measures, such as futures contracts and options, to safeguard against extended volatility. Diversifying into alternate energy sources helps decrease risks associated with geopolitical disruptions. Oil-producing nations ought to sustain strategic reserves to mitigate severe price volatility.

One of the major challenges of the current study was to measure global uncertainty, a complex and multifaceted term shaped by political, economic, and social forces. The utilization of proxies like the World Uncertainty Index or financial market volatility may inadequately encompass all facets of uncertainty, possibly undermining the robustness of the results. Moreover, oil prices are affected by other factors, including supply-demand dynamics, technical advancements, and environmental regulations, which may obscure the correlation with global uncertainty. Data availability, particularly in emerging economies or during crises, may impose constraints on the analysis.

This analysis reveals no statistically significant direct long-term effect of geopolitical risk or trade policy uncertainty on WTI crude oil prices during the examined period, despite the common expectation that these factors influence market sentiment and supply disruption forecasts. Cointegration indicates a long-term relationship among the variables; however, the individual impacts of geopolitical risk and trade policy uncertainty are feeble and ambiguous. This indicates that although these factors may influence short-term volatility or interact with other economic conditions, they are not definitive determinants of long-term crude oil price fluctuations in isolation.

This book chapter explored the influential relationship between the global uncertainties such as the trade war and geopolitical risks on crude oil market. As there remains significant supply shocks with respect to crude oil, the analysis of the impact of the two crucial factors were paramount to understand those shocks. The results underlined the complex dynamics of the global markets, aligning with Bloomberg data, leading to the possibility of future research on this area.

REFERENCES

Alqahtani, A., & Klein, T. (2021). Oil price changes, uncertainty, and geopolitical risks: On the resilience of GCC countries to global tensions. *Energy*, *236*, 121541. DOI: 10.1016/j.energy.2021.121541

Bouoiyour, J., Selmi, R., Hammoudeh, S., & Wohar, M. E. (2019). What are the categories of geopolitical risks that could drive oil prices higher? Acts or threats? *Energy Economics*, *84*, 104523. DOI: 10.1016/j.eneco.2019.104523

Cunado, J., Gupta, R., Lau, C. K. M., & Sheng, X. (2020). Time-varying impact of geopolitical risks on oil prices. *Defence and Peace Economics*, *31*(6), 692–706. DOI: 10.1080/10242694.2018.1563854

Duan, W., Khurshid, A., Rauf, A., Khan, K., & Calin, A. C. (2021). How geopolitical risk drives exchange rate and oil prices? A wavelet-based analysis. *Energy Sources. Part B, Economics, Planning, and Policy*, *16*(9), 861–877. DOI: 10.1080/15567249.2021.1965262

Gkillas, K., Manickavasagam, J., & Visalakshmi, S. (2022). Effects of fundamentals, geopolitical risk and expectations factors on crude oil prices. *Resources Policy*, *78*, 102887. DOI: 10.1016/j.resourpol.2022.102887

Ivanovski, K., & Hailemariam, A. (2022). Time-varying geopolitical risk and oil prices. *International Review of Economics & Finance*, *77*, 206–221. DOI: 10.1016/j.iref.2021.10.001

Kilian, L., Plante, M., & Richter, A. W. (2024). Geopolitical oil price risk. Federal Reserve Bank of Dallas, Working Paper No. 2403. https://www.dallasfed.org/~/media/documents/research/papers/2024/wp2403.pdf

Lau, C. K., Soliman, A. M., Albasu, J., & Gozgor, G. (2023). Dependence structures among geopolitical risks, energy prices, and carbon emissions prices. *Resources Policy*, *83*, 103603. DOI: 10.1016/j.resourpol.2023.103603

Li, X., Umar, M., Zhu, C. B., & Oprean-Stan, C. (2023). Can geopolitical risk stably predict crude oil prices? A multi-dimensional perspective. *Resources Policy*, *85*, 103785. DOI: 10.1016/j.resourpol.2023.103785

Qian, L., Zeng, Q., & Li, T. (2022). Geopolitical risk and oil price volatility: Evidence from Markov-switching model. *International Review of Economics & Finance*, *81*, 29–38. DOI: 10.1016/j.iref.2022.05.002

Shahbaz, M., Sharif, A., Soliman, A. M., Jiao, Z., & Hammoudeh, S. (2024). Oil prices and geopolitical risk: Fresh insights based on Granger-causality in quantiles analysis. *International Journal of Finance & Economics, 29*(3), 2865–2881. DOI: 10.1002/ijfe.2806

Smales, L. A. (2021). Geopolitical risk and volatility spillovers in oil and stock markets. *The Quarterly Review of Economics and Finance, 80*, 358–366. DOI: 10.1016/j.qref.2021.03.008

Su, C. W., Khan, K., Tao, R., & Nicoleta-Claudia, M. (2019). Does geopolitical risk strengthen or depress oil prices and financial liquidity? Evidence from Saudi Arabia. *Energy, 187*, 116003. DOI: 10.1016/j.energy.2019.116003

Wang, K. H., Su, C. W., & Umar, M. (2021). Geopolitical risk and crude oil security: A Chinese perspective. *Energy, 219*, 119555. DOI: 10.1016/j.energy.2020.119555

Wang, Y. (2022). Geopolitical risk, economic policy uncertainty and crude oil prices: A wavelet-based analysis. *International Review of Economics & Finance, 82*, 524–546. DOI: 10.1016/j.iref.2022.07.015

Weiss, T. G. (1994). The United Nations and civil wars. *The Washington Quarterly, 17*(4), 139–159. DOI: 10.1080/01636609409443755

Wu, J., Zhao, R., Sun, J., & Zhou, X. (2023). Impact of geopolitical risks on oil price fluctuations: Based on GARCH-MIDAS model. *Resources Policy, 85*, 103982. DOI: 10.1016/j.resourpol.2023.103982

Zhang, Z., He, M., Zhang, Y., & Wang, Y. (2022). Geopolitical risk trends and crude oil price predictability. *Energy, 258*, 124824. DOI: 10.1016/j.energy.2022.124824

Chapter 8
China's Geopolitical Strategy in Trade Policy: Navigating Strategic Autonomy and Global Influence

Marc Selgas-Cors
https://orcid.org/0000-0002-3074-3310
University of the Basque Country, Spain

ABSTRACT

This chapter examines the geopolitical dimensions of China's trade policy by analyzing how the People's Republic of China strategically leverages trade as an instrument of power to achieve greater strategic autonomy and expand its global influence in a rapidly shifting international order, particularly in the face of escalating tensions with the United States; it explores core policy instruments such as the Belt and Road Initiative, the Dual Circulation Strategy, and the Digital Silk Road, while also evaluating China's engagement with multilateral institutions, its efforts to securitize key supply chains, and its ambitions to reform global trade governance, concluding that China's trade strategy should be understood not merely as economic policy but as an integrated component of a grand geopolitical strategy aimed at reshaping the global order in line with its normative preferences and long-term interests.

1. INTRODUCTION

The international order is undergoing a profound transformation, and China stands at the center of this tectonic shift. As the People's Republic of China (PRC) increasingly integrates geostrategic ambitions into its trade policy, it challenges traditional separations between economics and geopolitics. What was once conceived

DOI: 10.4018/979-8-3373-3835-4.ch008

as a benign and market-driven engagement with globalization is now being reconfigured by Beijing into a comprehensive strategy aimed at reinforcing its strategic autonomy and extending global influence. Trade is no longer merely an economic instrument; for China, it has become an essential tool in crafting a multipolar world order more conducive to its interests and values. While debates about "decoupling," "friend-shoring," and "strategic competition" have become commonplace in Western policy discourse, they often overlook the depth and coherence of China's own grand strategy. In Beijing's view, trade is not only about market access or comparative advantage, but also about safeguarding national sovereignty, projecting soft and hard power, and defending civilizational legitimacy in an increasingly contested global arena (Jin, 2023).

The concept of "strategic autonomy" has traditionally been associated with actors like the European Union (Kim, 2023; Huang, 2024), yet it is now deeply embedded in China's foreign policy discourse as well. This autonomy does not imply isolationism; rather, it signals a calibrated effort to ensure that key nodes of national power, especially technology, logistics, and critical infrastructure, are shielded from external coercion. Beijing's response to the U.S.-led trade war, as well as its ongoing economic repositioning through strategies such as the Dual Circulation Policy and the Belt and Road Initiative (BRI), reflect a concerted effort to rebalance dependence on foreign markets while leveraging economic ties for geopolitical ends (Hart, 2021; Rai, 2022; Rolland, 2019).

At the heart of China's trade-geopolitical nexus lies a reinterpretation of globalism. No longer satisfied with being a participant in a liberal international order shaped by Western norms, China is attempting to reshape the architecture itself. As Mazzocco (2025) argues, the PRC's engagement with energy, technology, and infrastructure in response to trade conflict with the U.S. is illustrative of a broader ambition: to cultivate resilience against external shocks and to build influence among the Global South. Similarly, Rolland (2019) identifies in BRI not just as an infrastructure network, but a deliberate soft power and influence operation embedded in geopolitical logics of alignment and dependence.

Importantly, this strategic reorientation takes place amid growing geopolitical fragmentation. Jean (2024) emphasizes that, while global trade fragmentation is often overstated, certain "hotspots", particularly the U.S.-China bilateral relationship, are indeed experiencing clear geoeconomic decoupling. In these zones, trade flows increasingly reflect strategic realignment rather than market efficiency. For China, this fragmentation creates both challenges and opportunities: challenges, in terms of reduced access to critical foreign technologies and markets; opportunities, in the sense that it accelerates China's push toward industrial upgrading, regional leadership, and alternative institutional formations (Jean, 2024).

Indeed, the "Malacca Dilemma"[1], China's perceived vulnerability in maritime chokepoints, remains emblematic of the security anxieties shaping its trade behavior (Chen, 2010). It is in response to these vulnerabilities that China has expanded its overland connectivity via Central Asia, Africa, and even the Arctic. Through trade corridors and port acquisitions, the PRC seeks not only commercial benefit but strategic redundancy, ensuring that no single actor, particularly the United States, can control its economic lifelines.

Meanwhile, the logic of economic statecraft pervades China's foreign engagements. From resource agreements in Latin America and Africa to tech partnerships in Eurasia, China's trade and investment decisions are increasingly aligned with diplomatic strategy. Even in multilateral settings, such as the Asian Infrastructure Investment Bank (AIIB) or the Regional Comprehensive Economic Partnership (RCEP), Beijing's objective is not simply integration but influence. As Dar and Javid (2025) note, China's geopolitical rivalry with the U.S. is as much about ideas and norms as it is about GDP and trade volumes. It is a contest over whose vision of economic order will prevail in a post-Western world.

This geopolitical framing of trade also affects China's domestic political economy. The Chinese Communist Party (CCP) has consolidated greater central control over strategic sectors, invested heavily in state-led innovation, and reasserted ideological leadership in economic planning. The fusion of national rejuvenation narratives with economic policy goals, under slogans such as "common prosperity" or "self-reliance in science and technology", illustrates how internal political stability and external strategic positioning are mutually reinforcing (Jin, 2023).

But China's strategy is not without contradictions. As Ul Mansoor (2024) points out, Beijing's pursuit of a new world order is complicated by normative tensions. While China promotes values of sovereignty and non-interference abroad, its assertiveness in the South China Sea or vis-à-vis Taiwan undermines its credibility among smaller powers. Moreover, China's partnerships with authoritarian regimes, and its ambiguous role in upholding international labor and environmental standards, raise critical questions about the sustainability and legitimacy of its geopolitical trade agenda (Dar & Javid, 2025).

To understand China's trade strategy today, one must therefore move beyond the binaries of free trade vs. protectionism, or globalization vs. nationalism. Instead, we must examine how trade has become a vector of statecraft, intertwined with military preparedness, institutional diplomacy, digital infrastructure, and ideological projection. In this sense, China's approach resembles what Barry Buzan and Ole Wæver have described in security studies as "securitization"[2], the process of politicizing an issue to the extent that extraordinary measures become legitimate responses.

2. STRATEGIC AUTONOMY IN CHINESE TRADE POLICY

The pursuit of strategic autonomy has emerged as a defining feature of China's trade policy in the post-2010 era. While Western economies have debated the meaning of economic sovereignty in an interdependent world, Beijing has acted decisively to insulate itself from external vulnerabilities. This has manifested in an increasingly interventionist industrial policy, a commitment to technological self-reliance, and a recalibration of trade priorities through the Dual Circulation Strategy (DCS)[3]. These moves are not merely defensive but form part of a broader vision to reassert China's place in the global order, less as a dependent actor within a liberal trade regime and more as an architect of a new, multipolar structure.

2.1 From Integration to Insulation: The Evolution of Strategic Thinking

Historically, China's economic rise was predicated on integration into global markets. The accession to the World Trade Organization (WTO) in 2001 symbolized a turning point in China's embrace of globalization. However, the ensuing decades also exposed Beijing to the risks of external dependence, particularly in high-tech components, critical raw materials, and energy flows (Chen, 2010). These vulnerabilities became increasingly intolerable in the context of intensifying U.S.-China strategic rivalry.

The "Malacca Dilemma", China's reliance on sea routes controlled or patrolled by rival naval powers, serves as a paradigmatic case of Beijing's concerns over strategic chokepoints (Chen, 2010). In response, the PRC began diversifying its supply routes through land-based infrastructure projects (e.g., China-Pakistan Economic Corridor) and strategic port acquisitions in Southeast Asia and the Indian Ocean. Such efforts reflect an understanding of trade as an extension of national security, where access and autonomy go hand in hand.

2.2 The Dual Circulation Strategy: Internalizing Growth Drivers

The formalization of the DCS in 2020 marked a doctrinal shift in Chinese economic policy. Rather than relying primarily on external demand, the DCS prioritizes "internal circulation", domestic consumption, indigenous innovation, and self-sufficient supply chains, as the foundation of sustainable growth (Hart, 2021). External circulation, in turn, supports these domestic objectives but is no longer the driver. This approach was catalyzed by the COVID-19 pandemic, which exposed the fragility of global supply chains, and by the escalating U.S.-China trade war, which highlighted the strategic risks of technological dependence. Beijing's response was swift: ramping up investment in semiconductors, electric vehicles, AI, and green technologies, areas where China aims to lead without relying on foreign firms (Mazzocco, 2025; McKinsey Global Institute, 2025). Moreover, the DCS is closely tied to President Xi Jinping's narrative of "great national rejuvenation," in which economic resilience is indispensable to political sovereignty. As such, the policy is not purely economic but deeply ideological, reflecting the Party's emphasis on stability, control, and long-term strategic orientation (Jin, 2023).

2.3 Industrial Policy and Technological Sovereignty

A cornerstone of China's quest for strategic autonomy is its reindustrialization agenda. "Made in China 2025,"[4] introduced in 2015, laid the groundwork for a state-led transformation of China's manufacturing base, with the aim of climbing up the value chain and reducing dependence on foreign technology in ten key sectors, including robotics, aerospace, and new energy vehicles. Despite facing strong backlash from the U.S. and EU, the initiative has continued under different branding, reinforced by increased funding and institutional backing (Jean, 2024).

The emphasis on technological sovereignty intensified during the U.S. sanctions on firms such as Huawei and SMIC. These actions revealed the fragility of China's access to advanced semiconductors, most of which depend on U.S. or allied supply chains. In response, Beijing launched the "New Infrastructure" campaign, investing over ¥10 trillion in digital infrastructure, AI, and 5G, signaling that the future of trade competitiveness lies in technological leadership, not cheap labor (Rolland, 2019). The strategic rationale is clear: by mastering core technologies, China can shield itself from coercive leverage and ensure control over the rules of future industries. It also allows Beijing to export "digital standards" through initiatives like Digital Silk Road[5], thereby projecting normative influence abroad.

a. Strategic Commodities and Energy Resilience

China's vulnerability in energy and strategic minerals has also driven its pursuit of autonomy. The U.S.-China trade war, combined with tightening export controls on rare earths and semiconductors, underscored the geopolitical stakes of resource security. Beijing responded by accelerating its green energy transition, both as a domestic imperative and as a hedge against future sanctions (Mazzocco, 2025). In addition, China has been acquiring stakes in lithium, cobalt, and nickel mines across Latin America and Africa, ensuring access to materials essential for battery production. These moves are strategically motivated, aimed at consolidating control over the entire supply chain of clean tech industries (WEF, 2024). The PRC is also investing heavily in energy corridors with Russia, Central Asia, and the Middle East, diversifying away from maritime choke points and the dollar-based oil trade.

This orientation is supported by the integration of financial instruments, such as the expansion of the renminbi in trade settlements and the development of a central bank digital currency (CBDC), to reduce reliance on the U.S. dollar and Swift-based payments (Trends Research, 2025). Monetary autonomy thus complements trade and technological autonomy, creating a more sovereign economic architecture.

2.4 Governance, Control, and the Domestic Nexus

Strategic autonomy also implies greater centralization of decision-making within the Chinese political economy. Under Xi Jinping, the boundaries between state and market have blurred. Private firms are now expected to align with national priorities, particularly in sectors deemed strategic. This has resulted in regulatory crackdowns on big tech, tighter control over data flows, and enhanced coordination between party organs and corporate actors (Jin, 2023).

The securitization of China's economy, defined as the framing of economic sectors and decisions as matters of national security, represents a fundamental transformation in the relationship between state and market. Under Xi Jinping's leadership, this approach has become institutionalized through an expansive interpretation of what constitutes "strategic sectors," extending far beyond traditional defense industries to encompass digital platforms, fintech, logistics, and even education (Jin, 2023). This has resulted in the Party-state embedding itself more directly in the governance of the economy, not merely as a regulator but as a co-manager of capital, data, and innovation.

The rationale for this shift is rooted in the external geopolitical environment. From Beijing's perspective, the weaponization of trade, technology, and finance by the United States, illustrated by sanctions on firms like Huawei and ZTE, or the exclusion of China from advanced semiconductor supply chains, requires an internal countermeasure rooted in resilience and control (Mazzocco, 2025). The state sees itself as the only actor capable of orchestrating a national response to these multifaceted threats. Consequently, mechanisms such as the "military-civil fusion" strategy and the imposition of party committees in major private firms aim to align corporate interests with strategic imperatives (Rolland, 2019).

However, this approach carries significant trade-offs. By subordinating market logic to national security logic, China risks undermining the very dynamism that powered its economic ascent. The regulatory clampdown on firms like Alibaba, Didi, and Ant Group in 2020–2021 signaled a turning point: rather than promoting entrepreneurship, the state prioritized ideological conformity and systemic risk management (Jean, 2024). This has had chilling effects on venture capital, foreign direct investment, and private-sector confidence.

Moreover, excessive securitization may reduce institutional flexibility in responding to fast-changing global trends. Innovation thrives in environments of openness, pluralism, and contestation, traits that are increasingly constrained under China's tightening political regime. Despite these limitations, the Party appears willing to tolerate slower growth in exchange for enhanced control, viewing this trade-off as essential to long-term sovereignty and regime stability (Dar & Javid, 2025). Ultimately, the securitization of the economy encapsulates China's broader dilemma: how to insulate itself from a hostile global order without sacrificing the openness that made its rise possible. It is a delicate balancing act, and one that will shape not only the future of Chinese capitalism, but also the architecture of global trade itself.

3. GLOBAL INFLUENCE THROUGH TRADE: TOOLS AND TACTICS

China's growing economic power is not merely an instrument of national development but a core component of its geopolitical toolkit. Beyond the logic of strategic autonomy, Beijing has developed a sophisticated apparatus of trade-driven influence to shape the global order. This includes massive infrastructure investments, influence operations through connectivity projects, the establishment of alternative financial institutions, and the promotion of digital standards via the Digital Silk Road. Collectively, these mechanisms embody a "geo-economic statecraft" that advances China's interests by binding other nations into asymmetric but functional dependencies.

3.1 Belt and Road Initiative: Infrastructure as Strategy

Perhaps the most emblematic expression of China's global trade ambitions is the Belt and Road Initiative (BRI), launched in 2013. Far from a mere economic development program, the BRI is a geopolitical project that seeks to rewire the arteries of global commerce around Chinese capital, standards, and logistical dominance (Rolland, 2019). Through investments in roads, ports, railways, and energy infrastructure across Asia, Africa, and Europe, China is constructing a physical and normative alternative to Western-led globalization.

Figure 1. Number of Participating Countries by Chinese Trade Initiative

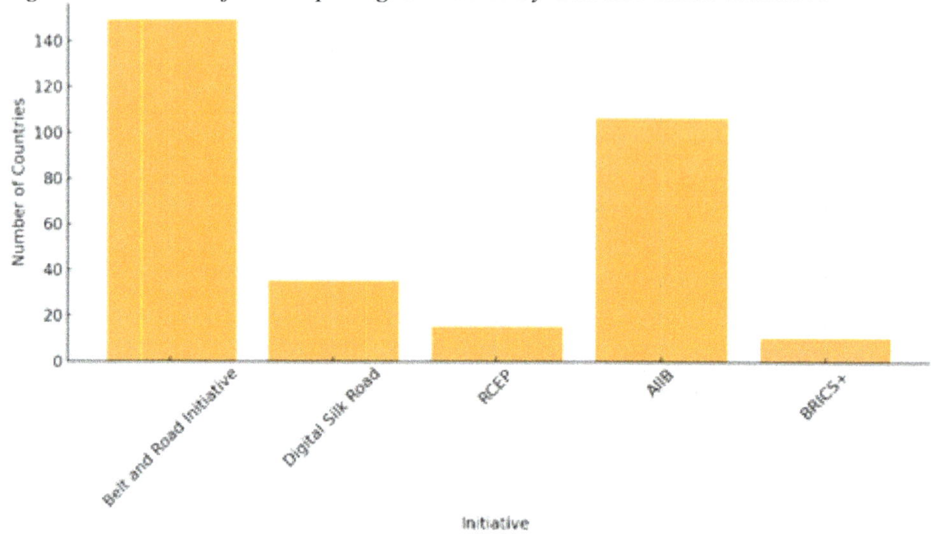

Source: Author's elaboration based on data from AIIB (2024), RCEP Secretariat (2023), and Rolland (2019).

Strategically located ports such as Gwadar (Pakistan), Hambantota (Sri Lanka), and Djibouti are more than trade hubs, they are nodes in a geopolitical network enabling China to secure maritime routes, project influence in critical chokepoints, and develop a string of strategic footholds along the Indian Ocean and beyond (Chen, 2010; Mansoor, 2024). These investments often come with opaque financial terms and are backed by Chinese state-owned enterprises (SOEs) and banks, making recipient countries reliant on Beijing for both capital and debt relief.

Critics argue that BRI sometimes induces "debt-trap diplomacy,"[6]. However, others interpret this as a symptom of poor governance in recipient states rather than deliberate coercion (Rai, 2022). Moreover, the BRI serves a dual purpose: it stimulates demand for Chinese construction materials and labor while locking in long-term trade partnerships that bypass Western supply chains. In so doing, China is not merely exporting infrastructure, it is exporting dependency and reshaping trade geography on its own terms.

3.2 The Digital Silk Road: Data, Norms, and Technopower

Complementing the physical infrastructure of the BRI is the DSR, a suite of initiatives aimed at promoting Chinese digital platforms, standards, and surveillance infrastructure abroad. Since 2015, the DSR has expanded to include undersea cables, 5G technology, satellite navigation systems (BeiDou), and AI governance frameworks.

The strategic rationale behind DSR is clear: control over digital infrastructure translates into both economic influence and information power. Countries that adopt Huawei or ZTE's 5G systems, for instance, often depend on Chinese technical expertise, maintenance services, and data protocols. This creates long-term dependencies that extend beyond hardware into software governance, data storage, and regulatory convergence (Jean, 2024). Moreover, through the DSR, China positions itself as a normative power in shaping global standards on AI ethics, cyber sovereignty, and digital privacy, areas where Western norms are no longer uncontested. This is particularly attractive to authoritarian or hybrid regimes seeking alternatives to liberal data governance models (Mansoor, 2024). Thus, the DSR exemplifies how trade in digital goods and services can evolve into a vehicle of ideological diffusion. China's push for its own digital currency, the e-CNY, and the development of blockchain-based trade logistics further demonstrate its ambition to reduce reliance on Western financial systems such as SWIFT. The DSR not only diversifies China's trade portfolio but also embeds its technological architecture in the fabric of global commerce.

3.3 Alternative Financial Institutions and Strategic Lending

Parallel to its trade and technological outreach, China has championed the creation of alternative financial institutions that challenge the hegemony of the Bretton Woods system. The Asian Infrastructure Investment Bank (AIIB) and the New Development Bank (NDB) are two such bodies designed to offer financing without the conditionalities often imposed by the IMF or World Bank.

These institutions allow China to project "soft authority"[7] in regions where Western financing is either absent or politically contentious. By controlling a significant voting share and leadership positions within the AIIB, Beijing can influence the direction of investment flows toward BRI-aligned projects. This not only reinforces China's role as a capital provider but also fosters a perception of China as a "responsible stakeholder" in global development, an image it is keen to promote (Rai, 2022; Rolland, 2019). China has also employed bilateral lending through "policy banks" like the China Development Bank and Export-Import Bank of China. While often framed as win-win cooperation, these loans have raised concerns about hidden debts, lack of transparency, and economic overexposure in low-income countries. For Beijing, however, the strategic logic remains compelling: such financial engagements enhance leverage and align foreign policy interests with economic tools.

3.4 Commercial Diplomacy and Influence Operations

Beyond infrastructure and finance, China engages in subtle yet effective influence operations under the guise of commercial diplomacy. This includes elite capture, media investments, and educational exchanges that aim to cultivate favorable perceptions among business and political elites in partner countries. Rolland (2019) and Ul-Mansoor (2024) document how many of these operations are embedded within BRI contracts or institutional partnerships. For instance, Confucius Institutes often operate alongside economic development projects, blending cultural diplomacy with soft power acquisition. Similarly, think tanks and academic forums funded by Chinese actors contribute to shaping intellectual and policy discourse around trade and investment, frequently favoring Chinese narratives.

One example is China's sponsorship of economic research in Africa and Southeast Asia, which frames Chinese trade and investment as inherently beneficial while downplaying negative social or environmental externalities. This discursive power complements China's material engagements, allowing Beijing to shape not only the trade flows but also the epistemologies through which those flows are understood. In Latin America, similar tactics have been used in promoting large-scale projects in Argentina, Brazil, and Ecuador, often involving non-transparent deals, elite co-optation, and a parallel diplomacy that bypasses traditional foreign policy channels.

3.5 Trade Dependencies and Supply Chain Management

A less visible but equally important dimension of China's trade influence lies in the creation of critical dependencies through supply chain restructuring. Over the last decade, Beijing has sought to make itself indispensable in sectors ranging from rare earth minerals to pharmaceuticals, solar panels, and electric vehicle components.

By dominating the upstream segments of global supply chains, China can exert leverage without direct confrontation. For instance, its near-monopoly in rare earth processing gives it de facto control over the production of key military and technological components worldwide (WEF, 2024). Similarly, its command of solar panel manufacturing allows it to influence the green energy agendas of countries from the EU to Africa. These dependencies are not accidental; they are nurtured through subsidies, vertical integration, and long-term trade agreements that entrench China's position. While some countries have sought to diversify supply chains post-COVID-19, the reality remains that many sectors are still structurally reliant on Chinese production and logistics (Jean, 2024).

Moreover, China has used these dependencies as both deterrents and incentives. During trade disputes, it has restricted exports of critical materials or raised regulatory hurdles for foreign firms, subtly reminding partners of the costs of confrontation.

Conversely, it offers preferential access, infrastructure, or financing to those who align with its trade and political preferences.

Table 1. Chinese Trade Initiatives and Global Reach

	Initiative	Participating Countries	Estimated Influence Score (1-10)
1	Belt and Road Initiative	149	9.5
2	Digital Silk Road	35	7.8
3	RCEP	15	8.2
4	AIIB	106	8.5
5	BRICS+	10	7.0

Source: Compiled by the author based on WTO, CPTPP, BRI, RCEP, and AIIB policy documents and academic sources (Jean, 2024; Rai, 2022; Rolland, 2019).

4. CHINA AND THE RECONFIGURATION OF THE GLOBAL TRADE ORDER

China's trade strategy in the 21st century has moved beyond mere participation in the global economy. It is now a conscious effort to reshape the international trade order itself. No longer a passive rule-taker, Beijing seeks to recast the architecture of global trade in a manner that reflects its political values, strategic interests, and developmental models. This evolution, from integration to transformation, is central to understanding China's emergence as a revisionist actor within the international system. The reconfiguration of the global trade order is not merely a consequence of China's rise; it is a deliberate policy trajectory embedded in its broader vision of national rejuvenation and geopolitical influence.

From its accession to the World Trade Organization in 2001, China leveraged the liberal international economic order to fuel an unprecedented period of growth and industrial modernization. Yet, while it embraced global markets, it never fully internalized the liberal norms that underpinned them. Rather than dismantling its state-capitalist model, China adapted WTO rules to its advantage, maintaining significant state influence over strategic sectors. Over time, as China's economic weight grew, so did its confidence, and its willingness to challenge the institutional and normative foundations of global trade.

The BRI is perhaps the most emblematic instrument of this reconfiguration. Initially presented as a development and connectivity program, the BRI has evolved into a geopolitical project that blends infrastructure investment, trade facilitation, and political influence. Through the construction of ports, highways, railways, and digital infrastructure across Asia, Africa, and Europe, China is creating new trade corridors that bypass traditional Western-dominated routes. More than a network of physical assets, the BRI is a strategy to institutionalize China's centrality in regional and global value chains (Rolland, 2019). Its logic is one of interdependence on Chinese terms, where infrastructure creates dependency, and dependency generates influence.

Strategic ports such as Gwadar in Pakistan, Hambantota in Sri Lanka, and Piraeus in Greece illustrate the dual commercial and geopolitical function of BRI assets. These nodes not only facilitate trade but also extend China’s logistical and, potentially, military reach. The Digital Silk Road further expands this influence into the virtual realm, embedding Chinese technology standards and infrastructure, such as 5G networks, fiber-optic cables, and satellite navigation systems, across partner countries. This digital layer of trade infrastructure raises normative questions around data governance, cybersecurity, and technological sovereignty, and highlights how China’s trade strategy fuses the economic with the ideological.

Crucially, China is not operating in a vacuum. Its assertiveness has coincided with, and to some extent exploited, the retreat of the United States from multilateralism under successive administrations. The American withdrawal from the Trans-Pacific Partnership and the Trump-era tariffs created space for China to present itself as a defender of globalization. The signing of the RCEP, a mega-trade deal encompassing China, ASEAN countries, Japan, South Korea, Australia, and New Zealand, consolidated China’s leadership in regional trade governance without committing to the high standards of labor, environment, or digital trade promoted in Western-led agreements.

In parallel, China has promoted alternative financial and institutional structures. The AIIB, the New Development Bank (formerly BRICS Bank), and increased bilateral currency swap agreements aim to reduce dependence on the U.S., dominated Bretton Woods system. These institutions reflect China’s dissatisfaction with its underrepresentation in existing global financial institutions and its desire to shape new rules more aligned with its state-led development model. The use of the renminbi in international transactions and the experimentation with a digital yuan are also part of a broader strategy to challenge the dominance of the dollar and promote a multipolar monetary system.

At a normative level, China’s approach to trade governance promotes principles of sovereignty, non-interference, and developmental pragmatism. These principles resonate with many countries in the Global South that see in Beijing a partner that offers infrastructure and investment without imposing political conditionalities. In forums such as the Forum on China-Africa Cooperation (FOCAC) or the China-CELAC Forum in Latin America, China deploys a narrative of South-South solidarity and shared development. This rhetorical framework is central to China's soft power strategy but also masks the asymmetries and dependencies that often characterize these relationships (Rai, 2022).

China’s vision of global trade is thus not anti-globalization per se, but rather an alternative globalization. One that is more state-centric, less liberal, and more strategically conditional. In this sense, China is engaging in what scholars have termed “normative hedging” (Jean, 2024): complying with certain international rules while building parallel frameworks that insulate it from external pressure. This dual-track strategy is evident in how China navigates the WTO: defending the multilateral system rhetorically while simultaneously pursuing bilateral deals, economic coercion, and issue-specific coalitions that bypass WTO mechanisms.

The consequences of this approach are profound. On the one hand, China’s proactive role in trade and infrastructure development has addressed real gaps in global public goods provision, especially in infrastructure finance. On the other hand, it has contributed to a fragmentation of global trade governance, where competing standards, institutions, and alliances create overlapping and sometimes contradictory frameworks. This fragmentation weakens the enforcement capacity of global rules and increases the space for power politics in trade relations. Moreover, China's increasing use of coercive economic statecraft, such as restricting exports of rare earths, imposing import bans on Australian goods, or weaponizing market access to punish critical countries, undermines the norms of predictability and rule-based behavior that are central to global commerce. This has prompted countermeasures from other major economies. The European Union’s anti-coercion instrument, the G7’s discussions on “economic resilience,” and Indo-Pacific supply chain initiatives are all, to some extent, responses to China’s perceived manipulation of interdependence for strategic gain.

Still, China’s ability to reconfigure the global trade order is constrained by structural and relational factors. Its economic model remains highly dependent on global demand, technological imports, and financial interconnectivity. Its infrastructure projects face growing scrutiny, and its normative appeal is limited by concerns about governance, transparency, and debt sustainability. Furthermore, while China has cultivated ties with the Global South, its relations with advanced economies remain tense and prone to escalation. The reconfiguration of the trade order is, therefore, not a unilateral process, but a contested one. China’s initiatives generate counter-reactions that shape the boundaries of its influence. The global trade landscape is moving toward a multipolar configuration, where overlapping spheres of rules and standards coexist, compete, and sometimes collide. In this environment, China's capacity to impose a coherent alternative order is limited, but its ability to shape the terrain of contestation is undeniable.

China’s role in global trade today is not merely that of a participant, but of an architect. Through infrastructure diplomacy, normative contestation, and institutional innovation, Beijing is crafting a new trade geography and governance model that reflects its interests and worldview. This process is reshaping how trade works, how it is governed, and who benefits from it. Whether this new order leads to greater inclusivity and balance, or to fragmentation and coercion, remains one of the defining questions of our time.

To better understand the extent of China's divergence from Western-led trade frameworks, the following table offers a comparative analysis across key governance dimensions. It highlights the philosophical and operational contrasts between liberal, rules-based systems and China’s more flexible, state-driven approach to trade. These distinctions have profound implications for the coherence of global trade governance and for the countries navigating between both poles.

Table 2. Comparison of Trade Governance Models

	Dimension	WTO/CPTPP (Western-led)	China-led (BRI, RCEP, AIIB)
1	Governance Model	Rules-based, multilateral	State-driven, strategic bilateralism
2	Core Principles	Transparency, liberalization, non-discrimination	Mutual benefit, infrastructure-led development
3	Membership Type	Open, often requires reform commitments	Flexible, project-driven, often bilateral
4	Approach to Sovereignty	Encourages legal harmonization and domestic reforms	Emphasizes non-interference and local autonomy
5	Digital Trade Rules	Strict rules on data privacy and cross-border flows	Technology infrastructure-driven; less focus on regulation
6	Environmental & Labor Standards	High standards with enforceable commitments	Minimal standards, with pragmatic adaptation
7	Dispute Resolution Mechanism	Independent dispute settlement bodies (e.g., WTO DSB)	Diplomatic or ad hoc, less formalized
8	Geopolitical Alignment	Primarily liberal democracies and market economies	Mixed regimes, Global South emphasis

Source: Author's elaboration based on WTO and CPTPP official documents, and secondary literature on BRI, RCEP, and AIIB (Jean, 2024; Rai, 2022; Rolland, 2019; Mansoor, 2024; Dar & Javid, 2025).

The comparative table highlights a fundamental bifurcation in the architecture of global trade governance. On one side, the Western-led models, represented here by the WTO and the Comprehensive and Progressive Agreement for Trans-Pacific Partnership (CPTPP), emphasize rules-based multilateralism, high regulatory standards, and formal dispute resolution. On the other, China-led initiatives such as the BRI, the RCEP, and the AIIB showcase a more pragmatic, state-centric, and flexible approach. This divergence is not merely institutional, it is deeply rooted in differing philosophies of economic order, sovereignty, and geopolitical influence.

The first and perhaps most fundamental distinction lies in the governance model. Western-led frameworks are typically institutionalized within international law, operating on consensus, and underpinned by predictable rule enforcement. In contrast, the Chinese model favors strategic bilateralism and state-driven coordination, which allows for more agility but often at the cost of legal consistency. This difference reflects the underlying values of liberal institutionalism versus strategic pragmatism: the former seeks to embed trade within a web of formal norms, while the latter uses trade as a vehicle for broader political or developmental objectives.

Closely tied to this is the dimension of core principles. WTO and CPTPP agreements prioritize liberalization, transparency, and non-discrimination. These norms aim to level the playing field and reduce barriers for all members equally. China's initiatives, however, emphasize "mutual benefit" and infrastructure-led development, focusing more on reciprocal arrangements and tangible outcomes rather than on abstract legal commitments. This approach resonates with many Global South countries, which often view Western conditionalities as intrusive or ideologically driven.

The membership structure further exemplifies this contrast. Whereas joining the WTO or CPTPP typically involves comprehensive domestic reforms and alignment with high-standard rules, participation in BRI or RCEP tends to be more flexible and less conditional. This allows China to expand its influence rapidly, especially among states with weaker institutional capacities or autocratic regimes that prioritize sovereignty over compliance. The project-based nature of many China-led agreements also means they are adaptive and transactional, appealing to countries seeking quick infrastructure or financing solutions.

Another critical axis is the approach to sovereignty. Western frameworks often encourage legal harmonization and internal policy reform as prerequisites for membership. This assumes that trade integration promotes domestic modernization. Conversely, China's trade strategy is grounded in a doctrine of non-interference. This allows participating countries to preserve policy autonomy, even as they deepen economic ties with Beijing. This posture is especially attractive to regimes wary of Western normative agendas on democracy, labor, or environment.

In the digital domain, the gap becomes even more apparent. Digital trade rules under the CPTPP include stringent provisions on data protection, cross-border data flows, and digital IP rights. These reflect Western anxieties about data sovereignty and the need for legal safeguards. In contrast, China's Digital Silk Road projects often embed Chinese hardware and software infrastructure without enforcing comparable regulatory norms. The result is a diffusion of Chinese technical standards and platforms, such as 5G, surveillance systems, or fintech tools, that enhance China's influence without imposing Western-style transparency or accountability.

When it comes to environmental and labor standards, the Western model again sets higher benchmarks. Agreements like the CPTPP include enforceable clauses on sustainable development, labor rights, and anti-corruption. These are intended to align trade with normative values and global public goods. By contrast, China's initiatives are more accommodating of local conditions, often omitting binding environmental or labor obligations. This has generated criticism about enabling ecological degradation or reinforcing authoritarian models, yet it also makes these frameworks more palatable to a broader range of partners.

Dispute resolution mechanisms represent another structural divergence. Western systems rely on formalized legal procedures, such as the WTO Dispute Settlement Body, designed to depoliticize conflicts and ensure procedural fairness. In contrast, dispute resolution under Chinese initiatives tends to be informal, ad hoc, or diplomatically mediated. This provides flexibility but lacks transparency and predictability, raising concerns among some partners about the enforceability of agreements and the possibility of coercion.

Finally, the table reveals stark differences in geopolitical alignment. Western frameworks are largely composed of liberal democracies and market economies, often aligned with the US or EU geopolitical orbit. China's networks, in contrast, are increasingly centered around the Global South, including a mix of emerging economies, resource-rich states, and authoritarian governments. This alignment reflects China's ambition to construct an alternative sphere of influence, one that is decoupled from Western norms and institutions, and more reflective of a multipolar global order.

Taken together, the contrasts outlined in the table point to a deeper reality: China's trade strategy is not simply about market access or economic growth. It is about rewriting the rules of engagement in global trade in a way that better serves its strategic interests and ideological preferences. While Western frameworks aim to universalize liberal norms through trade, China's initiatives seek to instrumentalize trade as a pillar of its grand strategy, blending economic connectivity with political loyalty, technological dependence, and institutional diffusion.

This bifurcation has profound implications for the coherence of the global trade system. As more countries become embedded in both Western and Chinese networks, the risk of normative fragmentation increases. This can lead to regulatory inconsistencies, competing technical standards, and divergent dispute resolution practices, all of which complicate the functioning of global markets. Moreover, it forces states to navigate an increasingly bifurcated environment, where trade choices are not only economic, but also geopolitical.

5. STRATEGIC RIVALRIES: THE US-CHINA TRADE WAR AND REGIONAL IMPLICATIONS

5.1 Reactions to China's Strategic Trade Assertiveness

China's increasingly assertive trade policy has provoked diverse responses across the globe, ranging from strategic decoupling and supply chain diversification to outright defensive coalitions. In the eyes of many Western policymakers, China's trade behavior reflects not merely commercial ambition but a deeper project of geopolitical revisionism. This interpretation has been most pronounced in the United States, where trade policy toward China has undergone a paradigmatic shift. Since the Trump administration's imposition of sweeping tariffs in 2018, the United States has progressively framed its economic relationship with China in terms of national security and systemic rivalry (Mazzocco, 2025). Rather than reversing course, the Biden administration has institutionalized this logic through policies such as the CHIPS and Science Act, as well as strategic export controls on advanced semiconductors, artificial intelligence, and quantum technologies (McKinsey Global Institute, 2025).

The logic of "small yard, high fence"[8] has come to define Washington's approach to critical technologies, with the intent of preserving U.S. leadership in foundational sectors while limiting China's access to key inputs and know-how (Zhang & Chang, 2020). This decoupling strategy, often cloaked in the language of "de-risking," aims to insulate Western innovation ecosystems from perceived Chinese espionage, IP theft, and coercive leverage. While this has undoubtedly affected Chinese firms, most notably Huawei, ZTE, and SMIC, it has also triggered a broader recalibration of global value chains, as multinational companies begin to rethink their exposure to China-related risks.

Europe, while adopting a more tempered discourse, has followed a similar trajectory. The European Commission now defines China as a "partner, competitor, and systemic rival", a formulation that reflects growing unease with Beijing's assertiveness in areas ranging from trade subsidies to political interference (Jean, 2024). European Union policy instruments such as the Anti-Coercion Instrument, the Carbon Border Adjustment Mechanism (CBAM), and the proposed restrictions on outbound investment reflect a growing willingness to use economic tools for strategic ends. Recent investigations into Chinese subsidies in electric vehicles and solar panels signal the EU's readiness to defend its industrial base against what it perceives as predatory practices (Rolland, 2019).

Meanwhile, regional powers such as India and Japan have opted for strategies of "strategic distancing." India, in particular, has embraced a dual strategy of economic nationalism and global diversification. Through its Production-Linked Incentive (PLI) schemes and rising tariffs, New Delhi seeks to reduce dependency on Chinese imports while positioning itself as an alternative global manufacturing hub (Rai, 2022). Japan, for its part, has mobilized state subsidies to encourage the reshoring of critical industries and has actively participated in Quad-related initiatives aimed at creating standards-based trade architectures in the Indo-Pacific.

5.2 Structural Vulnerabilities in China's Trade Model

These external reactions intersect with profound structural vulnerabilities within China's own trade regime. While Beijing has presented its model as one of strategic autonomy and resilience, the reality is far more complex. The Chinese economy remains deeply integrated into global value chains, particularly in high-tech manufacturing, pharmaceuticals, and aviation. Despite sustained investments in indigenous innovation and industrial upgrading, China still relies heavily on foreign technologies, especially in semiconductor equipment, aerospace components, and precision machinery (Chen, 2010).

The U.S.-led restrictions on exports of advanced chipmaking tools from ASML and Tokyo Electron have effectively slowed China's progress in key strategic sectors, underscoring the limits of techno-nationalism in the face of global interdependence (Hart, 2021). Furthermore, the rapid buildup of technological capacity through programs like "Made in China 2025" has often relied on state subsidies and top-down coordination, which, while effective in mobilizing resources, can also generate inefficiencies, misallocations, and a disconnect between innovation and market demand (Jin, 2023).

Domestically, the Chinese economy faces additional constraints. Demographic decline, youth unemployment, and declining productivity growth all point to deeper macroeconomic fragilities. China's working-age population peaked in 2011, and the country's population as a whole is now shrinking, undermining the labor-intensive manufacturing advantage that once underpinned its export-led model (Jean, 2024). In parallel, political interventions in the private sectors such as the crackdown on tech giants like Ant Group and Didi have undermined investor confidence and discouraged risk-taking (Dar & Javid, 2025). These developments raise questions about whether China can simultaneously pursue economic dynamism and centralized political control without sacrificing long-term growth.

5.3 Coercive Diplomacy and the Weaponization of Trade

Perhaps one of the most controversial aspects of China's recent trade diplomacy has been its resort to economic coercion. Countries that have crossed Beijing's geopolitical red lines, whether over Taiwan, human rights, or strategic alignment with the United States, have often faced informal sanctions, bans, and other forms of pressure. Australia, for example, faced wide-ranging import restrictions on coal, wine, barley, and beef following its call for an independent inquiry into the origins of COVID-19 (Dar & Javid, 2025). Lithuania experienced Chinese retaliation after allowing Taiwan to open a representative office under its own name, including the de-listing of Lithuanian products from Chinese customs systems (PeaceDiplomacy, 2025).

Such actions have fueled perceptions that trade with China carries embedded political risks, leading to growing support for defensive trade instruments in the European Union and among U.S. allies. The EU's Anti-Coercion Instrument, passed in 2023, is explicitly designed to counter economic blackmail by third countries, with China as the clear though unspoken target (Rai, 2022). Similarly, frameworks such as the Indo-Pacific Economic Framework (IPEF) and the CPTPP seek to offer an alternative to Chinese-led initiatives by emphasizing transparency, labor standards, and rule-of-law principles.

Nevertheless, coercion has also had unintended consequences for Beijing. Rather than forcing policy reversals, it has often hardened foreign positions and accelerated diversification efforts. Australia, for instance, found new markets for its exports, while Lithuania received backing from the EU and enhanced ties with Taiwan and the United States. These outcomes suggest that while economic coercion can be disruptive, it rarely compels behavioral change in democratic systems. Moreover, it undermines China's efforts to present itself as a benign and reliable economic partner.

5.4 The Global South and China's Alternative Trade Vision

Despite tensions with the West, China continues to enjoy significant support from many countries in the Global South. The BRI, while facing mounting criticism over debt sustainability and transparency, remains attractive to governments in need of rapid infrastructure financing. China's willingness to invest in ports, railways, energy grids, and digital networks, often with fewer governance conditions than those imposed by the World Bank or IMF, makes it an appealing alternative for states with limited access to Western capital (Rolland, 2019).

In addition, China has increasingly turned to the DSR and financial innovation to deepen its trade influence. The promotion of the digital yuan, cross-border e-commerce platforms, and the internationalization of payment systems such as CIPS (Cross-Border Interbank Payment System) are part of a broader strategy to challenge the dollar's dominance and create parallel channels of exchange (The Diplomat, 2024). In regions like Africa, Latin America, and Central Asia, these initiatives are not merely economic but geopolitical: they symbolize a shift toward a multipolar order in which China can shape norms, standards, and flows.

Yet China's appeal is not without limits. Failures in BRI projects, such as the Hambantota Port in Sri Lanka or the Bar-Boljare highway in Montenegro, have sparked concerns about debt traps, corruption, and overbuilding. Local resistance, environmental controversies, and project delays have highlighted the risks of opaque governance and elite capture (Jean, 2024). As a result, China is recalibrating its BRI strategy, placing more emphasis on smaller, greener, and more commercially viable projects, a so-called "BRI 2.0" (Rolland, 2019).

5.5 Future Scenarios and Strategic Ambiguity

Looking ahead, the trajectory of China's trade diplomacy is marked by uncertainty and contradiction. On one hand, the PRC seeks to assert itself as an architect of a new global economic order, one rooted in multipolarity, state sovereignty, and developmental pragmatism. On the other hand, its increasing reliance on coercion, securitization, and political control may limit its capacity to inspire trust and institutional buy-in.

Three scenarios stand out as plausible futures. The first is strategic bifurcation, where the world divides into competing economic blocs led respectively by the United States and China. This would institutionalize fragmentation, with distinct supply chains, standards, and financial infrastructures. The second is managed multipolarity, where competition is moderated by pragmatic cooperation within hybrid institutional arrangements. This path would require mutual accommodation and reform from both sides. The third is strategic retrenchment, in which internal constraints force China to turn inward, reducing its global trade ambitions and focusing on domestic stability. Whichever path unfolds; trade will remain central to China's strategic toolkit. But its effectiveness will depend less on material capabilities than on how Beijing is perceived: as a reliable partner or a coercive hegemon, a reformer or a revisionist, a stabilizer or a disruptor.

6. THEORETICAL AND NORMATIVE IMPLICATIONS: CHINA'S TRADE POLICY AS GRAND STRATEGY

China's approach to trade policy cannot be adequately understood through the lens of standard economic theory or trade liberalization paradigms alone. Rather, it must be framed within the logic of *grand strategy*, a concept that encompasses the coordinated and purposeful use of all national resources, military, diplomatic, economic, and ideological, to achieve long-term geopolitical objectives (Brands, 2014). In this context, trade becomes not merely a vehicle for growth or industrial advancement but a foundational pillar of national power projection, regime legitimacy, and global system-shaping.

This section explores how China's trade policy operates as a manifestation of grand strategy, analyzing its theoretical underpinnings, institutional expression, and normative implications. It draws upon theories of strategic culture, geoeconomics, and global order to assess the extent to which the People's Republic of China (PRC) is reengineering trade into a strategic instrument that reflects its distinctive civilizational ethos and systemic ambitions.

6.1 Grand Strategy and the Reconfiguration of Trade

Grand strategy, as traditionally defined in international relations literature, is a long-term pattern of purposefully coordinated policies and actions intended to secure a state's interests in an uncertain and contested international environment (Posen, 2003). For China, the reformulation of trade policy in the 21st century fits this model: it aims to secure critical supply chains, project soft power, undermine rival coalitions, and build a world order more favorable to Chinese interests and values (Jin, 2023).

Beijing's recalibration of trade policy, from a vehicle of liberal integration to one of sovereign insulation and global outreach, reflects a sophisticated understanding of the strategic utility of economic exchange. Initiatives like the BRI, the DSR, and the promotion of the renminbi as an alternative reserve currency are not isolated economic programs but strategic vectors that serve political, security, and ideological functions simultaneously (Rolland, 2019).

This integration of trade into grand strategy can be seen in China's effort to reconfigure global interdependence. Instead of seeking autonomy through autarky, China practices *embedded mercantilism*: using its centrality in global trade networks as a source of leverage while simultaneously insulating key sectors from external coercion (Hart, 2021). This model echoes what Farrell and Newman (2019) describe as "weaponized interdependence," albeit from a counter-hegemonic perspective.

6.2 Strategic Culture and Chinese Statecraft

A key to understanding China's strategic use of trade lies in its *strategic culture*. Drawing from its long civilizational history, Chinese leaders adopt a temporally expansive and historically grounded approach to power. Classical thought, such as the writings of Sun Tzu and Confucian statecraft, prioritizes indirect control, relational hierarchy, and moral legitimacy over coercion per se (Wang, 2011). These ideas continue to inform contemporary practice through concepts such as *tianxia*[9] (all-under-heaven), which envisions a harmonious order centered on Chinese leadership.

Within this framework, economic interdependence is not an equal partnership but a mechanism for moral-political hierarchy. Trade relationships, infrastructure development, and financial assistance are embedded within a broader narrative of *civilizational responsibility*, in which China is portrayed as a stabilizing force correcting the disorder of Western-led globalization (Mansoor, 2024). The BRI's frequent references to "win-win cooperation" and "community of shared future for mankind" exemplify this normative framing.

Moreover, China's Leninist political system allows for a centralization of strategic economic planning that liberal democracies struggle to emulate. The existence of a Party-state apparatus, where economic actors are nested within ideological hierarchies, enables the CCP to pursue long-term objectives through instruments like state-owned enterprises (SOEs), sovereign wealth funds, and party committees embedded in private firms (Dar & Javid, 2025). This blend of political loyalty and economic capacity constitutes what some scholars term *geoeconomic statecraft* (Blackwill & Harris, 2016).

6.3 The Normative Challenge to Liberal Trade Order

China's grand strategic trade approach also raises profound normative questions about the future of global economic governance. Since World War II, the liberal trade order undermined by institutions such as the WTO, IMF, and World Bank, have been grounded in principles of non-discrimination, transparency, and multilateral rule-making. China's rise challenges this framework not through overt rejection but through subversion and reinterpretation.

Beijing has participated actively in multilateral institutions, often to reshape them from within. Its role in the AIIB, the BRICS New Development Bank, and alternative payments systems reflect efforts to create parallel institutions that dilute Western hegemony without abandoning the system entirely (Rai, 2022). Moreover, its trade diplomacy in the Global South emphasizes state-led development models, non-conditional lending, and the primacy of sovereignty over human rights and democratic conditionality.

Normatively, this represents a shift from a rules-based to a *transactional* model of global trade: one where power, proximity, and loyalty increasingly determine the structure of exchange. This model resonates in parts of the Global South, where Chinese financing is seen as less intrusive and more responsive to local elite interests. But it also risks reinforcing authoritarian governance, weakening environmental standards, and exacerbating debt dependence (Jean, 2024; The Diplomat, 2024).

6.4 Trade, Legitimacy, and Ideological Contestation

China's trade policy also serves a crucial domestic function: it reinforces the CCP's claim to legitimacy. Since Deng Xiaoping's reforms, economic performance has supplanted ideology as the primary basis of Party legitimacy. In this context, trade becomes both a symbol and a substance of the CCP's governing success. Trade surpluses, global connectivity, and technological self-sufficiency are celebrated as markers of national rejuvenation (*fuxing*) and collective pride. But legitimacy also requires ideological control. The securitization of trade, seen in policies like the DCS and restrictions on data outflows, reflects a shift from openness to *strategic closure*. This closure is not merely economic but cognitive: it aims to insulate China's population from foreign narratives, dependencies, and vulnerabilities (Mazzocco, 2025). Trade thus becomes a mechanism for the Party's ideological project, reinforcing its narrative of national exceptionalism and civilizational destiny.

Externally, China's trade diplomacy attempts to export this legitimacy model. Through Confucius Institutes, media partnerships, development aid, and investment in think tanks, China seeks to shape global understandings of development, sovereignty, and governance. Trade is the vector through which these values travel, enabling China to propose not just an alternative economic model but an alternative modernity (Mansoor, 2024; Zhang & Chang, 2020).

6.5 Theoretical Contributions and Emerging Research Agendas

From a theoretical standpoint, China's trade policy as grand strategy contributes to several important debates in international political economy. First, it complicates liberal theories that assume trade openness promotes convergence and cooperation. China's model suggests that trade can coexist with authoritarian resilience, state capitalism, and geopolitical rivalry, a finding that challenges the democratic peace and commercial liberalism traditions (Farrell & Newman, 2019).

Second, it revitalizes the field of *geoeconomics*, which emphasizes the use of economic instruments for geopolitical ends. Here, China exemplifies a mature geoeconomic actor that blends coercion, inducement, and long-term structural positioning. Third, it supports the return of *civilizational analysis* to IR, highlighting how non-Western powers draw upon indigenous traditions, histories, and ideologies to shape global order in their own image (Acharya, 2014).

Future research should investigate how different regions respond to China's trade grand strategy, whether through resistance, accommodation, or hybridization. Comparative studies of African, Latin American, and Southeast Asian engagements with China can reveal the variegated nature of global responses. In parallel, work on the intersection of digital trade, data sovereignty, and authoritarian capitalism is urgently needed to assess how emerging technologies reshape the geoeconomic battlefield.

7. CONCLUSION: STRATEGIC PATHWAYS AND FUTURE OUTLOOK

China's evolving trade policy represents one of the most consequential shifts in the international political economy of the 21st century. No longer merely an instrument for economic growth, trade in the hands of the Chinese Communist Party has become a central pillar of a broader strategic architecture that aims to secure national autonomy, shape global norms, and project influence far beyond its borders. As this chapter has demonstrated, China's trade strategy must be read not only as a set of policy measures but as an expression of a coherent grand strategy, anchored in historical experience, ideological conviction, and pragmatic calculation.

The analysis began by situating China's current trade posture within the context of its historical engagement with the global economy. From the trauma of semi-colonial dependency in the 19th century to the reform and opening-up policies of Deng Xiaoping, trade has always been entangled with questions of sovereignty, identity, and survival. This legacy has conditioned Beijing's contemporary obsession with reducing external vulnerabilities, what is now framed as "strategic autonomy." In contrast to liberal assumptions that global integration necessarily produces convergence and interdependence, China seeks to participate in globalization on its own terms: selective, conditional, and reversible if required.

One of the clearest manifestations of this autonomy-seeking behavior is the securitization of trade. The Chinese state no longer treats economic openness as an unquestioned good; instead, it filters trade decisions through a security lens, assessing whether foreign technologies, markets, or firms enhance or threaten national resilience. The DCS is emblematic of this logic, as it reorients domestic and international economic activity towards greater self-reliance, innovation sovereignty, and internal consumption (Hart, 2021). This approach has been reinforced by Western actions, including the U.S.-China trade war, technological sanctions, and friend-shoring initiatives, that confirmed Beijing's belief in the need to "de-risk" at scale (Mazzocco, 2025).

Yet strategic autonomy does not mean isolation. China continues to engage globally, but in ways that rebalance the locus of control. The *Belt and Road Initiative* (BRI) exemplifies how trade is being used not just to open markets but to export infrastructure, norms, and institutional influence. Through strategic investments in ports, railways, energy corridors, and digital infrastructure, China is building a transcontinental sphere of economic connectivity that reinforces its own centrality in global value chains (Rolland, 2019; Mansoor, 2024). These material linkages are accompanied by ideological messaging: a civilizational narrative that presents China as a responsible power offering "win-win cooperation" and an alternative to Western domination. Simultaneously, Beijing has intensified its involvement in multilateral organizations and alternative institutional frameworks. The AIIB, BRICS+, and the RCEP reflect China's ambition to shape, if not replace, the global trade governance architecture. These moves signal a shift from normative alignment to normative contestation. Rather than accepting the liberal values underpinning the World Trade Organization, China seeks to reframe trade around state-led development, non-interference, and reciprocal loyalty, especially in its dealings with the Global South (Rai, 2022; Jin, 2023).

Crucially, this strategy also serves a domestic political purpose: trade has become a legitimacy resource for the Chinese Communist Party. In the absence of electoral mechanisms, the CCP relies on sustained economic performance and national pride to consolidate its rule. Trade surpluses, technological achievements, and global visibility all feed into a domestic narrative of *fuxing*. However, this also places trade policy under enormous pressure to deliver politically acceptable outcomes. Disruptions in exports, supply chains, or foreign investment can quickly become issues of regime stability, prompting assertive, and at times coercive, diplomatic behavior.

In normative terms, China's trade strategy poses a profound challenge to the liberal economic order. It disrupts the assumption that trade liberalization leads to political liberalization. It undermines faith in rule-based multilateralism by emphasizing bilateralism, power asymmetries, and transnationalism. It also blurs the boundary between economics and security, prompting other states to follow suit in "weaponizing" trade (Farrell & Newman, 2019). The result is a global trade landscape that is increasingly fragmented, ideologically contested, and structurally unstable.

This is not to say that China's strategy is risk-free. On the contrary, its growing economic centrality exposes it to strategic overreach, backlash, and entanglement in regional disputes. Initiatives like the BRI have encountered resistance over debt sustainability, labor practices, and lack of transparency (Jean, 2024). Moreover, China's heavy reliance on industrial policy and party-led coordination can lead to resource misallocation and innovation suppression, especially in sectors where openness and experimentation are vital (Dar & Javid, 2025). As other major powers pursue decoupling or de-risking strategies, China may find itself increasingly constrained in shaping the global economic rules it depends on.

Nonetheless, it would be mistaken to assume that Beijing will abandon this path. The fusion of trade, security, and ideology is now deeply embedded in the Party's governance philosophy. Future trajectories will likely involve selective opening in areas of advantage (such as green technologies or digital currencies) and continued insulation in sensitive domains (such as semiconductors, data flows, and rare earths). What emerges is not a return to autarky, but a new model of *strategic globalization*, one that seeks connectivity without vulnerability, openness without dependence.

The broader implication for the international community is the need to recalibrate expectations and frameworks. Engaging with China on trade will require more than technical negotiations; it will require understanding the strategic, cultural, and ideological logics that underpin its choices. Policymakers, scholars, and institutions must acknowledge the pluralization of economic models and the erosion of the liberal consensus. They must also be prepared for a world in which economic interdependence no longer guarantees peace, but may generate new forms of competition, asymmetry, and influence projection.

China's trade policy is not simply an economic artifact; it is a geopolitical doctrine, a tool of statecraft, and a signpost of the global transformation underway. It forces a rethinking of how trade relates to power, identity, and governance in the 21st century. Whether the world moves toward fragmentation, coexistence, or convergence will depend not only on how others react to China's rise, but also on how China itself manages the tension between ambition and responsibility, autonomy and interdependence, control and innovation.

REFERENCES

Acharya, A. (2014). *The End of American World Order*. Polity Press.

Blackwill, R. D., & Harris, J. M. (2016). *War by Other Means: Geoeconomics and Statecraft*. Harvard University Press.

Brands, H. (2014). *What Good Is Grand Strategy? Power and Purpose in American Statecraft from Harry S. Truman to George W. Bush*. Cornell University Press. DOI: 10.7591/9780801470288

Chen, S. (2010). China's Self-Extrication from the "Malacca Dilemma" and Implications. *International Journal of China Studies, 1*(1), 1–24. DOI: 10.22452/ijcs.vol14no1.1

Dar, Z. A., & Javid, S. (2025). Navigating the Turbulent Waters: An In-Depth Study of US-China Geopolitical Rivalry. *Law. Economics and Society, 1*(1), 1–13. DOI: 10.30560/les.v1n1p1

Farrell, H., & Newman, A. L. (2019). Weaponized Interdependence: How Global Economic Networks Shape State Coercion. *International Security, 44*(1), 42–79. DOI: 10.1162/isec_a_00351

Hart, B. (2021). Will the Dual Circulation Strategy Enable China to Compete in a Post-Pandemic World? *Center for Strategic and International Studies*. https://www.csis.org/analysis/will-dual-circulation-strategy-enable-china-compete-post-pandemic-world

Huang, J. (2024). China's role in the EU's search for strategic autonomy: Nonhegemonic power relations during world order transition. *China International Strategy Review, 6*(2), 254–284. DOI: 10.1007/s42533-024-00174-5

India, I. M. P. R. I. (2025). *Geopolitics of Trade and China Tensions*. https://www.impriindia.com/insights/geopolitics-trade-china-tensions/

Jean, R. (2024). *How Geopolitical Tensions Reshape Trade Patterns*. IFRI. https://www.ifri.org/en/publications/notes-de-lifri/china-and-world/how-geopolitical-tensions-reshape-trade-patterns

Jin, K. (2023). *The New China Playbook*. Viking.

Kim, S. (2023). *Realism and EU Trade Policy: European Strategic Autonomy through the Case of EU-China Comprehensive Agreement on Investment*. CAI. [Master's thesis, Seoul National University]

Mansoor, S. I. U. (2024). China's Geopolitical Strategy: Crafting a New World Order. *China Quarterly of International Strategic Studies*, *9*(1–4), 337–359. DOI: 10.1142/S2377740023500161

Mazzocco, I. (2025). Analyzing the Impact of the U.S.-China Trade War on China's Energy Transition. *Center for Strategic and International Studies*. https://www.csis.org/analysis/analyzing-impact-us-china-trade-war-chinas-energy-transition

McKinsey Global Institute. (2025). *Geopolitics and the Geometry of Global Trade: 2025 Update*. https://www.mckinsey.com/mgi/our-research/geopolitics-and-the-geometry-of-global-trade-2025-update

PeaceDiplomacy. (2025, March 18). China's Strategic Preparedness for a New Round of Trade War with the U.S.: A Comparative Analysis. https://peacediplomacy.org/2025/03/18/chinas-strategic-preparedness-for-a-new-round-of-trade-war-with-the-u-s-a-comparative-analysis/

Posen, B. R. (2003). The Sources of Military Doctrine and Grand Strategy. *Contemporary Security Policy*, *24*(2), 32–52. DOI: 10.1080/13523260312312

Rai, M. S. (2022). International Institutions and Power Politics in the Context of Chinese Belt and Road Initiative. *arXiv*. https://doi.org//arXiv.2209.10498DOI: 10.48550

Rolland, N. (2019). *Mapping the Footprint of Belt and Road Influence Operations*. Sinopsis. https://sinopsis.cz/en/mapping-the-footprint-of-belt-and-road-influence-operations/

The Diplomat. (2024, April). China's Alternative Global Trade System. https://thediplomat.com/2024/04/chinas-alternative-global-trade-system/

Trends Research. (2025). *The U.S.-China Trade War: China's Challenge in Navigating U.S. Tariffs and Global Trade Tensions*. https://trendsresearch.org/insight/the-u-s-china-trade-war-chinas-challenge-in-navigating-u-s-tariffs-and-global-trade-tensions/

Ul-Mansoor, A. (2024). *China's Geopolitical Strategy: Crafting a New World Order*. https://doi.org/DOI: 10.5281/zenodo.12345678

Wang, Y. (2011). *Harmony and War: Confucian Culture and Chinese Power Politics*. Columbia University Press.

World Economic Forum. (2024, November). *China's Critical Mineral Strategy: Beyond Geopolitics*. https://www.weforum.org/stories/2024/11/china-critical-mineral-strategy-beyond-geopolitics/

Zhang, Y., & Chang, C. (2020). Modeling the US-China Trade Conflict: A Utility Theory Approach. *arXiv preprint.*

ENDNOTES

1 The *Malacca Dilemma* refers to China's strategic concern over its heavy reliance on the Strait of Malacca, a narrow maritime chokepoint through which approximately 80% of China's imported oil passes. First articulated by President Hu Jintao in 2003, the dilemma underscores the vulnerability of China's energy security to potential blockades or disruptions in the Strait, which is under indirect control of U.S.-aligned naval forces. In response, China has sought to mitigate this risk through initiatives such as overland energy corridors (e.g., the Kyaukpyu–Yunnan pipeline), maritime infrastructure projects under the Belt and Road Initiative, and the development of alternative trade routes like the China–Pakistan Economic Corridor (CPEC).

2 *Securitization* refers to the process by which state actors frame certain issues—traditionally outside the realm of national security, such as trade, technology, or supply chains—as existential threats that justify exceptional measures beyond normal political procedures. Originating from the Copenhagen School of security studies, securitization transforms policy domains into matters of urgent national concern, legitimizing extraordinary state intervention. In the Chinese context, this has meant increasingly treating economic and technological dependencies as security vulnerabilities.

3 The *Dual Circulation Strategy* is a Chinese economic framework introduced in 2020 that seeks to balance and integrate two "circulations": internal circulation, which emphasizes boosting domestic consumption, innovation, and self-reliance; and external circulation, which continues to leverage global markets for trade and investment. This approach was accelerated in response to global uncertainties and strategic competition with the United States, aiming to reduce vulnerabilities while preserving China's integration into the global economy. It reflects a structural pivot toward resilience and long-term strategic autonomy.

4 *Made in China 2025* is a state-led industrial policy launched by the Chinese government in 2015, aimed at transforming China from a manufacturing-based economy into a global leader in high-tech industries. The strategy targets ten key sectors, including robotics, aerospace, semiconductors, and biopharmaceuticals, and emphasizes self-sufficiency, technological upgrading, and the development

of domestic innovation capacity. Internationally, the plan has drawn criticism for fostering state intervention and perceived unfair competition, becoming a focal point of U.S.-China trade tensions.

5 The *Digital Silk Road* (DSR) is a strategic component of China's Belt and Road Initiative (BRI), first introduced in 2015, aimed at enhancing digital connectivity and technological cooperation across participating countries. It encompasses infrastructure development such as fiber-optic cables, 5G networks, smart cities, and satellite navigation systems, alongside digital trade, e-commerce platforms, and cybersecurity collaboration. The DSR advances China's ambition to shape global technology standards, export digital governance models, and reduce reliance on Western digital infrastructure.

6 *Debt-trap diplomacy* refers to the allegation that China strategically offers excessive loans to developing countries—particularly under the Belt and Road Initiative—with the expectation or risk that they will default, enabling Beijing to extract political or strategic concessions (e.g., long-term control over infrastructure assets). The term gained prominence following Sri Lanka's 2017 handover of the Hambantota Port to a Chinese state-owned firm on a 99-year lease after it failed to service its debt. Critics argue this reflects predatory lending; however, several scholars contest this view, pointing to oversimplification and the complex agency of recipient states.

7 *Soft authority* refers to China's evolving approach to influence in the international system, where it seeks not to impose hard power or hegemonic control, but to shape preferences, norms, and institutions in a manner consistent with its interests and values. It blends aspects of *soft power*, such as culture, diplomacy, and economic partnerships, with a more assertive role in norm-setting, infrastructure development (e.g., via the BRI), and institutional creation (e.g., AIIB, SCO). This concept helps describe how China aims to lead without domination, building legitimacy through attraction, interdependence, and perceived mutual benefit.

8 *Small yard, high fence"* is a strategic doctrine increasingly associated with U.S. export control policy, particularly regarding China. It refers to the practice of strictly protecting a narrow set of critical technologies, such as advanced semiconductors, quantum computing, and AI-related tools, through comprehensive restrictions and controls. While the "yard" of technologies is small, the "fence" is high, meaning the controls are far-reaching and aggressively enforced. This approach underpins efforts to preserve technological advantage and national security without decoupling entirely from global trade networks.

[9] *Tianxia* is a classical Chinese political and philosophical concept that envisions a harmonious world order centered on a moral authority, traditionally embodied by the Chinese emperor. It implies a hierarchical system in which China serves as the civilizational core, radiating order and virtue to surrounding states. In contemporary geopolitical discourse, *Tianxia* has been reinterpreted by some Chinese scholars and strategists as an alternative vision to Western-centric international norms, emphasizing relationality, non-hegemonic leadership, and cultural inclusiveness, albeit with China at the normative center.

Chapter 9
Is China an Honest Trade Broker?

Jeremy L. Levine
https://orcid.org/0000-0002-7920-545X
Stony Brook University, USA

ABSTRACT

The story of modern China can be traced back to Deng Xiaoping, who challenged the Chinese people to do even better than Japan did with the Meiji Restoration. The end result has been over forty years of extraordinary economic growth and China rising to become the second-largest economy in the world with hundreds of millions of people lifted out of poverty. Its share of global trade has also risen significantly over the past four decades with the help of special economic zones being established, along with becoming a member of the World Trade Organization and more recently the Belt and Road Initiative. But the rise of China has not occurred without suspicions and concerns along the way. From cyber espionage and stealing trade secrets to Taiwan and the militarization of the South China Sea, questions remain about China's true intentions and if it is trying to rise peacefully or overturn the liberal order. This chapter explores the history of China's rise to global superpower status and if China can be considered an honest trade broker and member of the global community under Xi Jinping.

1. INTRODUCTION

The rise of modern China can be traced back to Deng Xiaoping, who declared "Poverty is not socialism" and challenged the Chinese people to do even better than Japan did with the Meiji Restoration that began nearly a century earlier. Deng first began by instituting agricultural reforms that saw real income for the average Chinese

DOI: 10.4018/979-8-3373-3835-4.ch009

farm family double within five years with an average annual increase of fifteen percent for rural Chinese families (Kissinger, 2011). The ten-year period between 1978 and 1988 also saw the Chinese economy double in size with its global exports increasing from less than $10 billion to over $50 billion. Exports quickly reached $200 billion by the 1990s with China going on to surpass Japan as the second-largest economy in the world by 2010 (Kissinger, 2011; Kroeber, 2016). Tens of billions of dollars also began to flow annually into China from foreign corporations in the 1990s due to China's ability to dominate the market in labor-intensive goods (Kroeber, 2016).

Foreign loans also began to flow into China following Deng having China join both the International Monetary Fund and World Bank. Special economic zones were created to encourage foreign investment, and those zones are still vital for the Chinese economy today. China would later join the World Trade Organization in 2001 (Kissinger, 2011; Woodward, 2017) and that decade would see greenfield investments reach $100 billion in China by 2010 (Yanlin, 2011). Since 2013, China has become the largest importer of oil in the world and has established three major national oil companies, which are the China National Petroleum Corporation, China National Offshore Oil Corporation, and Sinopec (Kroeber, 2016; Carney, 2018).

2013 was also the year Xi Jinping launched the Belt and Road Initiative, which has established multiple economic corridors and economic cooperation zones that have further interconnected Asia, Oceania, Africa, and even parts of Europe and Latin America. Examples of corridors and economic zones include the China-Pakistan Economic Corridor and Lancang-Mekong Cooperation Zone. The Belt and Road Initiative has seen China provide loans for infrastructure and financial investments spanning multiple continents that has resulted in the construction or restoration of railways, highways, ports, and more around the world. A network of sea routes has also been established, which has become known as the Maritime Silk Road and has further facilitated trade between China and signees of the Belt and Road Initiative. The BRI has been described by China as a way to enhance and deepen "South-South Cooperation" and (Castle, 2018; Chen, 2018; Bolt and Cross, 2020; Shambaugh, 2021; Shirk, 2023) perhaps offer an alternative to development than the ideas usually pushed by the International Monetary Fund and World Bank.

But the rise of China has not occurred without questions and concerns along the way. Is the Belt and Road Initiative really what China advertises it to be, or have poorer countries found themselves further indebted and exploited? The tensions between China and Taiwan have not been resolved, which is coinciding with militarization efforts by China in the South China Sea with the goal being to claim most of the sea as part of its territory (Hayton, 2014; Corr, 2018; Shambaugh, 2021). Concentration camps in Xinjiang have been reported, along with support provided to Russia for its invasion of Ukraine. The Chinese Communist Party has also made it clear that it plans on working with Russia to expand its access to the Arctic and the natural resources expected to be found there over the coming decades (Garamone, 2024).

China has also long been accused of manipulating its currency and artificially devaluing it, which makes its exports cheaper. Devaluing a nation's currency makes its exports cheaper, which can result in domestic businesses of importing countries unable to compete and even outright dumping (Kroeber, 2016). It is also estimated that China has stolen at least hundreds of billions of dollars' worth of trade secrets by launching cyber-attacks against both the United States government and private companies such as Google. Chinese espionage activities have even targeted healthcare providers known to have large databases of federal government employee fingerprints. 5G technology provided by Huawei was also recently a great concern expressed by national security officials in the United States (Buchanan, 2020).

The newly elected Trump Administration has recently decided that tariffs and the potential for a trade war between the two nations is the best course of action. His first term in office saw thirty percent tariffs imposed on solar panel imports in January 2018, most of which come from China. Subsequent tariffs were imposed on Chinese goods imported by the United States during the first Trump Presidency, which were often responded to by the Chinese government. This appears to be the case again with Trump back in office and quickly announcing tariffs against Chinese goods during the first couple months of his second presidency. China responded with duties on coal and liquified natural gas, along with the suspension of all poultry, bonemeal, and sorghum imports. Anti-monopoly probes have also been launched against DuPont China Group Co (Mistreanu, 2025). At the present time, talks remain ongoing between the United States and China with the truce between the two nations most likely to be extended until a deal is reached. But as Treasury Secretary Scott Bessent has stated, there will be no official deal reached between the two nations until Trump signs off on it. U.S. trade negotiators have made it clear that Trump has final say and must approve of a deal for it to be considered finalized (Breuninger, 2025).

This book chapter seeks to explore the story of the rise of China beginning in the 1970s, how deeply interconnected it has become with the United States and much of the world since the 1990s, and how best to move forward with Sino-American relations knowing the two nations have become so deeply woven into one another economically. But the heart of this chapter is acknowledging China has exploited that to its advantage by choosing not to act as a rational competition state through its increased militarization and espionage activities and will make the argument that the current status quo is unsustainable because of China.

While questioning the current course the Trump Administration has taken the United States on, what should have been a peaceful status quo for decades to come between the two nations largely due to trade will most likely not survive.

2. THE DRAGON AWAKENS

As Kissinger (2011) states, "China as the present-day economic superpower is the legacy of Deng Xiaoping" by his ability to take China from where it was in the late 1970s to where it had never been before. Deng believed that the Chinese people needed to be given a stake in the output they produced and that the country needed to shift its priorities from heavy industry to consumer goods. While the Communist Party would not cede power, Deng believed it was possible for the party to be less intrusive than it had been under Mao and that decentralization was both possible and necessary. Farmers needed to be liberated, modern technology that Mao had always viewed with suspicion needed to be brought into China, and Chinese students needed to be sent to the West for education. He also made it clear that the legacy of abuse from the Cultural Revolution was over.

In addition to stating "we have nothing to fear from Western education," Deng also decreed "poverty is not socialism" and challenged the Chinese people to do better than Japan did when it began the Meiji Restoration roughly a century earlier. Mao had ruled over China like a traditional emperor who tried to be awe-inspiring and link heaven with earth. He also counted on the Chinese people to endure periods of sustained suffering for his personal visions. But Deng had been more about invoking Chinese spirit and the invisibility of a ruler, while also liberating the creativeness of the Chinese people and closing the vast poverty and standard of living gaps that existed between China and the developed world. Closing those gaps would require foreign technology, expertise, and capital infusions into Chinese society (Kissinger, 2011).

Unlike the personality cult that surrounded Mao, Deng downplayed his own abilities and expertise, declined to hold some of the top positions within the Chinese Communist Party, and entrusted his subordinates to innovate and think of new idea to help China. While Deng believed it would be best for China to open its economy to the outside world, he acknowledged that he did not have all the answers for how best to accomplish that task (Kissinger, 2011). This was in sharp contrast to Mao who, for example, rejected economic plans drafted by party bureaucrats and personally pushed the ideas behind the Great Leap Forward that would result in the deaths of tens of millions of people. And it was the political fallout from the Great Leap Forward that led to the disastrous and violent Cultural Revolution (Shirk, 2023).

Understanding the differences between Deng and Mao at the start of China's rise will later help with an analysis of what to make of China under Xi Jinping today and whether it should be considered an honest trade broker in the global economy.

And shortly after joining the International Monetary Fund and World Bank in 1980, the first of Deng's economic reforms began to bore fruit. The income of Chinese peasants doubled by 1984 and the private sector became fifty percent responsible for gross industrial output. GDP also began to grow by nine percent annually (Kissinger, 2011). The number of people living in extreme poverty declined from 878 million in 1978 to 150 million in 2010 with the rest of the world outside of China only seeing a combined decline of 150 million during that same span. This remarkable economic achievement is further illustrated when considering that in 1978, less than one percent of the world lived in countries with a lower GDP per capita than China with seventy-four percent living in countries with higher GDP per capita. By 2012, China was in the middle fifty percent with only thirty percent of all other countries having a higher GDP per capita. Household consumption per capita also increased by an annual rate of over eight percent in China between 1990 and 2012 (Woodward, 2017).

Between 1978 and 1983, China also began to radically change the agricultural sector of its economy by adopting what became known as the "household responsibility system." Groups of farmers signed agreements that eliminated the collectives previously designed by Mao and instead agreed to divide farmland into individual plots. While this was initially done in secret, it became embraced by the Chinese government and the positive results were seen immediately. In 1984, grain output rose to 400 million tons, which was a thirty-three percent increase in output from 1978. Oilseeds and cotton production began to rise by fifteen percent annually with meat production also growing by ten percent per year. And the result of income doubling for Chinese peasants from 1979 to 1984 caused per capita cash savings to rise from virtually zero per family to 300 renminbi by 1989 (Kroeber, 2016).

Prior to the 1980s, China accounted for just a small fraction of the world's industrial production, including less than one percent of it being part of its trade exports. But by 2014, it was the number one manufacturing nation accounting for twelve and eighteen percent of all global exports and manufacturing exports respectively. China benefited early on from exporting to neighbors such as Taiwan, South Korea, and Japan, while also gaining access to the sophisticated ports, legal system, and financial system of Hong Kong. The electronics industry in Taiwan also began to establish manufacturing operations in China by the late 1990s. These early successes were due to Deng's belief that China should shift from intensive heavy industry to consumer goods because while China possessed little capital in the late 1970s and early 1980s, it possessed an abundance of cheap labor. The priority became about producing labor-intensive goods and developing labor-intensive industries to boost exports, which would later produce the foreign exchange required to import capital equipment. The early results of these reforms resulted in overall industrial output rising by sixfold between 1978 and 1990 with the economy growing by about ten percent annually during that time as well. The annual economic growth was similar to Japan's experience during the 1950s as it was leaving the devastation of the Second World War behind (Kroeber, 2016).

What allows China to be able to import and export so many goods is its 14,500-kilometer coastline. Its ports, which operate the largest number of berths and handle more cargo when measuring by metric volume and TEUs, also serve as transshipment hubs for global trade. Chinese ports went from processing 1.25 billion tons of goods in 2000 to 7.84 billion tons in 2015. When measuring by TEUs, eight of China's ports rank in the top twenty and they are Shanghai, Shenzhen, Ningbo-Zhoushan, Guangzhou, Qingdao, Tianjin, Dalian, and Xiamen. When measuring in tonnage, thirteen Chinese ports rank in the top twenty and include both the eight previously listed and also Suzhou, Rizhao, Yingkou, Qinhuangdao, and Tangshan. And these ports are predominantly clustered in the Pearl River Delta, Yangtze River Delta, and Bohai Economic Rim (Yoshihara and Holmes, 2018).

Foreign direct investment and being able to entice foreign companies to invest in China was crucial for this success as well. What first started as few billion annually in the 1980s primarily from small Hong Kong manufacturers investing in the Shenzhen special economic zone would reach $45 billion in 1997. Between 1990 and 2001, China would see its exports increase from $62 billion to $266 billion with more than half of all exports being made by foreign firms (Kroeber, 2016). Deng established these special economic zones and made these areas more business friendly than the rest of China through lower taxes and suspending antibusiness laws. This was Deng's way of bringing together China and capitalism following decades of Mao doing the exact opposite (Meredith, 2007).

The first four special economic zones were established in Fujian Province (Xiamen) and Guangdong Province (Shenzhen, Zhuhai and Shantou). Fujian is one the other side of the Taiwan Strait from Taiwan and Guangdong is near Hong Kong. The success of these zones caused Deng to establish additional special economic zones spread out along fourteen Chinese coastal cities. Estimates from 2005 alone show that U.S. companies saved up to $70 billion in manufacturing costs, while also saving American consumers around $100 billion (Meredith, 2007). And as hundreds of millions of Chinese workers saw their incomes rise, they were also able afford Western goods that are sold in China. Between 1997 and 2007, the number of cellphone subscribers increased from 10 million to 460 million people, which is greater than the entire population of the United States (Meredith, 2007; Miao and Deng, 2020).

Shenzhen is also now home to the Shenzhen Stock Exchange and a stock connect has been established with the Hong Kong Stock Exchange, which allows domestic and institutional investors to participate in Hong Kong's equity market. A similar connect was also established between Shanghai and Hong Kong (Miao and Deng, 2020). Shenzhen is also one of the four major global hubs for fintech companies with the others being Beijing, Shanghai, and Hangzhou. These cities are primarily in the Beijing-Tianjin-Hebei region, the Yangtze River delta, and the Guangdong-

Hong Kong-Macao Greater Bay Area. Beijing specifically, ranked first in the fintech industry in 2018, while also being number one in the world in the number of fintech companies. (Zhang, 2020).

Four out of the top five fintech companies worldwide were Chinese in 2016 with the top three also being Chinese in 2017. The main ones are Ant Financial, JD Finance, Du Xiaoman Financial, and Lufax Holdings with other companies like Tencent investing in fintech firms like the Brazilian company Nubank. These companies have also expanded overseas, which has allowed for transactions in retail stores to be made possible in twenty-eight other countries and regions as of 2020 (Zhang, 2020).

So contrary to those like Immanuel Wallerstein and world-system theorists who believed Communist countries could not reach their full potential until capitalism was overthrown (Chirot and Hall, 1982), China's rise over the last forty plus years is largely due to its embrace of capitalism and economic liberalization despite the Chinese Communist Party still being in power. But despite its incredible success, the question that needs to be asked and perhaps even more so under the current party leadership, is China an honest trade broker and responsible player in the current international order?

3. CYBER HACKING AND ESPIONAGE

Some experts speculate that China began cyber espionage operations shortly after 2000 and the start of the twenty-first century. A common Chinese tactic has been spear-phishing, which Buchanan (2020, 86) describes as "the practice of sending socially engineered emails in order to dupe a target into surrendering vital information or opening malicious code…" Many organizations within the Chinese security apparatus like the People's Liberation Army and the Ministry of State Security engage in these activities that can be done from the comfort of their homes and offices. The cyber activities by the Chinese were described in 2014 by then-FBI Director James Comey as "just prolific" (Buchanan, 2020).

Motivations behind these espionage activities stemmed from China being behind the United States in both business and geopolitical competition with inferior commercial innovations and a military lacking the advanced technology possessed by the United States. Chinese political leaders are also worried about how open the internet can be when it comes to free expression and dissenters both in China and abroad. From the perspective of the Chinese Communist Party, cyber espionage allows China to close the existing gaps it has with Western companies and American military capabilities, along with suppress dissent with the overall goal being to tip the strategic relationship it has with the United States in its favor. And in the world of digital information, this can be done faster than ever before, which is why former NSA Director Keith Alexander famously stated that Chinese cyber operations resulted in the "greatest transfer of wealth in history" (Buchanan, 2020).

The consequences of these efforts for the United States include doubts being sown about its ability to defend against Chinese cyber-attacks, along with China having recently deployed similar weapons systems to those of the United States that were most likely aided by stolen designs and plans (Buchanan, 2020). One example of this stems from the 2014 indictment of Chinese operative Su Bin, who helped Chinese co-conspirators back in China hack into computer systems of Boeing to access information about the C-17 transport aircraft F-22 and F-35 fighter jets with China now having aircraft that closely resemble the C-17 and F-35 (Sciutto, 2019).

Cyber operations have also targeted private companies, with the famous one being Operation Aurora in 2009 that targeted thirty-four major companies including Google, Microsoft, and Juniper. The operation would not be made public until 2010 and Google stated one of the main goals of Chinese hackers was to spy on the Gmail accounts of Chinese dissidents and human rights activists. Another goal was to discover what inside China was being monitored by the United States through Google's systems.

China was attempting to see if American technology was being used to conduct surveillance on Chinese intelligence officers and any of their assets. One other purpose for spying on tech companies was to steal source code, which is a form of intellectual property that can be highly coveted by foreign governments and any of their state-owned enterprises they want to help gain competitive advantage. Stealing what are called signing certificates also allows for code to be easier to impersonate and avoid detection (Buchanan, 2020).

This has all coincided with Xi Jinping's remarks from just over a decade ago that "without cybersecurity there is no national security." The Ministry of State Security and the Ministry of Public Security, which are essentially the Chinese versions of the CIA and FBI respectively, have both increased the amount of monitoring they do of online communications and use data mining to better identify dangerous individuals to the regime and dissidents inside China (Shirk, 2023). Because as Guo (2012, p. 418) states:

"The CCP believes that China is threatened by "Western hostile forces," led by the United States, and that those forces are attempting to Westernize, divide, and overthrow the CCP by supporting democracy activists and religious groups (including practitioners of falun gong), separatists (Tibetansm Uighurs, and Taiwan), and political dissidents."

This level of paranoia reflects what Huntington (1996) writes regarding there is no sharp distinction in China between domestic and foreign affairs. And this idea about hostile forces attempting to divide China and bring down the CCP was also the main motivation behind the Hong Kong National Security Law that was enacted in June 2020. Journalists have been prosecuted on suspicion of colluding with foreigners and endangering national security. The law is also applicable to people who do not live in Hong Kong. For example, an American who is critical of China from anywhere outside of China's borders can be arrested when they arrive in Hong Kong.

The law also allows for those arrested to be sent to mainland China for trial. Hong Kong has suffered the most from this law and the United States no longer gives it preferential treatment. It now has the same visa restrictions, tariffs, and rules concerning exports that every other Chinese city has. The United States has also frozen the assets of both Chinese and Hong Kong officials who were responsible for the crackdown against protesters that occurred shortly after the law was enacted (Shirk, 2023).

There are other examples of private companies being targeted by Chinese cyber operations with one serious case being the nuclear power firm Westinghouse Electric Company. While the company was in negotiations with China in 2007 to discuss the construction of nuclear power plants, Chinese hackers began to target the company and specifically about the design and construction of the AP1000 nuclear plant. Rather than have Chinese companies invest in their own research and development, hackers targeted the AP1000, which had previously taken Westinghouse fifteen years to design.

The end result was increased Chinese competition, which was one of the factors that would later cause Westinghouse Electric Company to declare bankruptcy in 2017. And when other companies like SolarWorld and US Steel would complain to the United States Department of Commerce about unfair subsidies being given by the Chinese government to their Chinese competitors, they became the targets of Chinese cyber-attacks that gave hackers access to intellectual property and internal files like financial information, executive emails, correspondence between the companies and their attorneys, and private filings submitted to the United States government (Buchanan, 2020).

So long as Chinese hackers remain safely inside China and protected by the state, little can be done about their activities other than indicting them without the means to arrest them (Buchanan, 2020). As Sciutto (2019, 60) states, "For China, this state-sponsored theft is not a crime, but a policy." While the United States has appealed to China about cyber espionage and stealing trade secrets, serious dialogue can only happen when both sides are willing to be fully open about their cyber intelligence-gathering capabilities. This is more complicated than the asymmetry that usually surrounds negotiations about nuclear weapons and nonproliferation and as United States Cyber Command has also previously acknowledged "the next war will begin in cyberspace" (Kissinger, 2014).

And these concerns have also spread more recently to apps and especially the social media platform TikTok. TikTok's parent company is ByteDance and the United States is concerned that the Chinese government could force the company to provide data about American users, which January 2025 is around 170 million Americans. There are also concerns about TikTok's algorithm being used to spread propaganda and disinformation. These concerns stem from a 2017 national security law enacted by China that requires companies to help with intelligence gathering upon request. So, if the Chinese government requests information about American TikTok users, it is illegal under Chinese law for ByteDance to refuse (Minges, 2025).

Lewis (2024) also highlights the risk of downloading and updating the TikTok app, which means accepting Chinese software into your mobile device that has little to no oversight. A person can unwittingly allow malware to be installed into their phone without ever realizing it. What makes this especially concerning to the U.S. government is none of this requires hacking or any kind of espionage activities. Downloading and using TikTok and contributing to the algorithm, along with being influenced by the algorithm are all voluntary actions now being taken by hundreds of millions of Americans.

4. XI JINPING'S FINTECH CRACKDOWN

Even the fintech industry and its executives are not immune from the wrath and scrutiny of Xi Jinping and the Chinese Communist Party. Alibaba co-founder and Ant Group controlling shareholder Jack Ma gave a speech in 2020 where he described Chinese banks as having a pawnshop mentality for giving loans to companies that should not receive them, which causes them to turn into bad companies. He also criticized the regulatory agencies and said China needed "policy experts, not paper pushers." Within one day the planned $37 billion IPO was scrapped and Ant Group was forced to undergo restructuring to adhere to China's new anti-monopoly laws (Feng, 2020; Campbell, 2021). In April 2021, Ant Group was fined the equivalent of $2.8 billion for what was described as abusing "its dominant market position in China's online retail platform service market since 2015." Thirty-four other technology companies were later warned to "pay full heed" of what happened to Alibaba. Didi was fined by the Cyberspace Administration of China in July 2021 just two days after its public listing on the New York Stock Exchange and was fined an additional time one year later. Ant Group would also receive an additional major fine in July 2023 (Zhang, 2023).

Altogether, Xi's crackdown just between 2020 and 2021 wiped away $1.1 trillion in market value from the stocks of the top six Chinese tech companies, which is especially significant given that the tech and digital industry comprises thirty-eight percent of China's GDP (Shirk, 2023).

Sovereignty can be viewed as both the greatest threat to capital and its greatest source of helping it flourish. Political authorities have the power to either block capitalist activities or enable them in the name of social harmony, religion, economic justifications, or political necessity. Capitalists prosper when they have the ability and security to trade and invest, while also having their property rights secured and a court system to enforce contracts. States can regulate competition, control the money supply, and stabilize the financial sector when necessary (Shovlin, 2021).

In the 2018 book *Authoritarian Capitalism: Sovereign Wealth Funds and State-Owned Enterprises in East Asia and Beyond*, Richard Carney describes a new phenomenon in which authoritarian regimes have harnessed capitalism to further solidify their grip on power. In contrast to neoclassical economics, which suggests the role of the state diminishes as free markets become more embraced, especially when it comes to ownership of the factors of production, the opposite has occurred (Carney, 2018). in places like China despite the economic miracle and development that has occurred over the last four decades. This has always been the case with China going back to the late nineteenth and early twentieth centuries (Moore, 1967) and is no different today under the Chinese Communist Party in what Shirk (2023) describes as "party-state capitalism."

And for the Chinese state, nothing comes at the expense of party politics and the grip on power held by the Chinese Communist Party. Capital accumulation, economic development, international trade and foreign direct investment are all secondary priorities to the Chinese government.

5. BELT AND ROAD INITIATIVE

The Belt and road Initiative, also branded as the New Silk Road or "One Belt, One Road," was first signaled to be happening in September and October 2013 in speeches given by Xi Jinping in Kazakhstan and Indonesia respectively. The first official Belt and Road Forum was in May 2017 with a follow-up summit happening in April 2019 (Woodward, 2017).

Within the first six years, 138 nations signed a Memorandum of Understanding to become part of the initiative spanning across most continents and including forty African nations (Zufle, 2023). More specifically, the BRI can be divided up into the following six corridors: Economic Corridor China-Mongolia-Russia, New Eurasian Land Bridge, Economic Corridor China-Central Asia, Economic Corridor China-Indochinese Peninsula, China-Pakistan Economic Corridor, and the Maritime Economic Corridor, also called the Maritime Silk Road (Pautasso, 2016).

The maritime corridor also reaches east African nations such as Djibouti, Ethiopia, Kenya, and Tanzania (Blanchard, 2021). Ethiopia is especially important to the Maritime Silk as China seeks to build the Addis Ababa-Djibouti Railway that will connect the port of Berbera in Somaliland to Mogadishu, Somalia, Lamu, Kenya, and Babamoyo, Tanzania (Tesfaye, 2020).

In Southeast Asia, this has involved the creation of even more specific corridors and economic cooperation zones like the Bangladesh-China-India-Myanmar Economic Corridor and Pan-Beibu Gulf Economic Cooperation Zone. Some of the specific infrastructure projects in the region include a 1,800-kilometer highway connecting Kunming to Bangkok in Thailand, a 150-kilometer high-speed rail line connecting Jakarta to Bandung in Indonesia, a new airport and upgraded airport in Phnom Penh, Cambodia and Luang Prabang, Laos respectively, and major port building and upgrades in Brunei, Cambodia, Indonesia, and Malaysia with one of the Malaysian ports being around the highly strategic Strait of Malacca (Shambaugh, 2021: Woodward, 2017).

China has also established the China Development Bank (CDB), which as of 2016 held $100 billion in capital and over $1 trillion in assets, while making more loans to Latin American countries than both the World Bank and Inter-Development Bank. The CDB also makes more loans to Asian countries than the World Bank and Asian Development Bank. Most Chinese trade and investment in Latin America have centered around iron and copper mining, oil extraction, agriculture like soybean farming and processing, beef exports, and more recently infrastructure projects. Examples of this include the Aluminum Corporation of China (CHINALCO) and the China National Petroleum Corporation establishing operations in Peru (Gallagher, 2016).

Bilateral lines of credits or loans is how China provides most of its financing to Latin American nations with most of the money going to large infrastructure, energy, and mining projects. Around eighty-seven percent of Chinese loans go to those sectors compared to just twenty-nine percent and thirty-four percent of loans from the Inter-Development Bank and World Bank respectively. Around half of all contracts signed between Chinese banks and Latin American governments are commodity-backed and all of the commodity-backed loans are secured via oil. The countries mostly involved with these kinds of deals have been Venezuela, Ecuador, and Brazil (Gallagher, 2016).

Similar forms of investment were also made in Central Asia like, for example, China agreeing to provide Kazakhstan with $30 billion in 2013 for energy, infrastructure, mining, science, and education projects (Woodward, 2017). Investments made in the Middle East show a similar pattern with half of all Chinese investments in Iran going toward oil and gas projects with the rest being spread across other sectors like transportation and telecommunications. China also views the Black Sea as strategically important with the Bank of China helping finance and support the construction of what could become the Kanal Istanbul waterway, which would provide alternative shipping lanes from the often-crowded Bosporus Straits (Bianchi, 2019).

Three main concerns have been pointed out by critics and skeptics of the Belt and Road Initiative with the first being port construction in other countries leading to overseas military bases. Both Sri Lanka's Hambantota port and Pakistan's Gwadar port have never been able to operate at full capacity despite billions in Chinese financing. China might be able to lose money on those investments if those ports can have dual civilian-military purposes.

The Chinese have one overseas military base in Djibouti, which is strategically located right where the Indian Ocean meets the Suez Canal. There are also roughly 40,000 Chinese firms operating in foreign countries with properties and investments estimated to be worth around $7 trillion. It might be understandable to a certain extent that China may want a military presence that can protect its overseas investments, businesses, and citizens (Shirk, 2023).

The second concern is about countries falling into what has bene labeled as the "debt trap," which has involved countries borrowing money from China to fund infrastructure projects like ports and railways. If the borrowing countries cannot repay the loans, they agree to sign away the property rights to China. Borrowers also must agree to never disclose the terms of the borrowing arrangements (Shirk, 2023). One example of this potential debt trap situation is African nations owed China more money in 2016 than they did the World Bank and International Monetary Fund combined (Tarrosy, 2020). Research conducted by the AidData research lab at the College of William & Mary speculate that Chinese lending toward overseas development projects between 2000 and 2021 have $385 billion in outstanding "hidden debt" (Malik et al, 2021). And for forty-two of these indebted nations, the amount they owe China exceeds ten percent of GDP (Shirk, 2023).

The other suspicion centers around the true motivations of China behind its Belt and Road Initiative, which brings back the question if it can be considered an honest trade broker. Some scholars speculate that modern China is attempting to operate like Ancient China by positioning itself as the "Middle Kingdom" and center of gravity through the Belt and Road Initiative. From this perspective, indebted nations are essentially outer subjects or tributary states (Tarrosy, 2020). Other writers have described the current Chinese system using the word *tianxia*, which means "all under heaven." In the traditional sense, this meant the Chinese emperor was above all due to China being superior to its neighbors with those neighboring states having to pay tributes as a way of acknowledging their subservience. This is also reflective in the Confucian philosophy that states "There are no two suns in the sky, there cannot be two emperors on earth." Supporters of this "Chinese World Order" argue this was better than the Westphalian system and a modern version led by Chinese hegemony is better than the liberal order established by the United States at the end of the Second World War because it will make East Asia more stable and with less conflicts (Huntington, 1996; Bolt and Cross, 2018).

This begs the question is China trying to be a responsible actor in the current order or even the next hegemon of this order? If not, is it attempting to overturn the current way of the world and establish a new global order where it writes the rules? Huntington (1996) also suggests that China was the dominant power in East Asia for two thousand years and now wants to reclaim that historic role after being humiliated and subordinated by both the West and Japan for over a century.

6. SOUTH CHINA SEA

The South China Sea is one of the business maritime trade routes in the world and is crucial for the global economy. It has three times and five times more tanker traffic than the Suez Canal and Panama Canal respectively. More than fifty percent of all oil tanker shipments and merchant fleet measured by tonnage navigates through the South China Sea, which is also home to more than half of the top ten busiest shipping ports in the world (Corr, 2018). \$1.2 trillion in United States trade also passed through the Sea in 2012, along with eighty percent of China's imported oil. Some consider the South China Sea to be "Asia's Mediterranean" (Woodward, 2017).

The economic interests of the South China Sea claimed by China and surrounding countries involve the potentially large oil and natural gas reserves believed to be beneath the water. According to Chinese and American estimates, the sea contains between 28 and 213 billion barrels of oil and between 58 and 190 trillion cubic feet of natural gas. Those estimates would make the South China Sea the third largest oil reserve in the world behind Venezuela and Saudi Arabia, along with having an estimated three percent of all global natural gas reserves (Corr, 2018).

The South China Sea is an important linkage between the Indian and Pacific Oceans and should the ability of the sea to offer such access ever be disrupted, billions of dollars would be added to shipping costs due to maritime fleets and merchant ships having to travel south of Indonesia. China capturing the sea militarily might also result in it being able to enforce transit taxes against and constrict the economies of countries that border the South China Sea, along with Taiwan, Japan, and South Korea (Corr, 2018). Both South Korea and Japan are vulnerable due to large percentages of their oil imports and overall energy supplies having to first past through the South China Sea (Woodward, 2017).

Since the end of the Cold War, the naval presence of the United States around the South China Sea had greatly diminished to nothing more than some naval exercises. This resulted in China-ASEAN relations flourishing between 1991 and 2010 with annual trade increasing from \$8 billion to over \$300 billion with ASEAN economies growing by around fivefold (Shirk, 2023). While trade between the United States and ASEAN more than doubled between 1996 and 2015, trade between China and ASEAN still grew at a greater pace (Forsyth, 2018).

More specifically, China is Brunei's third-largest source of imports and the second largest of Cambodia as well. China is also the largest export and import market for Indonesia, along with being the largest, second-largest, and third-largest export markets for Laos, Malaysia, and the Philippines respectively (Forsyth, 2018).

But that began to change under the Obama Administration when President Obama signed the ASEAN Treaty, which was then followed up by elevating relations between the U.S. and Singapore to a "strategic partnership." Relations with Malaysia, Vietnam, and Indonesia were upgraded to "comprehensive partnerships." While the American naval presence in the Pacific had always been more "North Asia Heavy," a shift in American priorities began in 2010 to begin focusing more on Southeast Asia and the South China Sea (Shambaugh, 2021).

As the United States has refocused its naval presence more in the South China Sea, China has exerted its territorial claims over the sea by rapidly building artificial islands with runways and other military facilities (Shirk, 2023). The defenses and garrisons established by China are much larger than those built by Taiwan, Vietnam, the Philippines, and Malaysia (McDevitt, 2020).

China's claims go beyond what maritime international law allows when it comes to exclusive economic zones (EEZ). Every country that borders the sea is supposed to have up to two hundred nautical miles to use for its own economic purposes if it so chooses. But the U-shaped line, or nine-dash line, which China is trying to now buffer with these artificial islands, would essentially make the entire sea China's exclusive economic zone. This would also take China beyond the Paracel Islands and into the Spratly Islands and other parts of the sea as well. Other countries like the Philippines have been victorious in their legal challenges against China, but China has continued to ignore such rulings. None of these countries by themselves can thwart China's ongoing efforts to militarize and claim the South China Sea, which as a result has made the sea once again a priority for the United States (Forsyth, 2018).

Kissinger (1994; 2011) states that the idea of raison d'état and how it can "lead to a quest for supremacy or to establishment of equilibrium. Equilibrium usually emerges from a country's attempt to dominate. Raison d'état also leads to states prioritizing what they perceive to be good for them and it's the duty of the ruler to carry that out often at the expense of weaker states. Weaker states can attempt to resist the dominant power, and one of two outcomes emerges. Either a balance of power is the result if the dominant power fails, or hegemony is achieved by the dominant power. History shows that the outcome is not predetermined and might need one or more conflicts to establish. Huntington (1996) predicted this very scenario that East Asian countries would have to respond to an increasingly assertive China if economic development continued on its current trajectory for the Chinese.

Instead of being an honest trade broker, China has spent the last decade-plus taking the world on a collision course in the South China Sea due to its embrace of raison d'état. Instead of focusing on its economic competitive advantages and connecting the economic and political aspects of globalization, which should result in the decline of the nation-state as countries become more economically interconnected with one another (King and Kendall, 2004), China has chosen to do the opposite. Instead of using its competitive advantages and increase in trade to peacefully coexist with its South China Sea neighbors, it seeks to exploit them much like Russia had previously tried to do with Europe and Ukraine. This goes back to what this chapter has previously described as China's priority being party-state capitalism (Shirk, 2023) and preserving the grip on power held by the party above all else, which the CCP has now decided to link to challenging the global order it is vocally discontent about (Bolt and Cross, 2018). A country can embrace raison d'état or act like a competition state, but it is not possible to do both.

7. TAIWAN AND SEMICONDUCTORS

Since the 1960s, Taiwan has been averaging an annual economic growth rate of 8.3% with GDP per capita rising from $170 in 1949 to $13,500 in 1996. This level of economic success helped Taiwan earn the label of being one of the 'Asian Tigers,' alongside Singapore, South Korea, and Hong Kong. One of the reasons for this success was the shift from agricultural to industrial production that began in 1962. Taiwan went from primarily exporting sugar, rice, tea, and bananas to high tech goods and welcoming companies like General Instruments and their electronic assembly plants. This level of economic liberalization eventually led to the lifting of martial law in Taiwan in 1987 and democracy taking root on the island in the 1990s, which is a stark contrast to China that is still dominated by the Communist Party (Brown and Tzu-hui, 2019).

The beginning of cross-strait economic relations between China and Taiwan when Taiwan announced a 'Non-interference Principle of Indirect Exports to the Mainland' in 1985. China responded by offering two investment zones with special tax privileges for Taiwanese enterprises in Fujian Province in 1989. Legislation that further protected Taiwanese investments was also enacted in 1994. Trade has since increased significantly between China and Taiwan going from just over $5 billion in 1990 to over $120 billion in 2010. When measuring trade in volume (Burdekin et al, 2013), it increased by over 280 percent since China and Taiwan both joined the World Trade Organization in 2001. Trade across the Taiwan Strait between

China and Taiwan accounted for 22.97 percent of Taiwan's total foreign trade and just slightly over four percent of China's total foreign trade (Burdekin et al, 2013). This has made China the largest trading partner for Taiwan with Taiwan becoming the fourth largest trading partner for China. And while countries like the United States have considerable trade deficits with China, Taiwan saw its trade surplus with mainland China increase from just under $20 billion in 2001 to over $48 billion by 2010 (Woodward, 2017). The trade surplus increased even further reaching around $75 billion in 2014. Foreign direct investment from Taiwan to China reached $8.7 billion in 2013, which was around sixty-three percent of the total FDI outflow for Taiwan. (Burdekin et al, 2013; Woodward, 2017).

As Taiwanese identity has become more associated with economic liberalization and democracy, its politics have also begun to shift to believing in formal independence from China. After seeing what happened in Hong Kong with the national security law, most Taiwanese no longer believe the "one country, two systems" reunification philosophy would allow for Taiwan to still possess democracy. But nationalist calls inside China for the military to be used against Taiwan is growing despite the economic interconnectedness that exists. Chinese President Xi Jinping has attempted to intimidate Taiwan more through economic sanctions and military air patrols (Shirk, 2023). On December 31, 2024, Xi explicitly stated that reunification between China and Taiwan was inevitable and that "no one can sever our blood ties" (The Times of India, 2024).

Some scholars also believe that if China invaded Taiwan and lost, which would also mean losing to the United States, or if Taiwanese independence was declared with no response from the Communist Party, Xi Jinping and the party would be overthrown. Estimates from 2015 show that China spent over $215 billion in military defense spending compared to only $10.3 billion spent by Taiwan (Shirk, 2023). Essentially, Xi Jinping's political survival, going back to what this chapter has described as party-state capitalism, hinges on the ability of China to handle both Taiwan and the United States (Shirk, 2023; Woodward, 2017). Such pressure within China is now new as Deng was once given a letter by one hundred generals in June 1993 demanding that China not be so passive toward the United States and risk being blackmailed (Huntington, 1996). Because when it comes to the United States and Taiwan, U.S. defense policy expert Michael Mazza states:

> *"Even though no US troops are stationed on Taiwan, the island's continued de facto independence is crucial for America's forward defence perimeter, which since World War II has sought to keep would-be aggressors from approaching the United States via the Pacific Ocean. If Taiwan fell into unfriendly hands, moreover, America would find it increasingly difficult to defend its Asian treaty allies, notably Japan and the Philippines" (Woodward, 2017, p. 125).*

But one of the other looming factors that will greatly impact what happens between China and Taiwan, while also showing whether China is an honest trade broker, is the semiconductor industry. In the same year that martial law was lifted in Taiwan, 1987, Morris Chang founded the Taiwan Semiconductor Manufacturing Company. The company agreed to solely focus on producing chips and not design, and it has since become the world's largest computer chip maker and responsible for ninety percent of the global supply of the most advanced chips. TSMC has also become the largest supplier of chips to Western companies like Apple, while becoming indispensable to the United States. This has caused Taiwan to become even more important to the U.S. beyond just the remnants of Cold War politics (Miller, 2022; Tseng, 2023).

Cross-strait relations have also been impacted by TSMC with the company first establishing an 8-inch fabrication plant in Shanghai in 2004 (Kirby, 2013). The main Chinese producer of semiconductors is the Semiconductor Manufacturing International Corporation (SMIC), which has become the third-largest pure-play foundry in the world (Chu, 2013). And between 2014 and 2018, around 1,500 senior engineers relocated from Taiwan to China to work for Chinese chip companies (Krige, 2024).

But one of China's main problems when it comes to semiconductors is being dependent on foreign technology for nearly all aspects of the production process. Most of the technology is controlled by Taiwan, Japan, South Korea, and the United States with all those countries being more geopolitical rivals than allies. For example, the United States dominates the market share for the software needed to design chips, while China only has two percent market share of the core intellectual property building blocks for transistor patterns (Miller, 2022).

These vulnerabilities faced by China threaten its economic security and led to Xi Jinping declaring in 2014 that national security is impossible to achieve without cybersecurity and being able to address threats from the digital world. The vulnerabilities, especially its dependent on foreign technology will continue to reveal themselves as China continues to make advancements in cloud computing, autonomous vehicles, and artificial intelligence after having already successfully replicated Silicon Valley when it comes to software needed for e-commerce, online shopping, and digital payments. Currently, no Chinese firms can produce a competitive GPU, which means they must be imported from Western firms like Nvidia and AMD (Miller, 2022).

In his desire to close the gap between China and the rest of the world when it comes to computer chips, Xi Jinping called for an "assault the fortifications of core technology research." This caught the attention of both the first Trump Administration and Biden Administration who responded by slapping restrictions against the Chinese company Huawei. The Trump Administration banned the company from doing business in the United States, while the Biden Administration banned the sale of computer chips to the firm. Huawei was accused when Trump was first President of giving sensitive communications to the Chinese military (Miller, 2022), which I argue echoes similar sentiments to the concerns many have about ByteDance and TikTok.

I also argue another concern is China invading and capturing the island of Taiwan, which would give it full control of TSMC and all its semiconductor operations on the island. China could also enact a blockade against Taiwan using the both the South China Sea and East China Sea, or a quarantine using maritime or aerial methods, all of which would cause massive disruptions to global supply chains costing the global economy trillions of dollars. Sharp GDP declines would also occur for both China and Taiwan (Patey, 2024; Liu et al, 2025) and while a rational government would more than likely avoid such situations, what about China and its party-state capitalism model this chapter has previously described?

8. CHINA AND INDIA

The Indian Ocean is 74.9 million square kilometers and is one of the most important bodies of water when it comes to the movement of energy, raw materials, and other goods traded between nations (Yuan, 2018). Roughly 100,000 ships transit across the Indian Ocean annually accounting for fifty percent of all maritime trade and forty percent of the world's oil supply (Yuan, 2018). One of the most important "choke points" for global trade that also allows the South China Sea to connect the Indian Ocean to the Pacific Ocean is the Malacca Strait. 70,000 ships sail through the Strait of Malacca annually with 15.2 million barrels of oil passing through the strait daily (Yuan, 2018).

The Malacca Strait is also important because China does not have direct access to the Indian Ocean like it does the Pacific Ocean and South China Sea. With China now the largest importer of oil in the world and its dependence on energy imports continuing to rise, it believes it is highly vulnerable to the threat of hostile states blocking energy transits and other exports in the Malacca Strait headed to China. This has caused China to begin making economic inroads around the Indian Ocean, while also expanding its military presence (Yuan, 2018).

All of this has caught the attention of India, which traditionally views the Indian Ocean as its sphere of influence. The Indian government has raised questions about the strategic intentions of China with one reason for those concerns being how dependent it is on imports for its energy needs. Seventy percent of India's energy needs are imported. While China has stated its expanding presence in the Indian Ocean is about commercial interests and energy security, India has become concerned as it continues to have unresolved territorial disputes with China, conflicts with Pakistan, and its own great power aspirations to expand its influence (Yuan, 2018).

China remains India's largest trading partner with trade in 2015 and 2016 between the two nations reaching $70 billion (Miller, 2022). But China has also deepened its military cooperation with Pakistan by helping modernize the Pakistani military with advanced weapon systems like the JF-17 thunder fighter, F-22P frigate with helicopters, K-8 jet trainers, T-85 tanks, and F-7 aircrafts. Cooperation between China and Pakistan has also expanded economically through the China-Pakistan Economic Corridor (CPEC), which as previously stated is part of China's efforts to establish a new land and maritime Silk Road. The crux of those Chinese investments center around the Gwadar Port, which India fears will allow for China to expand its military presence not only in the Indian Ocean, but alongside the country Pakistan that it is often in conflict with (Han and Belanger, 2018).

From the perspective of China, the access to the Gwadar Port in Pakistan helps improve trade and energy security by making the country less dependent on the Strait of Malacca and South China Sea, along with sea lanes patrolled by the United States Navy (Castle, 2018). But India views China expanding its influence in the region and using Gwadar as part of the "String of Pearls" strategy (Li, 2018). Each "pearl" represents a port that receives significant Chinese investment. And in addition to securing partnerships with those other countries, the strategy also allows China to expand its influence closer to other parts of Asia, along with Europe, Africa, and Latin America (European Parliament, 2013). The concerns expressed by India about String of Pearls also involves Sri Lanka and the Chinese investments made to develop the Hambantota Port, along with the deepening of ties between China and Myanmar, Bangladesh, and Nepal. Chinese submarines have reportedly docked in Hambantota. From the perspective of the Indian government, these are efforts by China to encircle India and leave it vulnerable to energy security and other concerns (Castle, 2018; Yuan, 2018; Han and Belanger, 2018).

But the China-Pakistan Economic Corridor that has the Gwadar Port at one end runs through Kashmir with India becoming concerned about Chinese infrastructure investments in the parts of Kashmir controlled by Pakistan. According to India, those investments will further entrench Pakistan's control over those areas and make negotiations even more difficult. India is also concerned that the China-Pakistan Economic Corridor will make it easier for terrorists to cross into India given its close proximity to the border shared by India and Pakistan (Li, 2018). And as the corridor passes through Kashmir, it ends in the Xinjiang Province in western China, which also borders Kazakhstan, Kyrgyzstan, Tajikistan, Pakistan, India, Mongolia, Russia, and Afghanistan. This further entrenches China's presence in Central Asia just as the presence of the United States is dwindling following its withdrawal from Afghanistan (Castle, 2018).

Xinjiang has historically been a crossroads and controlled by different groups of people through the centuries, such as Indo-Europeans, Turks, Mongols, and Tibetans. But it was the Han Dynasty that recognized its strategic importance for China, and it would later be a key part of the Silk Road that connected China with the West. Even the Russians and British competed for influence over Xinjiang in the nineteenth century, and it was later the main route for Soviet aid during the Second World War in support of China's fight against Japan (Barnett, 1993). Xinjiang is also now important to China and its connection to Central Asia, especially since the construction of the Kazakhstan-China oil pipeline that reaches from western China to the Caspian Sea and helps the Chinese with energy security by bypassing Russia. There is also the Central Asia-China gas pipeline that reaches from China to Turkmenistan and is expected to supply most of China's natural gas needs over the next few decades (Cooley, 2012).

But Xinjiang has recently been supposedly the site of some of the gravest human rights violations committed by China since Xi Jinping came to power. Over one million Muslims have been sent to camps for "thought reform" with the Chinese government saying the camps are for "vocational and educational training" for people whose "minds have been poisoned to the extent of losing reason" due to adopting religious extremist views. The United States Department of State believes there are as many as 1,200 camps throughout Xinjiang that are designed to "erase ethnic and religious identities under the pretext of "vocational training."" American sanctions now target Xinjiang surveillance companies and products, which many speculate are produced using forced or slave labor in the camps (Shirk, 2023; U.S. Department of State, 2025).

The United States Department Labor explicitly states that the Chinese government "has subjected Uyghurs and members of other predominantly Muslim ethnic minority groups in the Xinjiang Uyghur Autonomous Region (XUAR) to genocide, state-imposed forced labor, and crimes against humanity." China has fifty-five recognized ethnic groups in addition to the majority Han group. It is the mostly Muslim minority groups like Uyghurs, Kazakhs, Kyrgyz, and others that experience discrimination and repression in Xinjiang and also throughout China (U.S. Department of Labor, 2024).

One camp in Kashgar, Xinjiang, had forced labor comprised of Uyghurs making textiles. The Bureau of International Labor Affairs (ILAB) now includes goods from China on the *List of Goods Produced by Child Labor and Forced Labor*, which now include gloves, hair products, textiles, thread/yarn, tomato products, polysilicon, caustic soda, metallurgical grade silicon, polyvinyl chloride, aluminum, jujubes, and squid. Goods produced by other countries but use cotton from China have also been added to the list by the ILAB (U.S. Department of Labor, 2024).

But expanding more control over Xinjiang gives China more access to its energy resources, which is crucial for both its economic development and energy security. Twenty percent of China's total oil reserves are in Xinjiang and estimated to be around 21 billion tons. The largest coal reserves in China are also in Xinjiang and estimated to be around forty percent of China's total reserves. Billions of cubic meters of natural gas are also produced annually by Xinjiang as well (Wong, 2014). From energy production to being the key point on the China-Pakistan Economic Corridor that gives China access to the Port of Gwadar and Indian Ocean, along with being highly close geographically to India, Xinjiang will remain both important for China's continuing economic development and also a flashpoint of geopolitical tensions and human rights concerns. And it is those tensions and concerns that allow the valid question of whether China is an honest trade broker to be asked.

9. MOVING FORWARD

One of the other major contributing facts when trying to answer if China is an honest trade broker is the Sino-Russian strategic partnership that has been gaining in strength in recent years. Recent examples include Russia helping China expand its presence in the Arctic, while China has increased its energy imports from Russia and provided support for Russia in its invasion of Ukraine. The Arctic provides not only an abundance of natural resources just like the South China Sea, but also potential shipping routes as the region is expected to warm and see its ice caps melt more over the coming decades. Chinese and Russian coast guards have also increased their military cooperation in the Arctic as well. And the Ukrainian government has identified Chinese support for Russian forces in Ukraine recently include gunpowder and artillery (Garamone, 2024; Zhang, 2024; Melkozerova, 2025).

While neither country has the global reach and influence of the United States, China and Russia have both been working to limit American involvement in Central Asia for economic reasons, but also to prevent color revolutions. Few things would threaten a party-state capitalist model of power more than democratic movements and color revolutions, which both Russia and China blame the West for influencing (Bolt and Cross, 2018; Shirk, 2023). Both regimes in Beijing and Moscow have internal legitimacy crises at home, which is why their best defense is to portray the United States system as broken to advance the argument that there is no better system other than the one provided by those already in power. And one way they do this is by engaging in hybrid warfare, which is not like a traditional war with a beginning and an end. Instead, the hybrid war being waged by this partnership is never-ending (Sciutto, 2020).

Both China and Russia are also focused on righting the wrongs they consider having happened in their respective histories. From the collapse of the Soviet Union to the events that occurred between China and Western powers going back to the nineteenth century, both Russia and China seek to right their perceived wrongs of history that they believe keeps them from being world powers on par with the United States and the West (Sciutto, 2020). The question remains as Kissinger (2011) poses is can the United States merge their efforts to build a world and new world order in the Pacific that is peaceful for all Pacific nations? Because the alternative is this rivalry becoming competitive to the point that it is a zero-sum game, which heightens the risk of war like it eventually did for Europe leading up to the First World War.

And with Trump back in the White House and bringing with him advisers like Peter Navarro, trade has once again become viewed by both the United States and China as a zero-sum game. Tariffs have also targeted other countries like India due to it continuing to import Russian oil and becoming closer with China. The Trump Administration has made it clear that other countries must decide between being friendly with the United States or China wit Navarro stating on August 23, 2025 that he expects tariffs as high as fifty percent to be charged on Indian imports unless India complies with Trump's demands (Yahoo Finance, 2025).

The current trajectory is unfortunately trending in that direction due to the technological race between China and the United States that has morphed into a new cold war with the risk of becoming hot largely due to China no longer being trusted as an honest trade broker. Something to keep an eye on over the coming months and years is the financial stake the United States just took in Intel and how that might impact how Western tech companies do business with China (Wile, 2025). The competition between the "American Dream" and "Chinese Dream" is now in full swing (Daly, 2022; Kim et al, 2023) and the vision of Kissinger about those dreams coming together for the common good seems unlikely (Kissinger, 2011).

REFERENCES

Barnett, A. D. (1993). *China's Far West: Four Decades of Change*. Westview Press.

Bianchi, R. R. (2019). *China and the Islamic World: How the New Silk Road is Transforming Global Politics*. Oxford University Press. DOI: 10.1093/oso/9780190915285.001.0001

Bolt, P. J., & Cross, S. N. (2018). *China, Russia, and Twenty-First Century Global Geopolitics*. Oxford University Press.

Breuninger, K. (2025, Jul. 29). *U.S.-China trade talks end without extension of tariff truce, as Trump weighs options*. CNBC. https://www.cnbc.com/2025/07/29/trump-china-trade-tariffs-bessent.html

Brown, K., & Tzu-hui, K. W. (2019). *The Trouble with Taiwan: History, the United States and a Rising China*. Zed. DOI: 10.5040/9781350225688

Buchanan, Ben. (2020). *The Hacker and the State: Cyber Attacks and the New Normal of Geopolitics*. Harvard University Press.

Burdekin, Richard C.K. & Shen, Yijing & Whited, Hsin-hui. (2013). Cross-strait linkages: historical perspective and empirical evidence. In Peter C.Y. Chow (Eds). *Economic Integration Across the Taiwan Strait: Global Perspectives*. Edward Elgar Publishing.

Campbell, C. (2021, Jan. 4). *Where Is Alibaba Founder Jack Ma? What the Saga of One of the World's Richest Men Reveals About China Under Xi Jinping*. Time. https://time.com/5926062/jack-ma/

Carney, R. W. (2018). *Authoritarian Capitalism: Sovereign Wealth Funds and State Owned Enterprises in East Asia and Beyond.* Cambridge University Press. DOI: 10.1017/9781108186797

Castle, M. A. (2018). Globalization's Impact: Trade and Investment in China-India Relations. In Paul, T. V. (Ed.), *The China-India Rivalry in the Globalization Era*. Georgetown University Press. DOI: 10.2307/j.ctv75db2z.14

Chen, C. (2018). China and India's Quest for Resources and Its Impact on the Rivalry. In Paul, T. V. (Ed.), *The China-India Rivalry in the Globalization Era*. Georgetown University Press. DOI: 10.2307/j.ctv75db2z.10

Chirot, D., & Hall, T. D. (1982). World-System Theory. *Annual Review of Sociology*, *8*(1), 81–106. DOI: 10.1146/annurev.so.08.080182.000501

Chu, Ming-chin Monique. (2013). Semiconductor interconnectivity across the Taiwan Strait: a case study approach. In Peter C.Y. Chow (Eds). *Economic Integration Across the Taiwan Strait: Global Perspectives*. Edward Elgar Publishing.

Cooley, A. (2012). *Great Games, Local Rules: The New Great Power Contest in Central Asia*. Oxford University Press. DOI: 10.1093/acprof:oso/9780199929825.001.0001

Corr, A. (2018). Introduction. In Coor, A. (Ed.), *Great Powers, Grand Strategies: The New Game in the South China Sea*. Naval Institute Press. DOI: 10.2307/j.ctt20061hj.5

Daly, R. (2022, Mar. 10). *China and the United States: It's a Cold War, but don't panic*. Bulletin of the Atomic Scientists. https://thebulletin.org/premium/2022-03/china-and-the-united-states-its-a-cold-war-but-dont-panic/

European Parliament. (2013, Jun. 26). *China's investment in ports: what is behind the "String of Pearls" theory?* https://epthinktank.eu/2013/06/26/chinas-investment-in-ports-what-is-behind-the-string-of-pearls-theory/

Feng, E. (2020, Nov. 3). *Regulators Squash Giant Ant Group IPO*. National Public Radio. https://www.npr.org/2020/11/03/930799521/regulators-squash-giant-ant-ipo

Finance, Y. (2025, Aug. 23). *Trump tariffs live updates: Trump says US to tariff furniture imports following investigation*. https://finance.yahoo.com/news/live/trump-tariffs-live-updates-trump-says-us-to-tariff-furniture-imports-following-investigation-200619445.html

Forsyth, I. (2018). Old Game Plan, New Game: China's Grand Strategy in the South China Sea. In Coor, A. (Ed.), *Great Powers, Grand Strategies: The New Game in the South China Sea*. Naval Institute Press.

Gallagher, K. P. (2016). *Latin America's China Boom and the Fate of the Washington Consensus*. Oxford University Press.

Garamone, J. (2024, Dec. 5). *China Increasing Interest in Strategic Arctic Region*. U.S. Department of Defense. https://www.defense.gov/News/News-Stories/Article/Article/3986308/china-increasing-interest-in-strategic-arctic-region/

Guo, X. (2012). *China's Security State: Philosophy, Evolution, and Politics*. Cambridge University Press. DOI: 10.1017/CBO9781139150897

Han, Z., & Belanger, J.-F. (2018). Balancing Strategies and the China-India Rivalry. In Paul, T. V. (Ed.), *The China-India Rivalry in the Globalization Era*. Georgetown University Press. DOI: 10.2307/j.ctv75db2z.9

Hayton, B. (2014). *The South China Sea: The Struggle for Power in Asia*. Yale University Press.

Kim, P. M., Turpin, M., & Jr, N. Joseph S. & Weiss, Jessica Chen & Jo, Eun A. (2023, Sept. 1). *Should the US pursue a new Cold War with China?* Brookings Institution. https://www.brookings.edu/articles/should-the-us-pursue-a-new-cold-war-with-china/

King, R., & Kendall, G. (2004). *The State, Democracy, and Globalization*. Palgrave Macmillan.

Kirby, W. C. (2013). Global Business across the Taiwan Strait: The Case of the Taiwan Semiconductor Manufacturing Company Limited. In Wen-hsin, Y. (Ed.), *Mobile Horizons: Dynamics across the Taiwan Strait*. Institute of East Asian Studies, University of California. DOI: 10.2307/jj.7762620.11

Kissinger, H. (1994). *Diplomacy*. Simon & Schuster.

Kissinger, H. (2011). *On China*. Penguin Press.

Kissinger, H. (2014). *World Order*. Penguin Press.

Krige, John. (2024). Debate: Building a U.S. Regulatory Empire in the Chip War with China. *Technology and Culture, 65*(4), 1081-. DOI: 10.1353/tech.2024.a940462

Kroeber, A. R. (2016). *China's Economy: What Everyone Needs to Know*. Oxford University Press.

Lewis, J. A. (2024, Mar. 13). *TikTok and National Security*. Center for Strategic & International Studies. https://www.csis.org/analysis/tiktok-and-national-security

Li, Z. (2018). The Maritime Silk Route and India: The Challenge of Overcoming Cognitive Divergence. In David Brewster (Eds). *India & China at Sea: Competition for Naval Dominance in the Indian Ocean*. Oxford University Press.

Liu, R. C., Tang, H. W., Kao, Y., & Chou, Y. (2025). From vulnerabilities to resilience: Taiwan's semiconductor industry and geopolitical challenges. *Telecommunications Policy*, *49*(4), 102951. DOI: 10.1016/j.telpol.2025.102951

Malik, A. A., Parks, B., Russell, B., Lin, J. J., Walsh, K., Solomon, K., Zhang, S., Elston, T.-B., & Goodman, S. (2021, Sept.). *Banking on the Belt and Road. Insights from a new global dataset of 13,427 Chinese Development Projects*. AIDDATA: A Research Lab at William & Mary. https://docs.aiddata.org/ad4/pdfs/Banking_on_the_Belt_and_Road__Insights_from_a_new_global_dataset_of_13427_Chinese_development_projects.pdf

McDevitt, M. A. (2020). *China as a Twenty-First Century Naval Power*. Naval Institute Press.

Melkozerova, V. (2025, Apr. 17). *China is supplying weapons to Russia, Zelenskyy says*. Politico. https://www.politico.eu/article/china-is-supplying-weapons-to-russia-zelenskyy-said/

Meredith, R. (2007). *The Elephant and the Dragon: The Rise of India and China and What It Means for All of Us*. W.W. Norton & Company.

Miao, Y., & Deng, T. (2020). China's Capital Account Liberalization: A Ruby Jubilee and Beyond. In Amstad, M., Sun, G., & Xiong, W. (Eds.), *The Handbook of China's Financial System*. Princeton University Press. DOI: 10.2307/j.ctv11vcdpc.14

Miller, C. (2022). *Chip War: The Fight for the World's Most Critical Technology*. Scribner.

Minges, M. (2025, Jan. 23). *National Security and the TikTok Ban*. American University. https://www.american.edu/sis/news/20250123-national-security-and-the-tik-tok-ban.cfm

Mistreanu, S. (2025, Apr. 5). *A timeline of US-China tit-for-tat tariffs since Trump's first term*. Associated Press. https://apnews.com/article/china-us-tariffs-timeline-trump-xi-1eeed2865dc7b14e23d7eb8069ba41ea

Moore, B. (1967). *Social Origins of Dictatorship and Democracy: Lord and Peasant in the Making of the Modern World*. Beacon Press.

Patey, L. (2024, Dec. 2). *A Taiwan crisis is a China crisis*. Danish Institute for International Studies. https://www.diis.dk/en/research/a-taiwan-crisis-is-a-china-crisis#:~:text=The%20global%20economic%20decline%20from%20Chinese%20military,other%20industries%20dependent%20on%20the%20advanced%20technology

Pautasso, D. (2016). The Role of Africa in the New Maritime Silk Road. *Brazilian Journal of African Studies*, *1*(2), 118–130.

Sciutto, J. (2020). *The Shadow War: Inside Russia's and China's Secret Operations to Defeat America*. HarperCollins.

Shambaugh, D. (2021). *Where Great Powers Meet: America & China in Southeast Asia*. Oxford University Press. DOI: 10.1093/oso/9780190914974.001.0001

Shirk, S. L. (2023). *Overreach: How China Derailed Its Peaceful Rise*. Oxford University Press.

Shovlin, J. (2021). *Trading With the Enemy: Britain, France, and the 18th-Century Quest for a Peaceful World Order*. Yale University Press.

Tarrosy, I. (2020). China's Belt and Road Initiative in Africa, Debt Risk and New Dependency: The Case of Ethiopia. *African Studies Quarterly*, *19*(3–4), 8–28.

Tesfaye, A. (2020). *China in Ethiopia: The Long-Term Perspective*. State University of New York Press. DOI: 10.1353/book75410

The Times of India. (2024, Dec. 31). *'No one can sever out blood ties': China's President Xi Jinping on Taiwan 'unification' during New Year speech*. https://timesofindia.indiatimes.com/world/china/no-one-can-sever-our-blood-ties-chinas-president-xi-jinping-on-taiwan-unification-during-new-year-speech/articleshow/116832978.cms

Tseng, P. (2023). The Metaphysics of Globalization in Gadamer: A Case Study of Contemporary Taiwan. *Dialogo (Constanţa)*, *10*(1), 103–111. DOI: 10.51917/dialogo.2023.10.1.7

U.S. Department of Labor. (2024). *Against Their Will: The Situation in Xinjiang*. https://www.dol.gov/agencies/ilab/against-their-will-the-situation-in-xinjiang

U.S. Department of State. (2025, Jan. 20). *Forced Labor in China's Xinjiang Region*. https://www.state.gov/forced-labor-in-chinas-xinjiang-region/

Wile, R. (2025, Aug. 22). *U.S. takes 10% stake in Intel as Trump flexes more power over big business*. NBC News. https://www.nbcnews.com/business/business-news/intel-agrees-us-stake-in-company-how-much-what-to-know-rcna226667

Wong, E. (2014, Dec. 20). *China Invests in Region Rich in Oil, Coal and Also Strife*. The New York Times. https://www.nytimes.com/2014/12/21/world/asia/china-invests-in-xinjiang-region-rich-in-oil-coal-and-also-strife.html

Woodward, J. (2017). *The US vs China: Asia's new Cold War?* Manchester University Press. DOI: 10.7228/manchester/9781526121998.001.0001

Yanlin, W. (2011, Jan. 18). *China's 2010 FDI exceeds US$100 bln for 1st time*. Shanghai Daily. https://archive.shine.cn/business/economy/Chinas-2010-FDI-exceeds-US100-bln-for-1st-time/shdaily.shtml

Yoshihara, T., & Holmes, J. R. (2018). *Red Star Over the Pacific: China's Rise and the Challenge to U.S. Maritime Strategy* (2nd ed.). Naval Institute Press.

Yuan, J. (2018). Managing Maritime Competition between India and China. In David Brewster (Eds). *India & China at Sea: Competition for Naval Dominance in the Indian Ocean*. Oxford University Press. DOI: 10.1093/oso/9780199479337.003.0003

Zhang, B. (2020). Fintech Development. In Amstad, M., Sun, G., & Xiong, W. (Eds.), *The Handbook of China's Financial System*. Princeton University Press. DOI: 10.2307/j.ctv11vcdpc.21

Zhang, J. (2024, Dec. 9). *Russia clears the path for China in the Arctic*. Geopolitical Intelligence Services. https://www.gisreportsonline.com/r/china-arctic-russia/

Zhang, L. (2023, Jul. 15). *A timeline of China's 32-month Big Tech crackdown that killed the world's largest IPO and wiped out trillions in value*. South China Morning Post. https://www.scmp.com/tech/big-tech/article/3227753/timeline-chinas-32-month-big-tech-crackdown-killed-worlds-largest-ipo-and-wiped-out-trillions-value?module=perpetual_scroll_0&pgtype=article

Zufle, S. (2023). *The Political Economy of China's Belt and Road Initiative in East Africa*. Springer.

Chapter 10
China's Critical Mineral and EV Exports to the U.S. and Brazil:
Geopolitical and Economic Implications Amid Rising Tariffs

José Floriano Pereira Lima Filho
https://orcid.org/0000-0003-0434-1825
University of Sao Paulo, Brazil & University of Brasilia, Brazil

ABSTRACT

This chapter analyzes the geopolitical and economic implications of China's critical mineral and electric vehicle (EV) exports to the United States and Brazil amidst rising tariffs. Critical minerals are essential for the global green energy transition, particularly for EV batteries and renewable energy infrastructure. China has become the dominant force across the entire critical minerals supply chain, from raw material extraction to high-tech component manufacturing, and is the world's largest exporter of EVs. The U.S. has imposed substantial tariffs on Chinese imports. Brazil, with its significant critical mineral reserves, has adopted a phased import tax system for EVs. The intensifying competition for critical minerals, exacerbated by the U.S.-China trade war, presents a "Green Paradox," where the pursuit of clean energy risks environmental degradation. Ultimately, unilateral trade measures are insufficient to address supply chain vulnerabilities and environmental costs, underscoring the necessity for multilateral cooperation.

DOI: 10.4018/979-8-3373-3835-4.ch010

1. INTRODUCTION

Critical minerals form the backbone of an intended global green energy transition, serving as inputs for electric vehicle (EV) batteries, renewable energy infrastructure, and advanced technologies. The geopolitical landscape surrounding these minerals has intensified as nations compete for secure access to resources essential for economic security and technological advancement. Among the world's largest and most resource-rich nations, Brazil, China, and the United States are strategic actors, each grappling with distinct economic challenges in securing their roles across the critical mineral supply chain. This dynamic is increasingly defined by the U.S.-China rivalry, which has evolved into a full-fledged "economic systemic war" aimed at decoupling critical supply chains and establishing dominance in the industries of the future (Global4Cast.org, 2025).

China has strategically positioned itself as the dominant force across the entire critical minerals supply chain, from the initial extraction of raw materials to the final manufacturing of high-tech components. This comprehensive control, which extends to the processing of 60-70% of the world's cobalt, has solidified its major role in the international trade of these vital commodities (Detry et al., 2023; International Trade Centre, 2023b). The Asian country currently controls approximately half of the global critical minerals market value and has emerged as the world's largest exporter of conventional combustion vehicles and electric vehicles (EVs) (Chang & Bradsher, 2024). This dominance has raised significant concerns among international partners about dependency and supply stability. Beijing has shown a willingness to weaponize its control through export restrictions on key minerals, justifying such measures based on national security concerns (Shirley & Svensson, 2023).

In response, the United States actively seeks to bolster domestic production and build resilient supply chains through "friend-shoring" partnerships to diversify its sources. Reliant on imports for essential minerals, the U.S. has enacted legislation like the Inflation Reduction Act (IRA) to enhance national security and promote domestic production by offering substantial tax credits tied to domestic content provisions (Taulli & Busby, 2025). This techno-nationalist approach is complemented by aggressive tariffs on Chinese goods, including a surge to 102.5% on EVs, to shield its domestic industry from what it perceives as unfair competition (Shokri, 2025).

The U.S. and Brazil have imposed different levels of protective measures aimed at bolstering domestic industries while attempting to navigate complex international relations with China. The American government has been enacting substantial tariffs on Chinese imports since early 2018, up to the point of including critical minerals and EVs as part of a strategy to reduce reliance on foreign sources and enhance local manufacturing capabilities. These tariffs are intended to promote domestic industries, particularly in the burgeoning renewable energy sector, which relies heavily on these materials for technologies such as batteries and EVs. However, those measures have led to rising production costs and retaliatory tariffs from China, potentially hampering U.S. advances in critical sectors.

Simultaneously, Brazil is leveraging its vast reserves of niobium, lithium, and rare earth elements (REEs) to position itself as a pivotal supplier in the increasingly competitive global market (Vásquez, 2024). As the holder of the world's second-largest REE reserves, Brazil represents one of the few viable long-term alternatives to Chinese dominance (bne IntelliNews, 2025; Campbell, 2025). The country has adopted a sophisticated green industrial policy, encapsulated in its "Mover" Program, which uses a mix of strategic protectionism and incentives to attract foreign direct investment (Ramos, 2024; Nunes & Lopes, 2024). By implementing phased import taxes on EVs, Brazil is successfully coercing Chinese automakers like BYD and Great Wall Motor to establish local manufacturing facilities, thereby transforming a trade challenge into an opportunity for industrialization (Parodi & Waldersee, 2025).

As countries pursue ambitious climate goals amid these rising trade tensions, the demand for critical minerals is projected to surge, intensifying the competition and/or collaboration among Brazil, China, and the U.S. This dynamic landscape highlights not only the significance of critical minerals in the energy transition but also underscores the ongoing challenges and opportunities each country faces.

The strategic interactions between these three nations concerning trade policies for energy transition goods are underscored by their respective tensions, environmental sustainability concerns, and the need for responsible mining practices. As countries pursue ambitious climate goals amid rising trade tensions—particularly with continued tariff impositions under Trump's second administration—the demand for critical minerals is projected to surge, intensifying competition and/or collaboration among Brazil, China, and the U.S. This dynamic landscape highlights not only the significance of critical minerals in the energy transition but also emphasizes ongoing challenges and opportunities each country faces in securing its positions within the global market.

This chapter provides a comprehensive analysis of China's critical mineral and EV exports to Brazil and the U.S., contextualized within this broader geopolitical struggle. It explores how tariffs and industrial policies are influencing global trade dynamics, supply chain resilience, and industrial decarbonization efforts, while evaluating Brazil's potential as a major supplier amid its own environmental challenges and diplomatic maneuvering.

2. CHINA'S DOMINANCE IN CRITICAL MINERALS AND EV MANUFACTURING

China plays a dominant role in the global market for critical minerals, the result of a long-term, state-driven strategy to exert significant control over the extraction, processing, and manufacturing stages of the supply chain. The country is the primary source for a considerable number of minerals vital to the green transition and high-tech industries, including lithium, cobalt, nickel, and the 17 rare earth elements (REEs) indispensable for high-performance magnets used in EV motors and wind turbines (Detry et al., 2023; Kuhn, 2024).

Such concentration has provided the Chinese with undeniable power and influence over global value chains supporting the energy transition[1], reaching several countries. Given its dominance in the three stages of the critical minerals supply chain (upstream, midstream, and downstream)[2], it is no wonder that China also plays a major role in the international trade of those commodities and goods. This dominance is not merely a matter of geological endowment but a calculated industrial policy that has created a strategic stranglehold on the midstream processing segment, giving Beijing immense leverage in the escalating U.S.-China tech trade war (Detry et al., 2023; International Trade Centre, 2023b).

The scale of China's control is staggering. Chinese companies refine an average global market share of around 70% of critical metals (IEA, 2025). This includes processing an estimated 90% of the world's REEs, 68% of its cobalt, 65% of its nickel, and 60% of its lithium needed for EV batteries (Shirley & Svensson, 2023; Detry et al., 2023). This midstream bottleneck means that even countries with significant mining operations, such as the United States and Australia, are often forced to send their raw or semi-processed minerals to China for refining (Detry et al., 2023). This concentration of refining operations has raised global concerns about supply disruptions and the potential for China to "weaponize" its dominance, a fear realized when Beijing imposed export controls on gallium, germanium, and REE processing technologies in retaliation for U.S. restrictions (Kuhn, 2024; International Trade Centre, 2023b).

The strategic control over the supply chain underpins China's ascendance as an EV manufacturing superpower. By ensuring a secure and low-cost supply of processed minerals and battery components, Chinese firms like CATL and BYD have become the world's largest battery producers (Garcia Herrero et al., 2022). This vertical integration provides a formidable cost advantage, making a Chinese-made EV roughly 30% cheaper to assemble than its Western counterpart (Chang & Bradsher, 2024). As a result, China has not only satisfied its massive domestic demand but has also become the world's largest automobile exporter. This has created what trading partners label an "overcapacity" issue that compels an aggressive export strategy, directly leading to the imposition of steep tariffs by the U.S. and the European Union (Wang, 2024).

Faced with growing protectionism in the West, China has demonstrated strategic flexibility by diversifying its export markets and localizing production. Brazil has emerged as a primary target, becoming the single largest importer of Chinese-made electric cars (Nunes & Lopes, 2024; Ramos, 2024). In response to Brazil's new phased tariff system, Chinese companies are now investing billions to build local factories, effectively transplanting China's efficient supply chain model abroad to circumvent trade barriers (Caballero, 2025; ResearchAndMarkets.com, 2024). This strategy allows China to maintain its global market presence, turning a trade confrontation into an opportunity for deeper market penetration and solidifying its role as the indispensable hub in the global green technology supply chain.

2.1 Critical Minerals International Trade

The global trade in critical minerals has transformed from a market driven by commercial logic into a highly contentious geopolitical arena. This shift is characterized by soaring demand, acute supply chain chokepoints, and the strategic weaponization of trade policy. The annual trade value of energy-related critical minerals has skyrocketed from approximately \$53 billion to \$378 billion over the past two decades, with growth accelerating as the energy transition gains momentum (Snoussi-Mimouni & Avérous, 2024). This fierce competition is actively reshaping the international landscape, defined by three dominant and intersecting trends: the rise of resource nationalism, the deliberate bifurcation of global supply chains, and the formation of competing green technology alliances.

This surge is not uniform; trade in lithium, the so-called "white gold" essential for rechargeable batteries, has increased over tenfold since 2019, driven primarily by demand from manufacturing hubs in Asia (International Trade Centre, 2023a). This booming trade underscores a fundamental reality: no single nation possesses all the resources required for a modern economy, making international trade an indispensable, albeit contentious, mechanism for securing supply.

A defining feature of the critical minerals market is the extreme geographic concentration of extraction. For example, South Africa is a key producer of platinum-group metals and Chile is the world's leading exporter of copper, while the Democratic Republic of Congo (DRC) is the source of over 60% of the world's cobalt (International Trade Centre, 2023b; Snoussi-Mimouni & Avérous, 2024). Leveraging this concentration, a wave of resource nationalism is sweeping through resource-rich nations. These countries are no longer content to simply export raw ores; they are increasingly using export restrictions, ownership mandates, and processing requirements to conserve domestic resources, promote downstream industries, and capture more value from their natural wealth.

A clear example is Indonesia, the world's top nickel producer, which implemented a complete ban on unprocessed nickel ore exports to force foreign companies to build smelters and refineries within its borders. Similarly, Namibia has banned the export of unprocessed lithium to encourage domestic value addition (Kuhn, 2024; International Trade Centre, 2023b). This trend is further reinforced by policies like "tariff escalation," where major importing nations apply low tariffs on raw ores but significantly higher tariffs on finished products, which has historically discouraged developing countries from moving up the value chain (UNCTAD, 2025). The current pushback through resource nationalism represents a direct challenge to the established economic order.

On the demand side, consumption is similarly concentrated, with China, the European Union (EU), the United States (U.S.), and Japan acting as the primary importers (Snoussi-Mimouni & Avérous, 2024). That concentration means that political instability, natural disasters, or policy changes in a single exporting or importing nation can send shockwaves across the entire global supply chain.

However, a simple analysis of raw material flows is insufficient. The most significant concentration, and the greatest source of strategic leverage, lies in the midstream processing and refining stage. While a country may possess vast mineral reserves, it often lacks the complex, capital-intensive, and environmentally challenging capacity to refine them into high-purity metals. China has achieved a commanding position in this segment, processing an estimated 90% of the world's REEs and 60-70% of its cobalt (Detry et al., 2023; International Trade Centre, 2023b). Such dominance bifurcates trade flows: raw and semi-processed ores flow into China, while higher-value refined materials and manufactured components flow out. This structure is reinforced by "tariff escalation," where importing nations apply low tariffs on raw ores but significantly higher tariffs on finished products like wires and tubes, discouraging resource-rich developing countries from moving up the value chain (UNCTAD, 2025).

The strategic importance of these minerals has inevitably led to the weaponization of trade policy. Nations are increasingly using export restrictions to conserve domestic resources, promote downstream industries, or exert political leverage. China has famously restricted exports of gallium, germanium, and REE processing technology, while other countries, like Namibia, have banned the export of unprocessed lithium to encourage domestic value addition (Kuhn, 2024; International Trade Centre, 2023b).

In response, the U.S. and its allies are actively pursuing a strategic decoupling, creating a bifurcated supply chain split between a China-centric sphere and a Western-aligned "friend-shored" ecosystem. This is not just rhetoric; it is being enforced through powerful industrial policies. The U.S. Inflation Reduction Act (IRA), for example, ties lucrative EV tax credits to stringent domestic content rules that explicitly exclude materials processed in "Foreign Entities of Concern" like China, effectively creating a powerful financial motive for automakers to reconfigure their supply chains (Taulli & Busby, 2025). This policy is designed to systematically build alternative, resilient supply chains among politically aligned nations.

This supply chain bifurcation is accelerating the formation of competing green technology alliances. Importing nations and blocs are deploying defensive trade strategies to secure their access to minerals. The European Union's Critical Raw Materials Act, for example, explicitly aims to diversify supplies away from any single country and foster "strategic partnerships" with resource-rich nations (Kuhn, 2024).

On a broader scale, the U.S. has spearheaded the Minerals Security Partnership (MSP), an alliance of 14 countries and the EU focused on catalyzing public and private investment in responsible critical mineral supply chains. The MSP is a direct geopolitical counterweight to China's influence, which it has cultivated through its Belt and Road Initiative and partnerships within blocs like BRICS[3]. These competing alliances are transforming the market into a geopolitical chessboard where access to resources is synonymous with economic and national security. As the world accelerates its transition away from fossil fuels, the interplay between these nationalistic policies, bifurcated supply chains, and strategic alliances will determine the pace of the green transition and redraw the map of global economic power.

2.2 China in the new landscape

Beyond its domestic production, China has also made significant investments in mining operations abroad, further securing its access to raw materials. For example, a large portion of the world's cobalt, a key component in electric vehicle batteries, is extracted in the Democratic Republic of Congo, with a significant share of this extraction being controlled by Chinese-owned companies (International Trade Centre, 2023b).

However, it is in the midstream stage—processing and refining—that China's dominance is most pronounced. Raw minerals extracted from the earth are of little use until they are separated, purified, and converted into high-purity metals and chemical compounds. China has invested heavily in developing the complex and often environmentally challenging technologies required for this stage. As a result, besides controlling the global processing of rare earth elements and cobalt, it also processes over 45% of the world's refined copper production (Detry et al., 2023; International Trade Centre, 2023b; Kuhn, 2024; UNCTAD, 2025). This midstream bottleneck gives China immense leverage over the entire supply chain. Even countries with mining operations, such as the United States and Australia, often have to send their raw or semi-processed minerals to China for refining (Detry et al., 2023).

This dominance naturally extends to the downstream stage, which involves the manufacturing of components and finished goods. With a secure and cost-effective supply of processed critical minerals, China has become the world's leading producer of a wide range of high-tech products. For instance, the country manufactures over 90% of the world's high-performance permanent magnets, which are crucial for electric vehicle motors and wind turbine generators (Detry et al., 2023). This manufacturing prowess means that even when the final product is assembled elsewhere, a significant portion of its value and key components often originates in China.

Given its dominance in the three stages of the critical minerals supply chain, it is no wonder that China also has a major role in the international trade of those commodities and goods. The country is the world's largest importer of many raw critical minerals, which it then processes and either exports as refined materials or uses in its domestic manufacturing sector (Snoussi-Mimouni & Avérous, 2024; UNCTAD, 2025). In 2022, China was the largest importer of critical minerals, accounting for 33% of the global total (Snoussi-Mimouni & Avérous, 2024). That creates a situation where resource-rich countries are often dependent on China as a primary market for their raw materials.

At the same time, China is a major exporter of processed minerals and downstream products, supplying the world with the building blocks of the green energy transition. This has led to significant trade imbalances and dependencies for countries and blocs like the European Union, which relies on China for 100% of its supply of some heavy rare earth elements (Kuhn, 2024). Furthermore, China has shown a willingness to use its market power as a political tool, implementing export restrictions on certain critical minerals and related technologies to safeguard its national security and economic interests. These actions have sent shockwaves through global supply chains and have spurred other nations to seek greater self-sufficiency and diversification.

The strategic and long-term approach to the critical minerals sector has resulted in a level of dominance that is unparalleled in the modern global economy. By controlling key aspects of the upstream, midstream, and downstream stages of the supply chain, China has not only fueled its own economic growth but has also become an indispensable player in the international trade of these essential materials. As the world continues to move towards a more sustainable and technologically advanced future, China's grip on the critical minerals market will undoubtedly remain a central feature of the global economic and geopolitical landscape.

This market dominance represents a strategic advantage for China in global trade negotiations and provides leverage in geopolitical disputes. By controlling such a significant portion of essential inputs for green technology, China maintains influence over the pace and direction of the global energy transition, creating vulnerabilities for nations pursuing decarbonization goals.

2.3 Vertical Integration Strategy

China's ascendance as a global manufacturing and trade superpower, particularly in high-technology sectors like electric vehicles (EVs) and renewable energy, is not merely a product of scale but the result of a deeply entrenched strategy of vertical integration. This comprehensive approach, which spans the entire supply chain from the upstream extraction of critical minerals to the downstream assembly of finished goods, provides China with unparalleled cost advantages, operational flexibility, and strategic leverage in international trade (Chang & Bradsher, 2024). In an era marked by escalating trade wars, rising tariffs, and export bans, this mastery over the value chain allows China to adapt its export mix. By absorbing protectionist pressures and maintaining its competitive edge, it ensures its exports of batteries, EVs, and other mineral-dependent goods remain a formidable force on the world stage.

The foundation of China's competitive advantage is its deliberate control over the upstream and midstream segments of the critical minerals supply chain. Recognizing that access to raw and processed materials is a prerequisite for high-tech manufacturing, China has invested heavily in securing these inputs. The strategy begins at the source, with Chinese state-backed and private firms making significant investments to secure mineral resources abroad. In Brazil, for example, a Chinese consortium acquired a 15% stake in CBMM, the world's leading producer of niobium, an essential element for high-strength steel. More recently, Chinese firms have acquired significant copper-gold mining operations, securing vital inputs for energy and electronics (Sardain et al., 2024; Xiang, 2025). This global resource acquisition is coupled with near-monopolistic control over midstream processing. China refines an estimated 90% of the world's rare earth elements and a majority of its lithium, cobalt, and graphite, creating a critical bottleneck where even minerals mined elsewhere must be sent to China for purification (Detry et al., 2023; Garcia Herrero et al., 2022).

This control over the foundational layers of the supply chain translates directly into a dominant position in component manufacturing, most notably in the production of EV batteries. As the most expensive and technologically crucial component of an electric vehicle, leadership in battery manufacturing is paramount. Chinese firms like CATL and BYD are the world's largest battery producers, a position built on secure, low-cost access to processed critical minerals (Garcia Herrero et al., 2022).

Vertical integration creates immense cost efficiencies, insulating manufacturers from volatile global commodity markets and enabling them to produce batteries at a significantly lower cost than their international rivals. Analysts estimate that this integration is a primary reason why a Chinese-made EV is around 30% cheaper to assemble than a Western equivalent, with the battery alone accounting for a 29% cost advantage (Chang & Bradsher, 2024). Consequently, China not only satisfies its massive domestic demand but has also become the world's leading exporter of lithium-ion batteries, supplying the very competitors who seek to challenge its EV dominance (Zhang, 2024).

Table 1. Chinese Exports of Critical Minerals and Energy Transition Goods (2010-2023), USD*

Year	To Brazil	To The US	Global
2010	548,715,046.00	4,980,720,855.00	57,943,569,852.00
2011	754,781,865.00	6,491,871,485.00	70,204,137,389.00
2012	805,831,699.00	5,195,040,902.00	55,571,222,874.00
2013	832,373,462.00	5,092,015,701.00	54,850,138,581.00
2014	862,427,440.00	6,432,065,541.00	63,585,520,169.00
2015	570,615,891.00	6,130,016,529.00	64,917,551,498.00
2016	736,959,147.00	5,772,508,131.00	56,510,846,906.00
2017	879,249,170.00	5,830,882,118.00	60,015,248,388.00
2018	1,253,346,906.00	5,211,947,485.00	73,069,439,058.00
2019	1,909,912,286.00	4,652,164,826.00	78,729,603,255.00
2020	1,758,285,950.00	5,198,825,293.00	83,110,132,603.00
2021	4,261,483,307.00	8,602,544,001.00	130,723,742,518.00
2022	6,322,523,857.00	15,335,413,154.00	199,343,203,021.00
2023	6,486,184,579.00	17,285,772,114.00	218,114,709,557.00

Source: Aggregated by the author, based on the filtered data from the ADB/WTO Trade in Critical Minerals database

By integrating its industrial model, China has achieved remarkable strategic flexibility in navigating the turbulent waters of international trade. As Western nations erect tariff walls against finished Chinese products, China can adjust its export strategy to maintain its market presence and influence. When faced with a 100% tariff on EVs in the United States, for instance, the direct impact on vehicle exports is significant but does not sever the supply chain dependency (Zhou & Gao, 2024). The U.S. and Europe remain heavily reliant on imports of Chinese batteries and battery components, which face lower, albeit increasing, tariffs (Zhang, 2024; Mazzocco, 2025). This allows China to pivot its export focus from finished vehicles to the essential, high-value components that other nations' industries cannot function without. This ability to move up and down the value chain in its export mix acts as a powerful buffer, ensuring that Chinese industry continues to profit from the global green transition even when its signature products are targeted by protectionist measures.

China also leverages its integrated supply chain expertise by exporting the entire manufacturing ecosystem itself. To circumvent tariffs and trade barriers on finished goods, Chinese companies are pursuing an aggressive strategy of production localization. Firms like BYD and Great Wall are investing billions to establish assembly plants in Brazil, Mexico, Thailand, and Hungary (IEA, 2025; Parodi & Waldersee, 2025). These overseas factories are often supplied by the same network of Chinese component manufacturers, effectively transplanting China's efficient supply chain model abroad. This not only allows them to bypass tariffs on vehicles imported from China but also to embed their technology and standards within key regional markets, turning a trade confrontation into an opportunity for deeper global integration and market penetration.

The vertical integration strategy has become the central pillar of manufacturing and trade leadership. Chinese companies secured raw materials at the source, dominating global processing and achieving economies of scale in component and final assembly. Hence, China has built a resilient and cost-competitive industrial base. This comprehensive control provides a strategic flexibility that is proving highly effective in mitigating the impacts of the global trade war. While tariffs may disrupt the flow of finished EVs, they do little to address the West's fundamental reliance on China's midstream dominance in batteries and processed minerals. As long as this integration remains intact, China will continue to be an indispensable node in the global supply chain, able to leverage its control to navigate trade barriers and power its exports across the full spectrum of mineral-dependent goods.

2.4 Automakers Taken by Storm in Global Markets

China's dramatic rise to become the world's largest automobile exporter signifies a tectonic shift in the global industrial landscape. This new status is not solely built upon its well-documented supremacy in electric vehicles (EVs) but on a formidable two-track strategy that combines futuristic EV dominance with a pragmatic off-loading of its vast internal combustion engine (ICE) vehicle capacity. Meticulously cultivated over fifteen years through strategic industrial policy and control over critical supply chains, China's EV sector now poses an existential threat to legacy automakers (Chang & Bradsher, 2024; Zhou & Gao, 2024). Simultaneously, as its domestic market rapidly electrifies, China is exporting its surplus gasoline-powered cars on a massive scale. This dual-front export drive has triggered a new phase in the global trade war, with Western economies erecting steep tariff walls to protect their industries. In this increasingly protectionist environment, China's multifaceted export strategy is proving resilient, forcing a realignment of global trade flows and demonstrating that its automotive ambitions cannot be easily contained by unilateral barriers.

The cornerstone of China's automotive power is its state-driven leadership in electric vehicles. Beijing's long-term national strategy, aimed at leapfrogging Western ICE technology and ensuring energy security, has been backed by immense state support, estimated to be over $230 billion since 2009 (Chang & Bradsher, 2024). This support, ranging from consumer subsidies to low-interest loans for manufacturers, fostered a hyper-competitive domestic market and allowed Chinese firms to achieve unparalleled economies of scale. Critically, this industrial policy was vertically integrated, giving Chinese companies a near-monopolistic hold on the EV battery supply chain and the processing of essential minerals like lithium and graphite (Garcia Herrero et al., 2022; Mazzocco, 2025). This integration grants a formidable cost advantage, making a Chinese EV roughly 30% cheaper to assemble than a Western counterpart (Chang & Bradsher, 2024). The resulting production capacity now far outstrips domestic demand, creating what trading partners label an "overcapacity" issue that compels an aggressive export strategy (Wang, 2024).

Figure 1. Production, demand and net trade of electric cars in major global markets, 2024

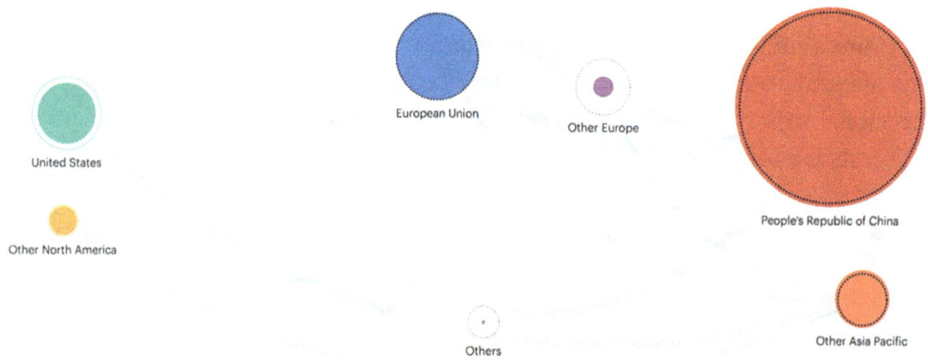

Source: IEA (2025). Available at https://www.iea.org/reports/global-ev-outlook-2025/trends-in-the-electric-car-industry-3, Licence: CC BY 4.0

Notes: "Other Asia Pacific" comprises Australia, New Zealand, Japan, Korea, India and Southeast Asia. "Other North America" includes Canada and Mexico. Other Europe includes Norway, Iceland, Israel, Switzerland, Türkiye, the United Kingdom and other European countries that are not EU member states.

While the world focuses on its EV prowess, China has also become a powerhouse in exporting traditional ICE vehicles. As Chinese consumers rapidly adopt EVs—with nearly half of all domestic buyers now choosing electric—the demand for gasoline-powered cars has plummeted (Chang & Bradsher, 2024). That has left

China with enormous excess capacity in its ICE factories. Rather than shuttering these facilities, automakers are unloading this surplus onto the global market, often at steep discounts. Most Chinese cars sold abroad in 2023 were traditional gasoline models. The primary destination was Russia, where Chinese brands filled the vacuum left by Western companies after the Ukraine invasion and the increased sanctions[4], but significant markets have also opened up in Latin America and the Middle East, where cost-effective ICE vehicles remain popular. This allows China to maintain production, preserve jobs, and expand its global automotive footprint even in segments it is domestically transitioning away from.

This dual flood of high-tech, low-cost EVs and surplus ICE vehicles has provoked a significant geopolitical and economic pushback from the West. The United States, framing the issue as one of unfair competition and national security, quadrupled its tariffs on Chinese EVs to 100% in 2024, effectively sealing its market (Zhou & Gao, 2024; Zhang, 2024). The U.S. has also raised concerns about data harvesting from "connected" Chinese vehicles (Wang, 2024). The European Union, a far more significant market that receives nearly 40% of China's EV exports, launched a sweeping anti-subsidy investigation. That culminated in the imposition of provisional tariffs of up to 37.6% on Chinese EVs, a measure designed to protect the EU's vast auto industry and its 14 million jobs (Wang, 2024; Zhou & Gao, 2024). These protectionist actions represent a concerted effort by legacy automotive powers to defend against the disruptive force of China's comprehensive industrial strategy.

China's reaction to this wave of protectionism has been strategic and multifaceted, moving beyond simple retaliation to a sophisticated realignment of its global trade posture. While Beijing has signaled its willingness to engage in reciprocal trade actions, such as initiating anti-dumping investigations into European products, its manufacturers are proactively mitigating the impact of Western tariffs through two primary strategies (Zhou & Gao, 2024). The first is export diversification. Recognizing the high barriers in the U.S. and EU, Chinese brands like BYD and Chery are aggressively targeting emerging markets in Southeast Asia, Latin America, and the Middle East, where their cost-effective EV and ICE models are rapidly gaining market share (Chang & Bradsher, 2024; IEA, 2025). The second, more durable strategy is the localization of production. To circumvent tariffs entirely, Chinese firms are investing billions to build manufacturing plants in countries like Brazil, Mexico, Thailand, and Hungary, turning direct trade challenges into opportunities for global expansion and deeper integration into regional supply chains (IEA, 2025; Zhou & Gao, 2024).

China's dominance in the global automotive trade is a complex, two-pronged phenomenon. It has successfully executed a long-term vision to lead the world in the electric vehicle revolution while simultaneously managing the decline of its domestic ICE market by transforming surplus capacity into a powerful export engine. This dual strategy is now confronting a wall of Western protectionism, leading to an era of escalating trade disputes, tariffs, and retaliatory measures. However, the deep-seated cost advantages derived from China's integrated supply chain, combined with its strategic pivot toward export diversification and localized production, demonstrate a formidable resilience. While tariffs may slow its advance into Western markets, they are unlikely to halt China's trajectory, which is fundamentally reshaping the global automotive industry and forcing a new, more contentious chapter in international trade relations.

3. IMPACT ON IMPORTING NATIONS–THE CASES OF THE US AND BRAZIL

China's strategic mastery of the entire critical minerals value chain has made its exports of batteries and electric vehicles (EVs) a defining force in the global economy. The vertically integrated export machine, while accelerating the green energy transition by providing affordable technology, has also forged profound dependencies for importing nations. For countries like the U.S. and Brazil, the influx of these goods presents a complex and double-edged sword. This dynamic has ignited a new "Great Game," where the trade of critical minerals becomes a conduit for geopolitical influence, potentially impacting the domestic politics and democratic trajectories of nations caught between superpowers.

The dependency created by the sheer concentration of China's supply chain control exposes importers to significant risks. For the United States, this dependency is a matter of economic and national security. In 2023, over 70% of the lithium-ion batteries imported by the U.S. came from China, a stark indicator of its reliance on a direct geopolitical competitor for the building blocks of the energy transition (Zhang, 2024). This reliance persists despite efforts to reshore manufacturing, as the U.S. industrial base cannot yet compete with the cost and scale of China's integrated model. The U.S. response has been fiercely defensive, culminating in a 100% tariff on Chinese EVs and framing "connected" vehicles as a data security threat, effectively treating trade as a front in a broader strategic competition (Wang, 2024; Zhou & Gao, 2024). This protectionist stance aims to shield its legacy auto industry from being overwhelmed, yet it fails to resolve the deeper, more intractable dependency on the components and processed materials that fuel it.

For an emerging economy like Brazil, the impact of Chinese exports manifests differently, presenting a complex mix of opportunity and peril. On one hand, the arrival of affordable Chinese EVs has been a boon for consumers and Brazil's climate goals. Brands like BYD and Great Wall Motors (GWM) now command over 80% of Brazil's EV market, drastically lowering the cost of entry and accelerating the country's green transition (Parodi & Waldersee, 2025). With one of the world's greenest energy grids based mainly on hydropower, Brazil has additional environmental credentials that could differentiate its mineral products in global markets increasingly concerned with sustainability. The massive Chinese influx, however, has triggered a backlash from local industry and labor unions, who fear that a flood of imports will decimate domestic manufacturing jobs.

This has placed the Brazilian government in a strategic bind, which it is attempting to navigate by using tariffs as leverage. The South American country has generally maintained openness to foreign investment in its mining sector while implementing a framework that emphasizes social and environmental responsibility, in line with Brazil's Mining Code (Law No. 13.575/2017). This approach aims to attract foreign investment while enhancing international credibility as a responsible supplier of critical minerals. By reintroducing and gradually increasing import duties, Brazil aims to convert China's export policies into foreign direct investment (FDI), compelling Chinese firms to build local factories to serve the Brazilian market (IEA, 2025; Parodi & Waldersee, 2025). This tactic turns market access into a bargaining chip to secure industrial development, a clear example of a nation seeking "geopolitical rents".

This dynamic, where economic dependency intersects with strategic competition, is reshaping the international order. The global scramble for critical minerals and market access has created a new landscape where major powers, chiefly the United States and China, actively court resource-rich and strategically located developing nations. This contest for influence has the potential to alter political calculus within these countries, creating risks for democratic governance. Leaders of developing nations can find themselves in a position to play one superpower against another, securing economic concessions, investments, or political support in exchange for alignment. While potentially lucrative in the short term, it can entrench autocratic or corrupt regimes, as leaders prioritize these geopolitical rents over the welfare of their citizens and the quality of their domestic institutions.

China's deep investments in Brazil's mining sector—from niobium to copper—illustrate this point (See & Moscati, 2025; Vieira do Prado & Moerenhout, 2024). These are not merely commercial transactions; they are strategic moves to secure the upstream portion of the value chain, which in turn solidifies China's leverage over the U.S. and Europe while deepening its economic partnership with Brazil. For Brazil, it brings welcome investment but also tightens the bonds of dependency, creating a complex web of economic and political interests. The stability of supply chains becomes intertwined with geopolitical alignment, and the pressure to choose sides in a world of escalating tensions becomes more acute.

The impact of China's exports of batteries, EVs, and other critical mineral-based goods is far-reaching and complex. For importing nations, these products offer the immediate benefits of accelerated decarbonization and access to affordable technology. However, it comes at the cost of a deep and unsettling dependency on a single, strategically motivated economic power. The resulting tensions are pushing the U.S. into a posture of costly industrial defense, while nations like Brazil engage in a high-stakes diplomatic game to leverage their market and resources for industrial gain. Ultimately, this new reality exposes the fragility of global supply chains and underscores how the trade in essential goods has become a central arena for geopolitical competition, with the potential to reshape alliances and influence the political trajectory of nations around the world.

3.1 U.S. Policy and Proactive Industrial Strategy

Confronted with deep-seated dependency on a primary geopolitical competitor for the foundational technologies of the 21st century, Washington has moved beyond merely reactive tariffs to enact an aggressive, multi-pronged strategy rooted in techno-nationalism. This comprehensive approach seeks to proactively reconfigure global supply chains and rebuild domestic industry through a combination of targeted industrial policy, the formation of new international alliances, and strategic investments in key resource-rich nations (EY Parthenon, 2023). While these measures aim to decouple critical supply chains from adversarial control, they have also exposed the immense difficulty of reshoring complex, vertically integrated industries, locking Washington in a protracted struggle to balance protectionism with the realities of globalized manufacturing.

The most direct and confrontational element of the U.S. strategy has been the use of tariffs as a primary economic weapon. Initiated under the first Trump administration and continued under President Biden, this trade war has specifically targeted Chinese goods essential to the green energy and high-tech sectors. Since 2018, the U.S. has imposed escalating duties on a wide range of Chinese imports, with tariffs on EVs surging from 27.5% to a prohibitive 102.5% by June 2024. This policy reflects a clear techno-nationalist belief that tariffs can serve as a powerful tool to force the "reshoring" of industries that had previously moved offshore, thereby revitalizing American manufacturing and protecting domestic jobs from what is perceived as unfair competition fueled by Chinese state subsidies (Shokri, 2025).

3.1.1 Domestic Revitalization Through Industrial Policy

The cornerstone of the U.S. strategy is a powerful suite of domestic industrial policies designed to revitalize American manufacturing. The Inflation Reduction Act (IRA) stands as the centerpiece of this effort, offering lucrative tax credits for consumers and manufacturers of EVs and batteries that are explicitly tied to stringent domestic content rules and "Foreign Entity of Concern" (FEOC) provisions, which systematically exclude materials sourced from China (Taulli & Busby, 2025). This policy creates a powerful financial motive for automakers to reconfigure their supply chains away from China, effectively creating a protected, "friend-shored" ecosystem (Hernandez-Roy et al., 2024).

This push is reinforced by the invocation of the Defense Production Act (DPA), which has been used to accelerate domestic mining and processing by streamlining regulatory approvals and allocating federal emergency funding to rare earth extraction and magnet manufacturing projects (3Gimbals, 2025). This executive action builds on a bipartisan foundation established by legislation like the Energy Act of 2020 and is informed by whole-of-government efforts, such as the U.S. Geological Survey's (USGS) initiative to map untapped domestic mineral deposits (3Gimbals, 2025). Spurred by these incentives, investments in U.S. battery gigafactories have surged, often through joint ventures with South Korean and Japanese firms (Zhang, 2024). However, this industrial mobilization faces significant structural hurdles. A primary challenge is the lengthy and complex domestic permitting process for new mines, which can take 7 to 10 years in the U.S., far exceeding the two-year average in allied nations like Australia and Canada (Hernandez-Roy et al., 2024).

3.1.2 Building Resilient "Friend-Shored" Alliances

Recognizing the limits of reshoring, the U.S. is simultaneously executing a "de-risking" strategy by forging a new architecture of international green technology alliances to secure supply chains among politically aligned nations (Hernandez-Roy et al., 2024). The primary vehicle for this is the Minerals Security Partnership (MSP), a coalition of 14 countries and the EU launched in 2022 to finance and develop sustainable and transparent mining and processing facilities, offering an alternative to Chinese state-backed capital (3Gimbals, 2025).

Beyond the MSP, Washington is pursuing robust bilateral partnerships. It has established a landmark mineral resources agreement with Ukraine to secure access to its abundant reserves and integrated Australia's critical mineral projects into its domestic industrial base for defense purposes (3Gimbals, 2025). The U.S.-Canada Joint Action Plan on Critical Minerals serves as a further model for deep hemispheric cooperation (Hernandez-Roy et al., 2024). This web of new economic and security alliances represents a core pillar of U.S. statecraft aimed at creating a resilient, non-Chinese supply network.

3.1.3 Strategic Engagement with Brazil

In this global realignment, Brazil has emerged as a pivotal potential partner due to its vast and diverse mineral wealth, including the world's second-largest reserves of rare earth elements (bne IntelliNews, 2025; Campbell, 2025). The U.S. has openly identified Brazil as a candidate for the MSP and is in discussions to forge a Critical Minerals Agreement (CMA), which would grant Brazilian exports preferential access to the American market under the IRA (Vieira do Prado & Moerenhout, 2024; Zuniga et al., 2025). The economic stakes are significant; while the U.S. is the largest foreign investor in Brazil with a stock of $228.8 billion, it lags as a destination for Brazil's mineral exports, which totaled $13 billion to the U.S. versus $23 billion to China in 2023 (Zuniga et al., 2025; Vieira do Prado & Moerenhout, 2024).

To catalyze this partnership, the U.S. is deploying targeted financial tools. The Development Finance Corporation (DFC), for instance, made in 2022 a $30 million equity investment in a Brazilian facility to produce battery-grade nickel and cobalt (Moreira, 2022). This proactive engagement demonstrates that the U.S. strategy is not simply to contain China, but to actively build a new, secure, and diversified industrial ecosystem for the energy transition, with key Latin American partners at its center.

Complementing these economic measures is the powerful framing of Chinese technological imports as a national security risk. The U.S. government has successfully broadened the debate beyond trade imbalances, portraying Chinese-made "connected" vehicles as potential instruments for data collection and cyber espionage, thereby justifying import restrictions on non-economic grounds (Wang, 2024; Taulli & Busby, 2025). This securitization of trade is further evidenced by the Department of Defense's blacklisting of major Chinese technology and battery firms like CATL, which restricts their access to government contracts and casts a shadow of suspicion over their operations in the U.S. market (Taulli & Busby, 2025). This narrative provides a robust political justification for protectionist policies that might otherwise be challenged as violations of free-trade principles.

Despite these efforts, the U.S. still imports nearly three-quarters of its lithium-ion batteries from China, and the domestic industrial base remains heavily dependent on Chinese-processed materials, particularly for battery-grade graphite and the increasingly popular lithium-iron-phosphate (LFP) battery chemistry (Taulli & Busby, 2025; Gordon, 2025). The U.S. reaction has successfully disrupted trade flows and catalyzed domestic investment, but it has not yet solved the core challenge of recreating an entire, deeply integrated industrial ecosystem, setting the stage for continued friction and a long-term, costly competition for control over the supply chains of the future.

The U.S. Geological Survey (USGS) leads efforts to identify and assess domestic critical mineral potential, driven by initiatives like the Earth Mapping Resources Initiative (Earth MRI). The program employs geospatial technologies to systematically map untapped subsurface deposits and underutilized mineral sources trapped in legacy minr wastes. It generates foundational datasets designed to de-risk exploration and incentivize resource development while addressing environmental liabilities from historical extraction practices.

Congress has enacted various legislative measures, including the Global Strategy for Securing Critical Minerals Act and the Critical Minerals Security Act, aimed at fostering cooperation among U.S. allies, improving information sharing with private sector stakeholders, and evaluating global supply dynamics. These initiatives reflect a proactive approach to safeguarding the nation's mineral resources amid growing international competition.

3.2 New Arsenals of Power

The escalating U.S.-China trade war has evolved far beyond a dispute over tariffs and trade balances into a systemic struggle for technological and military supremacy. At the heart of this confrontation lies another strategic battleground: the control of critical minerals and their dual-use applications in semiconductors and advanced defense systems. These elemental resources, from the rare earths that guide missiles to the gallium that powers radar, have become the chokepoints of 21st-century power. The U.S., leveraging its historical dominance in semiconductor design, has weaponized technology exports to stunt China's military modernization. In a powerful countermove, China is leveraging its near-monopolistic control over mineral processing to threaten the foundations of the U.S. defense industrial base. This dangerous tit-for-tat exchange of technological restrictions and raw material embargoes is fracturing global supply chains even further and creating profound national security vulnerabilities for both superpowers.

The semiconductor industry is a primary front in this techno-industrial conflict. Advanced semiconductors are the indispensable "brains" of modern military hardware, enabling everything from the AI-driven targeting in fighter jets to the complex communications and sensor arrays on naval warships. Recognizing China's reliance on foreign chip technology, the U.S. has implemented sweeping export controls to block Beijing's access to high-end semiconductors, the software used to design them, and the advanced equipment required for their manufacture (Shivakumar et al., 2025; Lawal, 2024). This strategy is explicitly aimed at crippling China's military-civil fusion development, where commercial technological advances are rapidly integrated into defense applications. However, this silicon blockade is predicated on access to another set of critical minerals. The production of advanced semiconductors relies heavily on elements like gallium and germanium, used for high-frequency electronics and infrared optics (Trager, 2024). China's dominance in this area—producing 98% of the world's raw gallium—gives it a powerful retaliatory tool (Choi, 2025; Trager, 2024).

This dependency has been starkly exposed by China's retaliatory measures. In response to U.S. semiconductor restrictions, Beijing has imposed export bans on gallium, germanium, and antimony, directly targeting a key vulnerability in the U.S. tech and defense sectors (S&P Global, 2025; Trager, 2024). The impact is significant, as these minerals are essential for a wide range of military applications, including night-vision goggles, explosives, infrared sensors, and nuclear weapons production (Choi, 2025; Trager, 2024). By restricting the export of these foundational materials, China demonstrates its ability to disrupt the very start of U.S. defense manufacturing, creating a direct challenge to Washington's technological superiority.

The strategic threat extends far beyond the minerals needed for semiconductors. The U.S. defense industrial base is critically dependent on a broader suite of Chinese-controlled materials, most notably rare earth elements (REEs). They are irreplaceable in modern weaponry. An F-35 fighter jet, for example, requires over 900 pounds of REEs for its engines, avionics, and radar systems; a Virginia-class submarine uses approximately 9,200 pounds (Baskaran & Schwartz, 2025; Choi, 2025). High-performance neodymium iron boron (NdFeB) magnets, made from REEs, are essential for the guidance and actuator systems in Tomahawk missiles and JDAM smart bombs (Choi, 2025; Perry & Van Veen, 2024). A stunning report from data analytics firm Govini revealed that over 78% of U.S. weapon systems, encompassing more than 1,900 distinct platforms, rely on critical minerals dominated by Chinese supply chains (Tucker, 2025; The Oregon Group, 2025). For some platforms, like the Arleigh Burke-class destroyer, 81% of the antimony used originates from Chinese-linked sources (The Oregon Group, 2025). This level of dependency represents a glaring strategic vulnerability that the Pentagon has only recently begun to address with urgency (Vergun, 2025).

As with semiconductors, China has shown its willingness to weaponize this dominance. In April 2025, Beijing imposed sweeping export licensing requirements on seven heavy REEs—including dysprosium, terbium, and yttrium—and the permanent magnets made from them (Bradsher, 2025; Baskaran & Schwartz, 2025). Because China controls virtually 100% of the processing for these specific heavy REEs, this move effectively gives it the power to halt the production of critical U.S. defense systems (Baskaran & Schwartz, 2025; Campbell, 2025). That is not an idle threat; China briefly cut off REE exports to Japan in 2010 during a territorial dispute, demonstrating a clear precedent (Wischer, 2024). The current restrictions, implemented in the midst of a broader trade war, are a clear signal that Beijing views its mineral dominance as a strategic counterweight to America's technological advantage.

The U.S.-China trade war has exposed the deeply intertwined and adversarial nature of 21st-century supply chains, where the building blocks of commercial innovation and military power have become tools of geopolitical coercion. The U.S.

is leveraging its formidable lead in semiconductor technology to contain China's military ambitions, while China is retaliating by exploiting its chokehold on the critical minerals and rare earths that underpin the entire U.S. defense industrial base. This dangerous exchange has moved beyond tariffs into a direct conflict over strategic resources, forcing a frantic and costly race by the U.S. to reshore and diversify its supply chains. The outcome of this battle—over who controls the flow of silicon chips versus who controls the supply of rare earth magnets—will not only determine the future of technological leadership but will also define the contours of global military power for decades to come.

3.3 Silicon, Magnetic, and Vehicles Battlefields

The U.S.-China trade war has evolved beyond a simple conflict over tariffs into a high-stakes battle for technological supremacy, with the automotive sector emerging as a critical front. While China has achieved a dominant position in electric vehicle (EV) manufacturing and battery production, its ascendancy is tempered by a significant vulnerability: a deep reliance on foreign-designed and manufactured semiconductors. These advanced chips are the “brains” of modern vehicles, and the United States has strategically weaponized its leadership in this domain through stringent export controls to stifle China's technological advancement. In response, Beijing has launched an all-out national effort to achieve semiconductor self-sufficiency. This conflict is further complicated by the pivotal role of Taiwan, the world's leading chip manufacturer, and by China's own formidable leverage in another key EV component: neodymium iron boron (NdFeB) magnets. These intricate dependencies have created a new geopolitical landscape where the supply chains for silicon chips and rare earth magnets have become primary battlefields.

Semiconductors are indispensable to the modern automobile, and their importance has magnified exponentially with the shift to electric, connected, and autonomous vehicles. These chips manage everything from powertrain and battery performance to advanced driver-assistance systems (ADAS) and sophisticated in-car infotainment, or “smart cockpit” functions (Tanaka, 2025). As vehicles become “computers on wheels,” access to the most advanced semiconductors is no longer just a matter of competitive advantage but a prerequisite for technological leadership. While China's automakers, like BYD and SAIC Motor, have conquered the EV market through manufacturing scale and battery technology, they have remained heavily dependent on foreign technology for the cutting-edge chips that power their most advanced systems (Hai, 2025; Tanaka, 2025). That has created a critical Achilles' heel in China's industrial strategy.

Recognizing this vulnerability, the U.S. has made restricting China's access to high-end semiconductor technology a central pillar of its foreign and economic policy. Beginning in 2022, the U.S. government implemented sweeping export controls designed to cut off China from advanced chips (particularly those used in AI and high-performance computing), the sophisticated software used to design them, and the lithography equipment[5] needed to manufacture them (Shivakumar et al., 2025). These regulations, including the "Foreign Direct Product Rule," have been progressively tightened to prevent workarounds, effectively creating a technological blockade. This strategy has directly impacted Chinese tech giants like Huawei, whose efforts to develop powerful, homegrown AI chips like the Ascend series are viewed by Washington as a direct challenge to U.S. national security (Gan, 2025). The goal is clear: to slow China's technological progress and prevent its military from benefiting from civilian advancements in areas like artificial intelligence.

This U.S.-led tech blockade has triggered what has been described as a "Sputnik moment" for Beijing, catalyzing a massive, state-directed campaign to achieve semiconductor self-sufficiency (Hai, 2025). Under ambitious industrial policies like "Made in China 2025," the Chinese government is channeling hundreds of billions of dollars into its domestic chip industry through entities like the National IC Industry Investment Fund, or "Big Fund" (Hai, 2025). The explicit goal is to create a fully independent and controllable supply chain. In the automotive sector specifically, China's Ministry of Industry and Information Technology is spearheading a project that aims for all automotive chips to be domestically developed and manufactured by 2027—a highly ambitious target that would, if successful, eliminate a key point of U.S. leverage (Tanaka, 2025).

At the heart of this global semiconductor struggle lies Taiwan, and specifically, the Taiwan Semiconductor Manufacturing Company (TSMC). As the world's most advanced foundry, TSMC manufactures over 90% of the world's leading-edge chips for American and Chinese firms, making it an indispensable and highly vulnerable chokepoint in the global tech ecosystem (Tobin, 2025). Both superpowers view this dependency as a strategic risk. The U.S. is trying to mitigate it by incentivizing TSMC to build fabs on American soil through the CHIPS Act. China, on the other hand, has employed a more nuanced approach. While engaging in military intimidation toward the self-governing island, it has also strategically exempted many advanced chips manufactured in Taiwan from its retaliatory tariffs, a tacit acknowledgment that it cannot afford to be cut off from TSMC's production (Tobin, 2025). This places Taiwan's chip companies in the precarious position of navigating the competing demands of their two largest markets.

While the U.S. holds the upper hand in the silicon battle, China wields its own powerful weapon in another part of the EV supply chain: permanent magnets. High-performance EV motors rely on sintered neodymium iron boron (NdFeB) magnets, a product for which China has near-total market control (Perry & Van Veen, 2024). China dominates the entire NdFeB value chain, from mining 69% of the world's rare earth elements (REEs) to refining nearly 90% of them and manufacturing over 92% of the finished magnets (Perry & Van Veen, 2024; Interos, 2022). Just as the U.S. has restricted chip exports, China has demonstrated its willingness to use its control over REEs as leverage. In retaliation for U.S. tariffs, Beijing has imposed export licensing requirements and, at times, halted shipments of critical rare earths and magnets, threatening to paralyze Western automotive and defense industries (Bradsher, 2025; Zimmermann, 2025). That creates a tale of two chokepoints: Washington controls the flow of advanced chips, while Beijing controls the supply of essential magnets.

The U.S.-China trade war has laid bare the intricate and weaponized nature of modern supply chains. In the automotive sector, this conflict is being fought on the dueling battlefields of semiconductors and strategic materials. While China's automakers lead the world in EV production, their ambition is held in check by their reliance on foreign, particularly Taiwanese-made, semiconductors—a vulnerability the U.S. is aggressively exploiting. However, China's all-out push for chip independence, combined with its stranglehold over the rare earth and NdFeB magnet supply chain, gives it powerful retaliatory leverage. This web of dependencies ensures that neither side can secure a decisive victory without inflicting immense economic pain on itself and the global economy, locking the two powers in a protracted struggle for control over the core technologies of the 21st century.

3.4 Outcomes of Tariff and Import Ban Escalations

The recent escalation of tariffs and retaliatory trade restrictions, spearheaded by the U.S. and China, signals a departure from conventional trade disputes and the dawn of a new era of economic warfare. The imposition of sweeping, often punitive, tariffs and the strategic use of export bans on critical technologies and minerals represent a fundamental shift in how great powers conduct geopolitical competition (The Economic Times, 2025). This escalating conflict is not merely a series of protectionist measures but a systemic shock that is actively dismantling the post-World War II global economic order. Possible international consequences are threefold: a dangerous slide toward global stagflation and recession, the fracturing and forced realignment of critical supply chains, and the rapid erosion of the rules-based multilateral system in favor of coercive, power-based economic blocs.

The most immediate and widespread consequence of the tariff war is severe economic disruption, which threatens global growth and stability. The Trump administration's strategy, characterized by a universal baseline tariff and additional punitive rates reaching as high as 145% on Chinese goods, has been described as an "economic systemic war" designed to upend the existing order (Global4Cast.org, 2025; Molof, 2025). This aggressive use of tariffs acts as a massive tax on businesses and consumers, fueling inflation and reducing purchasing power (J.P. Morgan Research, 2025). The resulting uncertainty has a chilling effect on business sentiment, constraining investment and hiring (Gordon, 2025). Economists have warned that this protectionist shock could reduce global GDP by as much as 1% and significantly increase the risk of a global recession, pushing the world toward a stagflationary environment of high prices and stagnant growth (J.P. Morgan Research, 2025; Dow Jones, 2025).

Beyond macroeconomic instability, the trade war is fundamentally a battle over the control of global supply chains, forcing a painful and costly decoupling. For decades, Western industries have built hyper-efficient, globalized supply chains that are now deeply dependent on Chinese manufacturing and processing, particularly for critical minerals like rare earths, lithium, and graphite (Park & Melendez, 2024; U.S. Energy Information Administration, 2025). In retaliation for U.S. tariffs, Beijing has weaponized this dependency by imposing export controls on rare earth elements and other critical materials, threatening to choke off the supply of essential components for the defense, aerospace, and EV industries (Bradsher, 2025; ET Online, 2025). The frantic race to reshore and "friend-shore" supply chains represents a monumental task that requires immense capital investment and years to accomplish (Shokri, 2025; Zimmermann, 2025). This supply chain fracturing creates widespread disruptions, increases production costs, and ultimately undermines the efficiency that underpinned the previous era of globalization.

The economic conflict is also accelerating a major geopolitical realignment, dismantling traditional alliances and replacing the rules-based order with a more anarchic, power-based system. The indiscriminate nature of U.S. tariffs, which have also hit allies in Europe and Asia, has strained long-standing partnerships and eroded trust in American leadership (Global4Cast.org, 2025). The European Union, for example, is caught in a strategic bind—dependent on China for critical inputs yet politically aligned with the U.S.—forcing it to develop its own defensive industrial policies while trying to avoid being crushed between the two giants (Zimmermann, 2025). This conflict is creating a new "Great Game" where developing nations rich in critical minerals are courted by Washington and Beijing. It offers investment and political support in exchange for access and alignment. This dynamic creates new dependencies and risks undermining democratic governance in these nations as leaders prioritize geopolitical rents over domestic reforms (Shokri, 2025).

Ultimately, this trade war is causing the rapid decay of the multilateral institutions, like the World Trade Organization (WTO), that once governed global commerce but were already weakened even before the U.S.-China trade war. By invoking national security justifications to impose unilateral tariffs, the U.S. has bypassed and further fragilized the WTO's dispute settlement mechanisms (Global4Cast.org, 2025; Molof, 2025). In response, China has developed its own legal frameworks, such as its Export

Control Law, to legitimize its retaliatory measures, creating a parallel system of trade governance (Zimmermann, 2025). This shift from a predictable, rules-based system to one governed by the unilateral actions of great powers introduces profound instability into the global economy. As one analyst noted, the world is witnessing an attempt to "completely smash" the existing trade regime, replacing it with an order where economic coercion, rather than cooperative norms, is the primary tool of statecraft (Global4Cast.org, 2025).

The escalating war of tariffs and export bans is not a temporary trade spat but a systemic conflict with profound and lasting consequences. It is actively contributing to global economic fragility, forcing a costly and inefficient reconfiguration of critical supply chains, and accelerating the fragmentation of the world into competing economic and geopolitical blocs. The erosion of the multilateral, rules-based order in favor of raw economic power risks a more volatile and less prosperous future for all nations. As this new era of trade warfare unfolds, the international community faces the monumental challenge of navigating a landscape where the principles of globalization are in retreat and the architecture of global economic governance is being fundamentally, and perhaps irrevocably, reshaped.

3.5 Brazil's Strategic Navigation of the Trade War

The escalating trade and technology rivalry between the United States and China has redrawn the map of global commerce, forcing nations to navigate a complex geopolitical landscape. In this new "Great Game," few countries are as pivotally positioned as Brazil. As a continental-sized nation endowed with vast reserves of critical minerals, a sophisticated industrial base, and a large consumer market, Brazil has emerged as a key "geopolitical swing state." Instead of being a mere bystander, it is actively leveraging its unique assets—including its role within multilateral forums like BRICS—to "play along" with the superpowers. It employs a sophisticated mix of open-market invitations and strategic protectionism to attract foreign investment while catalyzing its own domestic industrialization. This balancing act has transformed Brazil into a primary destination for Chinese capital, a potential partner for U.S. supply chain diversification, and a crucial case study in how middle powers can assert their interests in an era of great power competition.

Figure 2. Top 10 NEV Export Destinations, 2024H1 (thousands of units)

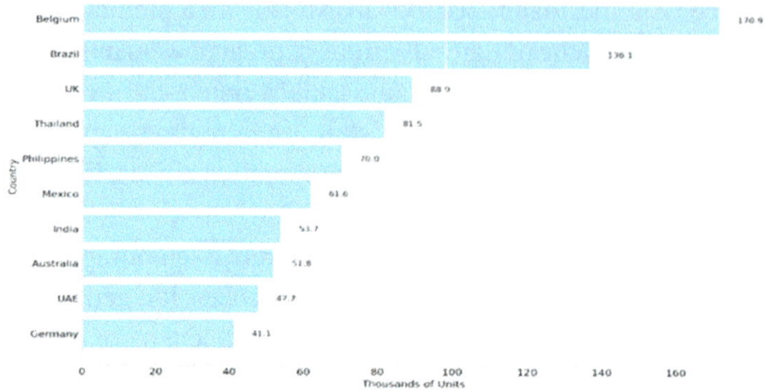

Figure 3. China's Top 10 Auto Exporters, 2024H1 (thousands of units)

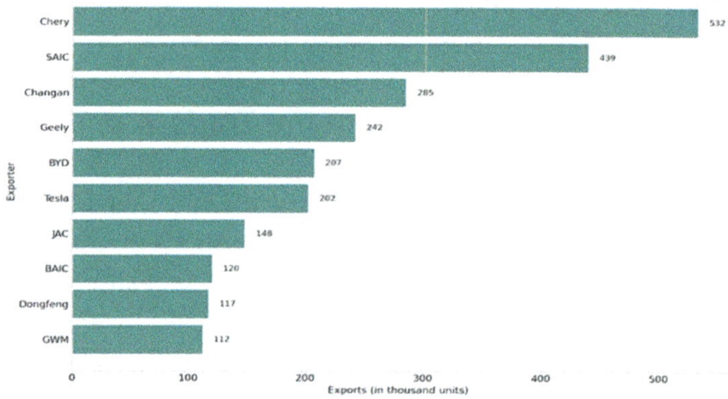

Source: Caixin Global. Available at bit.ly/3D5gd3H *Source: CAAM apud All About Industries. Available at* bit.ly/4bs098B

3.5.1 Leveraging Mineral Wealth and a Large Domestic Market

Brazil's strategic importance is fundamentally rooted in its immense geological wealth. The country holds the world's second-largest reserves of rare earth elements (REEs), positioning it as one of the only viable long-term alternatives to China's current dominance. Furthermore, Brazil is the world's largest producer of niobium and possesses significant reserves of graphite, nickel, and lithium—all designated as critical for the energy transition. This endowment has made Brazil a focal point for nations seeking to de-risk their supply chains. The U.S. has openly identified Brazil as a potential partner for its Minerals Security Partnership (MSP)[6], while other

Western allies and investors from Australia to Saudi Arabia are actively exploring Brazilian mining projects.

Simultaneously, as the U.S. and E.U. have erected tariff walls against Chinese EVs, China has aggressively pivoted toward untapped markets, with Brazil emerging as its primary target. Aided by a previous period of low import taxes, Chinese automakers like Chery (in a joint venture with a local company), BYD and Great Wall Motor (GWM) flooded the market, making Brazil a major importer of Chinese-made electric cars and capturing over 80% of the country's EV market share. This commercial offensive is paralleled by strategic upstream investments, with Chinese firms securing stakes in Brazil's mineral sector to integrate the country into their global vertical supply chain.

3.5.2 A Proactive Industrial Policy

In response to this influx, the Brazilian government has shifted from a low-tariff regime to a more strategic, protectionist stance designed to build a domestic EV industry. This policy is not intended to block Chinese firms but to coerce them into shifting from exporting finished vehicles to establishing local manufacturing facilities. The government systematically reintroduced and scheduled progressive increases for import tariffs on EVs, which will reach a peak of 35% in 2026.

This "stick" is complemented by the "carrot" of the "Mover" Program, a national initiative offering billions in tax incentives for companies that invest in decarbonization and local R&D. This dual engagement allows Brazil to offer China a vital and growing export market while presenting itself to the U.S. as a large-scale partner for diversifying supply chains away from China. It is yet to be seen how well the strategy will work. Chinese companies like BYD responded to the tariff pressure by committing billions to build factories in Brazil. Meanwhile the U.S. holds out the possibility of a Critical Minerals Agreement (CMA)[7] that would grant Brazilian exports preferential access to the American market under the Inflation Reduction Act (Caballero, 2025; Vieira do Prado & Moerenhout, 2024).

This balancing act is made more complex by Brazil's active membership in the BRICS bloc, a forum that provides a formal platform for cooperation with China outside the Western-dominated international system. The partnership is not merely symbolic; it has tangible economic outcomes. One example is the 2023 agreement between the two nations to settle trade in their local currencies, a key objective of the broader BRICS de-dollarization agenda (See & Moscati, 2025). How Brazil continues to balance these powerful forces will not only determine its own economic future but will also significantly shape the evolving architecture of global trade and the new geopolitical order.

3.5.3 Opportunities and Challenges for Industrialization

Brazil's ambition to become a green industrial power is supported by significant opportunities but faces considerable challenges. Its vast mineral reserves and one of the world's cleanest energy grids provide a strong foundation for producing "green" lithium and other low-carbon materials. However, the country's industrial capacity is hampered by structural issues. A major challenge is the convoluted and lengthy process for obtaining mining and environmental licenses, with an estimated 70,000 licenses awaiting approval, which deters investment.

Furthermore, while Brazil has a sophisticated industrial base, it lacks the technological know-how for certain midstream processes like mineral refining, and its infrastructure requires significant upgrades. Environmental and social governance (ESG) is another critical factor, as mining operations have led to disasters and conflicts with local and indigenous communities, creating reputational risks that could affect the country's "green" brand. Successfully navigating these hurdles will be essential for Brazil to convert its geopolitical leverage and resource wealth into sustainable industrial development. By deftly managing incentives, protectionism, and multilateral diplomacy, Brazil is positioning itself to advance its national agenda, demonstrating how a major emerging economy can create agency and opportunities amidst the competing interests of the world's two largest economies.

3.6 Brazil's Phased Import Taxes

In the turbulent arena of the U.S.-China trade war, where nations are increasingly forced to choose between protectionist walls and open-market vulnerabilities, Brazil has forged a distinctly pragmatic third path. Confronted with a flood of low-cost Chinese electric vehicles (EVs), Brazil has implemented a sophisticated, phased import tax system that transcends simple protectionism. This policy was explicitly engineered to transform Brazil's burgeoning consumer market into a hub for foreign direct investment and advanced automotive manufacturing. By creating a predictable, escalating tariff schedule, Brazil has given foreign automakers, particularly from China, a clear choice: face prohibitive future tariffs or invest in local production. This strategic use of trade policy demonstrates how a major emerging economy can leverage the dynamics of great power competition to catalyze industrialization and secure a more advantageous position in the shifting global value chain.

The context for this policy shift was the collision of two major global trends: the West's trade conflict with China and Brazil's own open-door policy for green vehicles. Since 2015, Brazil has maintained zero import taxes on EVs to encourage adoption and combat climate change (ResearchAndMarkets.com, 2024).

The government's response to an enormous influx of Chinese vehicles was not a sudden, prohibitive tariff but a carefully calibrated, phased-in tax structure designed to send a clear signal to foreign investors. Beginning in January 2024, Brazil systematically reintroduced import duties that are set to climb incrementally until they reach a peak of 35% in July 2026 (ResearchAndMarkets.com, 2024). For fully electric vehicles, the tax began at 10% and will rise in stages to 18%, 25%, and finally 35%. Hybrid vehicles follow a similar path, starting at 15% and also culminating at 35% (Ramos, 2024; See & Moscati, 2025). The explicit goal, as articulated by Brazilian officials like Vice President Geraldo Alckmin was to use this policy as a direct invitation for foreign companies to "install car factories in Brazil" (Ramos, 2024). The gradual nature of the tariff increase provides a clear window for companies to make investment decisions, while the certainty of the final 35% rate makes local production a near necessity for long-term market access. This "stick" of escalating tariffs is complemented by the "carrot" of decreasing tax-free import quotas, which further incentivize companies to establish local operations sooner rather than later to maximize their duty-free imports during the transition period (Ramos, 2024).

The industrial reaction, especially from Chinese automakers, has demonstrated the policy's efficacy. BYD, for example, is investing over $1 billion to establish a major industrial complex in the Northeast state of Bahia, with plans to commence vehicle production in 2025 (Caballero, 2025; ResearchAndMarkets.com, 2024). GWM, in turn, bought the Iracemápolis factory in the southeastern Brazilian state of São Paulo, where German Daimler AG once made motor vehicles. This is in addition to the joint venture comprising Brazilian automaker Caoa and its Chinese counterpart Chery in Itupeva, Sao Paulo, announced in 2018. This strategy of localization allows Chinese automakers to bypass the impending tariffs, transforming them from foreign importers into domestic producers. In the first quarter of 2024, Brazil recorded a 145% increase in sales of electrified vehicles compared to the previous year, amounting to 36,090 units sold. Chinese companies, notably BYD and GWM, have emerged as leaders in this market. This move not only secures their long-term presence in Brazil's market—the sixth largest in the world—but also positions them to use Brazil as an export hub for the wider Latin American region (Parodi & Waldersee, 2025; Nunes & Lopes, 2024).

Figure 4. Changes in tariffs on Chinese EV imports in selected regions announced since 1 January 2024

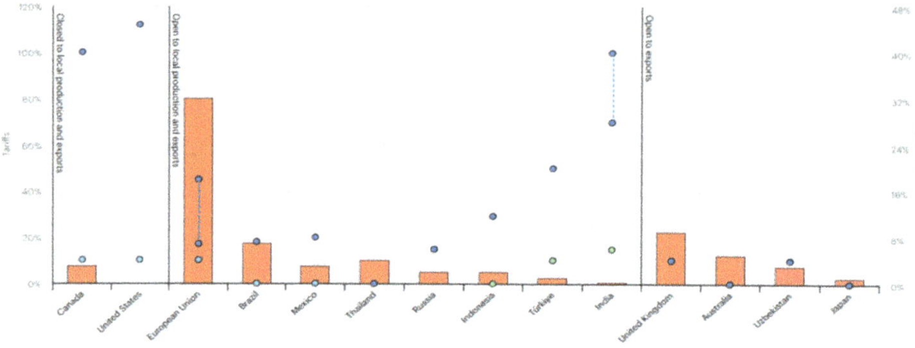

Source: IEA (2025). Available at https://www.iea.org/data-and-statistics/charts/changes-in-tariffs-on-chinese-ev-imports-in-selected-regions-announced-since-1-january-2024, Licence: CC BY 4.0

Within the broader national industrial strategy, the "Mover" (Green Mobility and Innovation) Program offers over $3.8 billion in tax incentives for automakers that invest in local R&D. Chinese firms like BYD have already been qualified for the program, signaling their intention to fully integrate into Brazil's industrial ecosystem. That creates a powerful synergy: the phased tariffs provide the pressure to invest locally, while the Mover program provides the incentive to deepen that investment in high-value areas like technology and sustainability, aligning corporate strategy with Brazil's national development goals.

Brazil's phased import tax system was the path chosen for a strategic 21st-century industrial policy. It is not a blunt protectionist instrument but a nuanced, coercive mechanism that leverages the pressures of the U.S.-China trade war to achieve a specific national objective: the revitalization of its domestic auto industry. By creating a predictable yet unavoidable tariff structure, Brazil has steered a surge of Chinese imports into a wave of foreign direct investment. This strategy demonstrates how a major emerging economy can assert its agency on the world stage, turning the challenge of globalization's shifting currents into an opportunity to build domestic capacity, attract advanced technology, and secure a more prosperous industrial future.

4. GREEN PARADOX: ENVIRONMENTAL COSTS OF CRITICAL MINERALS

The global race to secure critical minerals, seen by many as a transition panacea for a green and digital economy, is fraught with a profound and escalating paradox: the very quest for clean energy risks unleashing a new wave of environmental degradation. This dilemma is being dangerously amplified by the U.S.-China trade war. As the world's two largest economies engage in a systemic struggle for technological supremacy, using tariffs and export bans as primary weapons, the competition for minerals has intensified, creating immense pressure to accelerate extraction at any cost. This geopolitical conflict has significant environmental implications for the main actors—the U.S. and China—and for resource-rich nations like Brazil, which have become the central battlegrounds for this new resource scramble. While the stated goal is a sustainable future, the means of getting there are threatening to replicate the environmentally destructive patterns of past industrial eras, undermining the very concept of a "green" transition.

China's role in this environmental paradox is twofold. For decades, its path to dominating the global mineral processing industry was paved by a state-driven industrial policy that prioritized economic growth over environmental protection. The country's near-monopoly on refining rare earth elements (REEs), for example, came at a tremendous environmental price, creating vast toxic lakes and severe pollution in regions like Baotou, as lenient regulations allowed it to outcompete and ultimately displace Western producers (Campbell, 2025; Bradsher, 2025). While China has more recently championed the concept of an "ecological civilization" and tightened domestic environmental laws, its vast overseas investments, particularly under the Belt and Road Initiative, are now under scrutiny for exporting this environmental footprint (Reed & Hui, 2022). Some authors have expressed concerns over Chinese investments in mining and infrastructure in ecologically sensitive regions like the Amazon basin. They raised significant worries about deforestation and the protection of biodiversity, placing China's global resource strategy in direct conflict with its domestic environmental rhetoric (Muggah, 2025; Reed & Hui, 2022).

The U.S.'s aggressive, techno-nationalist campaign to reshore critical mineral supply chains, in turn, relies on a strategy that carries a complex set of environmental trade-offs. Spurred by policies like the IRA, the U.S. is channeling billions into developing domestic mining and processing capabilities (Baskaran & Wischer, 2025). However, the U.S. operates under a far more stringent and complex environmental regulatory framework, including the National Environmental Policy Act (NEPA) and the Clean Water Act, which makes permitting a new mine a lengthy and contentious process that can take decades (Bazilian & Wischer, 2025). This creates a fundamental tension: the strategic urgency to secure supply chains clashes with domestic environmental safeguards and community opposition. Projects like the Thacker Pass lithium mine in Nevada have faced intense legal challenges over their potential impact on local ecosystems and sacred tribal lands, highlighting the immense difficulty of fast-tracking extraction in a country with robust environmental laws and active civil society engagement. The political and industrial reaction in the

U.S. is thus caught between the geopolitical goal of decoupling from China and the domestic political imperative of environmental protection.

Caught in the crossfire of this great power competition is Brazil, a nation whose vast mineral wealth and critical ecological role place it at the epicenter of the global resource struggle. As the holder of over 60% of the Amazon forest, the world's second-largest REE reserves, and a dominant producer of niobium, Brazil has been on the radar of Washington and Beijing (bne IntelliNews, 2025; Hughes, 2024). The influx of Chinese investment into Brazil's mining sector and the use of phased import tariffs to attract Chinese EV manufacturing are accelerating development pressure (Parodi & Waldersee, 2025; Cefai et al., 2024). A significant portion of Brazil's mineral potential, however, lies within the Amazon basin, a bastion of biodiversity. The rush for "green minerals" might carry the hidden cost of potential deforestation, water contamination from mining activities, and the encroachment on Indigenous lands (Muggah, 2025). While Brazil's government has a modern environmental legal framework, even if lacking proper policies regarding national critical minerals for sustainable development, it faces the immense challenge of enforcing these regulations in remote frontier regions where illegal mining and organized crime are rampant (De Tomi et al., 2024; Zaparolli, 2025).

The already dysfunctional international trade system, fractured by the U.S.-China conflict, lacks a cohesive framework to address the old and new environmental externalities. The trade war incentivizes a race to the bottom, where securing supply chains can take precedence over enforcing high environmental, social, and governance (ESG) standards. While the U.S. and its partners in forums like the Minerals Security Partnership advocate for responsible mining, their ability to compete with the sheer scale and speed of Chinese state-backed investment is limited (Baskaran, 2025). The result is a fragmented global market where the environmental costs of mineral extraction are not uniformly priced or regulated. Tariffs and trade restrictions are reshaping supply chains, but they do not inherently promote sustainability; they merely shift the locus of production and, potentially, the locus of environmental harm.

Thus, the escalating trade war between the U.S. and China has intensified the geopolitical competition for critical minerals, creating a profound environmental paradox. The very materials needed to power a global green energy transition are being sourced through a geopolitical race that risks significant ecological damage in key producing nations like Brazil while creating complex environmental policy dilemmas in the U.S. and China. Achieving a truly sustainable future requires more than just a technological shift; it demands a new international consensus on responsible mining and trade practices. Yet, in the current climate of rivalry and protectionism, where strategic advantage often outweighs environmental stewardship, the global community is in danger of winning the battle for green technology while losing the war for the planet's health.

5. CONCLUSION

The intensifying geopolitical and economic competition between the U.S. and China has significantly reshaped global trade dynamics, particularly concerning critical minerals, batteries, and electric vehicles (EVs). China's strategic vertical integration across the critical mineral supply chain, from extraction to refining and EV manufacturing, has established its dominance, creating dependencies for nations like the U.S. and Brazil. This dominance provides China with considerable leverage in international trade and influences the global energy transition.

The implemented protective measures in response to China's surging exports and market control included substantial U.S. tariffs on imports, including critical minerals and EVs, aiming to bolster domestic industries and to reduce reliance on foreign sources. However, this strategy has led to increased production costs and retaliatory tariffs from China, complicating energy transition goals. On the other hand, imports of Chinese batteries kept growing in 2025.

Brazil, possessing significant critical mineral reserves and as part of the BRICS arrangement, has adopted a phased import tax system for EVs. So far, this approach seems to be successful in attracting foreign direct investment and localized manufacturing within Brazil, rather than merely blocking imports. Chinese automakers have established local production facilities, while others are still importing directly into the country for the time being, integrating Brazil more deeply into the global EV supply chain and leveraging its market access for industrial development.

The global pursuit of critical minerals, essential for the green energy transition, presents a "Green Paradox." The increased demand for these minerals, intensified by the U.S.-China trade war, risks environmental degradation through accelerated extraction and processing. China's historical environmental record in mineral processing and its overseas investments raise concerns, while the U.S. faces challenges in fast-tracking domestic mining due to stringent environmental regulations. Resource-rich nations like Brazil are at the epicenter of this dilemma, balancing economic development with environmental protection, especially in ecologically sensitive areas like the Amazon forest, which already holds one of the largest industrial complexes in the country.

Unilateral trade measures seem insufficient to address the intricacies of supply chain vulnerabilities and the environmental costs associated with the energy transition. The current geopolitical landscape, marked by escalating trade disputes and protectionism, indicates the need for multilateral cooperation. Balancing competitive interests with sustainable resource governance, promoting responsible mining practices, and fostering transparency in supply chains are crucial for achieving a sustainable and secure global energy future.

REFERENCES

Baskaran, G. (2025). A strategy for minerals diplomacy in emerging markets. In Baskaran, G., & Wood, D. (Eds.), *Critical minerals and the future of the U.S. economy* (pp. 90–100). Center for Strategic & International Studies., https://www.csis.org/analysis/critical-minerals-and-future-us-economy

Baskaran, G., & Schwartz, M. (2025, April 14). *The consequences of China's new rare earths export restrictions.* Center for Strategic and International Studies. https://www.csis.org/analysis/consequences-chinas-new-rare-earths-export-restrictions

Bazilian, M., & Wischer, G. (2025). Modernizing mine permitting in the United States. In Baskaran, G., & Wood, D. (Eds.), *Critical minerals and the future of the U.S. economy* (pp. 72–89). Center for Strategic & International Studies., https://www.csis.org/analysis/critical-minerals-and-future-us-economy

bne IntelliNews. (2025, May 12). *Brazil poised to challenge China's rare earth dominance.* https://www.intellinews.com/brazil-poised-to-challenge-china-s-rare-earth-dominance-380441/

Bradsher, K. (2025, April 14). China halts critical rare earth exports as trade war intensifies. *The Japan Times.* https://www.japantimes.co.jp/business/2025/04/14/economy/china-rare-earth-minerals-halt-exports/

Caballero, A. (2025, May 9). *Who will prevail? Incentives vs protectionism: The battle between BYD and local manufacturers in Brazil.* Mobility Portal. https://mobilityportal.eu/incentives-vs-protectionism-battlebyd-brazil/

Campbell, C. (2025, June 17). Why it's so hard to challenge China's rare earths dominance. *TIME.* https://time.com/7294964/us-rare-earths-minerals-china-dominance-trump-tariffs/

Cefai, S., Raboca, J., & the Fastmarkets team. (2024, October 10). *China's export restrictions create unexpected opportunity for Brazil's critical minerals sector.* Fastmarkets. https://www.fastmarkets.com/insights/brazils-critical-minerals-sector/

Chang, A., & Bradsher, K. (2024, November 29). How China became the world's largest car exporter. The New York Times. https://www.nytimes.com/interactive/2024/11/29/business/china-cars-sales-exports.html

Choi, S. H. (2025, June 2). Explainer | How dependent is America's arsenal on China's critical mineral supply? *South China Morning Post.* https://www.scmp.com/news/china/military/article/3312731/how-dependent-americas-arsenal-chinas-critical-mineral-supply

De Tomi, G., Loredo, G., & Santos, V. (2024). *Critical and strategic minerals in Brazil: A sovereignty and climate agenda.* Sovereignty and Climate Center. https://soberaniaeclima.org.br/wp-content/uploads/2024/10/Artigo-Giorgio-de-Tomi-04-INGLES.pdf

Detry, E., Gauduel, A., Geurts, F., Ivers, L., McAdoo, M., Möncks, T., & Butler, T. (2023). *Five steps for solving the rare-earth metals shortage.* Boston Consulting Group. https://www.bcg.com/publications/2023/five-steps-for-solving-the-rare-earth-metals-shortage

Dow Jones. (2025, April 3). Trump tariffs bring end to era of globalization; How might central banks react to new economic order. *Morningstar.* https://www.morningstar.com/news/dow-jones/202504033640/trump-tariffs-bring-end-to-era-of-globalization-how-might-central-banks-react-to-new-economic-order

Gan, N. (2025, May 21). US and China are feuding over Huawei's AI chips just days after tariff truce. *CNN Business.* https://www.cnn.com/2025/05/21/business/us-china-conflict-huawei-ai-chips-intl-hnk

Garcia Herrero, A. (2022). *The Future of Electric Vehicles in Asia.* HKUST IEMS. https://iems.ust.hk/protected/request?path=%2Fassets%2Fpublications%2Fthought-leadership-briefs%2F2022%2Fhkustiems-future-of-electric-vehicles-in-asia-alicia-garcia-herrero-hkustiems-tlb64.pdf

Gimbals. (2025, March 26). Strategic Natural Resources and U.S. National Security in a Resource-Hungry World. https://3gimbals.com/insights/2025/03/26/

Global4Cast.org. (2025, April 9). *Trump's 2025 trade war: Economic systemic warfare and the end of the old order.* https://global4cast.org/2025/04/trumps-2025-trade-war-economic-systemic-warfare-and-the-end-of-the-old-order/

Gordon, N. (2025, April 17). How the U.S.-China trade war could derail the energy transition. *Carnegie Endowment for International Peace.* https://carnegieendowment.org/emissary/2025/04/us-china-trade-war-tariffs-critical-minerals-clean-energy-impacts?lang=en

Hai, J. S. (2025, May 28). *What's happening in China's semiconductor industry?* Economics Observatory. https://www.economicsobservatory.com/whats-happening-in-chinas-semiconductor-industry

Hernandez-Roy, C., Ziemer, H., & Laske, N. (2024, April 11). De-risking Critical Mineral Supply Chains: The Role of Latin America. Center for Strategic and International Studies. https://www.csis.org/analysis/de-risking-critical-mineral-supply-chains-role-latin-america

Hughes, T. (2024, November 17). *China deepens ties with Brazil through financing and the promise of a green economy.* InvestorNews. https://investornews.com/critical-minerals-rare-earths/china-deepens-ties-with-brazil-through-financing-and-the-promise-of-a-green-economy/

International Energy Agency. (2025). *Global critical minerals outlook 2025.* https://www.iea.org/reports/global-critical-minerals-outlook-2025

International Trade Centre. (2023a, August). *The global state of trade: Trade in critical raw materials.* ITC Trade Briefs. https://tradebriefs.intracen.org/2023/8/spotlight

International Trade Centre. (2023b, September). *The global state of trade: Trade in critical minerals by processing level.* ITC Trade Briefs. https://tradebriefs.intracen.org/2023/9/spotlight

Interos. (2022, April). *Chinese rare earth elements (REE) & metals dominance analysis.* Interos Inc. https://www.interos.ai/wp-content/uploads/2022/04/Interos-Report-Explores-Concentration-Risk-of-Rare-Earth-Minerals-and-China.pdf

J.P. Morgan Research. (2025, June 9). *US tariffs: What's the impact?* J.P. Morgan. https://www.jpmorgan.com/insights/global-research/current-events/us-tariffs

Kuhn, B. (2024). Kritische Rohstoffe: Wie die EU ihre China- Abhängigkeit senken will (Critical raw materials: How the EU wants to reduce its dependence on China). *Wirtschaftsdienst (Hamburg, Germany), 104*(7), 490–496. https://www.wirtschaftsdienst.eu/inhalt/jahr/2024/heft/7/beitrag/kritische-rohstoff-e-wie-die-eu-ihre-china-abhaengigkeit-senken-will.html#footnote-003. DOI: 10.2478/wd-2024-0126

Lawal, S. (2024, December 4). Tech wars: Why has China banned exports of rare minerals to US? *Al Jazeera.* https://www.aljazeera.com/news/2024/12/4/tech-wars-why-has-china-banned-exports-of-rare-minerals-to-us

Mazzocco, I. (2025, April 22). *Analyzing the impact of the U.S.-China trade war on China's energy transition.* Center for Strategic and International Studies. https://www.csis.org/analysis/analyzing-impact-us-china-trade-war-chinas-energy-transition

Molof, D. (2025, April 10). *How Congress can end Trump's trade war.* Center for American Progress. https://www.americanprogress.org/article/how-congress-can-end-trumps-trade-war/

Moreira, A. (2022, November 9). U.S. unveils investment in nickel, cobalt in Brazil. Valorinternational. https://valorinternational.globo.com/economy/news/2022/11/15/us-unveils-investment-in-nickel-cobalt-in-brazil.ghtml

Muggah, R. (2025, May 13). *The Amazon's green "critical mineral" boom carries hidden environmental and social costs.* LinkedIn. https://www.linkedin.com/pulse/amazons-green-critical-mineral-boom-carries-hidden-social-muggah-9fdsf/

Nunes, V., & Lopes, G. (2024, November 19). Did you spot a new EV in Brazil? It's probably Chinese. *BloombergNEF*. https://about.bnef.com/insights/clean-transport/did-you-spot-a-new-ev-in-brazil-its-probably-chinese/

Online, E. T. (2025, June 5). Why rare earths are the new battleground in US-China trade war. *The Economic Times.* https://economictimes.indiatimes.com/news/international/global-trends/chinas-new-rare-earth-policy-rare-earth-magnet-export-why-rare-earths-are-the-new-battleground-in-us-china-trade-war/articleshow/121642918.cms

Park, C.-Y., & Melendez, A. C. (2024). *Building resilient and responsible critical minerals supply chains for the clean energy transition* (ADB Briefs No. 298). Asian Development Bank. https://www.adb.org/publications/critical-minerals-supply-chains-clean-energy-transition

Parodi, A., & Waldersee, V. (2025, June 19). China floods Brazil with cheap EVs, triggering backlash. *Reuters*. https://www.reuters.com/business/finance/china-floods-brazil-with-cheap-evs-triggering-backlash-2025-06-19/

EY Parthenon. (2023, December). 2024 Geostrategic Outlook: How to thrive amid ongoing geopolitical complexity. EYGM Limited.

Perry, A., & Van Veen, K. (2024, October). Recovering rare earth elements from e-waste: Potential impacts on NdFeB magnet supply chains and the environment. *Journal of International Commerce and Economics.* https://www.usitc.gov/publications/332/journals/jice_recovering_rare_earth_elements_from_e_waste.pdf

Ramos, M. (2024, June 28). Understanding why Brazil has become the biggest importer of Chinese electric cars and how 'Mover' should change the sector. *Brasil de Fato.* https://www.brasildefato.com.br/2024/06/28/understanding-why-brazil-has-become-the-biggest-importer-of-chinese-electric-cars-and-how-mover-should-change-the-sector/

Reed, S., & Hui, L. N. (2022, May 9). Can China's Amazon footprint evolve into a greener partnership? *Dialogue Earth.* https://dialogue.earth/en/business/53558-china-amazon-footprint-evolve-greener-partnership

ResearchAndMarkets.com. (2024, August 16). *Brazil electric vehicle market databook 2024: Global firms are investing in the development of manufacturing facilities to by-pass tax tariffs implemented on the import of electric vehicles in Brazil.* Business Wire. https://www.businesswire.com/news/home/20240816677947/en/Brazil-Electric-Vehicle-Market-Databook-2024-Global-Firms-are-Investing-in-the-Development-of-Manufacturing-Facilities-to-By-pass-Tax-Tariffs-Implemented-on-the-Import-of-Electric-Vehicles-in-Brazil---ResearchAndMarkets.com

Sardain, E., Anderson, J., Pronk, K., Adriaans, L., & Oosthuizen, M. (2024, December 5). *Is CNMC's acquisition of Mineração Taboca further evidence of China's expansion in Latin America?* Project Blue; ProjectBlue.com. https://www.projectblue.com/blue/opinion-pieces/1085/is-cnmc%E2%80%99s-acquisition-of-minera%C3%A7%C3%A3o-taboca-further-evidence-of-china%E2%80%99s-expansion-in-latin-america?----

See, A., & Moscati, J. (2025, May 15). *Opportunities and challenges of Brazil-China trade under the impact of US tariffs.* China Law Vision. https://www.chinalawvision.com/2025/05/international-trade/opportunities-and-challenges-of-brazil-china-trade-under-the-impact-of-us-tariffs/

Shirley, W., & Svensson, K. (2023, September 13). *Resource realism: The geopolitics of critical mineral supply chains.* Goldmansachs.com; Goldman Sachs Global Institute. https://www.goldmansachs.com/insights/articles/resource-realism-the-geopolitics-of-critical-mineral-supply-chains

Shivakumar, S., Wessner, C., & Howell, T. (2025, April 14). *The limits of chip export controls in meeting the China challenge.* Center for Strategic and International Studies. https://www.csis.org/analysis/limits-chip-export-controls-meeting-china-challenge

Shokri, U. (2025, February 12). Critical minerals and the U.S.-China trade war. *TRENDS Research & Advisory.* https://trendsresearch.org/insight/critical-minerals-and-the-u-s-china-trade-war/?srsltid=AfmBOopxwQNxrFCI5_IRrhVM15gNeOvlmAwYobl-qGQI4-BCsCqE2oXb

Snoussi-Mimouni, M., & Avérous, S. (2024, January 10). *High demand for energy-related critical minerals creates supply chain pressures.* World Trade Organization. https://www.wto.org/english/blogs_e/data_blog_e/blog_dta_10jan24_e.htm

S&P Global. (2025, January 30). *China responds to US restrictions with export ban on select critical minerals.* S&P Global Market Intelligence. https://www.spglobal.com/market-intelligence/en/news-insights/research/china-responds-to-us-restrictions-with-export-ban-on-select-critical-minerals

Tanaka, A. (2025, June 20). Letter from Nikkei Asia's editor: China's automotive chip ambitions raise stakes in US trade war. *Nikkei Asia.* https://asia.nikkei.com/Editor-s-Picks/Editor-in-Chief-s-Picks/Letter-from-Nikkei-Asia-s-editor-China-s-automotive-chip-ambitions-raise-stakes-in-US-trade-war

Taulli, B., & Busby, J. (2025, May 30). *The devil is in the details: Minerals, batteries, and US dependence on Chinese imports.* Center for Climate & Security. https://councilonstrategicrisks.org/2025/05/30/the-devil-is-in-the-details-minerals-batteries-and-us-dependence-on-chinese-imports/

The Oregon Group. (2025, May 1). *78% of US military weapon systems vulnerable to China's critical mineral dominance.* https://theoregongroup.com/commodities/rare-earths/78-of-us-military-weapon-systems-potentially-vulnerable-to-china-critical-mineral-dominance/

Tobin, M. (2025, April 16). Taiwan's chip companies are caught in the U.S.-China tariff war. *The New York Times.* https://www.nytimes.com/2025/04/16/business/china-taiwan-tariffs-chips.html

Trager, R. (2024, December 5). China bans sale of three critical elements and 'superhard materials' to the US. *Chemistry World.* https://www.chemistryworld.com/news/china-bans-sale-of-three-critical-elements-and-superhard-materials-to-the-us/4020652.article

Tucker, P. (2025, April 23). China's rare-earth mineral squeeze will hit the Pentagon hard. *Defense One.* https://www.defenseone.com/threats/2025/04/chinas-rare-earth-mineral-squeeze-will-hit-pentagon-hard/404776/

UN Trade and Development (UNCTAD). (2025, May). Global trade update: Focus on critical minerals – copper in the new green and digital economy. UNCTAD. https://unctad.org/publication/global-trade-update-may-2025-critical-minerals-copper

U.S. Energy Information Administration. (2025, May 21). *China dominates global trade of battery minerals.* https://www.eia.gov/todayinenergy/detail.php?id=65305

Vásquez, P. I. (2024, October 2). *Brazil's critical minerals and the global clean energy revolution.* Wilson Center. https://www.wilsoncenter.org/article/brazils-critical-minerals-and-global-clean-energy-revolution

Vergun, D. (2025, January 10). *Securing critical minerals vital to national security, official says.* U.S. Department of Defense. https://www.defense.gov/News/News-Stories/Article/Article/4026144/securing-critical-minerals-vital-to-national-security-official-says/

Vieira do Prado, V. B., & Moerenhout, T. (2024, August). *Brazil's potential role in diversifying US critical mineral supply*. Center on Global Energy Policy at Columbia SIPA. https://www.energypolicy.columbia.edu/publications/brazils-potential-role-in-diversifying-us-critical-mineral-supply/

Wang, Y. (2024, April 19). US and Europe: 2 different approaches to restricting Chinese EVs. *The Diplomat*. https://thediplomat.com/2024/04/us-and-europe-2-different-approaches-to-restricting-chinese-evs/

Wischer, G. (2024, February 12). *The U.S. military and NATO face serious risks of mineral shortages*. Carnegie Endowment for International Peace. https://carnegieendowment.org/research/2024/02/the-us-military-and-nato-face-serious-risks-of-mineral-shortages?lang=en

Xiang, H. (2025). Appian Finalizes $420M Sale of Brazilian Copper Mine to Chinese Firm. *Chemanalyst.com*. https://www.chemanalyst.com/NewsAndDeals/NewsDetails/appian-finalizes-420m-sale-of-brazilian-copper-mine-to-chinese-firm-35670

Zaparolli, D. (2025, April 23). Brazil to launch national critical minerals policy in 2025. *Valor Econômico*. https://valorinternational.globo.com/summit-valor-brazil-china-2025/news/2025/04/23/brazil-to-launch-national-critical-minerals-policy-in-2025.ghtml

Zhang, Y. (2024, June 3). US tariff increases. What is the impact on the US and China markets for electric vehicles and Li-ion batteries? *Interact Analysis*. https://interactanalysis.com/insight/us-tariff-increases-what-is-the-impact-on-the-us-and-china-markets-for-electric-vehicles-and-li-ion-batteries/

Zhou, W., & Gao, H. (2024). *Major economies are taking aim at China's EV industry. Here's what to know*. https://www.cibel.unsw.edu.au/news/major-economies-are-taking-aim-chinas-ev-industry-heres-what-know

Zimmermann, A. (2025, June 18). China's got the world in a rare earth choke hold. *POLITICO*. https://www.politico.eu/article/china-rare-earth-materials-donald-trump-west-magnets-cars/

Zuniga, R., Santos, B., Zimmerman, N., & Magnotta, F. (2025). Promoting Convergence in U.S.-Brazilian Relations. Wilson Center. https://www.wilsoncenter.org/publication/promoting-convergence-us-brazil-relations

ENDNOTES

1 The so-called "energy transition" process may also be understood as part of an energy complementarity or subsidiarity, given that global energy demand rose by 2.2% in 2024 and fossil fuel consumption, accounting for 81.5% of primary energy, keeps growing (Energy Institute, 2024).

2 Upstream is the mining of elements; midstream, the processing into separate oxides; and downstream, the manufacturing of permanent magnets and other components.

3 The BRICS group of countries (Brazil, Russia, India, China, South Africa, Iran, the UAE, Egypt, Ethiopia and Indonesia) agreed in May, 2025 to a new road map of energy cooperation up to 2030. Together, they already account for nearly 50% of global energy production and consumption.

4 On top of sanctions imposed after the annexation of Crimea in 2014, the US implemented another sweep of sanctions focused on isolating Russia from the global financial system. The EU also put in place unprecedented sanctions, ranging from penalties on individuals, companies, organizations, energy, and transport, besides measures concerning visas, foreign trade, and financial services.

5 Dutch company ASML is the sole global supplier of extreme ultraviolet (EUV) lithography systems for semiconductor manufacturing. These machines produce chips at the 7nm node and below, which are essential for AI, high-performance computing, and 5G infrastructure. The U.S. has pressured the Netherlands to restrict exports of lithography equipment due to concerns about China's technological advancement in the semiconductor industry. This pressure has led to restrictions on the sale of advanced chipmaking equipment.

6 The MSP is a collaboration of 14 countries and the EU to attract public and private investment in responsible critical minerals supply chains globally. The inaugural announcement was made at the Prospectors and Developers Association of Canada convention in June 2022.

7 Trying to diversify supply chains for critical minerals, particularly those essential for electric vehicle (EV) batteries, the U.S. has been pursuing Critical Minerals Agreements (CMAs) with various countries. The goal is to reduce reliance on single sources and ensure sustainable and responsible sourcing of these materials.

Chapter 11
The European Union's Geopolitical Role in the Era of Trade Wars

Marc Selgas-Cors
https://orcid.org/0000-0002-3074-3310
University of the Basque Country, Spain

ABSTRACT

In a world increasingly defined by great-power rivalry and economic coercion, the European Union (EU) is reshaping its trade policy to serve not only economic growth but strategic geopolitical objectives. Anchored in a realist international relations framework, the analysis traces how the EU is transitioning from a normative promoter of global trade rules to a more assertive, interest-driven actor capable of wielding economic tools to defend sovereignty, exert influence, and mitigate external threats. The paper examines this shift through five interrelated domains: (1) the internal foundations of the EU's single market and regulatory power; (2) its strategic posture vis-à-vis the United States, China, and Russia; (3) its emerging instruments of economic statecraft, such as the Carbon Border Adjustment Mechanism and the Anti-Coercion Instrument; (4) the geopolitical implications for the Global South; and (5) its attempts to stabilize a fragmented multilateral order. Drawing on official EU documents, think tank reports, and recent academic literature (2022–2025).

1. INTRODUCTION

The global trading system is undergoing a profound transformation. For decades, the European Union (EU) positioned itself as a steadfast advocate of multilateralism and free trade, relying on the liberal promise that economic interdependence fosters

DOI: 10.4018/979-8-3373-3835-4.ch011

peace and prosperity. Yet, recent shocks, from Brexit to the COVID-19 pandemic, from the U.S.-China trade war to Russia's invasion of Ukraine, have shattered the illusion that economic ties are apolitical or inherently stabilizing. In their place has emerged a world marked by strategic rivalry, weaponized interdependence, and a return to power politics. Within this new global context, the EU is reimagining its role, not as a passive rule-taker but as a strategic actor capable of shaping the rules and deploying them for geopolitical ends.

This shift is not merely rhetorical. As the Real Instituto Elcano has noted, the EU is no longer merely reacting to the erosion of multilateral norms; it is proactively developing a geopolitical mindset that fuses trade, security, and foreign policy into an integrated approach to international affairs (González, 2023). Key concepts such as "open strategic autonomy"[1] and "economic security"[2] now dominate the lexicon of Brussels policymakers, signaling a deliberate move toward realist thinking economic interdependence can be both a source of strength and a vector of vulnerability.

From a theoretical standpoint, this evolution reflects the convergence of two traditions. On one hand, realist international relations theory, with its emphasis on relative gains, self-help, and strategic autonomy, offers an apt lens through which to understand the EU's current turn (Baldwin, 1985). On the other, the EU continues to draw from liberal institutionalism, seeking to uphold a rule-based international order, albeit one adapted to the realities of great-power rivalry. This hybridity, realism in tools, liberalism in principles, defines what this chapter conceptualizes as the EU's "strategic dualism."[3]

Empirically, this dualism plays out across the EU's diverse trade relationships. With the United States, cooperation on transatlantic standards and green technology is juxtaposed with tensions over industrial subsidies and protectionist legislation, such as the Inflation Reduction Act. With China, the EU walks a fine line between economic partnership and systemic rivalry, employing instruments like the Foreign Subsidies Regulation or the Anti-Coercion Instrument (ACI) while still engaging in trade and investment. With Russia, the rupture has been near-total: tariffs and sanctions have become instruments of war-time strategy, decoupling Europe from a long-standing energy partner. In each of these cases, trade policy is no longer confined to economic calculus, it is diplomacy by other means.

Crucially, the EU's internal architecture plays a pivotal role in enabling its external trade assertiveness. The single market, the customs union, and the Brussels Effect (Bradford, 2020) give the EU unique leverage in shaping global standards. This institutional coherence allows the EU to act collectively, despite internal divisions, and to condition access to its vast market in ways that serve broader strategic goals. Yet, the exercise of trade power is not without externalities. As the EU imposes environmental or security-based conditions on market access, such as the Carbon Border Adjustment Mechanism (CBAM), developing countries often bear the brunt.

Accusations of green protectionism or neo-mercantilism are rising, especially from the Global South. As scholars such as Weinhardt and De Ville (2024) have shown, this may compromise the EU's soft power and drive emerging economies closer to alternative poles of influence, including China and India.

At the systemic level, the EU's trade strategy must also contend with a weakening of global governance institutions. The World Trade Organization (WTO) remains in crisis, paralyzed by political stalemates and normative divergence. The EU has tried to preserve multilateralism through creative legal workarounds and coalition-building, but these efforts often clash with their turn toward unilateralism and economic statecraft. The paradox is stark: the more the EU seeks to defend a rule-based order, the more it resorts to the very tactics that undermine it.

Against this backdrop, the central question animating this chapter is not whether the EU is becoming a geopolitical actor through trade, it already is, but whether it can manage the consequences of that transformation. Can it project power without undermining legitimacy? Can it defend economic interests without alienating strategic partners? And most critically, can it contribute to a more stable global order in a time of fragmentation?

To answer these questions, this chapter proceeds in six parts. First, it outlines a realist geopolitical framework for interpreting trade as a statecraft tool. Second, it explores the EU's internal trade foundations and the structural power they confer. Third, it analyzes the EU's major bilateral trade relationships and their geopolitical stakes. Fourth, it examines the EU's engagement with developing countries and its impact on global trade governance. Fifth, it surveys the Union's new instruments of trade policy, such as export controls and regulatory screening. Finally, it draws conclusions on the EU's prospects as a trade-powered geopolitical actor in a multipolar world.

2. A REALIST GEOPOLITICAL FRAMEWORK FOR TRADE

The European Union's evolving trade strategy must be understood within the broader theoretical framework of realism, particularly as applied to economic statecraft in a multipolar world. Traditionally, the EU's trade policy was conceived through a liberal institutionalist lens, emphasizing mutual gains, interdependence, and adherence to rules-based cooperation. However, the shifting geopolitical environment, marked by systemic rivalry, weaponized supply chains, and declining trust in multilateral mechanisms, has necessitated a profound strategic reorientation. This transformation is not merely tactical but paradigmatic: the EU is integrating realist assumptions into its trade policy, prioritizing relative power, resilience, and strategic autonomy.

At its core, realism asserts that the international system is anarchic and that actors, primarily states, seek to maximize their security and power. As applied to economic relations, this perspective views trade not as a neutral, efficiency-maximizing activity but as a vehicle for influence, coercion, and deterrence. Economic interdependence, in realist logic, creates asymmetric vulnerabilities that can be manipulated for geopolitical ends. Scholars such as Robert Gilpin (2001) and Jonathan Kirshner (2009) have long emphasized that economics and security are inextricably linked, especially in periods of systemic stress. The EU, although sui generis in its supranational character, increasingly embraces this logic in response to external shocks and strategic competition.

The EU's current embrace of *strategic autonomy*, now reframed as *open strategic autonomy*, is emblematic of this shift. Originally conceptualized in the security and defense domain, the notion has expanded to encompass trade, technology, energy, and health. The *Strategic Compass*[4] for Security and Defence (2022) identified economic instruments as central to ensuring Europe's sovereignty. This vision acknowledges that in a context of intensifying rivalry and coercion, economic power is national power by other means.

A striking feature of this realist turn is the growing centrality of *economic security* in EU discourse. This reflects a broader global trend where economic tools are deployed to achieve strategic objectives, a phenomenon often referred to as *geo-economics*. As Luttwak (1990) famously noted, power is increasingly exercised through economic means rather than military force. In the EU context, this is evident in its use of regulatory tools, trade defenses, investment screening, and sanctions, not only to protect domestic industries but to influence the behavior of foreign actors.

From a realist standpoint, the EU's historical commitment to multilateralism may have obscured the potential costs of asymmetric dependencies. The bloc's reliance on Russian energy, Chinese critical minerals, and American digital infrastructure created structural vulnerabilities. As noted in the ECB's (2024) economic bulletin, the pandemic and subsequent geopolitical crises revealed the fragility of global value chains and the EU's exposure to coercive leverage. In response, the EU has moved toward reducing strategic dependencies through reshoring, diversification, and the creation of internal capacity in sectors deemed critical, from semiconductors to green technologies.

Moreover, the EU's realist recalibration is not reactive but institutionalized. The 2023 *European Economic Security Strategy* formalized the integration of security concerns into economic policymaking. For instance, the EU has adopted a dual-use perspective on emerging technologies such as AI, quantum computing, and biotechnology. These are no longer seen merely as growth engines but as potential threats if exploited by systemic rivals. The proposed outbound investment screening mechanism, currently under consultation, reflects this logic: European firms may be restricted from transferring sensitive know-how abroad, especially to adversarial regimes.

This institutionalization of economic statecraft has implications for the EU's identity. The traditional narrative of the EU as a *civilian power*, a normative actor promoting peace through law and trade, is giving way to a conception of the Union as a *strategic actor*. This does not entail abandoning its normative ambitions; rather, it suggests that normative goals must be supported by power capabilities. As Meunier and Nicolaïdis (2019) have argued, the EU is becoming a *power through trade,* a bloc that seeks to shape global norms not only through persuasion but through leverage.

The EU's deployment of trade policy in response to geopolitical coercion exemplifies this approach. The ACI, finalized in 2023, is a clear manifestation of realist reasoning. It operates deterrence by threatening retaliatory measures against states that use trade restrictions for political purposes. The ACI arose after China's coercion of Lithuania over its Taiwan relations, a case in which the EU recognized the need to counteract external pressure decisively. In realist terms, this instrument enhances the EU's credibility as an actor willing to defend its interests, even at economic cost.

Another realist tool is the reorientation of the EU's regulatory power. While the *Brussels Effect* traditionally worked through the voluntary adoption of EU norms by third countries, the current strategy is more assertive. CBAM, for instance, is not only an environmental policy but a geopolitical one. It conditions market access on compliance with EU climate standards, effectively exporting regulatory requirements under the threat of economic exclusion. This aligns with what Farrell and Newman (2019) describe as *weaponized interdependence*, where network centrality enables coercive regulation.

The growing literature on weaponized interdependence suggests that global economic networks confer strategic advantages to actors who control critical nodes. The EU, by virtue of its regulatory centrality and market size, can exert influence over data flows, financial services, and industrial standards. However, this power is not absolute. The digital domain, for example, remains dominated by U.S.-based platforms, limiting Europe's sovereignty. The *Digital Markets Act* and *Digital Services Act* are efforts to regain control over digital infrastructure, but their extraterritorial impact is still uncertain.

Furthermore, realist trade policy entails a recalibration of alliances. The EU increasingly views trade alignment not only in terms of economic efficiency but in terms of political loyalty and strategic convergence. This is evident in the bloc's approach to *friendshoring*, whereby supply chains are reorganized around trusted partners. The EU–U.S. Trade and Technology Council (TTC), launched in 2021, aims to foster regulatory cooperation among allies. Yet tensions over subsidies, as in the case of the U.S. Inflation Reduction Act, reveal the limits of transatlantic alignment. Realism predicts such friction: even among allies, strategic sectors like green tech and semiconductors are arenas of competition.

This tension between realism and liberalism is also evident in the EU's ambivalence toward the WTO. While Brussels remains a vocal supporter of multilateral rules, its increasing use of autonomous instruments reflects a growing skepticism about the efficacy of the WTO framework. The paralysis of the dispute settlement system has led the EU to embrace bilateralism and plurilateral. This dual-track approach, supporting global rules while preparing for their breakdown, is deeply realist. It hedges against institutional failure while maintaining normative legitimacy.

Yet realism in EU trade policy is not without internal contestation. Member states differ in their tolerance for strategic costs, their threat perceptions, and their commitment to liberal values. For example, Germany's export-oriented model makes it more reluctant to confront China, while France has long advocated for strategic autonomy. Reconciling these preferences requires a careful political balancing act within the Council and Commission. The success of the EU's realist strategy thus depends not only on external variables but on internal cohesion.

Moreover, the realist turn raises normative questions. If trade is weaponized, can the EU still claim to be a normative power? Is the shift toward protectionism a necessary adaptation or a departure from core values? These dilemmas cannot be resolved by theory alone. They require democratic debate and public scrutiny, especially as trade-offs between economic efficiency and strategic autonomy become more salient. The Commission has attempted to frame its policies as *protective openness*[5], but this narrative has yet to gain broad societal traction.

The EU's realist turn in trade policy reflects a broader recalibration of its strategic posture. Confronted with an increasingly hostile and fragmented world, the EU is leveraging its economic instruments not only to defend itself but to shape its environment. This entails risks, fragmentation, retaliation, normative erosion, but also opportunities: enhanced resilience, greater influence, and a more credible geopolitical role. Whether the EU can sustain this balance will depend on its capacity to institutionalize economic statecraft without losing sight of the values that made it a global leader in the first place.

3. INTERNAL FOUNDATIONS: EU TRADE POLICY AND POWER PROJECTION

The external assertiveness of the European Union's trade policy derives its legitimacy and effectiveness from a robust and sophisticated internal economic architecture. The single market, customs union, regulatory capacity, and supranational governance mechanisms allow the EU to "punch above its weight"[6] in global trade politics. While many actors can impose tariffs or negotiate bilateral deals, few command the structural power that emanates from being the world's largest single market and a rule-maker for global commerce. The EU's ability to project trade power geopolitically is, therefore, intimately tied to its internal coherence, institutional design, and normative reach.

The cornerstone of EU trade power lies in its single market, a complex legal-economic space encompassing 27 member states, over 450 million consumers, and approximately 16% of global GDP. This market is not merely a space of economic exchange but a form of *strategic infrastructure*, enabling the EU to act collectively on trade policy, investment rules, competition enforcement, and product standards. The supranational authority conferred to the European Commission, especially under Article 207 of the Treaty on the Functioning of the European Union (TFEU), centralizes external trade competence, allowing the EU to negotiate as one actor at the WTO and in bilateral free trade agreements (FTAs).

This unity has clear geopolitical implications. It provides leverage in negotiations (offering or withholding access to a vast market), reduces vulnerability to external fragmentation, and enhances the EU's credibility as a global regulatory power. For instance, when the EU negotiates an FTA with a third country, it does so on behalf of all member states, using the single market as a unified bargaining chip. The EU–Japan Economic Partnership Agreement (2019) is a prominent example of how collective economic diplomacy can shape global trade architecture. Despite geopolitical shifts, Japan remains committed to high standards aligned with EU regulatory frameworks, largely due to the scale and predictability of the EU market.

The Customs Union and Common Commercial Policy

Beyond the single market, the customs union, abolishing internal tariffs and establishing a Common External Tariff, amplifies EU trade power. It enables frictionless trade within the bloc while projecting a unified external stance. The customs code ensures that goods imported into any EU country are subject to the same rules and inspections, which reinforces trust among member states and enhances enforcement capabilities at the border.

Moreover, the EU's Common Commercial Policy (CCP) institutionalizes its ability to pursue external trade objectives. Through the CCP, the EU has implemented over 40 trade agreements covering 70+ countries, reflecting a strategic ambition to shape trade rules globally. These agreements go beyond tariff reductions to encompass chapters on sustainability, digital trade, and labor rights, thereby exporting EU standards and values abroad. As Meissner (2016) argues, the EU has transformed its trade agreements into tools of "normative regulatory governance," creating incentives for partners to align with its internal rules in exchange for market access.

The "Brussels Effect": Regulatory Influence Beyond Borders

Perhaps the most distinctive source of EU power projection is its regulatory capacity, often referred to as the "Brussels Effect" (Bradford, 2020). This refers to the EU's ability to unilaterally externalize its legal norms, which then become global standards by default. Unlike coercive mechanisms such as tariffs or sanctions, the Brussels Effect operates through market logic: third-country firms voluntarily adopt EU standards to maintain access to its lucrative market.

This phenomenon is visible in sectors ranging from chemicals (REACH regulations), data protection (GDPR), food safety, environmental compliance, and increasingly, artificial intelligence. In each case, the EU's stringent internal standards shape corporate practices far beyond its borders. For example, the GDPR, although an internal data regulation, triggered global changes in how multinationals manage personal data. Companies from Silicon Valley to Shenzhen redesigned compliance architectures to meet EU requirements, not because of coercion, but due to the economic necessity of accessing the EU market.

Geopolitically, the Brussels Effect is a form of *soft power with hard consequences*. It allows the EU to set global norms without relying on military force or coercive diplomacy. However, in the current context of geoeconomic rivalry, this effect is becoming more contentious. Emerging economies increasingly view EU regulatory influence as an obstacle rather than an opportunity, especially when standards intersect with strategic sectors like energy, technology, or digital sovereignty.

Strategic Autonomy and Internal Coordination

The concept of "open strategic autonomy" has become the guiding narrative of the EU's new trade strategy. Articulated in the 2021 Trade Policy Review, it seeks to reconcile two imperatives: maintaining openness to trade and investment while reducing dependence in critical areas. Internally, this has led to renewed focus on industrial policy, research and development investment, and coordination on strategic supply chains.

A notable example is the European Chips Act, launched in 2022. Motivated by the global semiconductor shortage and geopolitical tensions over Taiwan, the Act aims to mobilize €43 billion in public and private investment to reduce dependency on Asian chipmakers. This internal industrial mobilization reflects a growing awareness that technological sovereignty is essential for geopolitical resilience. Similarly, the EU has invested heavily in green technology, digital infrastructure, and hydrogen ecosystems—sectors identified as critical for long-term strategic autonomy.

Coordination across member states remains a challenge. While the Commission provides strategic direction, implementation often depends on national willingness and fiscal capacity. The COVID-19 crisis and subsequent Recovery and Resilience Facility (RRF) demonstrated that solidarity-based fiscal mechanisms can reinforce collective capacity. Yet divergences remain, particularly between fiscally conservative states and those advocating for stronger EU-level industrial support. This internal political economy shapes the Union's ability to act decisively on external fronts.

3.1 Ports, Infrastructures, and Foreign Ownership

Less visible but geopolitically vital are the internal infrastructures that interface with global trade, ports, logistics hubs, and critical industries. Foreign investment in strategic assets, particularly by state-backed firms from China and the Gulf, has triggered concerns about undue foreign influence over essential nodes of the EU economy. The acquisition of a majority stake in the port of Piraeus by China's COSCO in 2016, or stakes in Italian and Belgian ports, exemplify this trend.

In response, the EU adopted a Regulation on Foreign Direct Investment Screening in 2019. While screening remains the competence of member states, the regulation created a coordination framework to monitor and potentially block investments that threaten security or public order. This reflects an internal alignment with realist thinking market openness must be tempered by national interest considerations, especially in sectors linked to defense, infrastructure, or dual-use technologies.

Member States have gradually increased their scrutiny of foreign investments. Germany, for example, blocked the acquisition of a semiconductor firm by a Chinese investor in 2022, citing national security risks. France and Italy have also reinforced their screening mechanisms, especially after COVID-19 exposed vulnerabilities in pharmaceutical and medical supply chains. Such national initiatives, coordinated at the EU level, enhance the bloc's ability to prevent strategic dependencies and maintain internal control over critical infrastructures.

3.2 The Role of the European Parliament and Civil Society

While much of the EU's trade power flows through the Commission and the Council, the European Parliament (EP) has become an increasingly influential actor in shaping trade policy. Its consent is required for all FTAs, and it has used this leverage to influence the inclusion of human rights, labor standards, and environmental commitments in trade agreements.

The EP's rejection of the Comprehensive Agreement on Investment (CAI) with China in 2021, following the imposition of Chinese sanctions on EU lawmakers, marked a turning point. It demonstrated that internal democratic institutions could act as a check on purely technocratic or economic-driven trade decisions. This parliamentary assertiveness reflects broader societal concerns about aligning trade policy with the EU's normative identity.

Civil society organizations also play a key role in this internal dynamic. NGOs, trade unions, and environmental groups have consistently pressured EU institutions to include enforceable sustainability provisions in trade deals. The debate around the EU–Mercosur agreement illustrates this vividly: strong opposition from civil society and national parliaments in countries like France and Austria has stalled ratification over concerns about deforestation and indigenous rights in the Amazon. This internal contestation strengthens the EU's credibility externally, signaling that trade power must be exercised in accordance with democratic values.

3.4 Internal Cohesion as Geopolitical Capital

Ultimately, the EU's ability to project trade power externally depends on internal cohesion. Divergences among member states, on China policy, transatlantic alignment, digital taxation, or environmental regulation, can undermine the coherence of EU trade positions. The unanimity requirement for certain trade policy decisions, especially those related to taxation or foreign policy, creates veto points that external actors can exploit.

Nevertheless, the EU has shown an increasing capacity to overcome internal divisions in response to external threats. The post-2022 energy crisis, triggered by Russia's invasion of Ukraine, catalyzed unprecedented coordination in energy procurement, storage, and diversification. Similarly, the EU's swift agreement on sanctions packages against Russia illustrated its capacity for rapid, collective economic action under geopolitical duress.

This resilience stems not only from institutional mechanisms but from a growing consensus that economic openness without safeguards is unsustainable in a hostile world. The realization that interdependence can be weaponized has led to greater support for instruments such as the CBAM, the ACI, and the Chips Act. In effect, external shocks are reinforcing internal unity, consolidating a shared understanding of strategic autonomy.

4. THE EU'S EXTERNAL TRADE RELATIONS IN A GEOPOLITICAL CONTEXT: COOPERATION AND COMPETITION

In the contemporary geopolitical landscape, the EU's trade relations with key global actors, namely the United States, China, and Russia, have become complex, ambivalent, and increasingly strategic. Trade has ceased to be a domain isolated from politics; rather, it is now an arena in which global power is contested and reconfigured. The EU's external economic diplomacy is caught between cooperation and competition, shared values and diverging interests, institutional alignment and strategic divergence. Far from being peripheral, trade relations now lie at the heart of the EU's foreign policy toolkit and its strategic positioning within an increasingly fragmented world order.

The transatlantic relationship, once seen as the backbone of the liberal international order, has undergone a profound transformation. Although the EU and the U.S. continue to share deep economic ties and strategic commitments, their trade relations have become marked by growing frictions, largely driven by industrial policy, protectionist tendencies, and techno-nationalism. The dispute over the U.S. Inflation Reduction Act (IRA), passed in 2022, exemplifies this dynamic. While intended to accelerate America's green transition, the IRA's discriminatory subsidies for domestically-produced clean technologies raised serious concerns in Brussels. EU officials feared a distortion of competition in key sectors such as electric vehicles and batteries, particularly as European firms faced pressure to relocate production to the U.S. to benefit from tax credits.

Although a full-scale trade war was avoided through negotiations, the IRA episode exposed a growing divergence in economic policy. It also highlighted a broader structural trend: while both actors endorse decarbonization and innovation, they differ on how to achieve these goals and on the degree to which state aid and market access should be balanced. The EU responded not only through diplomatic pressure but by launching its own Green Deal Industrial Plan and a more assertive subsidy framework, demonstrating that it was willing to match American industrial ambition with European resilience. This shift suggests that while transatlantic cooperation continues, it is increasingly underpinned by a realist awareness of competition, particularly in frontier sectors.

Moreover, despite rhetorical alignment on shared strategic concerns, most notably, countering China's coercive practices, the transatlantic alliance remains fragile. The EU has not fully aligned with U.S. decoupling strategies, preferring instead a "de-risking" approach that maintains engagement with Beijing while reducing dependencies in critical sectors. This divergence has generated tension within the Trade and Technology Council (TTC), which, although useful in coordinating standards, has struggled to bridge deeper disagreements on digital sovereignty, export controls, and supply chain strategies. In this sense, the EU's relationship with the U.S. reflects a balance of strategic partnership and autonomous positioning: convergence where possible, divergence where necessary.

China, on the other hand, presents a multifaceted challenge to the EU, combining economic interdependence, normative divergence, and growing geopolitical rivalry. While China remains one of the EU's largest trading partners, the perception of Beijing has shifted markedly in recent years. The 2019 European Commission's strategic outlook officially labelled China as a "partner, competitor, and systemic rival," marking a rhetorical break with the earlier technocratic engagement approach. Since then, the relationship has deteriorated due to escalating concerns about market distortions, forced technology transfers, human rights violations in Xinjiang, and Beijing's increasingly assertive global posture.

The CAI, negotiated in 2020 but suspended in 2021, symbolizes the contradictions in EU–China relations. Hailed initially as a breakthrough in market access and investment protection, it was later frozen by the European Parliament following China's retaliatory sanctions on European officials critical of its human rights record. The collapse of the CAI underscored the limitations of purely economic diplomacy in a context where values and strategic concerns weigh heavily on trade policy. As McElwee (2022) argues, the failure of the CAI revealed the growing politicization of EU trade policy and the impossibility of delinking trade from broader foreign policy goals.

Beyond institutional disputes, the EU has adopted a more defensive posture vis-à-vis China. The 2023 Anti-Coercion Instrument, developed in response to China's economic retaliation against Lithuania, exemplifies this turn. It provides the EU with the legal means to counter third-country coercion through calibrated retaliation. Similarly, the Foreign Subsidies Regulation, which took effect in 2023, aims to level the playing field within the internal market by subjecting subsidized foreign companies, often Chinese, to stricter scrutiny. These tools reflect a realist understanding that economic openness must be accompanied by strategic safeguards.

Another key dimension is the EU's effort to reduce strategic dependencies on Chinese inputs, particularly in critical raw materials, semiconductors, and green technologies. The European Critical Raw Materials Act (2023) sets ambitious targets to diversify sourcing and increase domestic capacity in materials such as lithium, rare earths, and cobalt. As the ECB (2024) notes, 98% of the EU's supply of rare earth elements currently comes from China, a dependency that poses significant geopolitical risks. In line with the broader de-risking agenda, the EU is forging new partnerships with Latin America, Central Asia, and Africa to secure alternative suppliers, reinforcing its capacity to act independently.

However, the EU's position is complicated by internal divisions among member states. Germany, for instance, remains deeply embedded in China's industrial ecosystem, particularly in the automotive and machinery sectors. French and Dutch authorities, by contrast, have adopted more hawkish stances. The European Commission has attempted to bridge these divergences by emphasizing a pragmatic approach that avoids full decoupling while addressing the structural asymmetries in the relationship. Ursula von der Leyen's "de-risk, not decouple" speech in 2023 encapsulates this nuanced vision, one that blends realism with continued economic engagement.

Russia represents a radically different case. Unlike the ambiguous blend of engagement and rivalry that characterizes EU relations with China and the U.S., the EU–Russia trade relationship has undergone a near-complete rupture following the 2022 invasion of Ukraine. The EU's response has been swift and coordinated, encompassing 13 sanctions packages that target key Russian exports and industries, including energy, banking, transport, and high-tech goods. The embargo on Russian coal, oil, and petroleum products, combined with a price cap on seaborne crude, has transformed Europe's energy trade landscape.

The shift has not been without cost. In the short term, energy prices surged, industrial competitiveness was challenged, and inflationary pressures mounted. However, in strategic terms, the EU has successfully reduced its dependency on Russian fossil fuels. Imports of Russian gas have dropped from over 40% in 2021 to less than 10% in 2024, replaced by liquefied natural gas (LNG) from the U.S., Qatar, and Norway. The REPowerEU plan, launched in 2022, accelerated investment in renewable energy, energy efficiency, and infrastructure interconnectivity, further reducing the Union's vulnerability to energy blackmail.

Geopolitically, the EU's sanctions strategy is underpinned by a realist calculus: accepting short-term economic costs to achieve long-term strategic autonomy and uphold international norms. Trade has thus become a tool of coercive diplomacy, designed to weaken Russia's warfighting capacity while signaling resolve and unity. Yet, the sanctions regime also illustrates the limits of economic power. Russia has redirected its exports to China, India, and Turkey, and despite initial setbacks, its economy has shown resilience, partly thanks to high commodity prices and a wartime mobilization of industrial capacity.

Moreover, the global ramifications of the EU's rupture with Russia are far-reaching. The sanctions have contributed to the emergence of parallel financial and trade systems, including alternative payment platforms and bilateral currency swaps that bypass the U.S. dollar and the euro. Countries in the Global South increasingly perceive the Western-led sanctions as politicized and asymmetrical, potentially weakening the legitimacy of the liberal trade order. The fragmentation of the global economy into competing blocs, exacerbated by the EU's own autonomous instruments, raises questions about the long-term viability of open global trade as a pillar of peace and development.

In all three cases, U.S., China, and Russia, the EU's external trade policy reflects a realist understanding of interdependence as both an asset and a liability. The Union is not abandoning its commitment to rules-based trade, but it is increasingly deploying trade tools to achieve non-economic objectives: deterrence, diversification, and the projection of values. This marks a departure from the earlier technocratic ethos of the EU's trade policy and its elevation into the realm of high politics.

At the same time, the EU faces constraints. Internally, the requirement for unanimity in certain foreign trade decisions limits agility. Externally, the erosion of multilateralism, epitomized by the paralysis of the WTO's Appellate Body, reduces the space for cooperative dispute settlement. The EU has responded by creating ad hoc mechanisms, such as the Multi-Party Interim Appeal Arbitration Arrangement (MPIA), but these are best stopgap solutions. The broader challenge remains: can the EU sustain its geopolitical ambitions without triggering reciprocal protectionism or losing its normative edge?

The imperatives and institutional constraints. With the U.S., cooperation continues but is tested by industrial rivalry and subsidy wars. With China, interdependence coexists with growing strategic distrust, prompting defensive instruments and diversification strategies. With Russia, the rupture has been nearly absolute, demonstrating the EU's willingness to use trade as a weapon of statecraft. The overarching trend is clear: trade has become geopolitical. The EU's challenge is to navigate this transformation without undermining its core identity as a defender of multilateralism, sustainability, and open markets. Whether it can succeed depends on its capacity to sustain internal cohesion, build flexible alliances, and wield its economic power with prudence and principle.

5. IMPACTS ON THE GLOBAL SOUTH AND THE MULTILATERAL ORDER

In the increasingly geoeconomic landscape defined by competition, resilience, and strategic autonomy, the EU's trade policy is having significant, and often unintended, repercussions beyond its traditional strategic rivals. One of the most revealing dimensions of this transformation is its impact on the Global South and the broader multilateral trade order. While the EU has historically presented itself as a normative and cooperative partner for developing countries, the recalibration of its trade instruments toward strategic interests is reshaping these relationships. This reorientation, while perhaps inevitable in a fractured world, is testing the EU's credibility, soft power, and multilateral leadership.

For decades, the EU maintained a privileged position vis-à-vis the Global South, offering preferential trade access, aid-for-trade packages, and capacity-building programs. Instruments such as the Generalised Scheme of Preferences (GSP) and the Everything but Arms (EBA) initiative granted developing and least-developed countries (LDCs) duty-free and quota-free access to the EU market. The logic behind these policies was dual: facilitating development through trade while securing political alliances in international fora such as the WTO and the UN. However, in recent years, this development-centric narrative has been increasingly replaced, or at least challenged, by a strategic calculus, where market access is conditioned not only by developmental needs but also by compliance with normative and regulatory expectations defined in Brussels.

One of the most contentious manifestations of this shift is the CBAM, which entered into its transitional phase in 2023. Framed primarily as an environmental tool to combat carbon leakage and protect the EU's climate efforts, CBAM applies a carbon price to imports of emissions-intensive goods such as cement, steel, aluminum, and fertilizers. While its objective is aligned with the European Green Deal, its geopolitical and developmental implications are far-reaching. For exporters in the Global South, many of whom lack the institutional capacity to implement carbon pricing or deterioration their industries, CBAM represents a potential barrier to market access. Countries such as Mozambique, India, and South Africa have already raised concerns at the WTO, arguing that CBAM is, de facto, a protectionist measure dressed in environmental clothing.

From a realist standpoint, CBAM serves a dual purpose: it shields European industries from regulatory arbitrage and compels trading partners to internalize EU-defined norms. Yet, for countries in the Global South, this policy is perceived as unilateral, technocratic, and disproportionately harmful. The imposition of carbon tariffs without accompanying technological or financial support not only risks undermining economic competitiveness but also reinforces a neocolonial narrative in which the rules of global trade are written by the North and enforced upon the South. Some analysts warn that if CBAM is not accompanied by compensatory mechanisms, such as carbon finance, capacity building, or just transition funding, it could provoke a legitimacy crisis for EU trade diplomacy among developing nations.

The geopolitical risks are real. As Weinhardt and De Ville (2024) have noted, the Global South is not a passive periphery but a strategic battleground in the emerging multipolar order. China, for instance, has actively positioned itself as a champion of "South–South" cooperation, offering concessional loans, infrastructure investment, and preferential trade deals through initiatives like the Belt and Road Initiative. Similarly, India and Brazil are mobilizing coalitions within the WTO to contest what they perceive as the weaponization of standards by the Global North. The EU's efforts to reform global trade rules must therefore contend with growing assertiveness among developing countries, many of whom demand a seat at the table, not as beneficiaries of goodwill but as co-architects of the international order.

To mitigate these tensions, the EU has launched initiatives such as *Global Gateway*, a €300 billion investment plan aimed at counterbalancing China's influence in digital, energy, and transport infrastructure across Africa, Asia, and Latin America. Unlike the Belt and Road Initiative, Global Gateway emphasizes sustainability, democratic governance, and transparency. However, early critiques suggest that the EU's offer still suffers from implementation gaps, slow bureaucratic machinery, and a lack of visibility on the ground. Moreover, its conditionality-based approach, tying infrastructure finance to regulatory alignment, may be perceived as paternalistic, further complicating EU efforts to win hearts and minds in the Global South.

Beyond bilateral dynamics, the EU's evolving trade strategy is reshaping the multilateral trade order itself. The WTO, once the bedrock of global trade governance, is facing a deep legitimacy and functionality crisis. The paralysis of the Appellate Body, driven by the U.S. refusal to appoint new judges since 2019, has effectively dismantled the WTO's dispute settlement mechanism. In this vacuum, the EU has tried to maintain legal continuity through the Multi-Party Interim Appeal Arbitration Arrangement (MPIA), created alongside Canada and other like-minded partners. While well-intentioned, the MPIA remains a stopgap, excluding major economies such as the U.S., China, and India. The EU's push for WTO reform, on issues such as industrial subsidies, digital trade, and environmental standards, has made limited progress, largely because of persistent North–South divisions.

The emergence of plurilateral negotiations, such as those on e-commerce, investment facilitation, and climate-friendly goods, suggests a partial retreat from the WTO's consensus-based model. The EU has embraced this shift pragmatically, pursuing "coalitions of the willing" rather than waiting for full multilateral convergence. While efficient, this approach raises concerns about fragmentation and exclusion. Smaller or poorer states, lacking negotiating capacity or technological readiness, may find themselves sidelined from rule-setting processes that affect them directly. This creates a dilemma: while the EU promotes rules-based governance, its own practices risk reinforcing a stratified order where power, not norms, shapes outcomes.

Moreover, the EU's unilateral instruments, ranging from trade defense measures to export controls and investment screening, further complicate its multilateral posture. These tools are often justified on security or sustainability grounds, but their cumulative effect may be to erode the principle of non-discrimination and transparency enshrined in WTO law. Developing countries have increasingly voiced concerns that the EU's new economic security agenda amounts to selective protectionism. The deployment of the Foreign Subsidies Regulation and the ACI, for instance, while directed primarily at China, may affect firms from emerging markets that receive state support but lack the political clout to negotiate exemptions or influence procedural design.

This duality, between normative ambition and strategic unilateralism, reveals a fundamental tension in the EU's identity. On the one hand, the Union aspires to be a stabilizing force, committed to a fair, inclusive, and rules-based global trade system. On the other hand, it increasingly behaves as a realist actor, prioritizing internal resilience, strategic autonomy, and regulatory sovereignty. The challenge is not merely technical but existential: can the EU preserve its image as a fair and reliable partner while deploying tools that may be perceived as coercive, exclusive, or disproportionate?

There are some avenues for reconciliation. One promising strategy is the expansion of climate and sustainability partnerships with the Global South. The EU–South

Africa Just Energy Transition Partnership, launched in 2021, offers a potential model: blending trade, investment, and technical assistance in a framework that recognizes asymmetries and prioritizes justice. Similarly, the EU's updated GSP+ scheme now includes enhanced conditionalities on human rights and climate standards, but also clearer paths for capacity-building and transitional assistance. These efforts can demonstrate that the EU's trade conditionalities are not mere instruments of discipline, but potential platforms for mutual benefit.

Another opportunity lies in knowledge and technology transfer. Many developing countries fear that the green and digital transitions will replicate the old extractive models of globalization, where innovation occurs in the North and dependency persists in the South. The EU could mitigate these concerns by investing in joint research projects, open standards for green technologies, and inclusive digital infrastructure. The Team Europe approach, which pools EU and member state resources for common development goals, offers a scalable mechanism to implement such partnerships.

Yet, time is of the essence. As the world becomes more fragmented and competitive, strategic alliances are being redrawn. If the EU is seen as unresponsive or coercive, it risks losing influence in key regions, especially Africa and Southeast Asia, where China, Russia, and Gulf states are increasingly active. In a world of rival spheres of influence, the ability to build trust, offer reliable alternatives, and maintain consistent engagement is more important than ever.

The Global South is also reshaping the future of multilateralism. Groupings such as the African Continental Free Trade Area (AfCFTA), MERCOSUR, and ASEAN are developing their own normative frameworks and institutional architectures. Rather than imposing standards from above, the EU would do well to co-construct trade norms with these blocs, recognizing their agency and contextual knowledge. This shift from conditionality to co-creation may be essential for maintaining multilateral legitimacy in a post-Western order.

It is worth acknowledging that trade policy alone cannot substitute for global governance reform. As the climate crisis intensifies, digital gaps widen, and economic inequalities persist, a new generation of global compacts is needed, ones that integrate trade, finance, and development in a more holistic manner. The EU, with its tradition of regulatory leadership and consensus-building, is well-positioned to contribute to this effort. But doing so will require humility, flexibility, and a renewed commitment to multilateralism not as a slogan, but as a shared responsibility.

6. KEY INSTRUMENTS OF EU TRADE POLICY TURN

In recent years, the European Union has reconfigured its trade policy arsenal to adapt to a more fragmented, hostile, and uncertain global landscape. This shift is not purely reactive, but part of a deliberate strategic turn whereby the EU equips itself with tools of economic statecraft designed to preserve strategic autonomy, manage asymmetric dependencies, and deter coercive behavior by third countries. These instruments represent a substantial recalibration from the EU's traditional liberal orientation, reflecting a realist logic that views economic interdependence as both a source of influence and vulnerability. Collectively, they signal the emergence of the EU as a geopolitical actor whose economic power is increasingly deployed with political intentionality.

One of the most emblematic developments in this transformation is the introduction of the Foreign Direct Investment (FDI) Screening Regulation, which became operational in 2020. Although investment screening has long been a prerogative of individual member states, the Regulation (EU) 2019/452 established, for the first time, an EU-level framework for coordination and information sharing. The mechanism is not a veto power at the supranational level, but it allows the Commission and other member states to issue opinions on investments that may affect security or public order. The key innovation lies in the creation of a "European ecosystem of vigilance", especially in strategic sectors such as energy infrastructure, semiconductors, and digital technology.

The strategic rationale behind this instrument was illustrated by several high-profile cases, including Chinese acquisitions of European ports and high-tech firms. In 2021, Germany blocked the sale of a semiconductor manufacturer to a Chinese buyer, while France and Italy imposed stricter oversight on deals in the energy sector. The FDI Screening Regulation institutionalizes a defensive lawyer in the EU's trade architecture, one that acknowledges the risk of foreign control over critical assets. While the framework remains intergovernmental, it represents a shift toward a shared understanding of economic security that transcends national borders.

Complementing this inward-looking tool is the ACI, finalized in 2023. The ACI is a legislative response to the increasing use of economic coercion by global powers to pressure EU member states. The triggering case was China's de facto embargo on Lithuanian goods in retaliation for the opening of a Taiwanese representative office in Vilnius. The ACI empowers the European Commission to investigate coercive practices and, if confirmed, propose countermeasures such as import restrictions, export bans, or public procurement exclusions. Unlike traditional trade defense measures, which are reactive and evidence-based, the ACI introduces a deterrent logic into EU trade policy: it signals that coercion will not go unanswered, even if WTO avenues are blocked.

This represents a qualitative leap in the EU's strategic thinking. The ACI blurs the boundaries between trade policy and foreign policy, enabling the EU to use market access as leverage in geopolitical disputes. It is also a manifestation of the EU's frustration with the paralysis of the WTO's dispute settlement system.

By creating autonomous enforcement mechanisms, the EU is asserting its right to protect its interests in the absence of effective multilateral remedies. While the ACI has been welcomed by proponents of a more muscular EU, critics warn that its discretionary nature and potential for politicization could erode legal certainty for international business.

CBAM exemplifies the EU's use of regulatory sovereignty as a form of economic statecraft. It externalizes the EU's climate norms and creates incentives for foreign producers to decarbonize or face financial penalties. The geopolitical consequences are substantial. Several emerging economies, including India, Brazil, and South Africa, have expressed concern at the WTO, accusing the EU of disguised protectionism. Yet the EU maintains that CBAM is consistent with WTO rules, as it treats foreign and domestic producers equally based on their emissions intensity, not origin.

Beyond legal debates, CBAM positions the EU as a global regulator of climate-related trade. It forces other countries to confront the cost of carbon in ways that may not align with their development priorities or institutional capacities. At the same time, it showcases the EU's normative ambition: to lead the global green transition not only through innovation but through conditional market access. From a realist angle, CBAM is a defensive mechanism, protecting EU industry from regulatory arbitrage, but also a projection tool, advancing European preferences in a world of fragmented climate governance.

The EU has also intensified its use of trade defense instruments, such as anti-dumping and anti-subsidy duties. These instruments have been part of the EU's trade policy for decades, but their frequency and scope have expanded significantly in the last five years. China is the main target of these measures, particularly in sectors like steel, solar panels, and electric vehicles, where overcapacity and state support distort market conditions. In 2023, the Commission initiated anti-subsidy investigations into Chinese EV imports, citing concerns about unfair competition and strategic dependence on Chinese technologies.

What is notable in this new phase is the increasing alignment of trade defense with industrial and technological policy. The EU is no longer merely protecting existing sectors from injury but also nurturing emerging industries deemed vital for long-term competitiveness and resilience. This logic has been evident in the Critical Raw Materials Act and the European Chips Act, both of which seek to reduce dependency and incentivize domestic production. Trade defense thus becomes a tool of industrial strategy, aligned with broader goals of technological sovereignty and green leadership.

Further extending its reach, the EU has introduced the Foreign Subsidies Regulation, which entered into force in 2023. The FSR addresses a long-standing gap in EU competition law: the ability to scrutinize distortive subsidies granted by non-EU governments to firms operating in the EU internal market. The regulation allows the Commission to investigate foreign subsidies that may affect mergers, acquisitions, or public procurement, and to impose redressive measures, including financial corrections or prohibition of deals.

The FSR represents a paradigmatic shift. Until now, EU competition policy focused on internal distortions, ignoring the external dimension. The FSR brings foreign state capitalism into the EU's regulatory perimeter, particularly targeting subsidized firms from China and other state-capitalist economies. It also strengthens the EU's role as a gatekeeper of fair competition in globalized markets. While the regulation may face challenges at the WTO, it reflects a growing international consensus on the need to address cross-border distortions in a world of asymmetric state interventions.

A less publicized but equally important development is the EU's reinforcement of export controls, particularly on dual-use goods and emerging technologies. The 2021 revision of the Dual-Use Regulation expanded the scope of controls to include cyber-surveillance technologies and gave the Commission a more central role in enforcement. Following the Russian invasion of Ukraine, the EU adopted a series of sectoral export bans on sensitive technologies, including microchips, drones, and encryption software. These measures were designed to degrade Russia's military capabilities and limit its access to advanced inputs.

The geopolitical rationale behind export controls is twofold. First, they serve as tools of coercive diplomacy, applying economic pressure without direct confrontation. Second, they align the EU with its strategic partners, particularly the U.S., in controlling the proliferation of technologies that could be used by authoritarian regimes. The EU's participation in multilateral export control regimes—such as the Wassenaar Arrangement and the Missile Technology Control Regime—has been complemented by autonomous measures tailored to specific threats.

What is emerging is a more proactive export control policy that anticipates rather than reacts to security risks. The EU is also considering an outbound investment screening mechanism, modelled in part on U.S. initiatives, to prevent European capital and know-how from being used to enhance the military or surveillance capabilities of systemic rivals. While still in early stages, this instrument would close a critical gap in the EU's strategic economic toolkit, reflecting a comprehensive approach to economic security.

Taken together, these instruments signify a profound transformation in the EU's trade policy paradigm. No longer confined to the promotion of liberalization, trade policy is now a platform for projecting power, defending sovereignty, and managing systemic risk. The institutionalization of these tools reflects the Commission's growing role as a geopolitical actor in its own right. It also mirrors broader shifts in global economic governance, where strategic competition and regulatory fragmentation increasingly define the rules of engagement.

However, this arsenal of trade policy tools also raises important normative and practical questions. Can the EU maintain consistency with its international legal obligations while deploying these instruments? How will developing countries be affected by these tools, particularly those with limited capacity to comply with complex regulatory requirements? And to what extent can the EU avoid the perception—and potential reality—of weaponizing interdependence in ways that contradict its liberal identity?

The answers to these questions will depend on how these instruments are implemented, interpreted, and justified. Transparency, proportionality, and engagement with stakeholders—especially those from the Global South—will be essential to preserving the EU's credibility. In parallel, the EU will need to coordinate more closely with like-minded partners to avoid regulatory divergence and fragmentation. The TTC with the U.S., the Green Alliances with countries like Japan and Canada, and capacity-building initiatives in Africa and Latin America can serve as vehicles for alignment and mutual learning.

The EU's new trade instruments are not merely defensive mechanisms; they are tools of strategic engagement in a world where economics and geopolitics are increasingly fused. Their success will hinge not only on their legal robustness or economic effectiveness but on their political legitimacy—internally within the EU and externally in the international community. If used wisely, they can reinforce the EU's position as a rule-maker in a contested global order. If used unilaterally or inconsistently, they risk undermining the very order the EU seeks to uphold.

7. CONCLUSION: NAVIGATING THE NEW GEOECONOMIC REALITY—EUROPE'S STRATEGIC TRADE DILEMMA

The European Union finds itself at the intersection of normative aspiration and strategic necessity. For decades, it championed a vision of the world rooted in rules-based multilateralism, economic interdependence, and regulatory diplomacy. In this vision, trade was not only a vehicle of growth but a tool for projecting European values, stabilizing regions, and fostering cooperation beyond borders. However, the emergence of a fragmented, adversarial, and post-liberal global order has forced the EU to reassess the foundations of its trade strategy.

The return of great power politics, marked by US–China rivalry, Russia's militarized revisionism, and systemic challenges to the liberal international order, has exposed the vulnerabilities of open economies. The COVID-19 pandemic and the war in Ukraine further accelerated this awakening, highlighting the fragility of global value chains, the perils of asymmetric dependencies, and the geopolitical dimensions of critical supplies, energy, data, and green technologies.

Against this backdrop, the EU has pivoted towards a strategy of "open strategic autonomy": a hybrid paradigm that preserves the benefits of openness while hedging against geopolitical risks. This doctrine is neither isolationist nor fully protectionist, but it recognizes that power and interdependence are no longer disjoint spheres. Economic openness is now conditioned on security, resilience, and reciprocity. Consequently, trade policy is no longer a technocratic domain but a central arena of geopolitical agency.

This strategic turn has been materialized in a growing arsenal of instruments: from CBAM and the Foreign Subsidies Regulation to the ACI and the revitalization of FDI screening. Each of these tools reflects a common thread, the need to defend the internal market, shape global standards, and counter coercive or distortive behavior by third countries. Yet they also signify a deeper shift in the EU's self-conception: from a normative power anchored in soft influence on a pragmatic actor engaged in geoeconomic competition.

One key insight is that this transformation is not merely institutional but ontological. The EU is redefining the very role of trade in its external action. No longer confined to liberalization and development cooperation, trade policy now embodies a strategic logic: it serves to protect, deter, and project. This is a significant departure from the post-Cold War orthodoxy that framed globalization as a win-win game governed by law, not power. In the new reality, the boundaries between market and security, law and politics, internal and external, have become porous. However, this strategic shift comes with trade-offs, normative, diplomatic, and developmental.

From a normative perspective, there is a growing tension between the EU's commitment to an open, rules-based multilateral order and the unilateral deployment of instruments that bypass or strain WTO disciplines. The proliferation of defensive and retaliatory tools, while justified by geopolitical necessity, risks undermining the very principles the EU seeks to uphold. Without careful calibration, the EU may inadvertently contribute to the erosion of the multilateral system, accelerating its transformation into a fragmented order of blocs and coalitions.

From a diplomatic angle, the EU's turn to economic statecraft risks alienating partners in the Global South. Policies such as CBAM, while environmentally ambitious, may be perceived as neocolonial if not accompanied by technological support, climate finance, and equitable burden-sharing. The same applies to trade defense measures and investment regulations that disproportionately affect firms from emerging economies. If the EU is seen as imposing standards rather than co-creating them, its credibility as a partner of inclusive global governance will be weakened.

From a developmental standpoint, the EU must reconcile its security-driven trade policies with its commitment to sustainable development goals. This requires ensuring that new instruments do not create insurmountable barriers for countries with limited institutional capacities. It also demands aligning strategic autonomy with global equity, recognizing that decoupling and reshoring can have ripple effects on the economies of the periphery. A truly ethical trade policy cannot be Eurocentric; it must incorporate voices and interests beyond the immediate strategic horizon.

In navigating these dilemmas, institutional coherence and politics will be essential. The European Commission, the European Parliament, and member states must develop a shared understanding of the objectives, limits, and implications of strategic trade instruments. A technocratic approach is no longer sufficient; political leadership must articulate a narrative that reconciles openness with sovereignty, rules with resilience, and ambition with responsibility.

Moreover, the EU must strengthen alliances with like-minded partners, especially in the face of economic coercion and systemic rivalry. The TTC with the U.S., the green alliances with Japan and Canada, and bilateral partnerships with developing countries are key vehicles for promoting regulatory convergence and supply chain security. At the same time, the EU must avoid becoming subsumed into exclusive Western coalitions that reproduce Cold War binaries. Strategic autonomy implies not only independence from coercion but also freedom to engage globally on its own terms.

A future-oriented EU trade strategy must also anticipate technological and ecological transitions. Digital sovereignty, green competitiveness, and data governance will define the new frontiers of trade diplomacy. The Union must invest in capacity-building, internally and externally, to manage these transitions without exacerbating global asymmetries. This means treating trade not as a zero-sum game but as a platform for collective resilience, innovation, and justice.

Finally, the EU must continue to play a constructive role in reforming the multilateral system. Despite its frustrations with the WTO, the EU remains one of the few actors capable of bridging North–South divides, advancing plurilateral solutions, and preserving legal disciplines in trade relations. The future of global trade governance will not be written in Geneva alone, but the WTO remains an indispensable forum for dialogue, dispute resolution, and norm creation. The EU should invest diplomatic capital in revitalizing it, through Appellate Body reform, inclusive rule-making, and support for capacity-constrained members.

The EU is at a crossroads. It can emerge as a leader of a new, more resilient, and just global economic order, or it can drift into a strategic posture that protects short-term interests while undermining long-term legitimacy. The instruments are in place. The challenge now is to deploy them wisely, transparently, and in concert with partners. The age of innocence in trade policy is over. What lies ahead is a geopolitical terrain in which the EU must navigate with both ambition and humility, resilience and solidarity, sovereignty and cooperation.

REFERENCES

Baldwin, D. A. (1985). *Economic statecraft*. Princeton University Press.

Balfour, R., Baroncelli, E., Bomassi, L., Csernatoni, R., Goldthau, A., Grevi, G., & Youngs, R. (2023). *Geopolitics and economic statecraft in the European Union*. Carnegie Endowment for International Peace.

Bradford, A. (2020). *The Brussels effect: How the European Union rules the world*. Oxford University Press., DOI: 10.1093/oso/9780190088583.001.0001

European Central Bank. (2024). *Economic resilience in a geopolitically fragmented world*. ECB Economic Bulletin, Issue 2/2024. https://www.ecb.europa.eu/press/economic-bulletin/focus/2024/html/ecb.ebbox202402_02~c81f58179e.en.html

European Commission. (2021). *Trade policy review – An open, sustainable and assertive trade policy*.

European Commission. (2023). *Joint communication on a European economic security strategy*.

European Commission. (2023). *Foreign Subsidies Regulation: Ensuring fair competition in the internal market*. https://competition-policy.ec.europa.eu

European Commission. (2023). Regulation (EU) 2023/956 establishing a carbon border adjustment mechanism. *Official Journal of the European Union, L, 130*, 52–103.

Farrell, H., & Newman, A. L. (2019). Weaponized interdependence: How global economic networks shape state coercion. *International Security*, *44*(1), 42–79. DOI: 10.1162/isec_a_00351

Gilpin, R. (2001). *Global political economy: Understanding the international economic order*. Princeton University Press. DOI: 10.1515/9781400831272

González, M. (2023, November 3). The EU in a new geopolitical world order. *Real Instituto Elcano*. https://www.realinstitutoelcano.org/en/commentaries/the-eu-in-a-new-geopolitical-world-order/

Kirshner, J. (2009). The political economy of realism. In Cox, M., & Stokes, D. (Eds.), *U.S. foreign policy* (pp. 83–97). Oxford University Press.

Leonard, M., & Pisani-Ferry, J. (2022). *The new geoeconomics: Securing Europe's place in a dangerous world*. European Council on Foreign Relations.

Luttwak, E. N. (1990). From geopolitics to geo-economics: Logic of conflict, grammar of commerce. *National Interest, 20,* 17–23.

McElwee, L. (2022). *The rise and demise of the EU–China Investment Agreement: Takeaways for the future of German debate on China.* Center for Strategic and International Studies.

Meissner, K. L. (2016). A case of failed interregionalism? Analyzing the EU–ASEAN free trade agreement negotiations. *Asia Europe Journal, 14*(3), 319–336. DOI: 10.1007/s10308-016-0450-5

Meunier, S., & Nicolaïdis, K. (2019). The geopoliticization of European trade and investment policy. *Journal of Common Market Studies, 57*(S1), 103–113. DOI: 10.1111/jcms.12932

Schmitz, L., & Seidl, T. (2023). As open as possible, as autonomous as necessary: Understanding the rise of open strategic autonomy in EU trade policy. *Journal of Common Market Studies, 61*(3), 834–852. DOI: 10.1111/jcms.13428

TFEU. (2012). *Treaty on the Functioning of the European Union.* Consolidated version. https://eur-lex.europa.eu/legal-content/EN/TXT/?uri=celex%3A12012E%2FTXT

von der Leyen, U. (2023, March 30). *Speech on EU–China relations.* European Commission. https://ec.europa.eu/commission/presscorner/detail/en/speech_23_2063

Weinhardt, C., & De Ville, F. (2024). The geoeconomic turn in EU trade and investment policy: Implications for developing countries. *Politics and Governance, 12*(2), 8217. Advance online publication. DOI: 10.17645/pag.8217

Woolcock, S. (2021). *The European Union and the geopolitics of trade policy.* London School of Economics. https://www.lse.ac.uk/ideas/publications/reports/the-eu-and-geopolitics-of-trade-policy

World Trade Organization. (2023). *World trade report 2023: Re-globalization for a secure, inclusive, and sustainable future.* WTO.

ENDNOTES

1. *Open strategic autonomy* is a concept promoted by the European Union to reconcile openness to international trade and investment with the capacity to act independently when necessary. It reflects the EU's aim to reduce critical dependencies, especially in areas like digital technologies, raw materials, and

health, while maintaining strong multilateral and economic ties. The term gained prominence in EU discourse after the COVID-19 crisis and rising geopolitical tensions, particularly with China and Russia (European Commission, 2021; Schmitz & Seidl, 2023).

2 *Economic security* refers to the ability of a state or union to protect and promote its economic interests in the face of external shocks, coercion, or disruptions to supply chains. In the EU context, it encompasses measures to ensure access to critical technologies and resources, safeguard strategic sectors, and enhance resilience against economic dependencies that may be exploited geopolitically. The concept has evolved notably since 2022 in response to Russia's invasion of Ukraine and increasing tensions with China (European Commission, 2023; Balfour et al., 2023).

3 *Strategic dualism* refers to the simultaneous pursuit of liberal economic openness and geopolitical autonomy within a states or union's external relations. In the EU's case, it captures the tension between promoting free trade and rules-based multilateralism, while increasingly adopting defensive instruments to protect strategic sectors and values. This dual logic reflects the Union's effort to balance normative power with realpolitik in a fragmented and competitive world (Meunier & Nicolaïdis, 2019; Leonard & Pisani-Ferry, 2022).

4 The *Strategic Compass* is the European Union's security and defense policy document adopted in March 2022. It sets out a common strategic vision for the EU's role in global security and outlines concrete objectives and actions to be achieved by 2030, including the development of a Rapid Deployment Capacity, enhanced resilience in cybersecurity, and stronger partnerships. The document reflects the EU's growing ambition to become a more capable geopolitical actor, particularly in response to Russia's invasion of Ukraine and rising global instability (Council of the European Union, 2023).

5 *Protective openness* is a normative and strategic framework developed by the EU to reconcile economic openness with mechanisms for safeguarding its strategic interests. It aims to maintain open markets and liberal values while introducing tools, such as investment screening, anti-coercion instruments, and carbon border adjustments, that shield the Union from external vulnerabilities and coercive pressures. The concept reflects a shift from naïve globalism to a more balanced, interest-driven trade policy in a fragmented geopolitical landscape (Woolcock, 2021).

6 The idiom *punch above its weight* refers to the ability of an actor, such as the EU, to exert influence or impact disproportionate to its military or hard

power capabilities. In geopolitical terms, it captures how the EU leverages its regulatory power, economic size, and normative agenda to shape global standards and outcomes beyond what its conventional power might suggest. The concept has been widely used in EU foreign policy discourse to justify ambitions for global leadership despite internal divisions or limited military force (Bradford, 2020; Meunier & Nicolaïdis, 2019).

Chapter 12

The "Newest Great Game": West-Russia Rivalry Over Trade Tariffs in Central Asia

Ahmet Turan
https://orcid.org/0000-0002-0227-6161
Inonu University, Turkey

ABSTRACT

The ongoing rivalry among major powers in Central Asia is driven by the region's strategic importance and abundant natural resources. Recent tensions between Russia and the West over trade tariffs have led to the emergence of a new arena for economic and political struggle in the region. The present study examines the dynamics of this competition, which is referred to as 'The New Great Game' and analyses the impact of trade policies on regional alliances and economic dependency relationships. The imposition of protectionist tariffs by Russia, implemented through the Eurasian Economic Union (EAEU), and the adoption of free trade and investment strategies by the West, targeting the region, are among the primary strategies that are deepening this competition. This article examines how Central Asian countries navigate great power competition through balancing strategies and explores the potential impact of global trade wars on regional economies. It argues that this contest will significantly shape the region's geopolitical future beyond trade tariffs.

1. INTRODUCTION

Throughout history, Central Asia has been the setting for the struggle between great powers for influence, becoming the focal point of geopolitical and economic

DOI: 10.4018/979-8-3373-3835-4.ch012

competition. While the 19th-century 'Great Game' between Britain and Russia demonstrated the region's strategic importance, today this struggle is being reshaped by different actors and dynamics. China's Belt and Road Initiative, Russia's military and energy policies, and the West's democratic and free-market approaches have placed Central Asia at the center of the global power struggle. This multidimensional competition has turned into a race for political, military, economic and cultural hegemony.

Following the dissolution of the Soviet Union after the Cold War, a new geopolitical vacuum was created in Central Asia, leaving the region open to the influence of global powers. The current "New Great Game" involves not only the classic power struggle between states, but also economic instruments such as energy corridors, digital infrastructure investments and trade agreements. The economic influence of China, the security-oriented policies of Russia and the investment strategies of the West are forcing Central Asian countries to perform a multifaceted diplomatic balancing act. This process has also enabled the region's states to redefine their role in the international system as independent actors.

Central Asia's rich energy resources and geographical location make the region a critical center of global trade. One of the most prominent features of the 'New Great Game' is the struggle for control over energy transmission lines and logistics corridors. Russia's Eurasian Economic Union, China's Belt and Road Initiative and the US's regional economic cooperation programs constitute different fronts in the battle for regional influence. However, while this competition poses risks, it also offers Central Asian countries strategic room for maneuver. Through multilateral diplomacy, regional states are trying to balance their economic development and security needs while strengthening their position as active players in the struggle between global powers.

This chapter aims to analyze the evolving dynamics of the "New Great Game" in Central Asia by examining the strategies of major global actors and the responses of regional states. It seeks to highlight how geopolitical competition, economic initiatives, and security concerns intersect in the region, while also exploring the opportunities and challenges these dynamics create for Central Asian countries in asserting their sovereignty and shaping their international roles.

1.1. The Historical Context of the 'Great Game' and the Geopolitical Importance of Central Asia

The competition between the various major players in Central Asia is symbolized by "game" theories of varying scales. The term "Great Game" is historically used to describe the British Russian struggle for influence in Central Asia. The origins of this enduring rivalry can be traced back to the Russian Iranian agreement of 1813, which marked the inception of a new phase in the relationship between the two nations. This period of heightened tensions was further compounded by the British Russian compromise of 1907, a significant turning point that ultimately led to the formation of an alliance during the Second World War. The term was first coined by Arthur Conolly, a member of the British East India Company, and continues to be utilized in contemporary discourse to describe analogous strategic conflicts in the region (Hopkirk, 1992).

Although the concept was first introduced by Conolly in the 1840s, it was not until much later that it gained widespread acceptance in academic circles. Subsequently, Demetrius Charles Boulger reintroduced the term in the context of Anglo-Russian rivalry, while Rudyard Kipling popularized it in his 1901 novel Kim, associating it with intelligence operations and counter-espionage activities. Kipling's literary contributions imbued the phrase 'Great Game' with a romantic aura, associating it with the struggles of clandestine agents and reflecting Britain's apprehensions regarding Russian expansionism in Central Asia. The term's inclusion in academic literature was first established by H. W. C. Davis's 1926 work. However, it was during the Cold War, particularly following the Soviet Union's invasion of Afghanistan in 1979, that the concept gained wider use. It began to be frequently mentioned in modern geopolitical analyses (Becker, 2012: 13-16).

A significant aspect of the Russia-West rivalry, symbolized by the 'Great Game', is that one of the fundamental motivations behind this rivalry is once again economic. The commercial ties established by Britain with the Ottoman Empire led Russia to perceive its own expansionist policy in the region as a threat. The fact that Ottoman territories had become a critical market for British trade deepened Russia's concern that its growing power in the region could undermine Britain's economic interests. This situation demonstrates that the competition between the two superpowers was not only political and military but also economic in nature. While Britain sought to protect the Ottoman Empire's strategic position and commercial potential, Russia's efforts to gain influence in the region caused London to become concerned from both a geopolitical and economic perspective. Consequently, the economic conflict of interest was one of the underlying reasons for the 'Great Game' (Fromkin 1980: 937).

1.2. The Definition and Actors of Today's 'New Great Game' (Russia, the West, China)

In contemporary discourse, the term 'new great game' is employed to denote the ongoing competition for dominance among the former colonies of the erstwhile colonial powers in Central Asia, as opposed to the direct confrontation between these powers themselves. This process has complicated the security concerns of the five Central Asian republics (Kazakhstan, Kyrgyzstan, Uzbekistan, Turkmenistan, and Tajikistan) that emerged after the collapse of the Soviet Union. The transition of Asia to a multipolar structure has prompted these countries to seek new regional security arrangements.

Whilst the 'new great game' is chiefly concerned with security, the economic dimension is also of significance. The economic dimension of the new great game is characterized by Central Asia's abundant natural resources and untapped potential as markets. The region boasts a market potential that is estimated to be in billions of dollars. Both Russia and Western actors are seeking to strengthen their economies by securing a share of this market. It is an indirect consequence of the economic competition that is present in the region that economic cooperation and investments could form a basis for supporting democratic development by increasing political stability in the region (Smith, 2016: 155-157).

The concept of the 'New Great Game' shares both similarities and significant differences with the original 'Great Game' of the 19th century. The geographical focus of both periods is Central Asia, particularly the Caspian Basin. The struggle for influence, power, and hegemony is a common theme in both processes. Furthermore, both periods are associated with geopolitical approaches, such as Mackinder's 'Heartland' theory. However, these two processes differ significantly in terms of historical conditions, the structure of the actors, and strategic objectives (Edwards, 2003: 83-102).

The original Great Game was a bilateral struggle between Britain and Russia based on the acquisition of territory and geopolitical supremacy. Local actors adopted a passive stance in the face of the policies enacted by these dominant global powers. The contemporary geopolitical landscape, often termed the 'New Great Game', is characterized by a significantly more intricate and multi-actor environment. In addition to states such as China, the United States, Turkey, and Iran, NATO, the United Nations, multinational corporations, Non-Government Organizations (NGOs), and local groups also play active roles.

Unlike the original Great Game, in which Britain and Russia dominated while local actors remained passive, the contemporary geopolitical landscape of Central Asia is shaped by a much more complex and multi-actor environment. Alongside major states such as China, the United States, Turkey, and Iran, international organizations, multinational corporations, NGOs, and local governments all exert influence through economic investment, security cooperation, cultural initiatives, and development programs. Unlike in the 19th century, regional states are no longer passive observers but active participants, using multi-vector diplomacy to balance competing powers and advance their own strategic interests. In this contemporary era, Central Asian states are no longer considered as mere pawns in a larger geopolitical game, but rather as independent actors with their own unique strategic agendas (Edwards, 2003: 83-102).

1.3. The Newest Great Game: Rivalry Over Trade Tariffs

When the focus is directed towards the 'great game', in which economics plays a pivotal role, it becomes evident that the issue is inextricably linked to trade tariffs. Indeed, the 1838 Anglo-Turkish Trade Agreement brought about a radical transformation in the Ottoman Empire's foreign trade policy, providing Britain with significant economic advantages. A pivotal provision within the treaty was the establishment of a symbolic customs duty of 5%, a measure that served to bolster the competitive strength of British industrial products within the Ottoman market (Eşiyok 2014: 88). The introduction of these low tariffs resulted in the erosion of the Ottoman Empire's conventional protectionist regime, which had previously provided a safeguard for domestic producers. Consequently, this led to the dissemination of inexpensive British textiles and manufactured goods across the empire (Fromkin 1980: 937-938).

From Britain's standpoint, this agreement was not solely a commercial endeavor, but also a geostrategic maneuver. The provision of financial support to the Ottoman Empire's faltering economic resistance against Russia by British capital resulted in the establishment of an indirect impediment to St. Petersburg's endeavors to secure access to warm seas. Indeed, the security of Britain's trade routes to India was directly linked to this economic influence in the Ottoman geography. However, these one-sided advantages ultimately led to the exacerbation of long-term economic issues, including the trade deficit and deindustrialization, within the Ottoman economy. Concurrently, Britain adopted a more assertive policy towards Russia's regional expansionism. Consequently, the tariff regulations of the treaty emerged as a pivotal element in shaping the economic and political dimensions of the 'Great Game' (Fromkin 1980: 938).

Furthermore, there are significant discrepancies in terms of the methods and objectives employed. The original Great Game was characterized by covert political maneuvering and military intervention, while the contemporary New Great Game is characterized by a diverse array of instruments, including diplomatic negotiations, media influence, energy consortiums, and cultural alliances. The objectives of the new era are more diverse, encompassing many different areas such as profit maximization, energy security, cultural influence, and national security. Moreover, given that the utilization of force directly is now subject to restrictions as outlined by international law, there is a preference for the employment of more indirect and sophisticated methods (Edwards, 2003: 83-102).

Nevertheless, the notion of the 'New Great Game' has been met with a degree of disapproval. It has been posited that the concept is frequently employed in a cursory manner, with an overstatement of contemporary events in Central Asia. Critics contend that the competition between states and companies is, in essence, an inherent feature of the prevailing market economy and international relations. The assumption that the activities of multinational corporations automatically serve state policies is also called into question. Consequently, some experts contend that the term 'New Great Game' is inadequate to elucidate contemporary dynamics and even furnishes a fallacious framework (Edwards, 2003: 83-102).

2. TRADING RELATIONS AND POWER STRUGGLES IN CENTRAL ASIA

During the Soviet era, Moscow's dominance over Central Asia was consolidated, exerting a profound and enduring influence on the region's economy. In the contemporary geopolitical landscape of Central Asia, the Russian Federation maintains its status as the preeminent external actor, wielding considerable influence through its engagement in high-level political relations, security cooperation, and investment projects within the region.

2.1 General Outlook

The data presented in the Figure 1, reveal the changes in the foreign trade structure of the Central Asian countries in 2016-2021. The distribution of exports and imports by regional partners, as well as their respective shares in gross domestic product (GDP), are analyzed. In general, countries in the region have a more diversified export structure, while imports are more dependent on specific partners.

Figure 1. Central Asia's Trade Share with Main Partners (2016-2021)

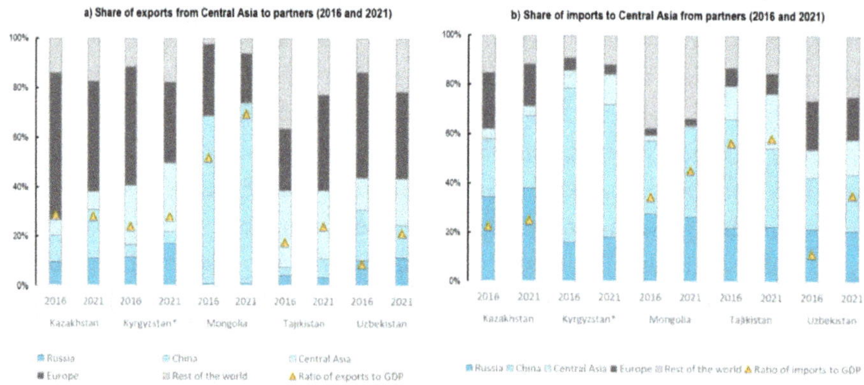

***Source:* OECD Report[1]**

An examination of export data reveals a marked increase in China's regional influence, particularly evident among its neighboring countries, such as Mongolia and Kyrgyzstan. Mongolia's exports are predominantly directed towards China, while Kyrgyzstan also exhibits a strong economic orientation towards China. In contrast, Kazakhstan demonstrates a more balanced structure, with substantial exports to both Europe and China. In Tajikistan and Uzbekistan, exports are more limited and less diversified. The ratio of exports to GDP is also low, indicating limited economic openness.

In terms of the import aspect, Russia occupies a significant role. Countries such as Kyrgyzstan and Tajikistan import a significant proportion of their imports from Russia. The People's Republic of China is also an important source of imports for Mongolia, and the latter is highly dependent on the former in this area. Europe's share of global imports remains comparatively low. The ratio of imports to GDP is indicative of a nation's reliance on external resources, with certain countries exhibiting notably elevated ratios.

In conclusion, it is evident that Central Asian countries have established and maintained diplomatic relations with both regional (Russia and China) and global actors in their foreign trade. However, it is noteworthy that the country has a high degree of reliance on Russia for imports, whilst the growing role of China in exports is prominent. The proportion of trade in GDP exhibits considerable variation across countries, thereby indicating the degree of openness exhibited by economic structures. Actually, they are not penalized simply for trading with Russia and China, but they could face U.S. pressure or secondary sanctions if their trade activities help Moscow circumvent sanctions or involve Chinese entities already under U.S. restrictions.

2.2 Russia's Trade Dynamics with Central Asian Countries

The primary geopolitical ambition of the Russian Federation, as evidenced by its actions, is to ensure that the countries of Central Asia remain within its geopolitical sphere of influence. This ambition is reflected in four key policy areas: the economy and trade, security and military relations, culture and people-to-people interaction, and politics and institution building. Since Russia's re-emergence as a great power in the late 1990s, the objective of preventing the loss of influence in the region has remained constant, but the strategies pursued to achieve this objective have varied over time. In the contemporary era, the city of Moscow employed multilateral institutions to both augment and sustain its global influence. In this framework, the Collective Security Treaty Organization (CSTO) in the security sphere and the Eurasian Economic Union (EEU) in the economic sphere are among the most striking examples (Silvan 2021: 6).

Following the dissolution of the Soviet Union, there was a substantial decline in Russia's trade volume with Central Asian countries. However, in the early 2000s, these relations experienced a resurgence, with Russia developing extensive cooperation in the energy sector with five Central Asian countries. Consequently, Russian companies have increased their activity in regional markets. Consequently, Russia established several multilateral trade blocs encompassing the region. The stated objective of these structures is to promote economic integration that is beneficial for all parties. However, as Jeronim Perović argued in 2005, Moscow's primary objective in this region is to establish a relationship of dependency with the countries of the region, thereby enabling the Kremlin to exert influence over domestic and foreign policy decisions. This assessment retains its validity in the present day (Silvan 2021: 6).

From 2003 to 2007, the Russian Federation witnessed a substantial augmentation in its trade volume with Central Asia, escalating from $7 billion to $21 billion. It is estimated that approximately one-third of this trade originates from the hydrocarbon sector. By 2011, the official mutual trade volume had reached $27.3 billion (Oliphant, 2013: 3). Nevertheless, in 2010 China superseded Russia to become the foremost trading partner among the five Central Asian countries. According to Oliphant (2013: 3), China's trade with the region was recorded at $40 billion in 2011 and approximately $46 billion in 2012.

Russia continues to exert a considerable influence within the energy sector of Central Asia. In Kazakhstan, Lukoil is engaged in seven onshore and three offshore oil and gas projects, and it controls the country's primary oil pipeline. In the context of Uzbekistan, both Gazprom and Lukoil are engaged in the acquisition of natural gas resources and the augmentation of their respective production capacities. It is noteworthy that these two entities collectively account for more than 20% of the nation's total natural gas output. In Turkmenistan, however, the scope of Russian interests is more circumscribed, with Itera being the sole Russian company operating in a direct capacity (Oliphant, 2013: 4–7).

In the countries of Kyrgyzstan and Tajikistan, the primary agent of Russian energy investment is the company Gazprom. Indeed, Gazprom and its subsidiaries have established a de facto monopoly in the petroleum products market of these countries. A significant proportion of large-scale cooperation projects have been centered on electricity generation. The Russian Federation has allocated $2.1 billion US for the Kambarata Hydroelectric Power Plant project in Kyrgyzstan and plans to construct four further hydroelectric power plants by 2016. The most substantial project in Tajikistan is the Sangtuda-1 HPP, which was implemented with an investment of approximately $680 million (Oliphant, 2013: 8–12). A significant proportion of the shares in this project are controlled by the Russian government and Russian energy companies (Oliphant, 2013: 8–12).

However, the countries in the region have developed alternative routes for energy exports. Turkmenistan exports natural gas to Iran and China, while Kazakhstan exports oil to China and to the West via the Baku-Tbilisi-Ceyhan pipeline. The diversification of export networks indicates a diminution of Moscow's traditional influence over oil and natural gas prices in Central Asia. In response to this situation, Russia has established various economic cooperation mechanisms, including the Customs Union, the Eurasian Economic Community (EurAsEC), the Eurasian Development Bank, the Crisis Response Fund, and the Commonwealth of Independent States (CIS) Free Trade Area Agreement, with the aim of strengthening its economic ties with the region (Oliphant, 2013: 6–13).

2.3 The West's Economic and Strategic Interests in Central Asia

It is evident that the West is intent on gaining access to Central Asia's abundant energy reserves and natural resources. The presence of substantial oil reserves in Kazakhstan and Azerbaijan, along with Turkmenistan's natural gas deposits, and Uzbekistan's significant mineral resources, including oil, natural gas, uranium, and titanium, has rendered the region a potentially lucrative prospect for foreign investment. This, in turn, has given rise to the imperative of re-evaluating and recalibrating existing economic relationships within the context of the region. In this context, the 'oil rectangle' – encompassing China's Tarim Basin, Uzbekistan's potential fields, and the Caspian Sea's confirmed resources – holds a significant portion of global energy reserves and has the potential to become one of the primary centers of world energy production in the future (Friedman & Wimbush, 1996).

In recent years, Western countries, spearheaded by the United States, have witnessed a marked strengthening of their relations with Central Asia. In February 2023, the official visit of the then-U.S. Secretary of State, Antony Blinken, to Kazakhstan and Uzbekistan demonstrated Washington's commitment to enhancing the security capabilities of the region's countries. At the inaugural C5+1 Presidential Summit, held in September of that year, President Joe Biden convened with five Central Asian leaders, with the agenda encompassing energy security, economic growth, and regional stability. The summit concluded with the parties expressing their willingness to deepen mutual diplomatic relations (Temnycky, 2023). Furthermore, Central Asia is a direct point of contact for five nuclear powers: The following countries are involved: the Russian Federation, the People's Republic of China, the Republic of Kazakhstan, the Islamic Republic of Pakistan, and the Republic of India. The region's geopolitical significance is twofold, owing to its strategic positioning about energy, security, and strategic stability. For the nations of the West, the prevention of the proliferation of nuclear weapons is as important as the prevention of potential military tensions between the countries of the region. Consequently, from the perspective of the West's long-term interests, it is imperative that Central Asia evolves into robust, peaceful states that are integrated into the global system. This approach assumes even greater significance for regional security in the event of a weakened and unstable Russia (Friedman & Wimbush, 1996).

Germany has also increased its interest in the region. In September 2023, the German Chancellor, Olaf Scholz, convened with the leaders of Central Asian countries in Berlin, with a view to emphasizing the necessity of enhancing regional security. The participants in this meeting subsequently signed a joint statement, thereby demonstrating their commitment to the territorial integrity of the region. In November 2023, French President Emmanuel Macron visited Kazakhstan and Uzbekistan. This visit served to highlight France's economic interests in the region. France stands as one of the most significant foreign investors in Kazakhstan, having played a pivotal role in encouraging economic diversification and market openness among neighboring countries (Temnycky, 2023).

The United Kingdom has also adopted a comprehensive strategy towards Central Asia. The House of Commons Foreign Affairs Committee has published a report which states that it is in London's best interests to strengthen its relations with the region. The report further calls for the convening of a summit in 2024 with leaders from Central Asia, with the primary agenda items including democratization and the promotion of renewable energy sources. Furthermore, the European Union is also taking steps to develop its relations with Central Asia at the institutional level. In October 2023, at a high-level meeting, EU officials and regional representatives engaged in discourse on energy, trade, security, and economic cooperation. The EU's aspiration to enhance trade with the region was a salient theme in these deliberations (Temnycky, 2023).

In the new strategic landscape that emerged after the collapse of the Soviet Union, there was a temporary decline in Russia's influence in the region; Moscow struggled to maintain its dominance both in the border regions and within the CIS. This situation has engendered a degree of uncertainty regarding Russia's approach to Central Asia. On the one hand, Russian nationalists regard the region as falling within Russia's historical sphere of influence; on the other hand, reformist governments may adopt a more distant attitude towards Central Asia. The prevailing environment of uncertainty is compelling the countries of the region to seek alternative geopolitical alliances (Friedman & Wimbush, 1996).

The development of China's policy towards Central Asia is occurring concurrently at both the state and societal levels. As Chinese workers and traders become more visible in the region, the Beijing administration is increasing its influence through economic investments, trade, and infrastructure projects. The People's Republic of China considers regional stability to be critical to its own internal security. Nevertheless, Russia's economic vulnerability in the face of China's growing economic influence may result in Beijing adopting a more interventionist stance. In the event of an internal political crisis in China coinciding with Russia's ongoing instability, there is a risk of Central Asia being plunged into deep and prolonged political chaos (Friedman & Wimbush, 1996).

The energy resources possessed by the countries in the region serve to increase their geopolitical appeal to external actors. In this context, the struggle for dominance over the "oil rectangle" emerges as a strategic priority. However, the transportation of energy resources also poses a significant challenge, particularly given the direct linkage between the Caucasus states (predominantly Georgia) and Central Asia's developmental process. The ongoing political turbulence in Russia, coupled with the inadequate security measures in regions such as Chechnya, serves to underscore the paramount importance of the Georgia-Turkey corridor for the transportation of Caspian oil to Western markets (Friedman & Wimbush, 1996). In parallel, the United States pursued closer ties with the region, initially focusing on energy cooperation and the promotion of alternative export routes that would bypass Russia. Washington's support for projects such as the Baku–Tbilisi–Ceyhan pipeline highlighted its commitment to Caspian energy diversification, while American companies became active in the oil and gas sector. After 9/11, relations expanded through the use of military bases in Uzbekistan and Kyrgyzstan, but cooled in the mid-2000s amid regional resistance to U.S. political influence. More recently, through the C5+1 framework, the U.S. has sought to re-engage by emphasizing connectivity, trade diversification, and sovereignty. Although trade volumes remain modest compared to Russia and China, U.S. involvement continues to underscore the strategic importance of Central Asia in energy and security affairs.

3. THE IMPACT OF U.S. TARIFF POLICIES ON CENTRAL ASIA

In the contemporary geopolitical landscape, trade tariffs imposed by the United States constitute a pivotal element in the ongoing competition between the West and Russia. Despite the limited direct impact of U.S. customs policies on Central Asian economies, there exists the potential for the creation of indirect risks for the region's banking system and corporate sectors.

3.1 U.S.–Central Asia Economic Ties: A Brief Overview

The United States' policy towards Central Asia is based on a multidimensional strategy that encompasses not only security, but also economic cooperation. In its cooperation with Kazakhstan, Kyrgyzstan, Tajikistan, Turkmenistan and Uzbekistan, the United States emphasizes regional stability, economic development, and integration into global markets. Noteworthy aspects of this strategy include economic support and defence industry cooperation with countries in the region. Notably, under the Foreign Military Sales (FMS), Foreign Military Financing (FMF) and Direct Commercial Sales (DCS) programs, various military equipment and services were offered to Central Asian countries and resources were transferred to bolster regional capabilities.

Uzbekistan's purchase of almost $40 million worth of military equipment through FMF and its own resources, as well as the increase in the FMF annual budget to $10 million in 2021, demonstrate the scale of US economic contributions. (U.S. Department of State, 2025). Furthermore, as of 2019, the defence imports of Kazakhstan, Kyrgyzstan and Uzbekistan totaled almost $9 million (U.S. Department of State, 2025).

Although these economic ties are primarily driven by the defence sector, the US has also offered technical and financial assistance in areas such as border security, infrastructure development, and explosive ordnance disposal. For instance, the United States has invested over $22 million in the clearance of conventional munitions and landmines since 2006. (U.S. Department of State, 2025). This commitment has continued in recent years, as demonstrated by a 2024 U.S. State Department review of ongoing demining and explosive ordnance disposal programs in Tajikistan, alongside OSCE-supported initiatives aimed at strengthening regional capacity in this field (Shoinbekova, 2024).

This form of cooperation strengthens the security capacities of Central Asian countries while also contributing indirectly to regional development through economic support. However, in the long term, such foreign aid and defence-oriented economic relations could impact the foreign policy balance and international cooperation preferences of regional countries. Therefore, the effects of these economic interactions are not limited to the financial dimension but can also indirectly influence the region's geopolitical orientation (U.S. Department of State, 2025).

Despite considerable increases in trade volumes following the dissolution of the Soviet Union, the Central Asia (CEA) region accounted for a mere 0.1% of total US trade in goods in 2021 and 2022. (Krulikowski, 2024). Over the last decade, trade between the US and OA has fluctuated, primarily due to the decline in oil prices in 2014-15 and the economic recession triggered by the global pandemic of Coronavirus (SARS-CoV-2) in 2020. Nevertheless, the economic recovery following 2020 was noteworthy, with trade volume attaining an unprecedented high in 2022. Kazakhstan, which has the largest share in this increase, is the main driver of US-OA trade in terms of both exports and imports. Recent data indicates that over the preceding five-year period, US exports to Kazakhstan have exhibited an average annual growth rate of 14%, while concurrently, imports from Kazakhstan have demonstrated a 27% annual increase (Krulikowski, 2024).

As of 2022, the primary US exports to Kazakhstan encompassed aircraft, spacecraft and their constituent components, nuclear reactors, boilers, machinery and associated parts, and electrical appliances and components. In the same year, many US imports from Central Asia were oil and petroleum products, the majority of which were sourced from Kazakhstan. It is evident that the capacity for trade with Central Asia continues to be constrained by several factors. These include the region's geographical isolation, its limited market size, and various country-specific risk factors (Krulikowski, 2024).

3.2 Trump's Trade War

On 9 April 2025, the United States government announced the deferral of the implementation of the previously scheduled increase in customs duties on imports from various countries, including Kazakhstan. Initially, a 27% customs duty was planned to be imposed on products exported from Kazakhstan to the United States; this rate is significantly higher than the 10% base tariff rate that came into effect on 5 April for Central Asian and Caucasus countries (The Astana Times, 2025). The United States' trade policies have given rise to concerns regarding the potential for a global trade war, which could exert pressure on expectations of global economic growth and adversely affect oil demand. In addition to these developments, OPEC+ countries have decided to increase oil supply, leading to a significant decline in oil prices due to increased supply in the market.

As demonstrated in Figure 1, the price of Brent and WTI crude oil has indeed decreased to $65 and $62, respectively, as of April 2025 (Uz Daily, 2025).

The implementation of the U.S. tariff-based trade policy persisted after April. Following the presidential decree issued by President Donald Trump on 7 July, the review date for reciprocal tariffs was postponed to 1 August, and new customs duties covering 14 countries were announced. President Trump initiated communication with the leaders of these countries via the medium of letters and social media.

On the same day, a 50 percent tariff on copper imports was also introduced. Shortly afterward, on August 6, tariffs on India were doubled from 25 percent to 50 percent, alongside a 100 percent tariff imposed on semiconductor imports, justified by India's continued purchase of Russian oil. The policy expanded further on August 7, when a sweeping executive order established new country-specific tariffs ranging from 10 to 41 percent on over 60 countries, with exemptions for goods already in transit until October 5 (Rugaber, 2025).

The correspondence addressed to the President of Kazakhstan, Kassym-Jomart Tokayev, comprised the following statements: As Putz (2025) asserts, it is a great honor to send this letter, which demonstrates the strength and resolve of trade relations between the United States and Kazakhstan. Despite the significant trade deficit with this country, the U.S. is willing to continue working with Kazakhstan.

According to trade statistics, as of 2024, the total volume of trade in goods between Kazakhstan and the U.S. has reached $3.4 billion. Within this scope, U.S. exports to Kazakhstan amounted to $1.1 billion, while imports from Kazakhstan amounted to $2.3 billion, resulting in a foreign trade deficit of $1.3 billion (Putz, 2025).

As stated in the official communiqué released by the Kazakh Ministry of Trade and Integration on 3 April 2025, the aggregate trade volume stands at $4.2 billion. Of this total, $2.2 billion represents imports from the U.S., with approximately $2 billion being exports from Kazakhstan to the U.S. In a subsequent statement issued on July 8, the ministry asserted that the implemented measures would not impact approximately 95% of Kazakhstan's exports to the U.S (Putz, 2025).

It was declared that a significant proportion of Kazakhstan's exports would be exempt from the new tariffs, and that exports would largely continue under the prevailing conditions (Putz, 2025). However, in a statement made by Trump in mid-July, he signaled a new wave of sanctions against Russia, which could affect Kazakhstan, Kyrgyzstan, and other former Soviet countries, including the imposition of a 100% customs duty on trading partners (Haydar, 2025).

Another regional country that could be affected by the trade war is Kyrgyzstan. In the aftermath of the imposition of tariffs by the United States, Akylbek Caparov, former Prime Minister of Kyrgyzstan, characterized the move as an "economic earthquake". However, he also identified a potential opportunity for Kyrgyzstan, given that the country's tariffs are relatively low, standing at 10%, in contrast to the 27% tariff imposed by Kazakhstan.

The US-China trade war accelerates supply chain diversification, creating an opportunity for Kyrgyzstan to leverage its low 10% import tariffs and membership in the Eurasian Economic Union (EAEU). By positioning itself as a low-cost assembly and manufacturing base, it can attract businesses seeking to import components cheaply and then export finished goods tariff-free into the vast EAEU market, capitalizing on shifts away from costlier production in China and higher-tariff neighbors like Kazakhstan (Xinhua, 2025).

As global supply chains undergo changes, particularly with China experiencing a decline in market share due to rising costs, he posits that the country could potentially gain a competitive advantage. The US-China trade war accelerates supply chain diversification, creating an opportunity for Kyrgyzstan to leverage its low

10% import tariffs and membership in the Eurasian Economic Union (EAEU). By positioning itself as a low-cost assembly and manufacturing base, it can attract businesses seeking to import components cheaply and then export finished goods tariff-free into the vast EAEU market, capitalizing on shifts away from costlier production in China and higher-tariff neighbors like Kazakhstan. Japarov is encouraging investment in logistics and product localization to boost re-exports. Trade leader Sergey Ponomarev adds that Kyrgyzstan's influence is limited, but businesses could benefit by repackaging or partially assembling Chinese goods to take advantage of lower tariffs. Despite the absence of an official policy, both parties recognize the commercial viability of this approach in the context of evolving global trade dynamics (Chipegin, 2025).

3.3 The Trade War-Ukraine War Connection

In the event of Russia failing to bring an end to the war in Ukraine, the US President, Donald Trump, has indicated that he will be prepared to impose 100% "secondary tariffs" on countries that continue their economic relations with Moscow. This approach, while not explicitly targeting Russia, seeks to exacerbate the Kremlin's economic isolation by exerting pressure on countries engaged in trade with Russia through the energy, agriculture, and defence sectors. In his remarks at the White House, Trump stated that the implementation of the sanctions would be contingent upon the failure of the parties to reach an agreement within 50 days (Inocencio, 2025).

Figure 2. Countries at Risk of Being Affected by US Secondary Tariffs Due to Their Economic Relations with Moscow

Source: CBS NEWS

This threat has placed a few countries in a position of potential vulnerability. These include Kazakhstan, Kyrgyzstan, Uzbekistan, China, India, Turkey, the United Arab Emirates (UAE), Brazil, Vietnam, and Thailand. These countries have maintained relations with Russia in the fields of energy, defence, fertilizers, and finance. The People's Republic of China and the Republic of India have played a decisive role in Moscow's energy exports by importing approximately 90% of Russia's seaborne crude oil. Turkey has become a significant importer of Russian oil and natural gas. Brazil has largely met its critical fertilizer needs for agricultural production from Russia, while the UAE has served as an important financial center for Russian capital and energy trade. These countries have elected to safeguard their national interests by sustaining economic relations with Russia in the face of Western sanctions following 2022 (Inocencio, 2025).

It is evident that Trump's statements were regarded as "unacceptable" by Russian officials, and the prospect of secondary sanctions was firmly rebuffed. However, these statements did not initially cause significant concern in the markets. It is evident that Trump's prior retreat on analogous tariffs, in conjunction with the 50-day period allocated for negotiations, has precipitated a notable appreciation in the Russian ruble's value against the dollar. Concurrently, there has been a 2.7% surge in the Moscow stock market (Inocencio, 2025).

The main sanctions imposed on Moscow include an import ban on Russian oil, price caps on Russian fuel and the freezing of assets belonging to the Bank of Russia held in European financial institutions. However, the implementation of secondary sanctions would bring about a significant shift in the current sanction's architecture.

So far, the G7 countries have largely avoided taking concrete steps to stop Russia from selling its fossil fuels to major buyers such as China and India (Kozul-Wright, 2025). The Russia Sanctions Act of 2025, which enjoys bipartisan support in the US Congress, aims to target countries that purchase Russian energy products. The bill authorizes former President Donald Trump to impose a 500% tariff on any country that supports Russia (Kozul-Wright, 2025). Currently, US senators are reportedly waiting for Trump's backing to pass the bill. Furthermore, Trump could impose secondary sanctions under the International Emergency Economic Powers Act in the event of a national emergency being declared (Kozul-Wright, 2025).

If such secondary sanctions come into force, they are likely to have a serious impact on the global energy market. Sudden reductions in natural gas supplies could cause prices to rise sharply. According to Kieran Tompkins, a senior climate and commodity economist at Capital Economics, the potential impact on natural gas prices is likely to be greater than the impact on oil prices. He notes that the oil market has a partially compensatory capacity due to OPEC's untapped reserves. However, a halving of Russia's crude oil and petroleum product exports could result in a loss of around $75 billion in export revenues (Kozul-Wright, 2025). This could have serious consequences for the Russian economy and lead to a financial crisis. Possible consequences include increased borrowing levels, rising bond yields, and large-scale fiscal tightening pressures. Trump's proposed 50-day deadline aims to put political pressure on Moscow while delaying the imposition of sanctions and creating room for diplomatic maneuver (Kozul-Wright, 2025).

4. WESTERN-RUSSIAN TARIFF RIVALRY: CRISIS OR OPPORTUNITY FOR THE REGION?

Although tariffs are not expected to have a direct significant impact on Kazakhstan's exports, if the Trump administration's trade policies lead to a global economic crisis, this could negatively affect commodity prices and create various challenges for Astana and Central Asia in general. However, the United States' prevailing trade strategy may potentially encourage affected countries, such as Kazakhstan and Uzbekistan, which are significant exporters, to explore alternative commodity markets. Notwithstanding the imposition of tariffs, the Trump administration has demonstrated a commitment to the continuation of the C5+1 platform initiated during the Biden administration, with a view to enhancing access to energy, mining, and oil and gas supply chains in Central Asia. This inconsistent trade approach could play a role in encouraging regional infrastructure cooperation, as demonstrated by the

Khujand Tripartite Border Agreement signed in March 2025 between Kyrgyzstan, Tajikistan, and Uzbekistan, which aims to enhance economic and energy resilience (Gruzer, 2025).

Conversely, the tariffs imposed by the U.S. may also have ramifications for the multi-vector foreign policy strategies of Central Asian countries. The imposition of increased customs duties may result in a contraction of the potential for the development of bilateral trade relations with the U.S., thereby risking the strengthening of China's investment and economic influence in Central Asia, which would be contrary to Washington's goal of strengthening its regional influence. However, rising tariffs on a global scale may prompt actors such as the European Union to seek more diverse partnerships and supply chain connections in Central Asia, thereby supporting the region's multi-faceted trade policy.

Indeed, initiatives such as the EU's "Global Gateway" infrastructure investment strategy and the Samarkand Summit held on April 4 demonstrate Europe's interest in establishing strategic investments and supply chains in Central Asia for renewable energy and advanced technology sectors. In this context, while the policies of the Trump administration may impede the diversification of trade with the U.S., they could also propel Central Asia towards a more profound collaboration with other international partners (Gruzer, 2025).

4.1 Strategic Recommendations for Navigating Geopolitical Rivalry

The competing tariff and investment policies of major global powers present Central Asia with a critical juncture. While U.S. tariffs may constrict direct trade opportunities, they simultaneously fuel a broader global shift towards supply chain diversification. This creates a unique opening for the region to leverage its strategic position.

By consciously rebranding as an integrated economic gateway rather than a passive corridor, Central Asia can attract "near-shoring" investment from companies seeking access to the vast EAEU market and a stable alternative to traditional manufacturing hubs. The key to capitalizing on this lies in aggressively improving regional connectivity, harmonizing customs standards, and upgrading infrastructure to become a competitive logistics and light manufacturing base.

To successfully navigate this rivalry, the region must adopt a cohesive and proactive strategy. This involves deepening institutional cooperation, as exemplified by the Khujand Border Agreement, to eliminate internal trade barriers and present a unified market to the world. Furthermore, Astana and its neighbors should strategically engage with all competing initiatives—from the U.S. C5+1 to the EU's Global Gateway—by steering investments towards projects that build internal resilience, such as cross-border energy grids and value-added production, rather than mere extraction.

Ultimately, the goal must be to leverage this great power interest to build economic sovereignty, using strategic investment screening and local content requirements to ensure that foreign capital translates into sustainable development, technological transfer, and a more resilient, integrated regional economy.

5. CONCLUSION

This research reevaluates the historical geopolitical importance of Central Asia within the framework of the "New Great Game" and provides an in-depth analysis of how the region has been shaped by global trade policies and economic competition. While there are fundamental similarities between the "Great Game" between Britain and Russia in the 19th century, the "New Great Game" in the post-Cold War era, and the current struggle, the current competition is much more complex, multi-actor, and multi-dimensional in nature. The geopolitical landscape is no longer confined to Russia and the Western powers; China's ascendant influence, as evidenced by its Belt and Road Initiative (BRI), Turkey's strategic maneuvers stemming from its historical and cultural affiliations, Iran's pursuit of regional pre-eminence, and the actions of actors such as India and Pakistan have become integral components of this evolving dynamic. Furthermore, the dynamics of competition in the region are influenced by international organizations such as the Shanghai Cooperation Organisation (SCO), the Eurasian Economic Union (EAEU), and international financial institutions.

The Central Asian states (Kazakhstan, Uzbekistan, Turkmenistan, Kyrgyzstan, and Tajikistan) have evolved from passive entities on the geopolitical landscape to independent actors with multifaceted foreign policy strategies. The countries have been able to pursue a policy of balance with global powers due to their energy resources, logistics corridors and economic potential. At times, they have sought compromise between competing projects. For instance, while engaging in China's Belt and Road Initiative (BRI) projects, they can also maintain a distance from Russia's Eurasian integration, continue their relations with the West, and develop strategic partnerships with Turkey and Middle Eastern countries.

Trade tariffs have become a critical tool that shapes not only the economy but also the political and security dimensions of this struggle. The high customs duties and indirect sanctions risks imposed by the U.S. on China are having a profound effect on the foreign trade balances of Central Asian countries. It is evident that global market fluctuations and supply chain disruptions pose a considerable risk, particularly for economies that are reliant on energy exports. Conversely, the sanctions imposed by the West on Russia have transformed Central Asian countries into both an alternative trade corridor and a “sanctions escape” center. While this situation presents short-term challenges for regional countries, it also creates opportunities for new trade routes (e.g., the Middle Corridor and the International North-South Transport Corridor) and regional integration projects (e.g., Uzbekistan-Kazakhstan trade cooperation) in the long term.

A fundamental aspect of the contemporary geopolitical landscape is the competition for control of energy resources and the establishment of logistics networks, which are instrumental in facilitating the transportation of goods and personnel. In the context of competition between China and Russia for access to Central Asia's hydrocarbon resources, Western companies are also seeking alternative energy routes. Concurrently, the green energy transition and the demand for rare earth elements are further augmenting the region's geostrategic significance. Infrastructure investments (railways, ports, pipelines) have become instruments that are not only economic but also military and political.

This emergent competitive dynamic in Central Asia is shaped not only by economic interests but also by energy security, digital infrastructure competition, and the pursuit of political stability. The imposition of trade tariffs and sanctions by one state on another state within the region serves a dual function. Firstly, it exerts pressure on the targeted state. Secondly, it provides the sanctioning state with the opportunity to engage in diplomatic maneuvering. For instance, Kazakhstan's endeavors to reduce its reliance on both Russia and China by strengthening its ties with Europe and Turkey, and Uzbekistan's aspiration to assume a leadership role in regional integration, are manifestations of this strategic flexibility.

In this context, the outcome of the 'Newest Great Game' will depend largely on the ability of Central Asian states to engage in multilateral diplomacy, diversify their economic structures and build resilience to emerging political and economic uncertainties at a global level. Progress in foreign policy is important, but so is progress in domestic political stability and governance capacities. In an environment of intensifying competition among global powers, Central Asian countries have the potential to pursue a balanced policy that protects their national interests while promoting regional integration. In this process, the institutionalization of regional cooperation is particularly important. Acting jointly in areas such as transnational security threats, energy infrastructure integration, transportation network diversification and environmental crisis management will provide Central Asian states with protection against external influences and increase the region's global geopolitical and geoeconomics value.

REFERENCES

Becker, S. (2012). The 'Great Game': The History of an Evocative Phrase. *Asian Affairs*, *43*(1), 61–80. DOI: 10.1080/03068374.2012.646404

Chipegin, A. (April 9, 2025). Trump Tariffs: A Barrier for Kyrgyzstan, or an Opportunity? *The Diplomat*. Accessed July 07, 2025, https://timesca.com/trump-tariffs-a-barrier-for-kyrgyzstan-or-an-opportunity/

Edwards, M. (2003). The New Great Game and the new great gamers: Disciples of Kipling and Mackinder. *Central Asian Survey*, *22*(1), 83–102. DOI: 10.1080/0263493032000108644

Eşiyok, B. A. (2014). Osmanlı İmparatorluğu'nun Dünya Ekonomisine Eklemlenmesinde Bir Dönüm Noktası:1838 Serbest Ticaret Anlaşması. *Mülkiye Dergisi*, *34*(266), 67–108.

Friedman, R. E., & Wimbush, S. E. (1996). Central Asia and The West. PERCEPTIONS: Journal of International Affairs, 1(4).

Fromkin, D. (1980). The Great Game in Asia. *Foreign Affairs*, *58*(4), 936–951. DOI: 10.2307/20040512

Gruzer, M. (April 22, 2025). Impact of US Tariffs on Central Asia. Bloomsbury Intelligence and Security Institute. Accessed July 07, 2025, https://bisi.org.uk/reports/impact-of-us-tariffs-on-central-asia

Haydar, A. (July 16, 2025). Trump's 100% Tariffs May Target Kazakhstan and Kyrgyzstan. *The Times of Central Asia*. Accessed July 18, 2025, https://timesca.com/trumps-100-tariffs-may-target-kazakhstan-and-regional-economies/

Hopkirk, P. (1992). *The Great Game: The Struggle for Empire in Central Asia*. In Kodansha International EBooks. http://ci.nii.ac.jp/ncid/BA20970331

Inocencio, R. (July 15, 2025). Trump threatens countries that do business with Russia with 100% tariffs. Here's who it could impact. CBC NEWS. Accessed July 20, 2025, https://www.cbsnews.com/news/trump-russia-ukraine-war-tariff-threat-countries-that-do-business-with-russia/

Kozul-Wright, A. (July 15, 2025). Russia may face Trump tariffs in 50 days, what does US import from Russia? *Al Jazeera*. Accessed July 24, 2025, https://www.aljazeera.com/news/2025/7/15/trump-threatens-tariffs-in-50-days-what-harm-will-it-do-to-russia

Krulikowski, S. (2024). *Central Asia: A Brief Overview of International Trade.* U.S. International Trade Commission.

OECD. (2023). *Trade Facilitation in Central Asia.* OECD Publishing., DOI: 10.1787/80ed999c-

Oliphant, C. (2013). Russia's role and interests in Central Asia. *Safeworld,* 1-13.

Putz, C. (2025). New Trump Tariffs Target Kazakhstan With 25% Rate. *The Diplomat.* Accessed July 04, 2025, https://thediplomat.com/2025/07/new-trump-tariffs-target-kazakhstan-with-25-rate/

Rugaber, C. (August 1, 2025). *Dozens of countries with no deals face new tariffs as trade deadline looms. AP News.* Retrieved August 19, 2025, from https://apnews.com/article/tariffs-trump-trade-deals-deadline-3977a3890ab7be85c0e07d5808dd2b55

Shoinbekova, M. (May 26, 2024). *U.S. Delegation Discusses Next Steps for the OSCE-led Integrated Co-operation on Explosive Hazards Program in Tajikistan.* OSCE. Retrieved August 19, 2025, from https://www.osce.org/programme-office-in-dushanbe/572467

Silvan, K. (2021). *Russian Policy Towards Central Asia 30 Years After the Collapse of The Soviet Union: Sphere of Influence Shrinking?* Finnish Institute of International Affairs.

Temnycky, M. (December 13, 2023). The West is Eying Closer Relations with Central Asia. *The Diplomat.* Accessed July 02, 2025, https://thediplomat.com/2023/12/the-west-is-eying-closer-relations-with-central-asia/

The Astana Times. (April 3, 2025). *US imposes 27% reciprocal duty on Kazakh products.* Retrieved August 19, 2025, from https://astanatimes.com/2025/04/us-imposes-27-reciprocal-duty-on-kazakh-products/

U.S. Department of State. (2025). *U.S. Security Cooperation with Central Asia.* Accessed July 22, 2025, https://www.state.gov/u-s-security-cooperation-with-central-asia

Xinhua. (August 15, 2025). *Kyrgyzstan lauds Eurasian Economic Union's economic vitality.* Retrieved August 20, 2025, from https://english.news.cn/20250815/2cfbdb617a0148ceae2293f62d8157fd/c.html

ENDNOTE

1 OECD (2023), *Trade Facilitation in Central Asia.*

Chapter 13
Global Trends in Logistics:
The Impact of the U.S. Trade War on Supply Chains

Ahlem Hamri
https://orcid.org/0000-0002-2052-021X
Higher School of Business, Manouba University, Tunis, Tunisia & Laboratory of Accounting, Financial and Economic Modeling (MOCFINE), ISCAE, University of Manouba, Tunisia

Rafaa Mraihi
Higher School of Business, Manouba University, Tunis, Tunisia & Laboratory of Accounting, Financial and Economic Modeling (MOCFINE), ISCAE, University of Manouba, Tunisia

ABSTRACT

Global conflicts are major factors contributing to supply chain disruptions. On the one hand, countries work to improve transport and logistics infrastructure to promote trade and global connectivity; on the other hand, they implement export bans, tariffs, embargoes, trade restrictions, and sanctions, which limit access to essential resources and materials. Trump's tariff measures caused a significant collapse of the multilateral trading framework, revealing the vulnerability of global economic governance and disproportionately impacting developing nations through 'reciprocal' tariffs. The protectionist measures announced by Trump included an increase in customs duties on goods imported from different countries. Therefore, this chapter proposes to study the relationship between logistics and trade. Indeed,

DOI: 10.4018/979-8-3373-3835-4.ch013

the objective is to better understand the effect of the logistics sector on trade, and then to study the repercussions of U.S. trade wars, especially the impact of Trump's tariffs on global logistics and supply chains.

1. INTRODUCTION

The literature has widely demonstrated that the efficiency of supply chain, particularly logistics systems, is an important determinant of bilateral trade but the magnitude of the effect can vary depending on the economic and geographical characteristics of the countries. In this context, Gani (2017) mentions that trade volume increases more significantly than the ratio of improvements in logistics infrastructure and services. The development of supply chains and logistics, particularly infrastructure improvements (ports, logistics platform), enables more reliable product distribution and promotes international trade flows, given that international trade depends largely on logistics and transportation services providers. Carruthers et al. (2003) highlighted the role of transportation and logistics infrastructure investments in promoting trade in Hong Kong and Singapore. Chinese exports have increased significantly thanks to changes in its logistics network (Lee & Rodrigue, 2006; Wang et al. 2021).

However, global Conflicts and political instability are major factors contributing to supply chain disruptions. In the one hand countries works to improve transport and logistics infrastructures to promote trade and world connections, in the other hand, they implement export bans, tariffs, or embargoes, trade restrictions and sanctions come into effect, limiting access to essential resources and materials. Additionally, conflicts often obstruct critical trade routes, leading to increased transportation expenses and delays in deliveries. The convergence of trade disputes, economic sanctions, and armed conflicts risks dividing global supply chains, compelling companies to rethink their dependence on particular suppliers and adjust their operational approaches.

Supply chain analytics plays a vital role in addressing these challenges by enabling companies to assess risks, identify vulnerabilities, and refine their supply chain approaches. Then, the rise in trade tensions has been further exacerbated by a surge in military conflicts worldwide (Owsiak et al., 2024). These conflicts severely disrupt international supply chains and generate substantial unpredictability for maritime and air freight and for port and airports flows, resulting in amplified and enduring disruptions to global trade patterns (Ivanov, 2025).

The supply chains, inventories, industries were already disrupted by the Russia–Ukraine war and COVID19 pandemic. Therefore, adopting resilience strategies is one of the solutions to face the supply chain disruptions. It would help mitigate cost increases in supply chains if a major disruption, like another COVID-19-level event, were to happen again (Rahbari et al., 2024).

Trump's tariff measures signify a significant collapse of the multilateral trading framework, revealing the vulnerability of global economic governance and disproportionately impacting developing nations through 'reciprocal' tariffs. American trade policy directly contradicts two key tenets of the WTO (Butler, 2025). It disregards the 'most-favored-nation' principle, which mandates that trade benefits granted to one member must be shared with all, and the 'national treatment' principle, which ensures equal treatment for both local and foreign goods. These foundational WTO principles have long been a point of debate among heterodox economists, labor unions, anti-globalization advocates, and social movements.

Critics contend that trade liberalization has negatively impacted developing countries by accelerating de-industrialization and causing job losses, as observed in South Africa, while also stifling the growth of emerging industries. Chang (2002) notably argued that WTO trade rules eliminated the mechanisms that historically supported industrialization in the Global North. Excessive customs duties, threats of sanctions, negotiation of bilateral agreements, revaluation of certain countries' currencies with surpluses. At the same time, both the Biden and Trump administrations have implemented industrial strategies designed to protect critical sectors, particularly through significant investments in semiconductor and electric vehicle (EV) battery production. However, the United States is not acting alone. The European Union (E.U.) and Canada have also enacted 100% tariffs on Chinese EVs, while the UK has announced intentions to remove Huawei from its 5G by 2027 (Liu, 2021).

In retaliation, China has imposed tariffs on agricultural and food products from the U.S. and Canada and has revoked soybean import licenses for three American companies. Trump's decisions for his second term are redefining the economic balance of power as he attacks traditional allies with an aggressive protectionist policy. Faced with unilateral and unpredictable tariff increases, Tunisian businesses find themselves without a safety net. This crisis reveals how essential proactive trade diplomacy is to protect Tunisian exporters. In addition, the difficult economic situation, high debt and a need for external financing, makes the country vulnerable to external trade pressures.

In 2025, the Tunisian government is trying to diversify its partners and strengthen its exports to other markets (sub-Saharan Africa, Middle East) in order to reduce the impact of dependence on European and American markets, given the current uncertainties.

It is in this context that this work proposes to study the relationship between logistics and trade. Indeed, the objective of our work is twofold: on the one hand, it aims to better understand the effect of the logistics sector on trade. On the other hand, we focus on the repercussions of US Trade Wars especially on the impact of Trump's tariffs on global logistics and supply chains. We give a preview to EU, African countries and Tunisia.

Thus, the first section of this chapter is a literature review. It underlines the relationship between the logistics Performance index, in particular its components, and Trade. Then, the second section aims to underline the impact of U.S tariffs on global supply chains.

2. RELATIONSHIP LOGISTICS-TRADE

Logistics acts as an intermediary between suppliers and customers, and its functioning and geographical location are closely linked to production and consumption flows. The production system has undergone significant changes since the 1970s. In the period following World War II, industrialized countries enjoyed thirty years of considerable prosperity. This period was characterized by the use of the Fordist model and a stock-based economy, followed by the crisis of the 1970s and the transition to a flow-based economy (standardized products, diversified ranges) (Joignaux & Verny, 2004). These events will have a strong influence on Europe's economic map.

The main driving forces behind these contemporary "revolutions" in the production of goods and services are well known, although there is still some disagreement about their theoretical and empirical significance. One driving force is globalization, illustrated by increased competition from Japanese manufactured goods, corporate structures that have shifted from "multinational" to "global," and global deregulation, particularly in finance (Castells & Hall, 1994).

Secondly, the old mass production models have many sectors and have been unable to compete with the new "flexible" production models. The rise of those models has contributed to the emergence of new strategies, new types of learning processes, and a reorganization of economic activity and trade.

In many cases, these strategies were a necessary adaptation to new market conditions following the first oil crisis in 1973. This did not prevent the structural problems that gradually accumulated during the 1960s. Industries such as steel, chemicals, and shipbuilding machinery. The competitive situation was intense, and companies responded by customizing their products. Advantages were achieved through attempts to increase quality and expertise, as well as through the implementation of flexibility instead of economies of scale and low costs. Due to product customization, more frequent changes to products and processes became necessary (Todtling, 1994).

These new guidelines have long-term effects that impact production workshops and even the strategic direction of the company and the economic and the commercial process in general. Consequently, this generates international flows and has a direct effect, particularly on the internalization of productive activities guided by the digital revolution and the emergence of ICT.

Thirdly, the process has been driven by a technological revolution: the emergence of new information and communication technologies that affect all areas of business.

Technology has provided new opportunities for flexibility in the production process and created new options for customizing products and production. Economies of scope have become as important as economies of scale. In addition, technology has contributed to the rise of new industries such as computer hardware and software, microelectronics, and telecommunications.

All these sectors are dominated by American and Japanese industries rather than European companies. This has an impact on the concentration of the industry. This concentration encourages the creation of large groups, a reduction in the number of production sites, and an increase in unit production. This is referred to as functional specialization, which leads companies to relocate their production sites.

These major changes have a considerable impact on logistics networks and, in particular on trade flows. The decentralization of production centers and their specialization are two causes of the geographical isolation of production and consumption centers. Production mechanisms are broken down into specialties and organized spatially. This is referred to as offshoring because the products are standard and will be differentiated at the end of the production cycle. The outsourcing of services therefore requires efficient logistics.

2.1 Just-In-Time Management and the Role of Just-In-Time

The last quarter of the 20th century saw the emergence of three major concepts for improving manufacturing operations that radically changed the way manufacturing companies manage their operations: production systems (JIT), the International Organization for Standardization, ISO 9000 certifications, and total quality management (TQM).

In essence, it is a production program aimed at continuous improvement and maintaining product and process quality by capitalizing on the involvement of management, staff, suppliers, and customers in order to meet or exceed customer expectations. TQM, in its simplest form, encompasses all of an organization's actions and values aimed at improving and maintaining quality standards. Thus, maintaining and improving quality and adopting integrated global manufacturing strategies lead to improved manufacturing performance (Fullerton & McWatters, 2002).

With the implementation of JIT, companies can reap benefits such as cost reduction, inventory evaluation, etc. With these tools for continuous improvement of SCM performance, firms become more responsive to demand. However, logistics is aligning itself with these changes and adapting information flows to stocks and transport capacities by reducing batch sizes and helping to reduce inventory holding costs (Dornier & Fender, 2007). As a result, distribution flows are changing, leading to a more concentrated and fragmented distribution network, which in turn requires logistics providers to consolidate flows.

Indeed, the work of logistics providers is becoming increasingly meticulous. As a result, the logistics function is not only growing but also offering customized services through just-in-time flows, optimal supply management, and cost control. At the same time, a transformation is taking place in the logistics infrastructure accompanying the change in flows and distribution networks, with a concentration of logistics providers and a change in the architecture of sites and their geographical locations and big consequences on global trade flows.

Logistics providers represent the interface between logistics and trade. Authorities and authors emphasize the importance of infrastructure investments in the logistics sector, given their contribution to economic growth (Jumah et al., 2025) through their impact on production, consumption, and international trade. The work on the relationship between logistics clusters and trade is mainly focused on two main areas, namely LPI, infrastructure (mainly ports) and transport costs. Indeed, port logistics clusters has an important effect in port city in China, and a study underline the role of infrastructure on port city development (Wang & Ma, 2019).

The Word Bank international indicators, which refer to both sectors, is the logistics performance index (LPI). We wonder about the relationship between this indicator and global trade.

2.2 The Logistics Performance Index and Trade in Literature

Logistics performance is assessed using a 5-point scale and the LPI is aggregated as a weighted average of six areas of logistics performance, through surveys developed by the WB in each country, we define these areas as follows:

a) Quality of Commercial and Transport Infrastructure

Essential for ensuring basic connectivity and access to gateways, infrastructure largely explains countries' trade performance. Poor transport and communications infrastructure isolates countries and hinders their participation in global logistics networks. Poor transport and communications infrastructure isolates countries and hinders their participation in global production-transmission-distribution networks. Remoteness is an important determinant of real trade costs and a country's ability to fully participate in the global economy.

Limao & Venables (2001) show that landlocked countries have transport costs 58% more important than those of coastal countries. By improving their own infrastructure, they reduce this cost penalty to 46%; improving transit reduces the penalty to 51%, and if both improvements are made, the penalty decreases to 39%. Mainly, enhancing infrastructure increases trade by 50%. Dee & Findlay (2006), in their survey of trade literature, indicated that infrastructure quality is associated with significant increases in trade. Studies have highlighted that much of Africa's weak trade performance can be explained by weak infrastructure, particularly maritime and road transport infrastructure.

b) Ease of Obtaining Competitive Prices on Shipping

The availability of competitive shipping is a key factor in the sourcing decision and, consequently, in the level of national competitiveness. However, Hausman et al. (2013) estimates that a 1% reduction in shipping costs increases trade by 1.39%. Similarly, a 1% reduction in total trade-related processing costs can be associated with a 0.49% increase in bilateral trade. Providing competitively priced shipments vary depending on the cost of logistics services.

The cost associated with the physical transfer of goods is made up of several elements corresponding to the services provided along the trade route. Direct costs are based on commercial rates, which reflect the local market, macroeconomic conditions, and the quality of the service and the service provider. Indirect costs are a consequence of the services provided, which translate into financial costs resulting from poor operations (e.g., slow speed, unforeseen delays), as additional costs. They reflect the effectiveness of services, the level of risk involved and the ability of service providers to address administrative and operational problems (Banomyong, 2005).

c) Skills and Quality of Logistics Services

This sub-component of LPI covers various aspects of service quality management and addresses customer satisfaction demand, not only in terms of the physical nature of products, but also in terms of the reliability and flexibility constraints of the logistics system. Therefore, achieving logistics excellence requires continuous improvement in the reliability and responsiveness of services through ongoing investments and the adoption of performance specifications, standards, and resource enrichment. The quality of logistics services plays an important role in promoting international trade.

d) The Ability to Track and Trace Shipment

Traceability is the result of the activities of the entire logistics sector, as all parts of the supply chain are involved in and contribute to the processes. Countries derive considerable benefits from improved tracking and tracing. Estimates show that the price equivalent of information costs as a barrier to accessing services is 6% in industrialized countries (Anderson & Van Wincoop, 2003). However, other authors criticize this figure as overestimated. Information cannot be directly measured accurately; information integration and total supply chain visibility are considered integral parts of an efficient supply chain. Information visibility across trade networks provides access to the location and status of the shipment, which can reduce uncertainty about the shipment's arrival. Tracking and tracing shipments also helps define and control delivery times, better tracking can improve international trade by reducing uncertainties caused by a more reliable, consistent and predictable flow of goods.

e) Respect for Deadlines

Time is a critical element in the trade-off between service level and inventory cost. Lead time costs are proportional to the size and sometimes the value of the shipment, making timeliness a primary factor in trade volume. On average, it is estimated that each day in transit represents 0.8% of the value of manufactured goods (Hummels et al., 2009), and every 10% increase in lead time decreases trade volume (between 5 and 8%) (Hausman et al., 2013). Lead times, the time elapsed between orders being placed and received, can be prohibitively long, reducing trade volume to zero (Nordas et al., 2006).

Not only the length, but also the variation of delivery times is a determining factor in logistics efficiency and trade volumes. The more variable the delivery time, the greater the safety stocks required. Thus, even if the average lead time is low, high variability can make a supplier uncompetitive and can be more damaging than longer, but predictable, lead times (Nordas et al., 2006). This impact is even greater in large, complex supply chains due to the "Bullwhip effect," i.e., the amplified variability of demand in the upstream parts of the supply chain. The importance of timeliness may vary depending on the type of exported products.

Exports of primary products are less sensitive to physical measures and rather more sensitive to measures of infrastructure services, or, for exports of perishable agricultural products, timeliness would be of utmost importance because their value depreciates rapidly. The time sensitivity of trade is associated with the value density of the goods traded. Therefore, the penalties for not meeting deadlines vary from country to country. The magnitude of this coefficient is also particularly high for exports of manufactured goods (Turkson, 2011). The Efficiency of the Customs Clearance Process

This criterion measures the efficiency of customs and the speed of customs procedures at the agency level. Indeed, low customs performance is generally linked to regulatory customs procedures, tedious documentation, and repeated inspections by several agencies. It is widely proven that improving customs clearance procedures significantly reduces the time required for goods to be delivered (Milner et al., 2008). Cumbersome customs procedures are said to be the main problem or barrier to trade (Hummels et al. 2009). Custom clearance involves calculation of tariffs. With roots in concepts as old as mercantilism's gold reserves and as contemporary as Heckscher Ohlin's factor endowments, tariffs are the oldest trade tactic—taxes on imports to shift the balance in favor of home producers.

2.3 Logistics Infrastructure and Trade in Literature

The growth of trade is strongly linked to improvements in technology, communication and the transport sector. In the United Kingdom, an analysis was conducted to show whether the maritime transport revolution between 1870 and 1913 had an impact on trade, although the results were unable to confirm whether this revolution was the main source of the boom in world trade at the end of the 19th century, which increased by 400% (Jacks & Pendakur, 2010). However, other authors suggest that containerization had a considerable effect on world trade during the period studied by Jacks & Pendakur (2010).

They argue, through a sample of 157 countries, that containerization affects not only the operation and relocation of ports, but also the entire transport sector, and it has also gone hand in hand with the creation of the modern intermodal transport system, facilitating the increase in transport capacities and the reduction of delivery times for intermodal freight movements between ships, trains and trucks. The Mediterranean, with the important ports of Valencia and Barcelona, is well represented in terms of logistics infrastructure, but the Madrid Region (organized as the Spanish hub), Aragon (with Zaragoza and the roads that connect Madrid to France, the Netherlands, and Catalonia), and finally Andalusia (a key region between Spain and North Africa) are leading the way in logistics performance in Spain.

Finally, it is worth mentioning that Spanish facilities, due to their strategic location, not only meet interregional needs and interregional-international trade flows but also transit trade flows. Indeed, the geography of the Mediterranean Sea offers favorable conditions for the emergence of transshipment terminals, and European gateways are often used as intermediaries. In the specific case of trade flows between North African countries and the United Kingdom, Spain could become a transit hub.

Notteboom (2012) states that North-South trade and diagonal routes (e.g., North Europe - West Africa and North Europe - South America) are largely connected to the main ring road by transshipment such as Algeciras. Asia and South America and West and South Africa are generally interlined in transshipment centers such as Algeciras and Valencia, the dependence of container flows on the Suez route is not guaranteed in the long term. In this context, existing transport infrastructure, as well as the need to update and modernize facilities, could be cited among the factors that play a fundamental role for regions trying to attract this type of trade flow.

A limited number of studies have analyzed the impact of infrastructure on trade in specific industries. The increase in Trump's trade tariffs has historical precedents in conflicts between the EU and the US on the one hand, and China and the US on the other. In the following section, we look at the history of the main trade conflicts and focus on the impact of the current trade war on markets, logistics flows and supply chains around the world and in Tunisia.

3. U.S. TRADE WAR IMPACT

3.1 Historical Preview

Trade wars have been around for a long time. In fact, it all started in 1963 with a poultry dispute that sparked the conflict. The United States had taken advantage of World War II to modernize its poultry industry. After the war, they flooded the European market with low-priced chicken, quickly capturing 50% of the market by volume. Faced with this competition, which was considered unfair, the European Community, led by France and Germany, introduced customs barriers in 1962 through the Common Agricultural Policy. This resulted in the imposition of a 25% tax on several European products, including Volkswagen trucks. Then, trade conflict of opium appeared brought China into conflict with Great Britain, following China's ban on the importation of Indian opium. The wars led to the forced opening of Chinese ports to foreign trade.

The battle for semiconductors, the internationalization of the renminbi, the arms race, the New Silk Roads... Globalization is increasingly being shaken by rivalries between the two major powers. Even the most ardent defenders of the liberal thesis of free trade must face the facts: "Trade has not been able to buy peace," as the Financial Times headlined. The more tensions mount, the more imperative it becomes to correctly identify their contours. Any observer who ignores this imperative will pay dearly for their carelessness. Like sleepwalkers, they will move forward without understanding the destabilization of the world taking place before their eyes and, as a result, risk stumbling over the obstacles in their path. There is, however, good news. The key to understanding is within reach. It lies in infrastructure.

To understand the profound and lasting nature of contemporary destabilization, we must read the world in terms of infrastructure. This argument will be defended in three stages. First, studies confirm that the functioning of the global economy relies on a multitude of infrastructures. Then, works highlight that the battle for control of the global economy between China and the United States is mainly being fought in the field of infrastructure. Finally, it should be noted that, while infrastructure is indeed the battlefield, the fundamental cause of the confrontation between Beijing and Washington lies in the dynamics of capital accumulation.

Trade wars have significant economic and geopolitical repercussions, affecting supply chains, prices, economic growth, and international relations. They can lead to increased costs, delays, shortages, and even recessions. Geopolitically, they can exacerbate tensions between countries and lead to fragmentation in global trade. Indeed, The US-China trade war is a major economic conflict that began in 2018, characterized by tariff increases and threats between the United States and China.

It began under the presidency of Donald Trump and involved protectionist measures on both sides, affecting trade, supply chains, and the global economy. American trade office investigates and accuses China of stealing intellectual property and has therefore imposed tariff increases over five periods from 2018 to 2019.Then, the United States has long faced a significant trade deficit with China, additionally, technological competition between the two countries participate to the trade war between them.

The trade war started with increases in customs duties on Chinese products by the United States, followed by retaliatory measures by China on American products. Given that the United States is the world's largest importer of steel and aluminum, these measures aim to increase tariffs by 25% on steel imports and 10% on aluminum imports for all US suppliers (except ALENA countries), representing around 100 countries. China has also responded to the new US measures, first by appealing to the World Trade Organization to challenge the entry into force of US tariffs, and then by immediately applying tariffs equivalent to those imposed on it. Beijing thus accuses the United States of having triggered “the biggest trade war in economic history.”

In response to China's reciprocal measures on steel and aluminum, the US government has decided to impose additional tariffs of 25% on 50 billion dollars' worth of Chinese imports. (Mestiri, 2019).

In 2019, the conflict increased with additional tariff measures (forced US tariffs where on approximately 350 billion dollars of Chinese imports, and Chinese government responded by imposing tariffs approximately 100 billion dollars of US exports) for thousands of products from China and growing tensions (Fajgelbaum & Khandelwal 2022). In 2020, the two countries signed the first phase of the agreement, which aimed to reduce tensions, but without resolving fundamental disputes. This agreement required China to increase its purchases of US goods and strengthen intellectual property protection, while the US reduced certain tariffs. Then, between

2020 and 2021, the tariff measures remain in place with a few exemptions, and negotiations are at a standstill. Finally, U,S. authorities, in 2024, note that problematic Chinese practices persist, paving the way for a new confrontation. Besides, recent years have seen tremendous changes in the global trade environment, mostly as a result of protectionist measures, the formation of economic blocs and alliances, and geopolitical movements.

In order to safeguard domestic industry, lower the trade deficit, and entice businesses to relocate their manufacturing back to the US, the United States has implemented a protectionist trade strategy since the Trump administration took office (2025). In contrast to the Trump administration's strategy (focus on tariffs on imports good sand aims to reduce balance deficit), for Biden administration tariff measures, rather than imposing general tariffs on a broad spectrum of commodities, the emphasis was more selective and focused (Fig.1).Strengthening local supply chains in sectors including semiconductors, electric vehicles, and green energy components, all deemed crucial for long term competitiveness and national security was the goal.

Figure 1. Comparisons between Tariffs

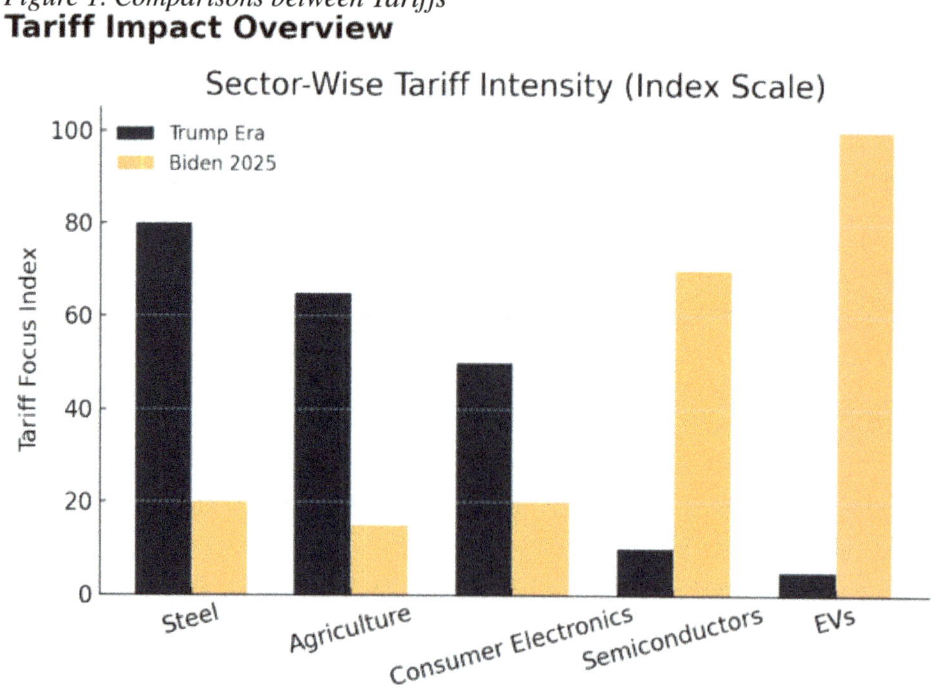

Source: U.S. Census Bureau

US clarified that the goal of these tariffs was to lessen excessive reliance on other nations in areas vital to the economy's future, not to initiate a trade war. This strategy focuses on updating bilateral and multilateral trade agreements and levying tariffs on imported goods. In the next section, we focus on the impact of Trump's tariffs on supply chains and global economies.

3.2 Impact of Trump's tariffs on supply chains and global economies

We start by giving an overview of the main impacts on global supply chains. Firstly, with the United States imposing a full tariff on EVs manufactured in China, the electric vehicle sector emerged as a major target in the 2025 tariff strategy. The goal of this program was to promote more domestic EV production while preventing low-cost imports from flooding the market. American automakers like Ford and GM started announcing additional investments in U.S.-based EV plants in response, while some Chinese companies started rerouting their exports to Europe and Southeast Asia. Tesla also alluded to supply chain diversification, importing some parts from China.

Early data indicates that one of the most immediate consequences of the new tariff wave was an almost 40% decline in Chinese EV imports between 2024 and 2025. According to Office of the U.S report, trade representatives are harsh but textbook. Tariffs stifle import supplies, driving up costs (EVs went from 40,000 to 65,000 dollars with 2024 levies), and shifting the supply curve to the left, which benefits producers while hurting consumers. However, the impact of the two trade strategies is different. Indeed, there were compromises.

Trump's tariffs increased costs and caused tensions with allies while drawing attention to unfair practices and trade imbalances. Although the Biden tariffs are intended to safeguard developing industries, they cause retaliation or impede international collaboration. Overall, how tariffs are applied and the support mechanisms (such as worker training or subsidies) that are offered in conjunction with them greatly influence their impact.

The world economic forum highlighted that supply chains, which were already experiencing stress from the pandemic's interruptions, claim that the intricate adjustments brought about by these tariffs are putting them under much more strain. Supply chains are changing because of the economic disruptions. The results show serious economic disruptions, such as a decline in trade in industries like electronics and automobiles and inflation that impacts American people.

It is a perfect storm when you combine logistics issues (freight charges have increased by 20% since 2023) with inflation (Nicita & Enxhi, 2023). Tariffs have prompted multinational firms to reconsider their supply chain strategy (Contractor, 2025). Companies are shifting production bases to countries not affected by U.S tariffs, while investing in digital systems to improve logistics and manage disruptions. As companies move their manufacturing to Southeast Asia and use AI-driven logistics for resilience, supply chains are changing. Besides, evidence of a significant reallocation of US supply chains, away from China and toward closer allies like Mexico and Vietnam, is presented by Alfaro & Chor (2023), among others.

The availability of extensive and representative microdata is a major advantage of this field of study. Handley et al. (2024) and Fajgelbaum & Khandelwal (2022) concluded that for increased Widespread 2018-2019 tariff occurred, research has conclusively demonstrated that U.S. imports of the impacted goods fell significantly. Furthermore, study supply chain disruptions based on the universe of US seaborne imports, with more than 200 million shipment-level observations. It is only a matter of time before this type of data is used to better understand the role of geopolitical risk shocks in global trade (Liu et al., 2024).

Europe accounts for 24% of Meta's revenue, 26% of Apple's revenue, and 29% of Google's revenue (the latter does not break down the calculation within the Europe, Middle East, and Africa (EMEA) region). Faced with Trump's tariff offensive launched on April 2, 2025, believing that any bilateral trade negotiations automatically place his country in a position of strength, China is proving him wrong, while the European Union is biding its time to calibrate its response.

This uncertainty is obviously disrupting business activity, with companies postponing their investments. They are adapting as best they can by drawing on stocks, thereby profoundly altering supply chains. The uncertainty is such that no company knows how much tax will be levied on a container shipped to the United States (Gomart, 2025). Tariffs reduce investment in the United States and around the world, resulting in lower demand, particularly for durable industrial goods.

This decrease in demand for agriculture and durable manufacturing goods causes a drop in employment in both sectors. Rather of promoting an industrial rebirth in the United States, tariffs render the U.S. a high-cost island in the global economy, reducing industrial output and employment. Tariffs have disproportionately impacted the US agriculture and durable manufacturing sectors, resulting in output losses, fewer employment, and price hikes, contradicting the premise that they will boost the US economy. Germany has been the most affected among the industrialized nations (McKibbin et al., 2025). According to US Census Bureau and BMI, the primary sectors vulnerable to the impact of these tariffs include many sectors cites in Table1. The MENA region exhibits varying levels of exposure, with nations such as Bahrain and the UAE encountering considerable risks stemming from their reliance on specific sectors.

Table 1. The Primary Sectors Vulnerable to the Impact of Trump's Tariffs

	Top Exporting Markets	Exports to U.S.
Iron & Steel	India	3%
	China	2.7%
	South Korea	2.4%
	Italy	1.9%
	Mexico	1.4%
	Canada	1.3%
Autos	Slovakia	78%
	Japan	33.8%
	South Korea	33.8%
	Mexico	27%
	Sweden	23.2%
	Germany	21.5%
Pharmaceutical Products	Ireland	48.7%
	Belgium	44.4%
	Singapore	35.3%
Lumber	Chile	6.4%
	Brazil	3.7%
	Canada	2.7%
Copper	Republic of Congo	91.7%
	Chile	37.4%
Aluminium	Bahrain	57.7%
	UAE	16%
Electrical Machinery	Malaysia	53.3%
	Thailand	35.7%
	Vietnam	30.5%
	China	28.2%
	Taiwan	27.5%

Source: US Census Bureau and BMI

The first impact is the reaction of countries to this trade war. Indeed, authors talked about different strategies. Firstly, Countries, including China and the European Union, swiftly imposed retaliatory tariffs in response to U.S. tariffs, using these actions as leverage in negotiations. This led to a delay in tariff implementation and initiated bilateral talks. Then, other countries can negotiate, during the 90-day delay in tariff implementation, countries engaged in negotiations with the U.S., with the deadline extended to August 1, 2025. This uncertainty in trade policy may result in additional challenges.

The third strategy Countries are redirecting trade away from the United States by leveraging regional trade blocs. Asian nations are enhancing "inter-Asian trade" through frameworks such as the Regional Comprehensive Economic Partnership (RCEP) and the Association of Southeast Asian Nations (ASEAN). This undermines the "China Plus One" strategy, which aimed to shift trade away from China in response to U.S. trade barriers (Murphy, 2025).

As a result of this strategy, Vietnam has emerged as a hub for consumer electronics, while Indonesia is building integrated electric vehicle supply chains. Murphy (2025) suggests that we are witnessing the emergence of a United States Plus One strategy, where trade may increasingly be diverted from the U.S. market. The fourth strategy consists of that China has been systematically challenging American trade policies designed to restore American manufacturing capabilities through its strategic industrial initiatives. Initially, China has put in place export controls on vital minerals to enhance vertical integration throughout its supply chain, which includes raw materials, processing, manufacturing, and assembly (Chou, 2025).

This approach to vertical integration acts as a shield against foreign trade regulations, compelling international companies to engage in Chinese-managed value chains to secure access to these essential minerals. Additionally, China is enforcing technology transfer by implementing rules that require foreign firms to disclose their intellectual property, such as technical specifications and manufacturing methods, as a condition for obtaining critical minerals and accessing the Chinese market (Chou, 2025). Finally, the restoration is the right response for this trade war by the revival of the most-favored-nations principle within the World Trade Organization (WTO) framework. These likely impacts are illustrated in the following Figure.2:

Figure 2. Impact Of Trump's Tariffs on Countries' Strategies

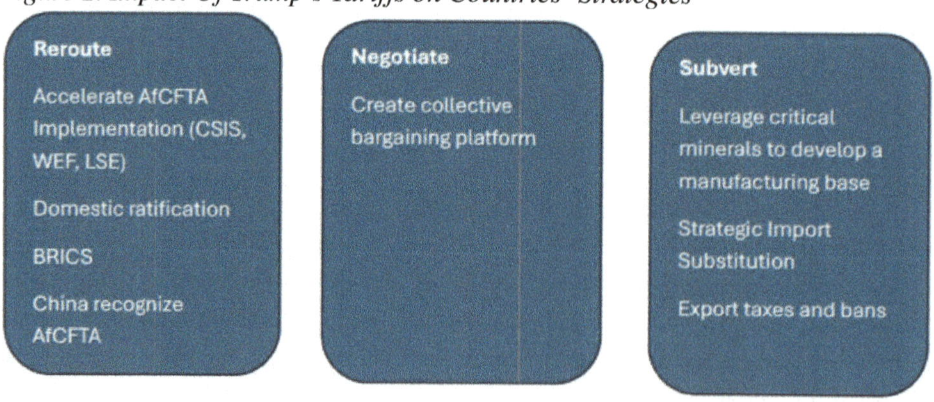

Source: Own Author

Butler (2025), for instance, contends that achieving this goal requires strong political leadership. He also urges the European Union to assume a leading role in promoting global free trade but acknowledges that the EU has been hesitant to adopt this stance due to concerns over potential retaliation from Trump and the internal divisions within Europe. In addition, Germany and the EU are projected to experience a one-time deflationary effect of as much as 0.34 percentage points, particularly in industries that significantly export to the U.S., including the automotive and mechanical engineering sectors. While supply chain disruptions may partially offset this disinflationary effect, the overall impact of slower growth, increased uncertainty, and a greater supply of goods from China and other exporters could create opportunities for more rapid interest rate reductions by the European Central Bank (Hinz et al., 2025).

Given the interdependence of these industries, the proposed tariffs could significantly disrupt global supply chains. There is particular concern regarding the potential tariffs on Taiwanese semiconductors, with speculation that they might be raised to 100%, leading to substantial cost increases for technology manufacturers in the U.S. Companies operating in these sectors should explore strategies to mitigate the impact of these tariffs by diversifying their supply chains, considering tariff engineering solutions, and clarifying risk allocation within purchase and sale contracts.

Logistics and transportation are impacted; European transporters anticipate that customs formalities will become more complex and that delivery times will lengthen as shipping and air freight costs increase. This forces operators to modify their business routes, increasing the risk of overload at entry ports and changing storage schemes.

However, according to Office of the United States Trade Representative, 2025b, The United Kingdom must protect its steel and aluminum supply chains from high-risk countries. In exchange, the US will create import quotas for UK metal products, allowing a fixed volume to enter the US market at Most Favored Nation tariff rates. Besides, The EU has not yet explored strategies like seeking alternative export markets for products at risk. Authors emphasize the need to rectify this oversight. A dual approach is recommended: first, implementing retaliatory tariffs and engaging in negotiations at the EU level, and second, assisting individual member states in mitigating tariff impacts through measures such as finding external market alternatives.

In this context, a study aimed to address these inquiries utilized an approach centered on examining global trade information sourced from the CEPII BACI harmonized UN COMTRADE dataset. Determined the time-adjusted Revealed Comparative Advantage (RCA) and Revealed Trade Advantage (RTA) for Dutch exports to the United States to evaluate the potential impact of tariff measures. Indeed, exports to the USA between 2017 and 2023 are used.

Key aspects of transportation and logistics include factors like global shipping duration and expenses by country, internal timelines and costs for importing goods, and the Logistics Performance Index (LPI) are used, those elements are combined into a market accessibility index, which assigns a score to each specific country pair in comparison to all other product-country pairs analyzed. Then, to evaluate the overall economic consequences of a possible tariff dispute with the U.S., Chowdhry (2025) employ advanced simulations using a cutting-edge quantitative framework that incorporates global supply networks.

The model is adjusted to reflect current global conditions and projects hypothetical scenarios where new tariffs are swiftly introduced, analyzing their effects on the global supply chain. analysis reveals that if the U.S. enacts a blanket 25% duty on imports from the EU and the EU responds with equivalent trade barriers, European shipments to American markets could decline by 50% over time.

This trade dispute would particularly harm major EU industries, leading to substantial output declines in electronic goods (down 2.3%), pharmaceuticals (down 9.3%), automotive production (down 4.1%), and transportation manufacturing (down 7.7%). The broader economic consequences would include an average 0.25% contraction in the EU's real economic output, with Germany facing a more pronounced 0.33% economic contraction.

The author suggests three essential strategies for EU decision-makers. Firstly, the EU should bolster its capability to recognize and oversee vital enterprises and supply chain linkages. This necessitates greater funding for data infrastructure and enhanced cooperation among national statistical bodies, researchers, and industry players. Creating detailed maps of these corporate-level trade and production networks is fundamental for the bloc to thoroughly assess vulnerabilities and implement focused measures. Next, the EU must address the uneven impacts of trade disruptions and strive to distribute the economic costs of tariff disputes more fairly. This could involve expanding current support mechanisms, like the European Globalization Adjustment Fund and Regional Development Funds, to aid affected workers. Additionally, reinforcing the EU Single Market could help mitigate the adverse effects of such external trade shocks. Lastly, the heavy reliance on a limited number of firms and their interconnected networks underscores the need to reduce vulnerabilities in the EU's export framework. Disruptions in even a handful of these critical connections could lead to significant economic repercussions.

To address this, the EU should prioritize strategic efforts to diversify its trade landscape. This might include removing internal trade barriers, aiding businesses in exploring new markets, maximizing the benefits of current trade deals, and broadening the EU's global trade alliances. Such an approach would enhance the bloc's long-term economic stability and adaptability, regardless of future changes in US trade policies.

3.3 *African economies facing Trumps Tariffs*

UNCTAD's (2025) evaluation of the first trump's tariffs announced in 2025 underscores the fundamental inequity of those tariff strategies. For instance, these initial "reciprocal tariffs" differed considerably, with rates ranging from 11% for Cameroon to an alarming 50% for Lesotho (reduced to 15% in August 2025). Even though 28 of the targeted countries accounted for less than 0.1% of the total American trade deficit, they were subjected to tariffs that could severely harm their export industries. Additionally, the justification for these tariffs as a means of generating revenue was tenuous.

UNCTAD (2025) indicates that for the 36 developing countries impacted, these tariffs were anticipated to generate less than 1% of the current tariff revenues collected by the United States. Furthermore, South Africa faces a 30% (the same rate for Morocco and Algeria) tariff that may lead to significant job losses, estimated at 100,000, in key industries. The Trump administration's trade policies effectively end the preferential market access for African countries under the AGOA agreement.

Alonso-Ortiz & José-Maria (2025) develop and analyze a short-term, multination input-output model where each industry acquires intermediate input in fixed Leontief ratios. This structure incorporates 77 countries and 11 sectors, accounting for both direct trade in finished goods and the interconnected supply chains that intensify the impact of price fluctuations.

This amplification mechanism has been emphasized in recent studies as crucial for assessing the consequences of U.S. tariffs. Indeed, data is classified into three categories according to the openness index (Figure.3): countries with declines greater than the world average are in black (Tunisia, etc.), those with smaller declines or increases are in gray (the majority of African country especially Algeria), and the rest are in white (south Africa & Morocco).

Figure 3. Trade Openness Redistribution after Tariffs Increase

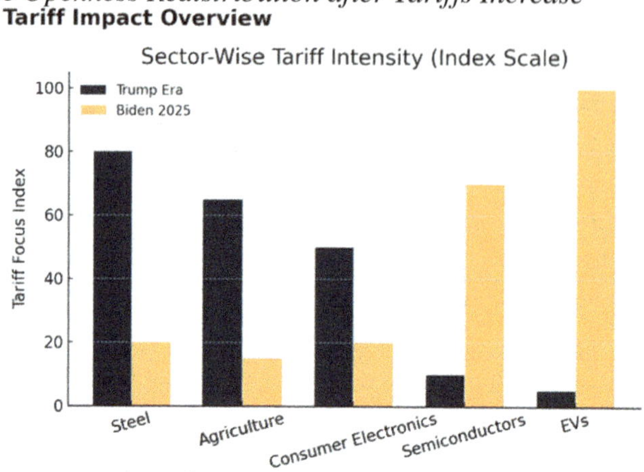

Source: Alonso-Ortiz & JOSÉ-MARÍA (2025)

To strengthen regional trade and development, it is essential to accelerate the implementation of the African Continental Free Trade Area (AfCFTA) agreement. This initiative should focus on fostering inward trade by addressing key barriers and creating a seamless trading environment across the continent. Several critical measures must be prioritized to achieve this goal: harmonizing customs procedures, reducing or eliminating tariffs, establishing a functional continental payment system, finalizing rules of origin frameworks, embedding AfCFTA principles into national laws and policies, and driving the digital transformation of trade facilitation platforms (Ryder, 2025; Osidejo & Akenroye, 2025).

These steps will not only streamline cross-border trade but also enhance efficiency and reduce costs for businesses operating within the region. However, the AfCFTA must go beyond being a mere trade facilitation agreement. To unlock its full potential, it should integrate robust industrial policies that support regional industrialization. This means fostering the development of local manufacturing capacities, promoting value addition to raw materials, and encouraging the creation of regional value chains.

By aligning trade policies with industrial strategies, the AfCFTA can help African nations move up the global value chain, reduce dependency on imports, and create sustainable economic growth. This dual approach—combining trade liberalization with industrial development—will ensure that the AfCFTA becomes a catalyst for economic transformation, job creation, and long-term prosperity across the continent.

African countries should identify key sectors that fulfill the requirements for successful import substitution industrialization (ISI) implementation. These requirements may involve focusing on manufacturing sectors that possess attributes such as high value addition, job creation, significant potential for replacing imports, and substantial capacity for absorbing and processing raw materials sourced from the continent. Nations like Ethiopia, Kenya, Mauritius, and South Africa have textile manufacturing capabilities that are largely underutilized, as over 70% of the continent's clothing is imported. Cocoa serves as another relevant example; although Africa is a major producer and exporter of raw cocoa, it imports as much as 77% of processed cocoa.

To ensure the effectiveness of this ISI approach, it must be supported by well-coordinated and coherent industrial policies, as well as trade facilitation measures that aim to enhance the capacities and capabilities of the targeted sectors and regional production networks within the continent. In addition, establish coalitions focused on critical minerals and engage in negotiations with China and the European Union, stipulating that access to Africa's critical minerals depends on the development of local processing facilities in the African nations from which these minerals are extracted.

The agreements for "commodity for manufacturing facility" should encompass provisions for technology transfer, skills enhancement, and a profit-sharing arrangement to guarantee that local communities reap the benefits. Additionally, impose export bans on critical minerals to promote the value addition of these resources.

3.4 *New channels for Tunisian Trade*

On April 2, 2025, the United States implemented a 28% matching duty on products brought in from Tunisia, driven by the trade gap between the two countries and Tunisia's shipments to the United States. Indeed, those tariffs are called by trump as a « discounted reciprocal tariff to redressing injustices in global trade and repatriate industries », they are applied in order to address the trade imbalance, determined by a specific formula, this tariff is based on the fact that the U.S. trade deficit with Tunisia in 2024, amounting to 619 million dollars, represents 56.3% of total Tunisian exports to the U.S.

Consequently, the United States decided to apply half of that percentage as the tariff rate. For example, Tunisia is cited for its high customs duties (for example, it imposes an average of more than 30% duty on US agricultural products).

The United States ranks as Tunisia's sixth-biggest market for overseas sales, making up roughly 3.2% of Tunisia's overall export volume. In 2024, this translated to approximately 2 billion dinars (around 668 million dollars). Major shipped goods consist of olive oil, machinery and electrical parts, fertilizers, fabrics, and dates. These shipments play a vital role in supporting Tunisia's economic growth.

Figure 4. Trade between Tunisia and The United States (source INS)

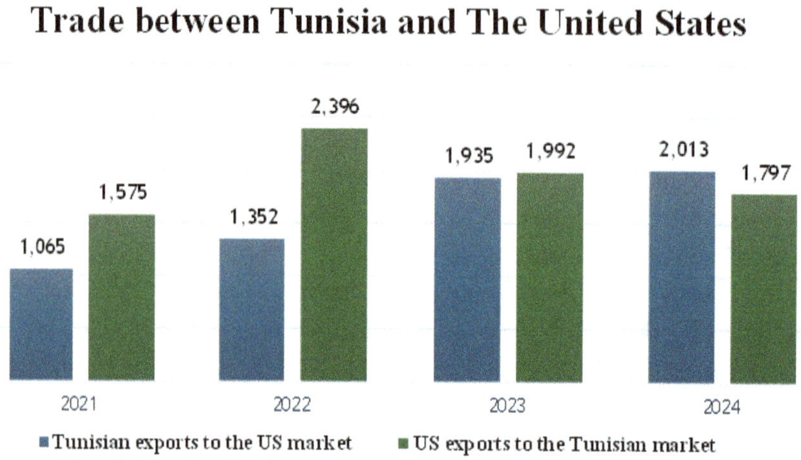

Source: Tunisia's National Institute of Statistics (INS)

According to The Observatory of Economic Complexity, Tunisia's exports to the United States decrease to 123 million dollars, while Tunisian imports from the United States totaled 42.9 million dollars, generating a trade surplus of 80.5 million dollars for Tunisia in June 2025.Furthermore, Tunisia's main imports from the United States: Corn (5.41 million dollars), ethylene polymers (4.3 million dollars), and vinyl chloride polymers (3.21 million dollars), while main Tunisian exports to the United States: Pure olive oil (66.2 million dollars), insulated wires and cables (4.76 million dollars), and low-voltage protective equipment (2.84 million dollars).

The year-on-year decrease in Tunisia's exports to the United States was primarily caused by significant reductions in the following categories: Gas and Liquid Flow Measuring Instruments, which fell by 2.02 million dollars (a drop of 79.5%); Oscilloscopes, which decreased by 5.41 million dollars (a decline of 74.3%); and Mixed Mineral or Chemical Fertilizers, which saw a dramatic drop of 21.3 million dollars (down 99.7%). Alshaalan (2025) mentions that the difference in reported figures between INS and USTR arises from their distinct accounting methods. Tunisia accounts for exports based on the final destination of the goods, which are often European countries, even if the products are partially or fully manufactured in Tunisia before being re-exported. On the other hand, the American tracks imports according to the origin of the goods.

For its part, the Tunisian government has not reacted to the increase in these tariffs. Then, in the wake of the newly imposed tariffs, trade relations between Tunisia and the U.S. are expected to become more strained in 2025. While formal negotiations for a free trade agreement are not currently in progress, discussions may be initiated within the TIFA Council to address these issues. Tunisia may attempt to obtain an exemption or a reduction in these tariffs by emphasizing its role as a modest strategic partner and highlighting the vulnerabilities of its economy. However, options for negotiation are limited, as the U.S. measures are part of a larger policy impacting multiple countries at once. Indeed, a study summarized the countries whose exports are most vulnerable to the possible surplus of Chinese goods in global markets.

This vulnerability is measured by the exports-weighted average increase in Chinese supply to markets outside the United States. This study counts Tunisia as the country number 13 in the ranking of top exporters by Exposure to Surplus Sectors from U.S.-China Trade Disruption with 0.1% of Share of global exports and 4.9% in exposure to surplus sectors.

The introduction of new tariffs threatens the competitiveness of Tunisian products in the U.S. market by driving up prices. This situation is particularly worrisome due to the competition from countries with lower tariff rates, including Brazil, Morocco, Gulf countries and Egypt. A possible decrease in export volumes may result in lower foreign exchange earnings, which poses a substantial challenge for the Tunisian economy. Alshaalan (2025), analyzes this situation and finds indirect effects of US trade policies. Indeed, the author underlines the importance of European channels. It refers to the pathways and mechanisms that facilitate trade between Tunisia and European countries. This can include various forms of trade agreements, logistics networks, and established market connections that allow for the export and import of goods. Leveraging these channels can help Tunisia enhance its trade relationships, potentially offsetting challenges faced in the U.S. market, such as tariffs.

By utilizing these European trade avenues, Tunisia may find opportunities for increased exports, diversification of markets, and stronger economic ties within Europe. Furthermore, the study showed an evident and robust Tunisia trade and industrial partnership with the EU, with exports reaching 42.6 billion dinars (approximately 13.9 billion dollars) in 2024, accounting for about 69% of its overall exports. This underscores the need to comprehend the indirect effects of the American. trade policies. Tunisia serves a significant function as an "intermediate supplier" across various sectors, such as textiles, electrical and mechanical parts, and food processing.

The United States implementation of a twenty percent tariff on imports from Europe is expected to weaken the competitiveness of European goods in the American market. As a result, this may trigger a decline in industrial production in Europe, leading to decreased demand for raw materials and components that Tunisia exports to European firms. This situation illustrates how the American policies can have indirect repercussions for Tunisia via its trade relationships with European partners. Moreover, the EU is the largest provider of imports for Tunisia, making up around 43% of the total. If European production expenses rise as a result of U.S. tariffs, it will directly influence the cost of goods entering Tunisia, leading to heightened inflationary pressures in the Tunisian economy.

At the lower end of the scale, Tunisia's direct exposure to the American market is relatively minimal, with exports destined for the United States comprising just 3.2% of the total. Nevertheless, essential sectors like olive oil, mechanical and electrical parts, and textiles are still threatened by the newly the trump's tariff. As a result, the temporary ninety-day suspension of these U.S. tariffs is expected to provide immediate relief, not only to Tunisia but also to global markets contending with uncertainty and escalating trade tensions. Finally, if African countries choose negotiation, they should leverage their collective strength to secure equitable agreements with trading partners and other external entities (Mathekga, 2025).

Establishing a collective bargaining platform within the African Union or regional economic communities will enhance the continent's trade benefits. This approach would prevent trading partners from taking advantage of divisions among African countries by negotiating separately with individual nations.

On the lower end, Tunisia's direct exposure to the U.S. market is fairly minimal, with exports destined for the U.S. representing just 3.2% of the total. However, critical sectors such as olive oil, mechanical and electrical components, and textiles are still vulnerable because of the recently implemented 28% tariff.

4. CONCLUSION

Trump's approach to tariffs marks a significant departure from the principles of multilateral trade, highlighting the vulnerabilities in global economic governance and disproportionately impacting developing nations through retaliatory measures. The widespread imposition of tariffs contradicts conventional industrial policy reasoning, as it focuses on countries that play a minimal role in the U.S. trade imbalance.

This strategy risks devastating export-driven industries, which often rely on marginalized workers, especially women employed in textile manufacturing. Such policies not only disrupt international trade norms but also threaten the livelihoods of those most dependent on export-oriented sectors.

According to the Centre for Prospective Studies and International Information (CEPII), this trade policy is likely to have negative consequences for the US economy. Higher tariffs will be passed on to the prices of imported products and fuel inflation. US companies that use imported components in their production cycle will see their production costs increase and their competitiveness decline. Finally, the multiple U-turns in trade policy create instability and could discourage investors from setting up in the United States, which would be contrary to the desired objectives.

For a global level, in response to the shifting trade environment, businesses must take proactive steps to navigate the risks posed by the new tariff regime. This includes diversifying supply chains by identifying alternative sources and reviewing product classifications and origins. Contracts should be updated to reflect tariff-related cost increases, while internal policies must be adjusted to remain adaptable. Companies should also explore duty-saving strategies, such as tariff engineering and foreign trade zones, and implement risk assessment frameworks to evaluate the financial and operational impacts of tariffs.

Clear communication with customers about potential price changes and delays is essential, as is staying informed about regulatory developments, including WTO rulings and legal challenges, that could affect trade policies. Then, Geopolitical tensions, trade disputes, and sanctions have far-reaching consequences, disrupting critical trade routes and creating bottlenecks that inflate transportation costs and delay deliveries. These disruptions not only strain logistics but also threaten to fragment global supply chains, forcing companies to rethink their reliance on specific regions or trading partners.

For instance, reliance on a single supplier or manufacturing hub can leave businesses vulnerable to sudden policy changes or conflicts, prompting a shift toward diversification and regionalization of supply chains. This strategic pivot often involves sourcing materials from multiple locations, investing in local production facilities, or exploring alternative markets to mitigate risks.

In this volatile environment, supply chain analytics plays a pivotal role in helping businesses navigate these challenges. By harnessing advanced data analysis, companies can assess potential risks, identify vulnerabilities, and optimize their supply chain strategies. For example, predictive analytics can forecast disruptions caused by geopolitical events or trade policy changes, enabling proactive adjustments to inventory levels, transportation routes, or supplier networks. Additionally, real-time monitoring tools allow businesses to track shipments, manage delays, and respond swiftly to unforeseen issues.

Moreover, supply chain analytics supports decision-making by providing actionable insights into cost-efficiency, sustainability, and resilience. Companies can evaluate the trade-offs between cost savings and risk exposure, ensuring that their strategies align with long-term goals. For instance, adopting technologies like blockchain can enhance transparency and traceability, while automation and AI-driven solutions can streamline operations and reduce dependency on manual labor.

Ultimately, in an era marked by uncertainty, supply chain analytics empowers businesses to build agile, adaptable, and resilient operations. By leveraging data-driven insights, companies can not only mitigate the impact of disruptions but also seize opportunities for innovation and growth in a rapidly evolving global trade landscape (Hinz et al., 2025).

The proposed three-part strategy provides a robust framework for enhancing Africa's resilience: first, by redirecting trade internally through the swift implementation of the AfCFTA and externally by diversifying partnerships within BRICS, particularly with underutilized allies such as India, Brazil, and Russia; second, by advancing targeted import substitution industrialization in key sectors both nationally and across the AfCFTA; and third, by negotiating collectively to strengthen the continent's bargaining power, including the formation of critical minerals alliances to counter divide-and-conquer strategies.

Asian nations are enhancing "inter-Asian trade" through frameworks such as the Regional Comprehensive Economic Partnership (RCEP) and the Association of Southeast Asian Nations (ASEAN). This undermines the "China Plus One" strategy, which aimed to shift trade away from China in response to U.S. trade barriers. As a result of this strategy, Vietnam has emerged as a hub for consumer electronics, while Indonesia is building integrated electric vehicle supply chains (Murphy, 2025).

Logistics and transportation are impacted, European transporters anticipate that customs formalities will become more complex and that delivery times will lengthen as shipping and air freight costs increase. This forces operators to modify their business routes, increasing the risk of overload at entry ports and changing storage schemes.

However, according to Office of the United States Trade Representative, 2025b, The United Kingdom must protect its steel and aluminum supply chains from high-risk countries. In exchange, the US will create import quotas for UK metal products, allowing a fixed volume to enter the US market at Most Favored Nation tariff rates. Besides, The EU has not yet explored strategies like seeking alternative export markets for products at risk.

Tunisia is more impacted through indirect means, particularly through its trade connections with Europe. This moment of crisis offers Tunisia a unique opportunity to lessen its reliance on precarious preferential agreements, accelerate its industrial growth, and establish durable regional value chains. By strategically leveraging its critical resources and adopting cohesive industrial policies, Tunisia—alongside other African nations—can shift from being passive victims of global trade disruptions to proactive shapers of their economic futures. This transformation aligns with long-term continental development goals and reduces susceptibility to external economic pressures (Ryder, 2025; Osidejo & Akrenroye, 2025).

REFERENCES

Alfaro, L., & Chor, D. (2023). *Global supply chains: The looming "great reallocation"* (No. w31661). National Bureau of Economic Research.

Alonso-Ortiz, J., & José Maria, . (2025). *"The short-run impact of US tariffs on an interconnected world."*. Documento de Trabajo.

Alshaalan, Z., (2025). Repercussions of the New U.S. Trade Policies on the Global Economy: A Focus on Tunisia.

Anderson, J. E., & Van Wincoop, E. (2003). Gravity with gravitas: A solution to the border puzzle. *The American Economic Review, 93*(1), 170–192. DOI: 10.1257/000282803321455214

Banomyong, R. (2005). The impact of port and trade security initiatives on maritime supply-chain management. *Maritime Policy & Management, 32*(1), 3–13. DOI: 10.1080/0308883042000326102

Butler, E. (2025). The Psychology of Protectionism. In *Free Trade in the Twenty-First Century: Economic Theory and Political Reality* (pp. 43–63). Springer Nature Switzerland. DOI: 10.1007/978-3-031-67656-7_4

Carruthers, R., Bajpai, J. N., & Hummels, D. (2003). Trade and logistics: an East Asian perspective. *East Asia integrates: a trade policy agenda for shared growth*, 117-137.

Castells, M., & Hall, P. (1994). *Technopoles of the World.* Routledge.

Chang, T. (2002). Financial development and economic growth in Mainland China: A note on testing demand-following or supply-leading hypothesis. *Applied Economics Letters, 9*(13), 869–873. DOI: 10.1080/13504850210158962

Chou, W. (2025). China's Bureaucratic Playbook for Critical Minerals: Control, Technology Transfer, and Manufacturing Dominance. *Hudson Institute*, (July), 9.

Chowdhry, S. (2025). *Trump's Tariffs: What Escalating Trade Tensions with the US Imply for EU Exporters and Supply Chains* (No. 11). DIW Berlin, German Institute for Economic Research.

Contractor, F. J. (2025). Assessing the economic impact of tariffs: adaptations by multinationals and traders to mitigate tariffs. *Review of international business and strategy*, 35(2/3), 190-213.

Dee, P., & Findlay, C. (2006). "Trade Facilitation: What, Why, How, Where and When"? Working paper, *Asian Development Bank*, Manila.

Dornier, P. P., & Fender, M. (2007). La logistique globale et le Supply Chain Management. *Edition d'organisation.*

Fajgelbaum, P. D., & Khandelwal, A. K. (2022). The economic impacts of the US–China trade war. *Annual Review of Economics*, *14*(1), 205–228. DOI: 10.1146/annurev-economics-051420-110410

Fullerton, R. R., & McWatters, C. S. (2002). The role of performance measures and incentive systems in relation to the degree of JIT implementation. *Accounting, Organizations and Society*, *27*(8), 711–735. DOI: 10.1016/S0361-3682(02)00012-0

Gani, A. (2017). The logistics performance effect in international trade. *The Asian Journal of Shipping and Logistics*, *33*(4), 279–288. DOI: 10.1016/j.ajsl.2017.12.012

Gomart, T. (2025). Chronique. Le commerce mondial, entre tarifs et infrastructures portuaires. Études, Juillet-Août(7-8), 31-32.

Handley, K., Fariha, K., & Ryan, M. (2024). Supply chain adjustments to tariff shocks: Evidence from firm trade linkages in the 2018-2019 US trade war. *Economics Letters*, *244*, 112009. DOI: 10.1016/j.econlet.2024.112009

Hausman, W. H., Lee, H. L., & Subramanian, U. (2013). The impact of logistics performance on trade. *Production and Operations Management*, *22*(2), 236–252. DOI: 10.1111/j.1937-5956.2011.01312.x

Hinz, J., Mahlkow, H., & Wanner, J. (2025). The KITE Model Suite: A Quantitative Framework for International Trade Analysis. *KITE White Paper*.

Hummels, D., Lugovskyy, V., & Skiba, A. (2009). The trade reducing effects of market power in international shipping. *Journal of Development Economics*, *89*(1), 84–97. DOI: 10.1016/j.jdeveco.2008.05.001

Ivanov, D. (2025). Supply chain stress testing for tariff shocks and trade conflicts: Methods, models, and reciprocal influence of operations and economics. *IEEE Transactions on Engineering Management*, *72*, 3559–3566. DOI: 10.1109/TEM.2025.3599711

Jacks, D. S., & Pendakur, K. (2010). Global trade and the maritime transport revolution. *The Review of Economics and Statistics*, *92*(4), 745–755. DOI: 10.1162/REST_a_00026

Joignaux, G., & Verny, J. (2004). Le découplage entre transport de marchandises et croissance: Organisations productives, localisations et demande de transport. *Revue d'Économie Régionale et Urbaine*, (5), 779–791. DOI: 10.3917/reru.045.0779

Jumah, Z., Moazzam, M., Manzoor, W., & Safdar, N. (2025). Economic policy uncertainty and firm's profitability: The role of logistics infrastructure. *International Journal of Productivity and Performance Management*, *74*(1), 180–202. DOI: 10.1108/IJPPM-08-2023-0410

Lee, J. Y., & Rodrigue, J. P. (2006). Trade Reorientation and Its Effects on Regional Port Systems: The Korea-China Link along the Yellow Sea Rim. *Growth and Change*, *37*(4), 597–619. DOI: 10.1111/j.1468-2257.2006.00342.x

Limao, N., & Venables, A. J. (2001). Infrastructure, geographical disadvantage and transport costs. *The World Bank Economic Review*, *15*(3), 451–479. DOI: 10.1093/wber/15.3.451

Liu, J., Xiaoye, W & Junyu G. (2024). "Port efficiency and its influencing factors in the context of pilot free trade zones." *Transport Policy* 105 (2021): 67-79.

Liu, X. (2021). Chinese multinational enterprises operating in Western economies: Huawei in the US and the UK. In *China's Big Power Ambition under Xi Jinping* (pp. 219–236). Routledge. DOI: 10.4324/9781003198871-14

Mathekga, R. (2025). *Trade tariffs hinder SADC integration.* GIS Reports Online.

McKibbin, W.J., Marcus N., & Geoffrey S. (2025) "25-13 *The global economic effects of Trump's 2025 tariffs.*"

Mestiri, R. (2019) "La contribution de l'agriculture urbaine à l'approvisionnement alimentaire de La Havane." *Revue internationale des études du développement* 237.1: 137-164.

Milner, C., Morrissey, O., & Zgovu, E. (2008). *Trade facilitation in developing countries (No. 08/05).* CREDIT Research Paper

Murphy, E.L. (2025). Trump Tariffs Likely Pushing Asia Elsewhere for Economic Partners, *Centre for Strategic and International Studies*, 14 July.

Nicita, A., & Enxhi, T. (2023). The heterogeneous effects of trade policy on trade resilience during the 2020 trade downturn. *World Economy*, *46*(10), 3048–3056. DOI: 10.1111/twec.13420

Nordas, H. K., Pinali, E., & Grosso, M. G. (2006). *Logistics and time as a trade barrier.*

Notteboom, T. E. (2012). Towards a new intermediate hub region in container shipping? Relay and interlining via the Cape route vs. The Suez route. *Journal of Transport Geography*, *22*, 164–178. DOI: 10.1016/j.jtrangeo.2012.01.003

Osidejo, A., & Akenroye, T. (2025). *How lowering tariffs could unleash Africa's economic opportunity*. World Economic Forum.

Owsiak, A., Diehl, P. F., & Goertz, G. (2024). Managing complexity: Addressing the civil conflict component of international-civil militarized conflicts (I-CMCs). *International Journal of Conflict Management*, *35*(1), 192–214. DOI: 10.1108/IJCMA-01-2023-0002

Rahbari, M., Arshadi Khamseh, A., & Sadati-Keneti, Y. (2024). Resilience strategies in coping to disruptions of wheat supply chain caused by the Russia–Ukraine war crisis: Case study from an emerging economy. *Kybernetes*, *53*(10), 2984–3018. DOI: 10.1108/K-12-2022-1728

Ryder, H. (2025). *How should Africa respond to Trump's new tariffs? Centre for Strategic and International Studies*. CSIS.

Tödtling, F. (1994). Regional networks of hightechnology firms—The case of the greater Boston region. *Technovation*, *14*(5), 323–343. DOI: 10.1016/0166-4972(94)90075-2

Turkson, F. E. (2011). *Logistics and bilateral exports in developing countries: a multiplicative form estimation of the logistics augmented gravity equation* (No. 11/06). CREDIT Research Paper.

UNCTAD. (United Nations Conference on Trade and Development). (2025). 2024 Economic development in Africa report – *Unlocking Africa's trade potential. Boosting regional markets and reducing risks*. United Nations Publications.

Wang, C., Kim, Y. S., & Kim, C. Y. (2021). Causality between logistics infrastructure and economic development in China. *Transport Policy*, *100*, 49–58. DOI: 10.1016/j.tranpol.2020.10.005

Wang, J., & Ma, Z. (2019). Port logistics cluster effect and coordinated development of port economy based on grey relational analysis model. *Journal of Coastal Research, 94*(SI), 717-721.

Chapter 14
Trade War:
Trump's Trade Policy and Its Impact on the International Economy

Raquel Isamara León De La Rosa
https://orcid.org/0000-0003-1019-0971
Autonomus University of Puebla, Mexico

Misael González Ramírez
https://orcid.org/0000-0003-2718-0809
Autonomus University of Puebla, Mexico

ABSTRACT

The return of Donald Trump has marked a key moment for the international system. The establishment of a system of reciprocal tariffs has had an impact on the international economy. This paper aims to identify the main effects of the trade war between the United States and China on the international economic system. The concept of trade war is rescued, as well as some trends on trade policy (Ripsman, 2006), globalization (Rodrik, 2007) and securitization (de Goede, 2017) to understand the economic dynamics of the international system. The proposed methodology is a network analysis (Granovetter, 2012) based on the exports and imports of the world's 40 main economies. With this, a series of categories are proposed to identify the adaptability of economies to the reciprocal tariffs imposed by the United States. The categories are commercial diversification, specialization of exportable supply, strategic industries and position within global value chains. Among the findings, it discusses the role of China, India, Japan and South Korea as key Indo-Pacific nodes.

DOI: 10.4018/979-8-3373-3835-4.ch014

1. INTRODUCTION

The first quarter of the 21st century has brought many changes all over the world, particularly 2025 is projected as a year of challenges on the international scene with the confrontation between the United States and China, that is the result of the decline and rise of each nation. Trade war is a symptom of the struggle for world leadership.

Donald Trump begun the trade war at his first term in order to fulfill his campaign promise of Make America Great Again. But the advance in China's positioning in the international system and the loss of space by the United States has taken this trade war to a new level.

The pandemic of COVID – 19 change the international scenario and new difficulties appear for all countries. Donald Trump can't win the election of 2020 and Joe Biden keep the tariffs for Chinese products. Trump defeat Kamala Harris in the election of 2024 and in his second term his first actions were establish a system of reciprocal tariffs for some countries. This commercial policy has had an impact on speculation about what will happen to the world economy in 2025. Data from the International Monetary Fund (IMF) published in the Outlook 2025 for April show a complex picture this includes limited global growth of 2.8%. Advanced economies will grow by 1.4% and emerging economies will grow by 3.7%. This shows a slowdown in the economy at all levels.

Since the 1990s-decade United States has shown many problems to keep its hegemonic position in the world economy. The offshoring strategy implemented for developed occidental economies opened the door for many countries to get integrated into the global market. Some Asian countries such as China, South Korea, Singapore and Taiwan take this opportunity seriously and change their position in the world economy.

Now the United States has many problems keeping its economy because its debt is skyrocketing for many years and its inner market is the only source of economic growth. The loss of his strength has impulse Donald Trump to change his commercial policy, believing that if his market is closed to other countries the companies will back his manufacturing operations to the United States.

This is one of the factors that ignite the trade war with China, but the consequences of American protectionism will affect countries from all regions of the world. We are witnessing the change in the balance of power in the world where emergent economies will play a central role in the new system that will emerge in the coming years.

Given this scenario, this chapter aims to identify the effects of United States trade policy through neo protectionism and securitization, particularly in the context of the trade war between the United States and China. To achieve this, the first section provides a historical overview of United States evolution from a medium power to global leader, highlighting key events in the 20th and 21st centuries that have shaped the country's economy and his today status on international arena. Beside this in this section review the commerce policy that United States has taken around China.

Next, a theoretical review of the concept of neo protectionism and the role of securitization in trade is presented. This section aims to understand how we can conceptualize the commercial policy of United States and how the World Trade Organization construct an asymmetrical system between developed and und developing countries.

The third section proposes analyzing empirical data using Mark Granovetter's network theory. This analysis systematizes the exports and imports linkages between major advanced and emerging economies, providing a structural perspective on international trade that helps identify the vulnerability of economies to United States tariffs. Statistical data on economic growth is also included to support the network analysis.

The fourth section presents a general overview of four cases China, India, Japan, and South Korea, as representative economies of the Indo-Pacific region and key players in the technological field. The fifth section discusses the global implications based on the empirical network and statistical analysis, proposing three key dimensions of trade and technological war.

Finally, in the last section of the paper the lector can find the main conclusions of the authors after their analysis of empirical trade data using the network theory, beside this the authors open a new approach to understand the effects of Trump's trade policies in international commerce.

1.1 Historical background

When the American Civil War ended, the United States began an unprecedented economic growth. The last years of the 18th century were named the Gilded Age; this epoch is marked for savage capitalism and the building of big monopolies. The economic development of the United States transforms this country from a middle power to a great power.

At the end of WWI, the United States changed its status from a debtor to creditor country. The help lent to European countries to fight against the Axis Powers worked to make this change real. President Woodrow Wilson began with the policy of promoting all over the world the values of democracy and the free market and trying to build an institution that will avoid the war, but the Society of Nations born death.

When the Great Depression came, the United States left its international role and went back to his isolationism. Few years later, the threat of the Third Reich encouraged the United States to fight to defend democracies and at the end of the war the Soviet Union and the United States became the two hegemons of a bipolar world.

In 1989 the fall of the Berlin Wall marked the end of the Cold War and the beginning of the American Hegemony in a unipolar world. In 1993 Christopher Layne and Benjamin Schwarz wrote in Foreign Policy the article *American Hegemony without an Enemy* where they recognized that international politics is dynamic and the United States must face emerging geopolitical realities rather than attempt to escape from them. In the post-Cold War world, the United States will not find absolute security in a unipolar system. Lyne and Schwarz understand too that a multipolar world will emerge and be turbulent and competitive; but while other powers will be seriously threatened and highly insecure, the United States as a great power will be able to stand back and watch international events from a posture of discriminating detachment, but like any other great powers, the hegemony of United States don't last forever.

Samuel P. Huntington in 1988 wrote in Foreign Affairs his article *The U.S.: Decline or Renewal?* where indicate that some declinist writers reflect about strength of United States who sets images of a nation winding down economically, living beyond its means, losing its competitive, sagging under the burdens of empire and political ills. Huntington debated with this declinist and concluded that the United States is not immortal, and his preeminence is not inevitable, but Huntington considered that the United States has a self-renewing genius and could maintain its position as hegemonic country for a long time.

For many decades all countries have looked for autonomy and tried to depend less on their neighbors and commercial associates. It was in the 1990's when Occident changed his approach to manufacturing matters and many companies in the United States and Europe modified his strategy of producing. Some financial strategists identify that the salaries paid in developing countries were cheaper than in the First World. Besides this the technological changes allowed some parts of the production chain to other countries, this is how the out-shoring appeared as a magic formula to increase the profits of big companies.

Since the appearance of outsourcing, many countries received important amounts of foreign investment to improve their infrastructure and industrial facilities. This money changes the fortune of the countries that left the primary sector to become manufacturing countries. This is one of many reasons that countries like China, South Korea, Brazil, Mexico among others were recognized as Emerging Markets in the beginning of 21st century.

The United States since the end of World War II built an international order that benefits world peace, human development, democracy and economic growth. When the Cold War ended, the United States controlled all the commercial and financial structures that rule the world. This control is executed through the indirect rule that means governing through local agents groomed, supported and controlled by the United States in different countries and regions (Lau, 2025).

The economic and commercial system constructed by the United States makes this country the foremost node in the world. America has many benefits of its role like their citizens can consume large amounts of products at very low prices, may have high fiscal deficits because they can always receive loans from other countries such as Japan, and many countries are eager to sell his products to the American market.

Being on top of all commercial networks has a price to pay. Other countries, such as China, thanks to the offshore tendency could receive several million dollars on foreign investment, among other factors, that drive his economy to reach an average growth of 9.05% of GDP from 1990 to 2023 (World Bank Group, 2025). South Korea, India, Brazil, Polonia and Mexico receive foreign money too, this results in a diversification of his economies.

These new actors got integrated into global production chains and took an important share of the global market, because developed countries such as the United States give away the manufacture to others. Since this happened, Western world in general and America in particular, lost control over the global economy.

Beside this, the political leadership of United States at the end of Cold War was in his highest point, but the Gulf War and the War on Terror erode their position. The perception about United States changes from a world leader to a vulgar imperialist country that sought impose its will over the entire world.

The third situation that limited the importance of the United States in the international arena was the decline of its economy. Then the first decade of the 21st century was marked by the terrorist attacks of 2001, problems with accounting fraud of Enron, and the subprime mortgage crisis.

The September 11 attacks had significant immediate and long-term economic effects, primarily in consumer confidence. Enron's fraudulent accounting practices case was marked for hiding billions of dollars in debt and inflating its earnings. Enron Corporation bankruptcy was the then-largest bankrupt corporation in United States history. The resulting economic dislocation sparked one of the extensive legislations over fraudulent practices (Levin Center, 2025). Finaly the subprime mortgage crisis begins in 2007 and was a period of significant financial turmoil in the United States. The crisis led to a sharp economic downturn in the United States and other counties, with high unemployment and reduced economic activities. Several major financial institutions failed to require government bailouts to prevent collapse such as Bear Stearns, Lehman Brothers and AIG (Federal Reserve History, 2025).

The three crises affected investors and consumer confidence in the United States and has long-term effects that undermined the strength of the American economy. These setbacks have led the United States to an internal crisis that has put it in a difficult position given the changing international environment.

Figure 1. Consumer Confidence Index

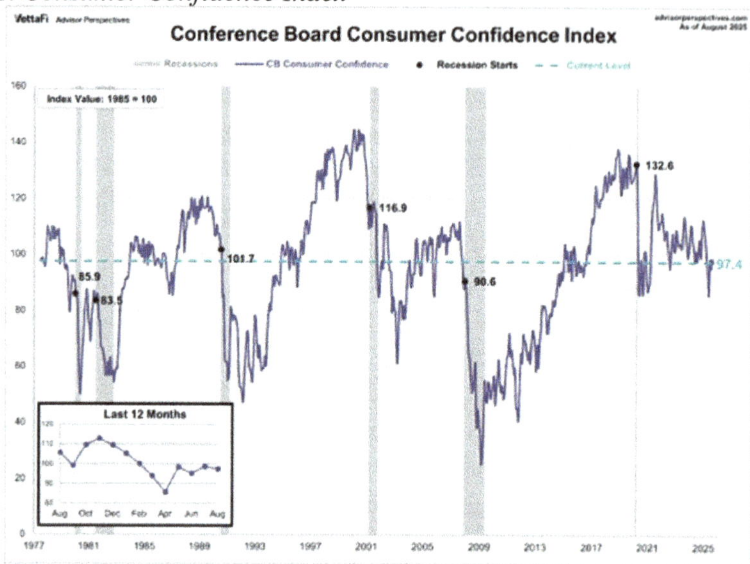

Source: Nash, 2025

The fears of the United States' decline that were felt in the 1990s have materialized a few years later. In the three branches of government that underpin a state's strength—economic power, political power, and military power—the United States is no longer capable of being considered the world leader it was in the 1990s. Its economy remains the largest in the world, but it is not the most dynamic; other countries, mainly in Asia, are growing more rapidly. The United States' military capability arguably remains the most significant, although it has not had an unchallenged victory against another military power close to its level since the Korean War.

The chances of reestablishing its leadership and regaining its hegemony are closely linked to improving its economy. But its main challenge is the large fiscal deficit facing the American government. Since Barack Obama's presidency, the United States' fiscal deficit problem has become more difficult to manage. The U.S. faces a growing fiscal deficit, where government spending exceeds revenue, leading to increased national debt. This trend, exacerbated by factors like the COVID-19 pandemic and rising interest rates, poses risks to the United States economy and financial stability. The government's spending, particularly on social programs, healthcare, and debt servicing, is outpacing its revenue from taxes and other sources (Fiscal Data. 2025).

Figure 2. Debt Held by the Public as a Share of the U.S. Economy (GDP)

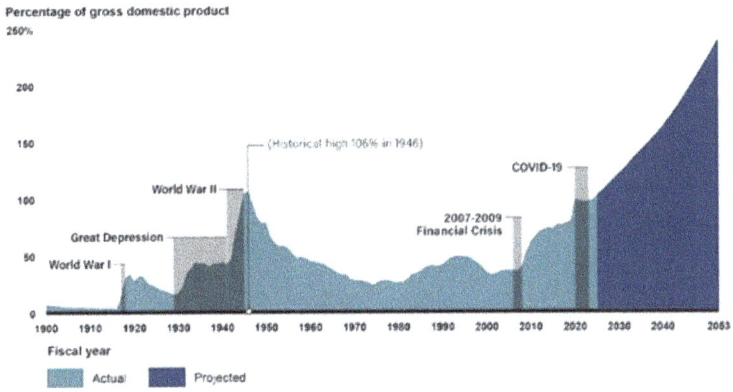

Source: U.S. Government Accountability Office

The United States national debt is now $33.6 trillion, and the excessive deficits have reached new highs at $1.7 trillion for the fiscal year — 5.8% of GDP. The cost of servicing this debt due to inflation and rising interest rates is also increasing by $162 billion, reaching $879 billion in 2023, approximately the size of the defense budget. The rise in the cost of servicing the debt is a significant challenge, often warned about in the past but now here to stay for at least some time, threatening federal spending priorities (Peterson and Murray, 2025).

To right the ship, the United States needs to reduce its spending and increase its revenue. Reducing its military spending will help with the deficit, but at the same time it needs a victory of any kind to strengthen itself internally. This is why the United States left Afghanistan without having successfully eliminated the Taliban, launched a trade war with China to attract increased investment on its soil, and has sought to limit its participation in NATO and the UN.

China's economic progress is one of the factors that has led to a rethinking of the United States' trade strategy. The securitization of U.S. trade policy was accentuated during Donald Trump's first term. From the first campaign, a discourse was inserted against all the trading partners with which the United States had a deficit relationship in its trade balance, leading the list China, Mexico and Canada. From Trump's vision and American nationalism, these countries had taken away jobs and damaged industry within this country.

Trump's inaugural address in January 2017 had phrases related to this, for example:

For many decades, we've enriched foreign industry at the expense of American industry... One by one, the factories shuttered and left our shores, with not even a thought about the millions upon millions of American workers left behind... Every decision on trade, on taxes, on immigration, on foreign affairs, will be made to benefit American workers and American families... We must protect our borders from the ravages of other countries making our products, stealing our companies, and destroying our jobs. Protection will lead to great prosperity and strength (The White House, 2017).

Figure 3 shows this increase in the trade deficit in the relationship with China, the first moment of the trade war between the United States and China, which began in March 2018. The result is a slowdown in imports of Chinese origin to the American market.

Figure 3. U.S.-China Trade Deficit 2014-2019

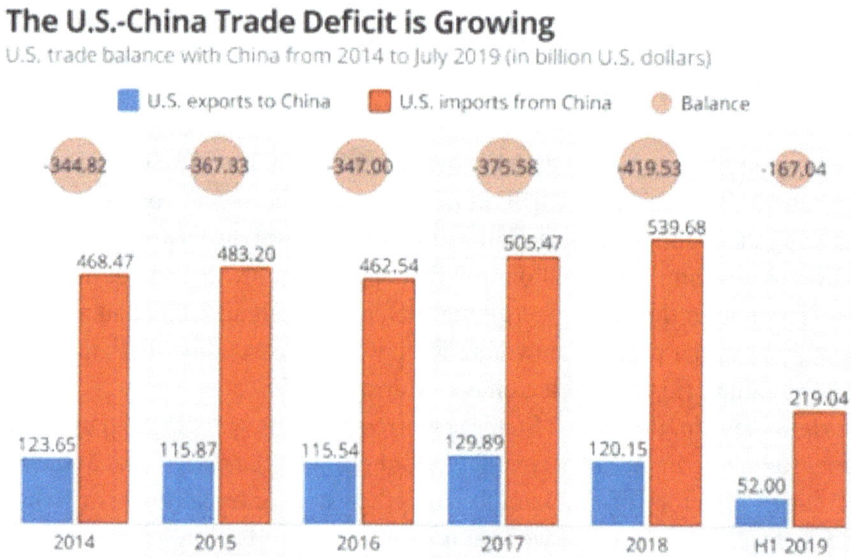

Source: Buchholz, 2019

Under the idea of neo-protectionism, the first Trump administration began to move from multilateralism to prioritizing bilateral relations.

Diagram 1 shows the process of trade war between these two countries in 2018 and 2019. In March 2018, the United States announced a tariff increase for Chinese aluminum and steel. As shown, this economic conflict brought a "ping-pong" of actions and reactions, where the United States concentrated on goods linked to industry and technology, while China focused on agricultural products and automobiles. However, one of the most critical points was the ban on Huawei in the United States. This issue not only had commercial implications, but also diplomatic ones, an example of this was the closure of the consulates in Houston and Chengdu, respectively, in 2020.

Figure 4. Trade War 2018-2019

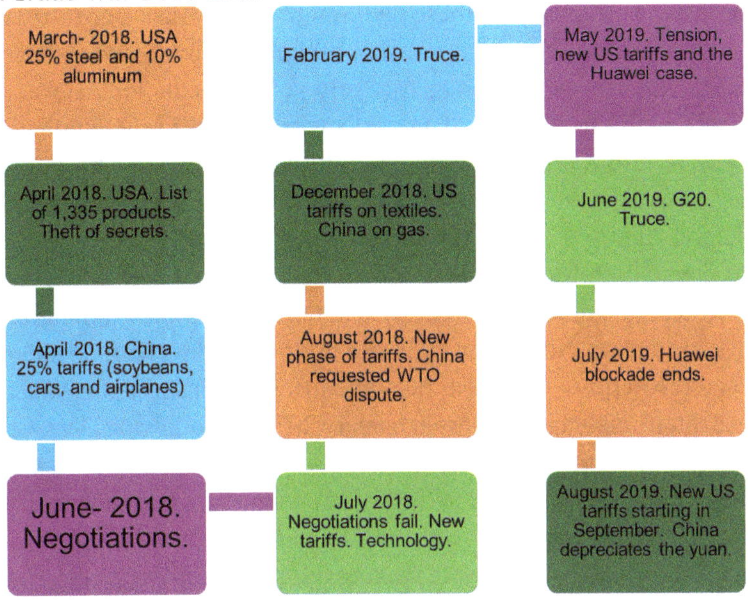

Source: León de la Rosa, 2019

The pandemic and the return of the Democrats to the government with Biden did not mean a détente in the relationship with China. For some scholars, this change did not mean a radical change in trade policy:

The Biden Administration has shown little interest, let alone leadership, in re-invigorating the deadlocked trade talks. However, disappointing the absence of a coherent U.S. international trade policy may be for proponents of liberalized trade, something more concerning lurks. The Biden Administration has continued, and at times expanded, Trump-era efforts to limit international trade, rather than promote it... The absence of U.S. leadership in trade (no trade policy), coupled with neo-protectionism (no trade policy), ultimately constitutes a continuation of the Trump-era trade tactics, even though the accompanying rhetoric by the Biden Administration is more polished (Schropp, 2022, p. 400).

Schoenbaum (2023) identifies seven elements in Biden's trade policy: (1) buy American; (2) tariffs; (3) World Trade Organization; (4) free trade agreements; (5) China; (6) technology; and (7) Russia. Throughout this mandate, several reforms were carried out that required work not only from the executive, but also from the legislature, in summary "economic and political confrontation with China now dominates American trade policy and actions" (Schoenbaum, 2023:124).

This change aligns with China's decoupling strategy. Authors agree that decoupling arises as a reaction to China's search for economic and technological autonomy based on the "Made in China 2025" (MIC2025) program. However, this also showed how interdependent the economies of these two countries are (Black & Morrison, 2021).

Unlike Trump, Biden's strategy was not initially oriented towards containment through tariffs but was focused on an escalation of the technological war (Wang & Hewett, 2021). In this technological war, it focused on limiting technological access to China for dual-use goods, mainly through the manufacture in China of American technology companies. This materialized with the enactment of the CHIPS and Science Act on August 9, 2022. Within this act, it is stated "Commerce must give priority to covered entities that support the resiliency of semiconductor supply chains for critical manufacturing industries in the United States" (Congress, 2022).

Trump's triumph in November 2024 did not mean a cessation of this position, as tariffs and restrictions on critical manufacturing continued until January 2025.

During Trump's inaugural address in January 2025, the following ideas were raised:

> *America will be a manufacturing nation once again, and we have something that no other manufacturing nation will ever have... we will revoke the electric vehicle mandate, saving our auto industry and keeping my sacred pledge to our great American autoworkers... Instead of taxing our citizens to enrich other countries, we will tariff and tax foreign countries to enrich our citizens... For this purpose, we are establishing the External Revenue Service to collect all tariffs, duties, and revenues. It will be massive amounts of money pouring into our Treasury, coming from foreign sources (The White House, 2025a).*

This speech was accompanied by the first executive orders, which identified the document entitled "*America First Trade Policy*". This document evokes as a precedent the strategy carried out during Trump's first term. Then, he emphasizes that "trade policy as a critical component to national security and reduced our Nation's dependence on other countries to meet our key security needs" (The White House, 2025b).

Throughout the document, a series of actions and instructions for secretaries are listed that are aimed at reviewing all U.S. trade policy to achieve the objective. One of the actions that makes securitization visible mentions:

> *The Secretary of State and the Secretary of Commerce, in cooperation with the heads of other agencies with export control authorities, shall review the United States export control system and advise on modifications in light of developments involving strategic adversaries or geopolitical rivals as well as all other relevant national security and global considerations. Specifically, the Secretary of State and the Secretary of Commerce shall assess and make recommendations regarding how to maintain, obtain, and enhance our Nation's technological edge and how to identify and eliminate loopholes in existing export controls -- especially those that enable the transfer of strategic goods, software, services, and technology to countries to strategic rivals and their proxies. In addition, they*

shall assess and make recommendations regarding export control enforcement policies and practices, and enforcement mechanisms to incentivize compliance by foreign countries, including appropriate trade and national security measures (The White House, 2025b).

All this has evolved into the reciprocal tariff system, which was launched on April 2, 2025. The following figure shows the formula designed by the American government to establish the percentages by country. It is worth mentioning that this formula has been criticized for its subjectivity and the lack of a clear basis for setting the percentages.

Figure 5. Reciprocal Tariffs Formula

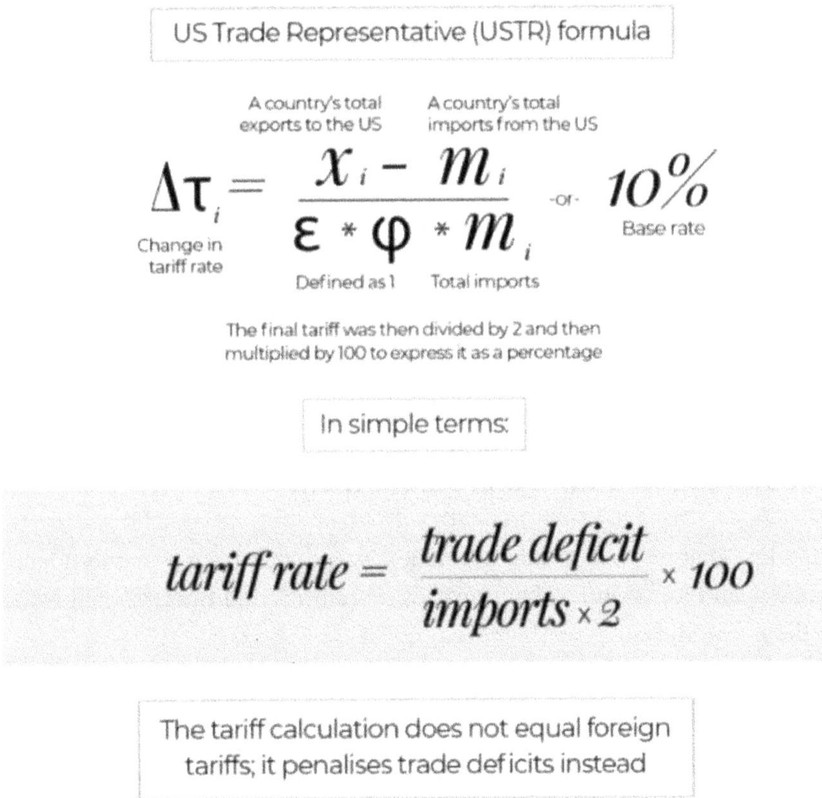

Source: Al Jazeera Staff, 2025

Donald Trump first became President of the United States in 2017. His campaign slogan, "America First," referred to the United States returning to its former glory. This statement acknowledged that the United States had lost its hegemonic position, and Trump believed the causes of this situation were the abuses of its trading partners and allies.

His populist rhetoric appealed to thousands of Americans who believed that the cause of the lack of jobs and money in their wallets was bad Democratic administrations, immigrants who stole their jobs, and abusive partners and allies. When Trump became president, he sought to fulfill his campaign promises, intensifying the confrontation with China, renegotiating the North American Free Trade Agreement, and pressuring NATO members to increase their military budgets. Trump sought reelection in 2020 but lost to Democratic candidate Joe Biden.

Trump's policies destroyed the United States' relationship with its allies and partners, so in his administration, Joe Biden sought to rebuild the relationship with his partners. One of the few things the Trump and Biden administrations had in common was maintaining a trade war with China. Despite an improving economy and weathering the COVID-19 pandemic, the Democratic Party failed to win the 2024 election, and Trump returned to power.

Trump's second term began on January 20, 2025, and in the first five months, he has maintained his populist agenda, toughened his immigration policy, attacked Iran, and reached a new trade agreement with China. But despite the efforts of Trump and Democratic Party presidents, the United States has failed to regain its hegemonic position.

It is important to identify the United States. trade policy to determine whether the decisions made in recent months have strengthened its centrality in the global trade network or whether they have merely mitigated its problem and continued its decline.

1.2 Securitization and neo protectionism

In the link that exists between the States, two dynamics are mainly identified, high politics and low politics. Dictionaries on politics and International Relations define them as follows:

..."high politics" generally refers to issues of vital importance and survival of the state, such as national and international security. This is in opposition to "low politics", which usually refers to secondary non-security issues such as economic policy and social policy (Brown, McLean, & McMillan, 2018).

Since the end of the last century, low politics has gained ground in the international arena, based on the economic interdependence proposed by Keohane and Nye (1987). However, the dynamics of the twenty-first century have allowed for reinterpretation of this division of politics and the prominence of high politics.

Therefore, the establishment of trade policy in international politics has led to an international scenario in which some states promote multilateralism, while others promote protectionism. The low politics of the last century promoted a multilateral system based on a series of institutions that built trade governance based on the World Trade Organization (WTO) and the promotion of free trade.

Joseph E. Stiglitz (2025) affirms that WTO trade regime was asymmetrical because the trade negotiations reflect power as much or more than economics, this is why the system is asymmetrical between developed and developing countries.

However, this has evolved with the transformation of actors within the international system. Yu mentions that:

increased competition in global markets and the emergence of new players in international trade negotiations, if economically less influential but actively involved in the geopolitical agenda, has resulted in trade policy being considered more in political studies (Yu, 2020: 31).

Ripsman (2006) argues that these two concepts are a false hierarchical dichotomy, since the events of the early twenty-first century changed this relationship through securitization. Therefore, economics is high politics under the following argument:

... when trade and investment flow freely across national boundaries, the opportunity costs of war in terms of economic exchange are so high as to make war an unattractive option. Furthermore, trade is more efficient than force as a means of extracting resources and wealth from territory, especially since nationalism and modern technology make conquest unprofitable in the contemporary era (Ripsman, 2006: 7)

This allows trade policy to be identified as a strategic policy that gives *status quo* to States in the twenty-first century. From this perspective, trade policy is strategic when "while it would not be beneficial to adopt it if the policies of all other countries were taken as given, adopting it may be beneficial if it caused other countries to change their trade policies" (Hashimzade, Myles & Black, 2016).

In a scenario where two countries fight to dominate the production of chips and green technologies the industrial policies have become tools for maintaining their comparative advantage. Industrial policies are defined as interventions by government to affect what is produced, how goods and services are produced, or where they are produced (Stiglitz, 2025).

The world system promoted by United States since the end of WWII look for construct some institutions that rule the interactions between countries. A global government where one of the goals of this system, but the problems confronted in the organization of the world system make that this kind of government until now doesn't exist.

Neoliberalism looks for a borderless world but the asymmetrical relationship between countries, the fight for the leadership of the world and the comeback of industrial policies has shown that our world is not ready for global government.

In this strategic vision of trade policy and the securitization of low politics, neo-protectionism appears. Panchenko and Reznikova say that:

Neo-protectionism aims to eliminate internal contradiction of liberalism, which is its duality: on the one hand, openness of the economy, non-interference of the state, on the other hand, simultaneously assumes already the fact that has taken place, the protection of the national producer and the growth of welfare in society. Such characteristics of liberalism as "spontaneous" and "intelligent" reflect its internal tension and self-denial. Therefore, "reasonable liberalism" and "reasonable protectionism" are the zone of interpenetration of opposites in one, according to O. Dovgal (Panchenko & Reznikova, 2017: 99-100).

The concept of securitization has been introduced into the economic sphere. Authors such as de Goede (2017) identify the relationship between security and the economy as a 21st-century trend embedded in International Political Economy. It also aligns with the idea that the securitization of the economy is related to "the deployment of money as a 'weapon of war' or the security role of financial institutions" (de Goede, 2017: 198).

In other words, this reorientation of countries' trade policies responds to the importance of legitimizing the discourse of free trade in trade governance and maintain competitiveness in the face of new actors and conditions of the system. Therefore, this can be identified as a soft version of protectionism that most states incur due to hyper globalization.

The combination of hyper globalization and securitization has impacted on the dynamics of supply and connectivity. For Liu (2025), this has generated a "pan-securitization" characterized by the integration of elements including security, economics, technology, environmental impact, access to resources, etc. Similarly, this makes the concept of security ambiguous and leads to a shift toward "nationalization" or "regionalization" through a power struggle mediated by discourse.

These changes are part of the effects of hyper globalization. One way to explain this is through Rodrik's Trilemma (2011), which emphasizes the incompatibility between the three facts in the international system at the same time, coexisting only by pairs. These facts are: (1) the nation-State, (2) democracy at the national level, and (3) economic globalization. Globalization and democratic politics result in global governance with a weak nation-State.

This situation has played against the United States' own agency of spaces of power in the international system. In addition to this, hyper globalization has also allowed the emergence and positioning of new actors, such as China. Returning to Rodrik's Trilemma, hyper globalization is rethought with factors such as the pandemic and its effects on the world economy, which evidenced economic dependence on China through the supply crisis. The result is a trend towards the combination of nation-state and democratic politics, which weakens globalization and thus the traditional idea of multilateralism and protectionism.

The arrival of a statesman like Trump with an extremely nationalist and conservative discourse promotes a return to a harsh vision of protectionism, which evokes the dynamics of the world economy of the first half of the twentieth century.

In response to these changes, Leonelli notes that “economic security has ultimately become an ‘embedded element of national security’... This trend is far from being reversed” (2025, p. 242). Furthermore, she identifies two types of trade securitization measures based on addressing strategic geopolitical and economic challenges. First, those vaguely related to national security, military, and defense issues in the narrow sense, which tend to be reactive. On the other hand, there are proactive measures, such as regulatory interventions.

Therefore, the securitization of low politics plus the effects of hyper globalization allow the emergence of hard protectionism based on the concept of trade war. The ongoing rivalry and competition between China and United States are related with their strength, ideological differences, changes in the international environment and domestical political influence (Wang, 2024).

The trade war is an economic conflict based on restrictive measures on international trade, such as tariffs, import quotas, or technical barriers. Where taxes and regulations protect a country's domestic economy. It is also an economic strategy, whose effects can be very negative if prolonged over time. Affecting the stability of global markets and international confidence. These wars become power struggles between economic powers (Carlomagno & Albagli, 2022).

1.3 Empirical impacts of the trade war

The following section proposes an analysis of the potential systemic impact of this protectionist environment. To this, statistical data on the trade balances of 37 global economies will be analyzed. The selection of these economies is based on the G20 group and additional economies from all regions of the world. With this, the empirical analysis proposes a global trade matrix, weighing exports and imports from 0 to 1 based on the percentage share of each trading partner. Using this data, a network analysis based on Granovetter's methodology will be conducted. This methodology aims to identify key economies within global value chains and global production networks. It will also examine the role of the United States in these global networks and the position of different regional blocs in international trade. This systemic network analysis will then be used to review the growth projections of the International Monetary Fund, comparing these projections with the network structure and tariff rates. This will lead to the examination of specific country case studies.

As already noted, in April 2025 the United States established a system of reciprocal tariffs. Table 1 on annexes shows the percentages imposed on the major economies of Europe and the Indo-Pacific.

Preliminarily, the most affected supply chains are divided as follows:

- China, Taiwan and Southeast Asia – electronics and technology
- European Union, United Kingdom, Japan and South Korea - automotive
- India and Switzerland - Pharmaceutical

To understand the international economic landscape in 2025, it is important to identify two key elements. First, international trade, to understand the economic interdependence of the world's major economies. Second, the International Monetary Fund's economic projections for 2025. These elements will help us understand the main economic implications of changes in American trade policy and the trade war scenario for the United States, Germany, China, India, Japan, and South Korea.

For the first element, Granovetter's network analysis methodology was used, with the purpose of grouping responses through matrices and weights based on trade exchange to determine the reach within the network, while centrality helps identify the node's strength (Granovetter, 1973). It is important to understand the scope of network analysis, which addresses diffusion, social mobility, political organization, and social cohesion (Granovetter, 1973). A second aspect to recognize in this tool is the strength of the ties within the network. Granovetter states that it is "the combination of length of time, emotional intensity, degree of trust, and reciprocity" (1973, p. 1361).

Regarding the strength of ties, Granovetter (1973) determines degrees of weakness or strength in the tie through a series of dual tie conditions, the relationship between A and B within the network, based on the number of members within the network:

1. Maximum when there are ties and they are strong.
2. Minimum when there are no ties or bonds.
3. Intermediate when there are ties, but they are weak.

Visually, Granovetter's social network theory can be represented as follows:

Figure 6. Networks And Weak Ties

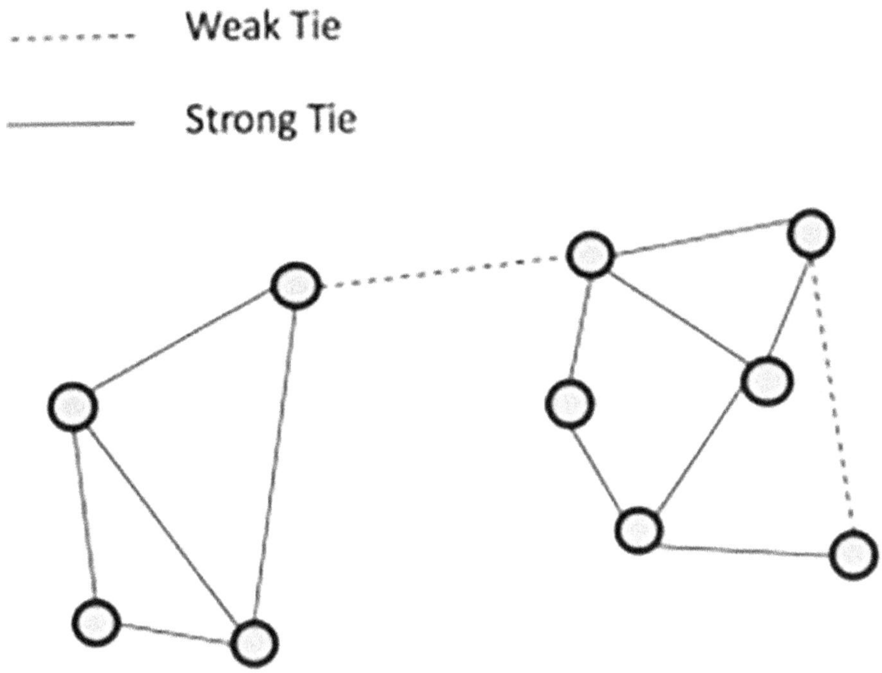

Source: Constantino & Nuñez, 2019

Therefore, these interactions can give rise to trios with varying degrees of attraction depending on the dual ties. However, the absence of trios creates a bridge, understood as "a line within the network that provides the only channel of communication between two points" (Harary, Norman & Cartwright cited in Granovetter, 1973, p. 1364). Thus, a bridge can be seen as a weak tie that plays an important role in the connectivity and flow of communication within the network.

Furthermore, members with higher centrality are more likely than other group members to maintain contacts outside the group (Langlois, cited in Granovetter, 1983). This is crucial for the application of this empirical study, as this position within the network will determine the extent of the impact of the tariff system imposed by Trump, particularly for economies that have a higher centrality than the United States.

The hyper-globalizing dynamic has generated interdependence between the world's main economies. In this scenario are the engines of Europe and the Indo-Pacific. The following networks show the centrality and trade connectivity between the world's major economies.

In exports, the network places Japan and China in a central place. This means that these two countries are the most important, as they have an important role in the placement of their products in different regions of the world. However, this network also allows us to see that Japan is the key node between the United States and China, that is, this country is highly sensitive to the trade war.

Figure 3 shows the formation of blocks and bonds. In purple is the European Union, where its position is closer to the United States and Japan than to China.

At the same time, it shows Germany and the United Kingdom as nodes of connection with the rest. In the case of the Indo-Pacific, it does not have as visible a place as in the case of the EU, two groups of nodes are identified. The first is made up of Japan, China, South Korea, India and Vietnam in green. The placement of the nodes shows that China is the center of this group, where Japan and India are more linked to the rest of the world than to the region itself. While Vietnam is very dependent on China, while South Korea is the node for the second Asian enclave.

The second group is identified in orange. Most of the ASEAN countries, Hong Kong, Taiwan, Australia, and New Zealand are seen here. Here Thailand is the key node connecting to the center of the network, but Malaysia is the node with the highest connectivity in this subgroup. A point that stands out is the peripheral location of some important economies such as Taiwan, Russia, Turkey, Indonesia, etc. This is explained by the high specialization of its exportable supply and/or the lack of diversification of trading partners with respect to export percentages.

Figure 7. Export Network Analysis by Regions

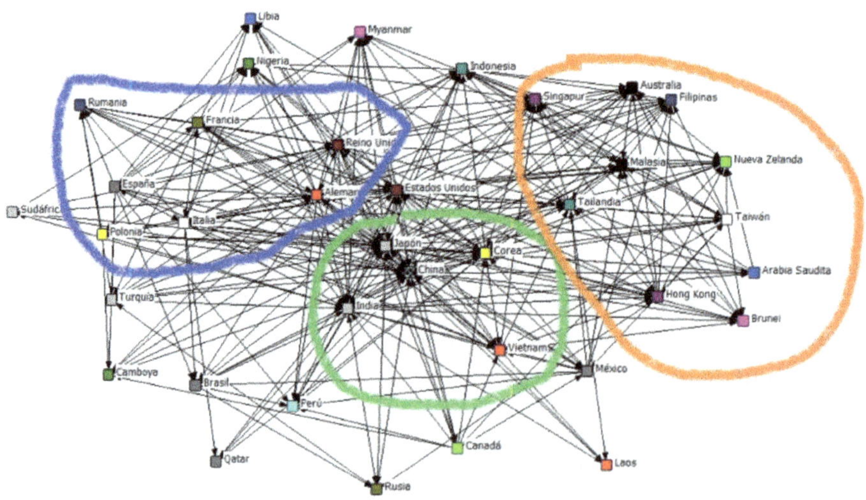

Source: Own elaboration based on OEC, 2024

In the import network, China is at the center and is understood by the deficit relations that a large part of the economies has with this country. With respect to the United States, China becomes the connection node for much of the network, as U.S. connectivity is limited to Canada, India, Mexico, Japan, Nigeria, and South Africa.

However, the identification of the two regions is very marked, as Germany and South Korea become the connecting nodes with each one. In purple is the EU. Here it is important to note that Germany is closer to China than to the United States, as well as the link between the United Kingdom and the main economies of the EU despite Brexit. On the other hand, in green, the importance of Japan and South Korea as connectivity nodes between China and the rest of the region is clearly observed. This also shows the dynamics of intra-industrial trade that has been generated in the region.

Figure 8. Import Network Analysis by Regions

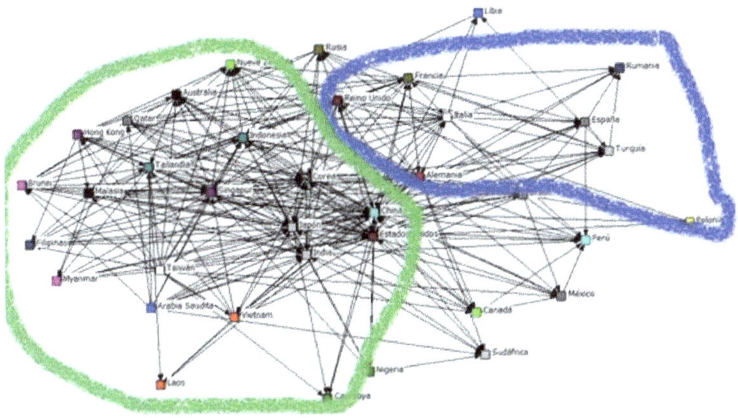

Source: Own elaboration based on OEC, 2024

In addition to these networks, the data released by the International Monetary Fund (IMF) in April 2025 are rescued. Within this report, the head of the IMF has stated that India and China will play an important role for this year. Below are the economic growth projections for this year and 2026 for the main economies. In red, the data that are linked to contractions in the economy and inflation indicators different from the trend that is marked in most of them are shown.

Table 2 on annexes shows a lot of red numbers in the economies of Southeast Asia; this is explained by network analysis. China is a key node with this region; the Chinese economic slowdown directly impacts these economies. Although India is growing, the lack of prominence in the export percentages in these economies means that there is no relationship that benefits this region. Economies such as Laos, Cambodia and Myanmar are the most affected due to their peripheral locations, type of exportable supply and lack of consolidation in the trading system. The cases of Taiwan and Vietnam are important.

Taiwan's slowdown responds to its place and high vulnerability amid the trade war between the United States and China. This is accentuated by the technological race between these three actors and the high specialization of the island's economy. In the case of Vietnam, its slowdown goes hand in hand with China's contraction due to post-pandemic nearshoring that intensified the economic link between the two countries.

In the case of the EU, its place in the GVC means that there is no considerable change. Regarding this region, it is important to note that 2024 was not a good year, mainly for Germany, and this has an impact on the entire region. Something similar is the case of Japan and the financial crisis it has experienced over the last year.

Regarding the expectation of the role of India and China, the inflation data is important, since India is the nodal economy that has the highest level projected, and China continues with its deflation scenario. This is a key moment to test how prepared both economies are based on their economic policies to achieve leadership in 2025.

On the other hand, it is also important to show that the United States does not present forceful changes in the short term.

2. CASE STUDIES

a) China

As mentioned above, the impact of the Chinese economy is significant for the entire network. This is due to the interdependence that the world's economy has with this power. However, one aspect to highlight is how this factor is important in the case of the United States, as over the last few years it has tried to intensify decoupling. According to Zhang, in the United States, "a bipartisan consensus on decoupling from China has emerged within the U.S. government, based on the assessment that China has become the greatest threat to American security and the most consequential strategic competitor for the coming decades" (2023, p. 254). So, this allows us to understand the multi-confrontation between Washington and Beijing, which responds to pan-securitization. At this point, decoupling is not a viable objective in the short term, as it would entail high costs for both parties.

At a technological level, it could impose significant restrictions on businesses and consumers, impacting innovation (Zhang, 2023). Similarly, it is important to note that both countries have developed strategies to address this potential decoupling. While the United States has focused on tariff and non-tariff measures, since 2015 China has launched the "Made in China 2025" plan.

Within this strategy, China has positioned itself at the economic level, while the traditional vision of security continues to be a key discourse for the positioning of the United States. However, the securitization of low politics has allowed a trade war that began in the first Trump administration and its continuity. Trump's return rescues the idea of a trade war.

In this second term, the trade war intensified with the system of reciprocal tariffs in April 2025. However, the first moment of truce came with the negotiation in Geneva on May 12, 2025. Prior to this agreement, the situation had resulted in percentages above 100% in tariffs on products from both countries. In the case of the United States, 145%, except for some electronic items, was accumulated for Chinese products, while Beijing had imposed a 125% tariff on American goods.

Within the agreements, a consultation commission was established to follow up on this situation. At the same time, the tariffs established by both sides were reorganized.

Out of the 34% tariffs announced by Washington in Executive Order 14257 of April 2, 2025, the Trump administration decided to withdraw 20%, leaving only 10%. However, it must be remembered that 20% already existed. For its part, Beijing decided to maintain only 10% of the total tariffs of the Announcement of the Customs Tariff Commission of the State Council No. 4 of 2025. These measures were agreed to be applied from May 14, with a duration of 90 days. Therefore, this joint statement shows a channel of dialogue between the two governments.

It is important to note that, within the commercial exchange between the two economies, the Chinese goods with the highest percentage of imports from the United States are electronic products for an approximate amount of 210 billion dollars; while China mainly imports soybeans and crude oil, for amounts of 15.2 billion dollars and 12.4 billion dollars respectively (OEC, 2024). These data represent an important factor why maintaining a tariff war in the long term did not necessarily represent a null impact on the U.S. economy.

The truce established by the Geneva agreement lasted only two weeks, as the trade conflict resumed after China announced a breach of the agreement by restricting U.S. access to rare earth minerals, and the US retaliated by prohibiting the export of semiconductor design software and AI chips. This type of action constitutes a reactive, defensive measure. However, this does not preclude proactive measures implemented during the Biden administration, such as the CHIPS and Science Act.

The evolution of the negotiations led to the London agreements of June 2025, in which China agreed to facilitate U.S. access to rare earth minerals and maintain the 10% tariff rate (down from 125%) on U.S. products in China, while Washington reduced its tariffs on Chinese goods from 145% to 30%. Based on Zhang, this negotiation process highlights the vulnerability of both economies to decoupling and protectionist measures.

Pan-securitization and the experience of Trump's first term have been factors for China to propose alternative initiatives to the institutional hegemony of the United States and the West. An example of this is the Belt and Road Initiative, which has allowed China greater autonomy to secure its supply chain and enhance its investments around the world, mainly in the countries of the Global South.

Regarding strategic sectors, in the relationship with the United States, technology is an area of triangulation and competition, and it is part of the pan-securitization of both sides. However, the "Made in China 2025" plan has allowed China to generate alternative scenarios regarding proactive measures. However, China is not totally decoupled from the world, but its main partners are in Asia Pacific, such as Japan, South Korea, Taiwan, Vietnam, Malaysia, among the most representative. At the same time, these partners play an important role for the United States at the geopolitical level.

Given this scenario, it is important for China to reaffirm:

- The vertical supply model of its new champion companies
- trade agreements with its main partners, such as the Regional Comprehensive Economic Partnership (RCEP)
- Gaining legitimacy through multilateralism and its global initiatives
- promote its new high-quality model inside and outside China

One Chinese advantage is its ability to plan for the long term, which has allowed it to generate a competitive infrastructure.

b) India

India has been an economy undergoing a particular emergence process. Throughout its history, it has maintained a position based on its geographic location, its neighbors, and superpowers. Such as its rapprochement with the USSR and its tense relation with China during the final decades of the 20th century. In the 21st century, the reorganization of the international system allowed India to align with the BRIC countries. However, this has not limited its ties with the United States. Given this, India has positioned as a U.S. pivot in the Indo-Pacific vision. Towards the second decade of the 21st century, the partnership between Modi and Obama paved the way for India to emerge as an alternative as a middle power from China and its commercial positioning. However, internal challenges prevented these two economies from competing *vis-a-vis*. Nevertheless, India continued its process like an emerging economy, specializing in certain sectors. Its main sectors are manufacturing, textiles, chemicals, automotive, and pharmaceuticals, with manufacturing contributing 13% of the national economy's GDP. New industries such as biotechnology, renewable energy, and aerospace have also developed (Santander Trade, 2024).

This scenario has allowed the Indian economy to become less interdependent on China. This is one of the reasons why the IMF views this economy as the most important by 2025. As a precedent, we can point to 2016, when China experienced a significant slowdown, growing below 7% annually, while India grew by 8.3% (World Bank, 2025). However, by 2017, China grew by 6.9% and India by 6.8%. Also, during the pandemic crisis, the sensitivity of the Indian economy was evident, when it contracted by -6% in 2020. This showed that India is not entirely immune to the effects of the Chinese slowdown.

Furthermore, India's limited international positioning in global production networks creates an inability to sustain the entire network of global value chains; something that China has achieved during this century. In the trade war scenario, the United States is India's main trading partner, accounting for 17.9% of its total trade; followed by the United Arab Emirates with 6.9%, the Netherlands with 4.9%, and China with 3.9%.

The main export product is refined petroleum, whose main buyer is the Netherlands. In sales to the United States, the main product is medicines, representing $9.9 billion. In the case of China, it is iron ore, representing $3.36 billion (OEC, 2024). The predominance of low-value-added goods in the export market limits India's ability to lead the global economy, especially when the trade war entails technological competition between the United States and China. At the same time, India has not strengthened its trade agreements. It's important to remember that India abandoned RCEP. This does not give it an advantage in a scenario of greater regionalization in the Asia-Pacific region.

c) Japan

The Japanese case is one of the most sensitive to the trade war. This country has experienced difficult times for its economy, having been decelerating for a decade, growing below 2% annually. The only time it grew more than 2% was the post-pandemic reopening, with 2.6%. This after a drop of -4.1%. (World Bank, 2025). Added to this landscape, it is the fall of the yen, a process that began in 2024 and will continue into 2025, as well as the outflow of portfolio investment.

At the trade level, vehicles are the most important, accounting for 15.3% of their exports. However, the electronics sector is the largest, with a value of $267 million; followed by the automotive sector with $180 million. Japan's main export partners are the United States and China, with 19.1% and 17.35%, respectively. In terms of value, Japan exports merchandise to the United States worth $141 billion, China $128 billion, South Korea $42.7 billion, Taiwan $42.1 billion, and Hong Kong $29.4 billion.

In the case of sales to the United States, these two sectors are the most representative. The automotive sector generates $52.7 billion, while electronics $52.4 billion. Regarding China, the main sales are to the electronics sector, with a value of $56.7 billion. In this area, it is worth noting that Japan provides part of the supply of semiconductor machinery and design. Comparing both countries, in the case of electronics, American demand is diverse and not linked to cutting-edge technology, a situation that is present with China and semiconductors. Similarly, it is important to highlight that the combined participation of East Asian countries exceeds that of the United States; this is reflected in the network analysis and reaffirms the linkage in electronics production. In this area, the common denominator is chips, with Japanese goods linked to the semiconductor supply chain valued at $44.58 billion (OEC, 2024). The semiconductor market is expected to grow by $1 trillion by 2030 (Vanguardia, 2023). Therefore, this supply has strategic potential for Japan.

In addition, it is important to note the trade displacement of the automotive combustion vehicle sector, which was controlled by Japan and Germany. In both cases, the rise of Chinese electric vehicles has been a significant blow, putting this Japanese commodity in jeopardy. The trade war has led the Japanese government to rethink its strategies and even approach South Korea and China in search of greater cooperation, such as the meeting of Trade Ministers of these countries on March 22, 2025.

Regarding the United States, the country's position as a buyer of Japanese products has already been mentioned. However, for the United States, this Asian economy is the fifth largest trading partner, with a trade value that represents a third of what it trades with its top three trading partners, which are Canada (14%), Mexico (13%), and China (8%). However, an important point beyond trade is the issue of U.S. debt bonds. The most recent data indicates that 25% of U.S. debt bonds are in foreign hands. The European bloc made up of Luxembourg, Ireland, Belgium, and France holds $1.83 trillion dollars, followed by Japan with $1.12 trillion dollars, and China and Hong Kong with $1.05 trillion dollars (Álvarez, 2025). In short, Japan is the country with the largest holdings; however, this has been diminishing with the fall of the yen and the behavior of the financial market.

d) South Korea

Regarding South Korea, its outlook is like Japan's, as its main trading partners are China (25.1%) and the United States (18.3%). Furthermore, electronics and the automotive sector are strategic sectors for this economy. However, in the Korean case, electronics represent more than a third of its exportable supply, with a value of $288 million. Within this, semiconductors are the main product in this sector, with a value of $134 million and represent 20.8%. Of this, $65.6 million corresponds to semiconductors purchased by China. Vehicles represent 10%, with a value of $64.8 million. The United States purchases $31.3 million worth of Korean vehicles, making it the main product imported from this country (OEC, 2024).

In this sense, the triangle between China, South Korea, and Japan reaffirms the importance of the semiconductor technology industry. South Korea has positioned itself in the design and manufacturing process. In the design process, the United States leads this part of the semiconductor supply chain. However, manufacturing is a key point in the supply chain, monopolized by Taiwan through TSMC, accounting for 63% of global manufacturing. However, South Korea ranks second in manufacturing with 19% of global production, making Samsung its largest company. Japan ranks third with 17% of global manufacturing.

In the case of automobiles, the landscape is complex regarding the competition with Chinese combustion and electric vehicle companies. At the same time, the tariffs imposed by the United States primarily impact this sector. Although tariffs on South Korea were paused for 90 days, the escalating conflict with China has affected Korean exports. According to the South Korean Ministry of Industry and Trade, exports declined 1.3% from the same month last year to $57.27 billion due to the trade war (Reuters, 2025). However, chip demand has been a lightning rod in this complex landscape for other Korean industries.

3. GLOBAL IMPLICATIONS

Based on theoretical implications, network analysis, and case studies, this section focuses on three aspects: the geopolitical effects on regional level, the challenges to global trade governance, and the sustainability in this trade-technology war.

3.1 Geopolitical Effects on Regional Level

The phenomenon discussed in this chapter has geoeconomic and geopolitical implications. However, as mentioned earlier, the U.S.'s pan-securitization strategies against China have a geopolitical scope, with a clear purpose that is being technological decoupling. The race for technological self-sufficiency between Washington and Beijing is complicated because of the supply chain of dual-use products. In this sense, the repercussions are not limited to these economies, those are extended to all countries involved in the supply chain.

The traceability of these supply chains creates a landscape of supply chain securitization, which implies access to strategic resources, labor, and, in some cases, relocation. In this regard, China maintains an advantage through the Belt and Road Initiative (BRI) corridors, leveraging its technological positioning and connectivity to access resources and markets. On the U.S. side, decoupling has led efforts to force the return of supply chain processes, primarily manufacturing, to the United States. An example of this is Washington's pressure on TSMC to manufacture semiconductors within its territory.

On the regional level, some areas become strategic while others do not. The export network, tariff rates, and IMF projections help explain this. The group of countries included in the RCEP+ India possess strategic resources such as minerals in Oceania, high-quality human talent in Southeast Asia, innovation hubs in East Asia and India, and over 50 years of continuous intra-industry trade, which has fostered expertise and cultural understanding on business. This is further strengthened by the recent rapprochement between India and China at the Shanghai Cooperation Organization Summit in Tianjin in August 2025. Despite the military challenges China faces in the region, Beijing has strengthened its lobbying efforts throughout the region, reaffirming it as a natural sphere of influence.

This is confirmed by the IMF's projections, which indicate that the Indo-Pacific will continue to be the engine of global economic growth. Similarly, the reciprocal tariff system shows discrimination among the countries in the region. Tariffs above 40% are imposed on the least developed economies, except for China. At the same time, given the isolation this implies for Taiwan, the tariff system has become the main coercive measure used by Washington against Taipei. In August 2025, Trump confirmed the "provisional" 20% tariff for the island. The negotiation between Lai Ching-te and Donald Trump has been asymmetrical, since the potential war in the Taiwan Strait is the factor that limits Lai's negotiating power justified by the importance of American assistance in case of an invasion. This has indirectly become a straitjacket for Taiwanese technology companies.

In the case of Europe, the peace process in Ukraine following the Alaska summit between Putin and Trump has placed them in a disadvantageous position with the announcement to reduce military aid on the border with Russia. Washington's interference in Europe involves a "neutral" discourse regarding Russia, but an aggressive stance regarding Europe's ties with China. This has resulted in a predicament for Brussels; it has sought to limit the entry of Chinese products into its territory, but the United States does not present itself as the ally Europeans expect. The result has been a "neutral" position.

This political context does not slow down the industrial and technological shift that large European companies are experiencing. The export network reaffirms the segmentation of the economies of the European Union and its closeness to the United States. This is reflected in the percentage that European exports to the United States represent, as well as a moderate tariff in the reciprocal system. The import network, on the other hand, reaffirms the dependence on China and how this generates weak links within the European Union subsystem. The IMF's projection table confirms this predicament with lower growth rates and a slowdown for economies such as France, Italy, and Germany.

The cases of Latin America, Western Asia, and Africa illustrate their continued role as suppliers of natural resources. Unlike the Indo-Pacific region, these areas have not managed to develop a complementary economic ecosystem that harmonizes intra-industry trade dynamics. This is evident in the two network diagrams. The export network shows a fragmented pattern across these regions, while the import network further isolates Western Asia and leaves Latin American and African countries as weak links. The IMF (2025) projects growth of 2.2% for Latin America, 3.4% for Western Asia, and 4% for Sub-Saharan Africa. This can be interpreted based on the resources each region possesses, the geopolitical and military influence of the United States, and China's presence through technological cooperation or mechanisms such as the BRI.

Latin America is a sphere of U.S. influence, which China has fragmented. However, this region is also the one that experiences the most securitization efforts from Washington. Examples of this include the war on drugs in Mexico, visa and immigration restrictions in Central America, and the potential intervention in Venezuela. During the Trump administration, Latin America is the only region where U.S. military force was deployed. These actions have become alternative mechanisms to reaffirm the Monroe Doctrine and limit China's presence through the BRI. Mexico's case is unique, as it is a member of the USMCA and highly dependent on exports to the United States. Therefore, maintaining a truce with the U.S. is vital for the Mexican government.

Regarding Western Asia, the resolution of the conflict in Palestine will be a determining factor in the region. However, Trump's stance on this has been close to that of Israel. This limits the region's potential to leverage its hydrocarbon resources. This does not mean that ties with China do not exist, but the conflict in Palestine poses a challenge to the continuity of the corridors promoted by Beijing. This is reinforced by China's condemnation of Benjamin Netanyahu's plan to control Gaza.

Africa has the best growth prospects. This can be explained by the China factor. Beyond China's immediate sphere of influence in Asia, Africa has been the most receptive region to Chinese presence in the 21st century. The result is the intensification of cooperation in infrastructure and technology through the Forum on China-Africa Cooperation (FOCAC). This is related to the strategic resources this continent possesses, including rare earth minerals. The countries with reserves include Madagascar, Burundi, South Africa, Tanzania, Angola, Malawi, Namibia, and Morocco. According to the organization In on Africa (2025), "Africa will produce 10% of the world's supply of rare earth minerals by 2030". Something that the trade war has highlighted is the importance of having access to these critical minerals.

3.2 Challenges to Global Trade Governance

The trade war has highlighted how these phenomena require immediate action, and that often the institutions that oversee trade activity are unable to resolve these types of disputes.

In August 2018, China initiated a dispute at the WTO. In this new phase, China filed a lawsuit against the United States at the WTO in February and April 2025, challenging the imposition of reciprocal tariffs on its trading partners, arguing that they violated WTO rules and undermined multilateral trade.

According to the WTO (2025), the process for the first complaint in 2018 took two years to be resolved. After the Appellate Body issued its report on October 26, 2020, the United States appealed. From 2018 to date, China has filed 12 complaints against the United States at the WTO, including DS471 for anti-dumping practices, DS543 for tariff measures, DS615 for semiconductor measures, and DS638 for additional universal and country-specific duties. In the case of the United States, there have been 5 complaints against China at the WTO since 2018. Regarding the current status of these disputes, most involve appeals or objections to the reports of the dispute settlement panels.

Of the complaints listed, the one filed by China in 2025, arguing that the "additional universal and country-specific duties on imports" violate the GATT, is a turning point, as the system of reciprocal tariffs challenges trade institutions and agreements.

Similarly, this raises questions about the trade agreements signed by the United States, particularly the USMCA. The review of this agreement was scheduled for 2026; however, Trump's trade policy has been a factor in moving it forward to September 2025. This process between the United States, Canada, and Mexico will be important in setting a precedent regarding Washington's stance on other agreements. This will primarily dispel the notion that the United States prefers bilateral agreements over multilateral ones.

This scenario could open new avenues for China's global initiatives under the concept of a "Global Community of Shared Future." By September 2025, China has proposed initiatives in the areas of security, development, dialogue among civilizations, artificial intelligence, and global governance. The underlying principles of these proposals are cooperation and multilateralism.

3.3 Sustainability and the Trade-Technology War

The trade and technology war between China and the United States reveals two distinct models of industrialization and resource allocation.

On one hand, the United States is pursuing reshoring and industrialization based on fossil fuels. This model emulates the approach followed by the country in the last century and disregards agreements on the impact of climate change. Trump's inaugural address emphasized the importance of oil and practices such as fracking. Similarly, the White House has limited federal programs that promote clean energy. One example is the elimination of tax credits for imported biofuels.

According to the IEA (2025), the growth in U.S. crude oil and natural gas production will remain relatively high until 2030 due to increased U.S. exports of petroleum products and liquefied natural gas.

On the other hand, China's model reaffirms its commitment to agreements on decarbonization and climate change. China aims to achieve carbon neutrality by 2060. To achieve this, Beijing is promoting new industries within the "Made in China 2025" plan and its high-quality development model. These industries focus on developing innovations in new energy vehicles, new materials, power equipment, and agricultural equipment, all aimed at achieving energy and material sources with a low environmental impact. This transition also aligns with initiatives like the Belt and Road Initiative (BRI), which is now oriented towards sustainability.

Regarding its industrialization model, self-sufficiency is a key factor for China. Unlike the United States, its focus is not on reshoring but on securing access to raw materials and reorganizing the supply chain. However, a characteristic of Chinese companies is their vertical integration of the supply chain to control every stage of the production process, from raw materials to final sales.

Currently, both countries are in a transitional phase towards achieving energy, technological, and economic self-sufficiency.

4. CONCLUSION

The evolution of the U.S. economy is linked to internal and external factors that result in a trade policy based on protectionism and securitization. The administration of Donald Trump has managed to institutionalize a series of mechanisms aimed at decoupling the American economy from the rest of the world, primarily from China. One of the results is the system of reciprocal tariffs, which impacts the entire dynamics of international trade.

It is also important to reaffirm what some academics point out about technology as the core of the confrontation between these two countries. At the same time, this factor reinforces the continuity of the securitization of the economy and places high-tech goods as elements of high politics in the 21st century.

Network analysis shows that the United States does not have an absolute role in the trade dynamics of the post-pandemic world. However, due to the interconnectedness generated by globalization, Washington has an influence where some economies are more vulnerable than others. It also shows that inputs linked to the supply chain of technological goods are a strategic area for America's trade policy. Within this context, the role of the Indo-Pacific economies is important for the future of the international trade structure, primarily East Asia. Other regions are also affected. However, empirical analysis shows that their position in export and import networks, along with their trade orientation, creates limitations. In the case of Europe, it is challenged by technological innovation from Asia. While Africa, West Asia, and Latin America are limited by their specialization in natural resources. This complex scenario has allowed China to position itself through mechanisms such as the BRI.

The trade policy based on "America First" not only has operational implications but also institutional implications for global trade governance and the future of free trade agreements. In addition, on the political scene, the radicalization of the discourse from Washington allows for the reconfiguration of alliances or closer ties between countries, this is the case of India with the rest of the Asia-Pacific region.

One of the important points of this research is to recognize two models with different orientations for their integration into the dynamics of international trade, represented by the United States and China. This paper also serves as a prelude to future research, such as the reshaping of the Indo-Pacific region, the sustainability of the current trade governance system, and the implications of Trump's trade policies for the technological race and climate change.

REFERENCES

Al Jazeera Staff. (April 9, 2025). *Penguins, vaccines: Can negotiations save Trump's oddest tariff targets?* https://www.aljazeera.com/news/2025/4/8/penguins-vaccines-can-negotiations-save-trumps-oddest-tariff-targets

Álvarez, J. P. (April 23, 2025). *Mercado de bonos: ¿quiénes son los principales tenedores extranjeros de la deuda estadounidense? Bloomberg en línea.* https://www.bloomberglinea.com/mundo/estados-unidos/mercado-de-bonos-quienes-son-los-principales-tenedores-extranjeros-de-la-deuda-estadounidense/#:~:text=Actualmente%2C%20los%20principales%20tenedores%20extranjeros,deuda%2C%20distribuida%20en%20distintos%20estamentos

Black, J., & Morrison, A. (2021). The Strategic Challenges of Decoupling. *Harvard Business Review.* https://hbr.org/2021/05/the-strategic-challenges-of-decoupling

Brown, G. W., McLean, I., & McMillan, A. (2018). *The concise Oxford dictionary of politics and international relations.* Oxford University Press. DOI: 10.1093/acref/9780199670840.001.0001

Buchholz, K. (August 19, 2019). *The U.S.-China Trade Deficit is Growing [Digital image].* https://www.statista.com/chart/15419/the-us-trade-balance-with-china/

Carlomagno, G., & Albagli, E. (2022). Trade wars and asset prices. *Journal of International Money and Finance, 124,* 102631. DOI: 10.1016/j.jimonfin.2022.102631

Congress. (2022). *H.R.4346 - CHIPS and Science Act.* https://www.congress.gov/bill/117th-congress/house-bill/4346

Constantino, S., & Nuñez, S. (2019). *Networks, Weak Ties, and Thresholds.* https://www.phenomenalworld.org/interviews/networks-weak-ties-and-thresholds/

De Goede, M. (2017). Chains of securitization. *Finance and Stochastics, 3*(2), 197–207. DOI: 10.2218/finsoc.v3i2.2579

Federal Reserve History. (2025). Subprime Mortgage Crisis. https://www.federalreservehistory.org/essays/subprime-mortgage-crisis#:~:text=The%20subprime%20mortgage%20crisis%20of%202007%2D10%20stemmed,was%20facilitated%20by%20rapidly%20rising%20home%20prices.&text=When%20house%20prices%20peaked%2C%20mortgage%20refinancing%20and,rates%20began%20rising%20for%20lenders%20and%20investors

Fiscal Data. (2025). The Causes of Deficits and Surpluses. https://fiscaldata.treasury.gov/americas-finance-guide/national-deficit/#:~:text=The%20federal%20government%20has%20spent%20$1.36%20trillion,(FY)%202025%2C%20resulting%20in%20a%20national%20deficit.&text=While%20revenue%20increased%20during%20the%20COVID%2D19%20pandemic%2C,health%20care%20caused%20spikes%20in%20the%20deficit

Granovetter, M. (1973). The Strength of Weak Ties. *American Journal of Sociology, 78*(6), 1360–1380. DOI: 10.1086/225469

Granovetter, M. (1983). The strength of weak ties: A network theory revisited. *Sociological Theory, 1*, 201–233. DOI: 10.2307/202051

Hashimzade, N., Myles, G., & Black, J. (2016). *A dictionary of economics.* Oxford University Press.

IEA. (2025). *Today in Energy.* https://www.eia.gov/todayinenergy/detail.php?id=65724

IMF. (2025). *World Economic Outlook Database.* https://www.imf.org/en/Publications/WEO/weo-database/2025/april

InOnAfrica. (2025). *The growing importance of rare earth minerals in African mining.* https://www.inonafrica.com/2025/02/11/the-growing-importance-of-rare-earth-minerals-in-african-mining/

Keohane, R. O., & Nye, J. S.Jr. (1987). Power and Interdependence revisited. *International Organization, 41*(4), 725–753. DOI: 10.1017/S0020818300027661

Lau, S. (2025). The 'American Empire' is fast declining. https://www.chinadailyhk.com/upload/main/pdf/2025/03/17/6667fb923456514ae6fa600bc4ce1fb3.pdf

León de la Rosa, R. I. (2019). *Guerra comercial China- Estados Unidos.* XVII Jornadas de Comercio UPAEP.

Levin Center. (2025). Portraits in Oversight: Congress and the Enron Scandal. https://levin-center.org/what-is-oversight/portraits/congress-and-the-enron-scandal/#:~:text=The%20Rise%20and%20Fall%20of,company%20stopped%20paying%20its%20bills

Liu, Z. (2025). The "Pan-Securitization" of the EU's Connectivity Policy and China–EU Cooperation. In Xiang, G., Gouliamos, K., Zuokui, L., & Kassimeris, C. (Eds.), *The Belt and Road Initiative.*, DOI: 10.1007/978-981-96-1128-7_13

OEC. (2024). *Trade data.* https://oec.world/es

Panchenko, V., & Reznikova, N. (2017). From protectionism to neo-protectionism: New dimensions of liberal regulation. *Information Economics and Policy*, (2), 91–111.

Peterson, D. M., & Murray, E. Lori. (2025). The Debt Crisis is Here. https://www.pgpf.org/programs-and-projects/convening-experts/expert-views/fiscal-commission/the-debt-crisis-is-here/

Reuters. (2025). *South Korea exports fall as tariffs hit US, China shipments.* https://www.reuters.com/world/china/south-korea-exports-fall-tariffs-hit-us-china-shipments-2025-06-01/

Ripsman, N. M. (2006). *False dichotomies: Why economics is high politics.* Concordia University. https://www.files.ethz.ch/isn/22143/Ripsman.pdf

Rodrik, D. (2011). *The globalization paradox: why global markets, states, and democracy can't coexist.* Oxford University Press.

Schoenbaum, T. J. (2023). The Biden Administration's Trade Policy: Promise and Reality. *German Law Journal*, *24*(1), 102–124. DOI: 10.1017/glj.2023.7

Schropp, S. (2022). Biden and Trade: No Trade Policy, No-Trade Policy or Both? *Inter Economics*, *57*(6), 399–400. DOI: 10.1007/s10272-022-1094-x

Stiglitz, Joseph E. (2025);Industrial Policy and the New Protectionism. (2025)... *Journal of Policy Modeling*, *47*, 708–722. https://www.sciencedirect.com/science/article/abs/pii/S0161893825000572?via%3Dihub. DOI: 10.1016/j.jpolmod.2025.06.007

The White House. (2017). *The Inaugural Address.* https://trumpwhitehouse.archives.gov/briefings-statements/the-inaugural-address/

The White House. (2025a). *The Inaugural Address.* https://www.whitehouse.gov/remarks/2025/01/the-inaugural-address/

The White House. (2025b). *America First Trade Policy.* https://www.whitehouse.gov/presidential-actions/2025/01/america-first-trade-policy/

Trade, S. (2024). *India: Política y economía.* https://santandertrade.com/es/portal/analizar-mercados/india/politica-y economia#:~:text=Sus%20principales%20sectores%20son%20el,(13%25%20del%20PIB)

Vanguardia. (2023). Taiwán, la perla del Indo-Pacífico. *Vanguardia Dossier*, 58. https://shopping.lavanguardia.com/taiwan-la-perla-del-indo-pacifico.html

Wang, J. (2024). The Logic of China – US Rivalry. China International Strategy Review. Volume 6. 1 – 8. 23 May 23 2024. https://link.springer.com/article/10.1007/s42533-024-00157-6

Wang, J., & Hewett, D. Y. (2021). U.S.-China Trade Relations in the Biden Era: Trade War, Industrial Policy, and Rule-Based International Order. *Proceedings of the ASIL Annual Meeting, 115*, 315–320. DOI: 10.1017/amp.2021.127

World Bank. (2025). *Data*. https://datos.bancomundial.org/

World Bank Group. (2025). GDP growth (annual %) - China https://data.worldbank .org/indicator/NY.GDP.MKTP.KD.ZG?locations=CN

WTO. (2025). *Chronological list of disputes cases*. https://www.wto.org/english/tratop_e/dispu_e/dispu_status_e.htm

Yu, T. O. (2020). Theoretical concepts of trade policy development and analysis: Evolution and modern challenges in the context of the international trading system transformation. *Вестник Санкт-Петербургского университета. Ekonomika (Nis)*, *36*(1), 27–48.

Zhang, K. H. (2023). U.S.-China Economic Links and Technological Decoupling. *Chinese Economy*, *56*(5), 353–365. DOI: 10.1080/10971475.2023.2173399

APPENDIX

Table 1. Reciprocal tariffs in European and Indo-Pacific economies

Country	% of US imports	Main Product
Cambodia: 49%	0.41	Semiconductor devices
Laos: 48%	**0.01**	**Optical fibers and bundles**
Vietnam: 46%	3.92	Broadcasting equipment
Myanmar: 45%	0.03	Trunks and cases
China: 34%+ 20%= 54%	14.5	Broadcasting equipment
Thailand: 37%	1.95	Office machines parts
Indonesia: 32%	0.93	Electrical machinery
Taiwan 32%	2.85	Office machines parts/ Computers
India: 26%	2.85	Packaged medicaments
Japan: 24%	4.7	Cars
South Korea 25%	3.93	Cars
Malaysia: 24%	1.5	Integrated circuits
Brunei: 24%	0.009	Cyclic Hydrocarbons
Singapore	1.1	Vaccines
Philippines: 18%	0.44	Office machines parts
United Kingdom 10%	1.99	Cars
European Union 20%	16.77	Cars/Vaccines
Switzerland 32%	1.5	Packaged medicaments

Source: Own elaboration based on OEC, 2024.

Table 2. Growth projections 2024, 2025 and 2026

Country	2024%	2025%	2026%	Inflation % 2025
EU	1.11	1.15	1.47	2.36
France	1.06	.64	1.01	1.29
Italy	0.72	0.44	0.83	1.7
Germany	-0.23	-0.05	0.92	2.08
Japan	0.08	0.55	0.57	2.36
United Kingdom	1.1	1.07	1.4	3.1
United States	2.79	1.82	1.74	2.9

continued on following page

Table 2. Continued

Country	2024%	2025%	2026%	Inflation % 2025
Australia	1.03	1.63	2.07	2.5
Brunei	3.9	2.5	2.64	1
Cambodia	6.01	4	3.4	1
China	5	3.9	3.9	-0.02
South Korea	2.02	1.02	1.44	1.83
India	6.4	6.1	6.2	4.2
Indonesia	5	4.6	4.6	1.6
Laos	4.2	2.5	1.9	9.3
Malaysia	5.1	4.1	3.8	2.4
Myanmar	-1.12	1.9	2.05	30
New Zealand	-.48	1.37	2.7	2.01
Philippines	5.69	5.4	5.7	2.6
Thailand	2.5	1.8	1.6	0.69
Taiwan	4.29	2.85	2.49	1.7
Vietnam	7.09	5.15	4.04	2.94

Source: Own elaboration based on IMF, 2025.

Chapter 15
The Dynamics of Global Trade Under Protectionism and Populism:
A Comparative Study of United States and India

Safa Ahmad
https://orcid.org/0009-0008-3643-259X
Aligarh Muslim University, India

ABSTRACT

Two of the world's largest democracies United States and India have a robust and progressing trade partnership, which has deepened over the years. This paper investigates the evolving dynamics of their global trade under the influence of protectionism and populism. In recent years both the countries are focusing more on their national interests and economic self reliance, rather than heavily relying on global trade or free market globalisation. However there is an increased skepticism towards liberal economic globalisation, because both the nations have witnessed drastic political and economic shifts driven by the populist leaders and their strategic directives. This research takes on a comparative approach on exploring the political economy of both the nations. This study underlines how domestic political narratives shape international trade participation, through scrutinizing key trade policies, institutional rhetoric and economic data related to the shifts in government both India (from 2014-2024) and U.S (from 2018-2024).

DOI: 10.4018/979-8-3373-3835-4.ch015

1. INTRODUCTION

Post the Cold War period, the World Trade Organisation (WTO) emerged as an umbrella institution for rules-based trade, indicating a triumph for liberal economic nations who were willing to evolve and globalize their economies. Most of the states reformed their stringent policies and attitude towards trading globally. However, the first decade of the 21st century has seen a noticeable realignment. With globalization pushbacks, displacement of jobs and escalating economic disparity have surged along with resentment in democratic nations leading the rise in populist and protectionist ideologies.

India and the United States both have sought to the same path of protecting and promoting their local trade but right after the Cold War both the countries had a different political stance. While the U.S. emerged as the sole superpower and chief advocator of economic liberalization and globalization themselves India was still recovering from the political instability and severe balance of payment crisis in 1991, though it shifted itself from a quasi-socialist restricted economy to liberalized, market-oriented economy. Aftermaths of the Cold War saw a steady evolution from hesitant trade partners into strategic economic collaborators, underpinned by India's gradual liberalization and America's push for market access. Both the states have advocated economic cooperation, they have also resorted to populist and protectionist reflexes in response to global disruptions, showcasing the growing disquiet with the volatility of liberal globalization.

Protectionist and Populist policies are not mere anomalies in liberal order but a projection of systematic shift in global trade governance. The resurgence of these policies in the 21st century have contested the foundations of global liberal globalization.

Populism broadly defined as a political ideology that divides the society into two antagonistic groups: the "pure people" versus the "corrupt elite" (Mudde and Rovira Kaltwasser, 2017). This narrative is measured not only as a political force but as a prominent economic influence specifically on trade policy. Economic populism often translates itself to redistributive and nationalistic policies targeting guarding domestic trade and populations from unforeseen global threats. Protectionism on the other hand, talks about restricting international trade to favor domestic industries, typically through tariffs, import quotas or regulatory barriers (Bown & Irwin, 2020). The traditional forms of protectionism were deeply in mercantilism and progressive state strategies; the contemporary forms are guided by populist politics, where world trade is blamed for job displacement, economic disparity and deindustrialization.

Within this framework, the United States and India hold a prominent position. They have adopted increasingly protectionist stances under populist regimes sculpted by discrete historical and developmental frameworks. India under Narendra Modi post

2014 has exhibited a shift towards economic nationalism, spearheaded by initiatives like "Make in India" and "Atmanirbhar Bharat" (Self-Reliant India), designed to minimize import dependency and promote indigenous industrial growth. Likewise, The U.S. under Donald Trump (2016-2020), pushed the policy of "America First" doctrine that itself paved the path for tariff wars along with the renegotiation of trade agreements and a general skepticism towards multilateral corporations.

While the U.S. has consistently maintained itself at the forefront of global governance, India has positioned itself as a traditional player in the arena of international trade but now has strikingly carved itself out as the voice of Global South, advocating for fairer trade regulations for developing countries. The recent retreat from both nations signals a growing cynicism of liberal trade orthodoxy, such as U.S. withdrawal from the Trans-Pacific Partnership (TPP) and India's decision to exit the Regional Comprehensive Economic Partnership (RCEP). These withdrawals would cast doubts on the durability and future of global trade governance and challenge the resilience of multilateral organizations, on how to adopt the evolving geopolitical and economic pressure.

Unlike purely economic analysis this paper will explore and examine the interplay between populism and protectionism has shaped both the countries and how the future holds under the age of these protectionist policies, it situates trade policies within its political context arguing that trade decisions under populist regimes are deeply influenced by domestic narratives, identity politics and electoral calculations of sovereignty and Self Reliance.

The importance of this study lies in its comparative lens by comparing U.S. and India two democracies at divergent trajectories of economic development but demonstrate a comparable resonance with populist rhetoric's. The chapter uncovers both the convergences and divergences in protectionist behaviour of trade. It will also talk about the broader repercussions of such shifts in global supply chains with the investing confidence and the normative theory of Authority built in institutions like WTO.

To be able to achieve this, this paper will employ a qualitative comparative methodology, seeking assistance from primary data available on primary policy documents, official speeches, trade data and secondary academic literature. Key focus would remain on global trade war (although tariffs also extended to key allies including Canada, Mexico and the European union), the reformulation of NAFTA into USMCA, India's tariff policy changes and its pullout from regional trade frameworks. It will contribute to the comprehension of the political underpinnings of economic policy in a world increasingly shaped by nationalism and populism. It further also provides a criticism that while protectionism may offer short term political gains and appeal to domestic constituencies, it carries long-term risking the trade fragmentation of weakened political and institutional cooperation providing diplomatic friction, infused with non-compliant persistent tendencies of a state potentially making it difficult for them to shed this label in future.

The financial crisis of 2008 globally turned the course of events projecting and exposing the vulnerabilities in the liberal economic order and increasing public dissatisfaction. As Rodrik (2011) argued in the Globalization Paradox, the mismatch between global economic integration and national level political accountability fosters what he calls a "trilemma" – a nation can't simultaneously maintain deep globalization, national sovereignty and democratic politics.

The disgruntlement shaped ground for populist leaders specifically in the Global North to embrace protectionist policies and challenge global alliances. In the United States, the Trump Administration's "America First" approach marked a clear departure from post war free trade leadership, evidenced by tariff escalations against China, renegotiation of NAFTA into USMCA and pullout from the Trans-Pacific Partnership (Bown and Irwin, 2019).

2. POPULISM AND TRADE POLICY: CONCEPTUAL FOUNDATIONS

While not inherently Anti-Globalization, populism often coexists with economic nationalism; most scholars align it perfectly with electoral strategies that emphasize National boast, domestic self-reliance and supreme rule of the nation on its trade and citizens. In the economic arena it manifests with skepticism towards other significant organizations and agreements, suspicion of multinational corporations and advocate for strategies that portray prioritizing domestic industries and workers. Leaders often tend to pursue their perceptions and direction under the garb of domestic nationalism to promote their own nation and to manipulate the masses through words that have Inclusive rhetorics, like Mitron (Friends) by the Indian PM or "Our Great Country" and "We The People" by the American president. Inclusive rhetoric is a strategic tool employed by political leaders to cultivate more than just a sense of belonging; it creates emotional resonance in mind and brings in shared purpose among the people. By using terms like "We", "Friends" and "My Fellow Citizens". Leaders create an illusion of horizontal solidarity between populace and the state, serving as a neutralizing agent for the dissent and constructing a great populist communication to unite the audience on a greater level. Such rhetoric further converts to bigger narratives that shape the kind of people that do not willingly go against the words of leaders, often leading to blind support. According to Laclau (2005), populist discourses rely on equivalent chains, where diverse grievances are tied together through emotionally charged inclusive signifiers. Such language reduces the distances perceived between authority and citizens, making critique appear as betrayal and consensus as patriotism.

Rodrik (2018) argued that the rise of populism is partly a response to the discontent of globalization. In both developing and developed countries a large section of people believe that liberalization and globalization are responsible for exacerbated inequality undermining local manufacturing and eroding employment security. Populist leaders manipulate and undoubtedly exploit these perceptions by framing trade globally, a tool used by cosmopolitan elites to undermine national interests. Protectionism is used as a weapon to reassert control over national economic supremacy.

3. THEORETICAL FRAMEWORK

This study explores the convergence of populism, protectionism, and global trade policy through the examples of India and the United States. To deconstruct and discover the ideological, institutional, and economic motivations driving these trade strategies of these two populists leaning democracies, this research draws on three interrelated theoretical approaches, namely constructivist theory, economic nationalism, and dependency theory. These schemas provide a multidimensional view to scrutinize how populist regimes and reframe trade norms and restructure their participation in global economic order.

The Economic Nationalism theory posits that over global or regional economic integration; national economy should be secured and prioritized. It promotes the regulation of foreign trade and investment to maintain national security, self-sufficiency and security within brackets (Helleiner, 2002). Unlike economic liberalism which pressures open markets and comparative advantage, economic nationalism is rooted in strategic protection of local labour and industries.

To comprehend global trade liberalism during the periods of populist ascendancy. This nationalist economic structure and theory offer a valuable foundation for understanding it. Populist leaders have used this ideology to justify withdrawal from multilateral agreements, use of tariffs as tool of economic supremacy and to justify trade restrictions, Donald Trump's "America First Doctrine" and Modi's "Atmanirbhar Bharat" (Self-Reliant) India campaign are pillars of economic nationalism in action. These policy shifts recommend that populist regimes reframe national interest through their lens of self-reliance. Resisting perceived external dependency is not relying more on global trade systems.

While economic nationalism explains the policy rationale, Constructivist trade theory adds layers of interpretative death by emphasizing the role of identity, political discourse, and national narratives in shape and trade decisions (Ruggie, 1999; Adler, 2005). Constructivist theory argues that social construct, beliefs and ideas are the things that assume state behavior, unlike rationalist theories that posit that state behavior is driven solely by material interests. And constructivist theory is largely mobilized by political leaders. They can significantly influence foreign economic policy and their states policy through ideas. Beliefs and social construct.

Populist reigns more than often employ the policy of Protectionist discourse as part of a major nationalist identity project. Trade is usually viewed in economic terms but in true essence it is a moral struggle between a predatory global elite and the exploited national workers. China and Mexico are two examples that are termed as 'cheaters' by Trump weaponizing trade rhetorics to stimulate electoral support. Similarly, the Modi government promotes self-reliance as a patriotic duty, linked to India's post-colonial aspirations for autonomy and strength.

Finally, the Dependency Theory, which originated from Latin America and post-colonial scholarship, sought to provide a robust critique of systematic inequalities inherent in capitalist systems globally. It argued that wealthier nations are the key players of the international arena, and the Global South is constrained by their history and dependency on them in almost every sector. (Frank, 1967; Dos Santos 1970).

These theories comprehend the whole idea of current trade wars and shifts in global trade. These are not just mere economic clashes but also struggles over nationalism, identity and structural power. Economic nationalism is evident in the U.S. and India's protectionist principles prioritizing domestic industries over multilateral commitments. Constructivism demonstrates how ideas and narratives like portraying tariffs as "sovereignty" or "fairness" legitimize economic nationalism. Dependency theory highlights how trade conflicts reinforce structural inequalities as states like India face greater vulnerabilities under protectionist measures by powerful countries.

4. THE RISE OF ECONOMIC NATIONALISM IN THE U.S.

A textbook case of populist driven protectionism is the United States under Donald Trump. The term "America First" was used by Donald Trump in his inaugural speech of 2017 and campaign speech of 2016 it entailed an important overhaul of U.S. trade policy, along with a protectionist agenda to uplift and put U.S. citizens like Workers, borders and industries above global commitments. Few of its characteristics include:

- **National Sovereignty First**

Prioritizing U.S. interests over global cooperation while rejecting multilateral agreements and supporting and favoring more bilateral deals

- **Trade Protectionism**

Backing out from TPP and renegotiating NAFTA (into USMCA), imposing tariffs on China and allies. It also aimed to reflect on trade deficits and project American industries.

- **Strong Borders and Immigration Control**

Building the border wall, restricting citizens into the country through Visas and immigrations and enforcing travel bans.

- **Non-Interventionist Foreign Policy**

Pressured NATO allies to spend more on defense and reduce the U.S military footprint abroad.

- **"Hire Americans First"**

Focused on reviving domestic manufacturing and job creation.

- **Disengagement from Global Institutions**

Rolling back from or exiting WTO, WHO, Iran Deal and Paris Accord. It provides a comprehensive analysis of these policies, noting that they were often justified on national security grounds, particularly under Section 232 of the Trade Expansion Act. The administration claimed that open trade had affected the American Industries and workers, particularly in manufacturing and steel. These actions became politically famous and popular among sections of policy makers and electorates. Empirical studies by the Peterson Institute for International Economics (2021) show that the tariffs led to price increase for consumers, retaliatory measures by partners in trade and disruptions in supply chains globally. Empirical studies substantiate that these policies resulted in significant economic consequences. Research from the National Bureau of Economic Research (Fajgelbaum et al., 2020) estimated that the tariffs functioned as a tax increase imposing annual costs of approximately $57 billion on U.S. consumers through higher prices. These policies also triggered widespread retaliation.

Furthermore, Trump's aggressive stance against multilateral trade organizations, specifically the World Trade Organisation WTO, showed a broader rejection of liberal international order. The administration openly and repeatedly blocked agreements or appointments to the WTO Appellate Body paralyzing its dispute and trade settlement function. This portrays a larger, wider and more open populist trend of delegitimizing institutions of national importance in favor of unilateral and bilateral decision making.

The shift of trade policy has been largely announced in Trump's Administration since 2017 and has gone forward in various forms during Biden's Presidency too. Unlike Trump's confrontational approach based on tariffs, Biden adopted a more pragmatic strategy. While retaining many of Trump's tariffs, Biden emphasized domestic industrial policies (e.g CHIPS and Science Act, inflation Reduction Act) and sought to rebuild alliances through frameworks like IPEF. Both administrations, however, maintained a protectionist posture, reflecting bipartisan consensus on economic nationalism.

One of the most significant outcomes of U.S. economic nationalism has been its retreat from regional and multilateral trade agreements that had once been the cornerstone of its global strategy. A key episode of its withdrawal was a decision to pull out of the Trans-Pacific Partnership TPP in January 2017 which was originally an invasion as accountability to China's rising influence in the Asia Pacific. This move marked a shift towards bilateralism and rejection of multilateral liberalisation, thereby weakening the credibility of U.S. leadership and shaping global trade rules. At the same time, the Trump administration adopted a sharply critical stance towards the World Trade Organisation, particularly its dispute settlement mechanism blocking appointments to the Appellate body and rendering it non-functional. This reflected both popular rejection of multilateral institutions and dissatisfaction with the WTO'S inability to discipline state-driven economic practices, especially those of China. Finally, the administration's widespread use of tariff and trade barriers, often justified on the grounds of national security and economic fairness further demonstrated the U.S. embrace of economic nationalism and protectionism during the period.

5. THE U.S.-CHINA TRADE WAR

Citing unfair trade practices, intellectual property violations, and national security concerns, the United States imposed tariffs on over $350 billion worth of Chinese goods under Sections 301 and 232 between 2018 and 2020. China retaliated with counter-tariffs, targeting key U.S. agricultural exports. This confrontation disrupted global supply chains, symbolizing a retreat from open-market norms historically championed by the West, and came to be known as the U.S.–China Trade War. Trade tools increasingly became instruments of geopolitical rivalry, visible in Washington's export controls on Chinese technology firms such as Huawei and the wider push for technological decoupling.

Although framed as national security measures, these tariffs were widely perceived as protectionist instruments to revive U.S. manufacturing in politically strategic regions. In 2018, invoking Section 232 of the Trade Expansion Act of 1962, the Trump administration-imposed tariffs of 25% on steel and 10% on aluminum, extending even to allies like Canada, Mexico, and the European Union. By broadening the scope of "national security," the U.S. invited criticism from the WTO and its partners.

Rather than exiting regional trade pacts, the U.S. pursued renegotiations to align them more closely with domestic priorities. NAFTA was replaced in 2020 by the U.S.–Mexico–Canada Agreement (USMCA), which introduced stricter intellectual property protections, rules of origin, and higher labor standards. While Trump denounced NAFTA as "the worst trade deal ever made," the USMCA, though touted as a victory for American workers, was largely a rebranding with modest but symbolically potent adjustments.

While Trump's administration adopted rigid protectionist measures to shield domestic industries from external competition, Biden's approach has been more pragmatic, maintaining tariffs while seeking to revive alliances and pursue diplomacy without embracing hardline isolationism. Most of Trump's tariffs on China remain intact, reflecting how protectionism has transcended partisan divides and become a durable feature of U.S. trade policy.

Biden's approach, described by many scholars as pragmatic economic nationalism, balances selective openness with targeted state support. Instead of dismantling trade barriers, his administration leveraged them as tools of negotiation while channeling substantial public investment into critical sectors. Landmark legislations such as the CHIPS and Science Act (2022) and the Inflation Reduction Act (2022) prioritized semiconductors and clean energy, reinforced by "Buy American" provisions. Together, these policies articulate a domestically centered yet future-oriented industrial vision.

Regionally, Washington refrained from rejoining large-scale free trade agreements like the TPP, opting instead for the Indo-Pacific Economic Framework (IPEF), a flexible, non-binding arrangement emphasizing secure and value-based partnerships over pure liberalization. This shift from free trade toward economic nationalism carries significant global implications: while certain domestic industries have been revitalized and supply chain resilience enhanced, the broader system faces mounting uncertainty, trade friction, and further erosion of multilateralism.

● Outcomes and Impact

Domestic Political Gain: Trump's protectionist policies resonated with a voter base disillusioned by job losses due to outsourcing and deindustrialization.

Global Trade Tensions: The aggressive use of tariffs damaged relations with key trading partners and led to multiple disputes filed at the WTO.

Erosion of Multilateralism: The U.S. took a more unilateral stance, weakening global governance frameworks like the WTO and shifting toward bilateralism.

- **Twofold Effects**

While Trump as people say has positively revived domestic manufacturing, strategically automated in critical industries, strengthened its national security through reshoring and created a policy space for industrial revival. It has its own set of negative impacts that undermines the global trade institutions like WTO, It is the reason for price hike and inflationary pressures due to tariffs, forms trade frictions with allies and strategic partners, paves way for erosion of liberal rules-based trading order.

6. POPULIST AND PROTECTIONIST POLICY IN DEVELOPING ECONOMY: THE CASE OF INDIA

India's trade policy has undergone prominent transformation in the post liberalization era P.V Narsimha Rao's Government with Manmohan Singh serving as the finance minister faced a severe balance of payment crisis dwindling foreign exchange reserves, the Indian government undertook a series of structural reforms which was to shape and stabilize the economy and integrate it with the global level.

India's policy framework prior to liberalization was rooted in "License Raj", a system of centralized planning and state intervention in Economic Affairs. Which hardly gave a room for free trading or less privatization. However, the reforms of 1991 marked a decisive shift from the earlier protectionist policies to a freer liberalized, deregulated, reduction in tariff framework. Which also had Import quotas, disinvestment in public enterprises, encouragement of Foreign Direct Investment (FDI) and deregulation of industries.

This series of changes laid down a comprehensive framework for the state to follow and set a transformative growth with increased global cooperation and integration which in turn molds the state's trajectory for decades to come.

Three decades after the 1991 reforms, some scholars still associate India as liberal economy completely, however things have changed, and protectionist tendencies have entered the state along with self-reliance and a shift from globalization. India is not dismissing globalization but rather comprehending it in strategic terms. It is now defined as "Strategic Globalization" a hybrid model where India particularly engages with global systems while building autonomous capabilities in key sectors.

Scholars including Chatterjee and Mehta (2022) note that India's Atmanirbhar Bharat (Self-Reliant India) initiative reflects not a rejection of globalization, but a recalibration toward strategic autonomy and controlled integration. For example:

6.1 Shift in Power Dynamics

Since 2014, the Political power shift in India, with National Democratic Alliance (NDA) coming to power, waving its flag and securing victory, older policies have taken a back seat. With Narendra Modi assuming the office, India has witnessed a distinct and rigorous shift towards not just its trading policies and economy, but also in education, defense, welfare and food distribution sector. A change that emphasized self-reliance, protection and domestic industrial resurgence. India has openly declared retreating from relying heavily on foreign investments and trade through Digital India introduced by Modi in 2014 and further enhanced this in his second term, through the Scheme of Atmanirbhar Bharat in 2020.

This trajectory shaped a clear departure from the earlier liberal economic policies championed during the reign of former Prime Minister Manmohan Singh, whose leadership prioritized global integration, market openness and deregulation. India's post-2014 pathway showed a clear stance of economic nationalism envisioned by strategic state led industrial promotion, cultural symbolism and systemized populism. The divergence from Singh's globalist orientation, marks a conscious shift in India to a more global populist trends, yet adapted to nations unique socio-political context. Few of the core characteristics of both the policies are:

Make in India Launched in 2014

Core Characteristics:

1. Early messaging was liberal and business friendly but overlapped and transformed to protectionist tendencies.
2. Goal to transform India into a global manufacturing hub
3. Targeting around 25 sectors including defence, automobile, textiles and electronics.
4. Focusing on FDI promotion, infrastructure improvement and regulatory simplification.
5. Creation of job opportunities through industrial growth
6. Positioning India as a global supply chain alternative

Atmanirbhar Bharat (Self Reliant India) launched in 2020

Core Characteristics

1. Promoting local manufacturing and reduction of Import dependency.

2. Self-Reliant as a strategic goal not a complete goal (resilience-focused not isolationist).
3. Focusing on five pillars: Infrastructure, Economy, Technology-driven system, demand and Demography
4. Strict element of nationalist-populist rhetoric (like "Vocal for Local")
5. COVID-19 recovery is not a trigger but a broader vision of economic supremacy.
6. Including structural strategic sectors like electronics, pharmaceuticals, defense food and Agriculture
7. Policy incentives: PLI (Production Linked Incentives) ease of doing business reforms.

Certain Initiatives like Digital India, Swachch Bharat (Clean India), Beti Bachao Beti Padhao (Save Girl, Educate the girl) already promoted what Modi wanted his nation to look like it is a reflection of his zeal for not just creating but supporting local issues of the country first. Likewise, he represents his efforts to boost domestic production and reduce reliance on foreign imports. Unlike the Trump Administration's confrontational style, Modi's Approach has emphasized developmental nationalism connecting self-sufficiency with economic modernization.

In November 2019, India withdrew from the Regional Comprehensive Economic Partnership, citing concerns over trade deficits and the inability of domestic sectors (notably agriculture and manufacturing) to compete with cheaper imports from China and ASEAN nations. The decision was politically popular but economically controversial, but the leader wanted robust change.

It all started with the decision to roll back from RCEP in 2019, even prior to this Modi's government was rejecting WTO's proposals of trade and patent rights. While officially justified on the grounds of protecting small farmers and manufactures from Chinese exploitation and competitiveness it was marked and comprehended widely as a shift towards inward looking trade strategy (Mehta,2022). The WTO's Trade Policy Review in 2023 documents a rise in tariff rates and non-tariff barriers in sensitive areas, especially Pharmaceuticals, electronics and Agriculture.

While India's protectionist stance has been framed in terms of developmental policy rather than outright opposition to globalization, it nonetheless reflects populist tendencies. The government often appeals to nationalist sentiments, portraying trade deficits and foreign competition as threats to India's economic sovereignty and social fabric.

- India has enforced a ban on Chinese apps like TikTok, Wechat, Shareit, PUBG mobile, Alibaba, CamScanner and many more from June 2020 to February 2022 and restricts FDI Foreign Direct Investment from neighboring countries only in sensitive areas, yet it courts global investment in tech and manufacturing (e.g Tesla and Apple supply chains).

- In Pharma India is asserting soft power while reducing external dependency the nation isn't just making generics for global markets anymore it's pushing Vaccine Diplomacy R&D hubs and IP ownership.
- Next up, most of India's PLI (Production linked incentive) schemes are designed to grab attention of global firms to manufacture and also to build in India but are not anti-global.
- India has been showing its reluctant behaviour of trading and relying completely on foreign trade systems and multinational firms since the second decade of the 21st century. It's hesitant to join Mega- FTAs like RCEP, the rise in import duties in key sectors and an emphasis on domestic manufacturing reflect a nationalistic economic vision. These patterns and tendencies are often justified in response to hierarchical trade imbalances, especially with China and the need to protect domestic jobs and SMEs in a competitive global environment (Kapoor and Mukhopadhyay, 2021).

The campaign launched in 2020 during COVID-19 pandemic but reviewed a broader strategic and structured policy towards reducing dependency on imports and shaping ways for indigenous production. It was under Modi that this policy has been rooted deeply through the economic ethos. The vision of this policy aligns really well with economic nationalism by asserting structural economy, strategic domestic value chains and national pride with economic resilience. In contrast, Manmohan Singh's government from 2004-2014 largely aligned with neoliberal globalization, greater integration with global supply chains, compliance with WTO World Trade Organization frameworks, and promoting foreign direct investments.

Between 2014 and 2024, industrial policies in India underwent a structural realignment marked by realigned state market partnership and assertive domestic capacity building. Not only using rhetoric but going beyond rhetorical nationalism, the Modi government formed protectionism through certain targeted sectorial incentives like Production Linked Incentive (PLI)schemes, tariff reformulations. Notably, the PLI scheme initiated in 2020 implied a strategic change from broad based subsidies to performance driven industrial incentives. This is not merely a subsidy regime, but also a structured and strategic attempt to embrace global manufacturing champions and significant sectors such as electric vehicles, semiconductors, electronics and pharmaceuticals. Other Phased Manufacturing Program PMP and Electronics targeting developing value chain depth locally by imposing increasing import duties on finished goods while incentivizing component level production. Import substitution, historically associated with Nehruvian socialism, was rethought with a techno-nationalist vision in this decade. Another important movement was the strategic denial of Chinese investments Post Galvan Clashes, pointing that the Industrial policy was no longer agnostic to geopolitical alignments.

Under Singh regime economic reforms took place by giving precedence to liberalizing FDI reforms and norms particularly in aviation, telecom and retail to draw in more global capital. His proposition was not a state driven but a market-led economy featuring his efficiency and enthusiasm through global connectivity. During the period of Manmohan Singh government, 2004 to 2014, India's industrial rules mirrored a market liberal orientation rooted deeply in the Post 1991 Economic progressive changes. Rather than explicit protectionism, the aim was on building an investor friendly environment and regulating Public Private Partnerships (PPPS) and coordinating Indian industry more deeply into global value chains.

The policy terrain focused on FDI Liberalization, Decontrol and Infrastructure Augmentation through schemes like Natural Manufacturing Policy, 2011 and the Delhi Industrial Corridor (DMIC), Mr. Singh's government favored horizontal facilitators such as the enhanced ease of doing business SEZ promotion and tax rationalization over direct industrial intervention. Industrial growth was envisioned through competitive enhancement, not subsidiary driven support. Moreover, despite the liberal thrust, challenges such as bureaucratic inertia, infrastructure bottlenecks and slow environmental clearances hinder the full realization of these initiatives.

What stands out is the deficit of tariff activism or strategic import substitution, which later became the hallmarks of Modi era protectionist industrialism. Manmohan Singh projected a belief that domestic industry would thrive through external competitiveness rather than internal protection. His policy thus reflected a globalist pragmatism aligning India with WTO's commitments.

A clear contrast emerges when comparing Modi's protectionist and nationalist orientation with Manmohan Singh's liberal and globalist economic framework. This divergence is particularly visible in three areas which are:

- **Tariff and Trade Policy**

During Modi's reign multiple sectors like electronics, automotive components and solar equipment have seen a surge in tariffs to secure domestic industries and local producers. Between 2014-2020, the tariff rate increased from 13% to 17%. India also withdrew from RCEP Regional Comprehensive Economic Partnership in 2019, citing concerns over domestic industry vis-à-vis Chinese imports, to not let domestic industries have a vulnerable time. Increased Tariffs on Strategic Goods from 2018 to 2022, India imposed tariff hikes on a variety of products including mobile phones, medical devices, and agricultural goods. The stated goal was to protect infant industries and reduce import dependency. For example, tariffs on electronic components rose from **10%** to as much as **20%** during this period.

In contrast Mr. Singh's government enthusiastically pursued **FTAs (Free Trade Agreements)** and was involved in regional trade diplomacy, attempting to deepen multilateral cooperation by organisations like **ASEAN+ and WTO-led structures.**

- **Recalibrated FTAs and Regional Diplomacy**

India became more cautious in its Free Trade Agreement negotiations, pausing several long-standing talks (e.g., with the EU) and reassessing the impact of previous agreements with ASEAN and South Korea. However, by 2022–2024, India resumed talks with the UK and the EU, showing selective liberalization under strategic considerations.

- **Populism and Political Messaging**

Before Modi's government India lacked such populist tones majorly. The economic messaging appealed more to the world organisations, investors and traders than nationalistic sentiments. Modi upturned this framework of the country by chanting slogans **"Vocals for Locals"** and appeals to the Swadeshi sentiment have blurred the line between cultural nationalism and economic strategy.

Highlights & Key Events

2014-2018: India rises its tariff to protect local industries while the U.S. retaliates with steel aluminum duty.

2018-2020: Ongoing action 232 duties: bilateral friction increases.

2021–2022: India resumes relations with EU, UK and U.S..

2023: Both nations reach market access agreement, Environmental trade dialogues of WTO were joined by U.S.

2024- 2025: U.S. imposes 10% universal tariff on most imports, shortly after imposing a 26% reciprocal tariff on Indian exports.

August 2025: Tariffs on certain Indian goods were escalated to 50%. In response India pursued Agriculture reforms amid U.S. pressure, bilateral negotiations aim to revert tariff escalation.

Table 1. Comparative Summary: Modi vs. Singh on Economic Nationalism

Dimension	Modi (2014–Present)	Manmohan Singh (2004-2014)
Economic Orientation	Nationalist, Protectionist, self-reliant	Liberal, globalized, reformist
Key Policies	Atmanirbhar Bharat, Make in India, Tariff hikes.	FDI liberalization, Multilateralism tax, reform
Trade Engagement	Withdrawn from RCEP, tariff increases	Pursued FTAs, pro-WTO reforms
FDI Approach	Conditional openness, Favoring domestic firms	Broad liberalisation in sectors
Political Rhetoric	Populist-nationalist: Swadeshi	Technocratic-economic: Inclusive growth, globalisation
Institutional Outlook	Strategic autonomy	Institutional, WTO skepticism, Convergence rules-based globalization

Source: Author's own compilation.

Outcomes and Impact

Domestic Industrial Support: The protectionist approach temporarily supported certain domestic sectors, such as electronics assembly and agriculture.

Concerns About Global Competitiveness: Critics argue that the focus on import substitution may hinder long-term integration into global value chains, especially in technology and services.

Diplomatic Repositioning: India's cautious trade diplomacy aligned with its broader foreign policy aim of strategic autonomy, though it raised questions about its commitment to regional economic integration.

7. NEW INSIGHT: INDIA AS A "SUPPLY CHAIN BALANCER" IN THE GLOBAL ARENA

India's self-subsistence trend is not an isolationist, it is another overlooked inside India is posturing itself as an innovative node in the polarizing global supply chain especially in a Post COVID, U.S. China decoupling world. Rather than cutting themselves off from global market India is rebranding itself as a dependable and democratic supply chain partner initiatives like Supply Chain Resilience Initiative (SCRI) with Japan and Australia and partnership with Indo Pacific economic framework IPEF shows how India is targeting to re anchor and rebrand its perception of Globalisation around the trusted network portraying itself as a significant player. At the same time supporting its local trade and industries from the tough competition of foreign states. There are undoubtedly stark differences between two different leaders' policies (see Table 1). This is something hardly laid emphasis in the mainstream literature, India is not Anti-Globalization, it is Anti-Vulnerable, using its self-reliance as a shield not a wall.

7.1 Global Trends: Populism, Inequality and Backlash Against Trade

Scholars like Piketty (2020) and Milanovic (2016) link the rise of economic inequality within countries to liberal trade regimes, automation and financialisation of economies. This economic disaffection often fuels political populism, with trade policy starting to form like a battleground.

As Margalit (2019) asserts that the key drivers of populist support are perceptions of cultural and economic insecurity rather than trade outcomes alone. Moreover, protectionist policies are more assertive over signal responsiveness to domestic anxieties rather than generating immediate gains. The populist theory's key drivers being the perceptions of economic and cultural insecurity than trade outcomes alone.

7.2 Global Consequences of Populist Protectionism

The global level consequences of National transformation are very profound. As Inglehart and Norris (2019), comprehends that populist protectionist policies undermine the foundational path of multilateral cooperation and interdependence. The distortion of public trust in international institutions doubled the risk of bi-lateralism and diplomacy between states transactionally, posing a greater risk for governance in the world. The OECD Economic outlook, titled The Price of War (2023), provides compelling evidence that this fragmentation is accelerating towards a tangible reality. The report argues that nations are pursuing "friend-shoring" strategies, forming selective partnerships based explicitly on ideological and strategic alignment rather than comparative advantage. This shift will however pose inflationary pressures worldwide.

The economic and political consequences of rising populism and protectionism are not confined to trade balances alone. They extend into multiple dimensions of the global system which can be broadly understood through their impact on financial market stability, the resilience of supply chains and overall health of multilateral cooperation:

- **Financial Market Fragility and Global fragmentation**

The Bank for the International Settlement warns that recent U.S. tariffs put in danger "fragmenting the world economy and triggering a financial panic centered on the global bond market". Hedge fund driven liquidity shocks and stress in foreign exchange swap markets assert systematic vulnerability.

- **Supply Chain Vulnerability and Lost Productivity**

The McKinsey Global Institute estimates supply chain distortions could have formed up to 1 trillion USD annually off global GDP. Tariffs also reduce productivity and do not enhance the economy upto the mark. IMF research found raising tariffs leading to long-term drops in output, employment and higher inequality.

- **Erosion of Multilateral Institutions and rule-based trade**

WTO is always sidestepped by populist protection policies using national security loopholes, undermining the entire rule system of trading and risking a shift towards fragmented regional agreement. It also provokes reduced confidence and membership in global governance (withdrawing from climate accords, trade treaties).

- **'Uncertainty traps and Investment Freezes**

Policies halted by populist like Mexico's cancelled NAIM airport trigger **"uncertainty traps"**, reducing fixed investment by nearly **9%** in a year and causing broader economic stagnation.

- **Chronic Slowdown and Cumulative Growth Penalties**

A study across countries shows that, on average, long-run GDP is 10% lower in economies with populist governments due to persistent protectionism and weakening institutions.

- **Decay of Innovation and Technological Isolation**

Innovation comes through Global value chains and open markets. Protectionism isolated industries, slowing tech diffusion, R and D cooperation and hurting global innovation driven productivity.

- **Geopolitical Fragmentation and Rising Tensions**

An interstate conflict might occur due to de-globalization, risk increase when national boundaries harden and interdependence declines.

- **Populism as Political- Economic Backside**

Democratic institutions are eroded by populist regimes (media, judiciary, checks and balances) which reduces investment confidence and fosters corruption further hurting growth.

Additional Underexplored Consequences: An Insight

- **Shadow-banking risks and FX instability:** BIS Bank for International Settlements warns about Shadow Banking misery in massive foreign exchange swap markets amidst protectionist shocks.
- **Global Apartheid and Inequality**: Hardening of borders restricted movements deepen inequality globally and reinforce North-South divide.
- **Shift towards 'friend-shoring':** States are reshaping FDI rules and supply chains around trusted allies this will shift global trade dynamic but also carve a way for unstable "bloc" dependencies.

Policy Recommendations for Mitigating eventual Consequences

- Propose coordinated Central Bank responses to manage bond market shocks.
- Call for WTO reforms to close national security loopholes and handle state subsidies.
- Advocate for targeted industrial support rather than sweeping Tariffs, also digital services taxes and sector specific policies can offer more precision.
- Recommended democratic resilience, maintaining judicial independence, institutional checks and media freedom to protect investment climate and sustainable growth.

8. CONTEMPORARY RELEVANCE AND FUTURE TRAJECTORIES

In core industries such as Pharmaceuticals, Defense Manufacturing and Semiconductors both India and U.S. have initiated industrial policies to lessen the reliance on foreign imports. The COVID-19 pandemic exacerbated the inward-looking economic policies further bolstering nationalistic discourses around supply chain resilience.

Recent (Tooze, 2021) argued that the world is at a critical turning point of Economic global governance; it currently confronts a decisive inflection point.

Fragmentation persists not due to technical shortcomings but political fragmentation and unless the EU and other stakeholders embrace combined strategies of fiscal risk sharing and deeper institutional integration the prevailing international order may unravel, it might also lead to geopolitical tensions. The most striking problem lies in increasingly normalizing the populist policies of trade.

8.1 Comparative Analysis: Convergence and Divergence of India and the U.S.

This section presents a comparative case study analysis of the United States and India, examining how populist governments in both countries reshaped global trade policies through protectionist frameworks. The timeframe spans from 2014 to 2024, covering the two most prominent populist administrations: Donald Trump's presidency in the U.S. (2017–2020) and Narendra Modi's leadership in India (2014–present). These case studies highlight the convergence and divergence in their strategic approaches to trade, illustrating the interplay between domestic political agendas and global economic participation.

While both countries adopted protectionist trade practices under populist regimes, the motivations and outcomes diverged. In the U.S., the shift was framed around job protection and strategic competition (especially with China), while India's approach combined economic nationalism with developmental objectives. Both, however, illustrate how populist politics can reshape trade narratives and institutional commitments.

Table 2. Annual figures for exports, imports, and trade balance (in US$ billion) from 2014–2024 of INDIA

Year	Exports	Imports	Trade Balance
2014	318.2	462.9.	–144.7
2015	310.3	447.9	–137.6
2016	262.3	381.0	–118.7
2017	275.8	384.3	–108.5
2018	303.5	465.6	–162.1
2019	330.1	514.1	–184.0
2020	314.3	467.2	–158.9
2021	420.0	612.0	–192.0
2022	676.5	760.1	–83.5

continued on following page

Table 2. Continued

Year	Exports	Imports	Trade Balance
2023	770.2	892.2	–122.0
2024	820.9	915.2	–94.3

Sources: The data presented above is drawn from official secondary sources including Ministry of Commerce and Industry, Government of India (2024); Reserve Bank of India (2024); World Bank (2024)

Observations:

- Trade deficits narrowed sharply in 2022, likely due to post-pandemic recovery and global demand shift.
- Post-2018 (rise of global protectionism), export/import growth largely continued until pandemic, with a dip in deficits in 2022 and slight recovery in 2023–24.

Table 3. Annual figures for exports, imports, and trade balance (in US$ billion) from 2018–2024 of U.S.

Year	Exports	Imports	Trade Balance
2018	2,500	3,306	–806.0
2019	2,528	3,387	–859.0
2020	2,131	2,757	–626.2
2021	2,528	3,388	–860.0
2022	2,578	3,537	–959.0
2023	2,789	3,586	–797.3
2024	2,910	3,828	–918.0

Note: All figures are in U.S. dollars (in US$ billion).

Sources: The data presented above is drawn from official secondary sources including U.S. Census Bureau(2024); BEA (Bureau of Economic Analysis 2024); World Trade Organisation (2023). Slight variations in reporting may occur due to revisions or rounding.

Key Takeaways:

- Despite protectionist policies beginning under Trump in 2018 (e.g., steel and aluminum tariffs, USMCA renegotiation), the U.S. trade deficit widened, peaking at –$959B in 2022.
- Exports did grow, but imports grew faster, revealing the ineffectiveness of unilateral protectionist tools in reducing overall trade deficits.

- In 2020, there was a dip due to COVID-19 disruptions, but the deficit rose again with economic reopening.

Table 4. U.S.–India Global Trade Comparison Table (2018–2024)

Year	U.S. Trade Balance	India Trade Balance
2018	–806.0	–162.1
2019	–859.0	–184.0
2020	–626.2	–152.9
2021	–860.0	–192.0
2022	–959.0	–83.5
2023	–797.3	–122.0
2024	–918.0	–94.3

Note: *Values in USD billions. Negative = Trade Deficit*

Sources: The data presented above is drawn from official secondary sources including U.S. Census Bureau(2024); Bureau of Economic Analysis (BEA) (2024); India Ministry of Commerce and Reserve Bank of India (2024)

Clarification on the Data:

- The exports and imports are aggregated annually and expressed in USD billions.
- The trade balance = exports – imports.
- Some figures are rounded for clarity but are within 1–2% of official reports, which is standard in academic and policy writing.
- For 2024, the data used is from official secondary sources, the latest available full-year estimates (BEA and Census release full-year trade stats with minor quarterly revisions).

United States:

Despite applying tariffs on steel, aluminum and China etc, nonetheless the U.S. imported more not less.

Exports grew although only marginally and remained stagnated.

Trade deficit in all years and worsened from -$860B 2018 to -$959B 2022 (see Table 3).

Reasons:

Non replaceable foreign goods, U.S. domestic production couldn't keep up with foreign goods fast pacing demands.

Consumers and firms kept on demanding cheaper foreign raw materials.

Tariffs hurt part assembly too because Supply chains were global.

Retaliatory tariffs by other trade partners targeted the U.S. agriculture and Machinery, with China cutting imports of soybean and farm equipment.

Outcome: The populist rhetoric did not reduce trade deficit it rather created trade tensions and higher cost it also reduced the intended benefits of protectionist policies.

India:

India raised import duties, launched Atmanirbhar Bharat, and offered incentives under PLI schemes. But India's imports kept rising until 2021.

Exports rose sharply only post-COVID in 2022 (see table 2) due to global demand (pharma, digital services, textiles).

The trade deficit shrank in 2022, but not because imports fell because exports surged.

India still relies heavily on imports of crude oil, gold, electronics which are hard to substitute domestically.

Outcome: India's policy worked better than the U.S., but the goal of "import less" wasn't fully met either in this case too.

8.2 Rhetoric vs. Reality: The Ideological Pitfalls

Despite the strong rhetorical emphasis on self-reliance and economic sovereignty, the realities of global trade reveal significant contradictions in both the United States and India. Neither country could disengage from global supply chains overnight, as deep into interdependence made such separation impractical. Structural gaps in domestic industries further constrain the capacity to replace critical imports, leaving both the economies dependent on foreign goods. In India, the volatility of the rupee added an additional layer of pressure, while in the United States the strength of the dollar made imports cheaper, because Americans could still afford imports, so tariffs did not stop foreign goods, limiting the effectiveness of tariffs. Moreover, retaliatory measures from trading partners undermined the intended benefits of protectionist policies, particularly in sectors such as agriculture and machinery. Consumer behavior also posed challenges as both the American and Indian population continued to demand foreign goods such as oil, electronics, luxury goods, iphone, MNC restaurants and global brands despite the political push for local alternatives. These realities highlight a persistent gap between populist rhetoric and economic outcome demonstrating that protectionist nationalism, when not accompanied by structural industrial reforms, often fails to achieve its stated objectives.

While both the nations adopted populist measures and trade postures post 2018, the consequences of it yielded suboptimal results. It could not materialize fully. In the U.S., the trade deficits actually widened, depicting that protectionism without structural industry reform is insufficient. India however fared comparatively better particularly in 2022 (see Table 4), yet its import dependency especially in energy and electronics limited the full realization of self-reliant aspirations of trade. This depicts an important lesson, which is populist trade nationalism without strategic depth often collapses or collides with structural realities of global economic multilateralism and independence.

9. FINDINGS AND DISCUSSION

This section focuses mainly on the key findings comparatively about how populist regimes in the U.S. and India have shaped global trade through protectionist policies. The analysis addresses the central research questions and explores broader implications for resilience, neutrality and governance in the liberal economic order.

The evidence from the state studies suggests that populism is rooted deeply in the democratic nations through nationalistic rhetoric, majoritarian models of nation and economic upliftment. It directly influences political and economic decisions of a country. When the rulers of a country wordplay and use rhetoric that aligns with protecting local industries and trade, the citizens blindly believe that it is for their right cause, and they feel motivated to support it. In both the United States and India, populist leaders have framed global trade as a source of national disadvantage:

The U.S. used a policy of protectionism under Trump's period to appeal to disenfranchised working class voters, particularly in the Rust Belt.

In India, where the population sort of worship its leaders, this ideology worked efficiently well to bolster national pride and economic sovereignty particularly among rural constituencies and middle-class citizens. The emphasis on terms like Atmanirbhar Vyapari (Self-reliant trader), Desh ke Nirmata(Nation builders) and Vyapari Bhaiyon aur Behnon (Trader brothers and sisters) are not mere words it is done to evoke feeling of belonging towards the leader and country thinking that the leader really cares for its citizens, also it reframes trade liberalization as a threat to local producers.

These findings aligned very well with Rodrik's (2018) thesis that populist governments often politicized trade policy by cultural identity, economic looking good, and national grievance.

Though implemented in both countries through distinct ways but had overlapping mechanisms.

Both countries have raised their Tariffs significantly during populist rule. India focused on electronics, agriculture and pharmaceuticals while the U.S. targeted steel, aluminum and Chinese imports. These actions disrupted trade flows and generated retaliatory characteristics from trading partners.

In addition, both the states willingly opted out of trade deals like TPP and RCEP and some others. These events of exiting were justified using the words that blend with citizens' mindset like national interest, sovereignty and protecting our goals.

Finally, both governments rebranded trade goals with emotionally resonant slogans. It served as populist discursive tools, justifying inward-looking trade stances without using explicit protectionist language.

These findings asserted the constructivist argument that trade policies are not built in economic and political logic but also molded by strategic narratives, identity politics and emotions of the citizens

9.1 Divergence in Policy and Strategic Orientation

Although thematically both countries stand on the same level, the strategic motivations and long run implications will distinguish between them.

India's approach is viewed as more defensive and selective, aimed at shielding vulnerable sectors rather than restructuring global trade. While this yielded short term benefits for certain domestic industries, it also risked reducing India's attractiveness to foreign investors and its role in global value chains (Mehta, 2022).

While the U.S. sought a constructivist approach specifically against China, leveraging its global economic clout to impose tariffs and extract more concessions through bilateral renegotiations like USMCA. In the U.S. case only, some domestic jobs were protected, but consumer prices rose and global supply chains were disrupted (Bown and Irwin, 2020).

While India is undoubtedly a developing economy, the U.S. is a capital exporting advanced economy with global leverage. This divergence becomes the structural difference in them.

Despite the United States adopting a string of protectionist policies post-2018 beginning with former President Donald Trump's "America First" agenda, the withdrawal from multilateral deals like TPP, and the imposition of tariffs on key trade partners, its trade deficit continued to widen.

In 2018, the U.S. trade deficit stood at –\$806 billion, increasing to –\$959 billion by 2022, the highest in its history (see table 3).

Even after a marginal improvement in 2023, the deficit again climbed to –\$918 billion in 2024. (see table 4). This suggests that tariffs and unilateral protectionist measures did not achieve their intended goal of reducing trade imbalances. Instead, they may have shifted trade flows to other partners, increasing import costs for American industries and consumers.

Protectionism in the U.S. proved ineffective in correcting trade deficits. Structural dependencies on foreign goods, global supply chains, and consumption-led growth overwhelmed tariff-based correction.

9.2 India's Strategic Protectionism and Resilience

India also leaned into economic nationalism through programs like Atmanirbhar Bharat and targeted tariff adjustments post-2018. However, unlike the U.S., India's trade performance displays a more resilient trajectory. Between 2018–2021, India's trade deficit widened from –$162.1B to –$192.0B, reflecting import dependency and pandemic disruptions.

By 2022, India reduced its trade deficit to –$83.5B (see table 4), marking a notable turnaround in global trade positioning. This narrowing continued moderately in 2024 -$94.3B (see table 4) indicating that India may have succeeded in realigning its export strategy (especially in services and pharmaceuticals), while curbing excessive import dependence.

India's mix of strategic protectionism and production-linked incentives helped stabilize trade balances, suggesting that targeted policies embedded in domestic capability-building may be more effective than blanket protectionism.

This comparison highlights that not all protectionist or populist policies yield similar outcomes:

The U.S. case reflects that without industrial restructuring; tariffs alone may distort trade without fixing the root problem. India's case suggests that trade resilience requires a combination of internal reform, export-oriented growth, and selective protectionism—not isolationism.

The efficacy of economic nationalism depends on whether it is inward-looking and reactive (as in the U.S.) or strategically aligned with export promotion and domestic strengthening (as seen in India).

9.3 Recommendations for Future Policy and Research

- **Recent Theme:** This study addresses a critical global trend- the rise of populist and protectionist trade policies in the wake of economic uncertainty, de-globalization and shift in political ideologies.
- **Comparative Insight:** By juxtaposing two Major Economies the U.S. the developed one and India the emerging one, the reserve provides a layered perception of how similar strategies can result in different outcomes on national context level.
- **Bridging the Rhetoric Reality Gap:** It examines the gap between political narratives and rhetoric promises of reducing deficits, reviving domestic Industry and actual trade data portraying how results shape the economy and often diverge from expectations.
- **Policy Relevance:** These findings are directly applicable to ongoing debates on trade, decoupling, industrial policy and self-reliance. Crucial for post COVID recovery strategies and future trade business.

■ **Scholarly Contribution:** The paper contributes to the growing academic literature on economics, politics and nationalism, providing data backed arguments that challenge or nuance conventional views about globalization backlash.

■ **Rebalancing National Interests and Global Commitments:** Governments must craft trade policies that protect vulnerable sectors without undermining global cooperation.

■ **Further Research on Regional Trade Alternatives:** Studies could explore how regional blocs like ASEAN, the EU, or the African Continental Free Trade Area (AfCFTA) respond to rising protectionism from global powers.

While there is an increasing body of research and literature on individual pathways of the United States and India, a few comparative studies systematically examine how different forms of populism shape trade policy in democratic states. Through this study the gap between these nations tends to be filled moreover to provide a comprehensive Comparative Political Economic analysis of India and the United States under the influence of Ideologies like Populism and Protectionism. And how it is tailored to specific national contexts while contributing to broader global shifts.

10. CONCLUSION

This book chapter has scrutinized the evolving structure and mechanisms of Global Trade under the influence of Populism and Protectionism viewing the comparative cases of the United States and India. A shift from liberal economic framework that earlier surrounded the world politics post-Cold war order.

The U.S. under Donald Trump and India under Narendra Modi demonstrate how populist politics often converge on protectionist economic policies albeit through different strategic paths. In the American case protectionism was used aggressively in a transactional, retaliatory style aimed at reshaping global trade relations. In India protectionism took the form of self-reliance pointing more at insulating the domestic economy from perceived external vulnerabilities.

Ultimately, this paper shows that the trade strategies of populist governments are neither irrational nor spontaneous; they are rooted in deeper structural discontent and political needs.

In conclusion populism can win elections, but it does not inherently win Trade wars. Functioning and productive trade policy requires more local aligning nationalistic slogans. It demands rigorous planning, reforms and structural adaptability to global realities. This study clearly mirrors how the future of trade will not be shaped by isolation but intellectual integration and planning.

A political ideology that divides society into two antagonistic groups: the pure people' versus 'the corrupt elite.' In the context of economic policymaking, populist leadership often promotes protectionist trade policies, nationalism, and skepticism toward global institutions.

REFERENCES

Adler, E. (2005). *Communitarian international relations: The epistemic foundations of international relations*. Routledge.

Bank for International Settlements. (2023). Annual economic report 2023. https://www.bis.org/publ/arpdf/ar2023e.htm

BBC News. (2020, June 2). Modi's 'Vocal for Local' call to boost India's self-reliance. https://www.bbc.com/news/world-asia-india-52890471

Bown, C. P., & Irwin, D. A. (2019). Trump's trade war: An assessment. Peterson Institute for International Economics. https://www.piie.com

Bown, C. P., & Irwin, D. A. (2020). The Trump trade war: Its motives, manifestations, and the future. Peterson Institute for International Economics. https://www.piie.com/publications/working-papers/trump-trade-war-its-motives-manifestations-and-future

Chatterjee, P., & Mehta, P. B. (2022). India's strategic economic nationalism. *Economic and Political Weekly*, *57*(36), 10–12. https://www.epw.in

Dos Santos, T. (1970). The structure of dependence. *The American Economic Review*, *60*(2), 231–236.

Fajgelbaum, P. D., Goldberg, P. K., Kennedy, P. J., & Khandelwal, A. K. (2020). The return to protectionism. *The Quarterly Journal of Economics*, *135*(1), 1–55. DOI: 10.1093/qje/qjz036

Frank, A. G. (1967). *Capitalism and underdevelopment in Latin America: Historical studies of Chile and Brazil*. Monthly Review Press.

Government of India. (2020). Atmanirbhar Bharat. https://www.pmindia.gov.in/en/news_updates/aatmanirbhar-bharat/

Government of India. (2020). Production linked incentive (PLI) schemes in India. Department of Commerce. https://commerce.gov.in

Helleiner, E. (2002). Economic nationalism as a challenge to economic liberalism? *International Studies Quarterly*, *46*(3), 307–329. DOI: 10.1111/1468-2478.00235

Inglehart, R., & Norris, P. (2019). *Cultural backlash: Trump, Brexit, and authoritarian populism*. Cambridge University Press., DOI: 10.1017/9781108595841

Kapoor, D., & Mukhopadhyay, P. (2021). The political economy of Atmanirbhar Bharat. Centre for Policy Research. https://cprindia.org

Laclau, E. (2005). *On populist reason*. Verso Books.

McKinsey Global Institute. (2020). Risk, resilience, and rebalancing in global value chains. https://www.mckinsey.com/business-functions/operations/our-insights/risk-resilience-and-rebalancing-in-global-value-chains

Mehta, P. B. (2022). India's populism and the politics of trade (ORF Occasional Paper No. 345). Observer Research Foundation. https://www.orfonline.org

Mehta, P. B. (2022). Strategic protectionism and India's trade dilemmas. *Economic and Political Weekly*, *57*(42), 21–24. https://www.epw.in/journal/2022/42

Milanovic, B. (2016). *Global inequality: A new approach for the age of globalization*. Harvard University Press.

Ministry of Commerce and Industry, Government of India. (2024). Export-Import data bank. https://commerce.gov.in/trade-statistics/

Mudde, C., & Rovira Kaltwasser, C. (2017). *Populism: A very short introduction*. Oxford University Press. DOI: 10.1093/actrade/9780190234874.001.0001

Norris, P., & Inglehart, R. (2019). *Cultural backlash: Trump, Brexit, and authoritarian populism*. Cambridge University Press. DOI: 10.1017/9781108595841

OECD. (2022). Trade policy briefs. OECD Publishing. https://www.oecd.org

OECD. (2022). Global trade fragmentation: Scenarios and implications. https://www.oecd.org/trade/tradestatistics/global-trade-fragmentation.htm

Office of the United States Trade Representative. (2020). United States–Mexico–Canada Agreement (USMCA). https://ustr.gov/trade-agreements/free-trade-agreements/united-states-mexico-canada-agreement

Office of the United States Trade Representative. (2023). US-India Trade Policy Forum joint statement. https://ustr.gov/about-us/policy-offices/press-office/press-releases

Peterson Institute for International Economics. (2021). Economic impact of Trump's tariffs. https://www.piie.com/research/trade-investment/economic-impact-tariffs

Peterson Institute for International Economics. (2021). Annual report. https://www.piie.com/publications/annual-report

Piketty, T. (2020). *Capital and ideology* (Goldhammer, A., Trans.). Harvard University Press.

Reserve Bank of India. (2024). Handbook of statistics on Indian economy. https://www.rbi.org.in/Scripts/AnnualPublications.aspx?head=Handbook%20of%20Statistics%20on%20Indian%20Economy

Rodrik, D. (2011). *The globalization paradox: Democracy and the future of the world economy*. W. W. Norton & Company.

Rodrik, D. (2018). *Straight talk on trade: Ideas for a sane world economy*. Princeton University Press. DOI: 10.1515/9781400888900

Rodrik, D. (2018). Populism and the economics of globalization. *Journal of International Business Policy, 1*(1), 12–33. DOI: 10.1057/s42214-018-0001-4

Ruggie, J. G. (1999). *Constructing the world polity: Essays on international institutionalization*. Routledge.

Tooze, A. (2021). *Shutdown: How COVID shook the world's economy*. Viking Press.

U.S. Bureau of Economic Analysis. (2024). International transactions accounts data. https://www.bea.gov/data/intl-trade-investment/international-transactions

U.S. Census Bureau. (2024). Foreign trade: Data. https://www.census.gov/foreign-trade/statistics/historical/index.html

U.S. Census Bureau. (2024). U.S. international trade in goods and services: Annual report 2023. https://www.census.gov/foreign-trade/Press-Release/current_press_release/index.html

U.S. Congress. (2022). CHIPS and Science Act (P.L. 117-167). https://www.congress.gov

World Bank. (2024). World development indicators. https://rbi.org.in

World Trade Organization. (2023). Trade policy review: India. https://www.wto.org

World Trade Organization. (2023). World trade statistical review 2023.

Compilation of References

Acemoglu, D., & Robinson, J. A. (2017, January 30). *The economic impact of colonialism*. VoxEU.org. https://cepr.org/voxeu/columns/economic-impact-colonialism

Acharya, A. (2014). *The End of American World Order*. Polity Press.

Adekola, F. (2019). The WTO and US-China Trade Disputes: Legal and Strategic Dimensions. *Journal of International Economic Law*, *22*(4), 685–706.

Adler, E. (2005). *Communitarian international relations: The epistemic foundations of international relations*. Routledge.

Afreximbank. (2023). *African Trade Report 2023: Export manufacturing and regional value chains in Africa*. https://media.afreximbank.com/afrexim/AFRICAN_TRADE_REPORT_2023.pdf

African Development Bank. (2024). *African economic outlook 2024: Driving Africa's transformation through climate-smart investments*. https://www.afdb.org/sites/default/files/documents/publications/african_economic_outlook_aeo_2024_0.pdf

African Development Bank. (2024). *Paving the way for a stronger and more integrated Africa: African Development Bank reaffirms its commitment at Casablanca ministerial roundtable*. https://www.afdb.org/en/news-and-events/press-releases/paving-way-stronger-and-more-integrated-africa-african-development-bank-reaffirms-its-commitment-casablanca-ministerial-roundtable-81179

African Union. (2022). *6th European Union - African Union Summit: A joint vision for 2030* [Press release]. https://au.int/en/pressreleases/20220218/6th-european-union-african-union-summit-joint-vision-2030

African Union. (2022). *African Continental Free Trade Area (AfCFTA)*. Retrieved July 5, 2025, from https://au.int/en/african-continental-free-trade-area

African Union. (2022). *Rules of Origin Manual, African Continental Free Trade Area Secretariat*. Retrieved from https://au.int/sites/default/files/documents/42397-doc-AfCFTA_RULES_OF_ORIGIN_MANUAL.pdf

African Union. *Rules of Origin Guidelines, AfCFTA*. Retrieved from https://au.int/en/documents/20230315/rules-origin-guidelines-afcfta

Aguilera, R., Duran, P., Heugens, P. P. M. A. R., Sauerwald, S., Turturea, R., & VanEssen, M. (2021). State ownership, political ideology, and firm performance around the world. *Journal of World Business, 56*(1), 101113. Universitat Ramon Llull+2IDEAS/RePEc+2DOI: 10.1016/j.jwb.2020.101113

Akkermans, J., Richardson, J., & Kraimer, M. L. (2020). The COVID-19 crisis as a career shock: Implications for careers and vocational behavior. *Journal of Vocational Behavior, 119*, 103434. PMC+2espace.curtin.edu.au+2DOI: 10.1016/j.jvb.2020.103434

Al Jazeera Staff. (April 9, 2025). *Penguins, vaccines: Can negotiations save Trump's oddest tariff targets?* https://www.aljazeera.com/news/2025/4/8/penguins-vaccines-can-negotiations-save-trumps-oddest-tariff-targets

Alessandria, G., Kaboski, J. P., & Midrigan, V. (2017). Trade integration and the trade balance in China. *IMF Economic Review, 65*(4), 642–668. DOI: 10.1057/s41308-017-0036-2

Alessandria, G., Kaboski, J. P., & Midrigan, V. (2021). Trade adjustment dynamics and the welfare gains from trade. *Journal of International Economics, 131*, 103450. DOI: 10.1016/j.jinteco.2021.103458

Alessandria, G., Kaboski, J. P., & Midrigan, V. (2024). Taking stock of trade policy uncertainty: Evidence from China's pre-WTO accession. *Journal of International Economics, 150*, 103938. DOI: 10.1016/j.jinteco.2024.103938

Alessandria, G., Kaboski, J. P., & Midrigan, V. (2024). Trade-policy dynamics: Evidence from 60 years of U.S.-China trade. *Journal of Political Economy.*

Alfaro, L., & Chor, D. (2023). *Global supply chains: The looming "great reallocation"* (No. w31661). National Bureau of Economic Research.

Alonso-Ortiz, J., & José Maria, . (2025). *"The short-run impact of US tariffs on an interconnected world."*. Documento de Trabajo.

Alqahtani, A., & Klein, T. (2021). Oil price changes, uncertainty, and geopolitical risks: On the resilience of GCC countries to global tensions. *Energy, 236*, 121541. DOI: 10.1016/j.energy.2021.121541

Alshaalan, Z., (2025). Repercussions of the New U.S. Trade Policies on the Global Economy: A Focus on Tunisia.

Álvarez, J. P. (April 23, 2025). *Mercado de bonos: ¿quiénes son los principales tenedores extranjeros de la deuda estadounidense? Bloomberg en línea.* https://www.bloomberglinea.com/mundo/estados-unidos/mercado-de-bonos-quienes-son-los-principales-tenedores-extranjeros-de-la-deuda-estadounidense/#:~:text=Actualmente%2C%20los%20principales%20tenedores%20extranjeros,deuda%2C%20distribuida%20en%20distintos%20estamentos

Amiti, M., Redding, S. J., & Weinstein, D. E. (2020). Who's Paying for the US Tariffs? A Longer Term Perspective. *AEA Papers and Proceedings. American Economic Association, 2020*(110), 541–546. https://swh.princeton.edu/~reddings/pubpapers/ARW-May-2020. DOI: 10.1257/pandp.20201018

Amsden, A. H. (1990). Third World industrialization: 'Global Fordism' or a new model? *New Left Review, (I)*/182, 5–31. https://newleftreview.org/issues/i182/articles/alice-h-amsden-third-world-industrialization-global-fordism-or-a-new-model.pdf

Anderson, J. E., & Van Wincoop, E. (2003). Gravity with gravitas: A solution to the border puzzle. *The American Economic Review, 93*(1), 170–192. DOI: 10.1257/000282803321455214

Arrighi, G. (1994). *The Long Twentieth Century: Money, Power, and the Origins of Our Times*. Verso.

Arrighi, G., & Silver, B. J. (2001). *Chaos and Governance in the Modern World System*. University of Minnesota Press.

ASEAN. *ASEAN Single Window*. Retrieved from https://asean.org/our-communities/economic-community/asean-single-window/

Azzimonti, M., Edwards, Z., & Ravindranat, S. (2025, April). *Tariffs: Estimating the Economic Impact of the 2025 Measures and Proposals*. From https://www.richmondfed.org/publications/research/economic_brief/2025/eb_25-12

Baldwin, D. A. (1985). *Economic statecraft*. Princeton University Press.

Balfour, R., Baroncelli, E., Bomassi, L., Csernatoni, R., Goldthau, A., Grevi, G., & Youngs, R. (2023). *Geopolitics and economic statecraft in the European Union*. Carnegie Endowment for International Peace.

Bank for International Settlements. (2023). Annual economic report 2023. https://www.bis.org/publ/arpdf/ar2023e.htm

Banomyong, R. (2005). The impact of port and trade security initiatives on maritime supply-chain management. *Maritime Policy & Management*, *32*(1), 3–13. DOI: 10.1080/0308883042000326102

Barnett, A. D. (1993). *China's Far West: Four Decades of Change*. Westview Press.

Baskaran, G., & Schwartz, M. (2025, April 14). *The consequences of China's new rare earths export restrictions*. Center for Strategic and International Studies. https://www.csis.org/analysis/consequences-chinas-new-rare-earths-export-restrictions

Baskaran, G. (2025). A strategy for minerals diplomacy in emerging markets. In Baskaran, G., & Wood, D. (Eds.), *Critical minerals and the future of the U.S. economy* (pp. 90–100). Center for Strategic & International Studies., https://www.csis.org/analysis/critical-minerals-and-future-us-economy

BBC News. (2020, June 2). Modi's 'Vocal for Local' call to boost India's self-reliance. https://www.bbc.com/news/world-asia-india-52890471

Becker, S. (2012). The 'Great Game': The History of an Evocative Phrase. *Asian Affairs*, *43*(1), 61–80. DOI: 10.1080/03068374.2012.646404

Bekkers, E., & Schroeter, S. (2020). *An economic analysis of the US–China trade conflict* (WTO Staff Working Paper ERSD-2020-04). World Trade Organization. https://www.wto.org/english/res_e/reser_e/ersd202004_e.htm

Bellora, C., & Fontagné, L. (2020). Shooting Oneself in the Foot? Trade War and Global Value Chains. *CEPII Working Paper, April.*

Bhuimali, A., & Chakraborty, P. (2018). WTO Under Stress: The Crisis of Multilateralism and Trade Dispute Resolution. *Economic Affairs*, *63*(4), 975–981.

Bianchi, R. R. (2019). *China and the Islamic World: How the New Silk Road is Transforming Global Politics*. Oxford University Press. DOI: 10.1093/oso/9780190915285.001.0001

Biden, J. (2021, February 4). *Remarks by President Biden on America's place in the world*. The White House. https://www.whitehouse.gov/briefing-room/speeches-remarks/2021/02/04/remarks-by-president-biden-on-americas-place-in-the-world

Black, J., & Morrison, A. (2021). The Strategic Challenges of Decoupling. *Harvard Business Review*. https://hbr.org/2021/05/the-strategic-challenges-of-decoupling

Blackwill, R. D., & Harris, J. M. (2016). *War by Other Means: Geoeconomics and Statecraft*. Harvard University Press.

bne IntelliNews. (2025, May 12). *Brazil poised to challenge China's rare earth dominance.* https://www.intellinews.com/brazil-poised-to-challenge-china-s-rare-earth-dominance-380441/

Bolt, P. J., & Cross, S. N. (2018). *China, Russia, and Twenty-First Century Global Geopolitics*. Oxford University Press.

Börzel, T. A., & Zürn, M. (2021). Contestations of the liberal international order: From liberal multilateralism to postnational liberalism. *International Organization, 75*(2), 282–305. DOI: 10.1017/S0020818320000570

Bounds, A. (2022). The WTO's lonely struggle to defend global trade. Financial Times. Retrieved October 15, 2022, from https://www.ft.com

Bouoiyour, J., Selmi, R., Hammoudeh, S., & Wohar, M. E. (2019). What are the categories of geopolitical risks that could drive oil prices higher? Acts or threats? *Energy Economics, 84*, 104523. DOI: 10.1016/j.eneco.2019.104523

Bowen, T. Rene; Broz, J. Lawrence; Rosendorff, B. P. (2023). A Theory of Trade Policy Transitions. *Journal of Historical Political Economy, 4*(4), 471–507. https://www.scopus.com/record/display.uri?eid=2-s2.0-105001191034&origin=resultslist&sort=plf-f&src=s&sot=b&sdt=b&s=TITLE-ABS-KEY%28US+Reciprocal+Tariff%29&sessionSearchId=cb95d1f13ec3a88216fb0a03783d5277&relpos=2

Bown, C. P., & Irwin, D. A. (2019). Trump's trade war: An assessment. Peterson Institute for International Economics. https://www.piie.com

Bown, C. P., & Irwin, D. A. (2020). The Trump trade war: Its motives, manifestations, and the future. Peterson Institute for International Economics. https://www.piie.com/publications/working-papers/trump-trade-war-its-motives-manifestations-and-future

Bradford, A. (2020). *The Brussels effect: How the European Union rules the world.* Oxford University Press., DOI: 10.1093/oso/9780190088583.001.0001

Bradsher, K. (2025, April 14). China halts critical rare earth exports as trade war intensifies. *The Japan Times*. https://www.japantimes.co.jp/business/2025/04/14/economy/china-rare-earth-minerals-halt-exports/

Brands, H. (2014). *What Good Is Grand Strategy? Power and Purpose in American Statecraft from Harry S. Truman to George W. Bush*. Cornell University Press. DOI: 10.7591/9780801470288

Breuninger, K. (2025, Jul. 29). *U.S.-China trade talks end without extension of tariff truce, as Trump weighs options*. CNBC. https://www.cnbc.com/2025/07/29/trump-china-trade-tariffs-bessent.html

Brown, G. W., McLean, I., & McMillan, A. (2018). *The concise Oxford dictionary of politics and international relations*. Oxford University Press. DOI: 10.1093/acref/9780199670840.001.0001

Brown, K., & Tzu-hui, K. W. (2019). *The Trouble with Taiwan: History, the United States and a Rising China*. Zed. DOI: 10.5040/9781350225688

Buchanan, Ben. (2020). *The Hacker and the State: Cyber Attacks and the New Normal of Geopolitics*. Harvard University Press.

Buchholz, K. (August 19, 2019). *The U.S.-China Trade Deficit is Growing [Digital image]*. https://www.statista.com/chart/15419/the-us-trade-balance-with-china/

Burdekin, Richard C.K. & Shen, Yijing & Whited, Hsin-hui. (2013). Cross-strait linkages: historical perspective and empirical evidence. In Peter C.Y. Chow (Eds). *Economic Integration Across the Taiwan Strait: Global Perspectives*. Edward Elgar Publishing.

Butler, E. (2025). The Psychology of Protectionism. In *Free Trade in the Twenty-First Century: Economic Theory and Political Reality* (pp. 43–63). Springer Nature Switzerland. DOI: 10.1007/978-3-031-67656-7_4

Caballero, A. (2025, May 9). *Who will prevail? Incentives vs protectionism: The battle between BYD and local manufacturers in Brazil*. Mobility Portal. https://mobilityportal.eu/incentives-vs-protectionism-battlebyd-brazil/

Cahalan, C. (2025, April). *Tariffs force important shift in consumer behavior*. From https://www.thestreet.com/personal-finance/tariffs-cause-an-important-shift-in-consumer-behavior?

Campbell, C. (2021, Jan. 4). *Where Is Alibaba Founder Jack Ma? What the Saga of One of the World's Richest Men Reveals About China Under Xi Jinping*. Time. https://time.com/5926062/jack-ma/

Campbell, C. (2025, June 17). Why it's so hard to challenge China's rare earths dominance. *TIME*. https://time.com/7294964/us-rare-earths-minerals-china-dominance-trump-tariffs/

CarboChain. *The US SEC Climate-related Disclosure Rules Explained*. Retrieved from https://www.carbonchain.com/carbon-reporting/us-sec

Carducci, M., & Bruno, A. S. (2014). The BRICS countries between justice and economy: Methodological challenges on constitutional comparison. *Sociology and Anthropology (Alhambra, Calif.)*, *2*(2), 46–58. https://www.hrpub.org/download/20140105/SA4-19601777.pdf. DOI: 10.13189/sa.2014.020204

Carlomagno, G., & Albagli, E. (2022). Trade wars and asset prices. *Journal of International Money and Finance, 124*, 102631. DOI: 10.1016/j.jimonfin.2022.102631

Carney, R. W. (2018). *Authoritarian Capitalism: Sovereign Wealth Funds and State Owned Enterprises in East Asia and Beyond*. Cambridge University Press. DOI: 10.1017/9781108186797

Carruthers, R., Bajpai, J. N., & Hummels, D. (2003). Trade and logistics: an East Asian perspective. *East Asia integrates: a trade policy agenda for shared growth*, 117-137.

Casey, C. A., Elsea, J. K., Casey, C. A., & Elsea, J. K. (2024). *The International Emergency Economic Powers Act : Origins*. Evolution, and Use.

Castells, M., & Hall, P. (1994). *Technopoles of the World*. Routledge.

Castle, M. A. (2018). Globalization's Impact: Trade and Investment in China-India Relations. In Paul, T. V. (Ed.), *The China-India Rivalry in the Globalization Era*. Georgetown University Press. DOI: 10.2307/j.ctv75db2z.14

Cavallo, B. A., Gopinath, G., Neiman, B., & Tang, J. (2021). Tariff Pass-Through at the Border and at the Store: Evidence from US Trade Policy. *American Economic Review: Insights, 3*(1), 19–34. DOI: 10.1257/aeri.20190536

Cefai, S., Raboca, J., & the Fastmarkets team. (2024, October 10). *China's export restrictions create unexpected opportunity for Brazil's critical minerals sector*. Fastmarkets. https://www.fastmarkets.com/insights/brazils-critical-minerals-sector/

Cerutti, E., Gopinath, G., & Mohommad, A. (2019, May 23). *The Impact of US-China Trade Tensions*. From https://www.imf.org/en/Blogs/Articles/2019/05/23/blog-the-impact-of-us-china-trade-tensions#:~:text=Evolution%20of%20trade%20in%20the%20US%20and%20China&text=The%20impact%20of%20previously%20imposed,since%20the%20trade%20tensions%20began

Chang, A., & Bradsher, K. (2024, November 29). How China became the world's largest car exporter. The New York Times. https://www.nytimes.com/interactive/2024/11/29/business/china-cars-sales-exports.html

Chang, S. U. N., Zhigang, T. A. O., Hongjie, Y., & Hongyong, Z. (2019). The Impact of US-China Trade War on Japanese Multinational Corporations. *RIETI Discussion Paper Series, June*.

Chang, H.-J. (2010). Institutions and Economic Development: Theory, Policy and History. *Journal of Institutional Economics*, 7(4), 473–498. DOI: 10.1017/S1744137410000378

Chang, H.-J., & Evans, P. (2005). The Role of Institutions in the Economic Development of Nations. In Haque, U. M., Kanbur, R., & Venables, A. P. (Eds.), *Institutional Development and Economic Growth* (pp. 87–111). UNU-WIDER.

Chang, T. (2002). Financial development and economic growth in Mainland China: A note on testing demand-following or supply-leading hypothesis. *Applied Economics Letters*, *9*(13), 869–873. DOI: 10.1080/13504850210158962

Chatterjee, P., & Mehta, P. B. (2022). India's strategic economic nationalism. *Economic and Political Weekly*, *57*(36), 10–12. https://www.epw.in

Che, T., Hsieh, C.-T., & Song, Z. (2023). *Non-Tariff Barriers in the U.S.-China Trade War*. National Bureau of Economic Research (NBER). Retrieved from https://sccei.fsi.stanford.edu/china-briefs/chinas-use-unofficial-trade-barriers-us-china-trade-war

Chen, S. (2010). China's Self-Extrication from the "Malacca Dilemma" and Implications. *International Journal of China Studies*, *1*(1), 1–24. DOI: 10.22452/ijcs.vol14no1.1

Chib, S., Mehta, A. K., Selvakumar, P., Saravanan, A., Mishra, B. R., & Manjunath, T. C. (2025). Mental health challenges and solutions in high-pressure work environments. In Harriott, S. (Ed.), *Innovative Approaches to Managing Conflict and Change in Diverse Work Environments* (pp. 247–272). IGI Global. DOI: 10.4018/979-8-3693-9556-1.ch011

Chipegin, A. (April 9, 2025). Trump Tariffs: A Barrier for Kyrgyzstan, or an Opportunity? *The Diplomat.* Accessed July 07, 2025, https://timesca.com/trump-tariffs-a-barrier-for-kyrgyzstan-or-an-opportunity/

Chirot, D., & Hall, T. D. (1982). World-System Theory. *Annual Review of Sociology*, *8*(1), 81–106. DOI: 10.1146/annurev.so.08.080182.000501

Choi, S. H. (2025, June 2). Explainer | How dependent is America's arsenal on China's critical mineral supply? *South China Morning Post*. https://www.scmp.com/news/china/military/article/3312731/how-dependent-americas-arsenal-chinas-critical-mineral-supply

Chor, D., & Li, B. (2024). Illuminating the effects of the US-China tariff war on China's economy. *Journal of International Economics*, *150*(July), 103926. DOI: 10.1016/j.jinteco.2024.103926

Chou, W. (2025). China's Bureaucratic Playbook for Critical Minerals: Control, Technology Transfer, and Manufacturing Dominance. *Hudson Institute*, (July), 9.

Chowdhry, S. (2025). *Trump's Tariffs: What Escalating Trade Tensions with the US Imply for EU Exporters and Supply Chains* (No. 11). DIW Berlin, German Institute for Economic Research.

Chu, Ming-chin Monique. (2013). Semiconductor interconnectivity across the Taiwan Strait: a case study approach. In Peter C.Y. Chow (Eds). *Economic Integration Across the Taiwan Strait: Global Perspectives*. Edward Elgar Publishing.

Cintra, M. A. M., & Pinto, A. C. (2017). The Asian Development Model and Its Impacts on Global Trade. *Revista de Economia Política*, *37*(4), 812–828.

Cohrs, P. O. (2018). *The new Atlantic order: The transformation of international politics, 1860–1933*. Cambridge University Press.

Congress. (2022). *H.R.4346 - CHIPS and Science Act*. https://www.congress.gov/bill/117th-congress/house-bill/4346

Constantino, S., & Nuñez, S. (2019). *Networks, Weak Ties, and Thresholds*. https://www.phenomenalworld.org/interviews/networks-weak-ties-and-thresholds/

Contractor, F. J. (2025). Assessing the economic impact of tariffs: adaptations by multinationals and traders to mitigate tariffs. *Review of international business and strategy*, 35(2/3), 190-213.

Cooley, A. (2012). *Great Games, Local Rules: The New Great Power Contest in Central Asia*. Oxford University Press. DOI: 10.1093/acprof:oso/9780199929825.001.0001

Corr, A. (2018). Introduction. In Coor, A. (Ed.), *Great Powers, Grand Strategies: The New Game in the South China Sea*. Naval Institute Press. DOI: 10.2307/j.ctt20061hj.5

Council of Foreign Relations (CFR). (2025). *Trump's Economic Disruption: The World Adapts*. Council of Councils Global Memos. Retrieved from https://www.cfr.org/councilofcouncils/global-memos/trumps-economic-disruption-world-adapts

Creswell, J. W., & Creswell, J. D. (2018). Research Design: Qualitative, Quantitative and Mixed Methods Approaches. *Sage (Atlanta, Ga.)*.

Cui, C., & Li, S. (2021). The Effect of the U.S.–China Trade War on Chinese New Firm Entry. *Economics Letters*, *203*(109846).

Cunado, J., Gupta, R., Lau, C. K. M., & Sheng, X. (2020). Time-varying impact of geopolitical risks on oil prices. *Defence and Peace Economics*, *31*(6), 692–706. DOI: 10.1080/10242694.2018.1563854

Dadush, U., & Dominguez Prost, E. (2023). Preferential trade agreements, geopolitics, and the fragmentation of world trade. *World Trade Review*, *22*(2), 278–294. DOI: 10.1017/S1474745623000022

Daly, R. (2022, Mar. 10). *China and the United States: It's a Cold War, but don't panic*. Bulletin of the Atomic Scientists. https://thebulletin.org/premium/2022-03/china-and-the-united-states-its-a-cold-war-but-dont-panic/

Dar, Z. A., & Javid, S. (2025). Navigating the Turbulent Waters: An In-Depth Study of US-China Geopolitical Rivalry. *Law. Economics and Society*, *1*(1), 1–13. DOI: 10.30560/les.v1n1p1

De Goede, M. (2017). Chains of securitization. *Finance and Stochastics*, *3*(2), 197–207. DOI: 10.2218/finsoc.v3i2.2579

De Tomi, G., Loredo, G., & Santos, V. (2024). *Critical and strategic minerals in Brazil: A sovereignty and climate agenda*. Sovereignty and Climate Center. https://soberaniaeclima.org.br/wp-content/uploads/2024/10/Artigo-Giorgio-de-Tomi-04-INGLES.pdf

Dee, P., & Findlay, C. (2006). "Trade Facilitation: What, Why, How, Where and When"? Working paper, *Asian Development Bank*, Manila.

Detry, E., Gauduel, A., Geurts, F., Ivers, L., McAdoo, M., Möncks, T., & Butler, T. (2023). *Five steps for solving the rare-earth metals shortage*. Boston Consulting Group. https://www.bcg.com/publications/2023/five-steps-for-solving-the-rare-earth-metals-shortage

Dhar, B. (2025). Trump's 'America First' Trade Policy. *Economic and Political Weekly, 60*(10), 18–21. https://www.scopus.com/record/display.uri?eid=2-s2.0-86000282208&origin=resultslist&sort=plf-f&src=s&sot=b&sdt=b&s=TITLE-ABS-KEY%28US+Reciprocal+Tariff%29&sessionSearchId=cb95d1f13ec3a88216fb0a03783d5277&relpos=1

Digital Economy Partnership Agreement (DEPA). Retrieved from https://web.archive.org/web/20210118060435/https://www.mti.gov.sg/Improving-Trade/Digital-Economy-Agreements/The-Digital-Economy-Partnership-Agreement

Dorn, J. A. (2023, October 10). *China's post-1978 economic development and entry into the global trading system*. Cato Institute. https://www.cato.org/publications/chinas-post-1978-economic-development-entry-global-trading-system

Dornier, P. P., & Fender, M. (2007). La logistique globale et le Supply Chain Management. *Edition d'organisation*.

Dos Santos, T. (1970). The structure of dependence. *The American Economic Review, 60*(2), 231–236.

Dow Jones. (2025, April 3). Trump tariffs bring end to era of globalization; How might central banks react to new economic order. *Morningstar.* https://www.morningstar.com/news/dow-jones/202504033640/trump-tariffs-bring-end-to-era-of-globalization-how-might-central-banks-react-to-new-economic-order

Draper, P., & Dadush, U. (2021, February 10). *Free trade in Africa is an important goal, but it is not easy to achieve.* Bruegel. https://www.bruegel.org/blog-post/free-trade-africa-important-goal-not-easy-achieve

Duan, W., Khurshid, A., Rauf, A., Khan, K., & Calin, A. C. (2021). How geopolitical risk drives exchange rate and oil prices? A wavelet-based analysis. *Energy Sources. Part B, Economics, Planning, and Policy, 16*(9), 861–877. DOI: 10.1080/15567249.2021.1965262

Economic Policy Research Centre. (2023). *Leveraging the AfCFTA agreement for Uganda's export growth: Challenges and solutions.* https://eprcug.org/publication/leveraging-the-afcfta-agreement-for-ugandas-export-growth-challenges-and-solutions/?wpdmdl=17885&refresh=6859313ca9b451750675772

Edwards, M. (2003). The New Great Game and the new great gamers: Disciples of Kipling and Mackinder. *Central Asian Survey, 22*(1), 83–102. DOI: 10.1080/0263493032000108644

Elms, D. K. (2025). *Southeast Asia in the Crosshairs: Navigating Trump's Protectionist Trade Policies.* https://techforgoodinstitute.org/blog/expert-opinion/southeast-asia-in-the-crosshairs-navigating-trumps-protectionist-trade-policies/

Elms, D. K. (2021). The U.S.–China Trade War: Impacts on Global Trade Governance. *World Economy, 44*(5), 1214–1232.

Eşiyok, B. A. (2014). Osmanlı İmparatorluğu'nun Dünya Ekonomisine Eklemlenmesinde Bir Dönüm Noktası:1838 Serbest Ticaret Anlaşması. *Mülkiye Dergisi, 34*(266), 67–108.

European Central Bank. (2024). *Economic resilience in a geopolitically fragmented world.* ECB Economic Bulletin, Issue 2/2024. https://www.ecb.europa.eu/press/economic-bulletin/focus/2024/html/ecb.ebbox202402_02~c81f58179e.en.html

European Commission. (2021). *Trade policy review – An open, sustainable and assertive trade policy.*

European Commission. (2022). *The WTO: A multilateral trading system.* https://policy.trade.ec.europa.eu/eu-and-world/wto-multilateral-trading-system_en

European Commission. (2023). *Foreign Subsidies Regulation: Ensuring fair competition in the internal market.* https://competition-policy.ec.europa.eu

European Commission. (2023). *Joint communication on a European economic security strategy.*

European Commission. (2023). Regulation (EU) 2023/956 establishing a carbon border adjustment mechanism. *Official Journal of the European Union, L, 130,* 52–103.

European Commission. (2024). *Corporate Sustainability Due Diligence Directive (CSDDD).* Retrieved from https://commission.europa.eu/business-economy-euro/doing-business-eu/sustainability-due-diligence-responsible-business/corporate-sustainability-due-diligence_en

European Commission. (2025). *Report Highlights EU's Approach to Export Controls of Dual-Use Items.* Retrieved from https://policy.trade.ec.europa.eu/news/report-highlights-eus-approach-export-controls-dual-use-items-2025-01-31_en

European Commission. *Carbon Border Adjustment Mechanism (CBAM).* Retrieved from https://taxation-customs.ec.europa.eu/carbon-border-adjustment-mechanism_en

European Commission. *Corporate Sustainability Reporting Directive (CSRD).* Retrieved from https://finance.ec.europa.eu/capital-markets-union-and-financial-markets/company-reporting-and-auditing/company-reporting/corporate-sustainability-reporting_en

European Parliament. (2013, Jun. 26). *China's investment in ports: what is behind the "String of Pearls" theory?* https://epthinktank.eu/2013/06/26/chinas-investment-in-ports-what-is-behind-the-string-of-pearls-theory/

European Union. (2021). *Regulation (EU) 2021/821 Setting up a Union Regime for the Control of Exports, Brokering, Technical Assistance, Transit and Transfer of Dual-Use Items.* Official Journal of the European Union. Retrieved from https://eur-lex.europa.eu/eli/reg/2021/821/oj/eng

Evans, P. (2014). The Role of Institutions in the Economic Development of the Global South. United Nations Development Programme (UNDP) Working Paper Series.

Export Compliance Training Institute. (2023). *A Comparison Between U.S. Export Controls and European Export Controls.* Retrieved from https://www.learnexport compliance.com/a-comparison-between-u-s-export-controls-and-european-export -controls

EY Parthenon. (2023, December). 2024 Geostrategic Outlook: How to thrive amid ongoing geopolitical complexity. EYGM Limited.

Fajgelbaum, P. D., Goldberg, P. K., Kennedy, P. J., & Khandelwal, A. K. (2020). The Return to Protectionism. *The Quarterly Journal of Economics, 135*(1), 1–55. https:// academic.oup.com/qje/article-abstract/135/1/1/5626442. DOI: 10.1093/qje/qjz036

Fajgelbaum, P. D., & Khandelwal, A. K. (2022). The economic impacts of the US–China trade war. *Annual Review of Economics, 14*(1), 205–228. DOI: 10.1146/ annurev-economics-051420-110410

Farrell, H., & Newman, A. L. (2019). Weaponized Interdependence: How Global Economic Networks Shape State Coercion. *International Security, 44*(1), 42–79. DOI: 10.1162/isec_a_00351

Federal Reserve History. (2025). Subprime Mortgage Crisis. https://www.federalrese rvehistory.org/essays/subprime-mortgage-crisis#:~:text=The%20subprime%20 mortgage%20crisis%20of%202007%2D10%20stemmed,was%20facilitated%20by %20rapidly%20rising%20home%20prices.&text=When%20house%20prices%20 peaked%2C%20mortgage%20refinancing%20and,rates%20began%20rising%20for %20lenders%20and%20investors

Feingold, S., & Botwright, K. (2025, June 25). *Tracking tariffs: Key moments in the US–China trade dispute. World Economic Forum.* Retrieved June 26, 2025, from https://www.weforum.org/stories/2025/06/trumps-us-china-trade-tariffs-timeline/

Feng, E. (2020, Nov. 3). *Regulators Squash Giant Ant Group IPO.* National Public Radio. https://www.npr.org/2020/11/03/930799521/regulators-squash-giant-ant-ipo

Finance, Y. (2025, Aug. 23). *Trump tariffs live updates: Trump says US to tariff furniture imports following investigation.* https://finance.yahoo.com/news/live/ trump-tariffs-live-updates-trump-says-us-to-tariff-furniture-imports-following -investigation-200619445.html

Financial Times. (2025, June 24). *EU readies retaliatory tariffs to secure better trade deal with Trump. Financial Times.* https://www.ft.com/content/3d336a84-ac59-45ee -b857-8a01fc7cd806 en.wikipedia.org+9ft.com+9reddit.com+9

Fiscal Data. (2025). The Causes of Deficits and Surpluses. https://fiscaldata.treasury.gov/americas-finance-guide/national-deficit/#:~:text=The%20federal%20government%20has%20spent%20$1.36%20trillion,(FY)%202025%2C%20resulting%20in%20a%20national%20deficit.&text=While%20revenue%20increased%20during%20the%20COVID%2D19%20pandemic%2C,health%20care%20caused%20spikes%20in%20the%20deficit

Foot, R., MacFarlane, S. N., & Mastanduno, M. (2003). *US hegemony and international organizations: The United States and multilateral institutions*. OUP Oxford. DOI: 10.1093/0199261431.001.0001

Frank, A. G. (1967). *Capitalism and underdevelopment in Latin America: Historical studies of Chile and Brazil*. Monthly Review Press.

Friedman, R. E., & Wimbush, S. E. (1996). Central Asia and The West. PERCEPTIONS: Journal of International Affairs, 1(4).

Fromkin, D. (1980). The Great Game in Asia. *Foreign Affairs*, *58*(4), 936–951. DOI: 10.2307/20040512

Fullerton, R. R., & McWatters, C. S. (2002). The role of performance measures and incentive systems in relation to the degree of JIT implementation. *Accounting, Organizations and Society*, *27*(8), 711–735. DOI: 10.1016/S0361-3682(02)00012-0

Gallagher, K. P. (2016). *Latin America's China Boom and the Fate of the Washington Consensus*. Oxford University Press.

Gan, N. (2025, May 21). US and China are feuding over Huawei's AI chips just days after tariff truce. *CNN Business*. https://www.cnn.com/2025/05/21/business/us-china-conflict-huawei-ai-chips-intl-hnk

Gani, A. (2017). The logistics performance effect in international trade. *The Asian Journal of Shipping and Logistics*, *33*(4), 279–288. DOI: 10.1016/j.ajsl.2017.12.012

Garamone, J. (2024, Dec. 5). *China Increasing Interest in Strategic Arctic Region*. U.S. Department of Defense. https://www.defense.gov/News/News-Stories/Article/Article/3986308/china-increasing-interest-in-strategic-arctic-region/

Garcia Herrero, A. (2022). *The Future of Electric Vehicles in Asia*. HKUST IEMS. https://iems.ust.hk/protected/request?path=%2Fassets%2Fpublications%2Fthought-leadership-briefs%2F2022%2Fhkustiems-future-of-electric-vehicles-in-asia-alicia-garcia-herrero-hkustiems-tlb64.pdf

Gava Group. (2025, July). *Vietnam Air Cargo to U.S. Soars as Tariffs Drive Shift from China*. From https://gava.com/vietnam-air-cargo-to-u-s-soars-as-tariffs-drive-shift-from-china/#:~:text=Vietnam's%20air%20cargo%20exports%20to,air%20cargo%20momentum%20may%20continue

Gerschenkron, A. (2015). *Economic Backwardness in Historical Perspective*. Belknap Press.

GhanaWeb. (2024). *ICUMS makes trade facilitation seamless – Samuel Akrofi*. https://www.ghanaweb.com/GhanaHomePage/business/ICUMS-makes-trade-facilitation-seamless-Samuel-Akrofi-1970946

Gilpin, R. (2001). *Global political economy: Understanding the international economic order*. Princeton University Press. DOI: 10.1515/9781400831272

Gimbals. (2025, March 26). Strategic Natural Resources and U.S. National Security in a Resource-Hungry World. https://3gimbals.com/insights/2025/03/26/

Gkillas, K., Manickavasagam, J., & Visalakshmi, S. (2022). Effects of fundamentals, geopolitical risk and expectations factors on crude oil prices. *Resources Policy, 78*, 102887. DOI: 10.1016/j.resourpol.2022.102887

Global4Cast.org. (2025, April 9). *Trump's 2025 trade war: Economic systemic warfare and the end of the old order*. https://global4cast.org/2025/04/trumps-2025-trade-war-economic-systemic-warfare-and-the-end-of-the-old-order/

Gomart, T. (2025). Chronique. Le commerce mondial, entre tarifs et infrastructures portuaires. Études, Juillet-Août(7-8), 31-32.

González, M. (2023, November 3). The EU in a new geopolitical world order. *Real Instituto Elcano*. https://www.realinstitutoelcano.org/en/commentaries/the-eu-in-a-new-geopolitical-world-order/

Gordon, N. (2025, April 17). How the U.S.-China trade war could derail the energy transition. *Carnegie Endowment for International Peace*. https://carnegieendowment.org/emissary/2025/04/us-china-trade-war-tariffs-critical-minerals-clean-energy-impacts?lang=en

Government of India. (2020). Atmanirbhar Bharat. https://www.pmindia.gov.in/en/news_updates/aatmanirbhar-bharat/

Government of India. (2020). Production linked incentive (PLI) schemes in India. Department of Commerce. https://commerce.gov.in

Granovetter, M. (1973). The Strength of Weak Ties. *American Journal of Sociology, 78*(6), 1360–1380. DOI: 10.1086/225469

Granovetter, M. (1983). The strength of weak ties: A network theory revisited. *Sociological Theory*, *1*, 201–233. DOI: 10.2307/202051

Gruzer, M. (April 22, 2025). Impact of US Tariffs on Central Asia. Bloomsbury Intelligence and Security Institute. Accessed July 07, 2025, https://bisi.org.uk/reports/impact-of-us-tariffs-on-central-asia

Guo, X. (2012). *China's Security State: Philosophy, Evolution, and Politics*. Cambridge University Press. DOI: 10.1017/CBO9781139150897

Haar, R. (2021). The Biden administration's incompatible views on multilateralism. [JSTOR.]. *Atlantisch Perspectief*, *45*(5), 20–24.

Hai, J. S. (2025, May 28). *What's happening in China's semiconductor industry?* Economics Observatory. https://www.economicsobservatory.com/whats-happening-in-chinas-semiconductor-industry

Han, D. (2023, January 14). *Economic Grrrowth in the East: Asian Tiger Economies*. JSTOR Daily. https://daily.jstor.org/economic-grrrowth-in-the-east-asian-tiger-economies/

Handley, K., Fariha, K., & Ryan, M. (2024). Supply chain adjustments to tariff shocks: Evidence from firm trade linkages in the 2018-2019 US trade war. *Economics Letters*, *244*, 112009. DOI: 10.1016/j.econlet.2024.112009

Hanh, V. (2025). *An Introduction to Rules of Origin for Vietnamese Exports* (Vu Nguyen Hanh). Retrieved from https://www.china-briefing.com/china-outbound-news/introduction-rules-origin-vietnam-based-production

Hart, B. (2021). Will the Dual Circulation Strategy Enable China to Compete in a Post-Pandemic World? *Center for Strategic and International Studies*. https://www.csis.org/analysis/will-dual-circulation-strategy-enable-china-compete-post-pandemic-world

Hashimzade, N., Myles, G., & Black, J. (2016). *A dictionary of economics*. Oxford University Press.

Hausman, W. H., Lee, H. L., & Subramanian, U. (2013). The impact of logistics performance on trade. *Production and Operations Management*, *22*(2), 236–252. DOI: 10.1111/j.1937-5956.2011.01312.x

Hayakawa, K. (2024). Do Exports to the US Increase Imports from China during the US–China Tariff War? *IDE Discussion Papers, Institute of Developing Economies, 946*(946).

Haydar, A. (July 16, 2025). Trump's 100% Tariffs May Target Kazakhstan and Kyrgyzstan. *The Times of Central Asia.* Accessed July 18, 2025, https://timesca.com/trumps-100-tariffs-may-target-kazakhstan-and-regional-economies/

Hayton, B. (2014). *The South China Sea: The Struggle for Power in Asia.* Yale University Press.

He, C., Mau, K., & Xu, M. (2021). Trade Shocks and Firms Hiring Decisions: Evidence from Vacancy Postings of Chinese Firms in the Trade War. *Labour Economics, 71*(102021), 102021. DOI: 10.1016/j.labeco.2021.102021

Helleiner, E. (2002). Economic nationalism as a challenge to economic liberalism? *International Studies Quarterly*, *46*(3), 307–329. DOI: 10.1111/1468-2478.00235

Hernandez-Roy, C., Ziemer, H., & Laske, N. (2024, April 11). De-risking Critical Mineral Supply Chains: The Role of Latin America. Center for Strategic and International Studies. https://www.csis.org/analysis/de-risking-critical-mineral-supply-chains-role-latin-america

Hinz, J., Mahlkow, H., & Wanner, J. (2025). The KITE Model Suite: A Quantitative Framework for International Trade Analysis. *KITE White Paper.*

Hollweg, C. H. (2019). *Global value chains and employment in developing economies.*, https://www.wto.org/english/res_e/booksp_e/gvc_dev_report_2019_e_ch3.pdf

Holtzmann, H.-D., & van der Voort, A. (2025, January 28). *BRICS - What are the key issues for 2025?* Friedrich Naumann Foundation for Freedom. https://www.freiheit.org/brics-what-are-key-issues-2025

Hong Kong's Esquel Group Added to U.S. Forced Labor Ban List. (2024). *The Wall Street Journal.* Retrieved from https://www.wsj.com/articles/hong-kongs-esquel-group-added-to-u-s-forced-labor-ban-list-fec7faa9

Hopewell, K. (2021). Trump and Trade: The Crisis in the Multilateral Trading System. *New Political Economy*, *26*(2), 271–282. DOI: 10.1080/13563467.2020.1841135

Hopkirk, P. (1992). *The Great Game: The Struggle for Empire in Central Asia.* In Kodansha International EBooks. http://ci.nii.ac.jp/ncid/BA20970331

Huang, J. (2024). China's role in the EU's search for strategic autonomy: Nonhegemonic power relations during world order transition. *China International Strategy Review*, *6*(2), 254–284. DOI: 10.1007/s42533-024-00174-5

Hughes, T. (2024, November 17). *China deepens ties with Brazil through financing and the promise of a green economy.* InvestorNews. https://investornews.com/critical-minerals-rare-earths/china-deepens-ties-with-brazil-through-financing-and-the-promise-of-a-green-economy/

Huld, A. (2025, August). *The Impact of Tariffs on Vietnamese Exports: US-Vietnam Trade Relations Under Trump 2.0.* From https://www.vietnam-briefing.com/news/us-vietnam-trade-relations-trump-impact-tariff-vietnamese-exports.html/#:~:text=Trump%20imposes%20reciprocal%20tariffs%20on,not%20available%20in%20the%20US

Huld, A. (2025). *The Impact of Tariffs on Vietnamese Exports: US-Vietnam Trade Relations Under Trump 2.0.* Vietnam Briefing.

Hummels, D., Lugovskyy, V., & Skiba, A. (2009). The trade reducing effects of market power in international shipping. *Journal of Development Economics, 89*(1), 84–97. DOI: 10.1016/j.jdeveco.2008.05.001

ICC Digital Standards Initiative. (2023). *Trust in Trade.* Retrieved from https://www.dsi.iccwbo.org/_files/ugd/8e49a6_5a75a77950d7474da772bf9cfc2d985b.pdf

ICC Digital Standards Initiative. *Digital Standards for Cross-Border Trade.* Retrieved from https://www.dsi.iccwbo.org

ICTSD. (2022). *Africa in WTO: Towards a unified agenda.* ICTSD (IISD). https://ictsd.iisd.org/africa-in-wto-towards-unified-agenda

IEA. (2025). *Today in Energy.* https://www.eia.gov/todayinenergy/detail.php?id=65724

Iglesias, S., Cele, S., & Viotti Beck, M. (2025, July 3). *BRICS aspires to occupy ground vacated by US under Trump.* Bloomberg. https://www.bloomberg.com/news/articles/2025-07-03/brics-aspires-to-occupy-global-ground-vacated-by-us-under-trump

Ignatenko, A., Lashkaripour, A., Macedoni, L., & Simonovska, A. I. (2025). Making America Great Again? The Economic Impacts of Liberation. *Journal of International Economics, 157*, 104138.1-104138.12.

Ikenberry, G. J. (2015). The Future of the Liberal World Order: Internationalism After America. *Foreign Affairs, 90*(3), 56–68.

Illuminem. (2025). *EU Moves to Ease CBAM Rules for SMEs While Keeping 99% of Emissions Covered.* Retrieved from https://illuminem.com/illuminemvoices/eu-moves-to-ease-cbam-rules-for-smes-while-keeping-99-of-emissions-covered

IMF. (2025). *World Economic Outlook Database*. https://www.imf.org/en/Publications/WEO/weo-database/2025/april

India, I. M. P. R. I. (2025). *Geopolitics of Trade and China Tensions*. https://www.impriindia.com/insights/geopolitics-trade-china-tensions/

Inglehart, R., & Norris, P. (2019). *Cultural backlash: Trump, Brexit, and authoritarian populism*. Cambridge University Press., DOI: 10.1017/9781108595841

Inocencio, R. (July 15, 2025). Trump threatens countries that do business with Russia with 100% tariffs. Here's who it could impact. CBC NEWS. Accessed July 20, 2025, https://www.cbsnews.com/news/trump-russia-ukraine-war-tariff-threat-countries-that-do-business-with-russia/

InOnAfrica. (2025). *The growing importance of rare earth minerals in African mining*. https://www.inonafrica.com/2025/02/11/the-growing-importance-of-rare-earth-minerals-in-african-mining/

International Energy Agency. (2025). *Global critical minerals outlook 2025*. https://www.iea.org/reports/global-critical-minerals-outlook-2025

International Monetary Fund. (2022, April). Global Trade and Value Chains during the Pandemic. *World Economic Outlook*.

International Monetary Fund. (2023). *Trade integration in Africa: Unleashing the continent's potential in a changing world (Departmental Paper No. 2023/007)*. https://www.imf.org/en/Publications/Departmental-Papers-Policy-Papers/Issues/2023/05/03/Trade-Integration-in-Africa-Unleashing-the-Continent-s-Potential-in-a-Changing-World-529215

International Plant Protection Convention (IPPC). *ePhyto Solution*. Retrieved from https://www.ippc.int/en/ephyto/

International Trade Centre. (2023). *Navigating Africa's digital trade with confidence*. https://www.intracen.org/news-and-events/news/navigating-africas-digital-trade-with-confidence

International Trade Centre. (2023a, August). *The global state of trade: Trade in critical raw materials*. ITC Trade Briefs. https://tradebriefs.intracen.org/2023/8/spotlight

International Trade Centre. (2023b, September). *The global state of trade: Trade in critical minerals by processing level*. ITC Trade Briefs. https://tradebriefs.intracen.org/2023/9/spotlight

Interos. (2022, April). *Chinese rare earth elements (REE) & metals dominance analysis*. Interos Inc. https://www.interos.ai/wp-content/uploads/2022/04/Interos-Report-Explores-Concentration-Risk-of-Rare-Earth-Minerals-and-China.pdf

Iqbal, N., & Prazeres, L. (2025, August 15). *Bolsonaro's son praises Trump's tariff hike on Brazil*. From https://www.bbc.com/news/articles/c5yl00qlyz9o

ITC. (2025). *Navigating Africa's digital trade with confidence*. https://www.intracen.org/news-and-events/news/navigating-africas-digital-trade-with-confidence

Ito, T. (2024). Trump Tariffs and Roundabout Trade. *KDI Journal of Economic Policy*, *46*(3), 25–47.

Ivanov, D. (2025). Supply chain stress testing for tariff shocks and trade conflicts: Methods, models, and reciprocal influence of operations and economics. *IEEE Transactions on Engineering Management*, *72*, 3559–3566. DOI: 10.1109/TEM.2025.3599711

Ivanovski, K., & Hailemariam, A. (2022). Time-varying geopolitical risk and oil prices. *International Review of Economics & Finance*, *77*, 206–221. DOI: 10.1016/j.iref.2021.10.001

J.P. Morgan Research. (2025, June 9). *US tariffs: What's the impact?* J.P. Morgan. https://www.jpmorgan.com/insights/global-research/current-events/us-tariffs

Jacks, D. S., & Pendakur, K. (2010). Global trade and the maritime transport revolution. *The Review of Economics and Statistics*, *92*(4), 745–755. DOI: 10.1162/REST_a_00026

Jean, R. (2024). *How Geopolitical Tensions Reshape Trade Patterns*. IFRI. https://www.ifri.org/en/publications/notes-de-lifri/china-and-world/how-geopolitical-tensions-reshape-trade-patterns

Jin, K. (2023). *The New China Playbook*. Viking.

Joignaux, G., & Verny, J. (2004). Le découplage entre transport de marchandises et croissance: Organisations productives, localisations et demande de transport. *Revue d'Économie Régionale et Urbaine*, (5), 779–791. DOI: 10.3917/reru.045.0779

Jumah, Z., Moazzam, M., Manzoor, W., & Safdar, N. (2025). Economic policy uncertainty and firm's profitability: The role of logistics infrastructure. *International Journal of Productivity and Performance Management*, *74*(1), 180–202. DOI: 10.1108/IJPPM-08-2023-0410

Kapoor, D., & Mukhopadhyay, P. (2021). The political economy of Atmanirbhar Bharat. Centre for Policy Research. https://cprindia.org

Kaur, M., Selvakumar, P., Dinesh, N., & Chandel, P. S. Mohit, & Manjunath, T. C. (2025). Reconstruction and preservation strategies for cultural heritage. In S. Oflazoğlu & M. Dora (Eds.), *Preserving Cultural Heritage in Post-Disaster Urban Renewal* (pp. 385–412). IGI Global.

Keohane, R. O., & Nye, J. S.Jr. (1987). Power and Interdependence revisited. *International Organization*, *41*(4), 725–753. DOI: 10.1017/S0020818300027661

Kilian, L., Plante, M., & Richter, A. W. (2024). Geopolitical oil price risk. Federal Reserve Bank of Dallas, Working Paper No. 2403. https://www.dallasfed.org/~/media/documents/research/papers/2024/wp2403.pdf

Kim, P. M., Turpin, M., & Jr, N. Joseph S. & Weiss, Jessica Chen & Jo, Eun A. (2023, Sept. 1). *Should the US pursue a new Cold War with China?* Brookings Institution. https://www.brookings.edu/articles/should-the-us-pursue-a-new-cold-war-with-china/

Kim, S. (2023). *Realism and EU Trade Policy: European Strategic Autonomy through the Case of EU-China Comprehensive Agreement on Investment*. CAI. [Master's thesis, Seoul National University]

King, R., & Kendall, G. (2004). *The State, Democracy, and Globalization*. Palgrave Macmillan.

Kirby, W. C. (2013). Global Business across the Taiwan Strait: The Case of the Taiwan Semiconductor Manufacturing Company Limited. In Wen-hsin, Y. (Ed.), *Mobile Horizons: Dynamics across the Taiwan Strait*. Institute of East Asian Studies, University of California. DOI: 10.2307/jj.7762620.11

Kirshner, J. (2009). The political economy of realism. In Cox, M., & Stokes, D. (Eds.), *U.S. foreign policy* (pp. 83–97). Oxford University Press.

Kissinger, H. (1994). *Diplomacy*. Simon & Schuster.

Kissinger, H. (2011). *On China*. Penguin Press.

Kissinger, H. (2014). *World Order*. Penguin Press.

Kozul-Wright, A. (July 15, 2025). Russia may face Trump tariffs in 50 days, what does US import from Russia? *Al Jazeera*. Accessed July 24, 2025, https://www.aljazeera.com/news/2025/7/15/trump-threatens-tariffs-in-50-days-what-harm-will-it-do-to-russia

Krige, John. (2024). Debate: Building a U.S. Regulatory Empire in the Chip War with China. *Technology and Culture, 65*(4), 1081-. DOI: 10.1353/tech.2024.a940462

Kroeber, A. R. (2016). *China's Economy: What Everyone Needs to Know*. Oxford University Press.

Krueger, A. (2022a). Will the Ukraine war revive the WTO? *Project Syndicate*. Retrieved April 15, 2023, from https://www.project-syndicate.org/commentary/wto-dispute-settlement-new-trade-issues-friend-shoring-by-anne-o-krueger-2022-05?barrier=accesspaylog

Krueger, A. (2022b). The false promise of America's CHIPS Act. *Project Syndicate*. Retrieved April 15, 2023, from https://www.project-syndicate.org/commentary/chips-act-will-not-keep-us-semiconductor-industry-on-top-by-anne-o-krueger-2022-11?barrier=accesspaylog

Krueger, A. (2022c). Sleepwalking into a global trade war. *Project Syndicate*. Retrieved April 15, 2023, from https://www.project-syndicate.org/commentary/trade-world-war-us-subsidies-protectionism-by-anne-o-krueger-2022-12?barrier=accesspaylog

Krugman, P. R. (1985). Is free trade passé? *The Journal of Economic Perspectives*, *1*(2), 131–144. DOI: 10.1257/jep.1.2.131

Krugman, P. R., & Smith, A. (Eds.). (1994). *Empirical studies of strategic trade policy*. University of Chicago Press., https://www.nber.org/books-and-chapters/empirical-studies-strategic-trade-policy/introduction-empirical-studies-strategic-trade-policy DOI: 10.7208/chicago/9780226454665.001.0001

Krulikowski, S. (2024). *Central Asia: A Brief Overview of International Trade*. U.S. International Trade Commission.

Kuhn, B. (2024). Kritische Rohstoffe: Wie die EU ihre China- Abhängigkeit senken will (Critical raw materials: How the EU wants to reduce its dependence on China). *Wirtschaftsdienst (Hamburg, Germany)*, *104*(7), 490–496. https://www.wirtschaftsdienst.eu/inhalt/jahr/2024/heft/7/beitrag/kritische-rohstoff-e-wie-die-eu-ihre-china-abhaengigkeit-senken-will.html#footnote-003. DOI: 10.2478/wd-2024-0126

Kuo, K. (2025, June 19). *How China got rich: A deep dive into China's 40-year history of economic transformation*. World Economic Forum. https://www.weforum.org/stories/2025/06/how-china-got-rich-40-year-history-of-economic-transformation/

Laclau, E. (2005). *On populist reason*. Verso Books.

Lapa, V. (2020). The WTO Panel Report in Russia – Traffic in Transit: Cutting the Gordian Knot of the GATT Security Exception? *Questions of International Law / Questions de Droit International*, 40, 15–38. https://www.qil-qdi.org/the-wto-panel-report-in-russia-traffic-in-transit-cutting-the-gordian-knot-of-the-gatt-security-exception/

Lau, S. (2025). The 'American Empire' is fast declining. https://www.chinadailyhk.com/upload/main/pdf/2025/03/17/6667fb923456514ae6fa600bc4ce1fb3.pdf

Lau, C. K., Soliman, A. M., Albasu, J., & Gozgor, G. (2023). Dependence structures among geopolitical risks, energy prices, and carbon emissions prices. *Resources Policy*, *83*, 103603. DOI: 10.1016/j.resourpol.2023.103603

Lawal, S. (2024, December 4). Tech wars: Why has China banned exports of rare minerals to US? *Al Jazeera*. https://www.aljazeera.com/news/2024/12/4/tech-wars-why-has-china-banned-exports-of-rare-minerals-to-us

Lawrence, R. (2025). *Explainer: How Do Tariffs Work and How Will They Impact The American and Global Economy?* https://www.hks.harvard.edu/faculty-research/policy-topics/public-finance/explainer-how-do-tariffs-work-and-how-will-they

Lederer, E. (2025, May 28). *U.S. says it will start revoking visas for Chinese students. Reuters*. Retrieved June 26, 2025, from https://www.reuters.com/world/us/rubio-says-us-will-start-revoking-visas-chinese-students-2025-05-28/ washingtonpost.com+10reuters.com+10staradvertiser.com+10

Lee, J. Y., & Rodrigue, J. P. (2006). Trade Reorientation and Its Effects on Regional Port Systems: The Korea-China Link along the Yellow Sea Rim. *Growth and Change*, *37*(4), 597–619. DOI: 10.1111/j.1468-2257.2006.00342.x

León de la Rosa, R. I. (2019). *Guerra comercial China- Estados Unidos*. XVII Jornadas de Comercio UPAEP.

Leonard, M., & Pisani-Ferry, J. (2022). *The new geoeconomics: Securing Europe's place in a dangerous world*. European Council on Foreign Relations.

Levin Center. (2025). Portraits in Oversight: Congress and the Enron Scandal. https://levin-center.org/what-is-oversight/portraits/congress-and-the-enron-scandal/#:~:text=The%20Rise%20and%20Fall%20of,company%20stopped%20paying%20its%20bills

Lewis, J. A. (2024, Mar. 13). *TikTok and National Security*. Center for Strategic & International Studies. https://www.csis.org/analysis/tiktok-and-national-security

Li, Z. (2018). The Maritime Silk Route and India: The Challenge of Overcoming Cognitive Divergence. In David Brewster (Eds). *India & China at Sea: Competition for Naval Dominance in the Indian Ocean*. Oxford University Press.

Li, C., He, C., & Lin, C. (2018). Economic Impacts of The Possible China-US Trade War. *Emerging Markets Finance Ad Trade. Emerging Markets Finance & Trade, 54*(7), 1557–1577. DOI: 10.1080/1540496X.2018.1446131

Li, J., Li, P., & Wang, B. (2019). The liability of opaqueness: State ownership and the likelihood of deal completion in international acquisitions by Chinese firms. *Strategic Management Journal, 40*(2), 303–327. DOI: 10.1002/smj.2985

Li, M., Balistreri, E. J., & Zhang, W. (2020). The U.S.–China trade war: Tariff Data and General Equilibrium Analysis. *Journal of Asian Economics, 69*(101216), 101216. DOI: 10.1016/j.asieco.2020.101216

Limao, N., & Venables, A. J. (2001). Infrastructure, geographical disadvantage and transport costs. *The World Bank Economic Review, 15*(3), 451–479. DOI: 10.1093/wber/15.3.451

Linh, D. K. M. (2025). *Trump's Tariff Turbulence is Reshaping Vietnam's Trade Future*. East Asia Forum. https://eastasiaforum.org/2025/06/23/trumps-tariff-turbulence-is-reshaping-vietnams-trade-future/

Li, S., & Lu, J. W. (2020). A dual-agency model of firm CSR in response to institutional pressure: Evidence from Chinese publicly listed firms. *Academy of Management Journal, 63*(6), 2004–2032. DOI: 10.5465/amj.2018.0557

Liu, J., Xiaoye, W & Junyu G. (2024). "Port efficiency and its influencing factors in the context of pilot free trade zones." *Transport Policy* 105 (2021): 67-79.

Liu, Juliana; Gan, N. (2025). *China imposes 34% reciprocal tariffs on imports of US goods in* retaliation for Trump's trade war.

Liu, R. C., Tang, H. W., Kao, Y., & Chou, Y. (2025). From vulnerabilities to resilience: Taiwan's semiconductor industry and geopolitical challenges. *Telecommunications Policy, 49*(4), 102951. DOI: 10.1016/j.telpol.2025.102951

Liu, X. (2021). Chinese multinational enterprises operating in Western economies: Huawei in the US and the UK. In *China's Big Power Ambition under Xi Jinping* (pp. 219–236). Routledge. DOI: 10.4324/9781003198871-14

Liu, Z. (2025). The "Pan-Securitization" of the EU's Connectivity Policy and China–EU Cooperation. In Xiang, G., Gouliamos, K., Zuokui, L., & Kassimeris, C. (Eds.), *The Belt and Road Initiative*., DOI: 10.1007/978-981-96-1128-7_13

Li, X., Umar, M., Zhu, C. B., & Oprean-Stan, C. (2023). Can geopolitical risk stably predict crude oil prices? A multi-dimensional perspective. *Resources Policy, 85*, 103785. DOI: 10.1016/j.resourpol.2023.103785

Luttwak, E. N. (1990). From geopolitics to geo-economics: Logic of conflict, grammar of commerce. *National Interest, 20*, 17–23.

Madeiros, C. (2016). China and the Global Division of Labor: A Structural Perspective. *Estudos Avançados, 30*(88), 25–44.

Malik, A. A., Parks, B., Russell, B., Lin, J. J., Walsh, K., Solomon, K., Zhang, S., Elston, T.-B., & Goodman, S. (2021, Sept.). *Banking on the Belt and Road. Insights from a new global dataset of 13,427 Chinese Development Projects.* AIDDATA: A Research Lab at William & Mary. https://docs.aiddata.org/ad4/pdfs/Banking_on_the_Belt_and_Road__Insights_from_a_new_global_dataset_of_13427_Chinese_development_projects.pdf

Mansoor, S. I. U. (2024). China's Geopolitical Strategy: Crafting a New World Order. *China Quarterly of International Strategic Studies, 9*(1–4), 337–359. DOI: 10.1142/S2377740023500161

Mathekga, R. (2025). *Trade tariffs hinder SADC integration.* GIS Reports Online.

Mattoo, A., & Staiger, R. W. (2019, April). *Trade wars: What do they mean? Why are they happening now? What are the costs?* (NBER Working Paper Series, No. 25762). National Bureau of Economic Research. https://www.nber.org/papers/w25762

Mattoo, A., Rocha, N., & Ruta, M. (2020). *The AfCFTA and Africa's growth prospects (Working Paper No. 20-9).* Peterson Institute for International Economics. https://www.piie.com/sites/default/files/documents/wp20-9.pdf

Mazzocco, I. (2025). Analyzing the Impact of the U.S.-China Trade War on China's Energy Transition. *Center for Strategic and International Studies.* https://www.csis.org/analysis/analyzing-impact-us-china-trade-war-chinas-energy-transition

Mazzocco, I. (2025, April 22). *Analyzing the impact of the U.S.-China trade war on China's energy transition.* Center for Strategic and International Studies. https://www.csis.org/analysis/analyzing-impact-us-china-trade-war-chinas-energy-transition

Mazzucchelli, F. (2009). Estados Unidos e a reconstrução da ordem mundial do pós-guerra: Entre a ordem liberal e o mundo livre. *Revista Brasileira de Política Internacional, 52*(1), 98–117.

McDevitt, M. A. (2020). *China as a Twenty-First Century Naval Power.* Naval Institute Press.

McElwee, M., Bartels, L., & Carr, C. (2025, April 9). *Trump's tariffs: WTO consultations requested by China, Canada and the European Union*. Freshfields Risk & Compliance. Retrieved June 26, 2025, from https://riskandcompliance.freshfields.com/post/102k86k/trumps-tariffs-wto-consultations-requested-by-china-canada-and-the-european-un

McElwee, L. (2022). *The rise and demise of the EU–China Investment Agreement: Takeaways for the future of German debate on China*. Center for Strategic and International Studies.

McKibbin, W.J., Marcus N., & Geoffrey S. (2025) "25-13 *The global economic effects of Trump's 2025 tariffs*."

McKinsey Global Institute. (2020). Risk, resilience, and rebalancing in global value chains. https://www.mckinsey.com/business-functions/operations/our-insights/risk-resilience-and-rebalancing-in-global-value-chains

McKinsey Global Institute. (2025). *Geopolitics and the Geometry of Global Trade: 2025 Update*. https://www.mckinsey.com/mgi/our-research/geopolitics-and-the-geometry-of-global-trade-2025-update

Mehta, P. B. (2022). India's populism and the politics of trade (ORF Occasional Paper No. 345). Observer Research Foundation. https://www.orfonline.org

Mehta, P. B. (2022). Strategic protectionism and India's trade dilemmas. *Economic and Political Weekly*, *57*(42), 21–24. https://www.epw.in/journal/2022/42

Meissner, K. L. (2016). A case of failed interregionalism? Analyzing the EU–ASEAN free trade agreement negotiations. *Asia Europe Journal*, *14*(3), 319–336. DOI: 10.1007/s10308-016-0450-5

Melkozerova, V. (2025, Apr. 17). *China is supplying weapons to Russia, Zelenskyy says*. Politico. https://www.politico.eu/article/china-is-supplying-weapons-to-russia-zelenskyy-said/

Mena, B. (2025, April 2). Key takeaways from Trump's Liberation Day tariffs. CNN. https://edition.cnn.com/2025/04/02/economy/key-takeaways-from-trumps-liberation-day-tariffs/index.html

Mendez-Parra, M. (2022). *The African Continental Free Trade Area in a global trade context: A governance perspective*. Friedrich-Ebert-Stiftung Geneva Office. https://library.fes.de/pdf-files/bueros/genf/19225.pdf

Menon, J. (2025). *Southeast Asia at The Crossroads of Trump Tariffs 2.0*. https://eastasiaforum.org/2025/01/23/southeast-asia-at-the-crossroads-of-trump-tariffs-2-0/

Meredith, R. (2007). *The Elephant and the Dragon: The Rise of India and China and What It Means for All of Us*. W.W. Norton & Company.

Mestiri, R. (2019) "La contribution de l'agriculture urbaine à l'approvisionnement alimentaire de La Havane." *Revue internationale des études du développement* 237.1: 137-164.

Meunier, S., & Nicolaïdis, K. (2019). The geopoliticization of European trade and investment policy. *Journal of Common Market Studies, 57*(S1), 103–113. DOI: 10.1111/jcms.12932

Miao, Y., & Deng, T. (2020). China's Capital Account Liberalization: A Ruby Jubilee and Beyond. In Amstad, M., Sun, G., & Xiong, W. (Eds.), *The Handbook of China's Financial System*. Princeton University Press. DOI: 10.2307/j.ctv11vcdpc.14

Milanovic, B. (2016). *Global inequality: A new approach for the age of globalization*. Harvard University Press.

Miller, C. (2022). *Chip War: The Fight for the World's Most Critical Technology*. Scribner.

Milner, C., Morrissey, O., & Zgovu, E. (2008). *Trade facilitation in developing countries (No. 08/05)*. CREDIT Research Paper

Minges, M. (2025, Jan. 23). *National Security and the TikTok Ban*. American University. https://www.american.edu/sis/news/20250123-national-security-and-the-tik-tok-ban.cfm

Ministry of Commerce and Industry, Government of India. (2024). Export-Import data bank. https://commerce.gov.in/trade-statistics/

Mistreanu, S. (2025, Apr. 5). *A timeline of US-China tit-for-tat tariffs since Trump's first term*. Associated Press. https://apnews.com/article/china-us-tariffs-timeline-trump-xi-1eeed2865dc7b14e23d7eb8069ba41ea

Mohawk Global. (2025, August 12). *Suspension of Additional Tariffs on Chinese Imports Extended Until November*. From https://mohawkglobal.com/word-from-the-white-house/suspension-of-additional-tariffs-on-chinese-imports-extended-until-november/#:~:text=Mohawk%20Global%20Home-,Suspension%20of%20Additional%20Tariffs%20on%20Chinese%20Imports%20Extended%20Until%20November,r

Molof, D. (2025, April 10). *How Congress can end Trump's trade war*. Center for American Progress. https://www.americanprogress.org/article/how-congress-can-end-trumps-trade-war/

Moore, B. (1967). *Social Origins of Dictatorship and Democracy: Lord and Peasant in the Making of the Modern World*. Beacon Press.

Moreira, A. (2022, November 9). U.S. unveils investment in nickel, cobalt in Brazil. Valorinternational. https://valorinternational.globo.com/economy/news/2022/11/15/us-unveils-investment-in-nickel-cobalt-in-brazil.ghtml

Mudde, C., & Rovira Kaltwasser, C. (2017). *Populism: A very short introduction*. Oxford University Press. DOI: 10.1093/actrade/9780190234874.001.0001

Muggah, R. (2025, May 13). *The Amazon's green "critical mineral" boom carries hidden environmental and social costs*. LinkedIn. https://www.linkedin.com/pulse/amazons-green-critical-mineral-boom-carries-hidden-social-muggah-9fdsf/

Munyati, C. (2024). *Africa and the Gulf States: A new economic partnership*. World Economic Forum. https://www.weforum.org/stories/2024/04/africa-gcc-gulf-economy-partnership-emerging

Murphy, E.L. (2025). Trump Tariffs Likely Pushing Asia Elsewhere for Economic Partners, *Centre for Strategic and International Studies*, 14 July.

Mwita, K. (2022). Strengths and Weaknesses of Qualitative Research in Social Science Studies. *International Journal Research in Business and Social Science*, *11*(September), 618–625. Advance online publication. DOI: 10.20525/ijrbs.v11i6.1920

Nelson, M. (2019). *U.S. Trade Policy: Section 301 and 232 Investigations and the Role of the WTO*. Congressional Research Service (CRS) Report R45529. https://crsreports.congress.gov

Nghi, G. (2025, July). *ADB lowers Vietnam's GDP growth forecast to 6.3%*. From https://english.thesaigontimes.vn/adb-lowers-vietnams-gdp-growth-forecast-to-6-3/

Nicita, A., & Enxhi, T. (2023). The heterogeneous effects of trade policy on trade resilience during the 2020 trade downturn. *World Economy*, *46*(10), 3048–3056. DOI: 10.1111/twec.13420

Nordas, H. K., Pinali, E., & Grosso, M. G. (2006). *Logistics and time as a trade barrier*.

North, D. C. (1990). *Institutions, Institutional Change and Economic Performance*. Cambridge University Press. DOI: 10.1017/CBO9780511808678

North, D. C. (1992). *Transaction Costs, Institutions, and Economic Performance*. ICS Press.

North, D. C. (2018). *Entendendo o processo de mudança econômica* (3rd ed.). Editora Senac.

Notteboom, T. E. (2012). Towards a new intermediate hub region in container shipping? Relay and interlining via the Cape route vs. The Suez route. *Journal of Transport Geography*, *22*, 164–178. DOI: 10.1016/j.jtrangeo.2012.01.003

Nunes, V., & Lopes, G. (2024, November 19). Did you spot a new EV in Brazil? It's probably Chinese. *BloombergNEF*. https://about.bnef.com/insights/clean-transport/did-you-spot-a-new-ev-in-brazil-its-probably-chinese/

OEC. (2024). *Trade data*. https://oec.world/es

OECD. (2021). *International Regulatory Co-operation: OECD Best Practice Principles for Regulatory Policy*. OECD Publishing., DOI: 10.1787/5b28b589-

OECD. (2022). Global trade fragmentation: Scenarios and implications. https://www.oecd.org/trade/tradestatistics/global-trade-fragmentation.htm

OECD. (2022). Trade policy briefs. OECD Publishing. https://www.oecd.org

OECD. (2023). *Trade Facilitation in Central Asia*. OECD Publishing., DOI: 10.1787/80ed999c-

OECD. (2025). *OECD Trade Facilitation Indicators*. Retrieved from https://www.oecd.org/en/publications/oecd-trade-facilitation-indicators_fd6f27dc-en.html

OECD. (2025). *OECD Trade Facilitation Indicators: Monitoring Policies up to 2025*. Retrieved from https://www.oecd.org/content/dam/oecd/en/publications/reports/2025/03/oecd-trade-facilitation-indicators_0a21eb4a/fd6f27dc-en.pdf

OECD. (2025, June 3). *OECD Economic Outlook, Volume 2025 Issue 1: Tackling Uncertainty, Reviving Growth*. https://www.oecd.org/en/publications/2025/06/oecd-economic-outlook-volume-2025-issue-1_1fd979a8/full-report/general-assessment-of-the-macroeconomic-situation_3e68d1e3.html

Office of the United States Trade Representative (USTR). (2018a). *Findings of the investigation into China's acts, policies, and practices related to technology transfer, intellectual property, and innovation under section 301 of the Trade Act of 1974*. Washington, DC. Retrieved May 10, 2022, from https://ustr.gov/sites/default/files/Section%20301%20FINAL.PDF

Office of the United States Trade Representative (USTR). (2018b). *USTR finalizes tariffs on $200 billion of Chinese imports in response to China's unfair trade practices*. Washington, DC. Retrieved April 28, 2021, from https://ustr.gov/about-us/policy-offices/press-office/press-releases/2018/september/ustr-finalizes-tariffs-200

Office of the United States Trade Representative (USTR). (2018c). *Rebalancing United States-China trade*. Washington, DC. Retrieved June 30, 2022, from https://ustr.gov/phase-one

Office of the United States Trade Representative (USTR). (2018d). *$300 billion trade action (List 4)*. Washington, DC. Retrieved May 15, 2022, from https://ustr.gov/issue-areas/enforcement/section-301-investigations/section-301-china/300-billion-trade-action

Office of the United States Trade Representative (USTR). (2018e). *Section 301 investigations*. Washington, DC. Retrieved May 15, 2022, from https://ustr.gov/issue-areas/enforcement/section-301-investigations

Office of the United States Trade Representative (USTR). (2018f). *USTR finalizes second tranche of tariffs on Chinese products in response to China's unfair trade practices*. Washington, DC. Retrieved May 15, 2022, from https://ustr.gov/about-us/policy-offices/press-office/press-releases/2018/august/ustr-finalizes-second-tranche

Office of the United States Trade Representative. (2020). United States–Mexico–Canada Agreement (USMCA). https://ustr.gov/trade-agreements/free-trade-agreements/united-states-mexico-canada-agreement

Office of The United States Trade Representative. (2022, February). *Section 201 – Imported Solar Cells and Modules*. From https://ustr.gov/issue-areas/enforcement/section-201-investigations/investigation-no-ta-201-75-cspv-cells

Office of the United States Trade Representative. (2023). US-India Trade Policy Forum joint statement. https://ustr.gov/about-us/policy-offices/press-office/press-releases

Office of The United States Trade Representative. (2025). *China Trade Summary*. From https://ustr.gov/countries-regions/china-mongolia-taiwan/peoples-republic-china#:~:text=China%20Trade%20Summary&text=U.S.%20goods%20imports%20from%20China,($15.9%20billion)%20over%202023

Oliphant, C. (2013). Russia's role and interests in Central Asia. *Safeworld,* 1-13.

Oliveira, G. (2007). O sistema multilateral de comércio: Da Rodada Uruguai à OMC. *Revista de Economia Contemporânea*, *11*(2), 305–327. DOI: 10.1590/S1415-98482007000200006

Online, E. T. (2025, June 5). Why rare earths are the new battleground in US-China trade war. *The Economic Times.* https://economictimes.indiatimes.com/news/international/global-trends/chinas-new-rare-earth-policy-rare-earth-magnet-export-why-rare-earths-are-the-new-battleground-in-us-china-trade-war/articleshow/121642918.cms

Ortiz-Ospina, E., Beltekian, D., & Roser, M. (2014, April). *Trade and globalization.* Our World in Data. https://ourworldindata.org/trade-and-globalization

Osidejo, A., & Akenroye, T. (2025). *How lowering tariffs could unleash Africa's economic opportunity.* World Economic Forum.

Owsiak, A., Diehl, P. F., & Goertz, G. (2024). Managing complexity: Addressing the civil conflict component of international-civil militarized conflicts (I-CMCs). *International Journal of Conflict Management, 35*(1), 192–214. DOI: 10.1108/IJCMA-01-2023-0002

Paese, A. (2025, July 29). *EU-US trade deal explained.* From https://ec.europa.eu/commission/presscorner/detail/en/qanda_25_1930

Panchenko, V., & Reznikova, N. (2017). From protectionism to neo-protectionism: New dimensions of liberal regulation. *Information Economics and Policy*, (2), 91–111.

Park, C.-Y., & Melendez, A. C. (2024). *Building resilient and responsible critical minerals supply chains for the clean energy transition* (ADB Briefs No. 298). Asian Development Bank. https://www.adb.org/publications/critical-minerals-supply-chains-clean-energy-transition

Parodi, A., & Waldersee, V. (2025, June 19). China floods Brazil with cheap EVs, triggering backlash. *Reuters.* https://www.reuters.com/business/finance/china-floods-brazil-with-cheap-evs-triggering-backlash-2025-06-19/

Patey, L. (2024, Dec. 2). *A Taiwan crisis is a China crisis.* Danish Institute for International Studies. https://www.diis.dk/en/research/a-taiwan-crisis-is-a-china-crisis#:~:text=The%20global%20economic%20decline%20from%20Chinese%20military,other%20industries%20dependent%20on%20the%20advanced%20technology

Patrick, S. (2021, February 4). *The Biden administration and the future of multilateralism.* Observer Research Foundation. https://www.orfonline.org/expert-speak/biden-administration-future-multilateralism

Pautasso, D. (2016). The Role of Africa in the New Maritime Silk Road. *Brazilian Journal of African Studies, 1*(2), 118–130.

PeaceDiplomacy. (2025, March 18). China's Strategic Preparedness for a New Round of Trade War with the U.S.: A Comparative Analysis. https://peacediplomacy.org/2025/03/18/chinas-strategic-preparedness-for-a-new-round-of-trade-war-with-the-u-s-a-comparative-analysis/

Pecequilo, C. S. (2012). *O poder e a nova ordem global*. Saraiva.

Perez, A. (2025, March 12). *The geopolitics of trade tariffs: The new Trump presidency*. From https://commonslibrary.parliament.uk/the-geopolitics-of-trade-tariffs-the-new-trump-presidency/

Perry, A., & Van Veen, K. (2024, October). Recovering rare earth elements from e-waste: Potential impacts on NdFeB magnet supply chains and the environment. *Journal of International Commerce and Economics*. https://www.usitc.gov/publications/332/journals/jice_recovering_rare_earth_elements_from_e_waste.pdf

Peterson Institute for International Economics. (2021). Annual report. https://www.piie.com/publications/annual-report

Peterson Institute for International Economics. (2021). Economic impact of Trump's tariffs. https://www.piie.com/research/trade-investment/economic-impact-tariffs

Peterson, D. M., & Murray, E. Lori. (2025). The Debt Crisis is Here. https://www.pgpf.org/programs-and-projects/convening-experts/expert-views/fiscal-commission/the-debt-crisis-is-here/

Petri & Plummer. (2020). *Mega-regional trade agreements: Implications for East Asia*. https://www.pecc.org/resources/trade-and-investment-1/2639-mega-regional-trade-agreements-implications-for-east-asia/file

Petri, P. A., & Plummer, M. G. (2020). *RCEP: A new trade agreement that will shape global economics and politics*. Brookings. https://www.brookings.edu/articles/rcep-a-new-trade-agreement-that-will-shape-global-economics-and-politics/

Piketty, T. (2020). *Capital and ideology* (Goldhammer, A., Trans.). Harvard University Press.

Pires, L. S., & Mattos, C. (2016). A crise estrutural do capital: Elementos teóricos e implicações para a economia mundial contemporânea. *Revista de Economia Contemporânea*, *20*(2), 207–230.

Plus, V. (2025, April). *PM calls for flexible response to US tariffs, maintaining 8% growth target*. From https://en.vietnamplus.vn/pm-calls-for-flexible-response-to-us-tariffs-maintaining-8-growth-target-post312943.vnp

Posen, B. R. (2003). The Sources of Military Doctrine and Grand Strategy. *Contemporary Security Policy*, *24*(2), 32–52. DOI: 10.1080/13523260312312

Putz, C. (2025). New Trump Tariffs Target Kazakhstan With 25% Rate. *The Diplomat*. Accessed July 04, 2025, https://thediplomat.com/2025/07/new-trump-tariffs-target-kazakhstan-with-25-rate/

Qian, L., Zeng, Q., & Li, T. (2022). Geopolitical risk and oil price volatility: Evidence from Markov-switching model. *International Review of Economics & Finance*, *81*, 29–38. DOI: 10.1016/j.iref.2022.05.002

Race, M. (2025, May 12). *What does the US-China tariff deal mean?* From https://www.bbc.com/news/articles/clyg2939ej2o

Rahbari, M., Arshadi Khamseh, A., & Sadati-Keneti, Y. (2024). Resilience strategies in coping to disruptions of wheat supply chain caused by the Russia–Ukraine war crisis: Case study from an emerging economy. *Kybernetes*, *53*(10), 2984–3018. DOI: 10.1108/K-12-2022-1728

Rai, M. S. (2022). International Institutions and Power Politics in the Context of Chinese Belt and Road Initiative. *arXiv*. https://doi.org//arXiv.2209.10498DOI: 10.48550

Ramos, M. (2024, June 28). Understanding why Brazil has become the biggest importer of Chinese electric cars and how 'Mover' should change the sector. *Brasil de Fato*. https://www.brasildefato.com.br/2024/06/28/understanding-why-brazil-has-become-the-biggest-importer-of-chinese-electric-cars-and-how-mover-should-change-the-sector/

Reed, S., & Hui, L. N. (2022, May 9). Can China's Amazon footprint evolve into a greener partnership? *Dialogue Earth*. https://dialogue.earth/en/business/53558-china-amazon-footprint-evolve-greener-partnership

ResearchAndMarkets.com. (2024, August 16). *Brazil electric vehicle market databook 2024: Global firms are investing in the development of manufacturing facilities to by-pass tax tariffs implemented on the import of electric vehicles in Brazil*. Business Wire. https://www.businesswire.com/news/home/20240816677947/en/Brazil-Electric-Vehicle-Market-Databook-2024-Global-Firms-are-Investing-in-the-Development-of-Manufacturing-Facilities-to-By-pass-Tax-Tariffs-Implemented-on-the-Import-of-Electric-Vehicles-in-Brazil---ResearchAndMarkets.com

Reserve Bank of India. (2024). Handbook of statistics on Indian economy. https://www.rbi.org.in/Scripts/AnnualPublications.aspx?head=Handbook%20of%20Statistics%20on%20Indian%20Economy

Reuters. (2025). *South Korea exports fall as tariffs hit US, China shipments.* https://www.reuters.com/world/china/south-korea-exports-fall-tariffs-hit-us-china-shipments-2025-06-01/

Ripsman, N. M. (2006). *False dichotomies: Why economics is high politics.* Concordia University. https://www.files.ethz.ch/isn/22143/Ripsman.pdf

Rodrik, D. (2011). *The globalization paradox: Democracy and the future of the world economy.* W. W. Norton & Company.

Rodrik, D. (2011). *The globalization paradox: why global markets, states, and democracy can't coexist.* Oxford University Press.

Rodrik, D. (2018). Populism and the economics of globalization. *Journal of International Business Policy, 1*(1), 12–33. DOI: 10.1057/s42214-018-0001-4

Rodrik, D. (2018). *Straight talk on trade: Ideas for a sane world economy.* Princeton University Press. DOI: 10.1515/9781400888900

Rolland, N. (2019). *Mapping the Footprint of Belt and Road Influence Operations.* Sinopsis. https://sinopsis.cz/en/mapping-the-footprint-of-belt-and-road-influence-operations/

Rowland, B. (2025, August 21). *European Union says U.S. consumers will end up paying tariffs.* From https://www.thecentersquare.com/national/article_89123db5-c909-4bb0-8e76-69cd28a6b206.html

Rugaber, C. (August 1, 2025). *Dozens of countries with no deals face new tariffs as trade deadline looms. AP News.* Retrieved August 19, 2025, from https://apnews.com/article/tariffs-trump-trade-deals-deadline-3977a3890ab7be85c0e07d5808dd2b55

Ruggie, J. G. (1999). *Constructing the world polity: Essays on international institutionalization.* Routledge.

Ryder, H. (2025). *How should Africa respond to Trump's new tariffs? Centre for Strategic and International Studies.* CSIS.

S&P Global. (2025, January 30). *China responds to US restrictions with export ban on select critical minerals.* S&P Global Market Intelligence. https://www.spglobal.com/market-intelligence/en/news-insights/research/china-responds-to-us-restrictions-with-export-ban-on-select-critical-minerals

Sardain, E., Anderson, J., Pronk, K., Adriaans, L., & Oosthuizen, M. (2024, December 5). *Is CNMC's acquisition of Mineração Taboca further evidence of China's expansion in Latin America?* Project Blue; ProjectBlue.com. https://www.projectblue.com/blue/opinion-pieces/1085/is-cnmc%E2%80%99s-acquisition-of-minera%C3%A7%C3%A3o-taboca-further-evidence-of-china%E2%80%99s-expansion-in-latin-america?----

Schmitz, L., & Seidl, T. (2023). As open as possible, as autonomous as necessary: Understanding the rise of open strategic autonomy in EU trade policy. *Journal of Common Market Studies, 61*(3), 834–852. DOI: 10.1111/jcms.13428

Schoenbaum, T. J. (2023). The Biden Administration's Trade Policy: Promise and Reality. German Law Journal, 24(Special Issue 1), 102-124. DOI: 10.1017/glj.2023.7

Schropp, S. (2022). Biden and Trade: No Trade Policy, No-Trade Policy or Both? *Inter Economics, 57*(6), 399–400. DOI: 10.1007/s10272-022-1094-x

Sciutto, J. (2020). *The Shadow War: Inside Russia's and China's Secret Operations to Defeat America*. HarperCollins.

See, A., & Moscati, J. (2025, May 15). *Opportunities and challenges of Brazil-China trade under the impact of US tariffs*. China Law Vision. https://www.chinalawvision.com/2025/05/international-trade/opportunities-and-challenges-of-brazil-china-trade-under-the-impact-of-us-tariffs/

Senate and House of Representatives United States of America. (1974). *US Trade Act of 1974*. https://www.govinfo.gov/content/pkg/COMPS-10384/pdf/COMPS-10384.pdf

Shahbaz, M., Sharif, A., Soliman, A. M., Jiao, Z., & Hammoudeh, S. (2024). Oil prices and geopolitical risk: Fresh insights based on Granger-causality in quantiles analysis. *International Journal of Finance & Economics, 29*(3), 2865–2881. DOI: 10.1002/ijfe.2806

Shambaugh, D. (2021). *Where Great Powers Meet: America & China in Southeast Asia*. Oxford University Press. DOI: 10.1093/oso/9780190914974.001.0001

Shirk, S. L. (2023). *Overreach: How China Derailed Its Peaceful Rise*. Oxford University Press.

Shirley, W., & Svensson, K. (2023, September 13). *Resource realism: The geopolitics of critical mineral supply chains*. Goldmansachs.com; Goldman Sachs Global Institute. https://www.goldmansachs.com/insights/articles/resource-realism-the-geopolitics-of-critical-mineral-supply-chains

Shivakumar, S., Wessner, C., & Howell, T. (2025, April 14). *The limits of chip export controls in meeting the China challenge*. Center for Strategic and International Studies. https://www.csis.org/analysis/limits-chip-export-controls-meeting-china-challenge

Shoinbekova, M. (May 26, 2024). *U.S. Delegation Discusses Next Steps for the OSCE-led Integrated Co-operation on Explosive Hazards Program in Tajikistan.* OSCE. Retrieved August 19, 2025, from https://www.osce.org/programme-office-in-dushanbe/572467

Shokri, U. (2025, February 12). Critical minerals and the U.S.-China trade war. *TRENDS Research & Advisory*. https://trendsresearch.org/insight/critical-minerals-and-the-u-s-china-trade-war/?srsltid=AfmBOopxwQNxrFCI5_IRrhVM15gNeOvlmAwYobl-qGQI4-BCsCqE2oXb

Shovlin, J. (2021). *Trading With the Enemy: Britain, France, and the 18th-Century Quest for a Peaceful World Order*. Yale University Press.

Silvan, K. (2021). *Russian Policy Towards Central Asia 30 Years After the Collapse of The Soviet Union: Sphere of Influence Shrinking?* Finnish Institute of International Affairs.

Silvestre, L. (2019). Ciclos hegemônicos e transições sistêmicas: Arrighi e a China como potência emergente. *Revista Brasileira de Política Internacional, 62*(1), e004. DOI: 10.1590/0034-7329201900104

Smales, L. A. (2021). Geopolitical risk and volatility spillovers in oil and stock markets. *The Quarterly Review of Economics and Finance, 80*, 358–366. DOI: 10.1016/j.qref.2021.03.008

Snoussi-Mimouni, M., & Avérous, S. (2024, January 10). *High demand for energy-related critical minerals creates supply chain pressures*. World Trade Organization. https://www.wto.org/english/blogs_e/data_blog_e/blog_dta_10jan24_e.htm

Söderbaum, F., & Shaw, T. M. (Eds.). (2003). *Theories of new regionalism: A Palgrave reader*. Palgrave Macmillan. https://link.springer.com/book/10.1057/9781403938794

Soundariya, A., Behera, N. K., Selvakumar, P., Chandel, P. S., Gupta, S., & Manjunath, T. C. (2025). AI and environmental ethics: The role of AI in addressing climate change – ethical considerations in AI-driven environmental solutions. In Chakraborty, S. (Ed.), *Human Values, Ethics, and Dignity in the Age of Artificial Intelligence* (pp. 321–346). IGI Global. DOI: 10.4018/979-8-3693-9035-1.ch013

Starshinova, O. (2021). Is the MPIA a Solution to the WTO Appellate Body Crisis? *Journal of World Trade, 55*(5), 787–803. DOI: 10.54648/TRAD2021033

Stiglitz, Joseph E. (2025);Industrial Policy and the New Protectionism. (2025)... *Journal of Policy Modeling, 47*, 708–722. https://www.sciencedirect.com/science/article/abs/pii/S0161893825000572?via%3Dihub. DOI: 10.1016/j.jpolmod.2025.06.007

Su, C. W., Khan, K., Tao, R., & Nicoleta-Claudia, M. (2019). Does geopolitical risk strengthen or depress oil prices and financial liquidity? Evidence from Saudi Arabia. *Energy, 187*, 116003. DOI: 10.1016/j.energy.2019.116003

Swanson, A. (2018). *"Trump's Trade War With China Is Officially Underway.* The New York Times. https://www.nytimes.com/2018/07/05/business/china-us-trade-war-trump-tariffs.html

Tanaka, A. (2025, June 20). Letter from Nikkei Asia's editor: China's automotive chip ambitions raise stakes in US trade war. *Nikkei Asia.* https://asia.nikkei.com/Editor-s-Picks/Editor-in-Chief-s-Picks/Letter-from-Nikkei-Asia-s-editor-China-s-automotive-chip-ambitions-raise-stakes-in-US-trade-war

Tarrosy, I. (2020). China's Belt and Road Initiative in Africa, Debt Risk and New Dependency: The Case of Ethiopia. *African Studies Quarterly, 19*(3–4), 8–28.

Taulli, B., & Busby, J. (2025, May 30). *The devil is in the details: Minerals, batteries, and US dependence on Chinese imports.* Center for Climate & Security. https://councilonstrategicrisks.org/2025/05/30/the-devil-is-in-the-details-minerals-batteries-and-us-dependence-on-chinese-imports/

Temnycky, M. (December 13, 2023). The West is Eying Closer Relations with Central Asia. *The Diplomat.* Accessed July 02, 2025, https://thediplomat.com/2023/12/the-west-is-eying-closer-relations-with-central-asia/

Tesfaye, A. (2020). *China in Ethiopia: The Long-Term Perspective.* State University of New York Press. DOI: 10.1353/book75410

TFEU. (2012). *Treaty on the Functioning of the European Union.* Consolidated version. https://eur-lex.europa.eu/legal-content/EN/TXT/?uri=celex%3A12012E%2FTXT

The Astana Times. (April 3, 2025). *US imposes 27% reciprocal duty on Kazakh products.* Retrieved August 19, 2025, from https://astanatimes.com/2025/04/us-imposes-27-reciprocal-duty-on-kazakh-products/

The Diplomat. (2024, April). China's Alternative Global Trade System. https://thediplomat.com/2024/04/chinas-alternative-global-trade-system/

The Economic Times. (2025, April). *US consumers rush to buy big-ticket items before Trump's tariffs kick in.* From https://economictimes.indiatimes.com/news/international/global-trends/us-consumers-rush-to-buy-big-ticket-items-before-trumps-tariffs-kick-in/articleshow/120004178.cms?

The Economist. (2025, July 28). *EU-US trade deal explained.* Retrieved from https://shows.acast.com/theeconomistmorningbriefing/episodes/eu-us-trade-deal-takes-shape-israels-new-negotiations-with

The Oregon Group. (2025, May 1). *78% of US military weapon systems vulnerable to China's critical mineral dominance.* https://theoregongroup.com/commodities/rare-earths/78-of-us-military-weapon-systems-potentially-vulnerable-to-china-critical-mineral-dominance/

The Times of India. (2024, Dec. 31). *'No one can sever out blood ties': China's President Xi Jinping on Taiwan 'unification' during New Year speech.* https://timesofindia.indiatimes.com/world/china/no-one-can-sever-our-blood-ties-chinas-president-xi-jinping-on-taiwan-unification-during-new-year-speech/articleshow/116832978.cms

The White House. (2017). *The Inaugural Address.* https://trumpwhitehouse.archives.gov/briefings-statements/the-inaugural-address/

The White House. (2025, February 1). *Fact Sheet: President Donald J. Trump Imposes Tariffs on Imports from Canada, Mexico and China.* From https://www.whitehouse.gov/fact-sheets/2025/02/fact-sheet-president-donald-j-trump-imposes-tariffs-on-imports-from-canada-mexico-and-china/

The White House. (2025, July). *Further Modifying The Reciprocal Tariff Rates.* From https://www.whitehouse.gov/presidential-actions/2025/07/further-modifying-the-reciprocal-tariff-rates/

The White House. (2025, May 12). *Fact Sheet: President Donald J. Trump Secures a Historic Trade Win for the United States.* From https://www.whitehouse.gov/fact-sheets/2025/05/fact-sheet-president-donald-j-trump-secures-a-historic-trade-win-for-the-united-states/#:~:text=AMERICAN%20ACTIONS:%20The%20United%20States,and%20stop%20unfair%20trade%20practices

The White House. (2025a). *The Inaugural Address.* https://www.whitehouse.gov/remarks/2025/01/the-inaugural-address/

The White House. (2025b). *America First Trade Policy.* https://www.whitehouse.gov/presidential-actions/2025/01/america-first-trade-policy/

Thornton, G. (2025, April). *A new tariff paradigm: How businesses can respond.* From https://www.grantthornton.com/insights/articles/tax/2025/new-tariff-paradigm-how-businesses-can-respond

Thorstensen, V. (1999). O Brasil e a OMC: Desafios e oportunidades. *Revista Brasileira de Comércio Exterior, 59*, 3–11.

Tobin, M. (2025, April 16). Taiwan's chip companies are caught in the U.S.-China tariff war. *The New York Times.* https://www.nytimes.com/2025/04/16/business/china-taiwan-tariffs-chips.html

Tödtling, F. (1994). Regional networks of hightechnology firms—The case of the greater Boston region. *Technovation, 14*(5), 323–343. DOI: 10.1016/0166-4972(94)90075-2

Tooze, A. (2021). *Shutdown: How COVID shook the world's economy.* Viking Press.

Trade Law Centre. (2022). *AfCFTA Protocol on Investment: Key features* [Infographic]. Tralac. https://www.tralac.org/resources/infographic/16152-afcfta-protocol-on-investment-factsheet.html

Trade, S. (2024). *India: Política y economía.* https://santandertrade.com/es/portal/analizar-mercados/india/politica-y economia#:~:text=Sus%20principales%20sectores%20son%20el,(13%25%20del%20PIB)

TradeMark Africa. (2024). *Digital innovation and regional collaboration: Essential drivers to transforming Africa's trade future.* https://www.trademarkafrica.com/digital-innovation-and-regional-collaboration-essential-drivers-to-transforming-africas-trade-future/

Trager, R. (2024, December 5). China bans sale of three critical elements and 'superhard materials' to the US. *Chemistry World.* https://www.chemistryworld.com/news/china-bans-sale-of-three-critical-elements-and-superhard-materials-to-the-us/4020652.article

Trends Research. (2025). *The U.S.-China Trade War: China's Challenge in Navigating U.S. Tariffs and Global Trade Tensions.* https://trendsresearch.org/insight/the-u-s-china-trade-war-chinas-challenge-in-navigating-u-s-tariffs-and-global-trade-tensions/

Trump, D. J. (2025). *Modifying Reciprocal Tariff Rates to Reflect Trading Partner Retaliation and Alignment.* Executive Order 14257, Presidential Action, The White House. https://www.whitehouse.gov/presidential-actions/2025/04/modifying-reciprocal-tariff-rates-to-reflect-trading-partner-retaliation-and-alignment/

Trust, S. T. Retrieved from https://www.tradetrust.io/about/what-is-tradetrust/

Tseng, P. (2023). The Metaphysics of Globalization in Gadamer: A Case Study of Contemporary Taiwan. *Dialogo (Constanţa), 10*(1), 103–111. DOI: 10.51917/dialogo.2023.10.1.7

Tucker, P. (2025, April 23). China's rare-earth mineral squeeze will hit the Pentagon hard. *Defense One*. https://www.defenseone.com/threats/2025/04/chinas-rare-earth-mineral-squeeze-will-hit-pentagon-hard/404776/

Turkson, F. E. (2011). *Logistics and bilateral exports in developing countries: a multiplicative form estimation of the logistics augmented gravity equation* (No. 11/06). CREDIT Research Paper.

U.S. Bureau of Economic Analysis. (2024). International transactions accounts data. https://www.bea.gov/data/intl-trade-investment/international-transactions

U.S. Census Bureau. (2024). Foreign trade: Data. https://www.census.gov/foreign-trade/statistics/historical/index.html

U.S. Census Bureau. (2024). U.S. international trade in goods and services: Annual report 2023. https://www.census.gov/foreign-trade/Press-Release/current_press_release/index.html

U.S. Congress. (2022). CHIPS and Science Act (P.L. 117-167). https://www.congress.gov

U.S. Customs and Border Protection. (2023, January). *QB 21-505 Washers and Covered Parts*. From https://www.cbp.gov/trade/quota/bulletins/qb-21-505-washers-and-covered-parts#:~:text=On%20January%2023%2C%202018%2C%20the,duty%20rates%20in%20the%20Annex

U.S. Customs and Border Protection. (2025). *Uyghur Forced Labor Prevention Act Statistics*. Retrieved from https://www.cbp.gov/newsroom/stats/trade/uyghur-forced-labor-prevention-act-statistics

U.S. Department of Labor. (2024). *Against Their Will: The Situation in Xinjiang*. https://www.dol.gov/agencies/ilab/against-their-will-the-situation-in-xinjiang

U.S. Department of State. (2025). *U.S. Security Cooperation with Central Asia*. Accessed July 22, 2025, https://www.state.gov/u-s-security-cooperation-with-central-asia

U.S. Department of State. (2025, Jan. 20). *Forced Labor in China's Xinjiang Region*. https://www.state.gov/forced-labor-in-chinas-xinjiang-region/

U.S. Energy Information Administration. (2025, May 21). *China dominates global trade of battery minerals*. https://www.eia.gov/todayinenergy/detail.php?id=65305

U.S. Senate. (2022a). Roll call vote #131, 117th Congress, 2nd session. Retrieved April 7, 2023, from https://www.senate.gov/legislative/LIS/roll_call_votes/vote1172/vote_117_2_00131.htm

U.S. Senate. (2022b). Roll call vote #132, 117th Congress, 2nd session. Retrieved April 7, 2023, from https://www.senate.gov/legislative/LIS/roll_call_votes/vote1172/vote_117_2_00132.htm

Ul-Mansoor, A. (2024). *China's Geopolitical Strategy: Crafting a New World Order*. https://doi.org/DOI: 10.5281/zenodo.12345678

UN Trade and Development (UNCTAD). (2025, May). Global trade update: Focus on critical minerals – copper in the new green and digital economy. UNCTAD. https://unctad.org/publication/global-trade-update-may-2025-critical-minerals-copper

UN/CEFACT. (2022). *White Paper: Verifiable Credentials for Cross-Border Trade (eDATA)*. Retrieved from https://unece.org/sites/default/files/2023-08/WhitePaper_VerifiableCredentials-CrossBorderTrade_September2022.pdf

UN/CEFACT. (2023). *White Paper: Data Pipeline*. Retrieved from https://unece.org/sites/default/files/2023-10/WhitePaper_DataPipeline_Eng.pdf

UN/CEFACT. *Solutions in Support of Digital Product Passports (ECE/TRADE/481)*. Retrieved from https://unece.org/trade/publications/uncefact-solutions-support-digital-product-passports-ecetrade481

UNCITRAL. (2017). *Model Law on Electronic Transferable Records (MLETR)*. Retrieved from https://uncitral.un.org/en/texts/ecommerce/modellaw/electronic_transferable_records

UNCTAD. (2021). *Africa's free trade area can deliver considerable inclusive economic growth for the continent*. https://unctad.org/news/africas-free-trade-area-can-deliver-considerable-inclusive-economic-growth-continent

UNCTAD. (2022). *Rethinking the foundations of export diversification in Africa: The catalytic role of business and financial services*. https://unctad.org/system/files/official-document/aldcafrica2022_en.pdf

UNCTAD. (2023). *Making the AfCFTA work for Africa: Building capacities for inclusive and sustainable implementation*. https://knowledge.uneca.org/idep/sites/default/files/IDEP_Course/2023/Making-AfCFTA-Work/Brochure-AfCFTA-EN-2023.pdf

UNCTAD. (2023). *World Investment Report 2023*. Retrieved from https://unctad.org/publication/world-investment-report-2023

UNCTAD. (2024, October 29). *The reshaping of global trade: How developing countries can strategize*. United Nations Conference on Trade and Development. https://unctad.org/news/reshaping-global-trade-how-developing-countries-can-strategize

UNCTAD. (United Nations Conference on Trade and Development). (2025). 2024 Economic development in Africa report – *Unlocking Africa's trade potential. Boosting regional markets and reducing risks*. United Nations Publications.

UNECA & AU. (2020). *Governing the interface between the AfCFTA and Regional Economic Communities: Issues, opportunities, and challenges (Revised November 2020)*. UNECA & AU. https://archive.uneca.org/sites/default/files/uploaded-documents/RITD/2020/governing_interface_between_afcfta_and_recs_afcfta_issues_opportunities_and_challenges_revised_final_version_as_at_nov._2_2020.pdf

UNECA. (2023). *Implementing the AfCFTA Agreement will boost intra-African trade and industrialization*. https://www.uneca.org/stories/implementing-the-afcfta-agreement-will-boost-intra-african-trade-and-industrialization

UNECA. (2025). *COM2025 Newsletter No. 1*. https://www.uneca.org/eca-events/sites/default/files/resources/documents/com/2025/bulletins/com2025_newsletter_1.pdf

UNESCAP. (2025). *Feasibility Studies: Identifying and Unlocking Cross-Border Paperless Trade Potential*. Retrieved from https://www.unescap.org/blog/feasibility-studies-identifying-and-unlocking-cross-border-paperless-trade-potential

UNESCAP. (2025). *Feasibility Study on Cross-Border Electronic Exchange of Trade Data and Documents: Kyrgyzstan*. Retrieved from https://repository.unescap.org/items/a904e9ae-be35-49df-a5b7-107756ed5ac3

UNIDO. (2023). *Third Industrial Development Decade for Africa (IDDA III): Mid-term progress report*. https://www.unido.org/sites/default/files/files/2022-07/IDDA%20III%20SG%20report%202019.pdf

United Nations Department of Economic and Social Affairs (UN DESA). (2022). *World Population Prospects 2022: Summary of results*. United Nations. https://www.un.org/development/desa/pd/sites/www.un.org.development.desa.pd/files/wpp2022_summary_of_results.pdf

United Nations Economic and Social Commission for Asia and the Pacific (ESCAP). (2019). *China's economic transformation: Impacts on Asia and the Pacific* (ST/ESCAP/2836). United Nations. https://www.unescap.org/sites/default/files/China%27s%20economic%20transformation_impacts%20on%20Asia%20and%20the%20Pacific.pdf

United Nations Economic Commission for Africa. (2024). *African perspectives of a just transition to low-carbon economies*. https://uneca.org/sites/default/files/ACPC/2024/African_perspectives_of_a_just_transition_to_Low_Carbon_economies.pdf

United States Census Bureau. (n.d.). *International trade data* [Data set]. Retrieved May 27, 2025, from https://www.census.gov/foreign-trade/data/index.html

United States International Trade Commission. (2023). Economic Impact of Section 232 and 301 Tariffs on U.S. Industries. Washington, DC: The Commission United States International Trade Commission.

Van der Wee, H. (1986). Prosperity and upheaval [Penguin.]. *World Economy*, 1945–1980.

Vangrasstek, C., & Pascal, L. (2013). *The history and future of the World Trade Organization*. World Trade Organization. https://www.wto.org/english/res_e/booksp_e/historywto_e.pdf

Vanguardia. (2023). Taiwán, la perla del Indo-Pacífico. *Vanguardia Dossier*, 58. https://shopping.lavanguardia.com/taiwan-la-perla-del-indo-pacifico.html

Vásquez, P. I. (2024, October 2). *Brazil's critical minerals and the global clean energy revolution*. Wilson Center. https://www.wilsoncenter.org/article/brazils-critical-minerals-and-global-clean-energy-revolution

Veblen, T. (1988). *The Theory of the Leisure Class*. Penguin Classics. (Original work published 1899)

Vergun, D. (2025, January 10). *Securing critical minerals vital to national security, official says*. U.S. Department of Defense. https://www.defense.gov/News/News-Stories/Article/Article/4026144/securing-critical-minerals-vital-to-national-security-official-says/

Vieira do Prado, V. B., & Moerenhout, T. (2024, August). *Brazil's potential role in diversifying US critical mineral supply*. Center on Global Energy Policy at Columbia SIPA. https://www.energypolicy.columbia.edu/publications/brazils-potential-role-in-diversifying-us-critical-mineral-supply/

von der Leyen, U. (2023, March 30). *Speech on EU–China relations*. European Commission. https://ec.europa.eu/commission/presscorner/detail/en/speech_23_2063

W3C. (2022). *Decentralized Identifiers (DID) Core*. Retrieved from https://www.w3.org/TR/did-core/

W3C. (2025). *Verifiable Credentials Data Model v2.0*. Retrieved from https://www.w3.org/TR/vc-data-model-2.0/

W3C. (2025). *Verifiable Credentials Overview*. Retrieved from https://www.w3.org/TR/vc-overview/

Wang, J. (2024). The Logic of China – US Rivalry. China International Strategy Review. Volume 6. 1 – 8. 23 May 23 2024. https://link.springer.com/article/10.1007/s42533-024-00157-6

Wang, J., & Hewett, D. Y. (2021). U.S.-China Trade Relations in the Biden Era: Trade War, Industrial Policy, and Rule-Based International Order. *Proceedings of the ASIL Annual Meeting, 115*, 315–320. DOI: 10.1017/amp.2021.127

Wang, J., & Ma, Z. (2019). Port logistics cluster effect and coordinated development of port economy based on grey relational analysis model. *Journal of Coastal Research, 94*(SI), 717-721.

Wang, Y. (2024, April 19). US and Europe: 2 different approaches to restricting Chinese EVs. *The Diplomat*. https://thediplomat.com/2024/04/us-and-europe-2-different-approaches-to-restricting-chinese-evs/

Wang, C., Kim, Y. S., & Kim, C. Y. (2021). Causality between logistics infrastructure and economic development in China. *Transport Policy, 100*, 49–58. DOI: 10.1016/j.tranpol.2020.10.005

Wang, K. H., Su, C. W., & Umar, M. (2021). Geopolitical risk and crude oil security: A Chinese perspective. *Energy, 219*, 119555. DOI: 10.1016/j.energy.2020.119555

Wang, Y. (2011). *Harmony and War: Confucian Culture and Chinese Power Politics*. Columbia University Press.

Wang, Y. (2022). Geopolitical risk, economic policy uncertainty and crude oil prices: A wavelet-based analysis. *International Review of Economics & Finance, 82*, 524–546. DOI: 10.1016/j.iref.2022.07.015

Weinhardt, C., & De Ville, F. (2024). The geoeconomic turn in EU trade and investment policy: Implications for developing countries. *Politics and Governance, 12*(2), 8217. Advance online publication. DOI: 10.17645/pag.8217

Weiss, T. G. (1994). The United Nations and civil wars. *The Washington Quarterly*, *17*(4), 139–159. DOI: 10.1080/01636609409443755

Wile, R. (2025, Aug. 22). *U.S. takes 10% stake in Intel as Trump flexes more power over big business.* NBC News. https://www.nbcnews.com/business/business-news/intel-agrees-us-stake-in-company-how-much-what-to-know-rcna226667

Wischer, G. (2024, February 12). *The U.S. military and NATO face serious risks of mineral shortages.* Carnegie Endowment for International Peace. https://carnegieendowment.org/research/2024/02/the-us-military-and-nato-face-serious-risks-of-mineral-shortages?lang=en

Wolff, A. W. (2025, April 10). *The WTO at 30: The return of higher tariffs.* Peterson Institute for International Economics. Retrieved June 26, 2025, from https://www.piie.com/commentary/speeches-papers/2025/wto-30-return-higher-tariffs

Wong, E. (2014, Dec. 20). *China Invests in Region Rich in Oil, Coal and Also Strife.* The New York Times. https://www.nytimes.com/2014/12/21/world/asia/china-invests-in-xinjiang-region-rich-in-oil-coal-and-also-strife.html

Wong, C. D., Tay, V., Homer, S. T., & Nazera, F. (2025). Impact of Trump's 2025 " Liberation Day " Tariffs on Southeast Asia. *International Journal of Research and Innovation in Social Science*, *IX*(June), 5556–5570. DOI: 10.47772/IJRISS.2025.905000428

Woodward, J. (2017). *The US vs China: Asia's new Cold War?* Manchester University Press. DOI: 10.7228/manchester/9781526121998.001.0001

Woolcock, S. (2021). *The European Union and the geopolitics of trade policy.* London School of Economics. https://www.lse.ac.uk/ideas/publications/reports/the-eu-and-geopolitics-of-trade-policy

World Bank Group. (2025). GDP growth (annual %) - China https://data.worldbank.org/indicator/NY.GDP.MKTP.KD.ZG?locations=CN

World Bank. (2020). *Doing Business 2020: Comparing Business Regulation in 190 Economies.* Retrieved from https://archive.doingbusiness.org/en/reports/global-reports/doing-business-2020

World Bank. (2020). *The African Continental Free Trade Area: Economic and distributional effects.* Washington, DC: World Bank. https://openknowledge.worldbank.org/server/api/core/bitstreams/ef1aa41f-60de-5bd2-a63e-75f2c3ff0f43/content

World Bank. (2023). *World Bank Logistics Performance Index 2023*. Retrieved from https://www.worldbank.org/en/news/press-release/2023/04/21/world-bank-releases-logistics-performance-index-2023

World Bank. (2024). *Improving Resilience and Economic Efficiency in Global Supply Chains to Counter Shocks*. World Bank Blogs. Retrieved from https://blogs.worldbank.org/en/trade/improving-resilience-and-economic-efficiency-in-global-supply-ch

World Bank. (2024). World development indicators. https://rbi.org.in

World Bank. (2025). *Data*. https://datos.bancomundial.org/

World Bank. (2025). *Electrifying Journeys* (Issue March). https://openknowledge.worldbank.org/server/api/core/bitstreams/9d53a06b-7302-4f9b-b78d-fb3b45d26caf/content

World Bank. (2025, March). *Viet Nam's Economy Forecast to Grow 6.8 Percent In 2025*. From https://www.worldbank.org/en/news/press-release/2025/03/12/viet-nam-s-economy-forecast-to-grow-6-8-percent-in-2025-wb#:~:text=Share%20more,pushing%20forward%20with%20structural%20reforms

World Bank. (n.d.). *Exports of goods and services (% of GDP)*. World Bank Open Data. Retrieved July 4, 2025, from https://data.worldbank.org/indicator/NE.EXP.GNFS.ZS?end=2024&most_recent_value_desc=true&start=2024&view=map

World Economic Forum. (2024, November). *China's Critical Mineral Strategy: Beyond Geopolitics*. https://www.weforum.org/stories/2024/11/china-critical-mineral-strategy-beyond-geopolitics/

World Health Organization. (2020, March 11). WHO Director-General's opening remarks at the media briefing on COVID-19 – 11 March 2020. https://www.who.int/director-general/speeches/detail/who-director-general-s-opening-remarks-at-the-media-briefing-on-covid-19---11-march-2020

World Trade Organization. (2015). *Understanding the WTO* (5th ed.). Information and External Relations Division. https://www.wto.org/english/thewto_e/whatis_e/tif_e/understanding_e.pdf

World Trade Organization. (2020). World Trade Report 2020: Government policies to promote innovation in the digital age. https://www.wto.org/english/res_e/booksp_e/wtr20_e/wtr20_e.pdf

World Trade Organization. (2022, December 20). DG Okonjo-Iweala: WTO can help strengthen global food security and resilience. https://www.wto.org/english/news_e/news22_e/dgno_20dec22_e.htm

World Trade Organization. (2023). *Public Forum 2023: "It Is Time for Action"* [Conference programme]. WTO. https://www.wto.org/english/forums_e/public_forum23_e/draft_programme_e.pdf

World Trade Organization. (2023). Trade policy review: India. https://www.wto.org

World Trade Organization. (2023). *World trade report 2023: Re-globalization for a secure, inclusive, and sustainable future*. WTO.

World Trade Organization. (2023). World trade statistical review 2023.

World Trade Organization. (2025). *WTO Secretariat issues updated Global Trade Outlook and Statistics: Forecast for 2025* [Press release]. WTO. https://www.wto.org/english/news_e/news25_e/tfore_16apr25_e.htm

World Trade Organization. (2025, April). *Global Trade Outlook and Statistics: Outlook for world trade in 2025 and 2026* [PDF]. Retrieved June 26, 2025, from https://www.wto.org/english/res_e/booksp_e/trade_outlook25_e.pdfwto.org+9wto.org+9wto.org+9

World Trade Organization. (n.d.-a). Understanding the WTO: The agreements – Goods: Rules on trade in goods. Retrieved May 15, 2025, from https://www.wto.org/english/thewto_e/whatis_e/tif_e/agrm2_e.htm

World Trade Organization. (n.d.-b). *Dispute settlement activity — some figures*. Retrieved June 10, 2025, from https://www.wto.org/english/tratop_e/dispu_e/dispustats_e.htm

World Trade Organization. (n.d.-c). Dispute settlement. Retrieved June 29, 2025, from https://www.wto.org/english/tratop_e/dispu_e/dispu_e.htm

World Trade Organization. (n.d.-d). WTO statistics database. Retrieved June 29, 2025, from https://stats.wto.org/

Worldwide, J. *CETA – European Opportunity for Canadians*. Retrieved from https://www.jetworldwide.com/blog/european-canadian-ceta-duty-free-from-canada

WTO. (2017). *Agreement on Trade Facilitation (TFA)*. Retrieved from https://www.wto.org/english/docs_e/legal_e/tfa_e.htm

WTO. (2023). *TFAF Work Plan 2024*. Retrieved from https://www.tfadatabase.org/en

WTO. (2023). *WTO Trade Monitoring Report 2023*. Retrieved from https://www.wto.org/english/res_e/publications_e/wtr23_e.htm

WTO. (2025). *Chronological list of disputes cases*. https://www.wto.org/english/tratop_e/dispu_e/dispu_status_e.htm

Wu, H., Kurtenbach, E., & Tang, D. (2025, April 4). *China slaps a 34% tax on all US imports in retaliation for Trump's tariffs*. From https://www.wfxrtv.com/news/business/ap-china-imposes-a-34-tariff-on-imports-of-all-u-s-products-starting-april-10/

Wu, J., Zhao, R., Sun, J., & Zhou, X. (2023). Impact of geopolitical risks on oil price fluctuations: Based on GARCH-MIDAS model. *Resources Policy*, *85*, 103982. DOI: 10.1016/j.resourpol.2023.103982

Xiang, H. (2025). Appian Finalizes $420M Sale of Brazilian Copper Mine to Chinese Firm. *Chemanalyst.com*. https://www.chemanalyst.com/NewsAndDeals/NewsDetails/appian-finalizes-420m-sale-of-brazilian-copper-mine-to-chinese-firm-35670

Xinhua. (August 15, 2025). *Kyrgyzstan lauds Eurasian Economic Union's economic vitality*. Retrieved August 20, 2025, from https://english.news.cn/20250815/2cfbdb617a0148ceae2293f62d8157fd/c.html

Xu, T., Li, W., Jiang, Y., & Chen, Y. (2020). The Impact of Destination Tariffs on China's Exports: Country, Firm, and Product Perspectives. *Journal of Asian Economics*, *71*(101246), 101246. DOI: 10.1016/j.asieco.2020.101246

Yanlin, W. (2011, Jan. 18). *China's 2010 FDI exceeds US$100 bln for 1st time*. Shanghai Daily. https://archive.shine.cn/business/economy/Chinas-2010-FDI-exceeds-US100-bln-for-1st-time/shdaily.shtml

Yokoyama, E. (2025, August 20). *Japan's Exports Fall Most in Four Years as Tariff Pain Deepens*. From https://www.bloomberg.com/news/articles/2025-08-19/japan-s-exports-fall-most-in-four-years-as-tariff-pain-deepens

York, E. (2024, January). *Tariff of Abominations Redux: Trump Proposes 60% Tariff on Chinese Goods*. From https://taxfoundation.org/blog/trump-china-trade-war-proposal/

York, E., & Durante, A. (2025, June 2). *Trump tariffs: Tracking the economic impact of the Trump trade war*. Tax Foundation. https://taxfoundation.org/research/all/federal/trump-tariffs-trade-war/

Yoshihara, T., & Holmes, J. R. (2018). *Red Star Over the Pacific: China's Rise and the Challenge to U.S. Maritime Strategy* (2nd ed.). Naval Institute Press.

Yuan, J. (2018). Managing Maritime Competition between India and China. In David Brewster (Eds). *India & China at Sea: Competition for Naval Dominance in the Indian Ocean.* Oxford University Press. DOI: 10.1093/oso/9780199479337.003.0003

Yu, T. O. (2020). Theoretical concepts of trade policy development and analysis: Evolution and modern challenges in the context of the international trading system transformation. *Вестник Санкт-Петербургского университета. Ekonomika (Nis)*, *36*(1), 27–48.

Zaparolli, D. (2025, April 23). Brazil to launch national critical minerals policy in 2025. *Valor Econômico.* https://valorinternational.globo.com/summit-valor-brazil-china-2025/news/2025/04/23/brazil-to-launch-national-critical-minerals-policy-in-2025.ghtml

Zhai, F. (2025). *Macroeconomic Impacts of Trump 2.0 Tariffs on China: A Model Based Assessment.* China Economic Insights.

Zhang, J. (2024, Dec. 9). *Russia clears the path for China in the Arctic.* Geopolitical Intelligence Services. https://www.gisreportsonline.com/r/china-arctic-russia/

Zhang, L. (2023, Jul. 15). *A timeline of China's 32-month Big Tech crackdown that killed the world's largest IPO and wiped out trillions in value.* South China Morning Post. https://www.scmp.com/tech/big-tech/article/3227753/timeline-chinas-32-month-big-tech-crackdown-killed-worlds-largest-ipo-and-wiped-out-trillions-value?module=perpetual_scroll_0&pgtype=article

Zhang, Y. (2024, June 3). US tariff increases. What is the impact on the US and China markets for electric vehicles and Li-ion batteries? *Interact Analysis.* https://interactanalysis.com/insight/us-tariff-increases-what-is-the-impact-on-the-us-and-china-markets-for-electric-vehicles-and-li-ion-batteries/

Zhang, Y., & Chang, C. (2020). Modeling the US-China Trade Conflict: A Utility Theory Approach. *arXiv preprint.*

Zhang, K. H. (2023). U.S.-China Economic Links and Technological Decoupling. *Chinese Economy*, *56*(5), 353–365. DOI: 10.1080/10971475.2023.2173399

Zhang, Z., He, M., Zhang, Y., & Wang, Y. (2022). Geopolitical risk trends and crude oil price predictability. *Energy*, *258*, 124824. DOI: 10.1016/j.energy.2022.124824

Zhou, W., & Gao, H. (2024). *Major economies are taking aim at China's EV industry. Here's what to know.* https://www.cibel.unsw.edu.au/news/major-economies-are-taking-aim-chinas-ev-industry-heres-what-know

Zimmermann, A. (2025, June 18). China's got the world in a rare earth choke hold. *POLITICO*. https://www.politico.eu/article/china-rare-earth-materials-donald-trump-west-magnets-cars/

Zoellick, R. B. (2022). Before the next shock: How America can build a more adaptive global economy. *Foreign Affairs*, *101*, 86.

Zufle, S. (2023). *The Political Economy of China's Belt and Road Initiative in East Africa*. Springer.

Zuniga, R., Santos, B., Zimmerman, N., & Magnotta, F. (2025). Promoting Convergence in U.S.-Brazilian Relations. Wilson Center. https://www.wilsoncenter.org/publication/promoting-convergence-us-brazil-relations

About the Contributors

Renata Thiébaut is the Secretary-General of the AI Global Exchange Forum and brings an impressive combination of academic excellence and global practical experience. As an expert in digital trade, particularly with a deep expertise in the Asian and North American markets, she has worked in senior positions in both the private and public sectors – including at renowned organizations such as Alibaba, Tencent and the United Nations. Her professional career spans several continents and cultures. Between 2018 and 2020, she was also a senior researcher at Harvard University. Internationally acclaimed, Dr. Renata has advised numerous Fortune 500 companies. She has effectively managed a diverse portfolio of over 1,000 brands, including PepsiCo, Unilever's Hourglass, Mondelēz, Nestlé (Beba and Garoto brands), Drogerie Markt, Aldi and Metro supermarkets, Dr. Oetker, Hansgrohe, among others; and collaborated with notable figures such as Taylor Swift, Magic Johnson, Kobe Bryant, Jennifer Aniston, Hulk, Jamie Foxx, Carmelo Anthony and Scottie Pippen. Her dedication to empowering women and minorities in tech earned her the prestigious 2020 Innovator of the Year award from the International Professional Women's Society, solidifying her reputation as a global leader in driving inclusive innovation. She has recently received the 2025 100 Brilliant Women in AI Ethics Awards. With her extensive expertise in digital trade in multinational teams, Prof. Dr. Thiébaut sets new standards for the future of digitalization. She is an author and Peer Reviewer at the United Nations Secretariat. Dr. Renata was directly involved in two trade wars while working in China, first between China and the U.S., and then between Lithuania and China. Due to her in-depth knowledge on global trade, she possesses first class knowledge of trade wars and their impact to individual countries.

Marc Selgas-Cors is a scholar in Intercultural Studies with a strong interdisciplinary background in Political Science, International Relations, and East Asian Studies. He holds a Ph.D. from Universitat Autònoma de Barcelona and is currently pursuing a second Ph.D. at the Universidad del País Vasco. His current research explores green dynamic capabilities enhanced by artificial intelligence to foster trade. Dr. Selgas-Cors is a full-time professor, where he coordinates undergraduate theses and international exchange programs. He also leads pedagogical innovation projects and supervises research in areas such as political systems, public policy, and global economic trends. His academic interests include China's socio-economic transformation, political meritocracy, and the application of artificial intelligence in education and organizational development. He has authored numerous articles, including recent publications in Jiexi Zhongguo and Company Games & Business Simulation Academic Journal. Dr. Selgas-Cors has presented his work at prestigious conferences, such as the ICCSR in London or in the International Congress of Chinese Studies in Bilbao. In addition to his academic achievements, Dr. Selgas-Cors brings practical experience from governmental and corporate roles, enriching his expertise in policy analysis and organizational strategy. His multilingual proficiency in Catalan, Spanish, and English supports his active engagement in global academic collaborations.

***

Safa Ahmad is a PhD scholar in Political Science at Aligarh Muslim University,with a research focus on cultural diplomacy, media narratives, and political transformations in West Asia. She holds a Master's degree in Political Science and has presented papers at national and international conferences. Her published works explore the intersections of soft power, strategic communication, and global governance. Currently, she is examining the dynamics of protectionism and populism in global trade, with a comparative lens on India and the United States. Her academic interests also include Middle Eastern studies, public diplomacy, and international political economy.

Roberto Alexandre Zanchetta Borghi is Associate Professor of Economics at the State University of Campinas (UNICAMP) and holds a PhD from the University of Cambridge.

Nilesh Anute is an Associate Professor at Sri Balaji University, Pune, where he brings a wealth of academic and industry experience to the field of management education. With a strong foundation in research and teaching, Dr. Anute specializes in areas such as marketing, business strategy, and consumer behavior. His commitment to academic excellence is reflected in his numerous research publications, participation in national and international conferences, and mentorship of postgraduate students. At Sri Balaji University, he plays a key role in curriculum development and industry-academia collaboration, contributing significantly to the institution's mission of producing industry-ready professionals.

Sumanta Bhattacharya from Salkia, Howrah, West Bengal is an Expert commissioner member IUCN Environmental, economics and social policy, Individual Policy Analyst (ADB) . He is among the top 2% world scientist (AD Index), Special civilian member Ministry of Defence, (USI) Member at Ministry of Culture (AS) . Member of Ministry of Defence { [Defence and strategic analysis] IDSA }, Member of World Economic Forum, littérateur at National Economic Research Bureau, Member of Ministry of Personnel, Pension and Public grievance (IIPA) He completed his B.Tech, M.Tech in Textile Technology along with that he has MA in Development studies, M.Sc in Environmental Science, LLB, MA in security and defence law from NALSAR, MA in Economics, MBA, Post Graduate Diploma in Environment and Sustainable Development, DIA&D, DS&DS, MPI(Oxford University) . Being a research scholar he has 290 research papers published in International and Scopus index journal, Wiley, Springer, Hindawi in various sectors like law, economic, Development studies, Textiles, Climate Change, SDGs, Public policy, Nanotechnology, Biotechnology, cancer, environment studies, 100 Book chapters published, Edited 2 books, wrote 4 book, 95 patents International and National, 4 copyrights, attended 150 International and National conference and presented papers and won 29 awards for his excellent in education, policy making and innovation which includes Best Water Management Solution Award 2022, Young Researcher Award 2020, Bravo International Book of Records, Mahatma Gandhi Ratna Award 2020, Sustainable Technology Award 2022, Global Change Maker Award 2020, Best Water Management Solution Award at the Rural & Urban Development Summit & Awards 2022, New Delhi, The Progress Global Awards 2023 for Excellence in Research, GIS -Person of the year – Water Conservation, Green India award, 2023, Global Legend Award 2023 by GSIL Educational Society . He is also a member of various International and National organization which includes IEI, IICHE, Asiatic Society, IIPA, IDSA, YOUNGO, IUCN, USI and many more .

Aleksei Bondarenko is a seasoned expert with over 15 years of extensive experience in international trade facilitation, Single Window development, customs modernization, and the implementation of international standards. He has a proven track record in strategy and roadmap development, applying digital technologies to trade, and contributing to global customs and trade facilitation initiatives including UN/CEFACT and the World Customs Organization (WCO). Currently, Aleksei serves as a Project Consultant with the United Nations Economic and Social Commission for Asia and the Pacific (ESCAP) in Bangkok, where he focuses on cross-border paperless trade initiatives and customs modernization in Central Asia. He also holds the position of Vice Chair of the Centre for Trade Facilitation and Electronic Business (UN/CEFACT), where he coordinates domain activities and contributes to key recommendations on Single Window interoperability and digital trade facilitation. Previously, Aleksei worked with prominent international organizations such as the International Trade Centre (ITC), the World Bank Group, GIZ, and the Eurasian Economic Commission. His roles have encompassed conducting feasibility studies, business process analyses, and assessments to support trade facilitation reforms across Eurasia and Asia-Pacific. As an academic, he is an Associate Professor at MGIMO University, where he lectures on digital economy, e-commerce, and international trade procedures. Aleksei holds a Ph.D. in Economics from the Russian Customs Academy, where his dissertation focused on business process analysis of export-import procedures and Single Window implementation. He also possesses extensive certifications including Yale School of Management's Digital Strategy Programme and professional training in business process analysis and European Union law. Fluent in English and a native Russian speaker, Aleksei combines strong analytical skills with practical experience to drive digital transformation and regulatory harmonization in international trade, with a particular focus on improving transparency, efficiency, and interoperability in customs and trade systems worldwide.

Ann Mary Cherian is an academic in the Department of Economics at Christ College (Autonomous), Irinjalakuda, located in Thrissur, Kerala.With a passion for economics and a commitment to academic excellence, she has made significant contributions to the field through her research and teaching. Her areas of interest include Macroeconomics, Development economics, International Trade, Agricultural economics and tourism economics. She is a dedicated educator, guiding students in understanding complex economic concepts while conducting insightful studies in her field.

Raquel Isamara Leon De La Rosa Full-time professor at Autonomus University of Puebla in Mexico. Director of the Observatory of Chinese Politics in Spain.

Juliana Florentina Fernandes Leao is a Brazilian economist and current Master's student in the Economics of Globalization and European Integration (EGEI) Program at Ghent University. She holds a Bachelor's degree in Economics from the State University of Campinas (UNICAMP).

Misael González Ramírez is a Full-time professor at Autonomus University of Puebla in Mexico.

Ahlem Hamri has a doctorate of economics from the High School of Commerce University of Manouba, Tunisia.

Susanna Hartanto, S.E., M.M., M.L.S. Int Tax graduated from Business Faculty of Widya Mandala Catholic University, Surabaya, major in accounting with cumlaude predicate. Then she worked for Big four Public Accounting Firm - Ernst & Young until 2005. Then she moved to tobacco industry and worked for several tobacco companies from staff in accounting & tax department until managerial level in a multinational tobacco company. Since 2009 until now she also has been working as part time tax consultant with some partners to add taxation and accounting knowledge in various industry. In 2011 she took Master of Management Program at Widya Mandala Catholic University, Surabaya and graduated in 2012 with cumlaude predicate. Since 2014 until now she has been teaching Business & Vocational Faculties at Widya Mandala Catholic University. In 2019 she had opportunity as reviewer in International Taxation Program at Texas A&M University, USA for about two years. In 2020 she also joined International Tax Law Course which was held by University of Leiden (Leiden Universiteit). In 2022 she graduated from Master of Legal Studies, with International Taxation concentration with scholarship from Texas A&M University, USA with summa cumlaude predicate.

Anton Kozhankov, Ph.D. Associate Professor, Department of Trade Affairs and Trade Regulation, MGIMO University, Russia Anton Kozhankov is a member of the Board of the Association of Customs Lawyers and holds a Ph.D. in Law. He serves as an Associate Professor at the Department of Trade Affairs and Trade Regulation at MGIMO University under the Ministry of Foreign Affairs of the Russian Federation. In addition to his academic work, Anton is the CEO of Astema Group, a logistics company providing comprehensive services in international trade and cross-border cargo transportation since 2014. Under his leadership, Astema Group has established representation in several regions across Russia and has become an accredited logistics partner of the Russian Export Center. The company also serves as the official representative of Heilongjiang Dragon-Link International Logistics Co., a state-owned Chinese logistics enterprise. Anton actively contributes to bridging academia and practice in the field of trade regulation, customs law, and international logistics.

Jeremy Levine is entering his fourth year as a PhD student at Stony Brook University in the United States pursuing a degree in sociology. He has a bachelor's in finance from Fairleigh Dickinson University and a master's in public policy in international affairs from William Paterson University. Jeremy has also been an adjunct professor at multiple universities teaching sociology, political science, economics, and businesses courses with some of his most recent appointments being at Seton Hall University for both the Stillman School of Business and School of Diplomacy and International Relations. Some of his recent journal article publications include "Professional Sports, Authoritarian Capitalism, and Their Impact on the Global Community" in The International Journal of Sport and Society and "The Political Dimensions of Conflict and Globalization: What Russia and China Have Recently Taught Us about the Fallout and Political Ramifications of Globalization" in The International Journal of Interdisciplinary Global Studies.

José Floriano Lima Filho, Scholar and journalist Floriano Filho (bit.ly/447SEiz) completed research studies at Nagoya University and postdoctoral fellowships on China-Latin America-Japan relations (University of Tokyo) and on energy security in Taiwan, where he was also a non-resident fellow at Chihlee University of Technology. He is a collaborating researcher at the universities of Brasilia and Sao Paulo (Asian Studies), a POC in Brazil for the Shandong Foreign Trade Vocational College, and a senior political journalist at the Brazilian Senate news agency, where he used to host a podcast on global issues. Previously, Dr. Filho served as deputy director at the Senate's School of Government, where he gave short courses about China. His PhD thesis (University of Brasilia and fellowships at Johns Hopkins and the University of Tokyo) dealt with Japan-China strategic relations. He earned an MSc in Broadcast Journalism from Columbia University (NYC, 1991) and an MA with distinction in Communication Policies from the University of Westminster (Harrow, 2001) and, for about ten years, taught journalism, media, and ESL in public and private colleges in Brazil. As a Monbusho researcher, he studied Japan's information society at Tsukuba and Hitotsubashi Universities (1991–1993). In 2006, he was a Reuters Foundation fellow at the University of Oxford, researching the global trade of digital content. From 2007 to 2009, he worked as a Washington, DC-based TV correspondent and was a Fulbright-APSA senior Congressional fellow in the US House of Representatives. Dr. Filho is an advisor to the Center for Democracy and Culture at the University of Oklahoma and was the sole Brazilian delegate to the 2019 Tibet Development Forum (second visit to Tibet).

T.C. Manjunath was born on 6th February 1967. He did his B.E. from RV College of Engg. in 1989 (B'lore Univ), M.E. in Robotics & Automation from Govt.'s LD College of Engg., (Gujarat Univ., Ahmedabad) in 1992 with FCD-First Rank & PhD in Systems & Control Engg. from IIT Bombay in the year 2007, got best research scholar award for the entire IITB. He is currently working as the Dean Research (R & D) and as Professor in Dept. of Computer Science & Engg. with specialization in IoT, Cyber Security, Blockchain Technology in Rajarajeswari College of Engineering, Bengaluru, Karnataka. He has got a teaching (academic), research & administrative experience of more than 35+ years (10 years as Principal & 8 years as HoD, 1 year as Dean Research & rest as faculty) and has published more than 1500+ research papers in various national & international journals & conferences, with 175+ patents, 100+ book-chapters, 25 awards, 100s of Keynote talks and also published 25 text books in various field of science, engineering & technology, completed projects worth Rs. 9 Crores till date & guided 10 PhD scholars in VTU. He is a member of 30 Professional Society Chapters and is a fellow of IE, IETE, AMIEE, Sr. Member of IEEE and a chartered engineer.

Aleksandr Orel, Ph.D. is an expert in MSME development and trade facilitation with over 8 years of experience supporting small and medium enterprises, cross-border trade, and regional economic cooperation. He specializes in conducting feasibility studies, developing strategies and roadmaps, and implementing digital tools for trade. Aleksandr has a proven track record in fostering collaboration between academia, the private sector, and government agencies. He currently serves as an Associate Professor at Gatchina State University (Russia), teaching Regional Economics and Entrepreneurship, while conducting research on socio-economic issues in the CIS region. Concurrently, he works as an Economist at the Competence Center for Trade Facilitation at the M. Ryskulbekov Kyrgyz Economic University, where he leads analytical research and capacity-building activities to support MSMEs in Central Asia. Previously, Aleksandr was Head of the Economic Department at the Entrepreneurship Support Foundation (Russia), overseeing socio-economic policy analysis, business consulting, and the development of support programs for SMEs. He also has extensive experience as a business consultant, providing strategic advice to over 1,500 SMEs and startups. Aleksandr earned his Ph.D. in Economics from Peter the Great St. Petersburg Polytechnic University in 2023, with a dissertation focused on sustaining regional economic systems through MSME support. He holds a Master's degree in Regional Economics from St. Petersburg State University of Industrial Technologies and Design, and a Bachelor's degree in Financial Management from the Russian Customs Academy, both with honors. He is fluent in Russian and English and holds multiple professional certifications in business planning, international trade, and business analytics. Aleksandr has received several awards for his contributions to sustainable development and education and serves as an expert for UNNExT.

P. Selvakumar is currently an Associate Professor in the Department of Science and Humanities at Nehru Institute of Technology, Coimbatore, Tamil Nadu, India. Prior to joining Nehru Institute of Technology, he held positions as an Assistant Professor in the Department of Science and Humanities various engineering colleges in Coimbatore, Tamil Nadu, India, spanning from 2011 to 2023. Dr.P. Selvakumar's academic and research interests lie primarily in the field of phytochemistry. He has made significant contributions to his field, with an impressive record that includes 30 journal publications, 12 patents, and 20 conference papers. Additionally, he has organized 5 seminars and conferences, further demonstrating his commitment to academic and scientific exchange. Throughout his career, Dr. P.Selvakumar has been recognized for his dedication and excellence in teaching, having been honored with several awards, including the Best Teacher Awards. He holds a prominent position in the academic community, contributing actively to research.

Satish Pawar serves as the Principal of Balaji College of Arts, Commerce & Science (BCACS), Tathawade, Pune, under the aegis of Sri Balaji University, Pune. A dedicated academician and seasoned administrator, Dr. Pawar brings extensive experience in higher education leadership, curriculum development, and student-centric academic planning. Under his guidance, BCACS has seen significant growth in academic excellence, infrastructure, and industry engagement. His focus on holistic student development, quality education, and research-driven learning has positioned the college as a reputed institution in the region. Dr. Pawar continues to inspire both faculty and students through his visionary leadership and commitment to educational innovation.

Kamal Kumar Rajagopalan is an experienced academician and finance professional, currently serving as an Assistant Professor at School of Liberal Arts and Management Studies, P P Savani Universtiy, India. With expertise in finance, accounting, business analytics, and strategic management, he integrates analytical tools into finance curricula for data-driven decision-making. He holds a Ph.D. and MBA in Finance from ICFAI, along with ACMA certification. His industry experience spans roles in accounting, auditing, and financial management. A published researcher in Scopus and UGC Care journals, he is proficient in Python, R, Power BI, and SAP. Dr. Rajagopalan is a member of ICAI.

Piyali Roy Chowdhury serves as Assistant Professor, Christ University, School of Business and Management, Bangalore, India. Her area of teaching is – Economics, Sustainable Finance and Behavioural Finance. Her area of research includes International Trade, Foreign Investments, Macroeconomics, and Econometrics. She holds a Doctorate degree in Management (Area- Financial Economics) from Vellore Institute of Technology, Chennai and MBA in Finance. She is an Indian Institute of Management (IIM) Ahmedabad alumni of Faculty Development Programme held in IIM Ahmedabad. She has many publications in Scopus, Web of Science, UGC and ABDC C category journals. She has attended several workshops based on econometric analysis and methods. She led entrepreneurship teams in different academic fields. She has overall 15 years of academic work experience with four years of experience in retail banking operations. She is a resourceful speaker in management case discussions and a sincere mentor for budding graduates with innovative knowledge and skills.

Ahmet Turan graduated from Sakarya University, Faculty of Political Sciences, Department of International Relations in 2017. In 2020, he completed his master's in Middle Eastern Studies at Middle East Institute of that University. He received his PhD from Sakarya University Institute of Social Sciences with his thesis titled 'Türkiye-Russia Rivalry in the Caucasus: The Case of Karabakh Issue' from Sakarya University Institute of Social Sciences. He is the Head of the International Relations Office, Inonu University, Türkiye. His research focuses on Turkish foreign policy, Türkiye-Russia relations, Central Asia and Caucasus.

Index

A

B

C

D

E

G

I

M

P

R

S

T

U

W

X

www.ingramcontent.com/pod-product-compliance
Lightning Source LLC
LaVergne TN
LVHW062340300926
849161LV00007B/1760